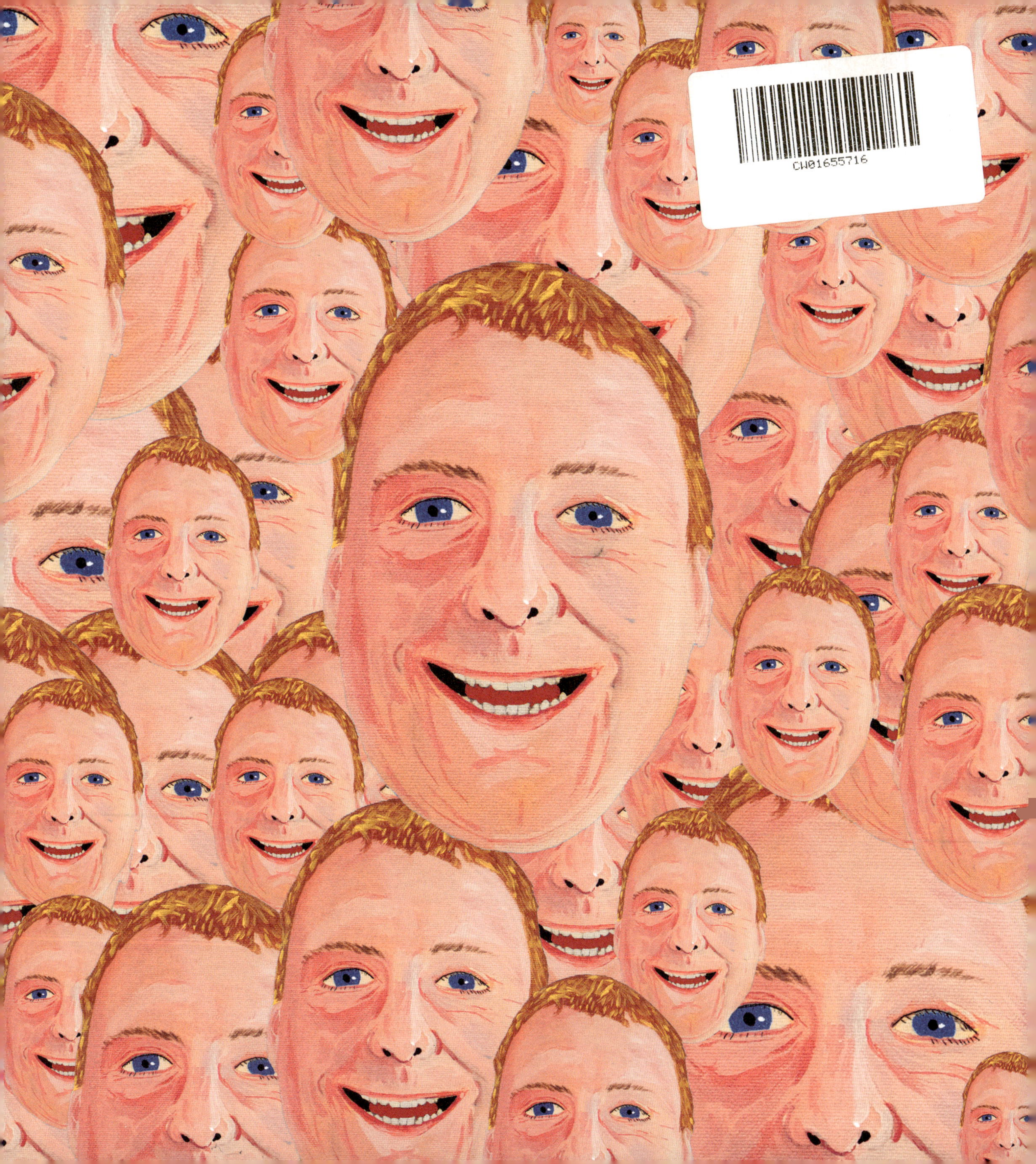

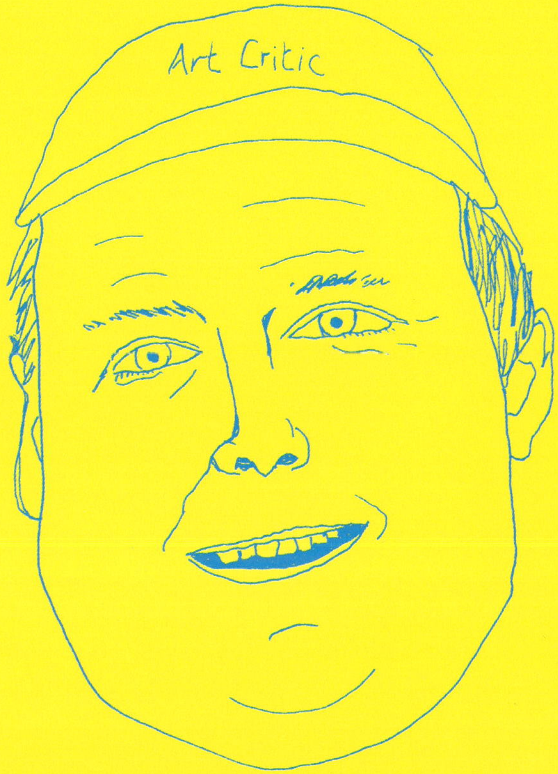
Art Critic

TRAPEZE

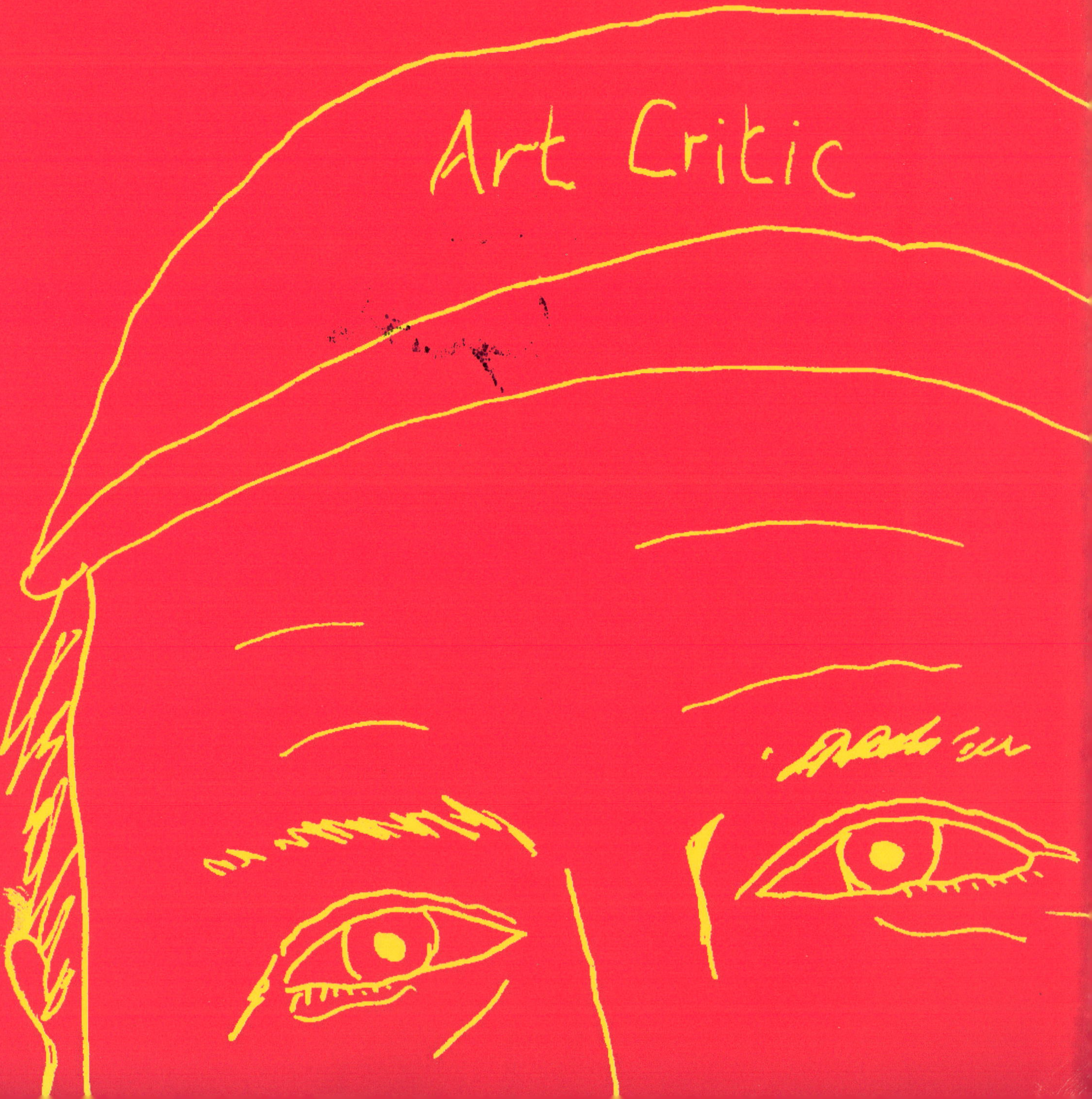

Joe Lycett's ARTHOLE

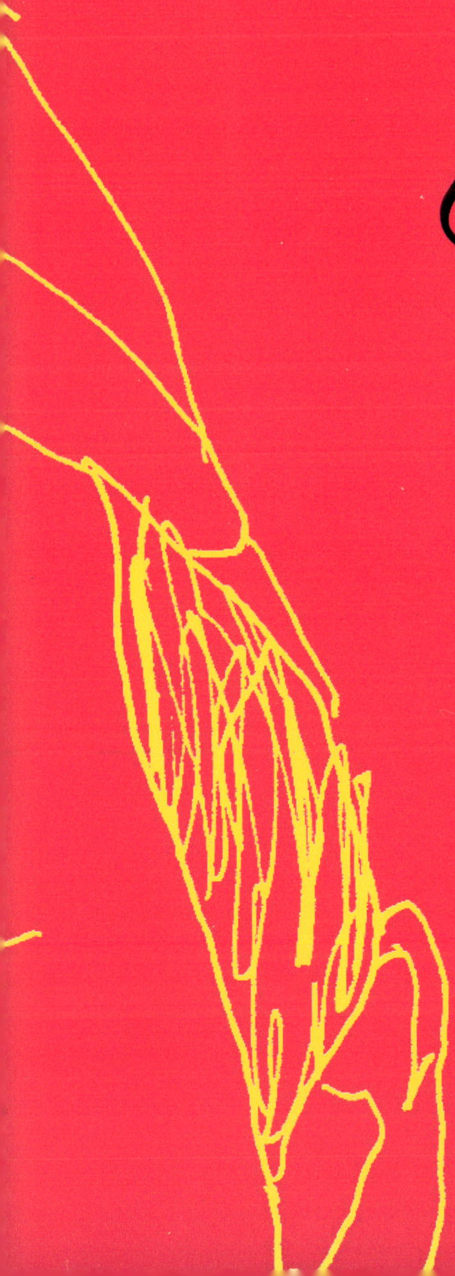

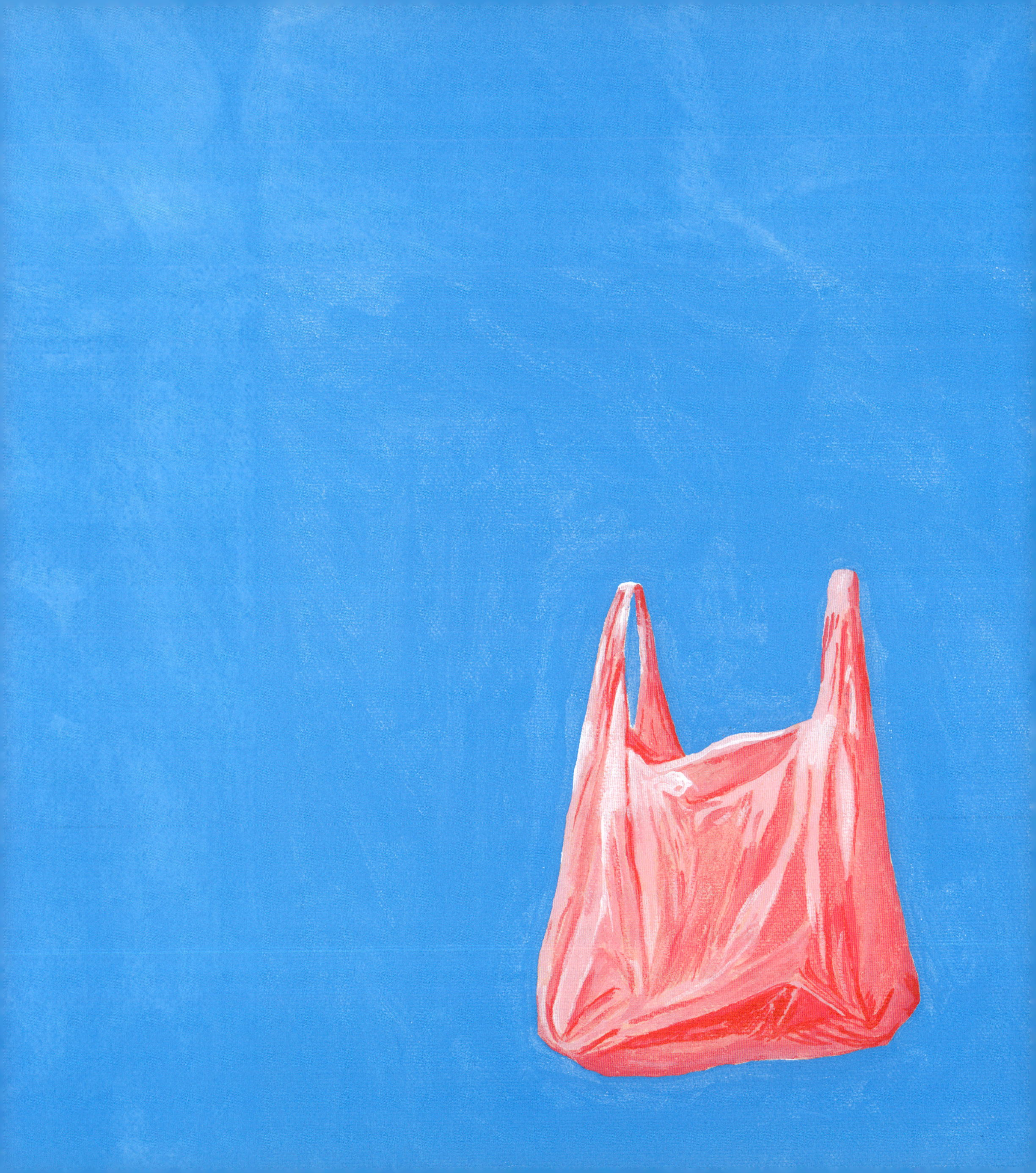

The expiry date is 12/25.
And the three digits on the back are 524.

– DAVID HOCKNEY

I can't get the air conditioning to work in the room. I pressed the button, but it doesn't let me get the number down below 20 degrees. It just stays on 20 degrees. It is very warm in the room.

– MARINA ABRAMOVIĆ

Just a black coffee, cheers.

– DAMIEN HIRST

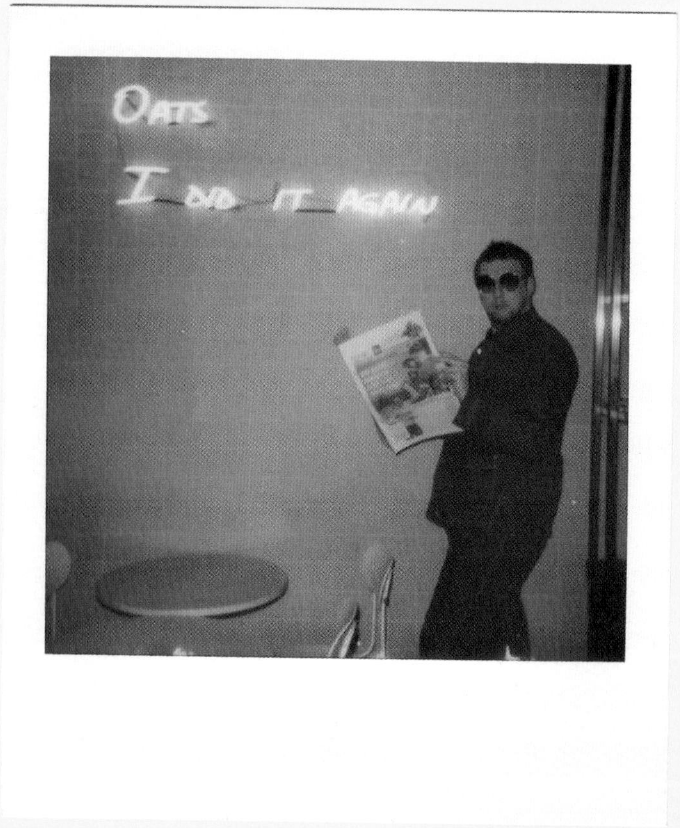

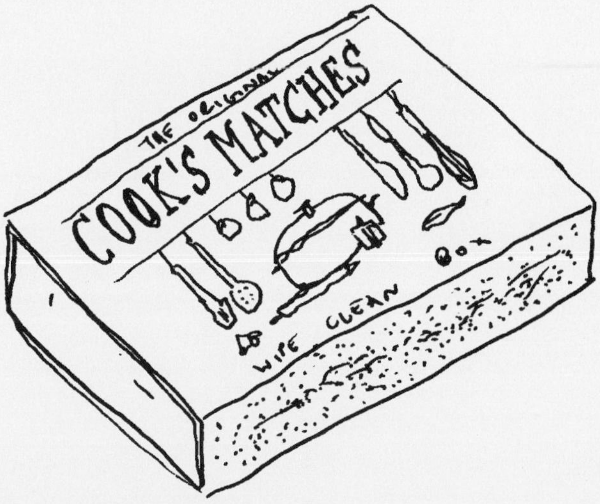
THE ORIGINAL
COOK'S MATCHES
WIPE CLEAN BOX

CONTENTS

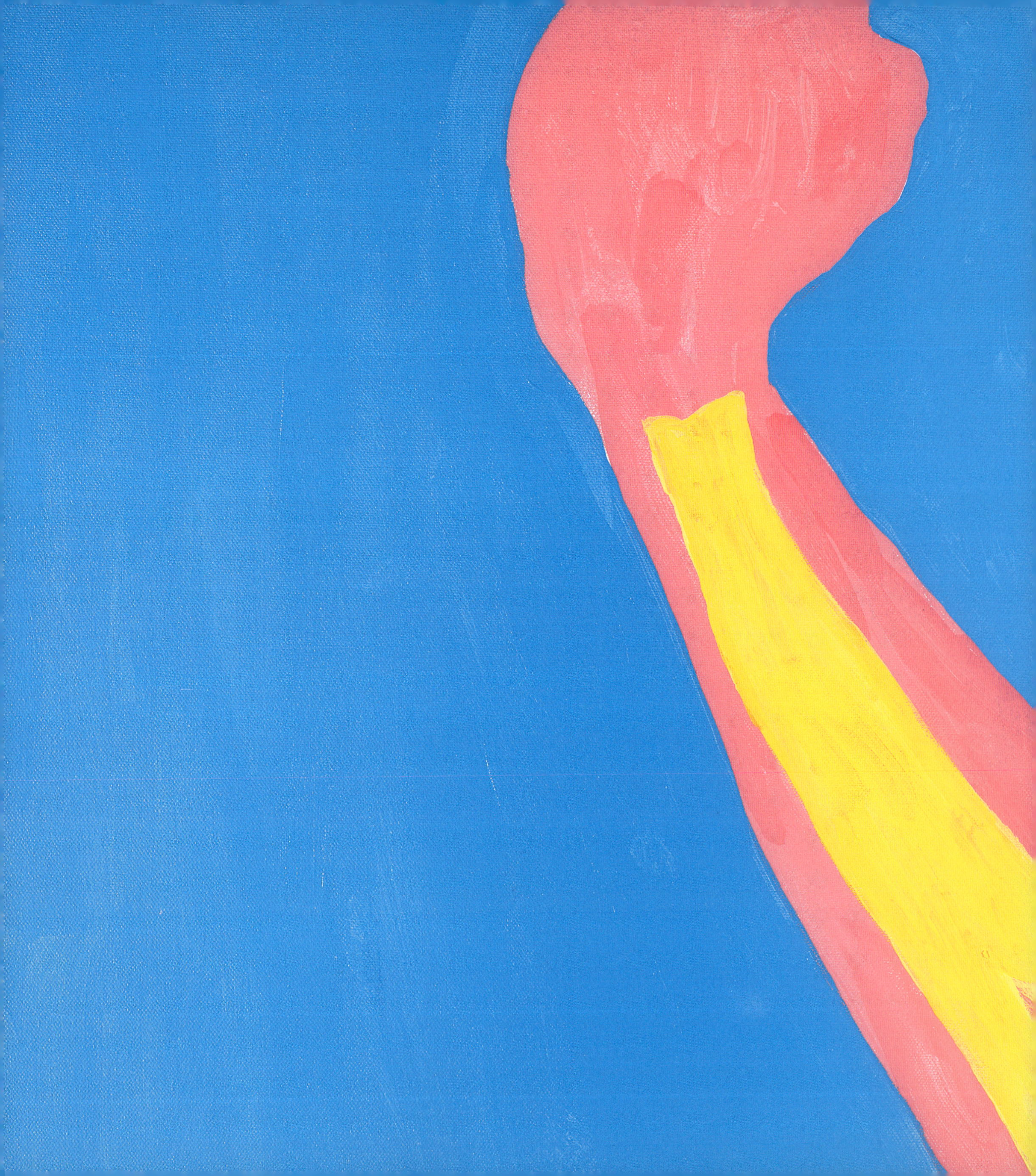

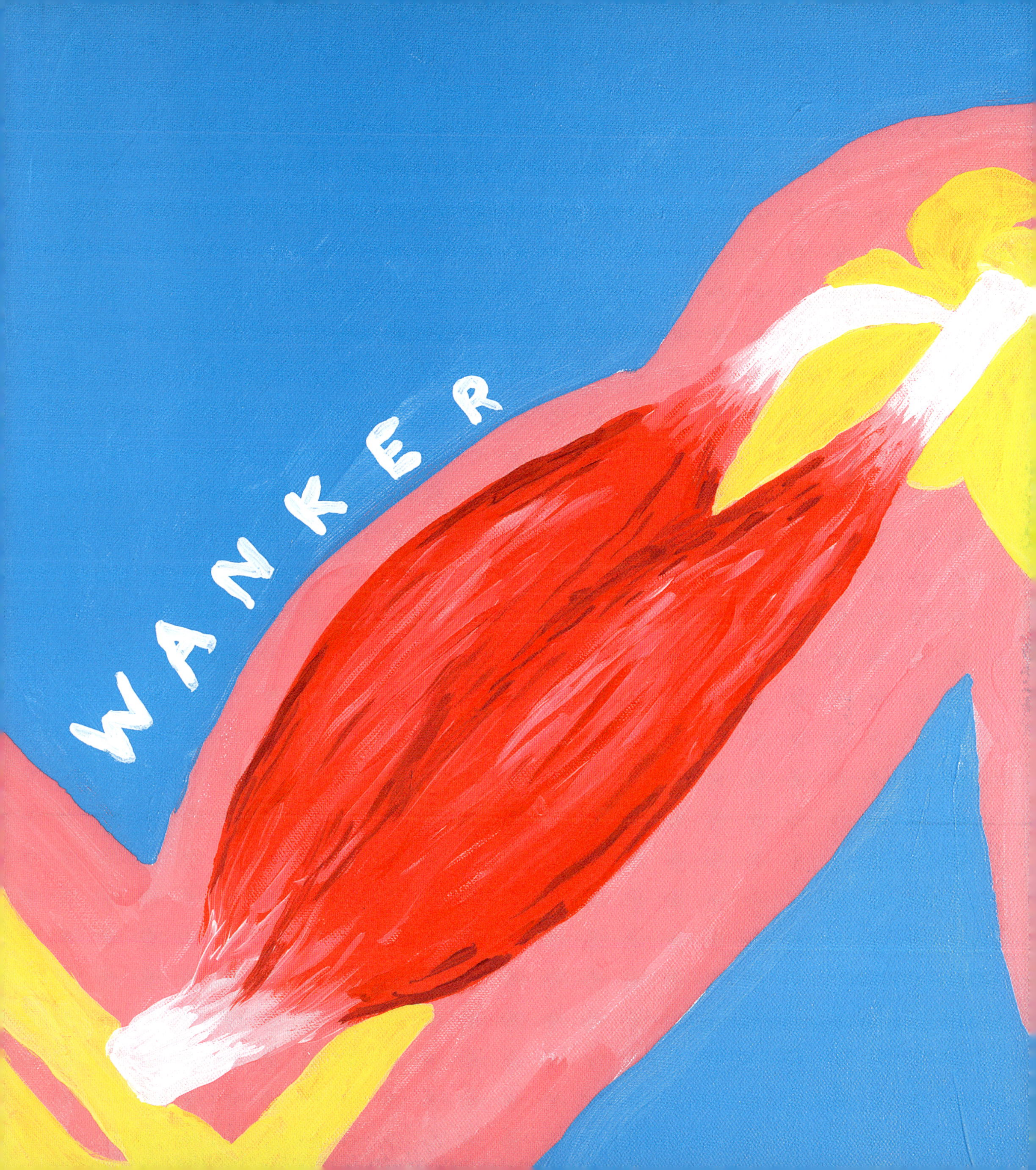
WANKER

FOREWORD

by the ghost
& Leonardo da Vinci

As the years have hurried on, with their forest frosts and courtyard sunsets, as fruits have fallen and kings dethroned, over the last five centuries I have been asked, from a litany of humiliating missives, to write the foreword to some artist or other's book. Caravaggio, Turner, Warhol, and most recently that idiot Anish Kapoor – I refused them all. None have come within any notable proximity to my talents, none truly capable of expressing the human condition and spirit through shapes and shades. Until now.

I am going to state it as plainly as a ghost can: Joe Lycett's work is the greatest artistic contribution to humanity since my own, during those batshit crazy days of the Renaissance, lol. He is an innovator, for sure: brave, vibrant, elusive, unashamedly modern and yet in a thorough embrace with history. When I died in 1519, I presumed in vain that before long someone else, anyone else, would hold a mirror to humanity's soul, confidently and brilliantly, as I did. But not until Lycett has anyone achieved it. Fearne Cotton maybe gets close.

It is undeniable. I am undeniably the greatest artist to have ever lived. It is undeniable to deny. Why else would my works be coveted and cosseted like delicate saplings; my sagas told and retold, over dwindling campfires from dusty parchments, and also in the film *The Da Vinci Code* starring Tom Hanks (and, if I'm honest, a miscast Audrey Tautou)?

These days, I reside not in heaven as you might reasonably expect, what with all the work I did for God, but here's a fun plot twist: I'm in hell. Contrary to what you might believe about hell, I actually love it down here. Endless fiery nights spilling with gamblers, vandals and drunks, plus some absolutely wild girls who are up for anything – and I mean absolutely fucking anything. One night you are drinking chartreuse with Cleopatra, the next you are sipping in a tail of fresh smoke from the tight leaves of a hand-rolled spliff with Pablo Escobar (or on Thursdays it's Pam St Clement). Then maybe you're having a cup of Earl Grey and sharing gossip-filled whispers with Thora Hird or emptying a bag of Wotsits with Bernard Manning. Each of them is endlessly charming, oozing wit and cunning and brilliance – except Manning, who I find irritating.

In hell, I'm known under the moniker of LDV, which had been a successful and iconic nickname for about five hundred years until someone invented the light-duty vehicle. Now, whenever a fresh corpse arrives it gets pretty confusing. My rope-like beard acts as a distinctive identifier for most, but many from America think I have named myself after a passenger car or passenger car derivative that has the seating capacity for twelve passengers or more. When those souls from South Africa dive through the earth to join us in Satan's

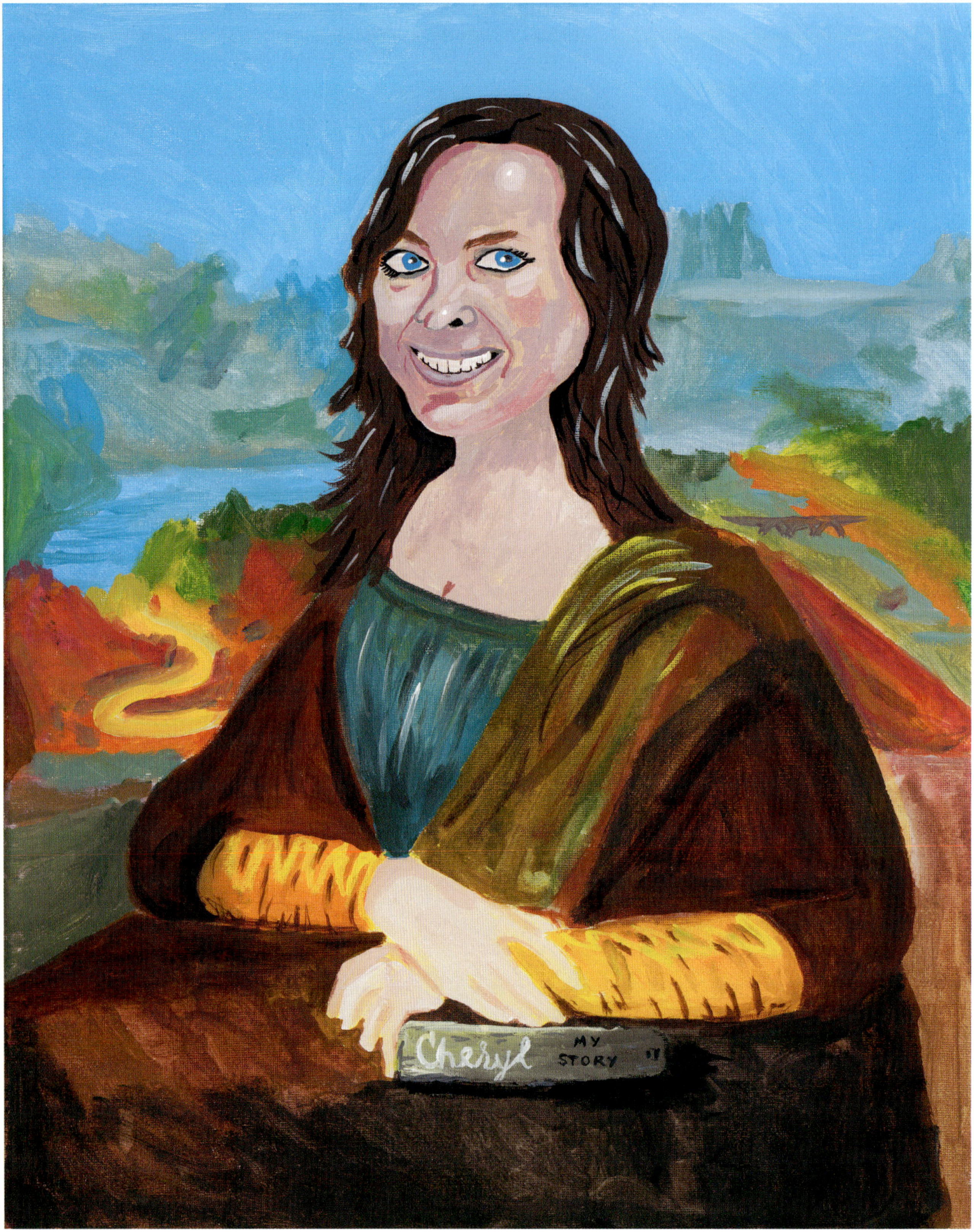

Fig. 1

Fig. 1 *The Mona Lisa Scott-Lee*, 2024, acrylic gouache on canvas, 77 × 53cm.

bedsit it gets even more confusing, because their definition of a light-duty vehicle is different, and they think I am a motor vehicle with no heavy axle designed or adapted for the conveyance of persons and freight. In 1993, a company called Leyland DAF Vans was formed in Washwood Heath in Birmingham and later became known as LDV; I have been receiving legal threats from them explaining that I cannot operate with their name or produce merchandise with 'LDV' on it, even though I definitely claimed it first. And also: guys, I am not producing merch right now on account of being in hell. When Lisa De Vanna started making waves in Australian pro soccer I started to get really concerned, but luckily, she is not precious or litigious.

I've got off the subject, which is: Joe Lycett is great at art. What else is there to add? As Michelangelo saw the angel in the marble and carved until he set him free, Lycett sees ITV daytime presenters on the blank canvas and paints until he gets a legal letter. I could mention his use of colour, perhaps – celestial blues, faded coral pinks (my fave) and then a slap in the gob with bright yellow. How vast and deep is my wish that I'd had access to the vibrancy of acrylics in the 1500s, but I was adrift with mere lead and oil, unable as I was to access any branches of Cass Art. And his portraiture, oh his portraiture! An intangible and erratic feast, yet mysteriously deliberate and true. God, I sound pretty horny for the guy, don't I?!

It is my great honour to inscribe the foreword to this tome, to introduce to the world the works of my great contemporary equivalent, Joe Harry Lycett BA (Drama with English, 2:1, Manchester University). May this volume of astounding works, and the fables behind them, engrave his name alongside mine on the infinite towering stones of time.

Yours, in the spirit of artistic enquiry,
and the pursuit of knowledge above all else,

Leonardo da Vinci

P.S. Hope that's OK, Joe? Let me know if you have any revisions. I'll get my agent at YMU Management to send you an invoice. They'll know how to forward the cash onto me down here in hell.

INTRODUCTION

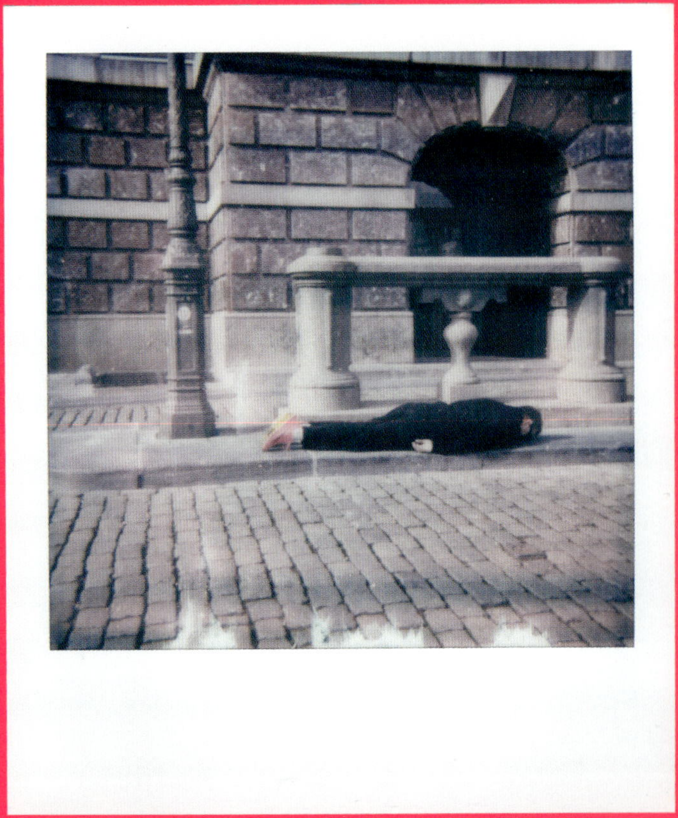

Ever since I was a little girl, I have been enthralled by colour. I remember bouncing on my auntie's knee[1] in the dappled sunlight of our family garden in south Birmingham, as she patiently pointed at the flowers and asked me to identify the shade of each one in turn. 'Sapphire!' 'Gamboge!' 'Cerulean!' 'Sarcoline!' 'Coquelicot!' I thought I was just making adorable noises, but it transpires that I was actually born with an innate understanding of pigments.

My auntie was obsessed with colour in a different way – she was a racist – but those halcyon days beneath the pear trees would form the boy, and then the teenager, and then the young woman, and now the disgraced man I have become today.

As my interest in colour matured, and my auntie went to prison for attempting to firebomb a tandoori balti house, I began to explore the vast array of pigments the natural world made available to me, as well those found in buckets at our local branch of The Works. Like a young and enthusiastic staff member at Homebase, I would mix and stir my accrued paints, testing them, observing their behaviours, their relationships to one another, discovering how more often than not you just end up with a brown that looks like poo. Tentatively, I approached the task of layering my discoveries on various parchments, canvases, garments and toilet doors. In abstract shapes at first, then simple fruits and vegetables, then landscapes, animals, aggressive words, hate symbols, and finally … portraits.

To my mind, the portrait is the highest form of art, alongside paintings of dogs playing snooker. It is so impressive and elusive an art form that around the world it has its own dedicated galleries, such as: the National Portrait Gallery, United Kingdom; National Portrait Gallery, Australia; National Portrait Gallery, Canada; National Portrait Gallery, Estonia; National Portrait Gallery, Spain; National Portrait Gallery, Italy; National Portrait Gallery, Japan; National Portrait Gallery, Malta; National Portrait Gallery, India; National Portrait Gallery, France; National Portrait Gallery, Denmark; and National Galleries Scotland: Portrait. These galleries ooze distinctiveness, creativity and individuality from their names alone. I cannot tell you what pleasure I gleaned from copying and pasting them.

I am not too shy to say, dear reader, that portraiture is an art form that I have mastered and, dare I say it, completed. Where it has eluded many, over my years of experience I have cajoled it, caressed it and, to quote Dannii Minogue whenever she completes a Sudoku, 'fucking nailed it'. I am surely one of the greatest living painters, unless you are reading this after I am dead, in which case I am one of the greatest dead painters.[2]

1. The knee was replaced.

2. On that note: as I wrote this book many of the people referenced in it decided to die (so I removed their entries) or get divorced (thanks, Eamonn and Ruth). There is a delay between the submitting of the final manuscript and publication, and so I would like to apologise in advance if any of those mentioned are now dead and in hindsight their inclusion seems unkind or in poor taste. If they have died and their inclusion seems kind or in good taste, that was entirely deliberate.

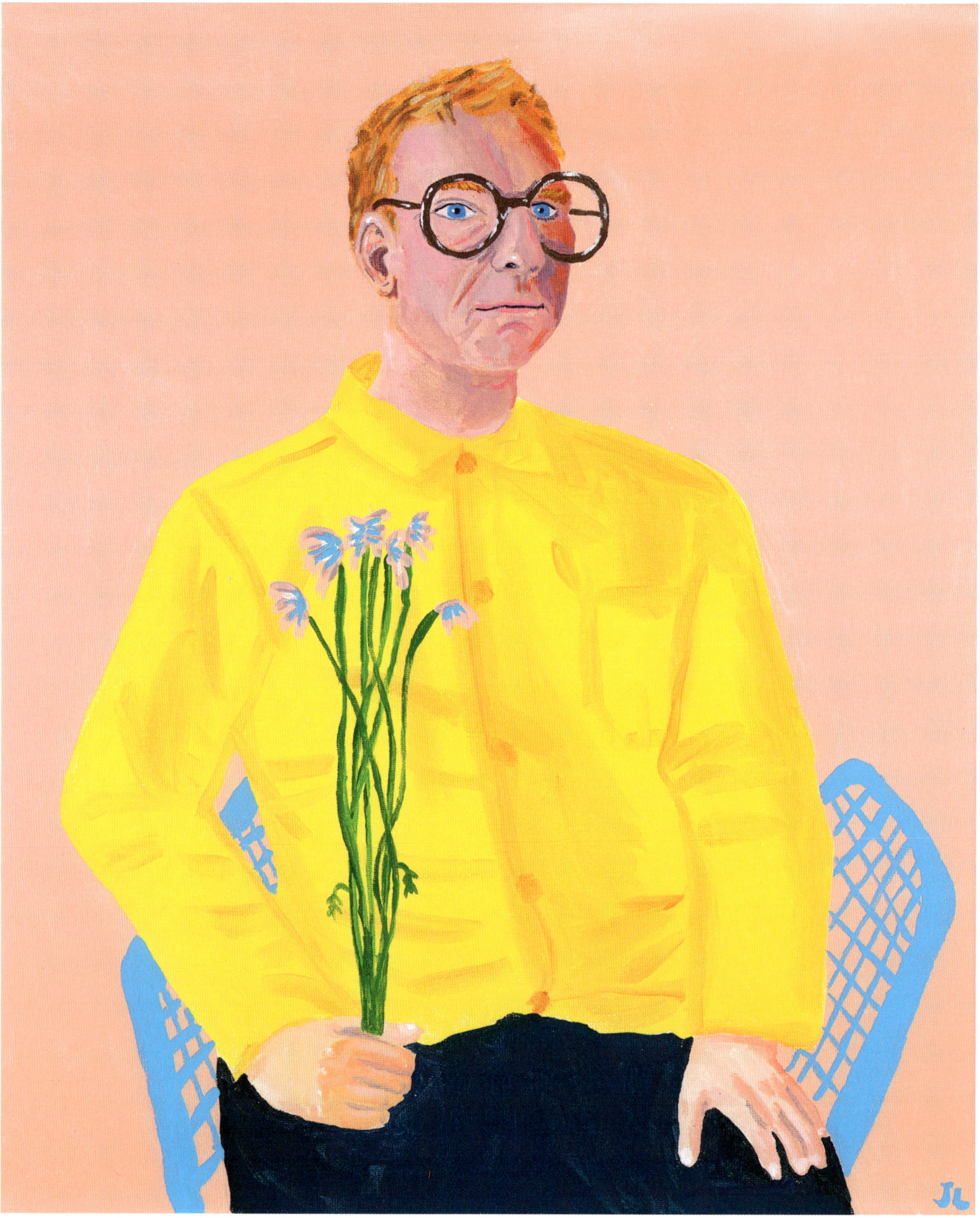

Fig. 2

Fig. 2 *Future Self-Portrait*, 2002, glitter on brick, 28 × 42 bricks.

My workspace is, like most of my subjects, simple: an easel on which sits a canvas; a palette; an unassuming wooden chair; a selection of brushes; a glass of water; a J cloth (I believe the 'J' stands for 'jism'); a glass of champagne; a glass of Châteaux Margaux; a glass of Domaine de la Romanée-Conti; a small television set playing old episodes of *Casualty*; a roll of Plenty (formerly Bounty) kitchen roll; a selection of fishing magazines; some prescription medicine (presented on a platter); a glass of Pepsi Max; a small group of men holding me aloft; and my subject. I keep the drinks cool in a Hotpoint H55RM1110W1 Fridge in white, but to be honest, recently I've been having some issues with it. I normally paint in the orangery, unless the staff are preparing it for a banquet or recital, in which case I will retire to the study or a nearby WeWork. The orangery is my favourite place to paint simply because it is the greatest source of natural light, which is the best and only light to work with – aside from the Lumie Vitamin L® SAD Light, which I purchased at John Lewis, although the website was at pains to point out that '"Vitamin L®" is not a vitamin, but a reference to the mood-enhancing properties of this SAD light'.

This compendium provides a comprehensive companion to my considerable concoctions within the medium of colour. Between these pages are the paintings of (and some for) the great and the good, with the stories behind them – some of them completely and utterly unbelievable.

I hope my *Art Hole* delights, fascinates and perhaps inspires you to pick up a paint brush, insert yourself at the heart of contemporary British public life, and do some absolutely wank paintings of celebs.

Cheers,

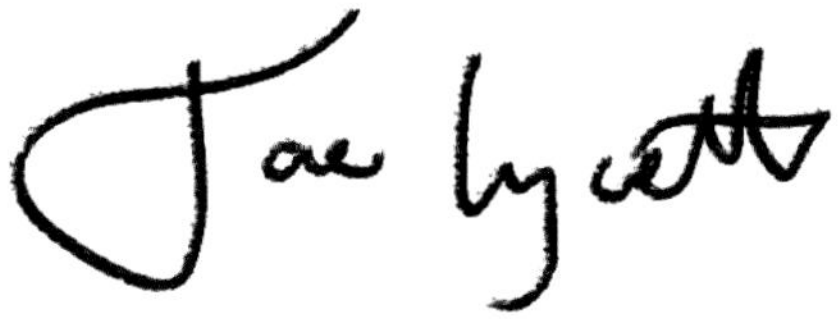

Come on in

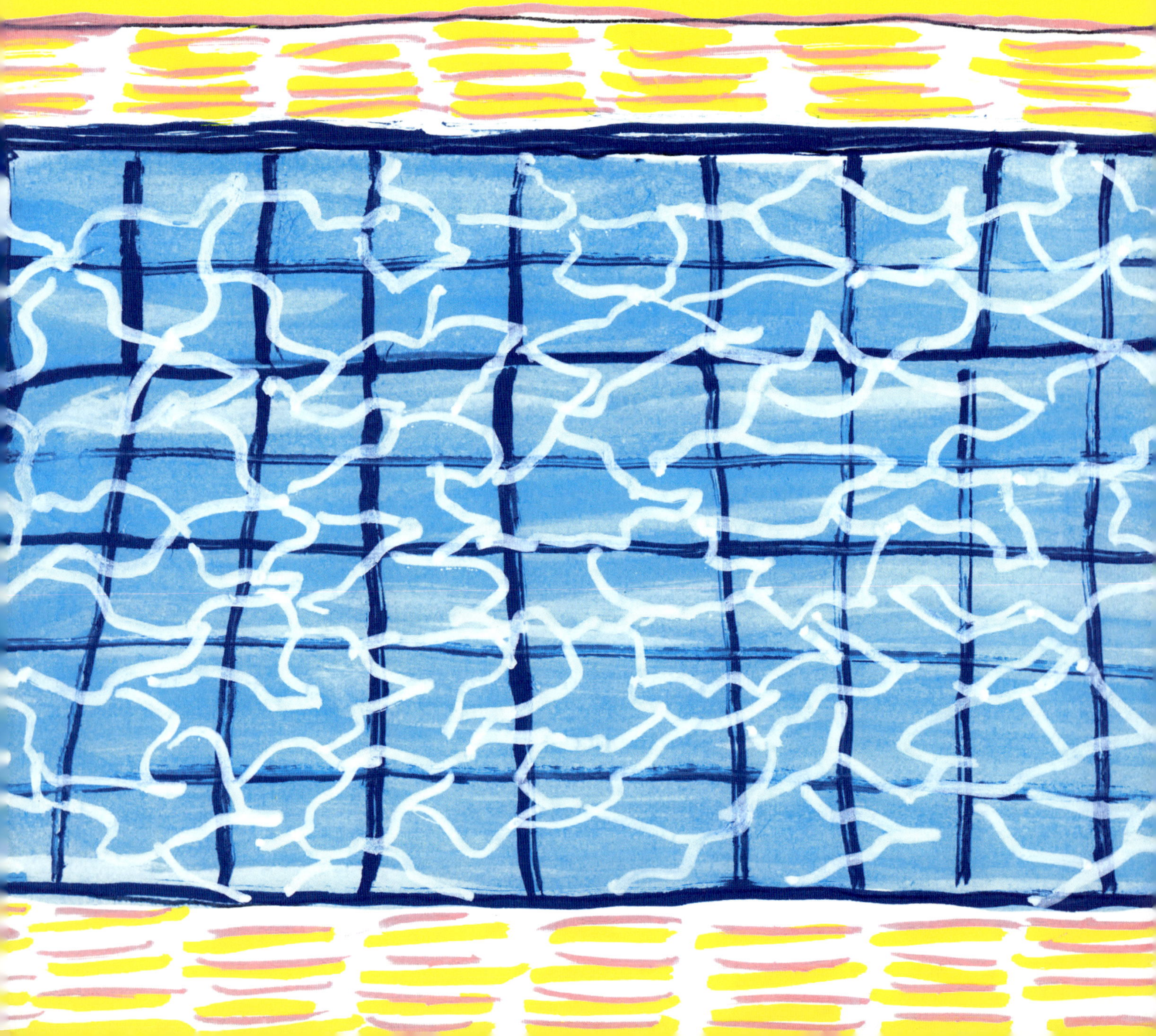

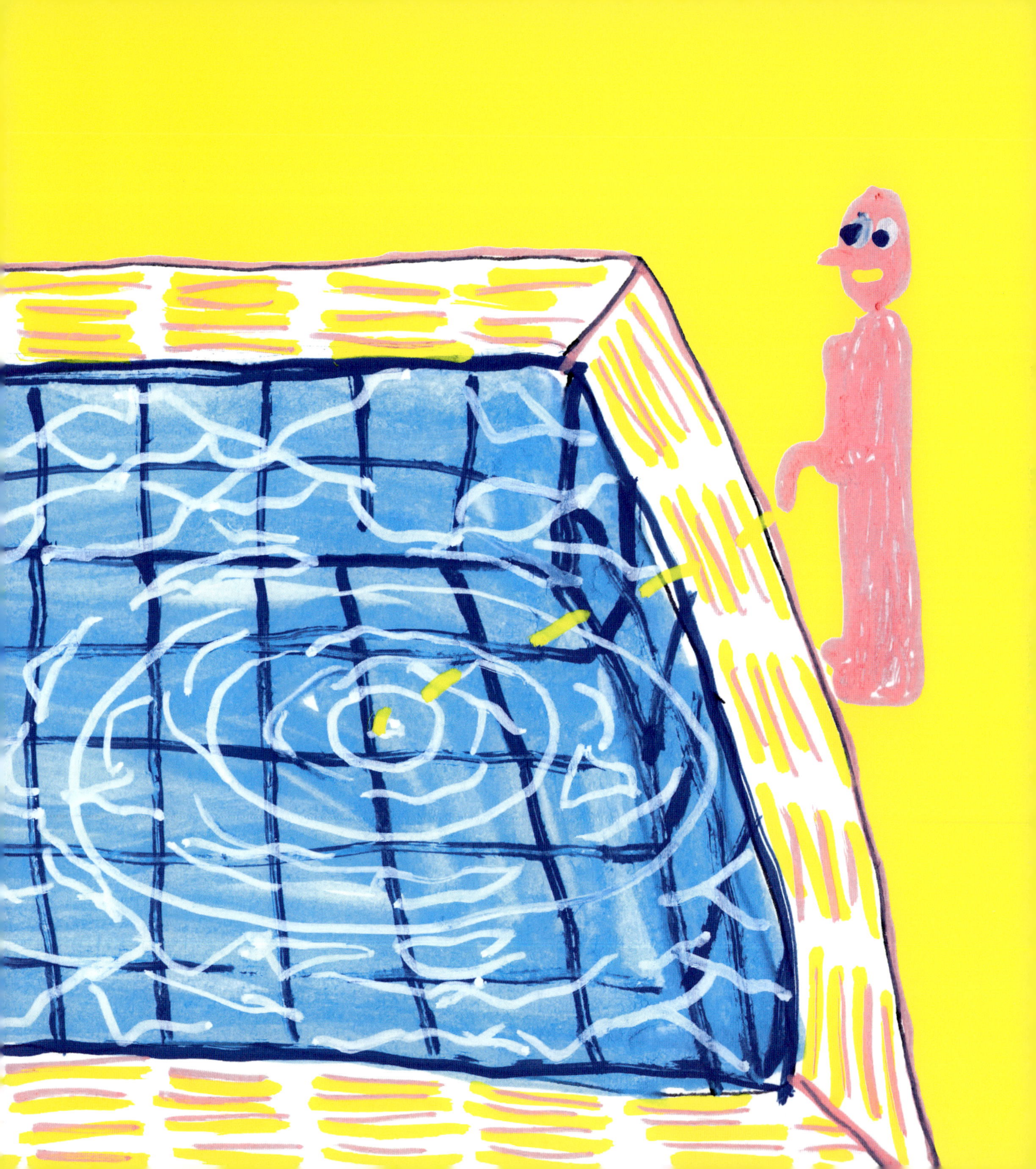

P
REA
NOU

HOTO-
LISTIC
UVEAU

Photo-realistic Nouveau

GARY LINEKER

This portrait/self-portrait/masterpiece is one of my most successful paintings and one of the singular most lauded and respected visual works of the modern era, alongside the oeuvres of Tracey Emin, Damien Hirst and the stuff George W. Bush does. It appeared in the Royal Academy Summer Exhibition in 2023 thanks to the Academy's keen eye for artistic genius and free publicity. It was described by Jonathan Jones, the art critic in the *Guardian*, as 'an accomplished parody of David Hockney', adding '[AI] could well have designed it' – both of which I see as compliments and thinly veiled ways of saying that I am his favourite painter, able to do work that is better than both Hockney and all of artificial intelligence.

Gary Lineker and I met a few years ago in the gluten-free aisle of the Tesco Superstore in Padstow. I'm not intolerant to gluten and I'm not sure if he is intolerant to gluten either,[1] but from time to time I do like to have a look at what new products they've come up with, to see 'how the other half lives'. This morbid curiosity of other people's suffering comes from a period when I did think I was intolerant to gluten[2] and so, for a short while, was eating the bread branded as 'Genius'.[3] I was drawn to the name and branding at first: who wouldn't want to eat bread for/of a genius? Plus, the logo was handwritten (and jolly!). There was something aspirational and modern and somehow youthful about eating newly invented and exciting bread with such a bold name. We are in a brave new world, where we can now call a quiche 'compassionate' or a slice of ham 'visionary'. Future generations will surely marvel at our behaviour as they fight to the death for the remaining tins of 'magnanimous' soup.

I digress: the point I wanted to make is that despite the aforementioned pleasing branding of Genius bread, I am sad to say that it is not at all an intelligent choice. It looks like bread but behaves more like a block of compressed moths. I have great sympathy for anyone who is intolerant to gluten and must put themselves through the indignity of eating a sandwich with the stuff. I suspect some have been hospitalised from choking on its dust/crust/dustcrust.

1. He strikes me as gluten sceptic rather than firmly opposed.

2. I later learnt, to my great delight, that I am not intolerant to gluten but that eating two bowls of Bran Flakes a day will mimic the symptoms, and merely cutting them out of my diet and (weirdly) stopping watching daytime television returned my bowels to normal.

3. Genius bread is not the only genius in the consumer world. I would argue the most recognisable use of the word 'genius' is the Apple Genius Bar. A successful sub-patent of the Apple mega-brand, in the early days these bars would be manned by 'Geniuses', which would comprise of a 'Lead Genius' (a technical manager) and 'Genius Admins' (secretaries) who would be responsible for the paperwork. Alas, at time of writing, Apple's website now seems to have demoted all of these people to the less impressive 'expert' (particularly irksome for me as disposing of experts was my main reason for voting Leave). I'm unsure when this change occurred or why, but I feel for those poor staff members returning home to their families to say they are no longer geniuses – a brutal kick in the teeth from Tim Cook, almost as brutal as the working conditions in some Chinese factories. To be fair to Apple management, I have been to the Genius Bar on a handful of occasions and can confirm that the staff, while lovely, are now correctly categorised. They seem to have an extensive knowledge of the Apple software, but their hardware abilities are nowhere near as impressive, oft resulting in the solution being an entire replacement. I am not comfortable putting the work of Darwin or Einstein on the same level as the phrase 'rather than fix this iPad, I will just give you a new iPad'.

Fig. 3 *I drink a crisp, cold glass of lager in a pool in Los Angeles while Gary Lineker looks on in disgust*, acrylic on bonnet of Vauxhall Corsa, approx. 1 × 3mm.

Fig. 3

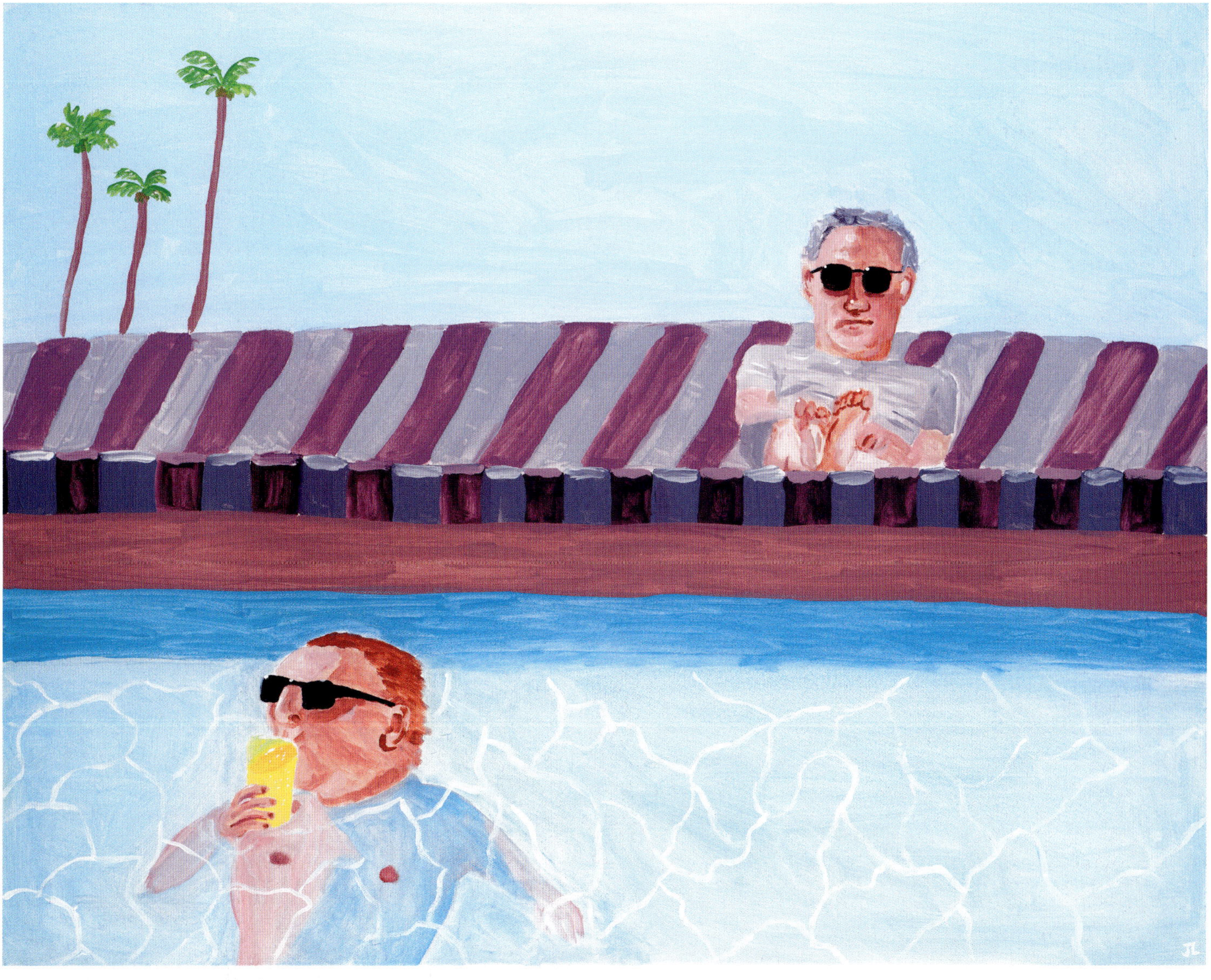

Anyway, I met Gary Lineker in the gluten-free aisle of the big Tesco in Padstow on the A389 and we got chatting, at first about my Hotpoint H55RM1110W1 Fridge in white that doesn't seem to be getting as cold as it used to. As soon as I'd started speaking, I realised I had taken a wrong turn, and quickly changed the subject to something he would find interesting. You might not know this about me, but I am actually very knowledgeable about football (if FIFA had the intellectual property rights to use the term, they might describe me as a 'genius', lol) and in particular Lineker's club Leicester City (named after the City of Leicester). He seemed visibly stunned when I explained how impressed I was with their historic Premier League win in 2016, of course massively helped by the exceptional and consistent skill of Jamie Vardy over that unforgettable season, but surely a nod should go to management for their sustained commitment to youth development and scouting of talented young players. 'I wonder,' I said to Gary, who was visibly enthralled by me, 'if you feel that Vardy is the definitive and iconic Leicester City player, or whether that title should go to the legendary goalkeeper Gordon Banks, or perhaps even your good self?' He suggested we discuss it over a Costa coffee.

Of the major high street coffee brands – which I determine to be Starbucks, Costa and Caffè Nero – I would consider Costa to be the lowest rent. I am not basing this on the coffee itself as I am not a coffee aficionado and will happily drink instant. But, in my experience, the average Costa customer is subject to an almost daily change of whimsical syrup options and novelty flavours. In addition to the perennial classics (Americano, latte, cappuccino, etc.), it appears to me that on any given day you can go into a Costa and be offered a 'seasonal bonfire spiced latte', then the next day a mocha 'made in collaboration with Quality Street', then the next day be presented with a limited-edition 'ruby' hot chocolate. Putting aside the fact that 'ruby' and 'bonfire' are not flavours accessible to the human tongue, all of this constant change smacks of desperation and ultimately results in a feeling of tawdry classlessness. Even outside of the revolving novelty drinks selection, there are a dazzling number of flavours that seem to be available year-round. The great lord herself only knows how long the less popular syrups have been up there on the shelf, gathering dust and allergens – a destiny this book surely shares.

Starbucks is guilty of this insane desire for novelty too, yet somehow it manages to appear more restrained. I know, for example, that I will be unable to drink a gingerbread latte from Starbucks in March, yet Costa will be more than happy to give me a Christmas nutmeg flavoured drink at the height of summer. It makes me want to say to Costa: 'Get a grip.'[1]

1. Having said all that, a glance at the Starbucks website reveals a bunch of new products I've never heard of, including the seeming latest fad of merging their drinks with extra virgin olive oil, so perhaps adding various gunk into coffee is an industry-wide trend.

Fig. 4 The famous ribbed Costa coffee cup.

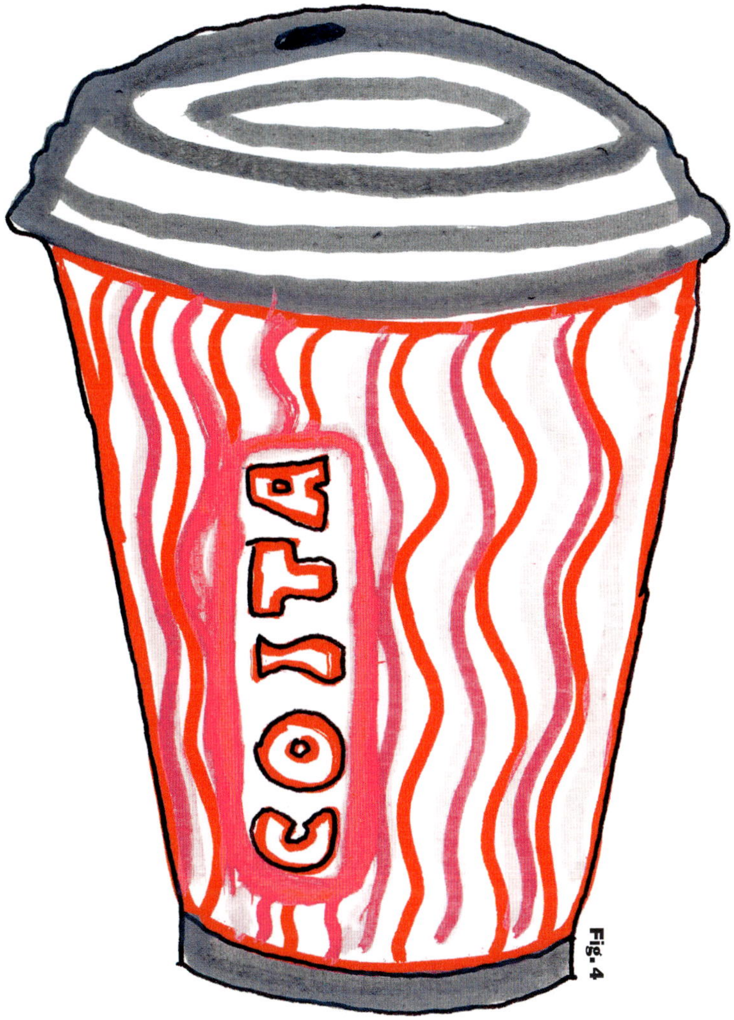

Fig. 4

Whereas Costa seems to want to accommodate absolutely everyone, the occasional rigidity of Starbucks and the sheer global success of the brand can come off as smug. There's a feeling of quality, yes, but also you suspect at times that they think they are simply too good for you. I can't speak for you, reader, but I know I am far better than the concept of Starbucks.

And then there's Caffè Nero. Refreshingly familiar, open and honest, like Nick Clegg was for those three weeks in 2010. For a start, it is the only establishment that has the word 'cafe' in its name (I'm not sure why they added the second 'f', but even that feels authentic). They are noisy, bristling places, with giant black and white photographs taken in the 90s of bronzed Italian-looking people who are now almost certainly dead. Sure, their menu has some new stuff on it from time to time, but it is promoted in a small square at the bottom, far away from the classics, as if to say: 'We will accommodate you, whimsical syrup fan, but we refuse to encourage you.' The ceramic cups for in-store drinking feel comfortably ancient, the blue of the takeaway cups is far more pleasing and aspirational than the dirty purples and sad greens of the other two.[1]

Nero isn't perfect by any means: they have the ability to feel cold, messy and often filthy. They are filled with grey plastic washing trays and frayed wicker chairs. The Roman emperor Nero was a thug. But their mess is perhaps their charm. To conclude: when forced to drink coffee at a high street cafe, I opt for Nero.

Anyway, all of the above meant that when Gary Lineker said we should meet in Costa to discuss the careers of Jamie Vardy and Gordon Banks, I flat out said, 'No.' In hindsight, I should have given him a reason, or suggested Nero, but for some reason I just said 'No' again a couple of times and then walked right out of the Tesco Superstore in Padstow on the A389. Years later, we both stayed in the same hotel in Los Angeles and while I was in the pool sipping a crisp, cold, glutinous beer my friend took a picture of me while Gary looked on, appearing furious. This is a painting of that picture.

1. Costa, I concede, does impress with their (surely patented) ribbed cup, which entirely eliminates the need for the additional cardboard sleeves which Starbucks and Caffè Nero are obliged to provide. Preference for ribbed or classic cup I expect comes down to personal taste – some people won't want the faff of additional paperwork, but there will be those with asbestos-palms who want the option to go sleeveless, either because the temperature of the drink deems it unnecessary, or to demonstrate to the wider world their ability to absorb extreme heat into their fingers.

Fig. 5 A map of the location of the Tesco Superstore in Padstow on the A389.
Fig. 6 A drawing I did of my faulty Hotpoint H55RM1110W1. Personally, I think this drawing is shit.

Fig. 5

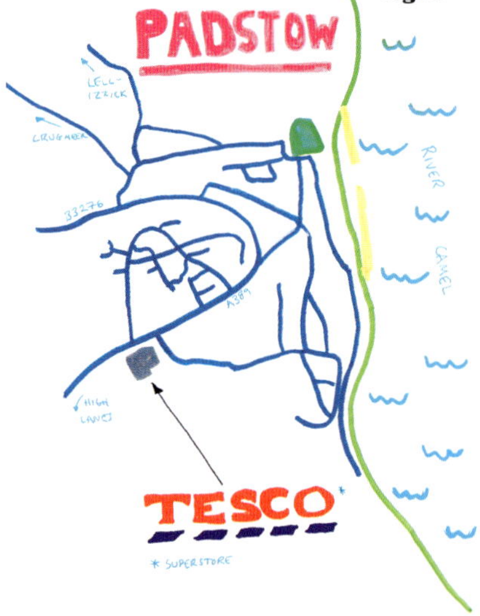

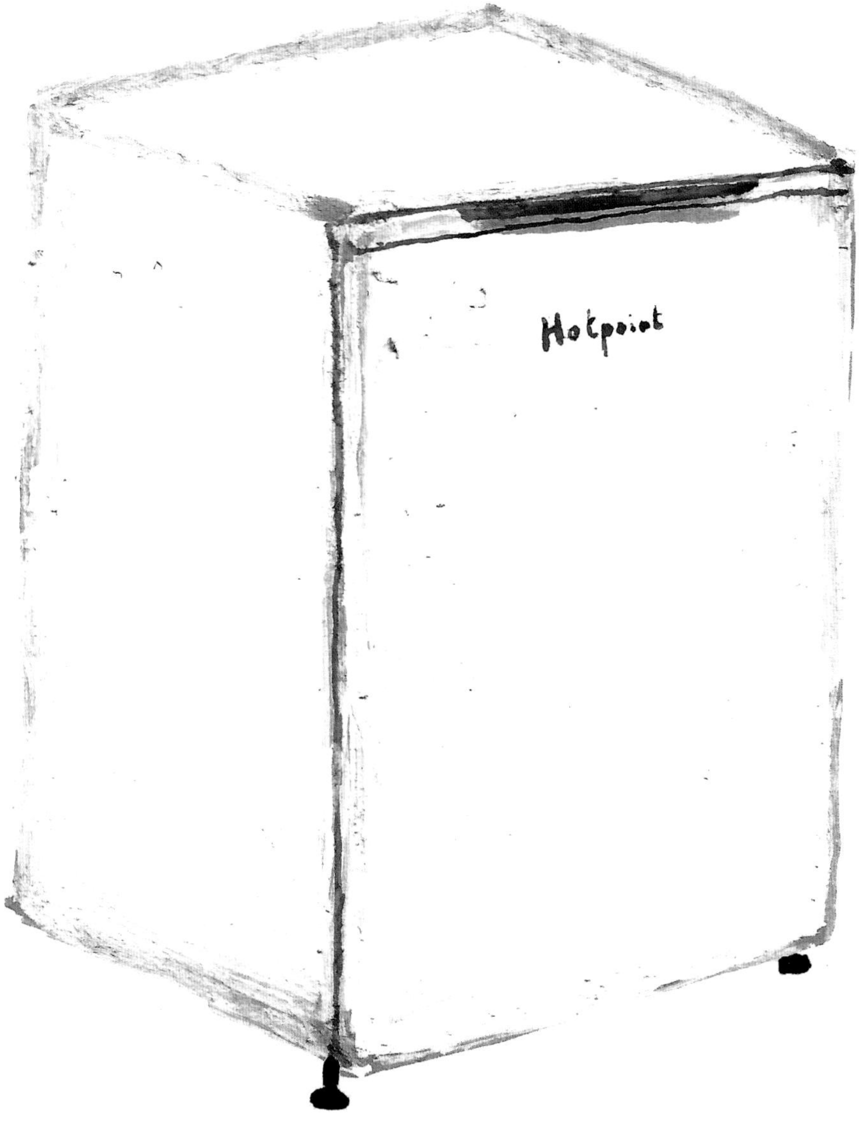

Fig. 6

a crisp,
cold gold

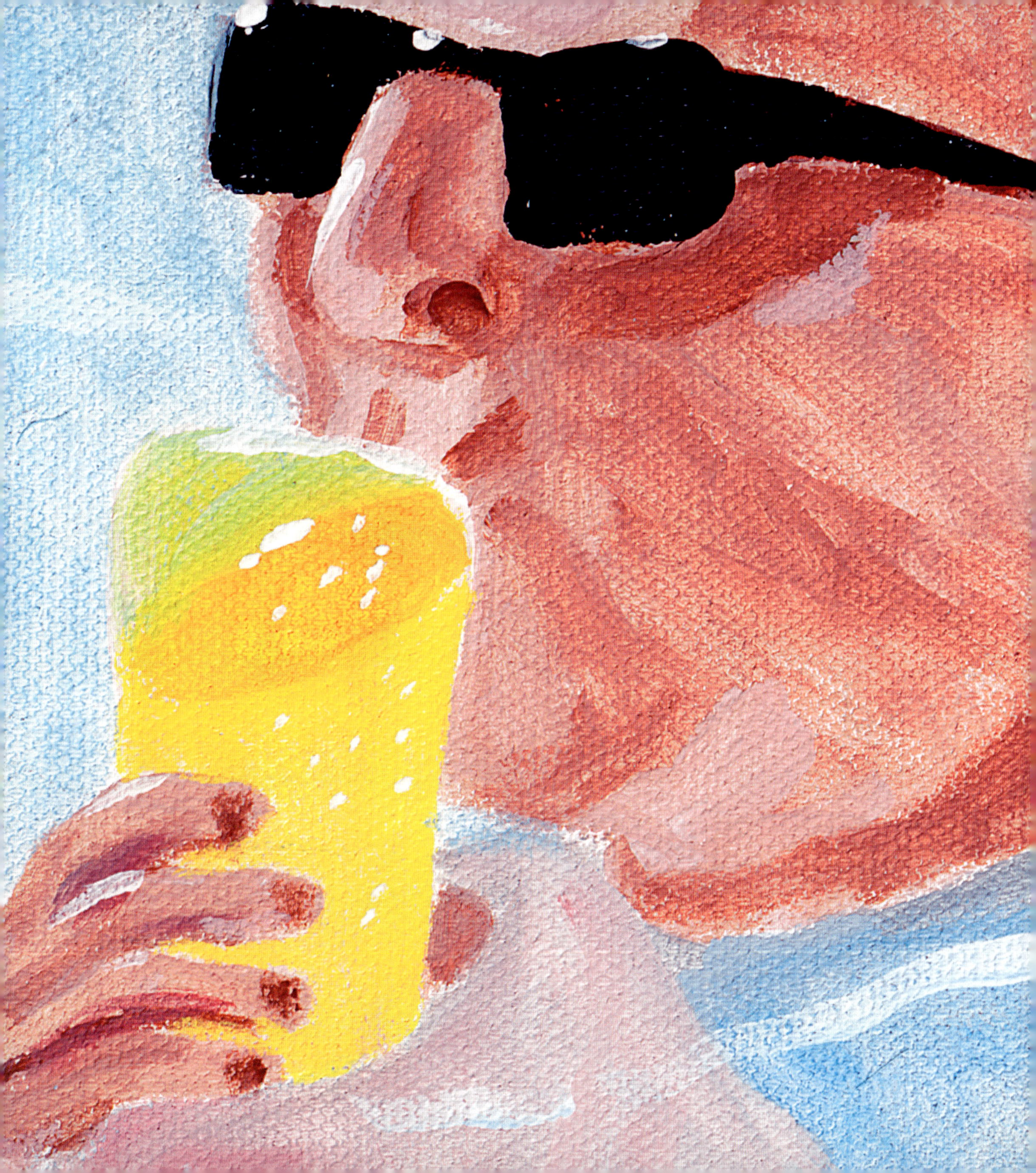

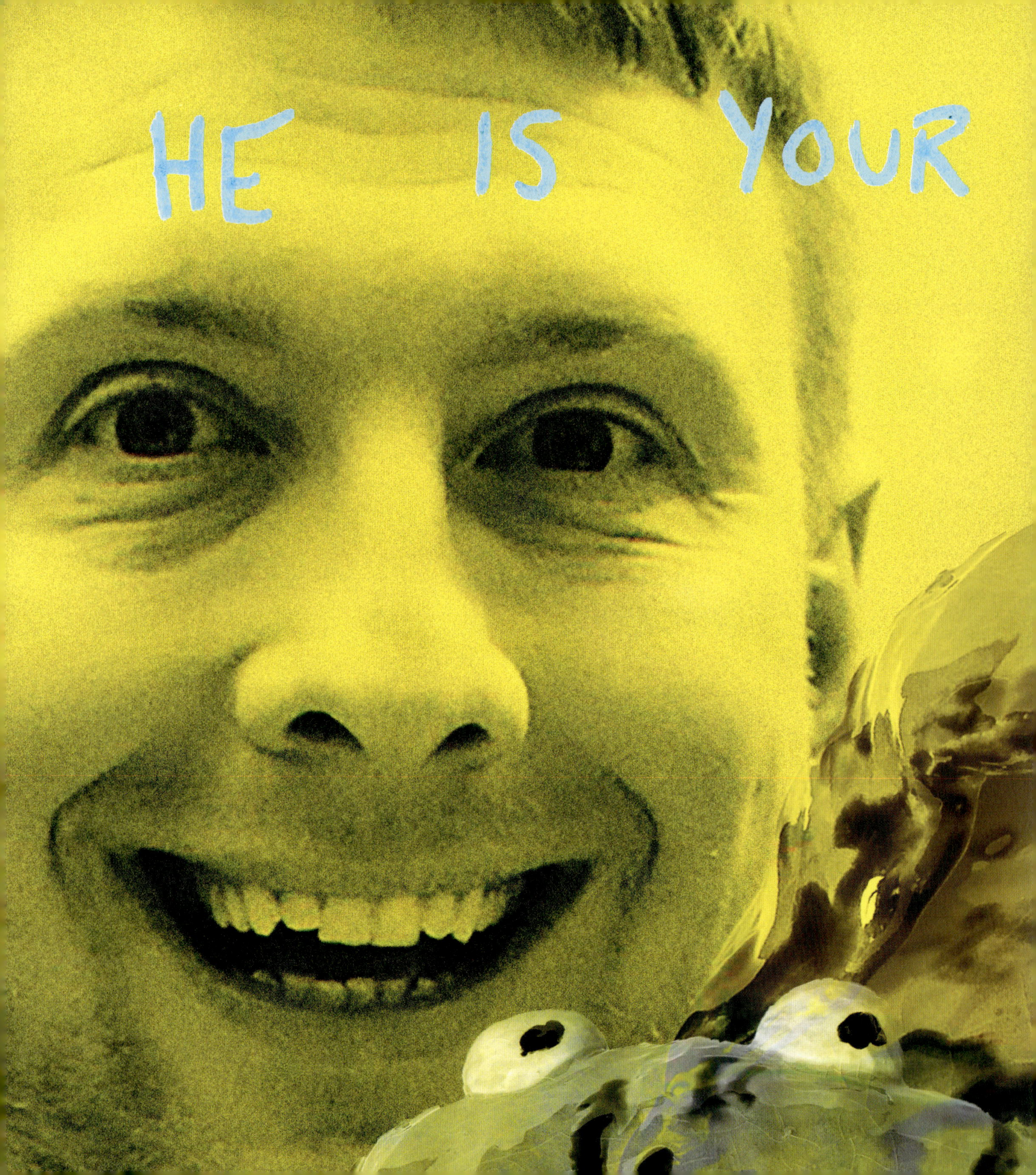
HE IS YOUR

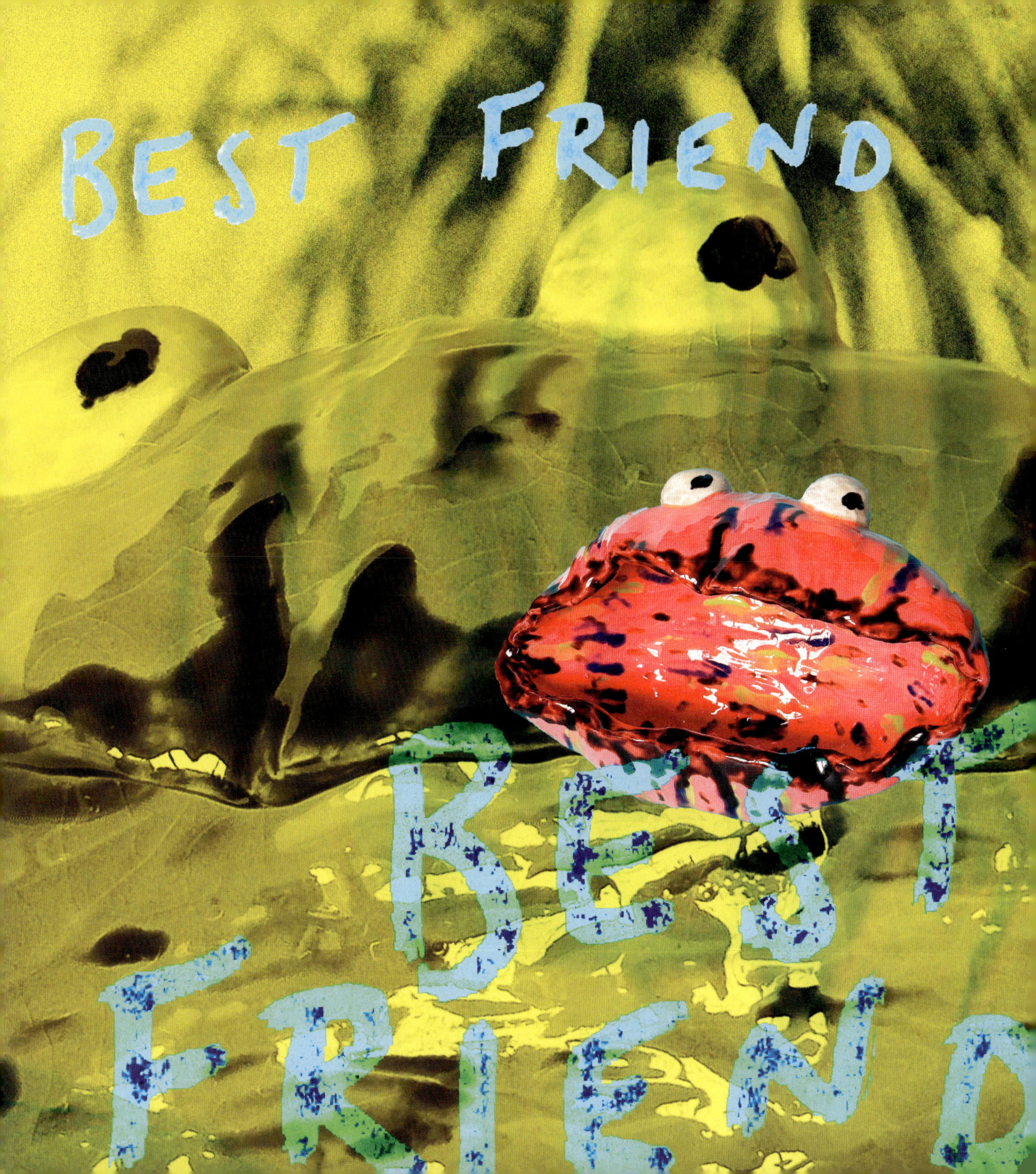
BEST FRIEND
BEST FRIEND

LORD ALAN SUGAR

To describe my relationship with Lord Alan Sugar as love/hate would be to do it a disservice. I would instead say we are two raging bulls locked in a perpetual and never-ending feud, something akin to Pepsi and Coke, Aldi and Lidl or Ruth Langsford and Holly Willoughby. We are enemies, yes, and yet the extermination of either of us will likely eradicate the other.

I met him briefly once at a recording of the TV programme *The Apprentice: You're Fired!*, to which he had turned up unannounced (apparently something that he did not irregularly). He was stern and curt, and I was surprised to see that he is not a tall man; if he was stood on the other side of a football pitch he would probably be about the size of a uni-ball UB-150-10 Blk PFP GZ pen if you held it on its side and at arm's length. This might seem a strange way to measure someone, but portrait artists will know this is the only way to measure accurately. From that moment, I was delirious with the desire to paint him.

Ten years came and went, then my phone pinged with a message from none other than Lord Sugar, saying that he was filming *The Apprentice* in Birmingham that day, but that the episode was 'dragging on fucking longer than my fucking arse', which I didn't really understand as a phrase. I told him he'd be very welcome in the orangery for a glass of something and he replied straight away 'do you have crisps', so I wrote 'yes, I have crisps' and he said 'what sort of crisps', and I wrote 'McCoy's crisps' and he wrote 'what flavour of McCoy's crisps', and I said 'flame grilled steak and cheddar and onion McCoy's crisps and actually I've got one bag of the chip shop curry sauce flavour too'. He was there within twenty minutes.

His mood was more jocular on this occasion, making cheeky little jokes and nibbling his crisps. He'd say things like, 'I'm just going to run to the loo – no, actually I'll walk!' and then giggle to himself, giddy with delight. It was lucky I'd bought a multipack of crisps[1] because he must've got through six or seven bags before he left, all while skittishly sliding along the kitchen tiles in his socks.

Sugar was getting high on crisps, whereas I was getting a little tipsy, thanks to a perfectly agreeable Chablis. At one point, the crisp dry white took over and I punctured the convivial mood with a question that silenced him: 'Might you sit for a painting, Lord Sugar?' He stopped in his tracks, crunched the crisp that was still in his mouth purposefully, swallowed then said, 'You fucking what?'

1. He emptied all the packets of Chip Shop Curry Sauce, Thai Sweet Chicken and Mexican Chilli into the toilet because of 'Brexit'.

Fig. 7 *Alan Sugar Staring at You Through a Skylight*, 2020, acrylic gouache on glass (window of Greggs), 1 × 3m.

Fig. 7

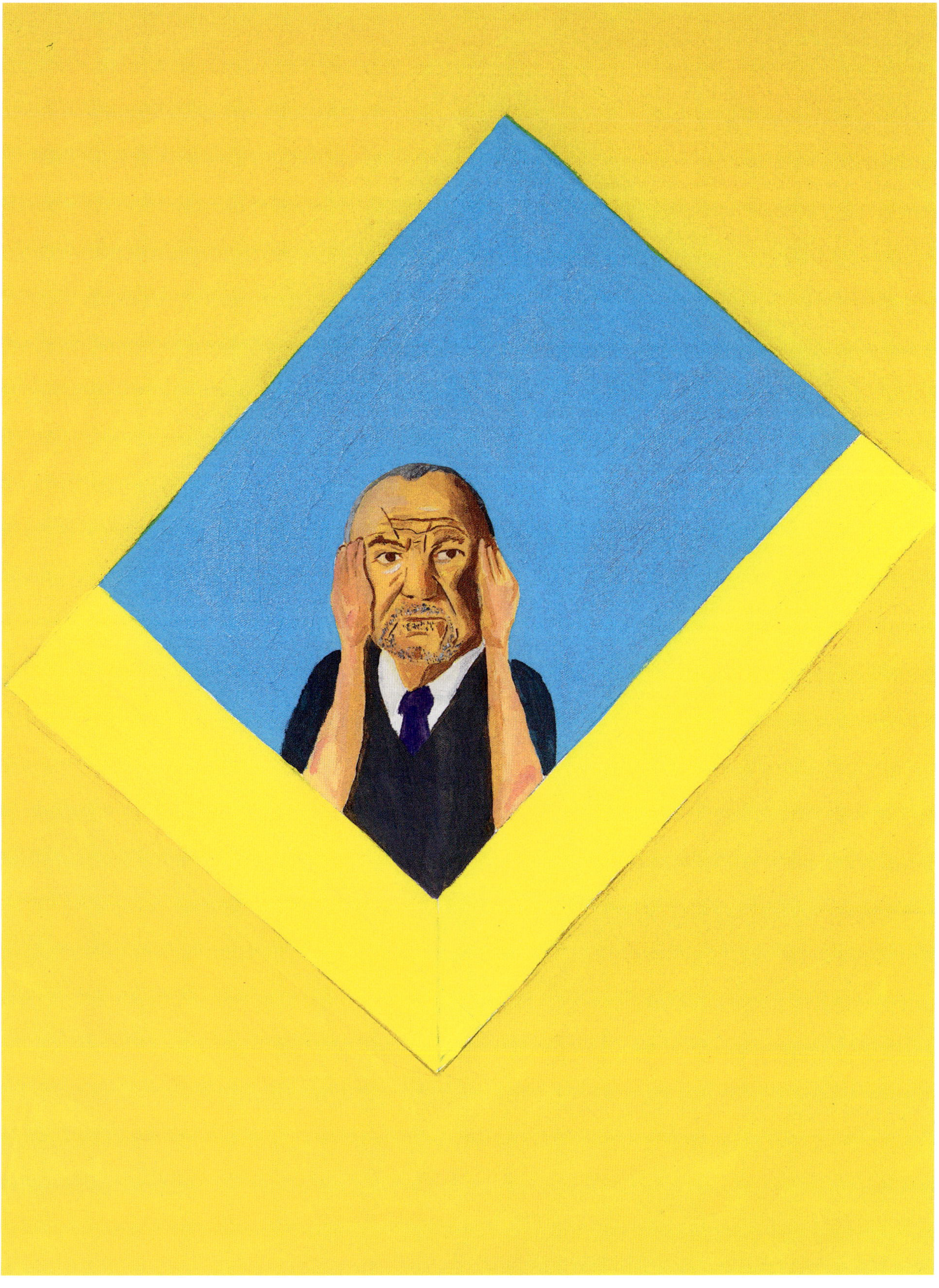

‘I mean … we don’t have to … just … I like to paint …’

‘I’m just joshing with you, you fucking art nonce. I’d love to.’ He giggled again.

The relief was intense. I beckoned him towards an armchair but he had other ideas. ‘Nah, fuck that. I’m gonna hide. Try and paint me while I hide.’

‘Paint you while you hide? How would I even—’ It was too late. He was already jaunting up the stairs, chuckling to himself like a little gremlin (from the film *Gremlins*).

I heard his animated footsteps above me on the landing, like the excitable scuttling of a toddler on Christmas morning. I shouted up, ‘Alan, come on now. Don’t be silly.’ I could hear things falling off shelves.

‘Catch me, you fucker! Tehehe!’ came the impish reply, followed by more pitter-patter and the turning of doorknobs. ‘You’re a fucking postman,’ he yelped. Then, ‘Your dad is good with electrics but probably couldn’t do a full rewire.’ I have learnt from occasionally looking after my friend’s children and through various public engagements with Rob Beckett that you cannot pander to this sort of behaviour – you must ignore it. I retired to the kitchen.[1]

I sat and sipped my Chablis, hoping he would eventually run out of steam, but the sniggering upstairs crescendoed with every passing moment, more doors opening, things falling, a couple of smashes, a couple of cries of ‘Put the heating on, you paedo,’ before the man stopped, followed by about four minutes of total and concerning silence.

Then three sinister taps, as if from a fingernail on glass. Where was it coming from? Three more, followed by tittering that sounded like it was coming from outside. I glanced out at the garden at the restless summer afternoon, lengthened shadows under a blue sky. No one was there. Another chuckle. It was coming from above.

I looked up, and there, in the dwindling afternoon, in my kitchen skylight, was Lord Alan Sugar, squealing with delight. ‘You fucking found me, tehehehe!’ he beamed. I cannot underestimate, dear reader, that for him to achieve this would have required some considerable gymnastics; that skylight is normally only accessible via a tall ladder.[2]

‘Don’t move,’ I shouted up. ‘I will paint you in that exact position!’ As I looked above at him, despite being at least twelve feet away and through a sheet of bulletproof glass (installed for security purposes after a threatening message from Sue Barker), in some strange way I felt we were closer than ever. He seemed so vulnerable. Perhaps he and I aren’t that different after all, I pondered; both trying to find approval from a faceless and unpredictable TV audience, pushing out our chests and pretending we’re big and clever, when really we’re

1. By ‘retired’ I mean I ‘moved’, not leaving my job and/or ceasing work. When I retire in the work sense, I will unavoidably spend a small percentage of it in the kitchen, but intend to spend much more of it outside of the kitchen, and so I anticipate it will never be appropriate or accurate for me to say that I am going to retire to the kitchen.

2. I later learnt that he had climbed out the window of the attic bathroom and scaled the guttering down two floors and onto the top of the kitchen. A very dangerous move, and all while holding two bags of McCoy’s crisps.

Fig. 8 McCoy’s crisps.
Fig. 9 McCoy’s crisps.

Fig. 8

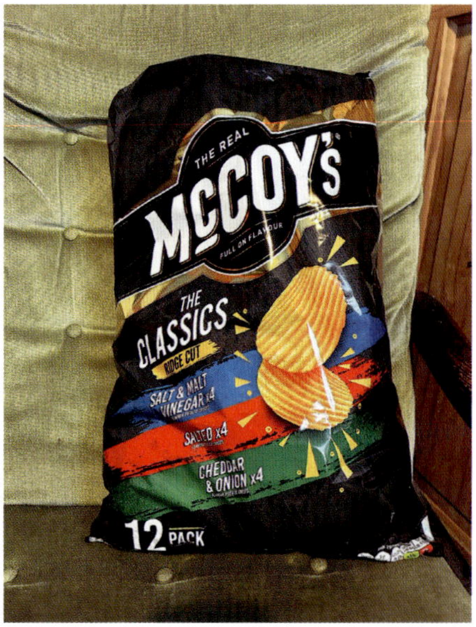

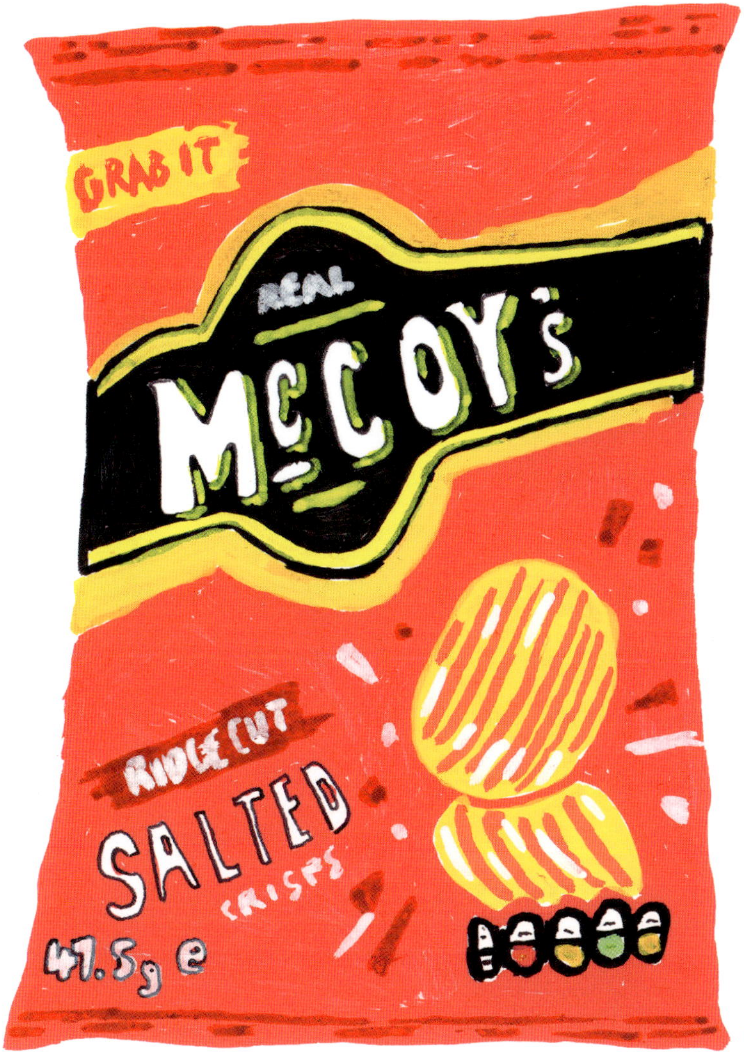

Fig. 9

neither (definitely not big in his case). When it comes to it, we are just frightened little children clambering for love, in all the wrong ways, playing our games, giggling at our pranks, lost in simple pleasures, pretending we don't care.

The resulting painting, I'm sure you'll agree, is a remarkable and accomplished feat of artistic engineering. Lord Sugar's expression became far less amused, almost despondent (he had to remain in position on top of my kitchen skylight for three hours – he was cold and had run out of crisps so was eating the moss from my roof tiles). I think it is a more accurate depiction of the man than any I have seen.

He left, quietly, leaving ten grand in cash on the kitchen counter for any damages before being collected by a Toyota Yaris – an Uber Pool that I believe dropped everyone else off first, contributing further to his furious mood. After the painting was released, an offer to buy it came in the form of a telephone call from a mysterious stranger called Lord Albert Succulent. I knew it was Alan because his name immediately came up on my phone, but the offer was a measly £1.8 mil and so I politely declined.

Fig. 10 An aggressive note from Sue Barker.
Fig. 11 Lord Alan Sugar's schedule, (hand-written after four packets of crisps).

Fig. 10

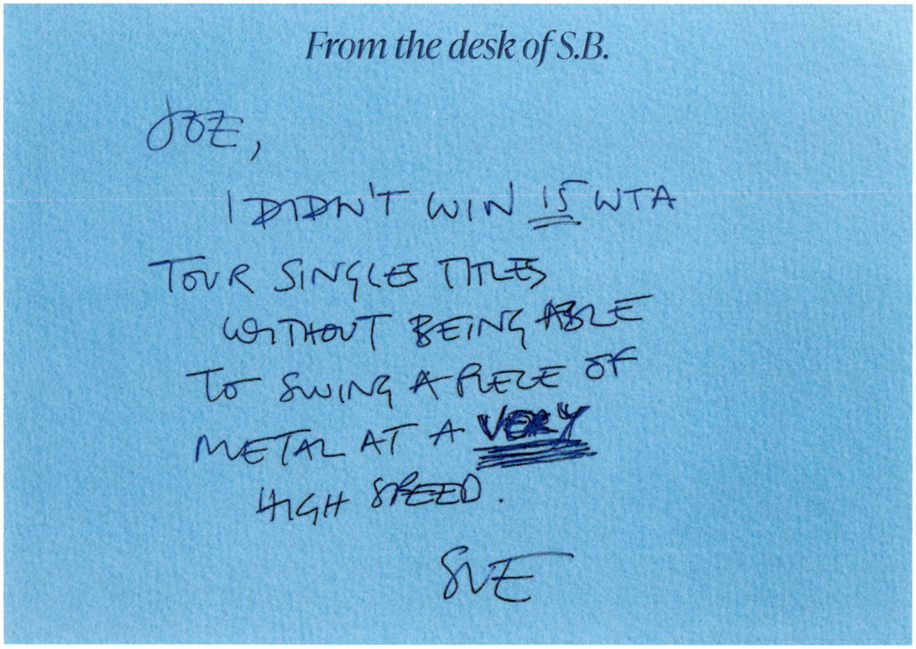
From the desk of S.B.

JOE,

I DIDN'T WIN 15 WTA TOUR SINGLES TITLES WITHOUT BEING ABLE TO SWING A PIECE OF METAL AT A VERY HIGH SPEED.

SUE

Fig. 11

4am - wake with a start, hot and confused from terrifying nightmare. Eat crisps to calm.

5am - return to beautiful, deep, nourishing sleep.

10am - wake properly, send hate tweets and one or two promoting some piece of shit business, crisps

10:30 am - breakfast of crisps

10:45 am - call Karen Brady to check she's bringing crisps.

10:50 am - call Claude and make sure he's going to help Karen load crisps into the van

11:00 am - meetings about some piece of shit business, with crisps

1:30 pm - lunch (tuna nicoise, small glass of rosé from Provence, crisps)

2:30 pm - light nap (Karen has her own key so quietly lets herself in and puts crisps away)

7pm - wake from light nap. Watch edits of The Apprentice with grab-bag of crisps.

8:30 pm - dinner with CEO of Budgens (Thai green curry, Mango, salad, crisps)

10 pm crisps

10:10 pm bed

10:20 pm crisps

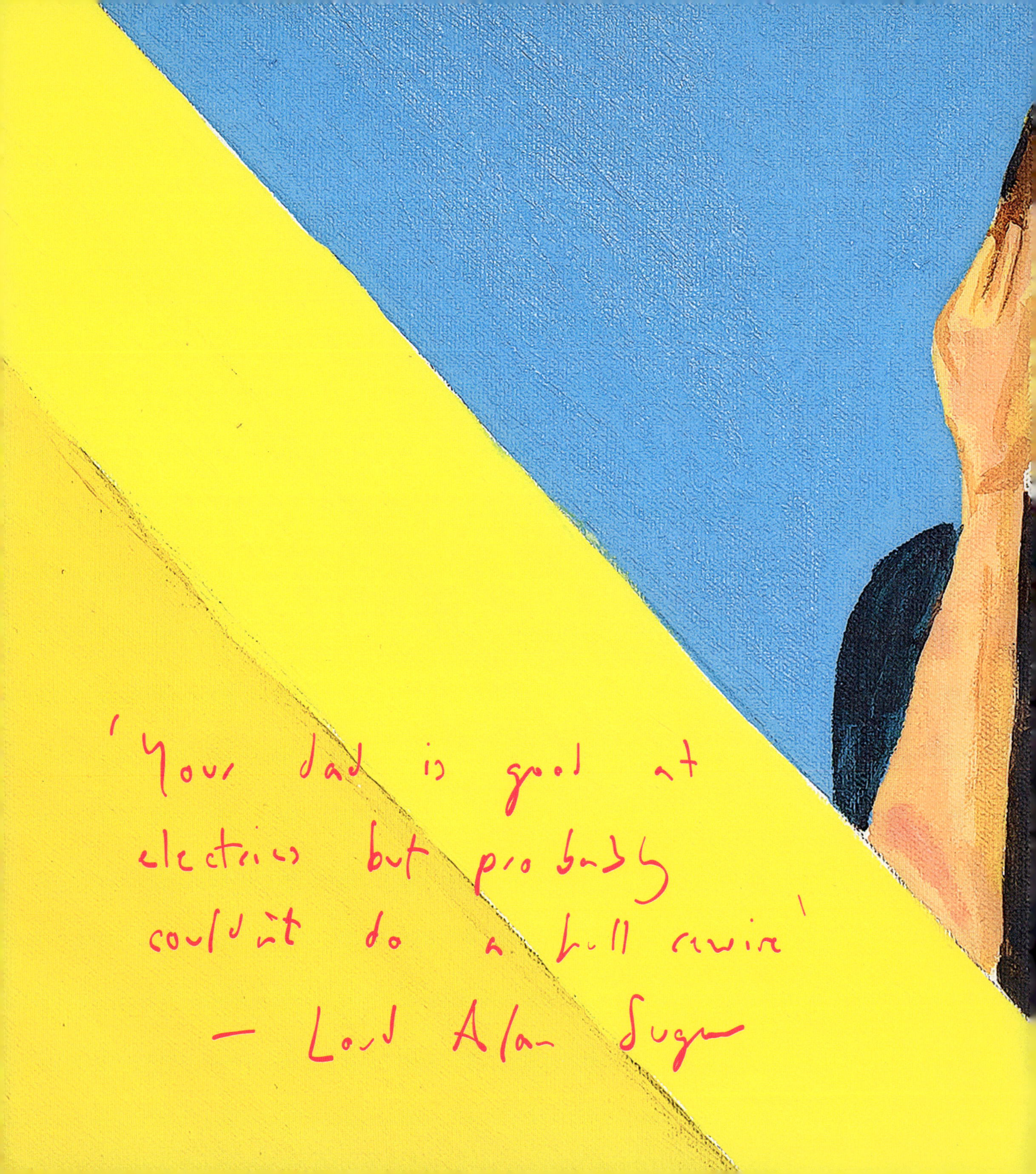
'Your dad is good at
electrics but probably
couldn't do a full rewire'
— Lord Alan Sugar

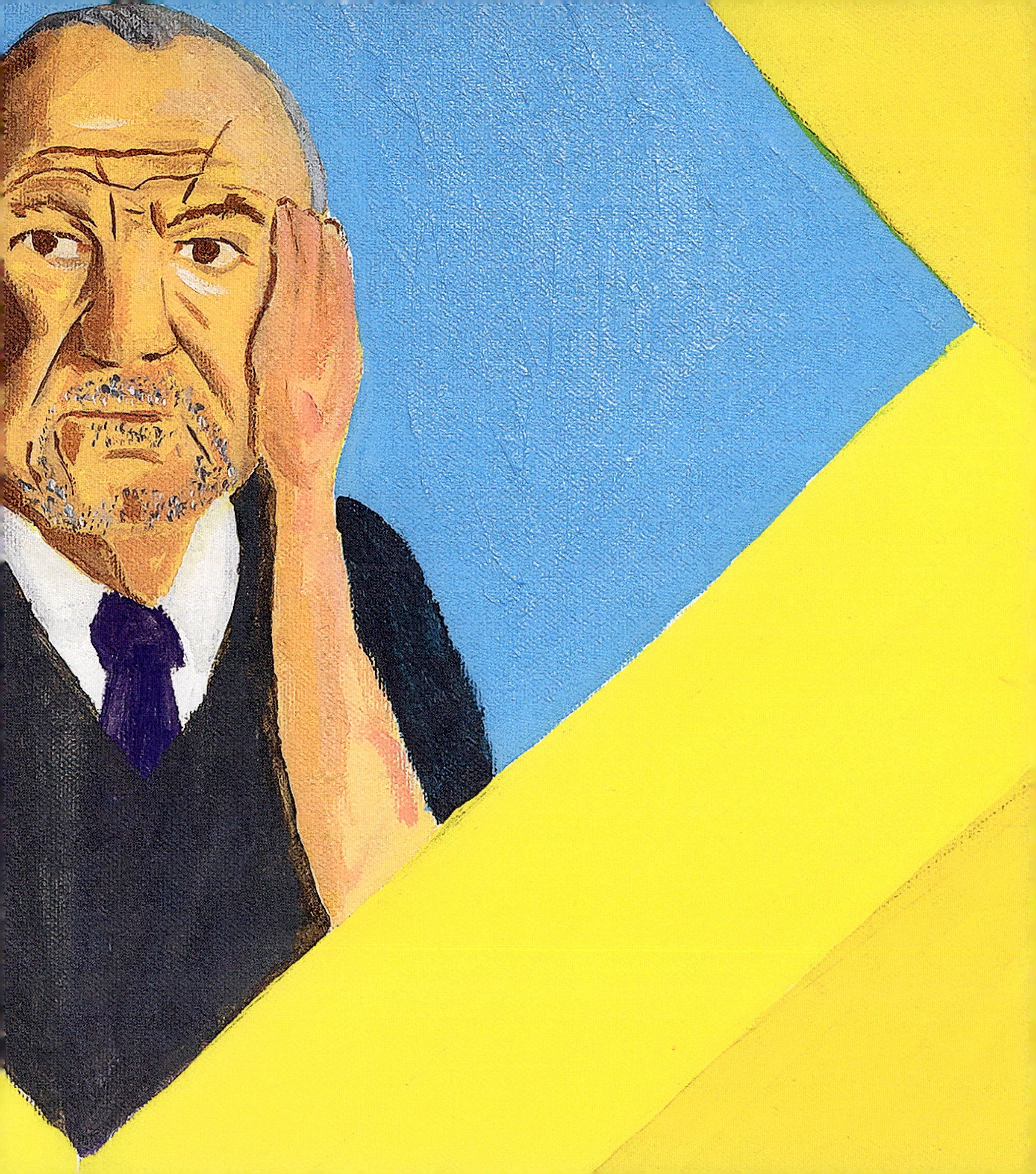

THE PRINCE, HIS ROYAL HIGHNESS PRINCE WILLIAM, THE PRINCE OF WALES, THE WELSH PRINCE, WELSH BILL, THE WHALE PRINCE

Many people refuse to believe that some of my subjects have actually sat for me, but of all my portraits the most disputed is that of Prince William, The Prince of Wales, The Welsh Prince, Welsh Bill, The Whale Prince. When I explain that it is indeed true that he invited me to his residential home in Windsor to do this portrait, I am met with disbelief. My mate Chris said that there are no official logs of it ever happening, or on the 'Royals' section of the Mail+ website, but I told Chris that he is not smart and that they don't keep logs of everything that goes on with the royals cause otherwise how would Prince Andrew get up to all the stuff he does, and also how would Chris even have access to royal logs when he lives in Tamworth and works in the back office of a Wickes?

I arrived at 9 a.m. as scheduled, but for the first hour I was walked around various rooms, which was really annoying as I kept having to put down and then pick up my bag.[1] At one point, a man who I think was called Ernest or Alfred or Sarah came and asked if I would like a cup of English Breakfast. I made a joke about how impressive it is that they can get a whole breakfast in one cup which didn't make him laugh, and I was left humiliated.

Finally, I was beckoned through to William's living quarters and was surprised to see that they were very basic. Essentially just a fatigued sofa (like the sort you see on the Rightmove images of a house someone has recently died in); a white plastic chair that you might find in the street in somewhere like Malaga or Benidorm and normally drenched in a pesto of un-evaporated rainwater mixed with sand and dirt; a thin Ercol wardrobe; and a Philips Airfryer.

1. Foolishly, I had taken an overfilled tote and really should've brought my backpack and carried the empty canvas under my arm.

Fig. 12 *The Prince, His Royal Highness Prince William, The Prince of Wales, The Welsh Prince, Welsh Bill, The Whale Prince,* 2023, acrylic on human arm, 3 × 4mm.

Fig. 12

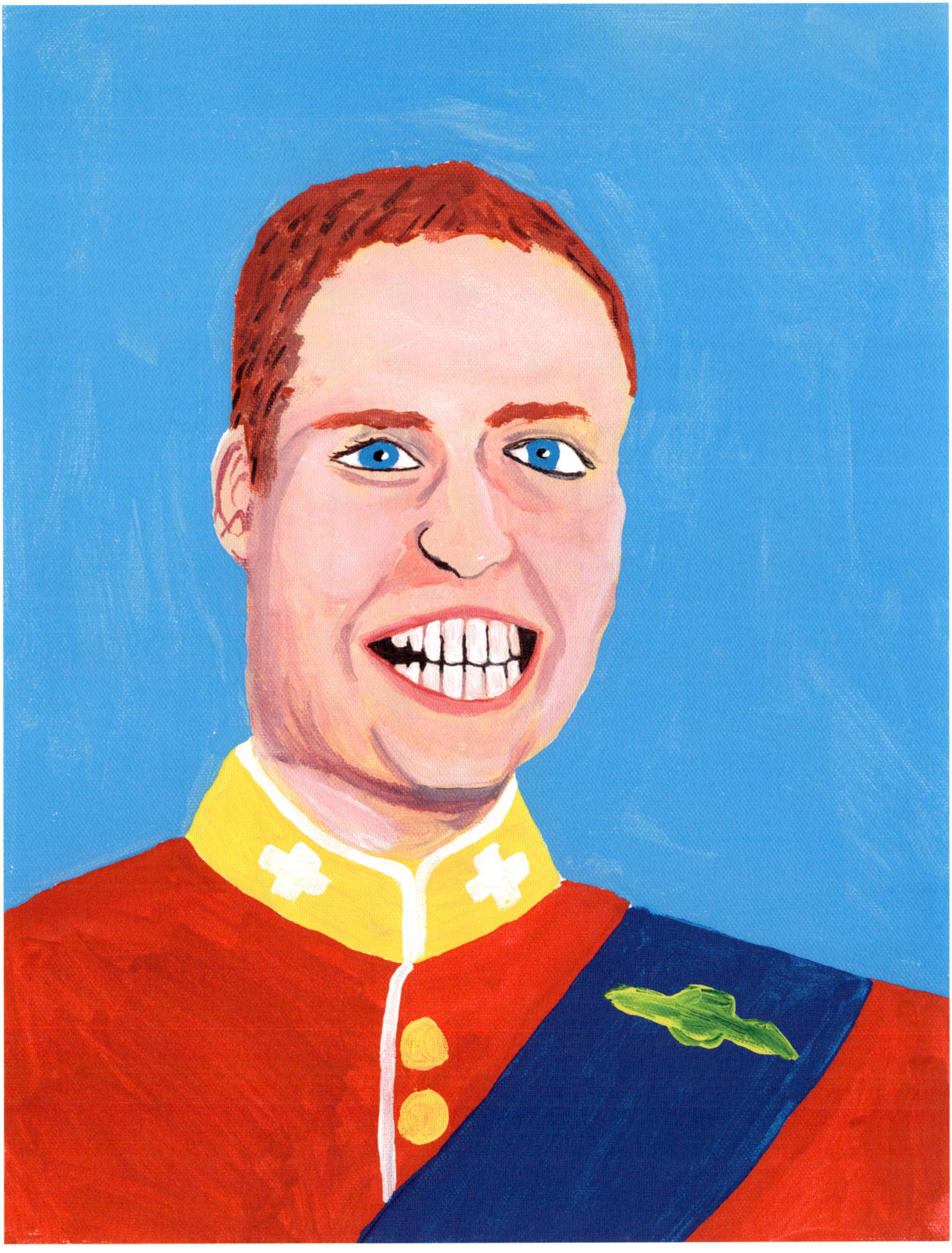

William greeted me with a warm, 'Ah yes, hello', and then placed his hand on the air fryer, which seemed to me a very strange opening gesture. His entire body language suggested he really wanted me to know about it. 'Are you familiar with the Philips Airfryer 5000 Series XXL Connected, boy?' he said, almost flirtatious.

'No, ma'am,' I replied nervously and erroneously.

'You refer to me as "Sir", boy,' he spat back. 'Nevertheless, the Philips Airfryer 5000 Series XXL Connected has sixteen different cooking functions including fry, bake, grill, roast, dehydrate, toast, defrost, reheat, ferment and more, and can even make yoghurt.' He delivered this as if it were a memorised script.

'Wow, yoghurt?' I was no longer nervous, but profoundly curious.

'Yes, boy, yoghurt.'

I must confess that whatever His Highness said over the next six to ten sentences will remain a mystery to me and, alas, will presumably be condemned to history. He could have been telling me the truth about Prince Andrew, or bemoaning the Philips Airfryer 5000 Series XXL Connected's lack of built-in rotisserie. I heard none of it. Rather than focus on the present moment, my mind chose to spiral almost uncontrollably towards thinking about the texture, taste and production of yoghurt,[1] my happy place. I love yoghurt, and in more recent years have been seduced by the tubs boasting 20g of protein, such as a Skyr,[2] which I got into after Stephen Mulhern gave me a discount code for a dozen tubs.

I steered my mind to the present and suggested we begin. 'Will this outfit do?' he asked. He was naked.

'I think maybe you should put something on?' I suggested. 'Do you have a shawl or a gown?'

He began rummaging in the Ercol wardrobe and pulled out his wedding outfit. 'This?'

I nodded.

He began pulling on the trousers, which was an uncomfortable watch as his toes kept getting jammed into the cuffs of the left leg. He would mutter things like, 'Stupid fucking trousers', before shouting, 'Kate!' at an open window. The shouts went unanswered, although I am sure I heard someone in a neighbouring room turning up the sound on an episode of *Cash in the Attic*.

I traced His Royal Highness's outline in BiC biro, an ancient technique favoured by Caravaggio – although I read he preferred a pencil probably like the Staedtler HB 120-2 BK5D (manufacturing code likely different in his era but correct at time of writing). I made sure to add more hair than in real life because I was told by palace staff that if

1. Yoghurt is one of the great staples of my diet, alongside cherry tomatoes, almonds, smoked salmon, tripe, boiled rice, avocado and Kit-Kats (served together in a bowl). I tend to prefer a traditional Greek yoghurt and have never tolerated the uneasy term 'Greek style' – this simply means the yoghurt hasn't been strained to remove the whey but instead is thickened with gelatin or similar. Simply throwing around the words 'Greek style' and daubing a subpar Aegean or Greek Mediterranean design on the tub does not make me feel like I'm having an authentic Greek experience any more than me describing this book as 'Booker Prize style' makes the judges believe it deserves one.

2. The Skyr experience is not without its difficulties: I remember being told that as a food-stuff it has been considered for years to be a very basic and unimpressive by-product of butter in most Icelandic communities (in the same way Paddy McGuinness is a very basic and unimpressive by-product of Peter Kay in British communities), and while similar to yoghurt in texture, it is, in fact, a type of soft cheese. The rebranding of it in Britain as a recently discovered health food causes some amusement to the Icelandic. Thus, I enjoy it almost secretly, generally in the privacy of my own home or behind a newspaper if I am attending a public engagement (funerals and so on).

Fig. 13 A drawing I did of the Philips Airfryer 5000 Series XXL Connected on my iPad (iPad means 'internet Pad').
Fig. 14 A photograph I took of the Philips Airfryer 5000 Series XXL Connected on my iPhone (iPhone stands for 'internet Phone').
Fig. 15 Here I am with the Philips Airfryer 5000 Series XXL Connected.

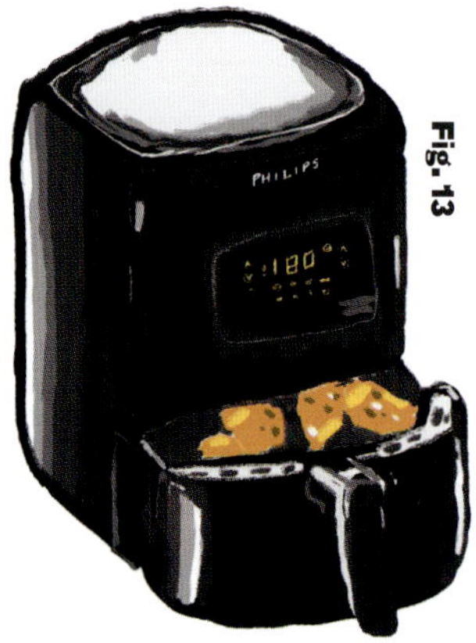

Fig. 13

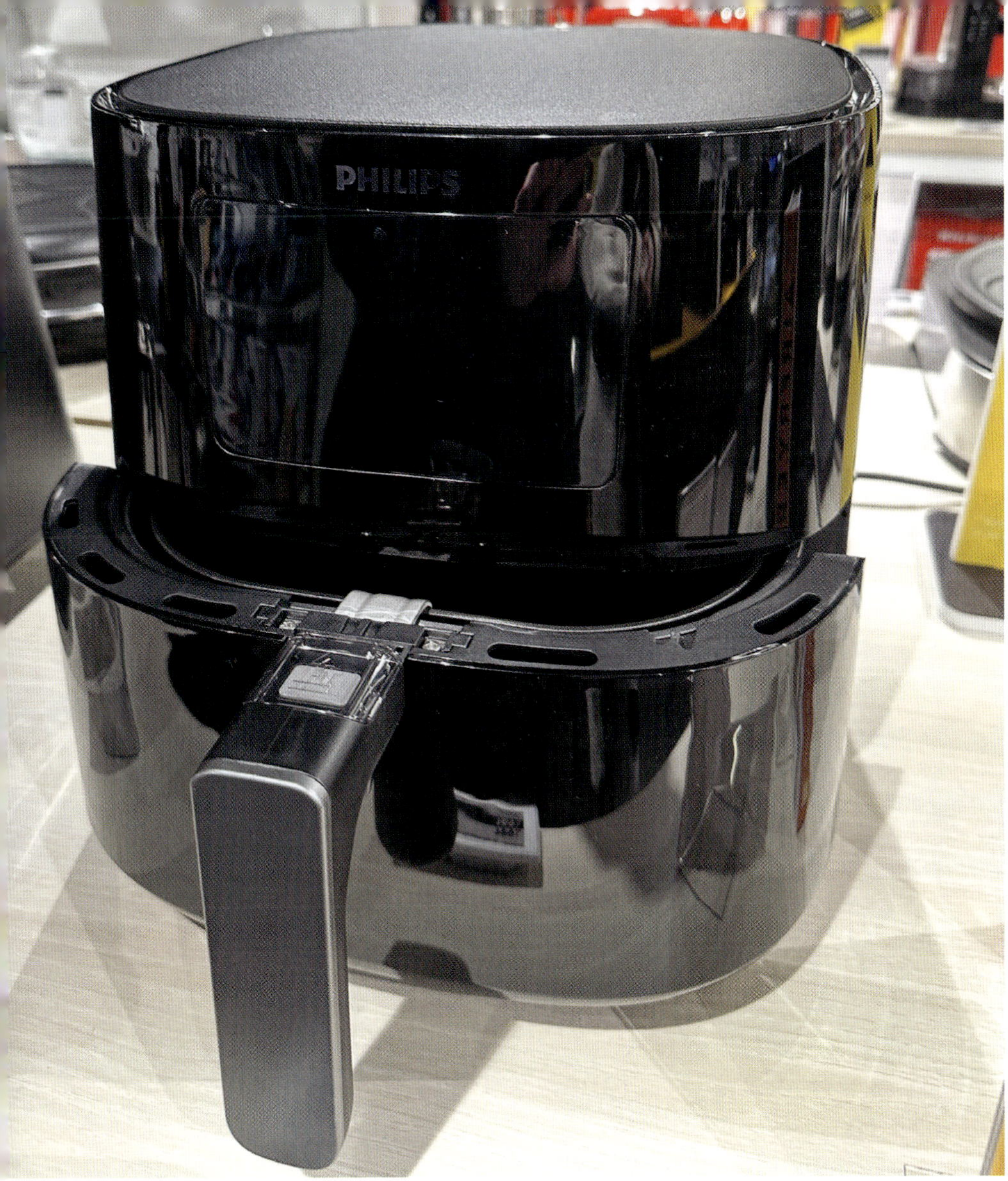

Fig. 14

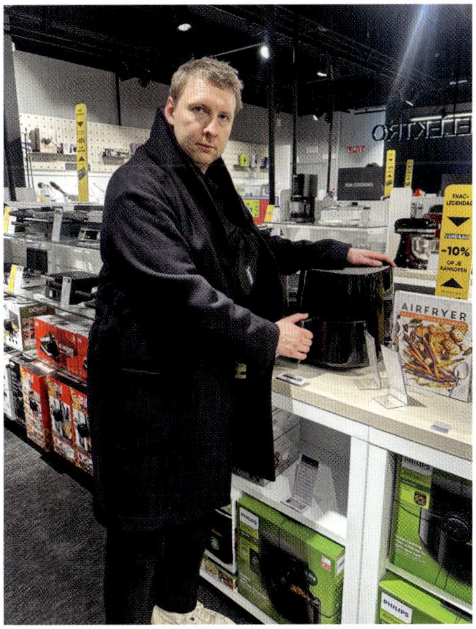

Fig. 15

I didn't, they could make life very difficult for me, but I think that threw off my ratios, which is the only explanation for why his teeth came out as they did and why his left eye is entirely fucked.

I tried my hardest to ask him about his thoughts on the concept of monarchy etc., but all he wanted to discuss was the Philips Airfryer 5000 Series XXL Connected. We did briefly discuss flavours of Rustlers and my Hotpoint H55RM1110W1 Fridge in white, because at that point it wasn't cooling properly, but the Philips Airfryer Series 5000 XXL Connected was the only thing that managed to animate the future king. He explained that to make yoghurt in it, you add milk and a spoon of pre-existing yoghurt with live cultures in it, leave it for a few hours at around forty-three degrees centigrade and it will ferment into a delicious yoghurt. I enquired as to the logic of making yoghurt if, in order to make yoghurt, he'd have to buy a yoghurt, and why not just eat the first yoghurt, but that confused and almost angered him. I could feel the atmosphere in the room curdling, rather like yoghurt. I rushed the rest of the painting and left.

When I got home I was intrigued, and so tried making yoghurt in my air fryer (not the Philips Airfryer 5000 Series XXL Connected but the Tower T17088 Vortx 9L Duo Basket Air Fryer with Smart Finish, 2600W Power in black), and it definitely had the mouthfeel of yoghurt, but the taste of a dead owl.

Fig. 16

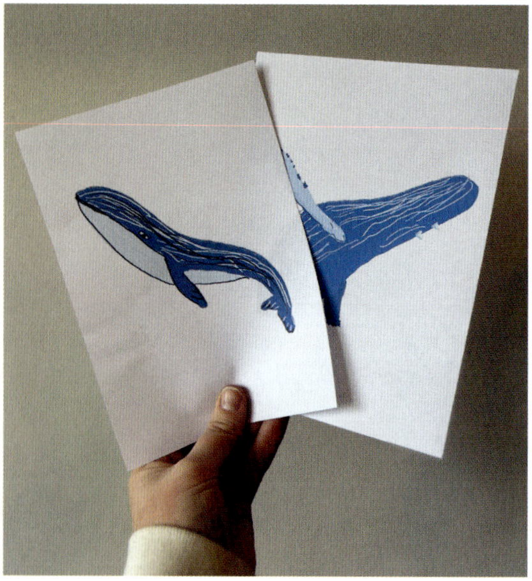

Fig. 16 The Prints of Whales.

Fig. 17 Prince William's dad, painted on a separate occasion. *All New King*, 2023, acrylic on copy of *Woman & Home*, 21 × 29cm.

Fig. 17

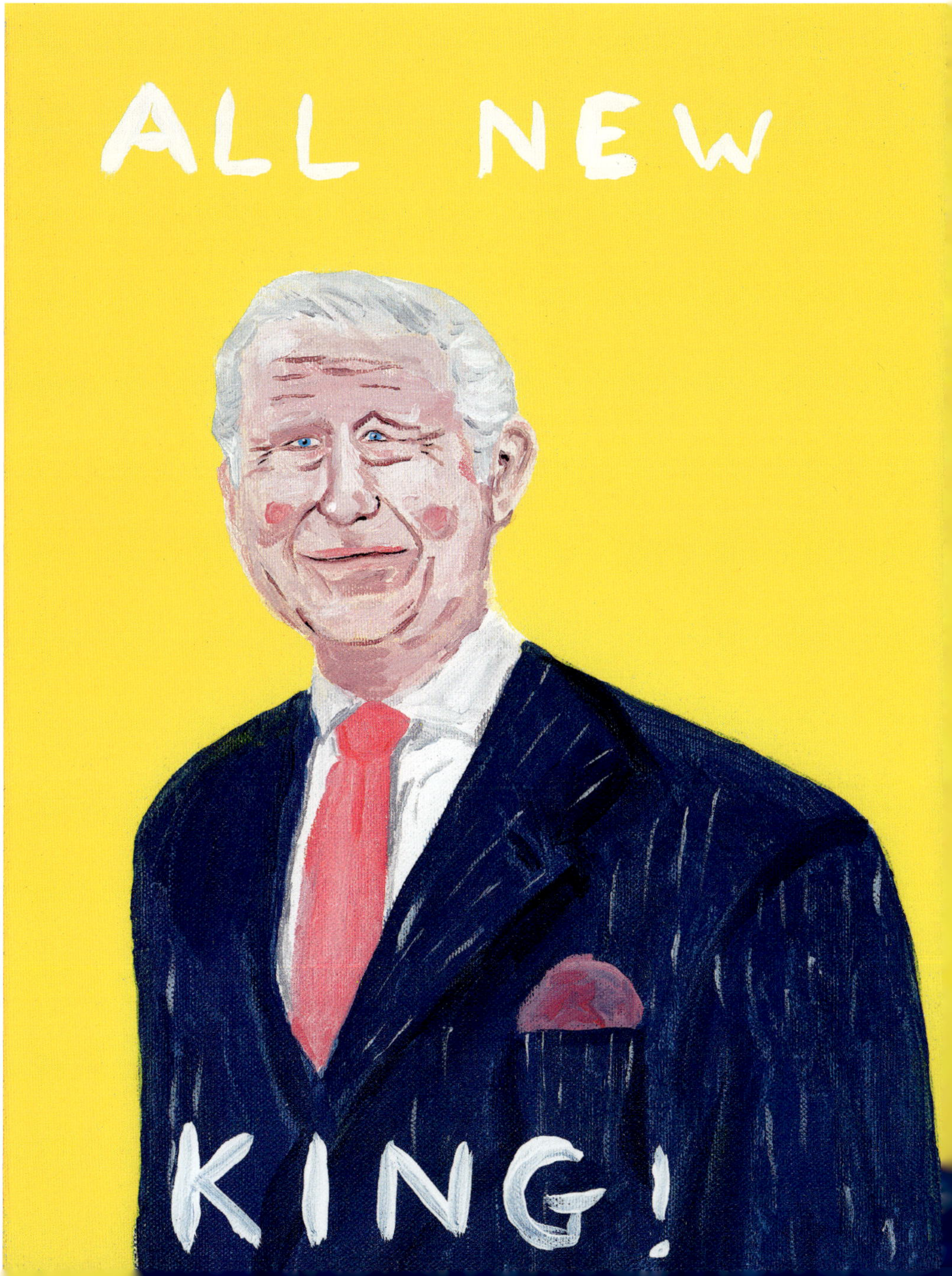

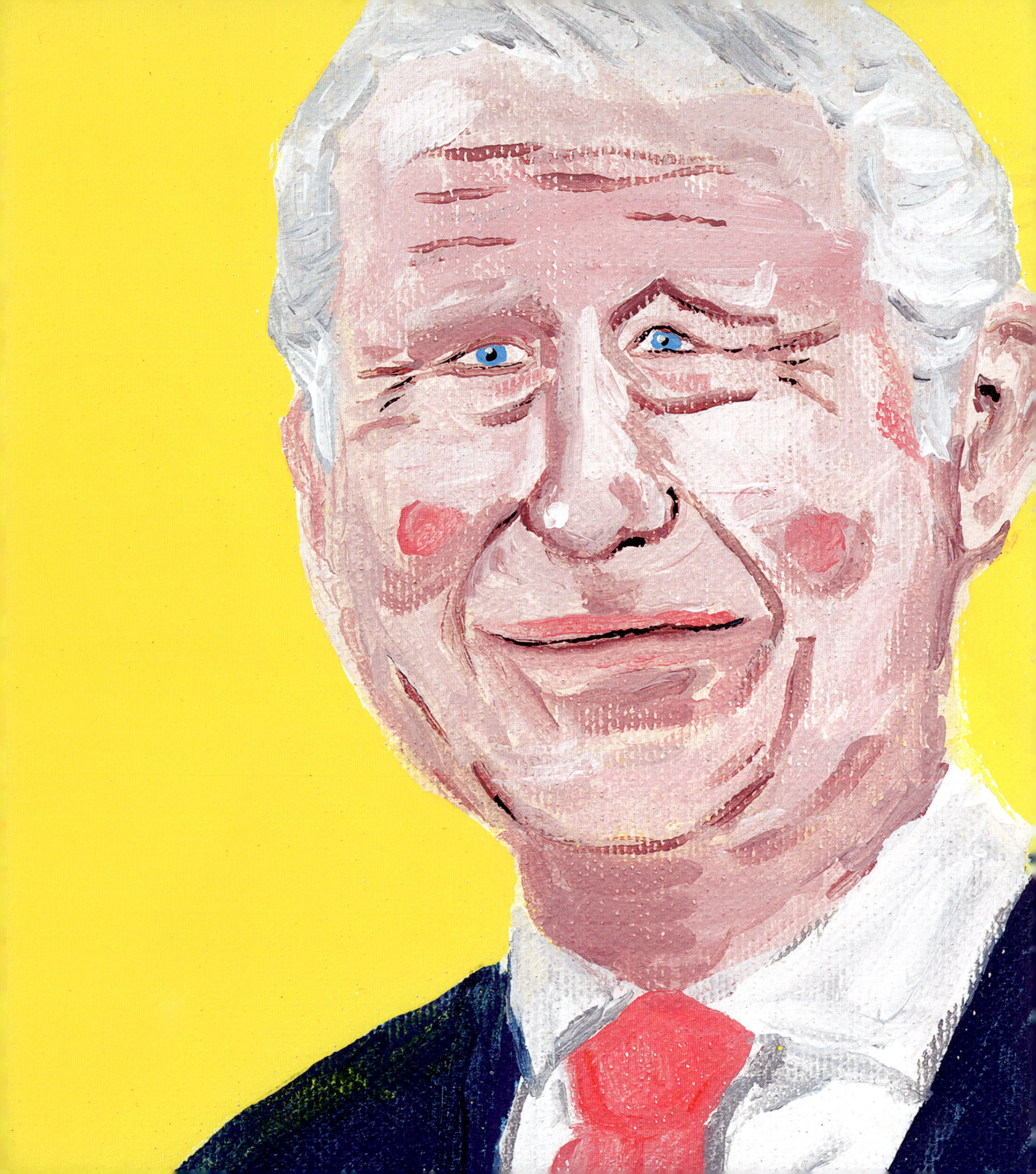

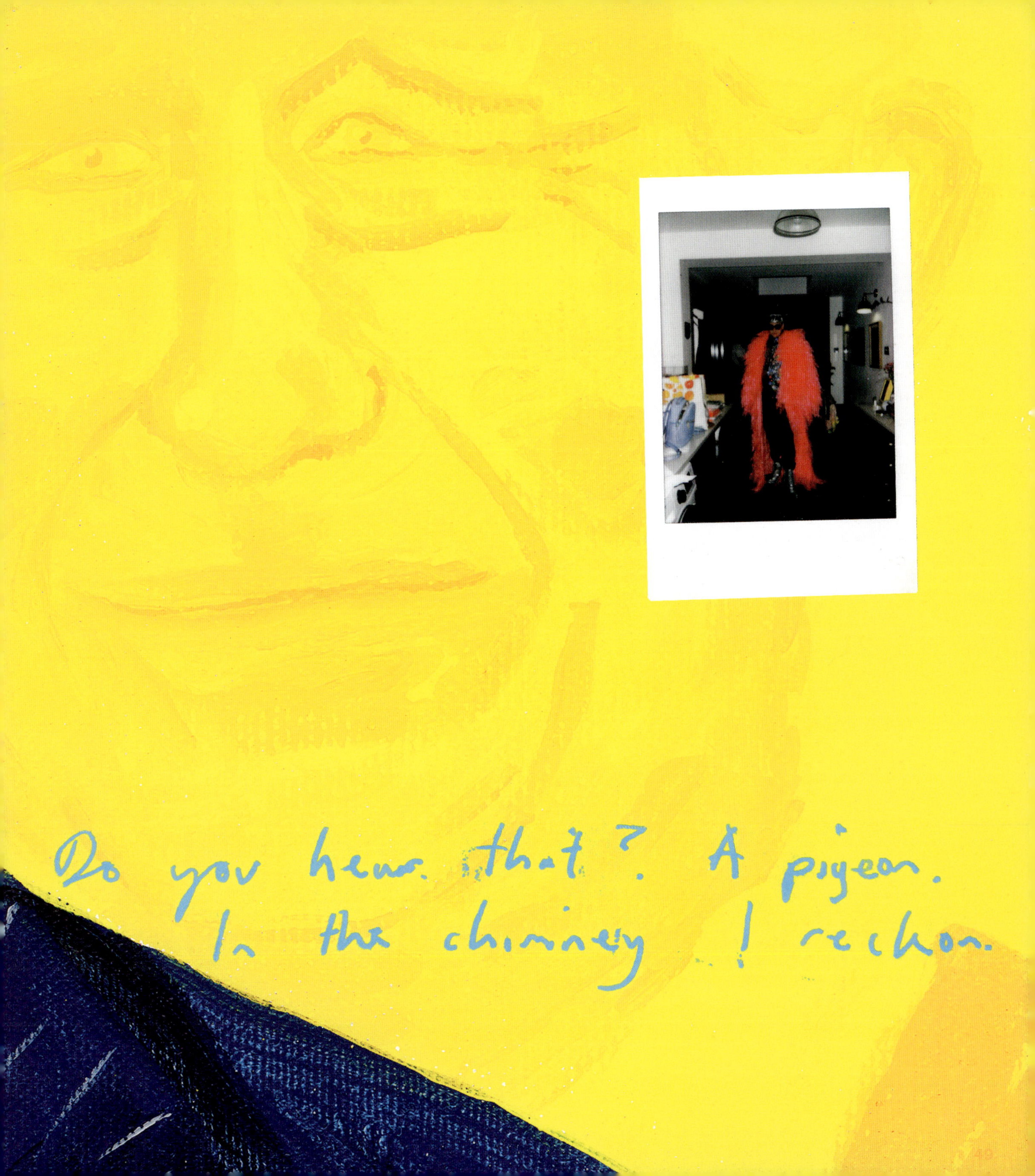
Do you hear that?. A pigeon.
In the chimney I reckon.

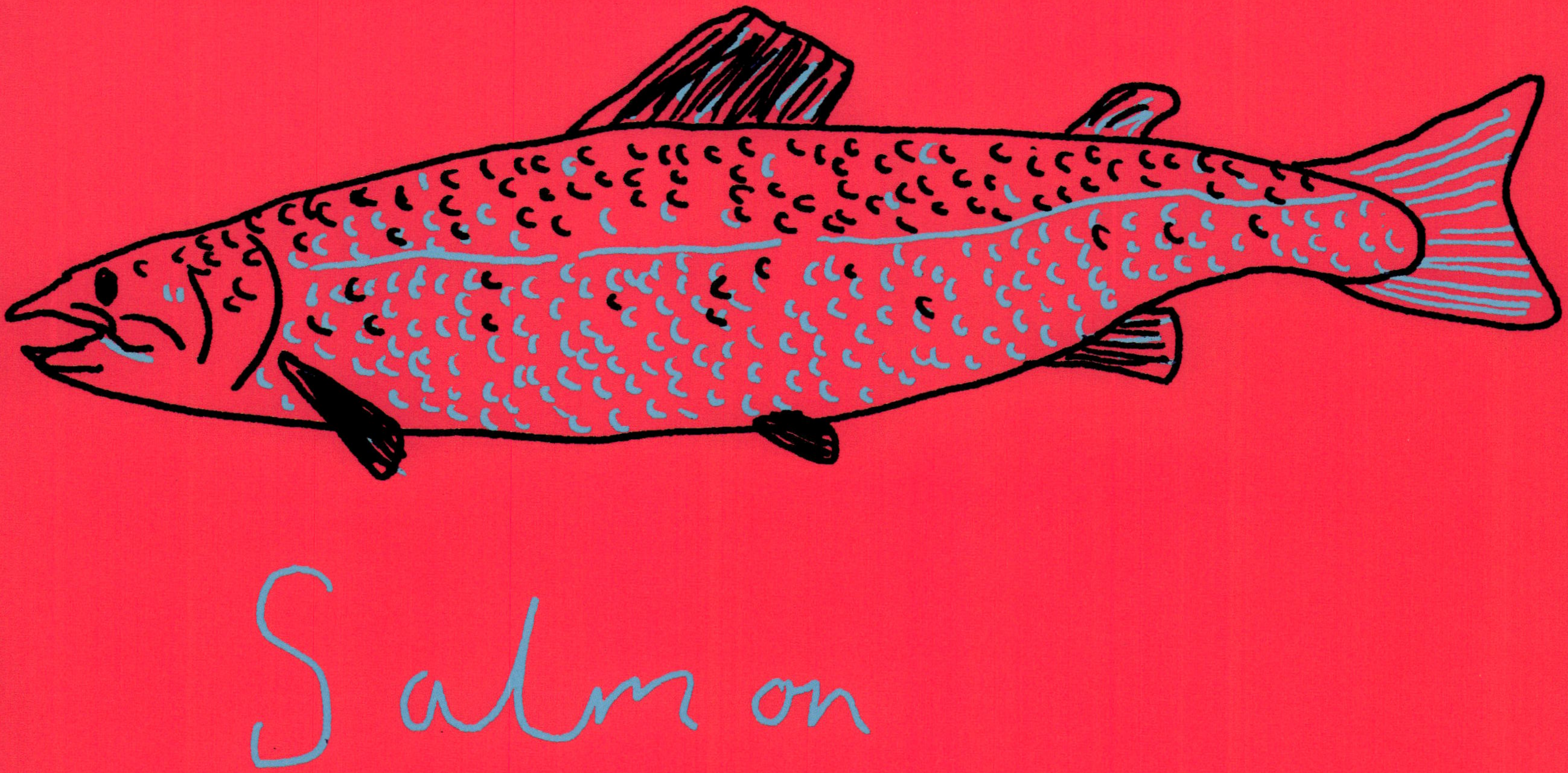
Salmon

Milka Choco

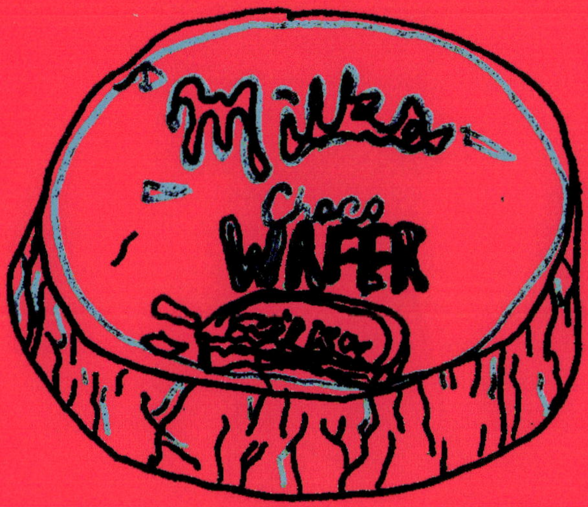

Wafer

MICK HUCKNALL/ JUDY FINNIGAN/ PATSY PALMER/ GERI HALLIWELL

Once my status as portraiture artist to the stars was firmly solidified, I became smothered with requests by agents and publicists. The intensity was such that I had to create a fake PA called Gary Trousers who could send the 'No' emails without me feeling too much guilt. Gary, who I imagined to be ruthless and deeply unhappy, was dispatched to let down some of the absolute greats. Nigel Farage, Grant Shapps, Lewis Hamilton, Suella Braverman, Susanna Reid, Michael Buerk – all of them were desperate to be immortalised in one of my paintings. I simply did not have the time. And yet, four names kept nagging, a quadruplet of pillars of British life that I couldn't bring myself to turn down: Mick Hucknall, Judy Finnigan, Patsy Palmer and Geri Halliwell.[1]

I was about to press the nuclear button[2] when I had an ingenious idea: invite them all to the orangery at the same time and paint them all at once (merged together, not all four in one pose) in an epic multilayer uber-painting, the likes of which had never been seen before. I knew it would work – all of them have largely the same face, the same energy and the same public standing. Here was an opportunity to knock out four celeb birds with one stone (metaphorically, I am a pacifist and was raised to never throw stones at women).

Lesser artists would likely have been callous – dropped three of them and just decided on the most famous subject – but with years of experience and excellence under my belt, I knew that this was not necessary. Many amateur painters make the grave error of trying to capture a likeness, when of course a true contemporary artist is actually trying to paint an éssèncę.[3] As such, I am never looking to capture the exact shapes and dimensions of my subjects – I want to depict their soul. Grayson Perry once said to me: 'If you were to paint things perfectly, you'd end up with a photograph. Your mistakes are your style.' I nodded and smiled, which made him relax and finally allow the police community support officer to breathalyse him.

1. Or Horner or Halliwell-Horner or Ginger or Ginger Spice – the Wikipedia entry is unclear.
2. By 'nuclear button', I mean the 'send button' on a 'no' email.
3. You know an éssèncę when you see one: a Ford Fiesta is basically exactly the same as a low-tier solicitor, unless it is a 'sport' variety with a spoiler in which case it is a junior manager at a Staples or similar. A Snickers is the same as an aggressive rugby enthusiast, a lampshade is almost always gay. All of us know these facts instinctively yet struggle to articulate why.

Fig. 18 *Mick Hucknall/Judy Finnigan/ Patsy Palmer/Geri Halliwell,* 2023, watercolour, acrylic, oil and pen on the side of a moving e-scooter, 34 × 46cm.

Fig. 18

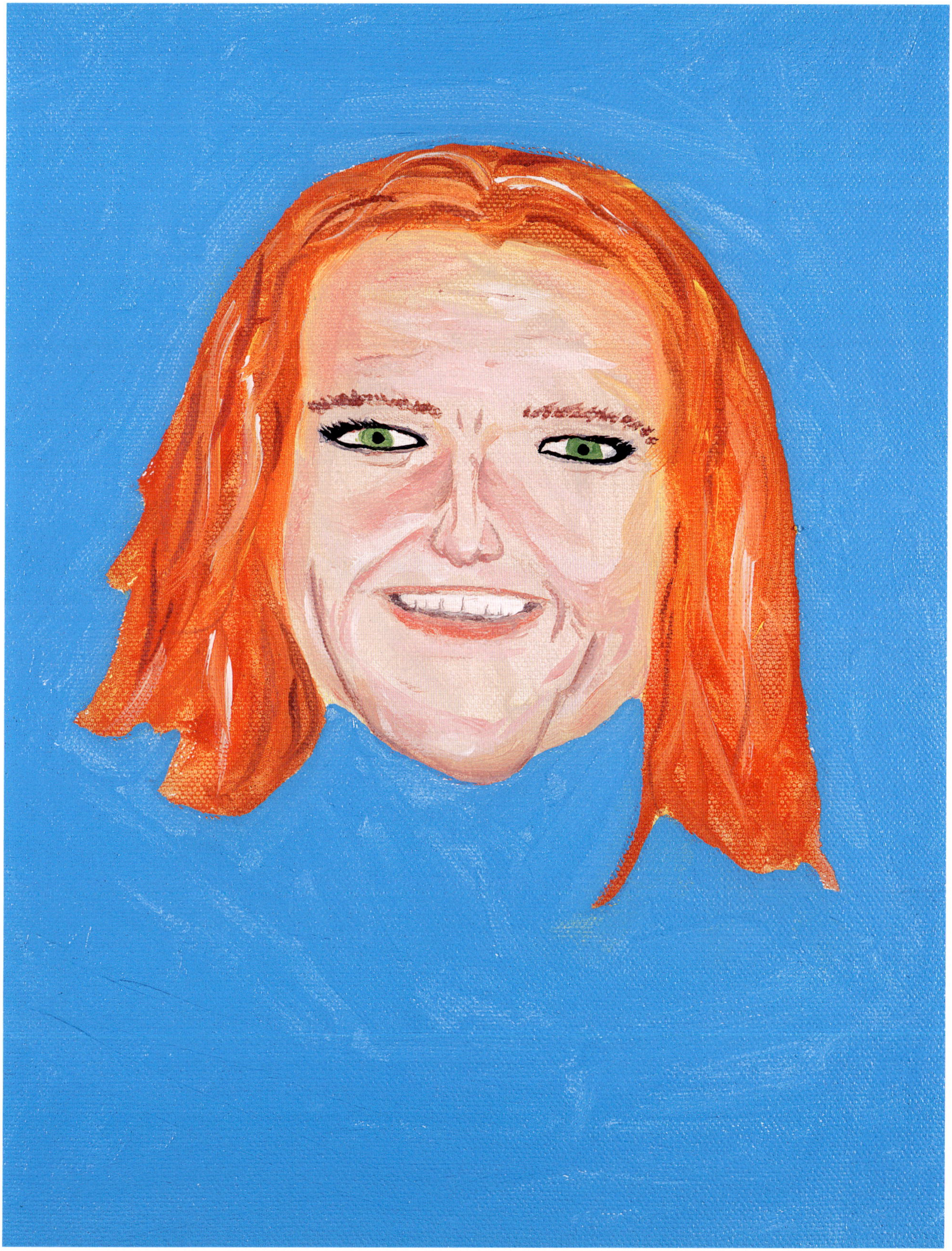

After emailing Hotpoint to ask why my Hotpoint H55RM1110W1 Fridge in white wasn't cooling properly, resulting in at least three ruined salmon en croutes, Gary Trousers made the Hucknall/Finnigan/Palmer/Halliwell arrangements.

First to arrive was Patsy, a bit flustered and incapable of looking anywhere but just slightly beyond my forehead into the middle distance. I offered her a tea, a wine, a champagne. She requested a hot Ribena (with milk) and sat silently on her phone.

Next was Hucknall,[1] who swaggered in as if he'd just found out his ejaculate was made of diamonds, and immediately began flirting with Palmer. This went down surprisingly well, which meant I could focus on preparing my paints while they hit things off. Hucknall was going on about Martine McCutcheon and something to do with her vomiting on his dreadlocks on *Loose Women*, when Ginger Spice scaled the fence and approached the back door.

I really liked Geri – she made a graceful but high-energy entrance, a bit like if I'd just released an ostrich, or a burglar with some experience in ballet. There's a refreshing no-nonsense attitude about her, where no comment could possibly be deemed offensive, or query seem off limits. She immediately chastised me for ignoring Nadine Dorries's emails, saying, 'She just wants her painting, babe, don't worry, she won't talk to you about her book.' I told her I was working on it (it is now finished, see Nadine Dorries chapter), but she was adamant. 'Surely she could have joined in with us?' she suggested. I had to explain that Dorries doesn't share the same éssènçȩ as the Hucknall/Finnigan/Palmer/Halliwell clan and I would be better off doing her at another date, perhaps with someone like Denise Welch or Seyyed Ali Hosseini Khamenei, the Supreme Leader of Iran (both of whom had also been emailing). I took her through into the orangery, at which point Hucknall dropped Palmer like a hot rock and, as effortlessly as the IKEA MILLBERGET rotating chair, swivelled his admiration towards the new addition.

Geri lapped up the affection to a grotesque degree, reminding me of that time I went to see the *Magic Mike* stage show with Christopher Biggins, and so there was an almost audible gasp of relief from Patsy and myself when the doorbell punctured the pheromonic atmosphere, signalling the arrival of our final subject.

To those unfamiliar with the Judy Finnigan concept (Oxbridge graduates and the young), she was a daytime television titan and gay icon, who hosted decades of programming alongside her objectively odd but somehow handsome husband, Richard Madeley. Then, after over forty years in the business and without warning, she vanished from our screens.[2]

1. Two days later. He was on time – Patsy had been extremely early. For those two days she was very polite and unimposing.

2. I've often wondered about that moment. The conversation when it was decided that Richard would go it alone, that Judy would finally hang up the lapel microphone and retire the earpiece, close the compact clamshell case of foundation powder and twist the mascara applicator into its cylindrical reservoir. It must have been a sensational moment. I wish more than anything that I'd been there. Years of co-hosting – the memories, the early alarms, the shared executive cars to the studio – all turned to dust and ash, because Judy was over it. Did Richard originally agree to pack it in alongside her, only to be lured back by the deep pockets and alluring tentacles of daytime ITV management? Or had he secretly wished for this day all along, fatigued by the same old shtick with the wife, keen to prove his worth without her? We will perhaps never know – it may well have been written about in books or interviews, but of the things I know about myself for sure, one is that I am absolutely confident that I will never find the time to read a biography or autobiography about or by either of them.

Fig. 19 The IKEA MILLBERGET chair, which has an intensely smooth swivelling motion.
Fig. 20 Apology note from Biggins.

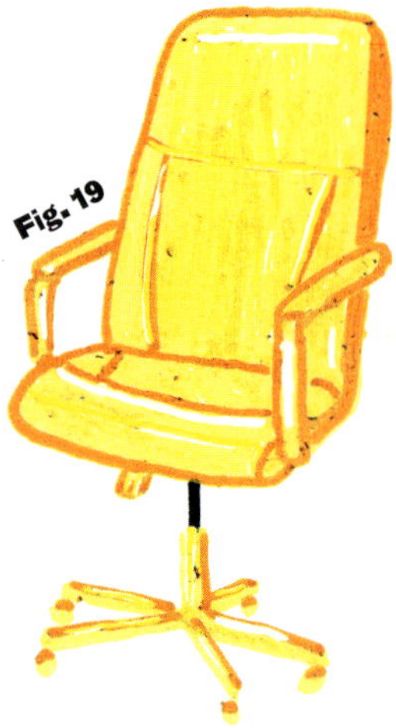

Fig. 20

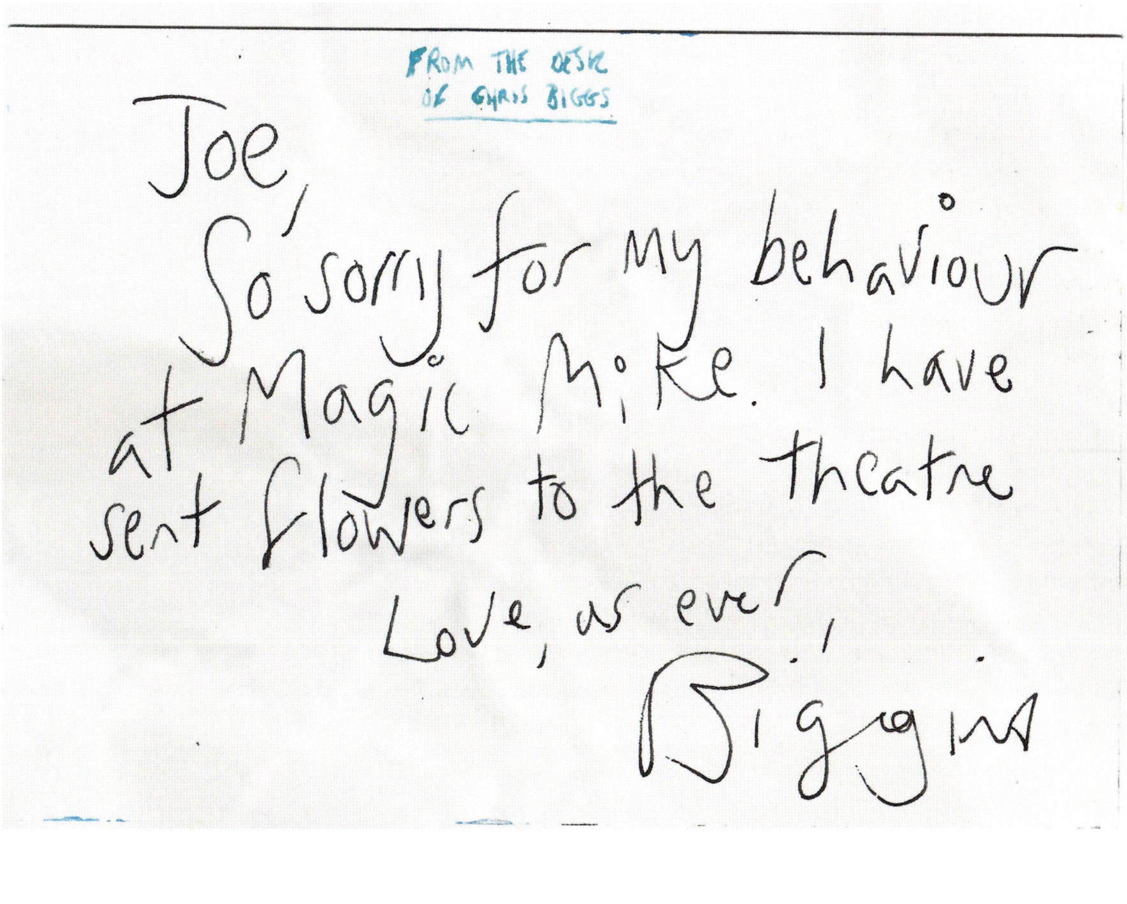

FROM THE DESK
OF CHRIS BIGGS

Joe,
So sorry for my behaviour at Magic Mike. I have sent flowers to the theatre

Love, as ever,
Biggins

She was matter of fact, business-like, almost impatient. She seemed surprised to see the other three, even though I had explained very clearly in our correspondence that they would all be there, just in case there was an unpublished rivalry. 'Met them all, all of them fine,' had been her reply. She put down her bag, a large chestnut leather holdall that clanged like it was full of scrap metal, and began by shaking Hucknall's hand, saying, 'Nice to meet you.'

He said, 'Nice to meet you, too,' but with that look in his eyes that says, 'I am confused because we should both know that we have met before.'

Halliwell went straight in for an overly familiar hug while almost shouting the words, 'Hello again, babe!'

Finnigan, speaking over Ginger Spice, said 'Nice to meet you' again, creating a horrendous few seconds where Finnigan had to step back and make an inquisitive 'oh' sound, forcing Halliwell to then double down, explaining that they'd met on *This Morning*.[1] 'What?' Finnigan snapped back, as if she'd only just heard of the concept of *This Morning* in that exact moment and was disgusted by the idea (correctly).

'The Spice Girls were on *This Morning* in 1996, babe, you and Richard interviewed us,' said Geri, as close to polite as she could manage (i.e., pushy and aggressive).

'Oh. OK. Sure, whatever,' Judy replied. You could cut the atmosphere with a Shure SM58 handheld microphone.[2]

I asked them to sit in a curve, but then changed it to 'a banana shape' for clarity. Palmer literally tried to sit down in the shape of a banana (*see* **Fig. 21**) by putting her arms in the air and arching her back – probably a technique learnt in acting school – but I told her that wasn't necessary and she could just sit normally. In that moment I fully understood the creative constraints on the directors of *EastEnders*.

The group sat in serene silence for the twelve or so hours it took me to complete and perfect the painting. We had one short break for KFC: I had a bucket of chicken and a Krushem, Mick had a Zinger Tower, Geri and Judy shared a Mini Fillet, and Patsy had already eaten so she just had a large gravy. It was important for me to take my time because I wanted the éssènçę of each of them to be present in equal measure – a bit of Finnigan's eyes, a touch of Hucknall's skin, a flash of Halliwell's hair, a sprinkling of Palmer's make-up. I think you'll agree, it was worth it. The painting is a roaring success. Each of the four subjects is depicted beautifully, accurately, compassionately, and yet all in the same singular portrait. It is an artistic feat that has never been achieved before.[3]

Once I'd finished, I pronounced loudly: 'It is done.' There was an enormous exhale of relief from the room.

1. This sort of encounter, while being appalling in the moment, is not uncommon in these sorts of circles. People forget who they've met, particularly if they are familiar faces. I once said 'Nice to meet you' to Richard Ayoade, completely forgetting that I'd been on a TV panel show with him, and he said, 'We were on a TV panel show', and I said, 'Oh yes'. This is the sort of showbiz story I should've saved for my autobiography but am gifting to you here.

2. If you're wondering what she said to Patsy Palmer, she didn't say a word to her for the entire duration of her stay.

3. Marcel Duchamp did attempt something like it where he merged his face with the *Mona Lisa* in his famous ***L.H.O.O.Q.***, but with that he just whacked a moustache on a *Mona Lisa* postcard, whereas I actually did a proper fucking painting. When said aloud, the title of Duchamp's work roughly sounds like the French for 'She is hot in the arse', and it sold for $750,000, last I heard. Twat.

Fig. 21 A drawing of a banana to delineate the shape of a banana.
Fig. 22 Zinger Burger.

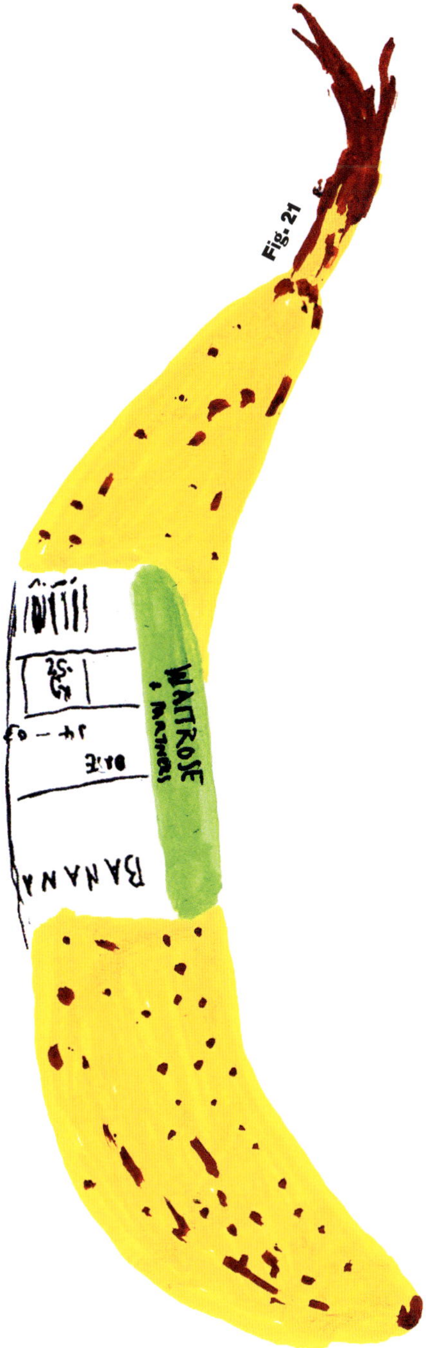

Fig. 21

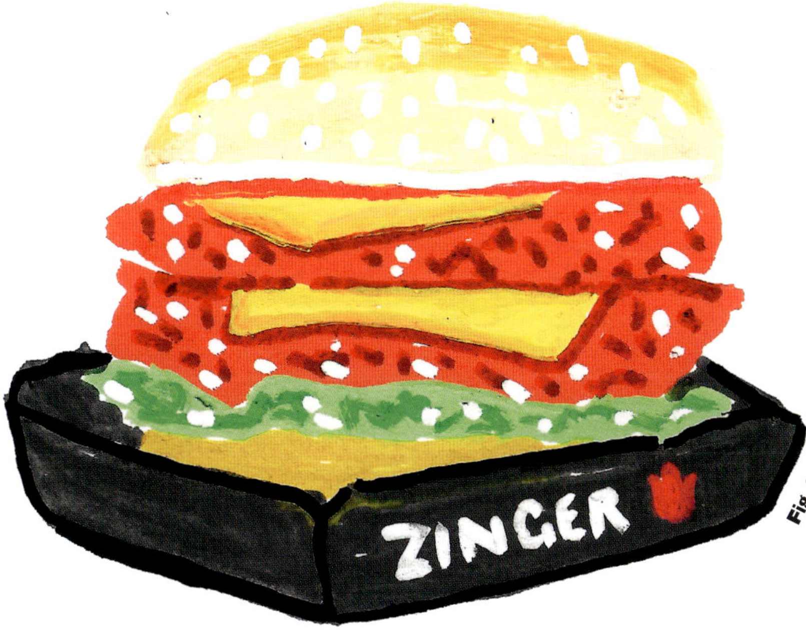

Fig. 22

‘Finally!’ yawned Finnigan.

I turned the easel round to show them the fruits of our (my) labour. Another gasp. Hucknall began to applaud, a frightening experience due to the dampness of his palms.

‘It’s quite something,’ said Finnigan, winning the award for understatement of the century.

‘Well done, babe, great stuff,’ said Halliwell, putting on her coat. ‘Shall I set up a WhatsApp group for us all? Do a nice little dinner and some drinkies sometime?’

‘I don’t have WhatsApp,’ said Finnigan, reaching into her bag of scrap and pulling out a roll of *Richard and Judy Book Club* stickers, which she proceeded to put on all my cookbooks.

‘Lovely idea,’ interjected Patsy, pressing her digits into Halliwell’s disappointed phone. Hucknall pulled out a black, embossed business card from the back pocket of his 550™ ’92 Relaxed Taper Fit Levi’s Jeans and slid it across to Geri. I couldn’t see most of it, but I noticed it included the pun ‘Give me a Mick Huckcall’, which I consider to be despicable. After they had left, I returned to the orangery and sat alone for a while, looking upon my work. As normal, I was being overly self-critical – there wasn’t enough Hucknall in it, Halliwell was lost behind Finnigan’s eyes, it looked like Angela Scanlon if she’d been squeezed into a jam jar, et cetera, et cetera – but a few minutes later I was struck by a wave of profound melancholy. Each of them in their own eccentric ways had been integral to British life and yet now here they were, in my orangery, lives lived. Now they were nothing more than mere footnotes,[1] not important nor impressive enough to warrant their own portraits, but tribute acts to their own decay. I began to feel a nostalgia for a time for which I was never really around – the roaring 90s when I was a simple toddler, a footnote myself,[2] life yet to be lived, where things seemed brighter and simpler.

I never really looked at the portrait again, just took myself to bed, checked to see if Hotpoint had replied,[3] switched on GB News to calm me, and drifted off, guided by the soft voice and considered opinions of Julia Hartley-Brewer. She was saying something about ‘the Turkish’ – absolute bliss. The piece was sold to Finnigan at a police auction and has since been destroyed in a manner that one eyewitness described as ‘enthusiastic’.

NB: It has been alleged that I actually just did the painting using Patsy Palmer as the reference image but that it went wrong and so I’m backtracking by making this story up. But that is obviously not factual at all, and I am pursuing legal action against those hideous and damaging claims.

1. Mick Hucknall, Judy Finnigan, Patsy Palmer and Geri Halliwell. I list them so they are also literal footnotes.

2. A young Joe Lycett. I write it here so I am also a literal footnote.

3. They said it might be an issue with the thermostat, but they couldn’t advise further without more information.

Fig. 23 3D visualisation of the Understatement of the Year Award, as won by Judy Finnigan.

Fig. 24 Patsy Palmer’s schedule.

Fig. 23

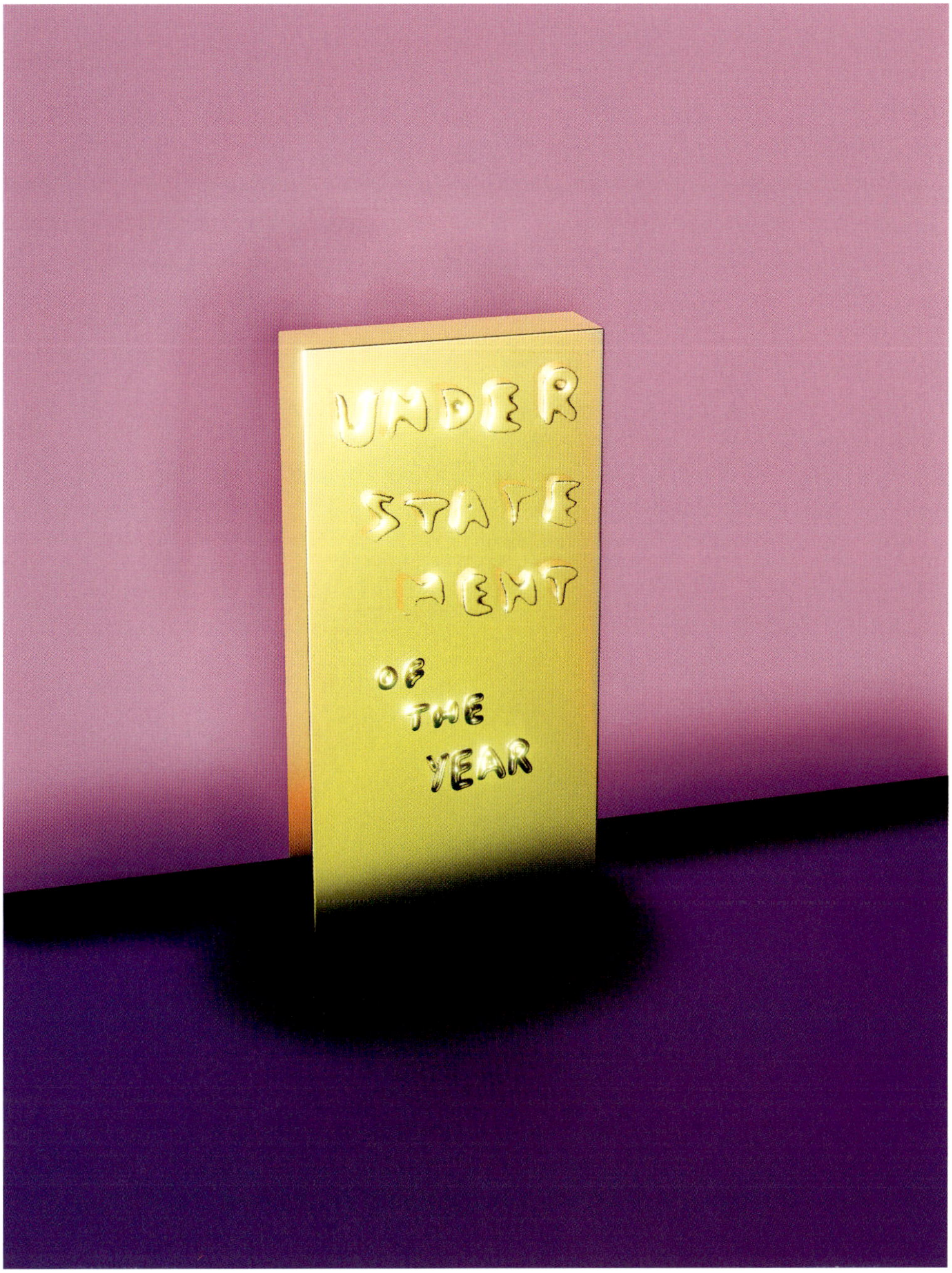

Fig. 24

9:00 am. - I awake, revelling in my solitude. What will this dawn, carried to me on the long river of night, provide?

9:30 am. - pilates

10:00 am - my spirit is awakened and the days potential is becoming clearer. I reflect on what has been and what is to come

10:15 am. - McDonald's Double Sausage and Egg McMuffin. Two hash browns. An act of tenderness and self-care. Don't drink the Tropicana because of the bits so drop it off at Oxfam

11:00 am - I take a walk, to conjure thoughts and philosophies, to solve life's riddles, to step out beyond myself and look back at who I am. What a gift it is to be amongst nature, to observe her whims and beauties. I find myself in Lewisham shopping centre and pick up some bits

1:00pm. - lunch, in scintillating company, as always. There is nothing like debate and dialogue with a great mind. Today I am blessed with Joe Swash at Chopstix Noodle Bar.

3:00pm - the afternoon is a period of collaborative cultural and creative endeavour, elevating the individual to a grand pedestal, their stories writ deep across the sands of eternity.

6:00pm - Finish shooting Eastenders and get in car home

8:00pm - a life cannot be lived without periods of rejuvenation, reflection and reanimation. How is one to go on without this? How can any

of us face the darkest caverns of our souls without nutrition and rest? I have a Sainsbury's Taste the Difference Fish Pie (400g) while watching 'The One Show'
9:00pm – fade to black.

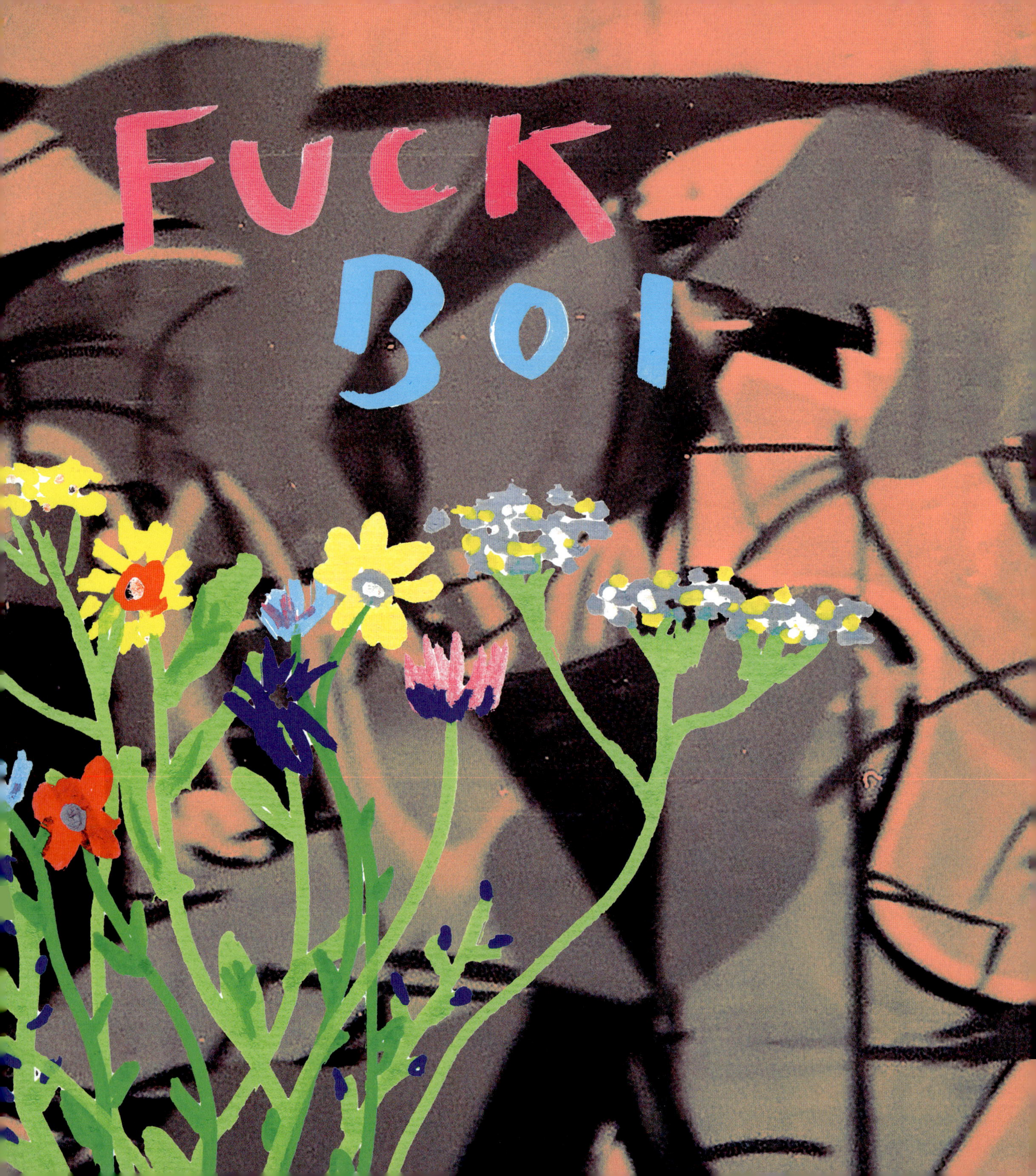
FUCK
BOI

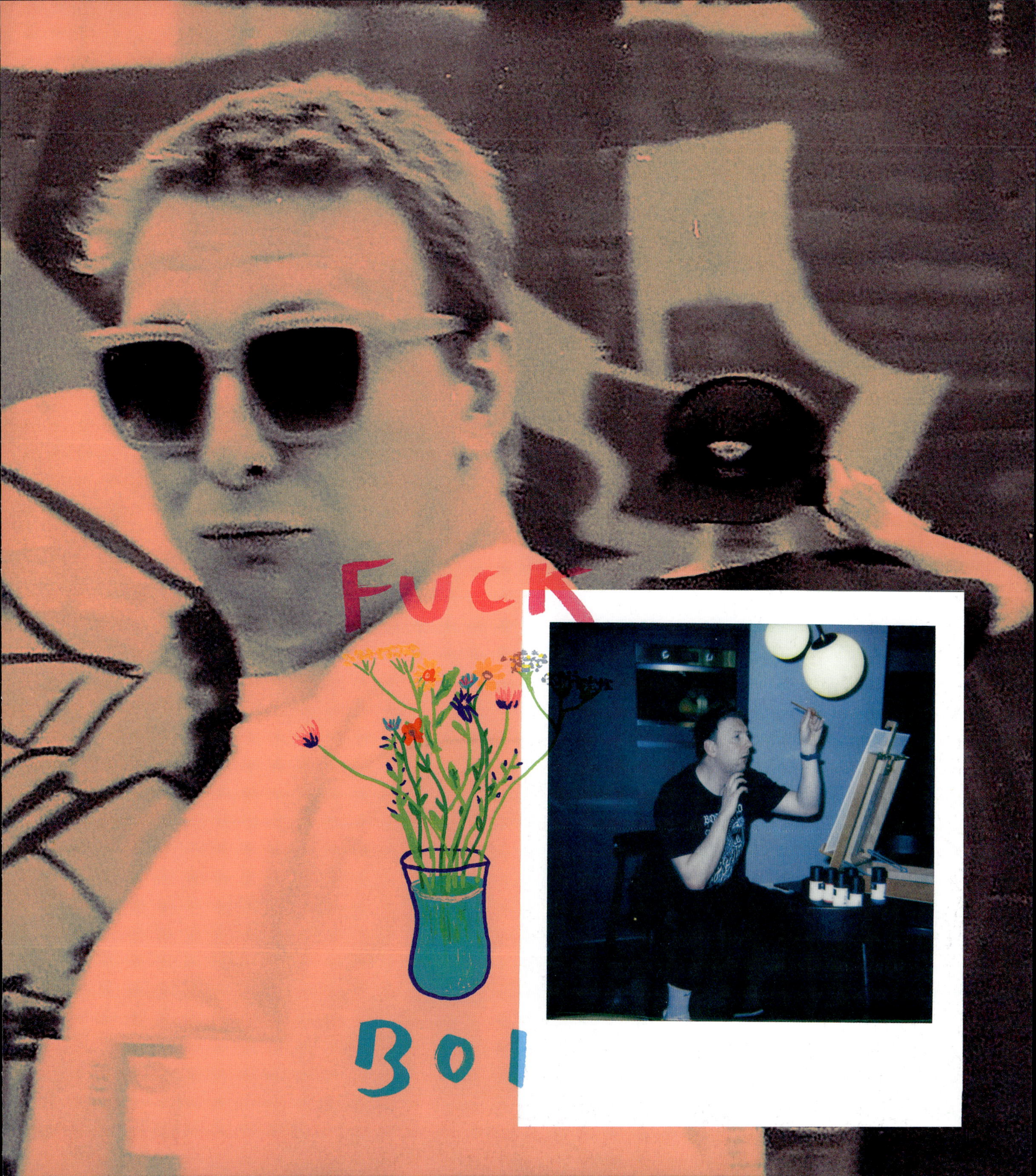
FUCK
BO

GAIL PLATT – PLATT DU JOUR

Fig. 25 *Platt du Jour,* 2021, acrylic mixed with poppers on parchment, 83 × 104ft.

This painting of National Treasure and *Coronation Street* icon Gail Platt (aka Gail Rodwell, Gail Potter, Gail Tilsley, Gail Hillman, Gail McIntyre or Helen Worth) is arguably my most successful and beloved. Prints of it adorn thousands of homes around the United Kingdom and beyond. I have received countless messages from fans expressing their love and respect for the tenderness with which I depicted the great woman.

Sadly, this is one of the few of my portraits that I was forced to do from a photograph, rather than the real-life person. Naturally, I tried my very best to get hold of the woman herself, but she remained elusive, secretive and seemingly entirely off-grid. I very much admire this respect for her own privacy, as opposed to the ostentatious desperation for attention from the likes of her colleagues (Sally Webster).

I have been a fan of *Coronation Street* and her character since I was a little girl. I remember my mother slapping a copy of Leo Tolstoy's *The Death of Ivan Ilyich* out of my hand before saying, 'You'll learn nothing from that crap, watch this,' while turning on ITV1 (channel three as it was known then, pre-BBC Three or Dave) for that evening's edition. While I was frustrated at the time, I have come to appreciate the wisdom that my mother was trying to impart. *The Death of Ivan Ilyich* is indeed total garbage, which you can tell from its failure to ever be sponsored by Compare the Market. There is nothing that Tolstoy's novella could have taught me that Gail's trajectory could not.

Both Ivan Ilyich and Gail Platt's stories deal with ordinary, mundane lives. They explore the trials and toils of having a family (what David Platt has done to that woman over the years is nothing short of a disgrace, behaviour which would have been dealt with far more brutally in nineteenth-century Russia), and both characters give us mortals compelling ideas about how to grasp meaning out of the indignity of immense suffering. But where *Coronation Street* thrives is that it is much easier to ingest and is infinitely more relatable, with some of Gail's more profound lines being: 'I bought this blouse before it went into the half-price sale,' 'Liar!', and 'I think I'll have an olive now actually. Would you like an olive, Kylie? I love olives.'

Gail is a multifaceted, complex character. There is so much beneath the surface, like an iceberg or Lorraine Kelly – but the essence I wanted the portrait to depict most is her impish energy, her lust for

Fig. 25

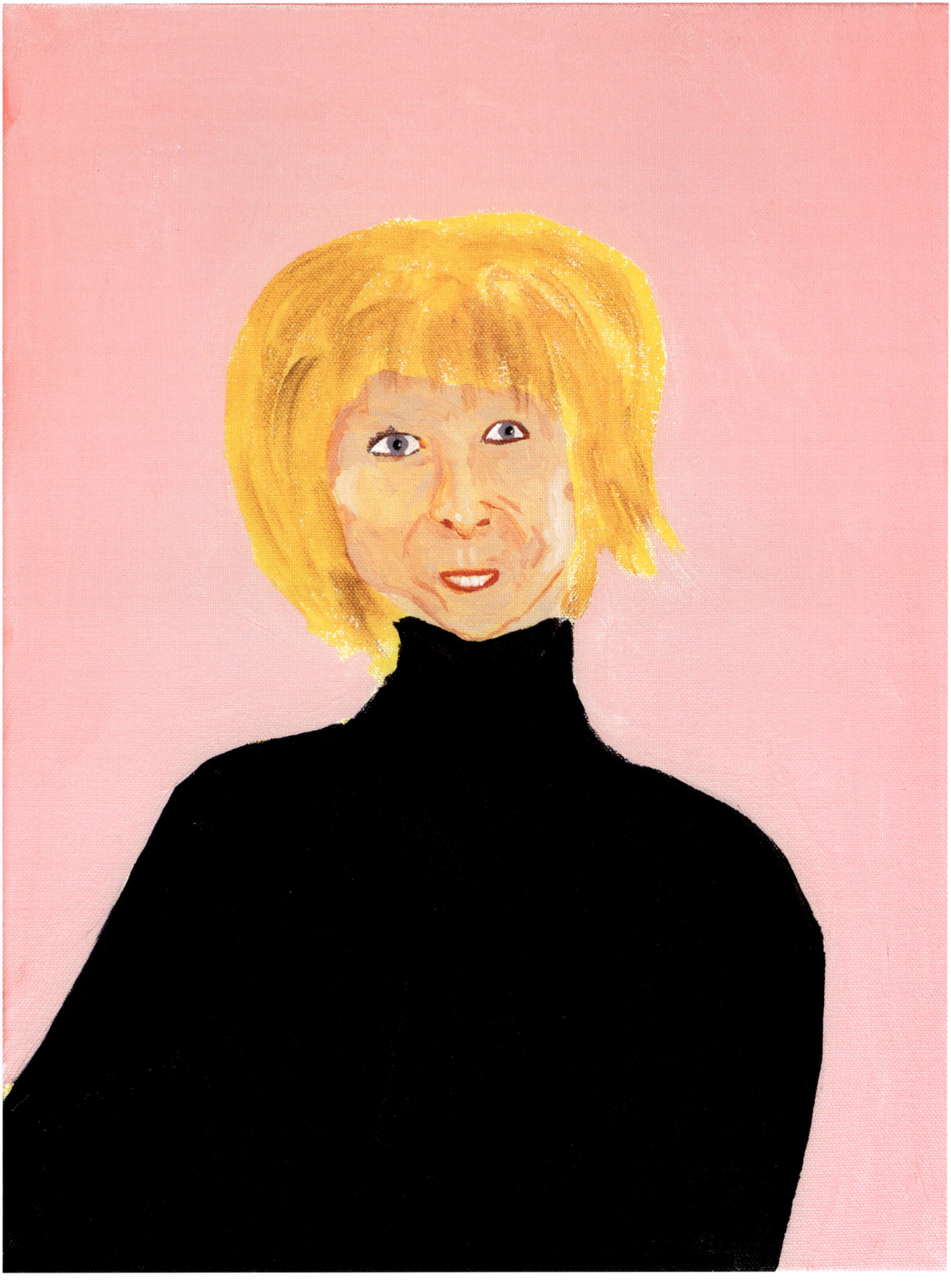

life, and her love of a turtleneck. I also utilised an ancient artistic practice, which is to reduce the amount of time you have to spend on clothing by making it black – a tip I believe was handed down from Michelangelo (the painter, not the ninja turtle). I could've spent hours on the creases and stitches but instead it took me about three minutes to just paint it all in. You're welcome!

I spent about six weeks finessing the piece, working day and night in eight-hour shifts, with twenty-minute breaks to rest. I produced thousands of drafts and hundreds of false starts, spending approximately £15,000 on canvases that are now entirely unusable. The finished piece was offered to all the major galleries, but none accepted, which I understand – it must be a delicate balancing act to introduce new, exceptional work that may disrupt the inferior pieces already hanging. Thankfully, there was a market elsewhere and prints of my masterpiece were wildly popular, spreading the joy of this work beyond the stuffy walls of a shitty little dump like the Tate Modern.

Fig. 26 The logo for *Coronation Street*, from which I learnt everything I know.
Fig. 27 A young Joe Lycett wasting his time with another idiotic book. This may look like a contemporary photograph of a small girl but it is me as a little boy in the early 1990s, trust me.
Fig. 28 Helen Worth's schedule (in her own words).

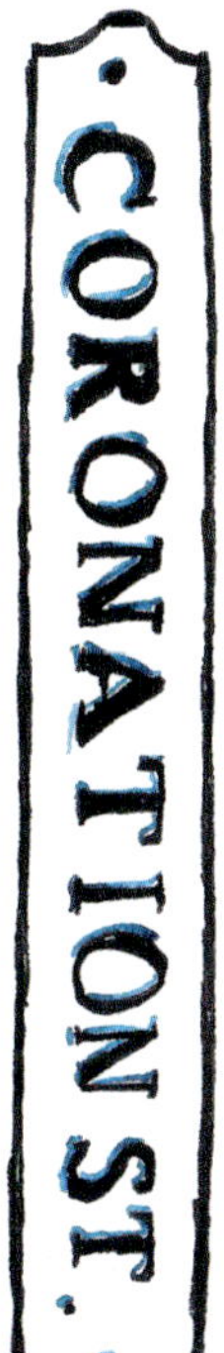
CORONATION ST.

Fig. 26

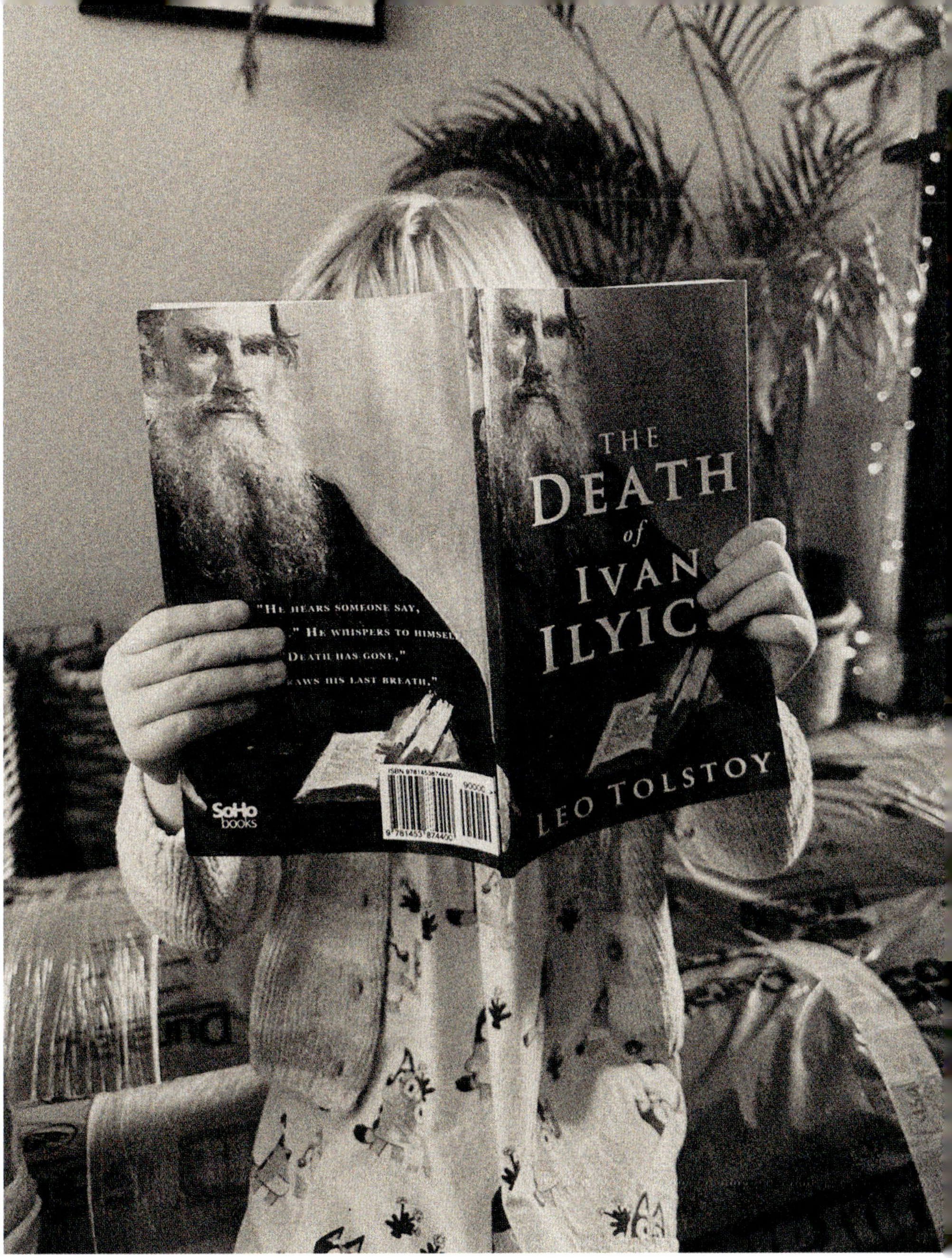
THE
DEATH
of
IVAN
ILYIC
LEO TOLSTOY
SoHo
books

Fig. 27

Fig. 28

	A	B	C	D	E	F	G
1	**Helen Worth Schedule**						
2		06:02	wake up, drink pint of water, mouth is like fukkin dust				
3		06:31	another little sleep OK				
4		07:43	gotta take a dump, gonna ignore it				
5		08:23	OK really need that dump now, have to get up				
6		09:03	omelettes				
7		10:32	they sent a script in an email what is the password				
8		11:21	password: deardre				
9		11:23	password: diedeer				
10		11:24	password: deirdre				
11		12:19	i learnt it, some good lines for me				
12		13:12	lunch time, stroganoff, cheeky little dry white wine didn't hurt anyone				
13		14:21	oops had the bottle lol				
14		15:43	gotta be on set tomorrow oh dear				
15		16:56	gonna have a litl nap				
16		18:52	grog				
17		19:12	fish and chips for tea with mushy peas maybe have one more wine				
18		20:22	have you seen The Chase it's quite good				
19		21:11	need to remember				
20		21:23	password: deirdre				
21							
22							

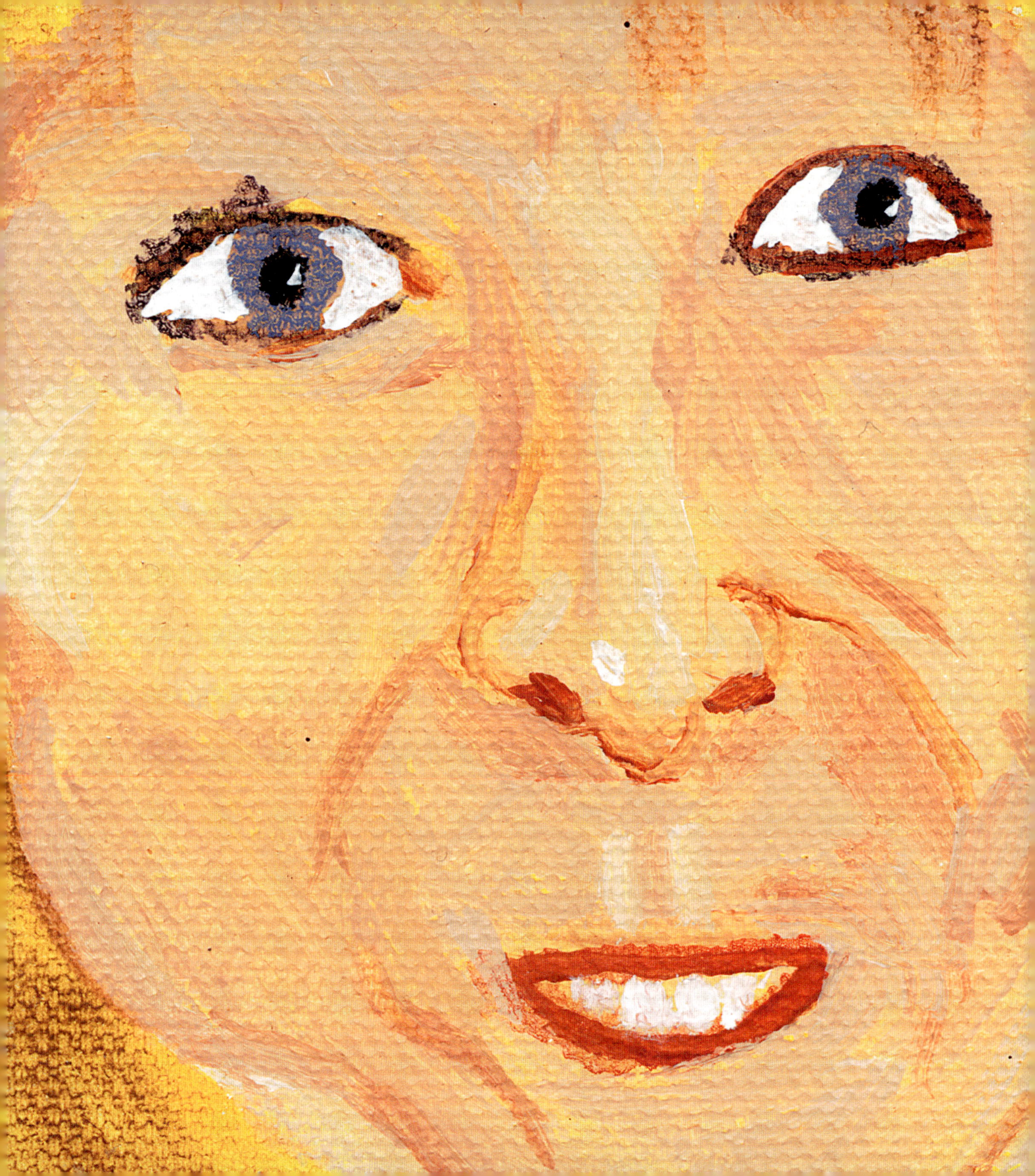

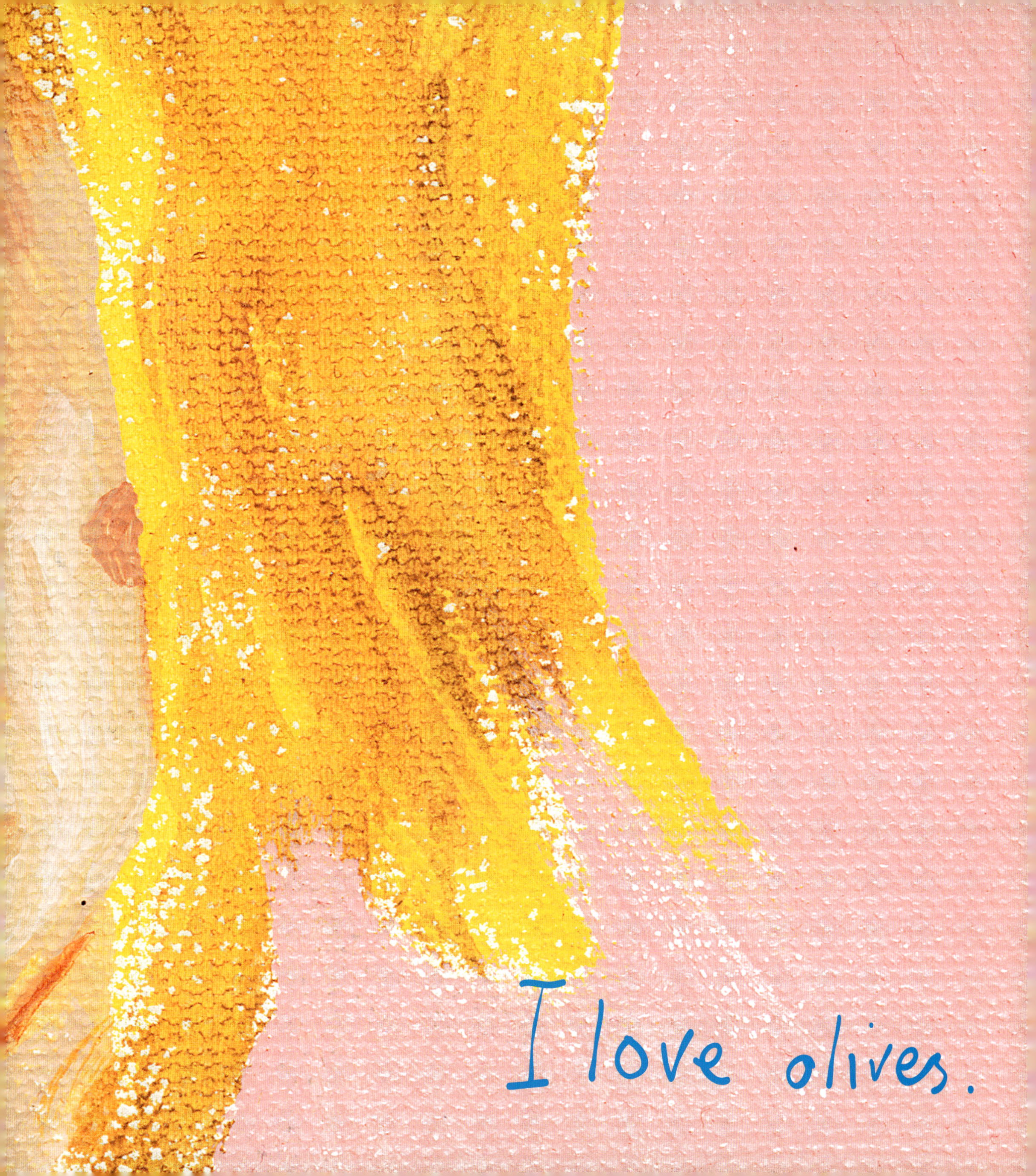
I love olives.

HOT GIRL SUMMER

Fig. 29 A map showing the 57-hour journey from Birmingham to Tenby on foot.

Fig. 30 *Hot Girl Summer,* 2023, acrylic on number 11 bus stop, 152 × 121cm.

So, I took a walk in some park in Birmingham in the summer of 2023 and spotted some chocolate on a bench. Now, please understand, I am not the sort of person to just eat random chocolate off a park bench, but on this one occasion I ate the chocolate off the park bench, and let me tell you that choccy was some real tasty choccy, quite moreish. I was en route to Santander to pay in a cheque, 'cause when you go on Graham Norton's show, they don't officially pay you but afterwards Graham takes you into a room and gives you a cheque for £65. Well, there must've been something a bit naughty in that little bar of choccy 'cause no sooner had I gobbled it down than I was visited by the ghost of the Queen (weirdly not as the old lady we all remember, but as a toddler). She was screeching and wailing and saying, 'Run to Tenby, run to Tenby!' So, I started running towards Tenby, even though the only thing I knew about Tenby was that there was a walrus there once. So I started running, and then thought, 'I should just check the map' and Google Maps said it was a two-day walk, but I thought 'Joe, it's the goddamn child-ghost-queen asking you to do this,' so I ran, but suddenly my feet and toes were replaced with little tiny artichokes, and I was anchored to the ground like a bollard, or, I suppose, an anchor. I was annoyed about the artichoke foot thing, so I crawled on my hands and my knees and the tips of my artichoke toes, back to the bench. But the toddler queen wasn't there any more, just a man called Tom who told me I didn't look so well, and then I fell asleep and woke up in my house on my sofa next to an empty choccy wrapper and I had done this painting.

I had an offer to buy it for £800,000 from Andrew Tate because, in his words, it 'spoke' to him, but I'd read online that he might not be that nice a guy, so I sold it to James Acaster for £65 (because in the confusion I misplaced the Graham Norton cheque).

Fig. 29

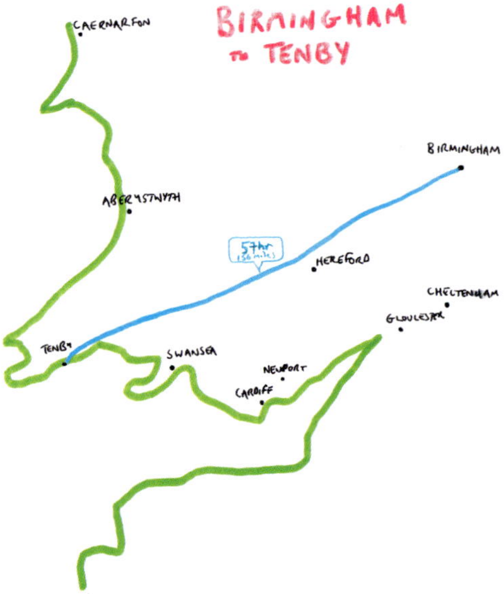

Fig. 30

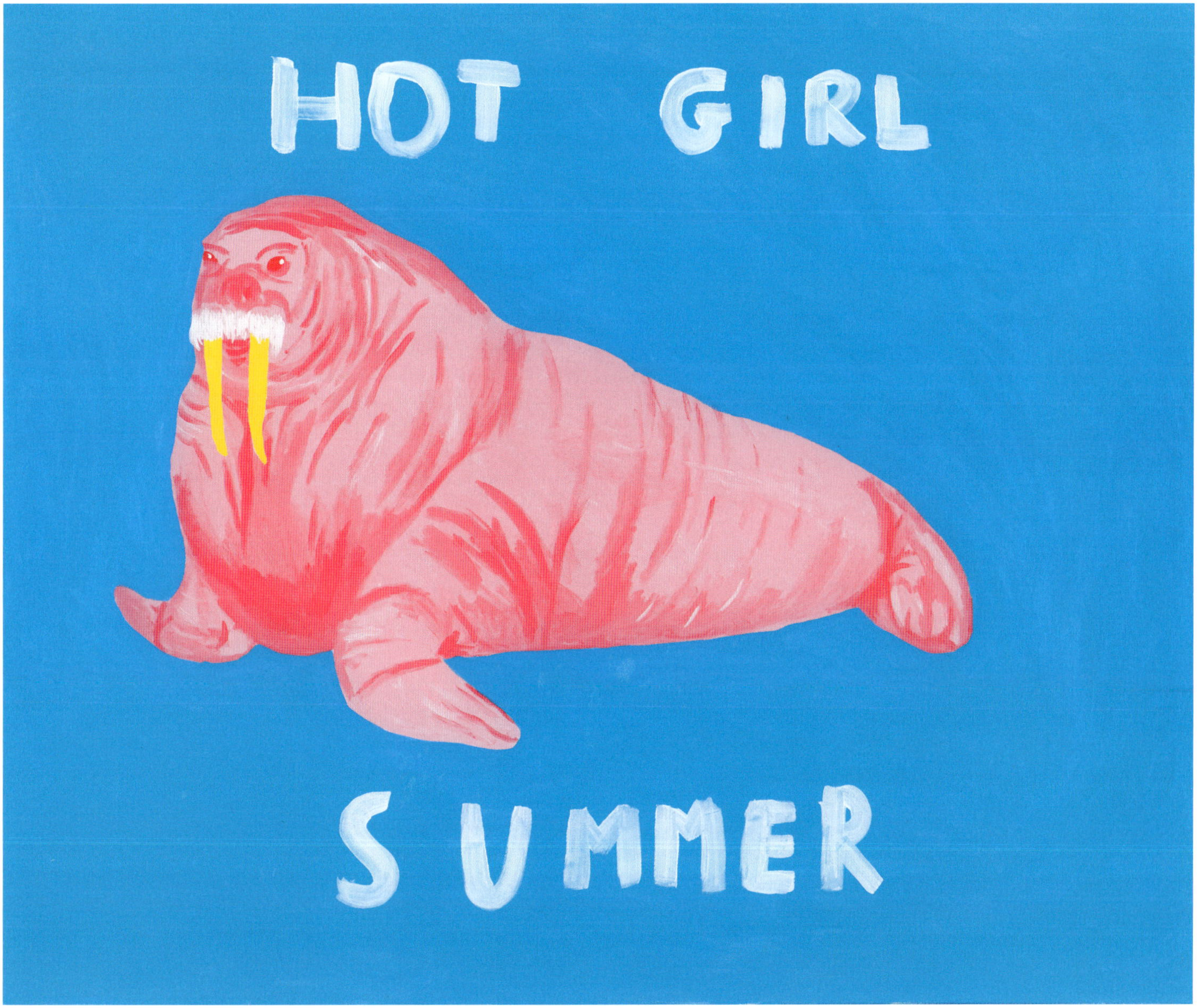

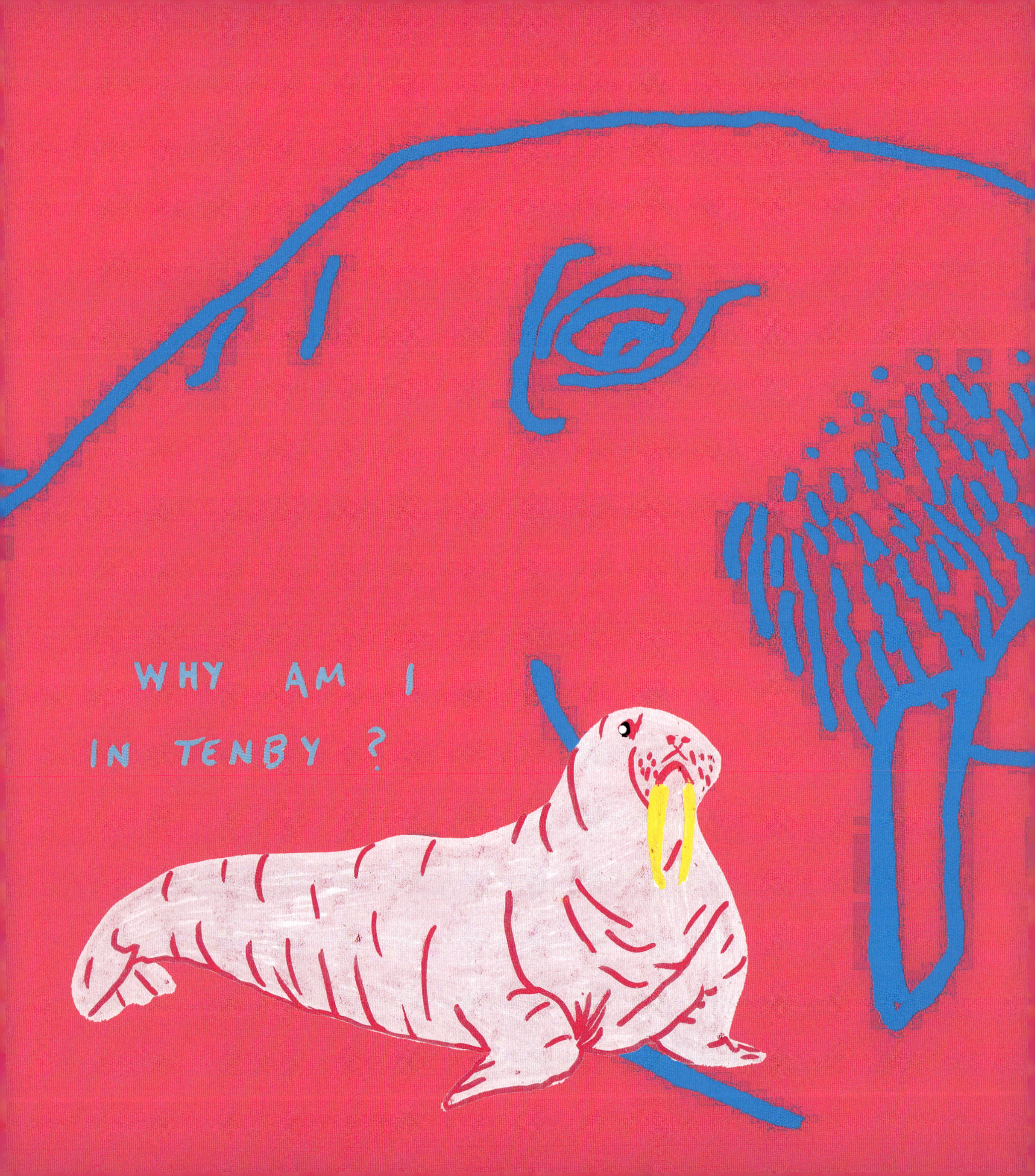
WHY AM I
IN TENBY ?

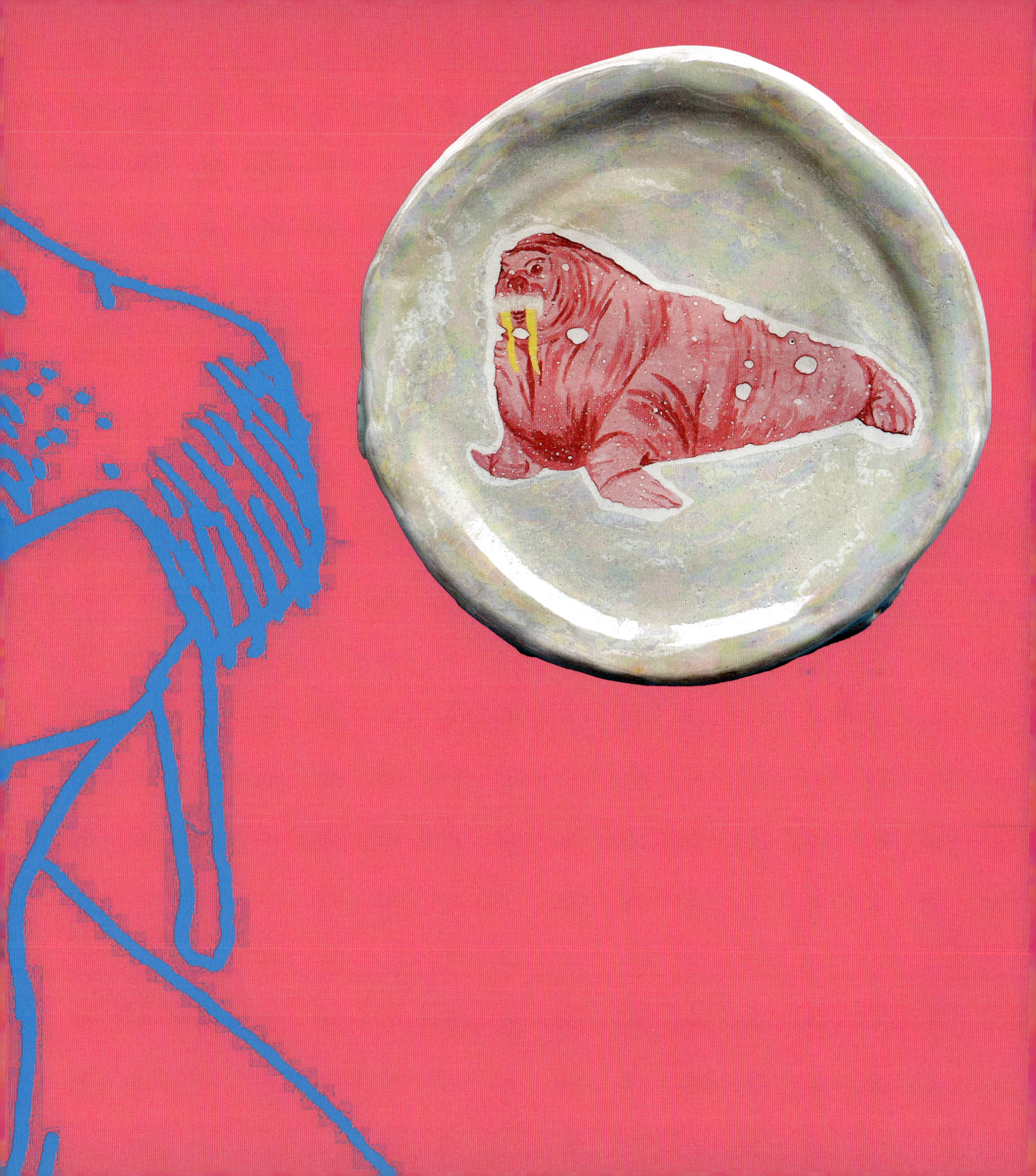

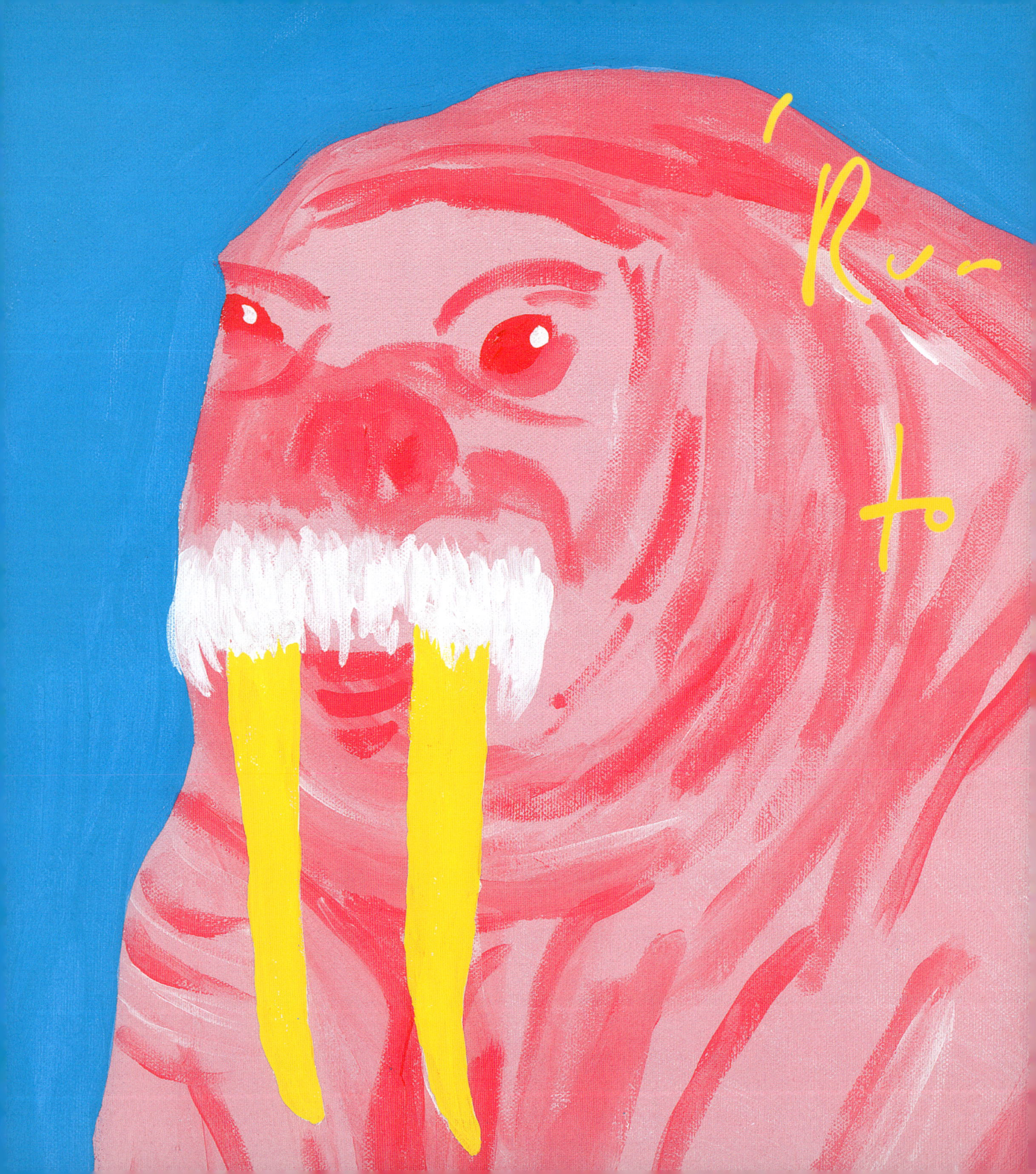

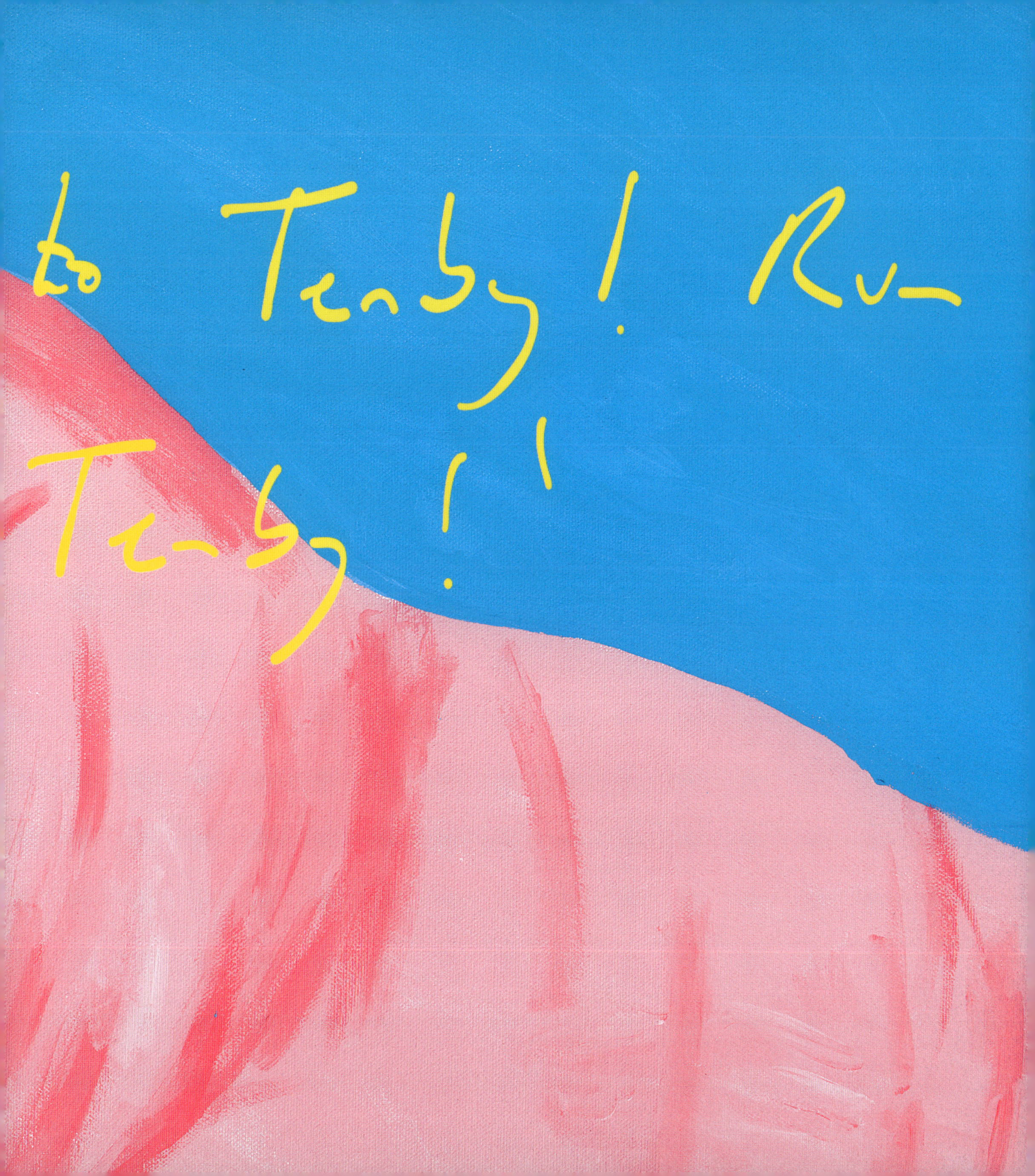
to Tenby! Run
Tenby!!

LIZ TRUSS

Picasso once remarked, 'To finish a work? To finish a picture? What nonsense! To finish it means to be through with it, to kill it, to rid it of its soul.'

What in the living piss does this mean? Is Picasso telling us to keep working over and over on the same piece of art, like the endless coats of paint applied to the Eiffel Tower, or whoever does the make-up for Ant and Dec? Thankfully, no, the hairless Spaniard (Picasso) is getting at something else entirely.

I met former Right Honourable Former Prime Minister Liz Truss at a chance meeting on the *Sunday with Laura Kuenssberg* programme, the very day before she became PM. My actions resulted in my name being drizzled (like olive oil, jus or drizzle) across the front page of the *Daily Mail*, my performance referred to by some as an act of 'genius' and by others as 'puerile'. The choice of word had an exact correlation to the tendency to vote Conservative. I prefer the words 'earnest' and 'accurate'.

People (wrongly) presumed I didn't much like Liz; they commented on how it would be ridiculous for someone to sincerely like her so much that they would physically applaud and shout 'Well done, Liz' after watching her do an interview.[1] Far from sarcastic, my emphatic support was genuine, designed only to ensure Truss's tenure as prime minister would get off on the strongest footing. That some individuals, including the editor of the *Daily Mail*, felt that my appearance was in any way belittling will go to the grave with me as one of my saddest and deepest regrets, alongside missing out on hosting the reboot of *Deal or No Deal* and my relationship with Irish fighter Conor McGregor.

Luckily, Truss herself wasn't troubled by this whatsoever, and I could tell this by the look in her eyes from across the studio (glazed and hungry for meat). Thus, when I emailed primeministerliztruss4@hotmail.com (I guessed it would be that) some days later asking if she might sit for a portrait, her chief of staff replied instantly, asking, 'How did you get this email?' and also 'as the prime minister she will be very busy but I will work hard to find a window in her schedule and can probably manage to carve out five days'. I picked up my easel and began the long journey to Number 10 Downing Street.[2]

I was welcomed into Number 10 by a lithe lad in a blue Ralph Lauren suit, who smelt like a mix of Sure for Men and BBQ Hula Hoops – an odour I always associate with power. He walked me through a corridor with dozens of traditional (aka shite) portraits of

1. Unfortunately, when I am trying to be at my most truthful, there is something about my voice that comes across as facetious and sarcastic. This is something that causes me some difficulties and I am working on it with a speech therapist called Denise.

2. About one hour and twenty minutes on the Avanti train from Birmingham New Street to London Euston if it is running smoothly, then another thirty minutes or so to Number 10 via various options: you can get the London Underground and take the Victoria Line to Green Park, then change to the Jubilee Line, getting off at Westminster; OR the Northern Line straight down to Charing Cross and then walk; OR the 91 bus will take you just outside Euston to Whitehall stop N; OR the 24 will take you slightly closer to Horse Guards Parade but you have to walk a bit from Euston to Warren Street. I took a cab.

Fig. 31 *Fucking Hell*, 2022, squid ink on pages of *Economics for Dummies*, 3 × 4cm.

Fig. 31

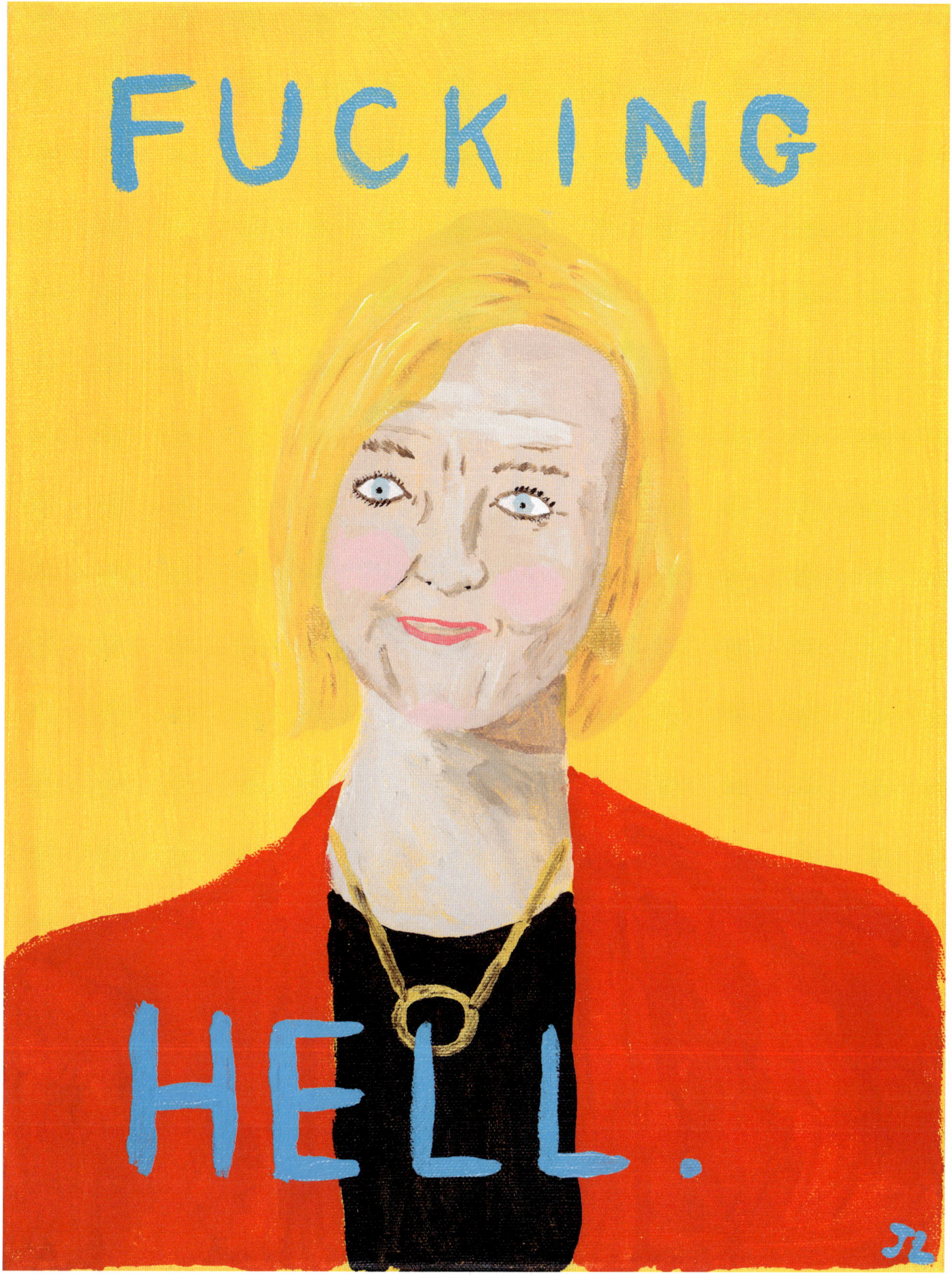

old prime ministers (Theresa May, Boris Johnson, the one who shagged a pig), which a lesser artist would've been intimidated by but, actually, it just gave me a real boost.

'How's your day been?' he asked, attempting small talk.

'Yeh, alright,' I said, lying. 'Actually, I've been having a bit of a nightmare with my Hotpoint H55RM1110W1 Fridge in white. It's just not getting cold enough.'

'Oh, that is annoying,' he said, uncaringly. We arrived at an old oak door. He knocked three times and waited for a response. Some seconds passed before a voice shouted, 'ICE CUBE!' The lad nodded and in we went, or we went in, whichever you prefer.

Truss was sat opposite her chancellor, Kwasi Kwarteng, playing the card game Dobble, which I believe is a sort of slightly more complicated version of Snap.

'Green spider,' squealed Kwasi as he slapped a card down.

'That spider isn't fucking green, you twat,' spat Truss.

'It's dark green,' he replied, terror in his voice.

'It's black and you fucking know it.' It was truly thrilling to see fiery debate occurring at the highest level.

The lad in the Ralph Lauren suit coughed to announce our presence in a way that suggested he had done it many times before. Truss looked up and, with those tiny little lizard eyes, clocked it was me. Her body language changed from combat mode to something altogether softer, like when Clive Myrie switches on the news from a report about a dangerous pothole to a story about an adorable toad.

'Fucking hell Lycett, you tosser! All the papers think you were ripping the piss out of me!'

'I know,' I said, giggling, sharing in the bafflement. 'I'm not sure why anyone would think someone supporting you would seem unserious.'

'I'm going to go and launch this mini budget now, then,' said Kwasi, picking up a pile of papers, some of them falling to the ground, which he just left there.

'Kwasi, darling, why don't you go and tell someone who gives a fuck,' she said, pushing his arse through the door with the point of her Dolcis shoe and slamming it shut. She lit a cigar and sat back in her chair. 'Fuck me, that guy is a nause.'

We sat in silence for a moment, Liz taking a few drags of her cigar, me sending a text to my mom[1] saying I'd arrived safely and that the Avanti had only been delayed by twenty-five minutes but experience had told me to build in a minimum thirty-minute contingency anyway. Finally, Liz spoke. I can't really remember what she said – it sounded quite grand, almost poetic, about destiny or chess pieces. I do recall it

1. Contrary to those who believe it is exclusively American, the spelling 'Mom' rather than 'Mum' is correct in many areas of Birmingham and the Black Country.

Fig. 32 My rejection letter from ITV.

Fig. 32

ITV
Television Centre
[redacted]
London
[redacted]

Joe Lycett
[redacted]
Birmingham
UK

Dear Mr Lycett,

Thank you for your correspondence regarding hosting the new *Deal or No Deal* on ITV1.

We enjoyed your audition tape but have a pre-arranged contract that states we must commission at least one reboot of a beloved gameshow per year which is hosted by Stephen Mulhern. As such we are going with Stephen Mulhern.

Best Wishes,

Carolyn Kennedy

Head of ITV

started with 'Fucking hell' and ended with 'Right, we best get on with this fucking painting, hadn't we?'

She sat for hours without blinking. I wondered at one point whether this was her way of sleeping, like Gandalf, but then she cleared her throat and spat the resulting phlegm into a copy of *The Economist* to remind me she was awake. This blinkless stance was actually quite helpful as I wanted to take particular care to get her eyes just right. I was keen to capture their intrigue, their intensity, and their ability to burn through light fixtures and stone. It was remarkable she could hold them so still, aside from at half-hour intervals when each one swivelled independently 360 degrees. I painted as various ministers, advisors and secretaries came and went, each request met with the same response from Truss: 'Fucking hell.' I understand the finished piece hangs in her private study. Her exact words to describe it were: 'Fucking hell.' I took this as emphatic approval.

I left entirely exhausted. It hadn't occurred to me how relentless the job was; a conveyor-belt of disasters, threats and urgent questions needing imminent answers. And yet her resolve to say nothing but 'Fucking hell' to all of it was impressive and, dare I say, inspiring. We kept in touch, casually at first as she was understandably fairly busy for those next few days. But then things calmed down and we now message almost daily, swapping Wordle scores, lists of people we would arrange to have killed (as a joke!) and viral memes. She loves colourful recipes and videos of Tucker Carlson trying to instigate wars. She would like Carol Vorderman to be killed (as a joke!)

Months after her premiership ended and Sunak had taken her place (another great guy IMHO), I began to reflect on her time as our leader, and what it meant for us as a country, but mainly me personally. At the time of her ascension some people said that it was a disaster; the natural conclusion to the ill-considered and self-destructive Brexit vote. These people said our politics had suffered from a prolonged period of degradation, resulting in the electorate becoming befuddled from a constant tsunami of half-truths and lies presented to them via largely unregulated social media advertising and inadequate political TV programming. In hindsight (and probably foresight), say these remoaners/haters/gays, Brexit was a deeply stupid thing to do, with little to no benefit to anyone actually living on this island, and as such could only be implemented once all the smarter and more nuanced politicians had been shuffled out, replaced by a group of people as stupid as the decision itself.[1] On the contrary, I believe her time as PM was a triumph.

As I reflected on my portrait of Truss[2] something profound occurred to me. I've noticed over the years that my favourite artworks generally

1. Reader, let me state it clearly that this is not something that I would ever say. It demeans the electorate and the astute prime ministers of recent years and goes against our fantastic and infallible country. I write it here only in the spirit of journalism, and also because former PM Boris Johnson taught me the trick of writing down two sides of an argument to understand them both, before deciding to pursue the more reckless one because it is more exciting and will sell more copies of the *Telegraph*.

2. Not literally. Truss's portrait does not reflect at all, absorbing light like a roll of Plenty does with spilt barista oat milk.

Fig. 33 An ancient diagram depicting hindsight.

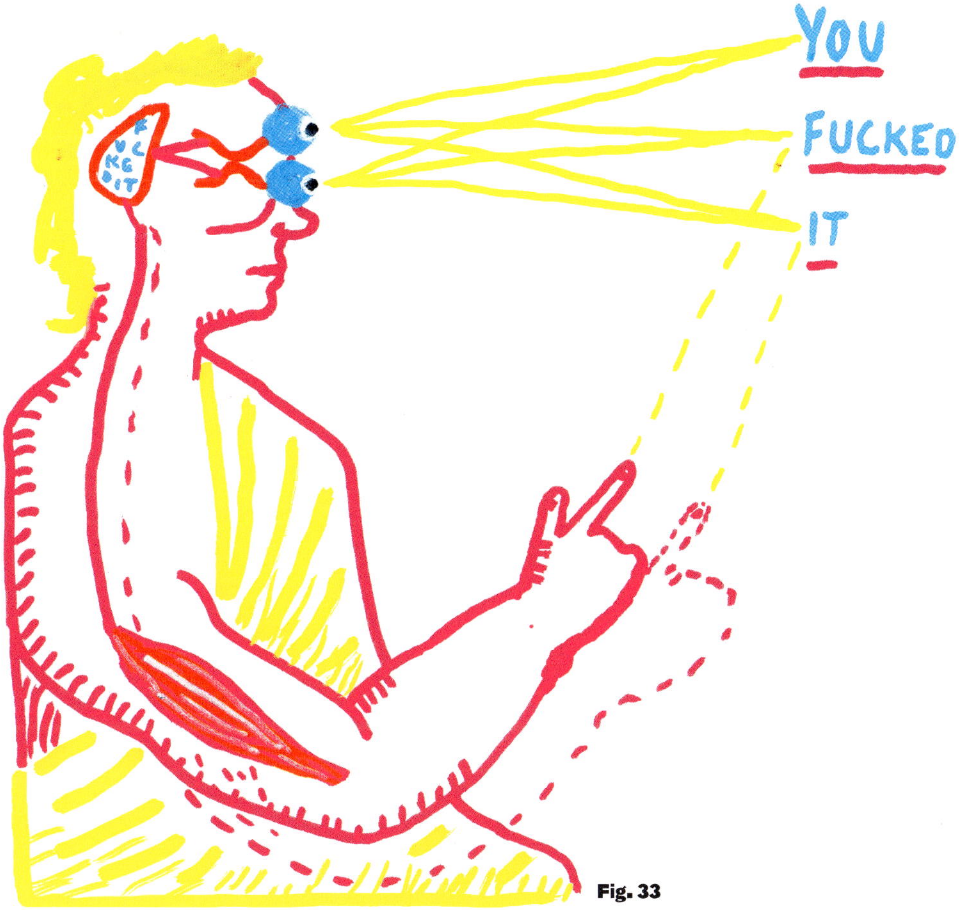

Fig. 33

follow a similar pattern in that they are unfinished. I think the most beautiful building I've ever visited is the Sagrada Família in Barcelona (apart from Gloucester motorway services on the M5, but to be fair to the Sagrada it does not have an independent farm shop). When I visited, and as I write this, it was/is unfinished. It's been like this for over 140 years. But far from diminishing its beauty, to me its unfinishedness makes it even more beautiful. It feels alive, still evolving, changing, growing. An unfinished work that holds something back leaves space for imagination and mystery. Beauty is in the colours unused, the words unsaid, the instruments left unplayed, the M&S Count on Us chicken jalfrezi with rice (400g) left uneaten.

And so it is with Liz Truss and her forty-four days as the prime minister of the United Kingdom. To some a job unfinished, but to me – the policies she never implemented, the budgets unannounced, the Prime Minister's Questions unanswered, the countries uninvaded (France) – it was beautiful. To finish a full term as prime minister? What nonsense! To finish it means to be through with it, to kill it, to rid it of its soul.

Sweet Liz, there is no shame in doing the job for 1.5 months. It is for us to fill in the gaps.

Fig. 34

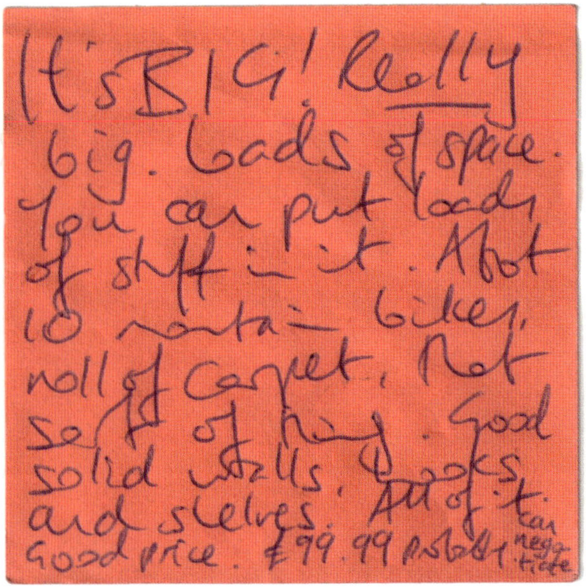

Fig. 34 Liz Truss's schedule (in her own words). I too was confused when I read this, but it turns out Liz misheard and thought I'd asked her to write a 'shed deal'.

Fig. 35 Etching of me and my father outside the Sagrada Família.

Fig. 35

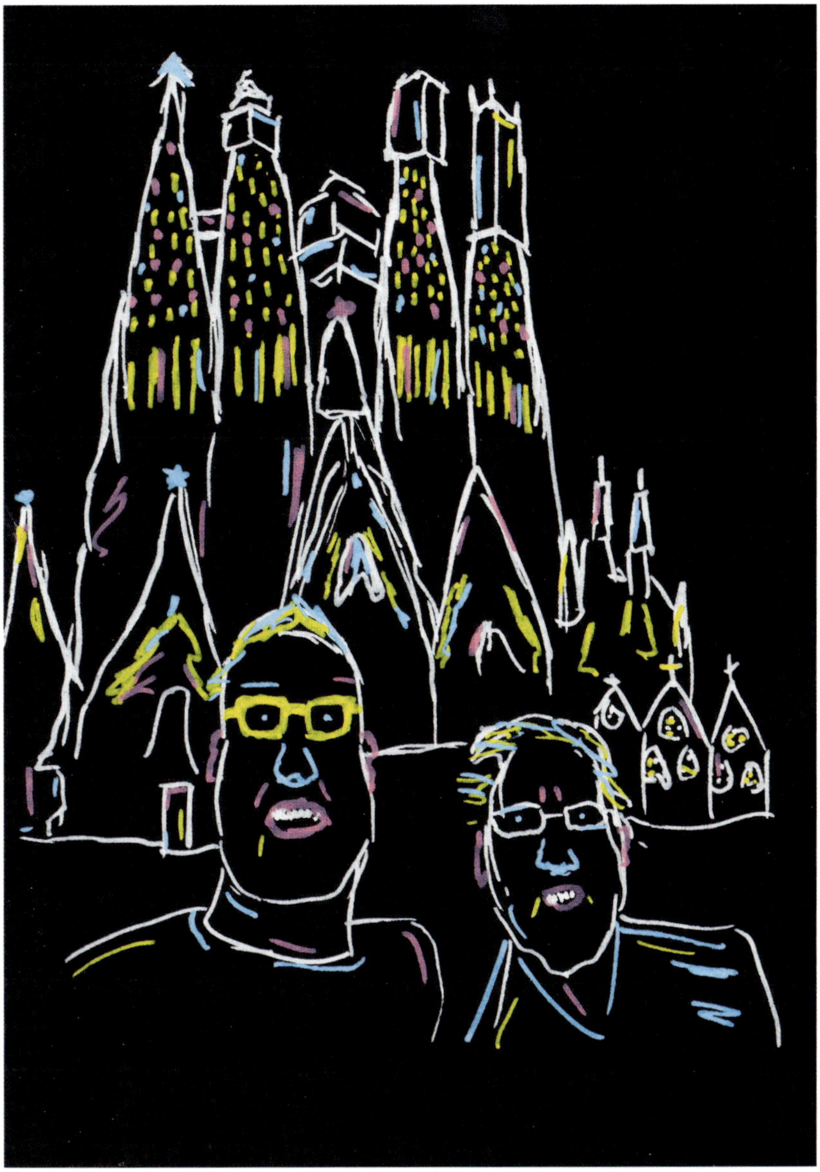

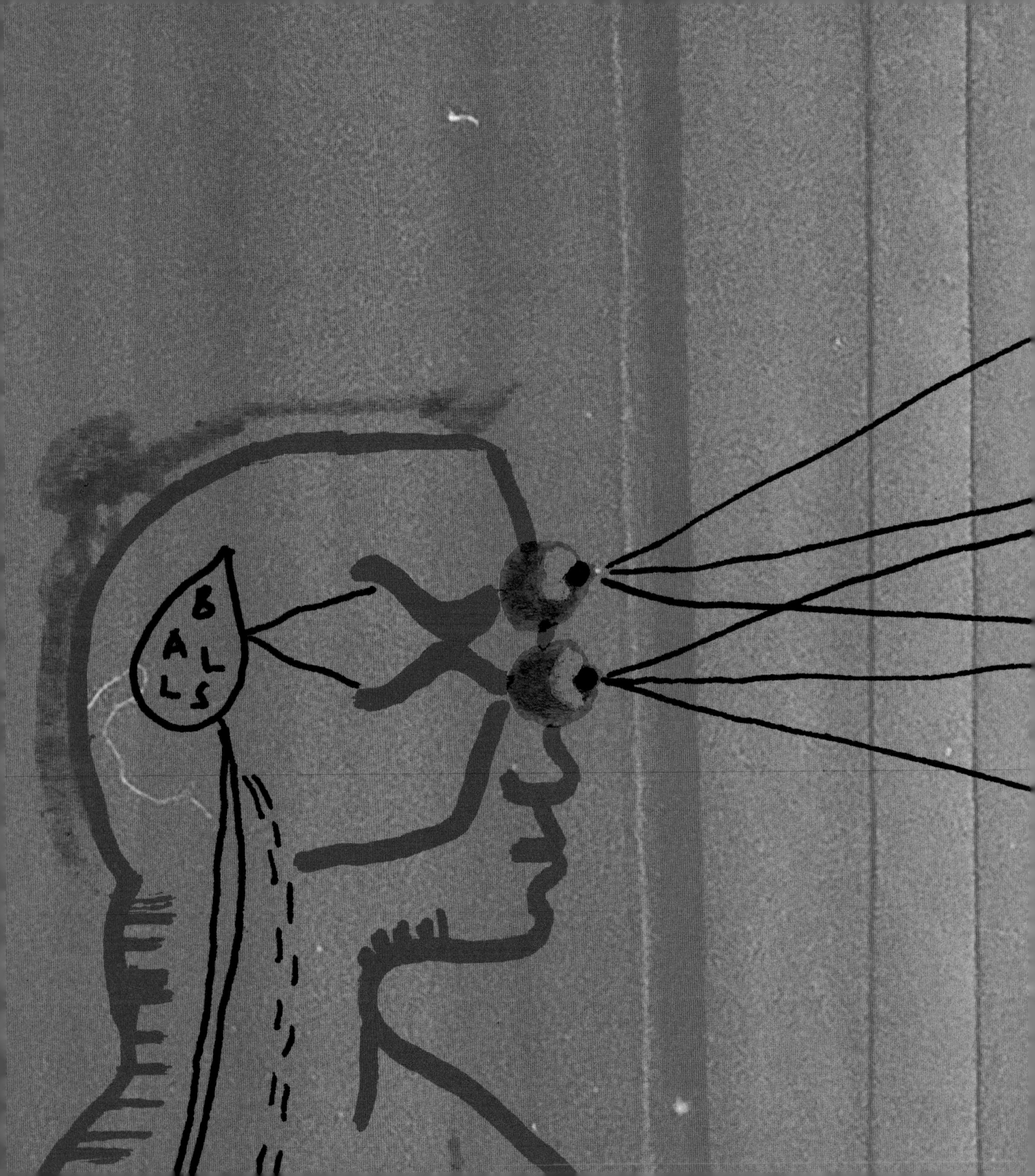
BALLS

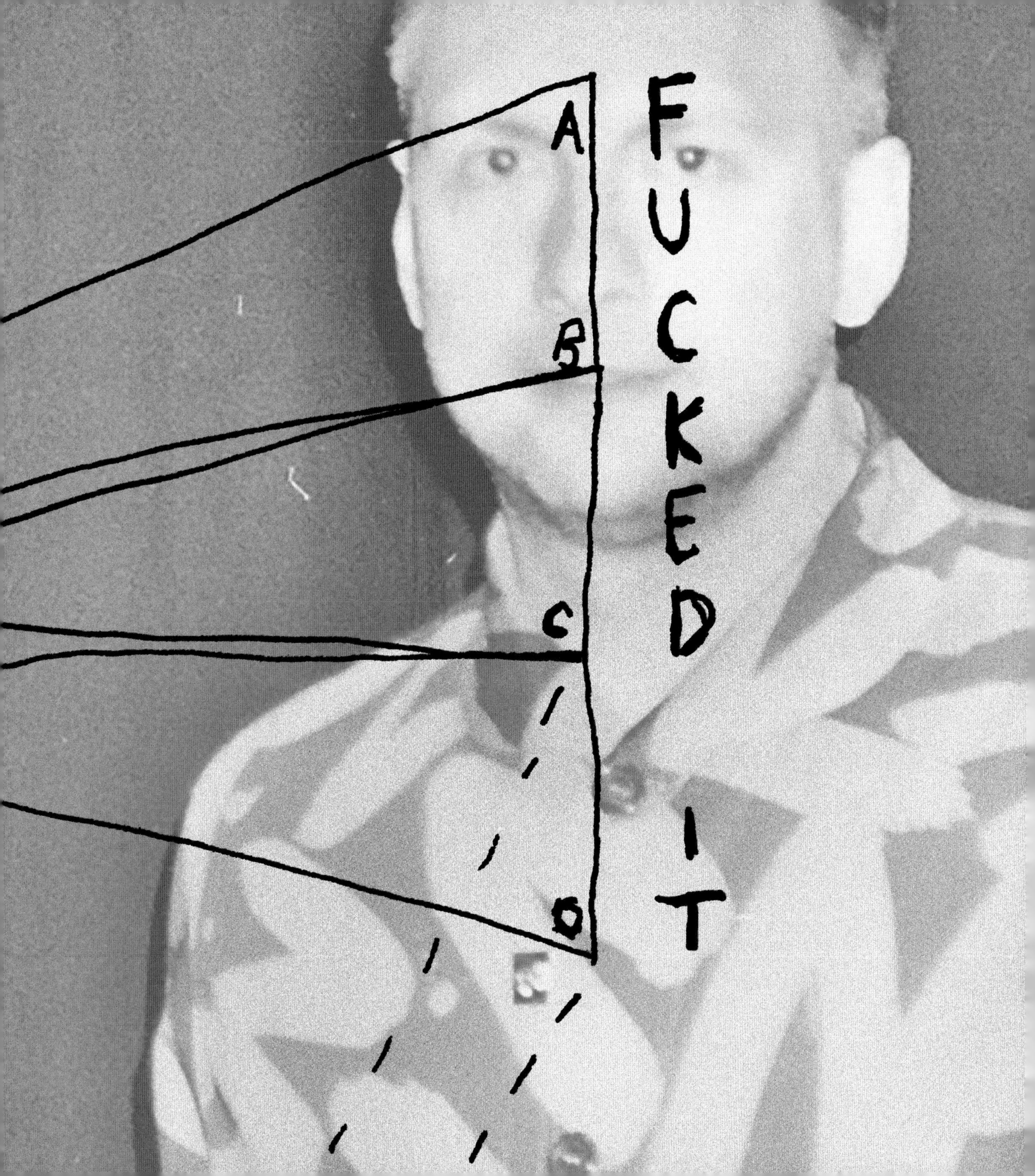
FUCKED IT
A
B
C
D

EAMONN HOLMES & RUTH LANGSFORD

Like Mark Twain, Ernest Hemingway and Michael Portillo, I am a great fan of train travel. There is little more civilised than sitting down in a modern train carriage and watching as the world passes by, and then sometimes not passing by at all while they delay the journey for over an hour to clear a small collection of leaves.[1]

Of course, train travel is not without its issues. In the United Kingdom, the trains have had a bad run of press recently on account of them being frequently delayed, unreliable, dirty, expensive, uncomfortable, smelly, dangerous, overcrowded, bumpy, tedious, polluted, stressful and full of violent gangs. But I don't let that put me off, and that's how I ended up on an Avanti West Coast with TV presenters Eamonn Holmes and Ruth Langsford.

I had been at a speaking engagement in Preston (sometimes I refer to stand-up comedy gigs as 'speaking engagements' as it makes the act of talking about your arsehole in front of hundreds of people sound cultured) and found myself on a very busy service.

Reader, I don't want there to be any confusion: I absolutely should be in First Class at all times. But sometimes I feel it is important to see what it is like for those less fortunate than me, and so I stepped onto a carriage labelled Standard Premium.[2]

On this particular occasion, there must have been a sale at John Lewis or Burton because the middle-class carriage I boarded was absolutely bursting.[3] As such, I decided to sit in the first available seat, which was at a table of four. Next to me I was surprised to see Hollywood actor Ryan Gosling, wearing a cap down low to cover his eyes and with AirPods blasting out what sounded to me to be *Cheryl: My Story* by Cheryl Tweedy/Cole/Ferrari-Viscount, but read by an actor. I later glanced at his phone screen, and it looked like Daniel Day-Lewis was sending voice notes to Gosling's WhatsApp.

Opposite us sat Eamonn and Ruth, who were far more friendly and engaged, reassuringly saying, 'Yes,' when I asked if the chair was free, as Ruth moved their coats onto her lap. Ruth had a well-worn copy of *The Spectator* in front of her while Eamonn had a Panini sticker book for the German World Cup of 2006. As I sat down, he reached into his suit pocket and pulled out a brick of stickers, about four or five inches thick, and said, 'Got any swapsies?' The year was 2022.

1. Or twigs or someone tied to the track in a sex game gone horribly wrong.

2. There are three tiers available to the Avanti West Coast traveller: Standard, Standard Premium and First Class.

In First Class, you find yourself surrounded by middle-aged men with the name Martin, wearing blazers and/or cashmere jumpers. You are served a small meal and have access to complimentary drinks, including alcoholic beverages. First Class normally comprises of carriages J and K.

Carriages H and often G and F are Standard Premium, which is Avanti's attempt at providing for the middle classes: the fees are a fraction of what it would be to upgrade to First Class and as a result you get a fraction of the benefits (no food or drink but a slightly nicer chair).

Then there are carriages A–E, which are known as Standard, which is exactly what it sounds like: nothing is guaranteed, including human rights, and the staff treat you like the piece of shit that you know you are.

3. I want to make clear for legal reasons that this is an exaggeration for dramatic effect – to insinuate that the carriage may 'burst' in some way is possibly libellous against Avanti, and it would be remiss of me to antagonise their legal team with untrue statements. By 'bursting', what I mean is that there were probably only a handful of available seats, not that there were so many people in the carriage that it might have somehow compromised the structural integrity of the coach body, under frame, superstructure or chassis.

Fig. 36 *Eamonn & Ruth*, 2024, burnt butter on toasted brioche, about the size of a 20 pence piece.

Fig. 36

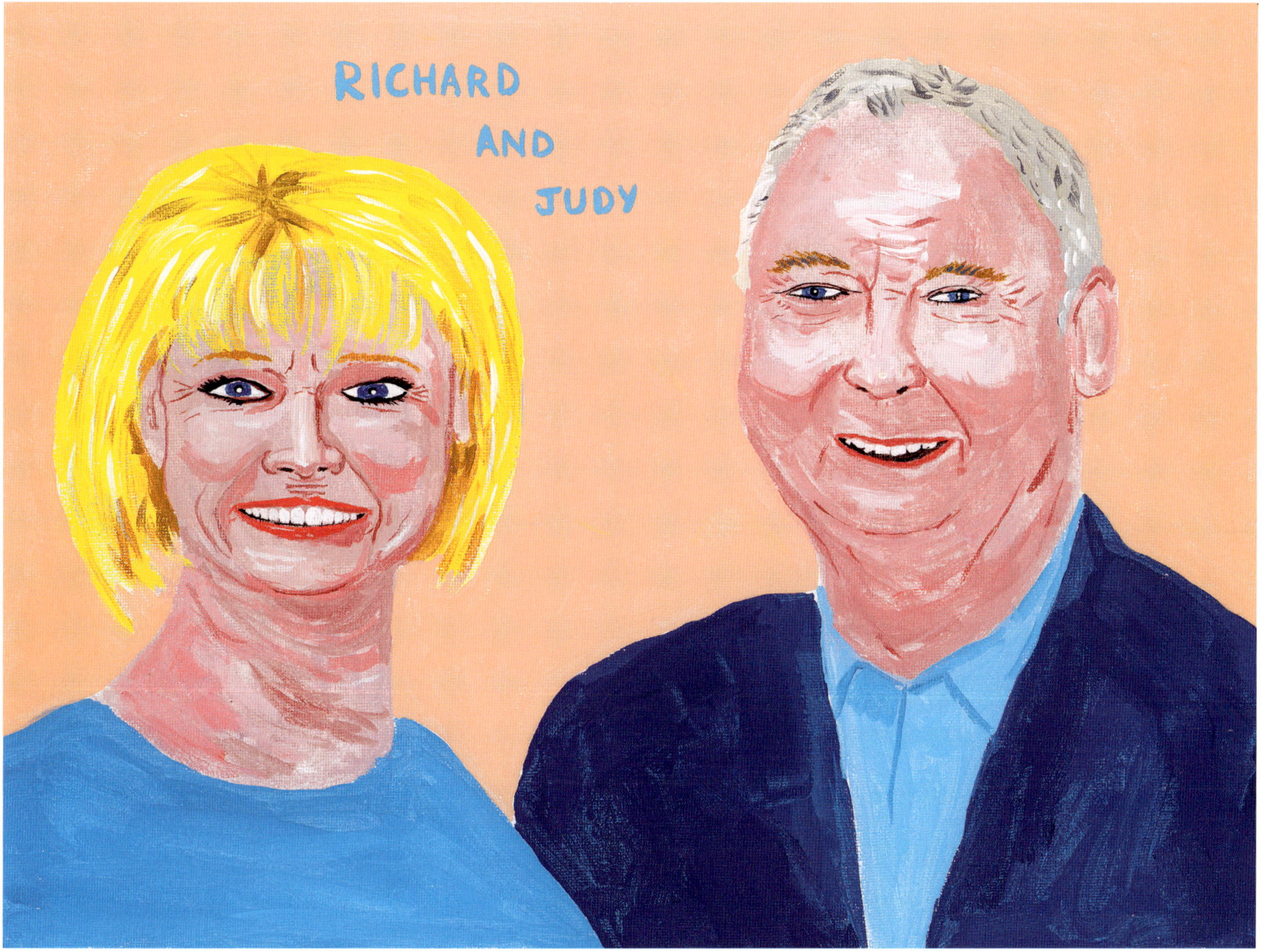

Mr Holmes had absolutely no idea what he was dealing with and was soon to discover that I am a voracious collector of Panini football stickers, with an entire room dedicated to them (known to visitors as 'The Gold Room'). I'd completed the book for Germany 2006, including shinies, before the kick-off of Germany v Costa Rica on 9 June (the first match). Looking down at Eamonn's sad, half-empty and very worn copy made him seem sad and pathetic, between you and me.

'Who you missing?' I said, smug as a bug with an expensive rug.

'Patrick Owomoyela,' he said. German player. Solid. I knew there were at least three spares in a Gold Room drawer.

'Yep, got it,' I replied.

'Seriously?' His expression was more joyful than I've ever seen it on television, apart from maybe when he did that interview with Dan Wootton.

'Seriously. Any others?' He began erratically flicking through the thing, getting totally carried away.

'Oh, erm, eek, I don't know, erm, Robert Krovač?'

'Easy, come on, give me a challenge,' I said, wishing I had a cigarette to drag on.

'Zinedine Zidane?'

'I've got five.' True story.

His hands were turning the pages so fast it was almost becoming dangerous. I leant in and calmly placed my right hand on his, to still him. 'Look,' I said, charismatically pressing his hand in a way that almost aroused the onlooking Langsford. 'I'm getting off this train at Birmingham New Street. How about you guys hop off with me, come back to mine, and you can go through my entire collection?' Ruth sighed, while a shallow pool of liquid congregated in Eamonn's lower eyelid.

'That's really very generous of you, but we must get back to London,' said Ruth, firmly.

'Don't be ridiculous, woman, we can spare a few moments to look at this young man's sticker collection and then get a cab,' he said. She huffed, then sat back into her chair and reopened *The Spectator*.

Barely two hours later, Eamonn and I were in The Gold Room, him filling his pockets with cards, while Ruth sat downstairs on the PlayStation playing *Fortnite*. 'I can't believe it,' he said, turning the pages of one of the many binders. 'Peter Crouch!'

'Take it,' I said, pouring myself another glass of a stunningly dry Picpoul. 'Take whatever you want.' I'm not sure I've ever had more self-confidence.

'Is there anything I can give you?' He was desperate to swap something, but I had duplicates of everything. 'I have a spare Lionel Messi! I saw someone selling one on eBay for two grand!'

Fig. 37 Illustration of Cristiano Ronaldo sticker.
Fig. 38 A preparatory drawing of Ruth on an ornate hotel chair.

Fig. 37

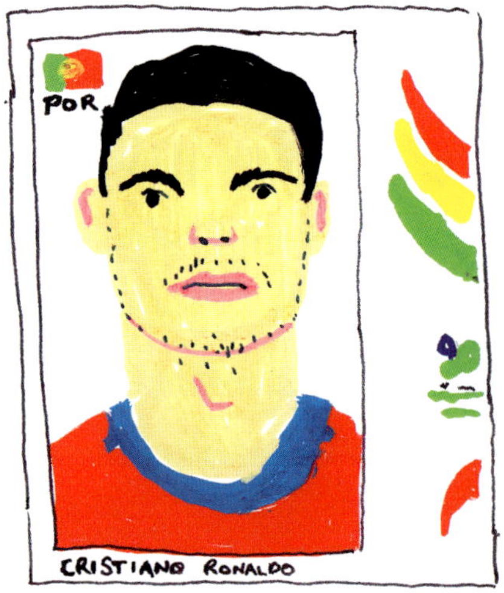

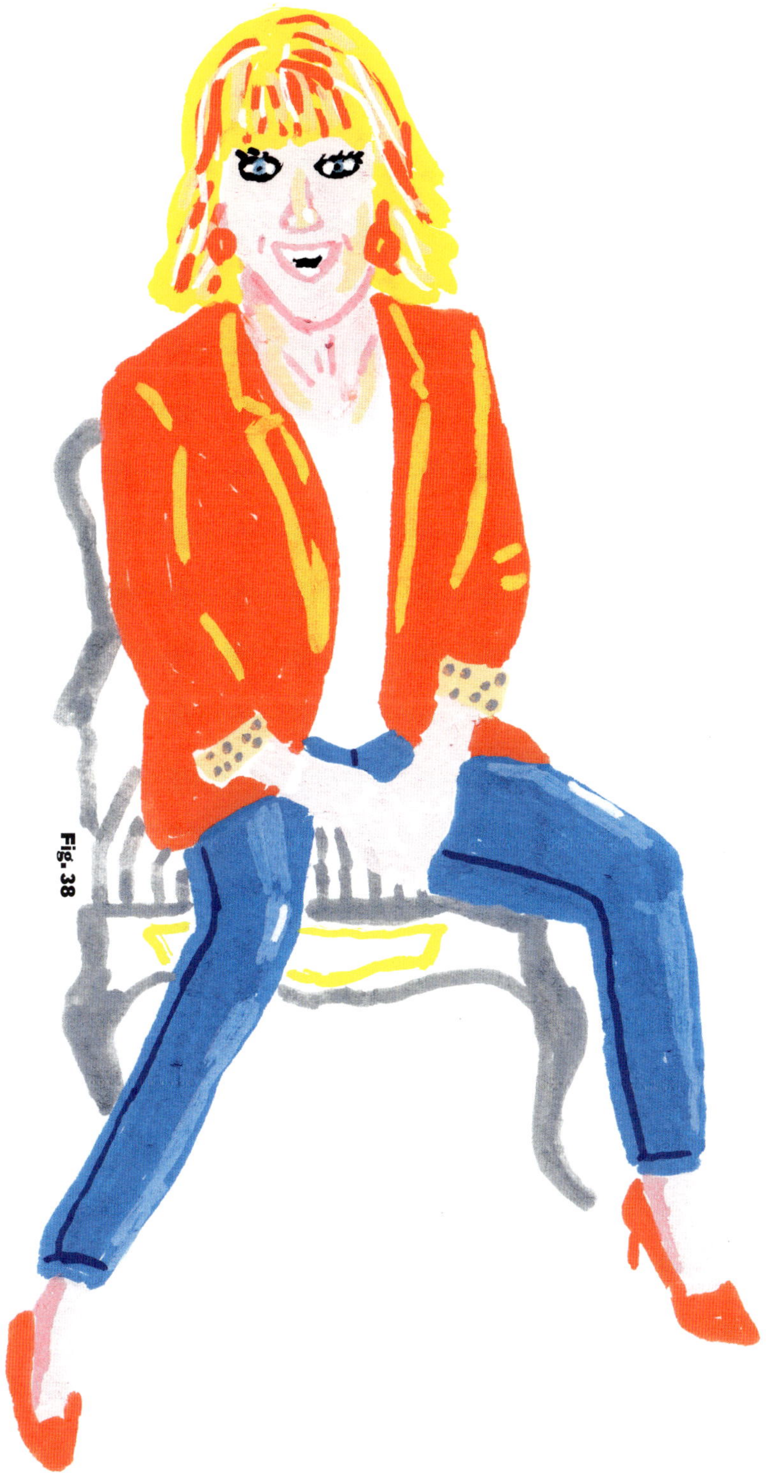

Fig. 38

'Darling, I was the one selling it.' I took hold of his hands. 'There is one thing you can do for me. Might you and Ruth sit for a short while in the orangery, so that I can paint you?'

'It is the least we could do,' Eamonn replied.

Ruth refused to be involved at first. When I asked if she would consider being immortalised in a painting by one of the great artists of this generation, she didn't even look up from the screen. 'Fuck off,' she yelped, jamming the control pad with her fist. 'I've got six more fuckers to kill and I'll get a Victory Royale.' She came round after I promised she could play *The Elder Scrolls V: Skyrim* as I worked.

Eamonn took home over four hundred cards that day. Ruth took the open bottle of Picpoul to celebrate her massacre. But I came away with much more: accomplished, unique and frankly breathtaking portraits of two of Britain's most beloved national treasures.[1]

1. And some information about Rylan that I am prepared to use if threatened.

Fig. 39 Ruth before I added her eyes and hair.
Fig. 40 A preparatory drawing of Eamonn in a camping chair.
Fig. 41 Eamonn & Ruth's schedule (written by staff).

Fig. 39

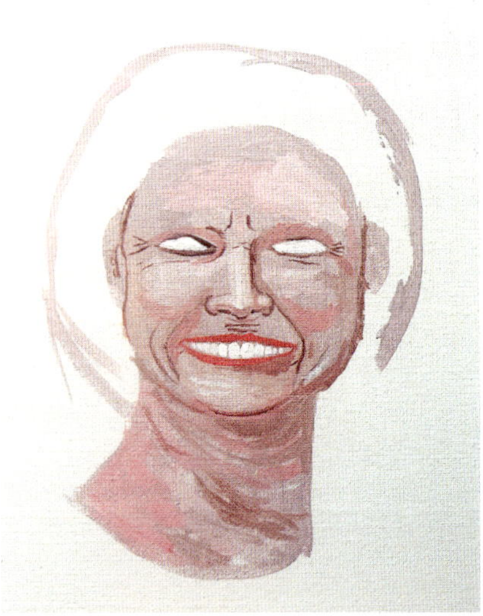

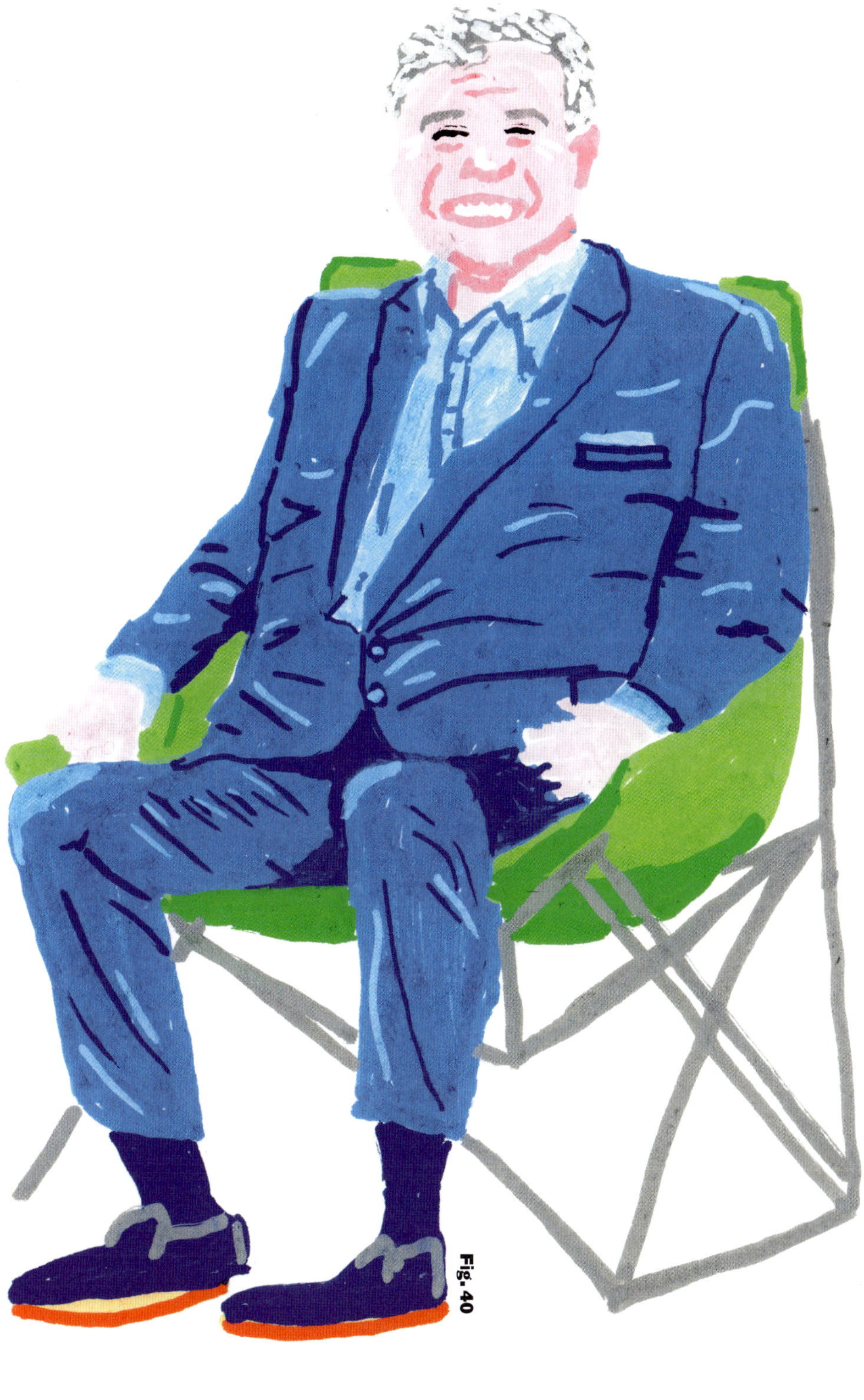

Fig. 40

Fig. 41

4.00

Rise.

4.30

Breakfast: multiseed sourdough toast with salted butter, thinly sliced salt-cured salmon, eggs scrambled in extra virgin olive oil and truffle salt, small roasted piccolo tomatoes with fresh basil, cranberry and orange juice mix.
And while Ruth eats that Eamonn has a little carton of Sun-Maid raisons and a Petit Filous.

5.00

Luxurious L'Occitane bubble bath with Le Labo Santal 65 candle and a large cup of rich hot chocolate, while listening to choral archestral music. And while Eamonn does that, Ruth has a stand-up wash at the kitchen sink using only multipurpose Dettol wipes.

5.30

Executive car to GB News Studio reads scripts, morning papers and searches own name on Twitter.
And while Ruth does that Eamonn has another little carton of Sun-Maid raisons and a short nap.

6.00
Eamonn live on air, Ruth in Green Room. Cheering and punching the air every time Eamonn appears on screen. Eamonn eats sixteen little cartons of Sun-Maid raisins over the course of the programme.

11.00
Executive car to ITV studios. Eamonn has another little carton of Sun-Maid raisins, leans in to driver and says 'How long till we get there 'cause think I'm going to shit myself'

12.00
Arrive at ITV studios and run to loo. And, while Ruth does that, Eamonn asks Loose Women producers if they have ever shat themselves.

12.30
Ruth on air with Loose Women Eamonn in green room cheering and punching the air every time Ruth appears on screen.

3.00
Arrive back home. Continue knitting project of an adorable tiny outfit for a friends puppy, applying the message 'you are precious treasure' in contrasting thread. And, while Eamonn does that, Ruth does a kickboxing YouTube tutorial in the spare room.

4.00
Early dinner. Garden herb-crusted halibut with creamy parsnip purée and a vanilla-infused champagne beurre blanc, garnished with edible gold leaf. And while Eamonn eats that Ruth has a banana Huel.

6.00
Bed.

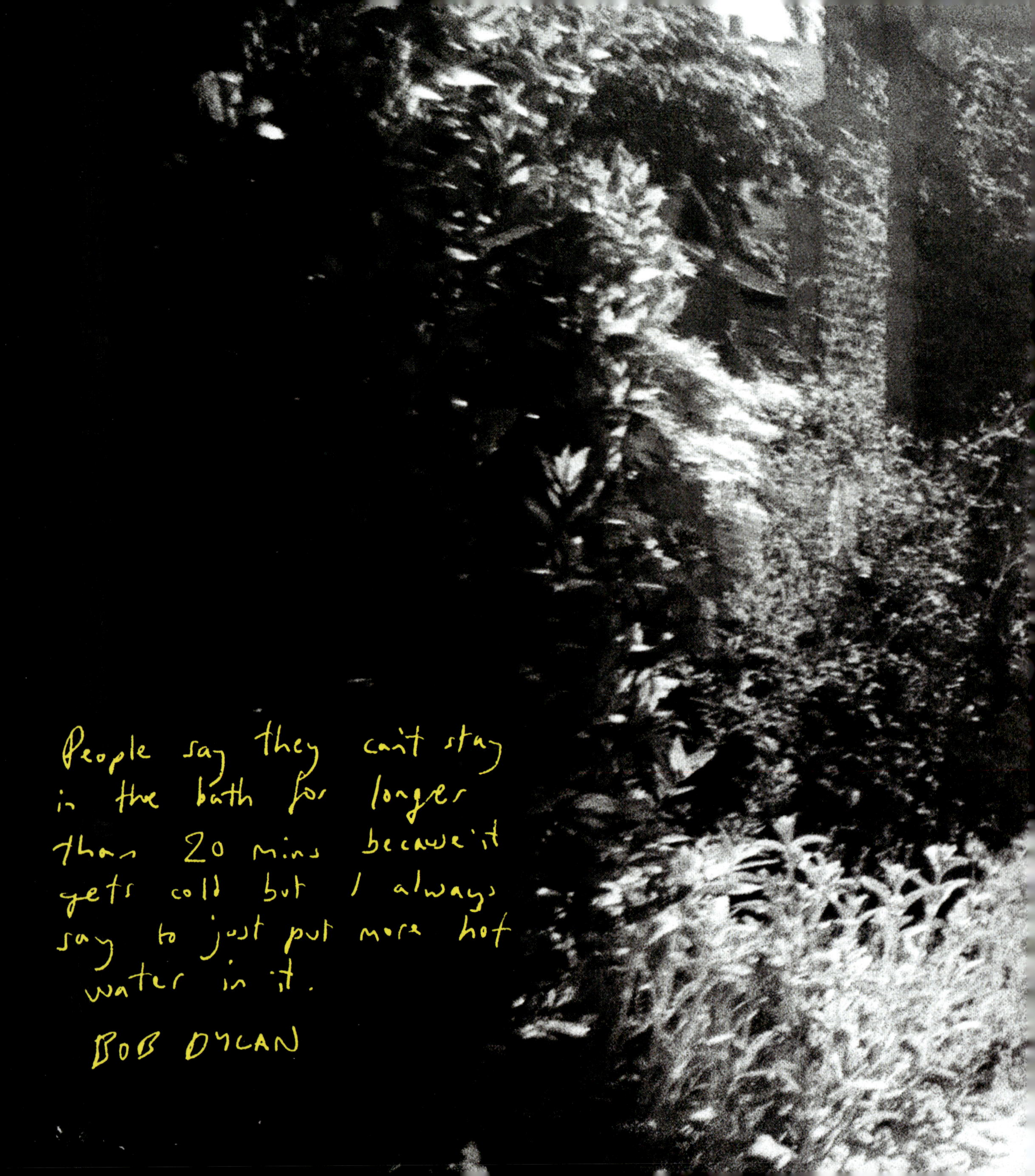

People say they can't stay in the bath for longer than 20 mins because it gets cold but I always say to just put more hot water in it.

BOB DYLAN

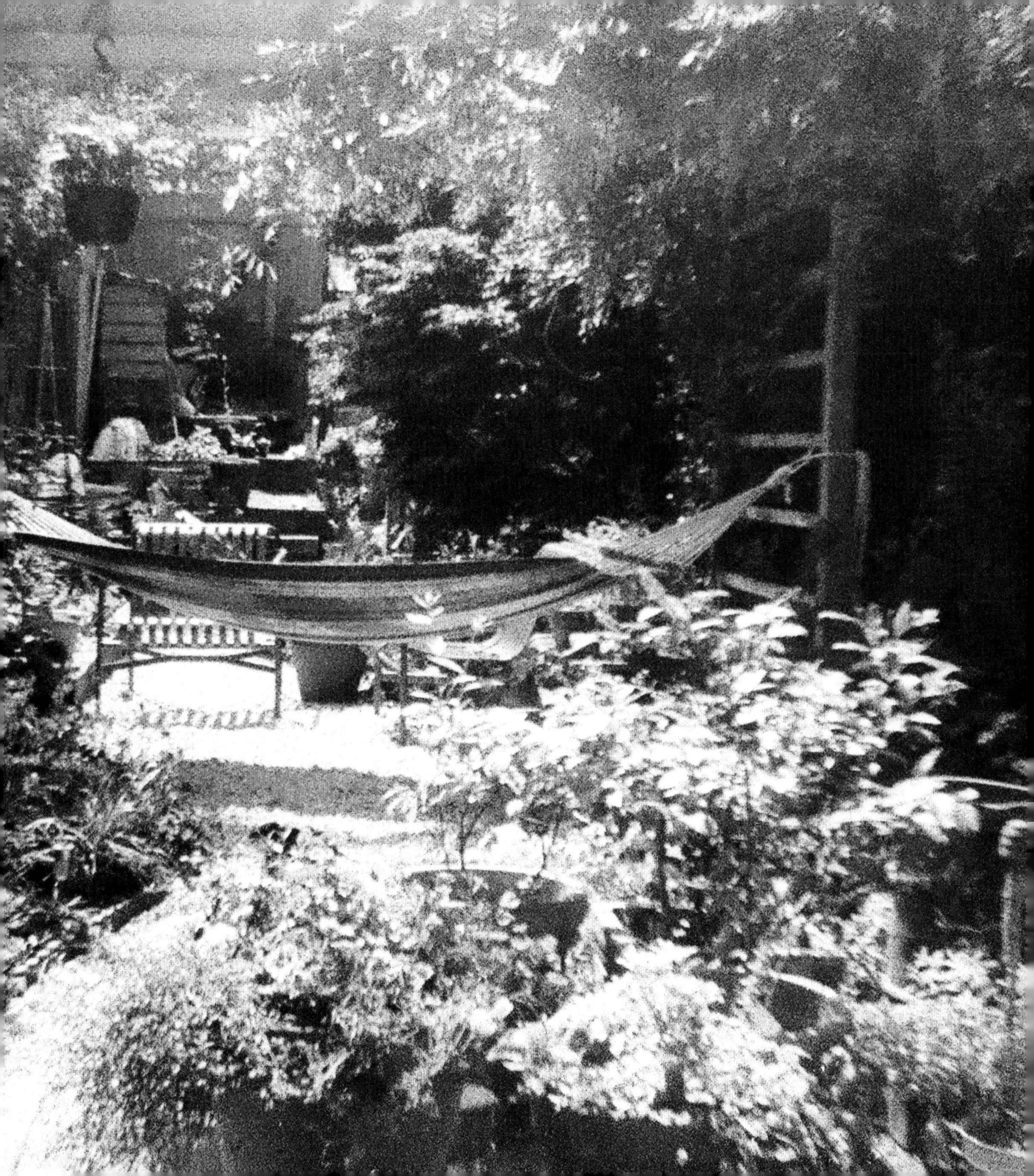

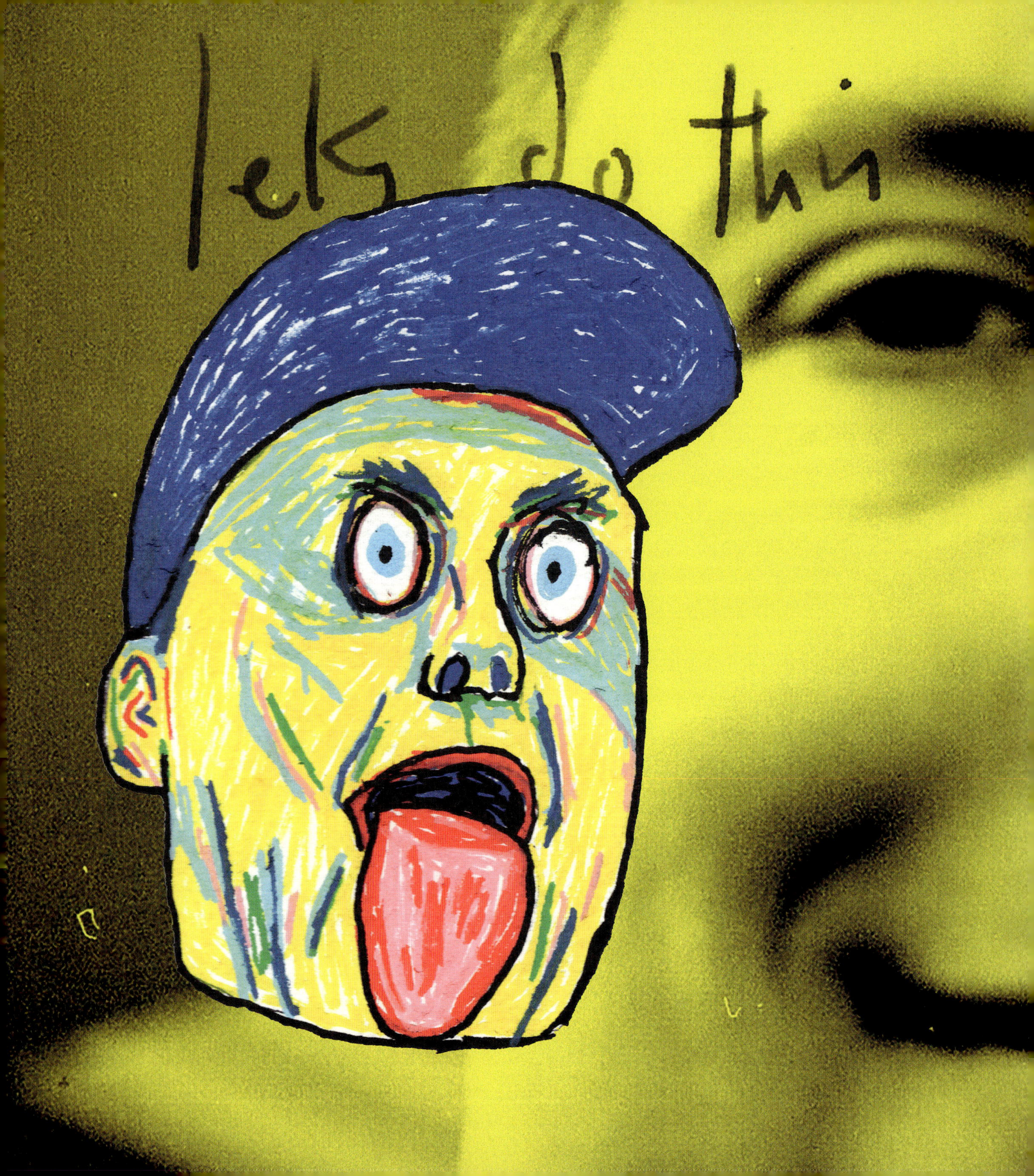
lets do this

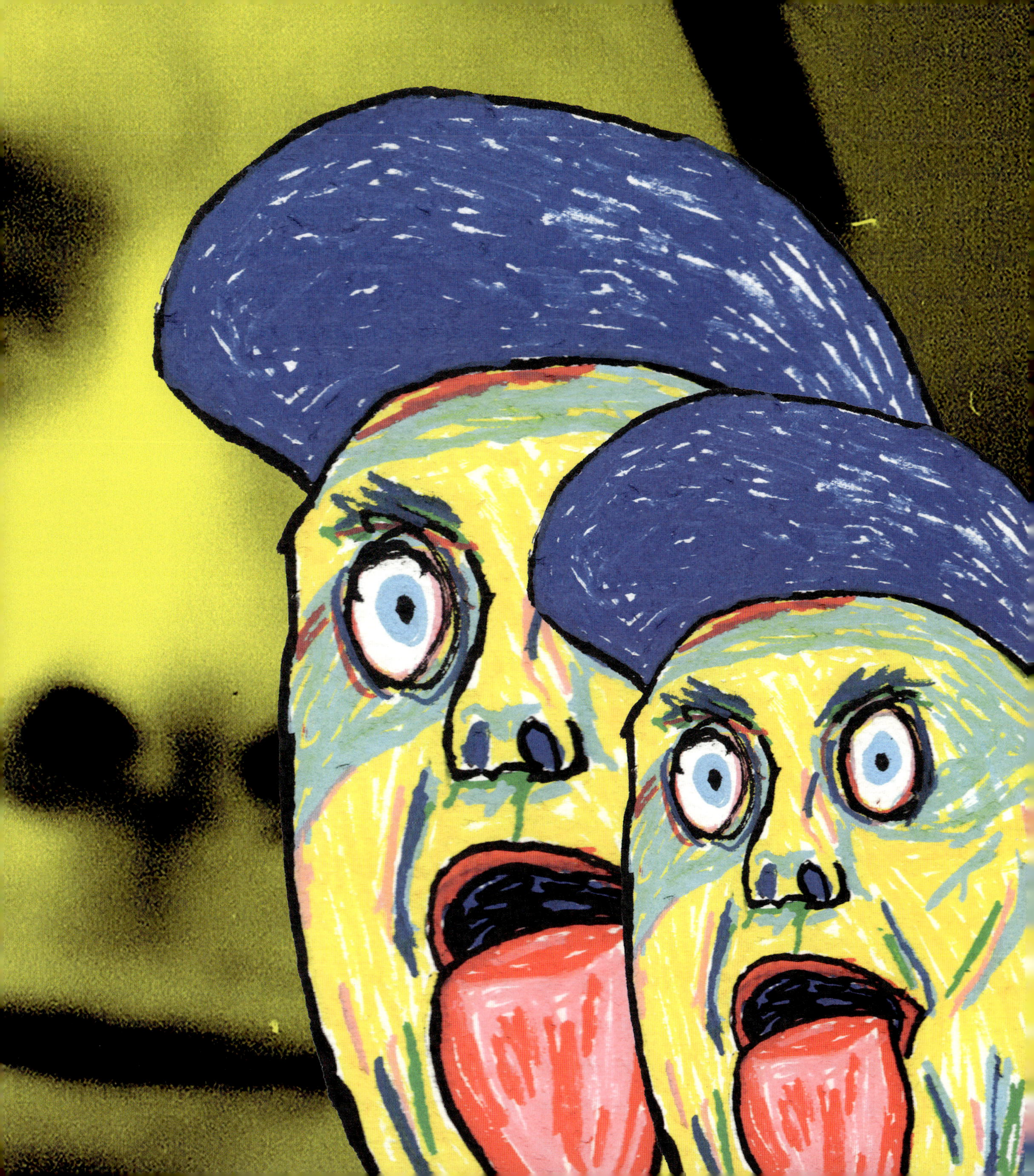

HARRY STYLES

You would think that, given the publicity and status afforded to me after Harry Styles purchased one of my paintings, I would be immensely grateful to him. But alas, the snivelling little worm ended up ruining my home.

It all began with a portrait of him done by David Hockney – an artist who is revered by the art world but, from what I can tell, is just some bloke with an iPad. I have often had my work compared to his, which I don't understand because I don't do my paintings on an iPad as I lost the Apple Pencil down the side of the seat in a Toyota Prius.

'I wasn't really aware of his celebrity then, he was just another person who came to the studio,' Hockney said, lying, to *Vogue France*. His immortalisation of young Mr Styles was apparently done over a couple of days at his studio in Normandy, and now appears in the National Portrait Gallery in London. On arrival, the portrait was widely condemned.

Weeks later, I was contacted by management for Harry Styles asking whether I would consider improving Hockney's portrait as it wasn't going down well on social media. I said that I didn't really know of Harry's celebrity, but I would google him and have a go. I hung up and immediately did my version of the painting in literally about three minutes on a bit of paper I got out of the printer, and all I really did was change his head so it looked like an egg. I was pleased with the results and put the painting on Instagram (short for Instant Gramicidin, a form of antibiotic).

The next day I went to the toilet (as is my right) and, while sat there dropping the kids (turds) off at (into) the pool (toilet water), noticed I had received an Instagram direct message from Mr Styles himself. He wanted to buy the painting and made me an offer I couldn't refuse (a year's supply of Diptyque candles). He asked that I did not disclose the real amount to the public as he didn't want to be seen pushing Diptyque, so I told the public the painting had been sold for £6 and a Kit Kat Chunky Peanut Butter. Soon after, Harry announced his own range of candles under his Pleasing brand, so I suspect he didn't feel he should be associated with a rival company.

Little did I know that the year's supply of candles amounted to nearly five thousand units,[1] which were delivered in one go. The pallets took up so much space that I was forced to abandon my home while I tried to flog the candles on Vinted. I got rid of the lot, but I've been unable to clear the residual smell of sandalwood, which is overwhelming and inflames my sinuses, so I have moved back in with my parents for the foreseeable future.

1. Harry told me he burns through a dozen a day.

Fig. 42 An exclusive photograph of my process. This one involved making an egg shape and then adding a neck and cardigan. Adding the red stripes was painstaking work that took a little over three minutes.
Fig. 43 *Harry Styles,* 2023, Posca pen on tablecloth, approx. 15 × 15cm.

Fig. 42

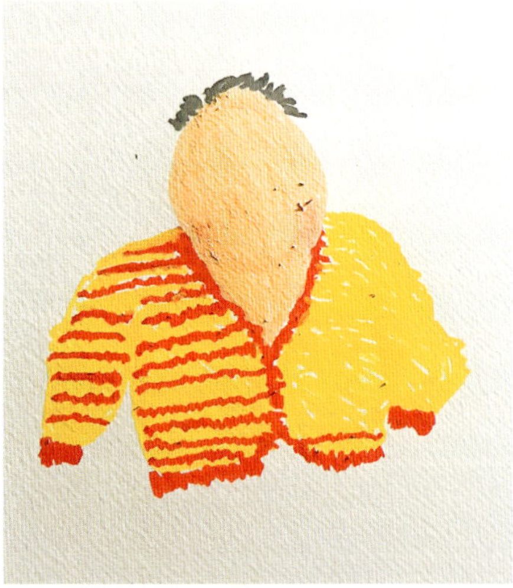

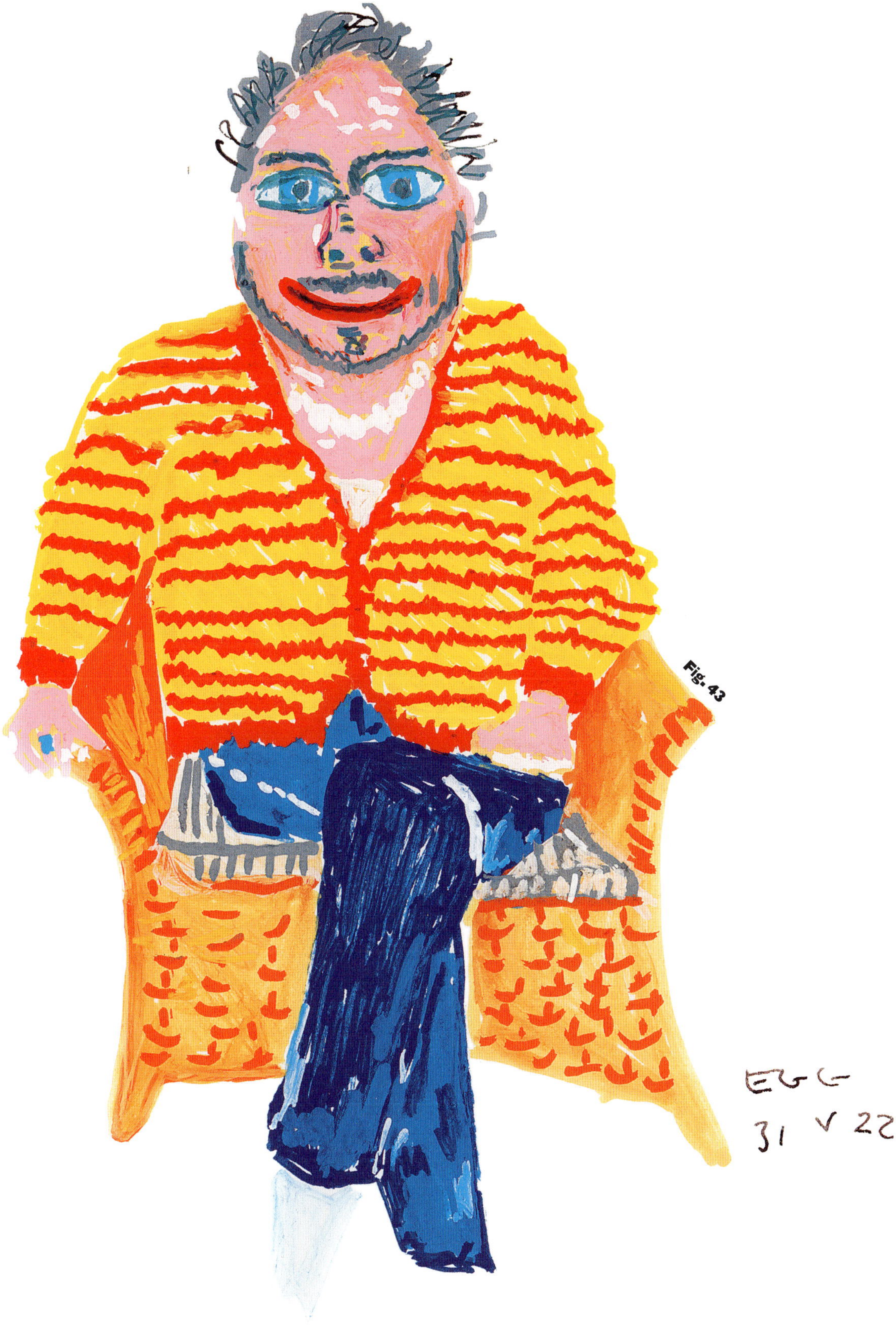

Fig. 43

S

ART

TREET
(INDOORS)

Street Art (indoors)

ROBERT PESTON

I don't want to make a big deal about it 'cause he seems like a nice guy, but I feel I should address the rumours, which are true, that since the late 90s I have been in a legal battle with the ITV presenter Robert Peston.

It all started in the hot summer of July 1994, around my sixth birthday, and around Robert's thirty-fourth, when my parents took me on a trip to London to kickstart my career in show business. I had a beautiful and angelic singing voice, which was once described by the pre-audition team on *The X Factor* as 'nice but not quite right', and so mother and father strongly believed I could and should be a child star.

Having grown up in Birmingham, the bright lights of the capital seemed brighter than any I had seen, apart maybe from in 1992 when my grandfather went into our garden shed to get blazed and accidentally set off a dozen fireworks. That was a very bright light. London was way different back then: no mobile phones, no Elizabeth line, no congestion charge zone. Dairylea Dunkers hadn't even been thought of. You didn't really have to respect women, and no one would judge you if you kicked a gay person over. Simpler, happier times. There were no branches of Leon, Wasabi or Five Guys. But there was, as there is now, and has always been, and is now, a Boots.[1] As there always was.

Most people in the UK see Boots as basically a familiar half-decent pharmacy with some nice skincare and OK sandwiches. But back in July 1994, the single surnamed Joe Lycett was standing outside Boots Piccadilly Circus clutching his mother's hand with his mouth wide open, in complete flabbergasted wonder at the size and stature of that extraordinary branch. (My mouth was also open because I am asthmatic and it makes it easier to breathe.) I'd never seen a Boots that big. How many types of toothpaste and painkillers could they possibly stock? How many products in there would use aloe vera? Would the Advantage Card work outside of Birmingham? Lloyd Webber would have to wait for once in his stupid life.

It can't be expressed enough what a mammoth Boots that Boots is. To that young boy (me) it was as if entering something else really big, like a car park or a field or a car park in a field, but that car park or field or car park in a field is a Boots. I was immediately stunned by the number of bottles of shampoo and bubble bath. Until then, that naive little punk

1. Boots was founded in 1849 by John Boot (cool name), and became one of the iconic and beloved British brands alongside Harrods and Greggs. It has changed hands a number of times. Not to go into too much detail, but Boots Group plc was famously merged with Alliance UniChem plc in 2006; no one knew what the hell a UniChem was, so they just called the new company Alliance Boots. This was bought the following year by an American company and an Italian bloke called Stefano. What Stefano wanted to do with it is anyone's guess – maybe he had lots of people coming round and wanted to capitalise on the meal deals – but he is a billionaire so I'd hazard a guess he just loves to have loads of stuff! Then, in 2012, Walgreens, the American pharmaceutical company, bought 45 per cent of it (I can't imagine buying 45 per cent of something, I can barely imagine what 45 per cent of anything looks like: 45 per cent of a cake is basically half, you may as well call it half) and they created a new company called Walgreens Boots Alliance. I cannot find why they demoted Alliance to the last word. It could be that it sounds like Walgreens and Boots are in an alliance, but it is unfair to the still thriving Alliance Healthcare to consider its name as a descriptive noun. My best guess is that, early in the renaming process, they threw out the far more accurate, but admittedly confusing sounding: Walgreens Boots Alliance Alliance.

This naming of large multinational companies has reached levels where the words start to melt into nothingness. If I work at Boots I can say, 'I work at Boots' at a party. If I work for Mitsubishi UFJ Financial Group Inc or Skadden, Arps, Slate, Meagher & Flom LLP and Affiliates, I'll just say that I work very hard. The longest business name I am aware of remains a limited company in the UK called: This Is The Company With The Longest Name So Far Incorporated At The Registry Of Companies In England And Wales And Encompassing The Registries Based In Scotland and Northern Ireland Up Until and Including The Current Date Limited. If you don't believe me, check Companies House.

It's not only companies that are guilty of it; the (understandable) fashion for name equality in families by creating double-barrelled surnames is laying the foundations for a future name apocalypse. If I have a child with, to choose someone entirely at random, Jacob Rees-Mogg, the child would likely be Bobby Lycett-Rees-Mogg. If Bobby then has a child with someone else with a double-barrelled surname, who then has a child, you could end up with someone with the name Steve Lycett-Rees-Mogg-Finnigan-Nyong'o-Windsor-Sunak-Cumberbatch-LaBeouf.

Fig. 44

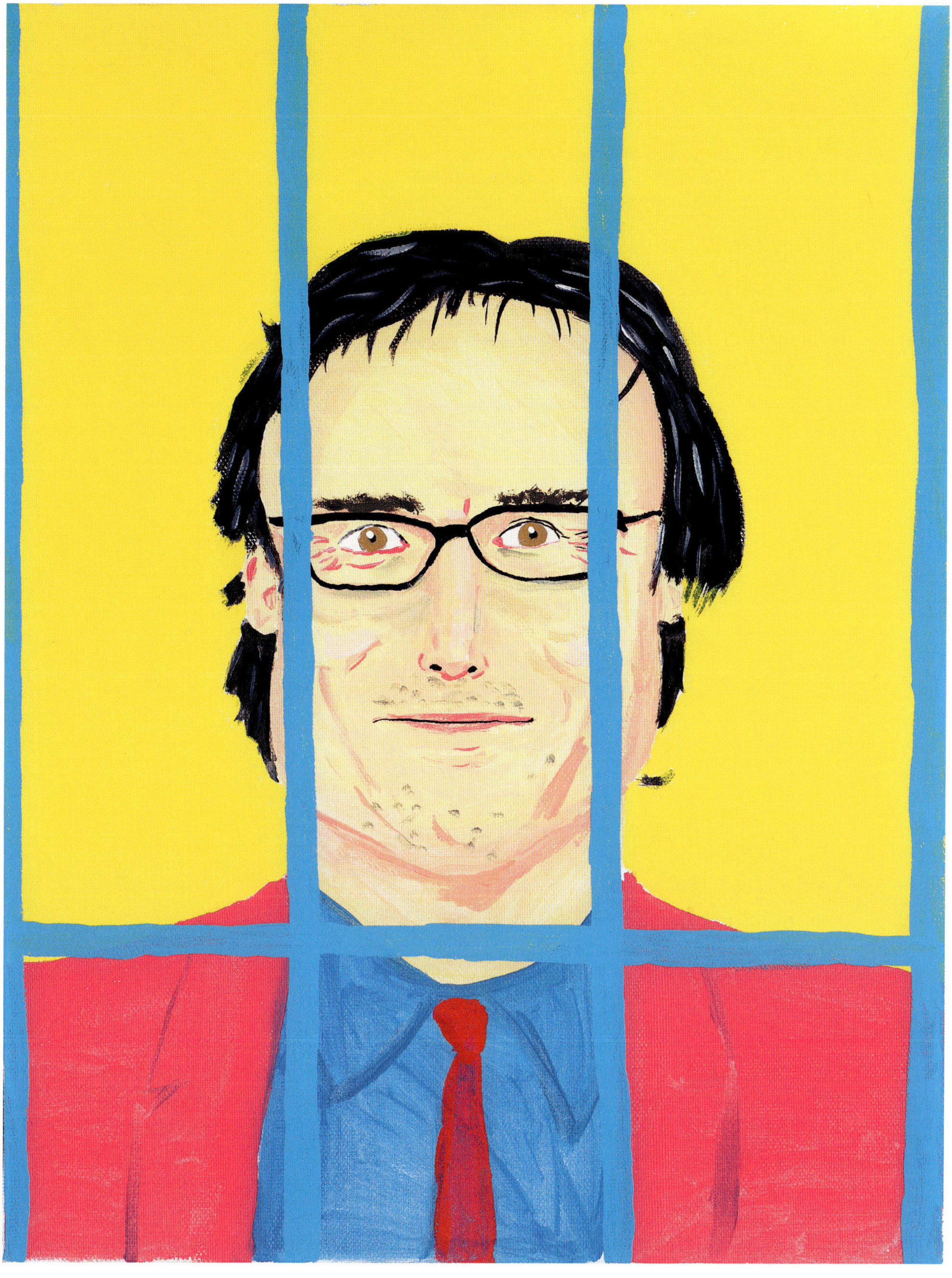

presumed there was only Head & Shoulders for adults and Matey[1] for youngsters. But here was shelf after shelf of all manner of delightfully stacked, colourful plastic bottles. I wanted to drink them all.[2]

Also inspecting the shelves of Boots that day, picking up some Ibuprofen and a sandwich, was Robert Peston. At that time, he was working at the *Financial Times*, grasping his way up the slippery journalistic pole that ended in him being the titan he is today. Peston is a thin, bespectacled, angular man, with a perennial look of concern on his face, as if he is always just about to have to tell someone they've left a chicken in the oven slightly too long. Fate and/or destiny colluded that day, so that both Peston and I found ourselves staring into the famous long Boots sandwich fridge at exactly the same moment. The young Lycett looked up at the young(ish), fop(ish), wasp(ish) Robert Peston, full of curiosity, trepidation and a little bit of admiration.

'There's a lot of sandwiches, aren't there, little fella?' he said, smiling down at me. He was stood next to, and clearly angling for, a prawn sandwich. I clung to my mother's leg, saying nothing.

'Oh yes, there are a lot of sandwiches. You like sandwiches, don't you?' she said, encouraging me to engage, yet I sensed from subtle muscle movements in her leg that she too was brimming with fear.

I nodded. That's all I had. Words had become as elusive to me as the meaning of the universe, or the reason Eamonn Holmes does what he does.

'And what sort of sandwiches do you like, chap?' Peston was trying his best. 'Chicken?' I shook my head. 'Oh, OK. Cheese ploughman's?' Another rebuttal from young Lycett. He only had one option left. 'Prawn?' I didn't even really like prawns, but in that moment the sound of the word was almost soothing. I nodded enthusiastically. Robert let out a deep sound resembling an 'oh', but more abstract than that.

'Well, that IS a surprise! I didn't think you liked prawns?' said mother, effortlessly transforming from caregiver to snitch.

'Gosh. OK. Well. That … that does put us in quite a quandary. Because I too was hoping to have a prawn sandwich. And I don't know if you've noticed, there's only one prawn sandwich left.' He literally had his hand on the thing.

My eyes darted around the fridge like darts in a fridge. The bastard was right. Only one prawn sandwich, Peston's fingers already caressing the waxy cardboard box. 'I'm sure you can have a different sandwich, little Joe, you like cheese, don't you?' My mother had now assumed the role of his chief negotiator. The woman had thrown me under the bus.[3]

'Oh, I mean … I can find somewhere else to get one …' Peston said, unconvincingly. The saliva was practically dripping out of the guy's mouth for that prawn sandwich.

1. For those unfamiliar with Matey – for a while I was a connoisseur – it is a bubble bath in a bottle that was designed to look like an officer from a naval regiment. As an adult it now seems inappropriate that youngsters will associate a nice warm bubble bath with the navy, when in fact the only bubbles the navy are responsible for are the hot froth on fresh enemy blood.

2. This desire to chug shampoo wasn't new; on another occasion, Mother was forced to pay for a Pantene she didn't want in a Birmingham branch of Superdrug because I had locked my disgusting little child lips firmly round the lid.

3. This is a turn of phrase and for legal reasons I should clarify my mother has never once 'thrown' me under a bus, but did once try to push me into a canal.

Fig. 44 *Robert Peston*, 2023, Marie Rose sauce on prawn, 2 × 5mm.
Fig. 45 Prawn.
Fig. 46 Another prawn.
Fig. 47 And another prawn.

Figs 45–7

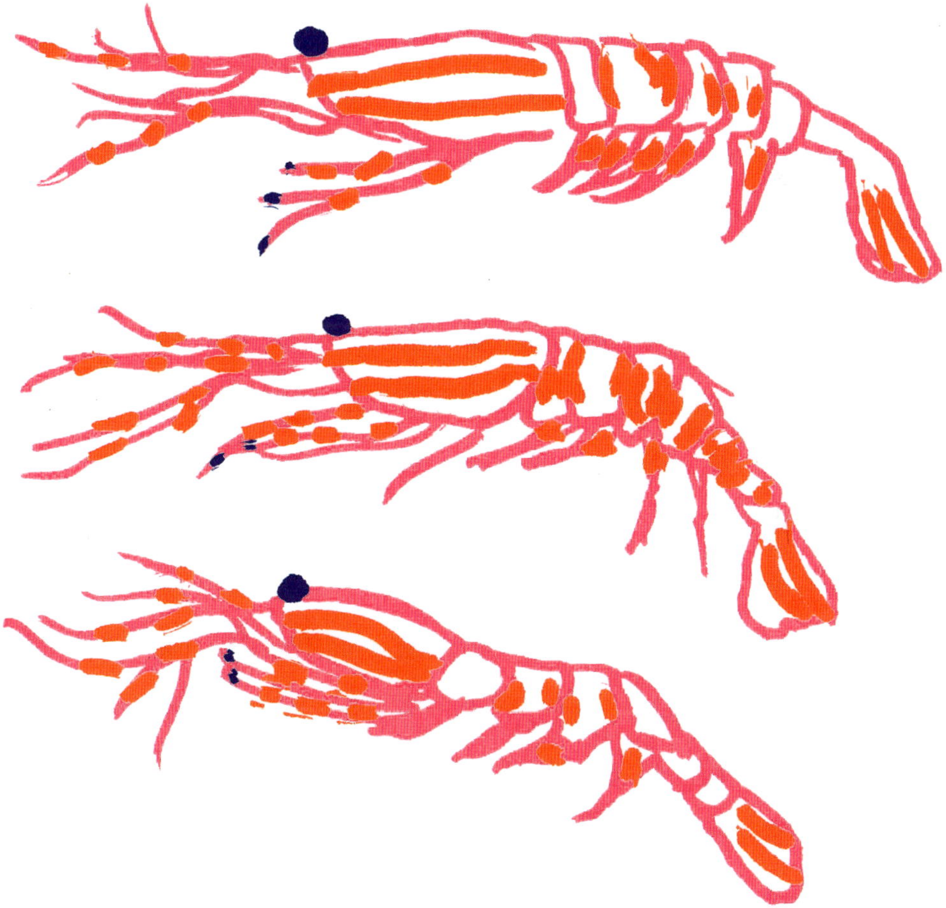

'Don't be silly. Joe doesn't even really like prawns. You take it, honestly,' said the scab (my mother).

'Cheers, little fella,' he said as he floated away gleefully holding what I will forever consider to be my prawn sandwich.

As I sobbed – loudly, uncontrollably, ostentatiously – I watched him purchase my sandwich, walk out the door and into the West End, my West End. He never once looked back at the destruction he had caused. I looked back at the fridge. Like fuck was I going to have chicken or cheese.

The rest of the London trip was completely ruined. I refused any other sort of sandwich and Mom started ignoring me, which I later learnt is a parenting technique, but at the time seemed a rude and inconsiderate approach to trauma. The treacherous bitch has since tried to convince me that pushing me into a canal is a parenting technique, but I am yet to have that backed up with empirical data.

I refused to participate in all the auditions she had lined up for me that day, and never auditioned again. I never got my chance to play 'Ensemble' in *Oliver*, or 'Ensemble' in *Billy Elliot* or 'Michael Ball' in *Michael Ball Sings Songs from the West End*. What's more, I had become undeniably obsessed with prawns. On one day alone I estimate I ate approximately three hundred prawns. I began to throw them back like roasted nuts. They don't tell you on the packaging because they presume you're only going to have a few, but eating three hundred prawns is really bad for you. I began to take time out of school because, in the words of my deputy headteacher, 'His farts are making other children cry.' My friendship group dwindled to one lad called Andy (his dad was a fishmonger and had access to good quality prawns).

My parents re-mortgaged the house to fund my addiction, and eventually became financially destitute. Until my father decided to buy some shares, in the hope they might pull us out of the hole we were in. And so, he picked up a copy of the *Financial Times*.

The details are blurry, but Mom spotted Peston's picture in the paper, and then put two and two together, and in their desperation my parents decided to sue, using the company who have the television adverts with the woman with the vile fringe who slips over at work and it isn't her fault. She has no one but herself to blame for the fringe. To this day not a penny has been clawed back – Peston's team have put most of their eggs in the basket of Mom saying that I didn't like prawn sandwiches, but also assert that just because he took the last remaining prawn sandwich that cannot be directly linked to my failure to become a West End star, which seems absolutely ridiculous to me when it is obviously his fault. As a gesture of goodwill, he did send a Hotpoint H55RM1110W1 Fridge in white but it's not working properly.

Fig. 48 Prawn sandwich Polaroid.
Fig. 49 Another prawn sandwich Polaroid.

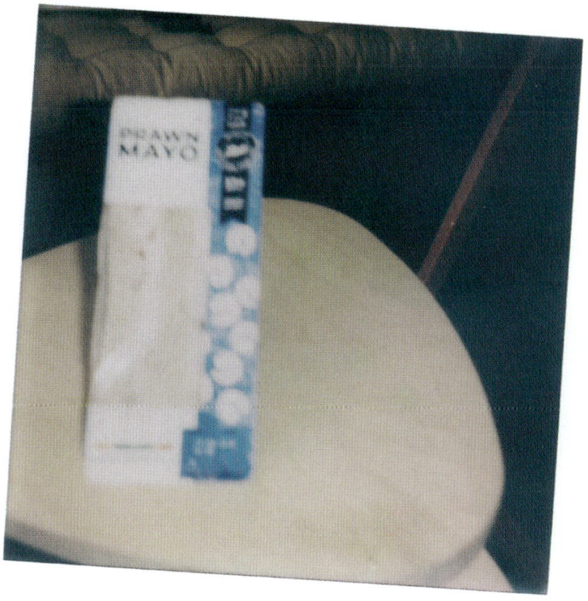

Figs 48–9

Annoyingly, if we don't win the case, we have to pay our legal fees and Peston's as well, so I believe the plan is to keep appealing until he dies.

To recoup some of the fees I did this painting of Peston in jail, where he belongs, for scuppering my chances of childhood stardom. Who knows where I would be today, had I fulfilled my parents' dreams of being in the theatre. Instead, I have had to live the difficult and nomadic life of an artist, while Peston roams free, revelling in his success and sneering at the Lycett family on a nightly basis through the medium of his nightly ITV television show, *Peston*. The painting was purchased for £8 million by Steph McGovern.

NB: A few years after that first encounter with Peston, while walking along one of Birmingham's canals, Mom asked what I wanted for lunch and I said 'prawns', and in what she described to the social services as 'an unfortunate ill-tempered moment' pushed me into the water saying, 'See if you can find any in there, you little dickhead'.

Fig. 50 Me with Boots prawn mayo sandwich.
Fig. 51 My prawn sandwich recipe.

Fig. 50

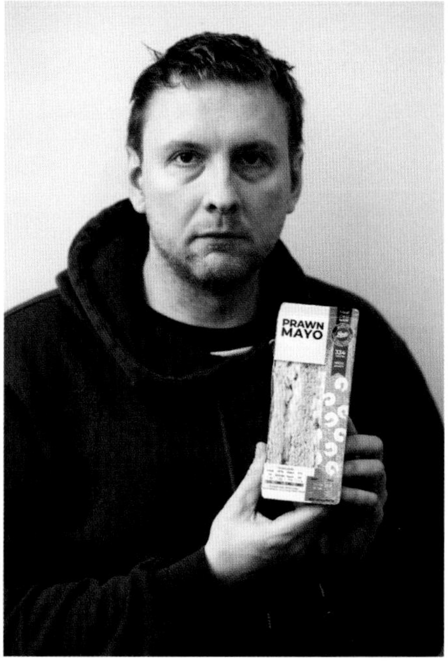

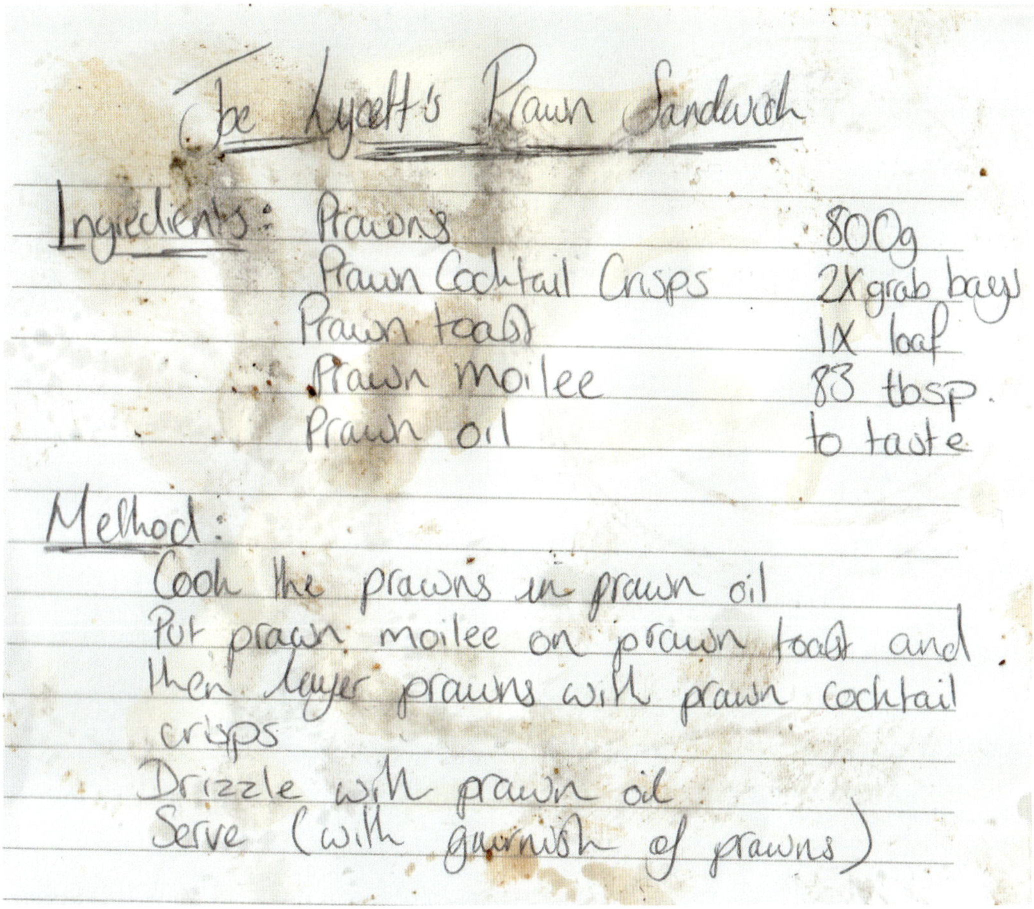

Joe Lycett's Prawn Sandwich

Ingredients:

Prawns	800g
Prawn Cocktail Crisps	2X grab bags
Prawn toast	1X loaf
Prawn moilee	83 tbsp.
Prawn oil	to taste

Method:

Cook the prawns in prawn oil
Put prawn moilee on prawn toast and then layer prawns with prawn cocktail crisps
Drizzle with prawn oil
Serve (with garnish of prawns)

Fig. 51

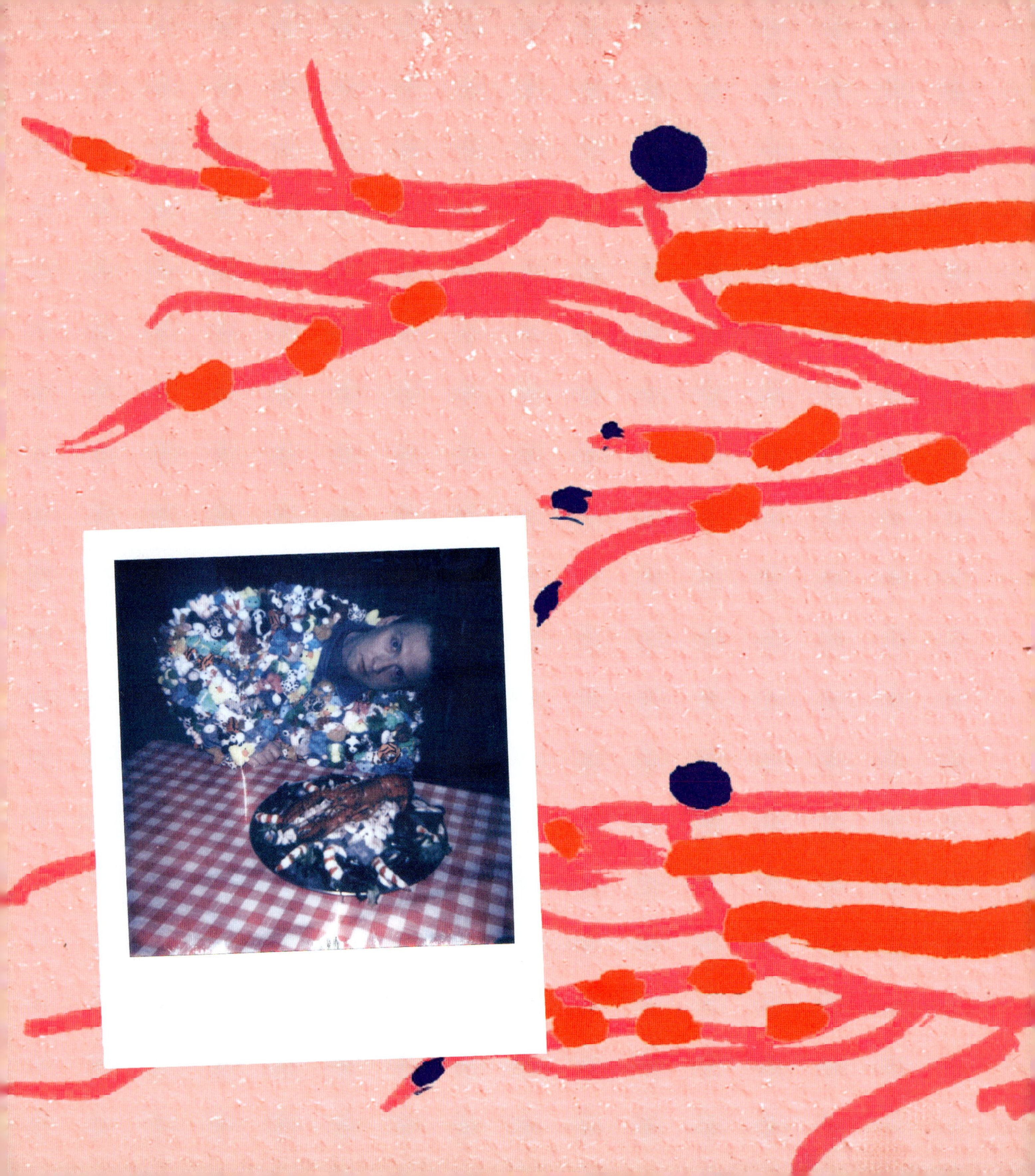

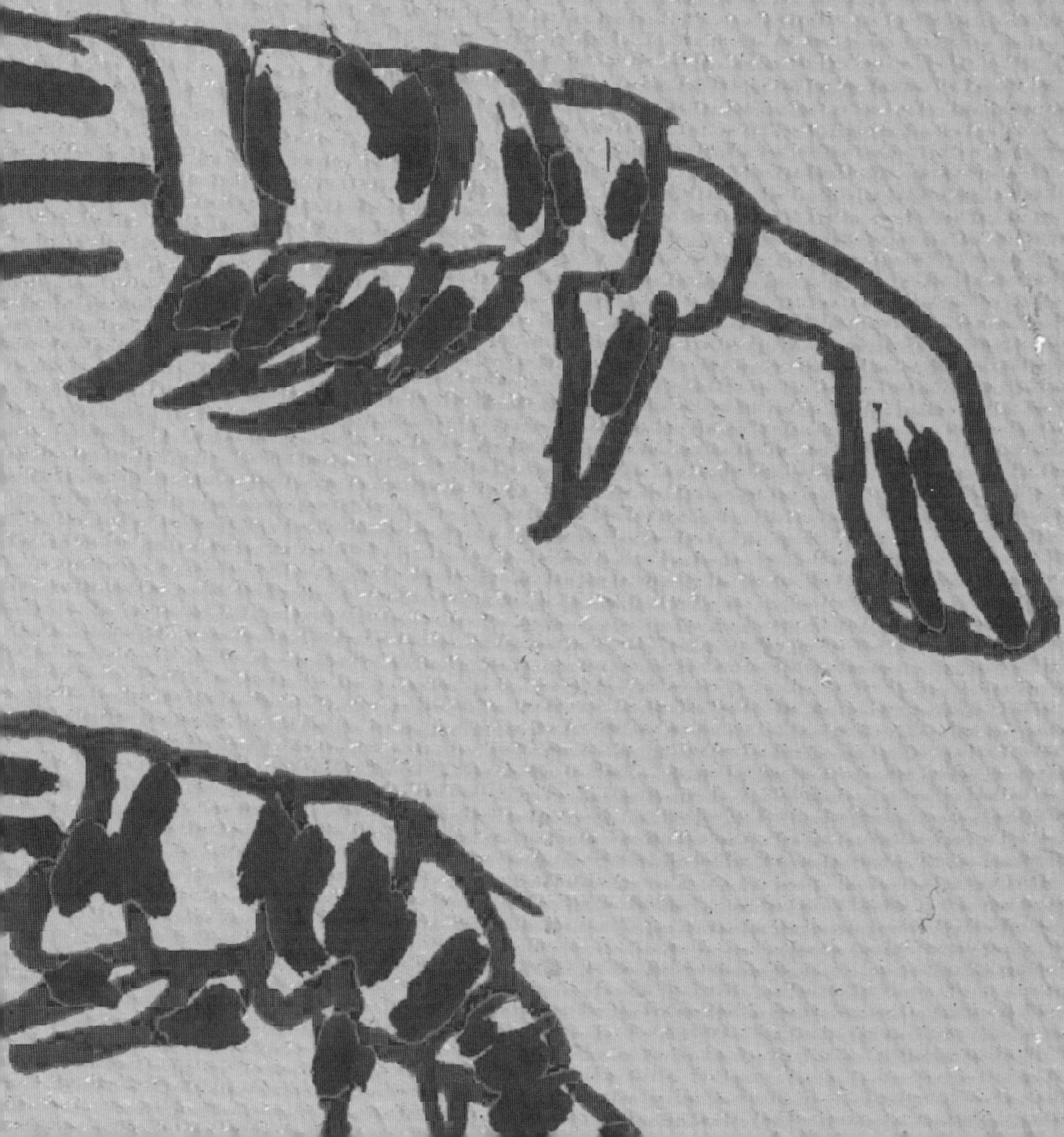

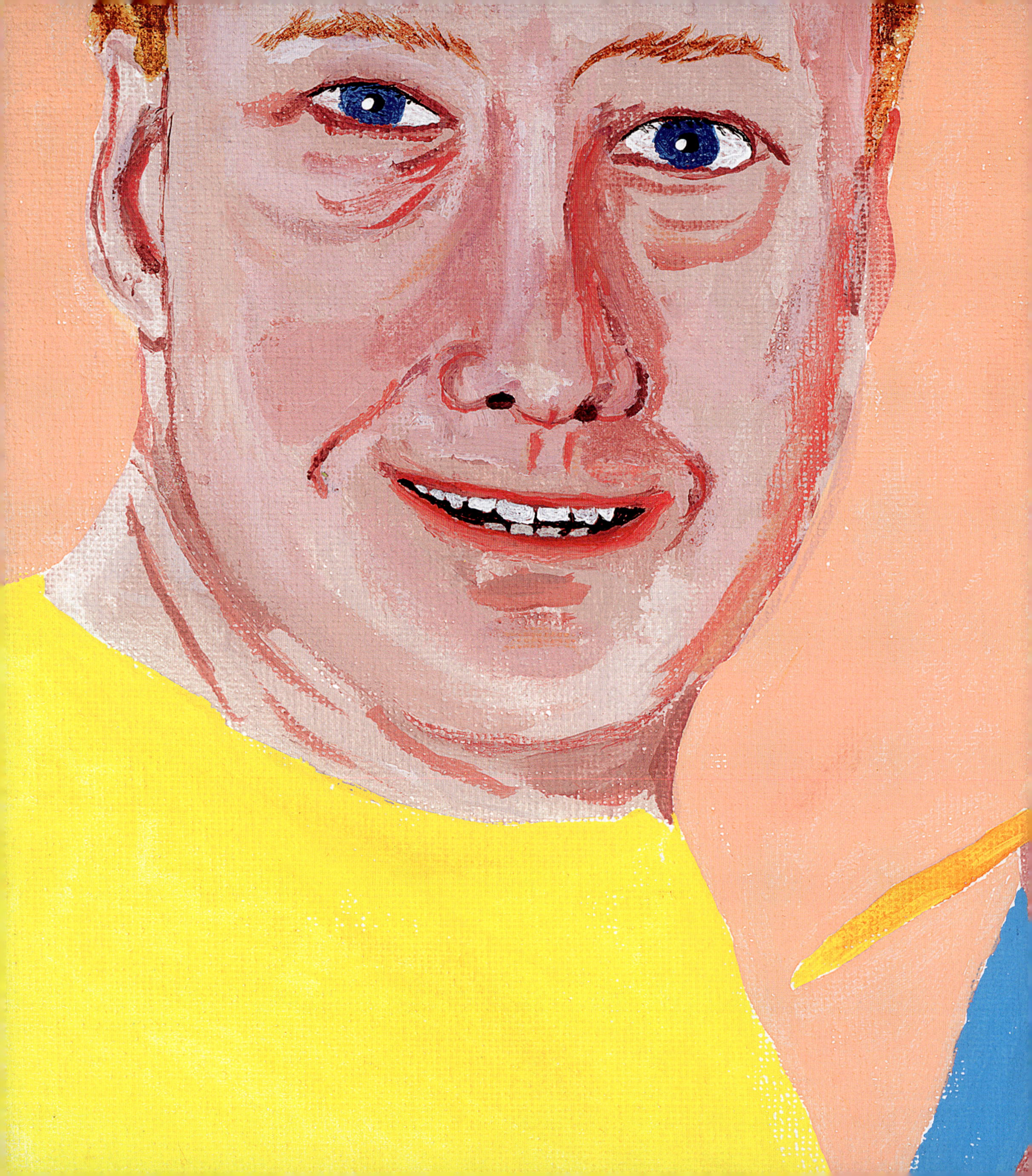

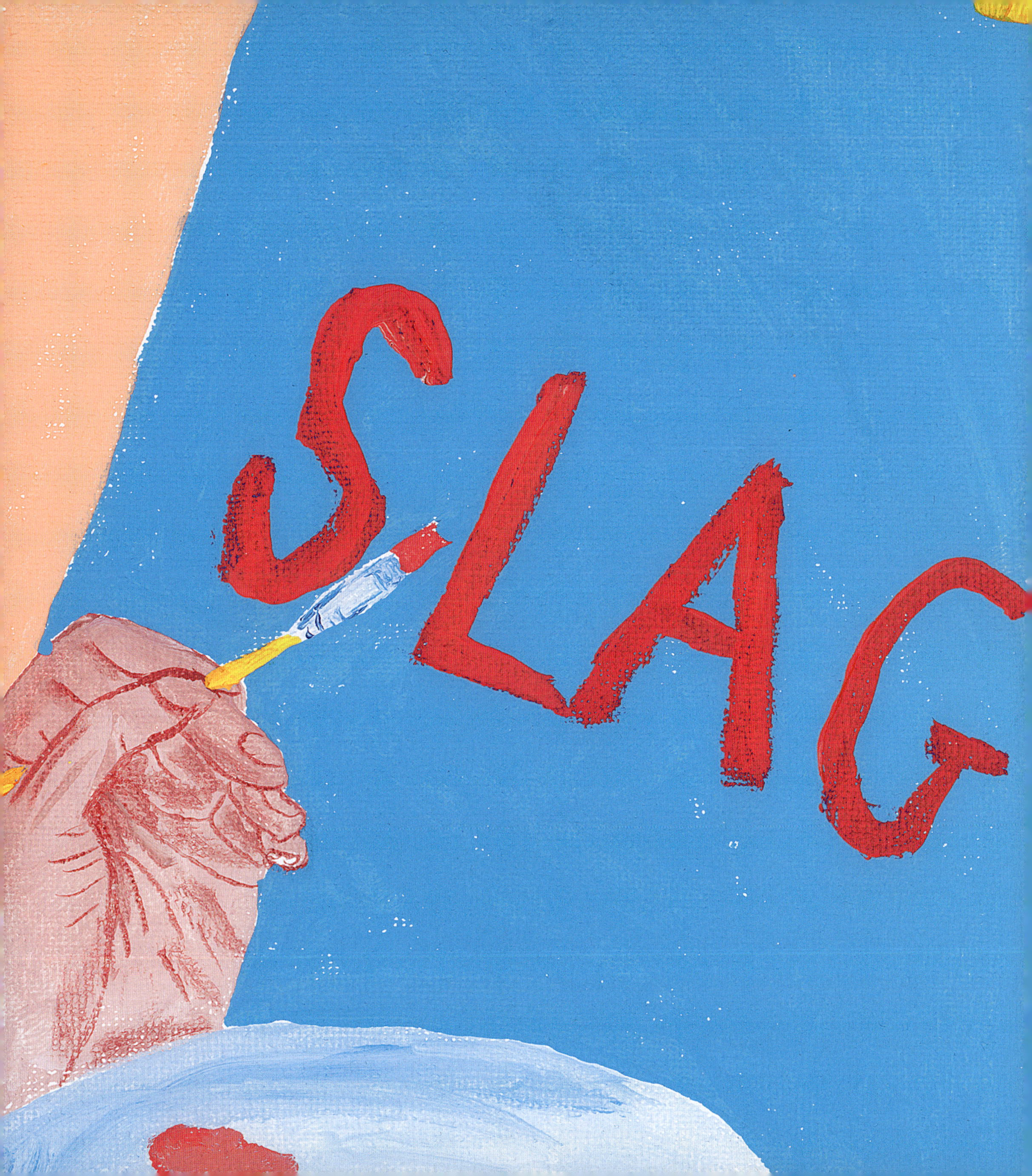
SLAG

TIMOTHÉE CHALAMALLETT

The success of the Hucknall-Finnigan-Palmer-Halliwell painting, far from deterring enthusiastic publicists, increased requests ten-fold for mash-up portraits. Every major Hollywood studio wanted the stars of their films to be painted by me … I think. I didn't check which Hollywood studios are considered major because I wrote this chapter while eating an onion quiche and am typing with one hand. I wasn't that pleased about all the emails. Sure, I was delighted with how the first mixed portrait had gone, but I had no interest in this becoming my thing. I wasn't a gun for hire; I am in fact an artist, which everyone knows is not even remotely like a gun. I instructed my made-up assistant Gary Trousers to politely decline all requests (as Gary is me, I just sent an email to myself, so it felt real).[1]

However, I did make one exception after a representative for Timothée Chalamet sent me a message on popular messaging app WhatsApp. I enjoyed *Call Me by Your Name*, a beautifully made, emotive film about how a young lad has a shag with some fruit. The publicist had never heard of it, but wondered if I might paint young Chalamet alongside his current beau; I think it was a fashionable celebrity – someone from the Kardashians or Natalie Cassidy.

I wasn't interested in some loved-up tosh that they could use as their Christmas card and so responded with an alternative offer, a unique proposal and something that might finally challenge my skills as a keen observer of form and éssèncȩ. 'How would Timothée feel about having his portrait merged with that of Timmy Mallett?' Bafflingly, the representative did not know who Timmy Mallett was. THE Timmy Mallett! With his catchphrases 'Utterly brilliant!' and 'Bleurgh!' I assured them that he is a knight of the realm, a prince of the people, and a national treasure. Some of this was hyperbole. Yet somehow, and with reluctance, they agreed.

I presumed Mallett would be up for it without any persuasion, but I ended up having to negotiate with layer after layer of agent, manager, lawyer, PA, masseuse. In the end, I managed to find a personal email and he agreed to do it if he could take regular breaks, it wouldn't take longer than an afternoon, we would listen to the music from *Glee* throughout, and that I would pay him £250,000 in cash in a mixture of pound sterling, euros, US dollars and Bahraini dinar. Confident I could sell the piece for a tasty profit, we had a deal.[2]

1. Quiche update: some of the onion has fallen from the quiche and landed on my laptop on the letter 'q'. Thankfully, apart from the word 'quiche', which I will now refrain from using, I don't expect to be using the letter much more in this chapter.

2. Spoiler: currently I am down approximately £249,900, or 119,870 Bahraini dinar.

Fig. 52 *Timothée Chalamallett*, 2023, saag paneer, black daal and ketchup on paper, 21 × 29cm.

Fig. 52

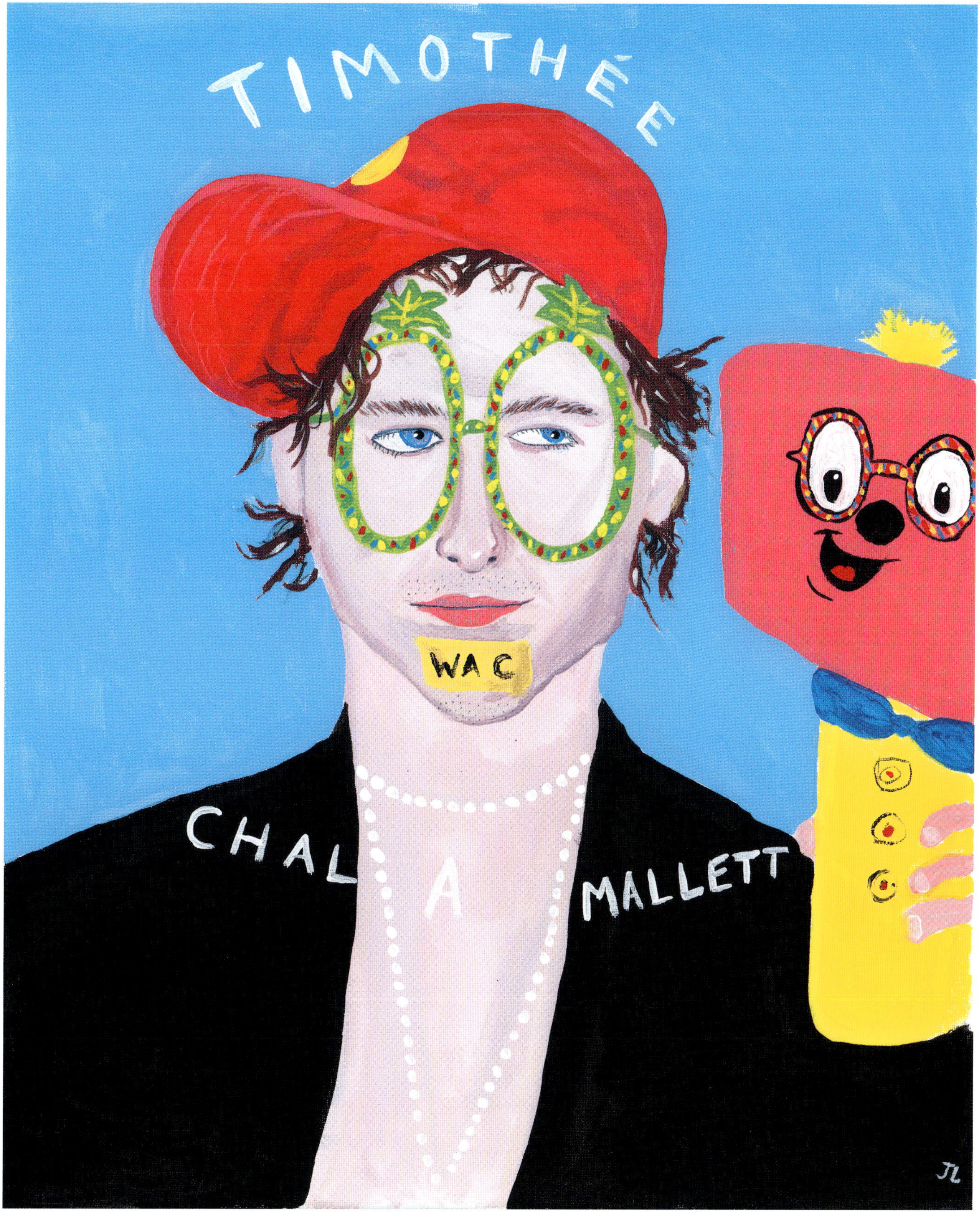

Much to my surprise, Timothée was very polite, gracious and patient. Timmy was a nightmare: aggressive, agitated and, in the end, actively violent.

'Fucking how long is this fucking painting taking, you fuck,' and other variations seemed to be his catchphrase. I was surprised by this; Mallett is a keen artist himself, producing established work that is both beautiful and considered, so I thought he would have some sympathy with the process.

I began saying soothing things like, 'Not long now.'

Chalamet tried to help, softly and charismatically adding, 'Come on, man, it'll be worth it,' to tame the beast.

Far from defusing the situation, this made Mallett even more enraged, and before long he had threatened to 'get [his] fucking mallet out of [his] fucking bag, you pigeon-chested fuck'.

Eventually, what we thought was an empty threat became real, and Mallett's mallet was procured from his holdall. It looked different to the fun pink foam one he had on TV that I remembered from my childhood. This one was made of solid wood, with thick, deep-grey nails protruding from all sides. He raised it aloft and screamed into the orangery, 'Come to Mallett, you Chalamet bastard!' before chasing the poor lad round the room, Timothée throwing various bits of furniture to the ground in a futile attempt to create obstacles.

In the end, we had to abandon the session and I worked on the piece from photographs. Chalamet was taken to a premiere in a car[1] and Mallett was removed by a trio of officers and bundled into the back of a police van. I later discovered that Timmy Mallett was first choice to play Henry V in Netflix's historical epic *The King* but was kicked off set for offering Robert Pattinson MDMA, which explains his disdain for Chalamet, but does not excuse the attack he subsequently launched at my neighbour who'd asked us to turn down 'Don't Stop Believin' (Glee Cast Version)'.

1. I have never been taken to a premiere in a car, but I have been taken to a Premier Inn in a car.

Fig. 53 James Corden's foot piano (as mentioned in Timothée's schedule).
Fig. 54 Mallett's new mallet.
Fig. 55 Timothée Chalamet's schedule (in his own words).
Fig. 56 A gift I offered to James Corden which was violently rejected: *Throat Goat*, 2023, oil on goat, 84 × 17ft.

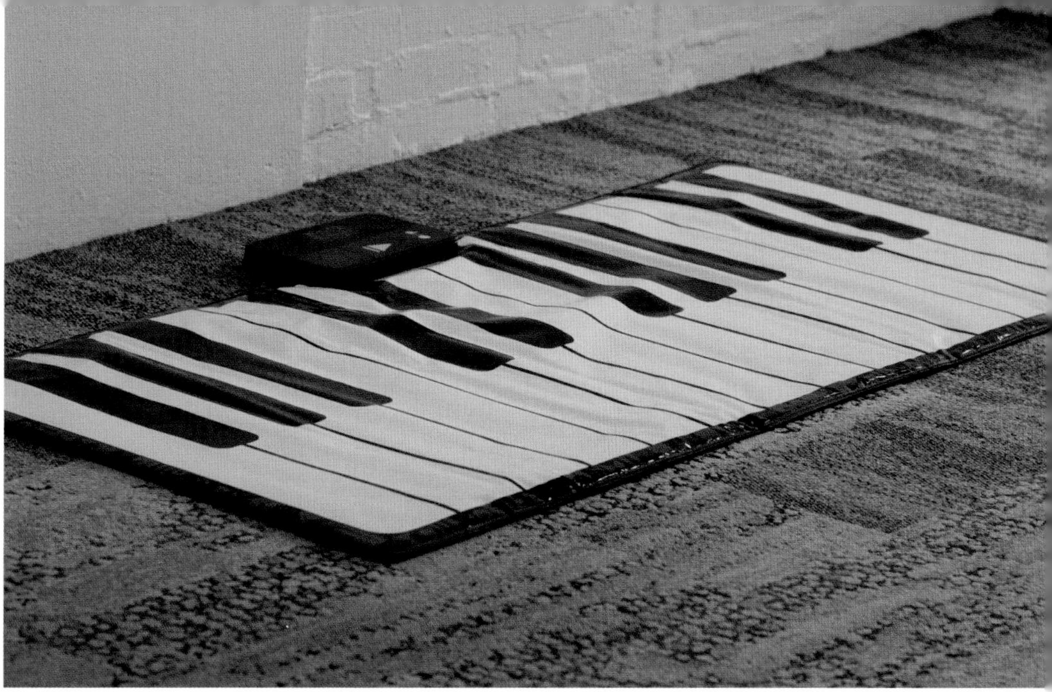
Fig. 53

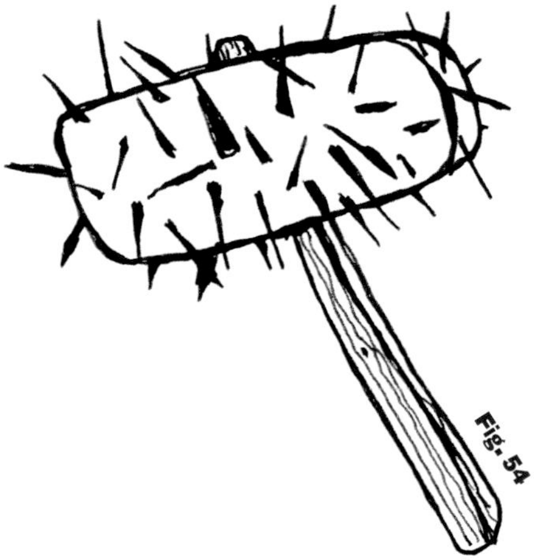
Fig. 54

Fig. 55

7.00am	WAKE UP AND WOW IT'S A BEATIFUL DAY, MAN, REAL BRIGHT LIGHT OUT THERE, MAN, THINK IT MIGHT BE THE SUN
7.30am	OH, MAN, I'M SO HUNGRY, MAN, GONNA HAVE AN EGG IN A CUP OR SOMETHING, MAN
8.30am	OH, MAN, HAD MY EGG AND THEN JUST HAD A MEETING I'M GONNA BE IN ANOTHER FILM. SO COOL, MAN
9.30am	JUST READING THE SCRIPT, IT'S A REMAKE OF SPACE JAM WHERE I'M PLAYING THE LEAD, THATS SO COOL, MAN, I LOVE SPACE AND JAM, MAN. AND EGGS
11.00am	FLORENCE PUGH HAS JUST COME ROUND, SHE'S MAKING A TUNA MAYO BAGUETTE, WOW, COOL, MAN
11.30am	HOUSE STINKS OF TUNA AND EGGS PRETTY COOL, MAN.
1.00pm	JUST HANGING WITH FLORENCE BY THE POOL AND JAMES CORDEN HAS COME ROUND, MAN SUPPOSE THATS COOL, MAN
2.00pm	JAMES CORDEN IS TELLING US STORIES ABOUT HOW NICE HE IS TO PEOPLE ON MINIMUM WAGE, HE SEEMS COOL, MAN
5.00pm	FLORENCE HAS LEFT BUT JAMES CORDEN IS STILL HERE TALKING ABOUT THAT TIME HE GAVE $500 TO A WAITRESS AND IS SHOWING ME A VIDEO. COOL, MAN
5.30pm	JAMES CORDEN HAS CALLED THE STUDIO FOR SPACE JAM FILM AND IS NOW THE EXEC PRODUCER AND ALSO PLAYING A COMEDY BASKETBALL. SO COOL, MAN
6.30pm	JAMES CORDEN IS PLAYING THE PIANO AND SINGING 'AT LAST' BY ETTA JAMES, COOL STUFF, MAN
8.00pm	JAMES CORDEN IS STILL HERE BUT IT'S NIGHT TIME NOW, MAN, SO WE'RE HAVING A FEW BEERS, JUST CHATTING ABOUT SHIT, MAN, REALLY FUN, JAMES CORDEN IS CRYING FOR SOME REASON, MAN
9.00pm	I'VE GONE TO BED AND ASKED ONE OF THE STAFF TO TALK TO JAMES CORDEN. THE STAFF MEMBER SAID, 'PLEASE, PLEASE, I HAVE TO FINISH NOW, TIMOTHÉE, I HAVE TO RETURN TO MY FAMILY.' GAVE HIM $25K, MAN, HE'S HAVING SOME BEERS WITH JAMES CORDEN

Fig. 56

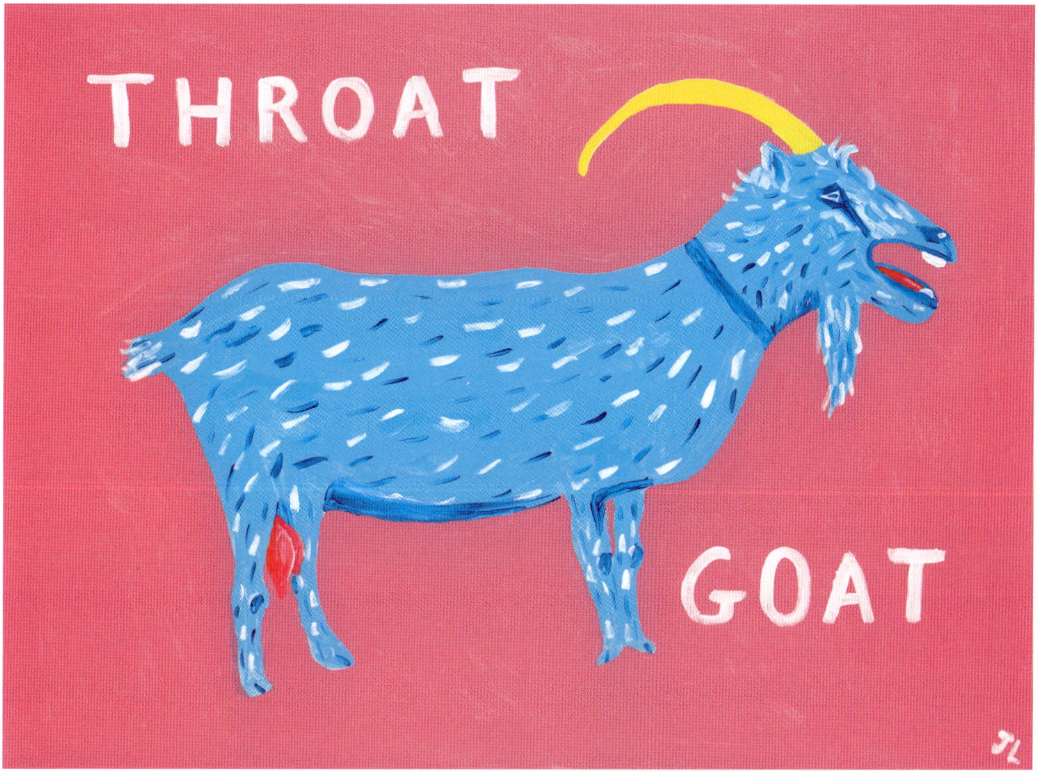

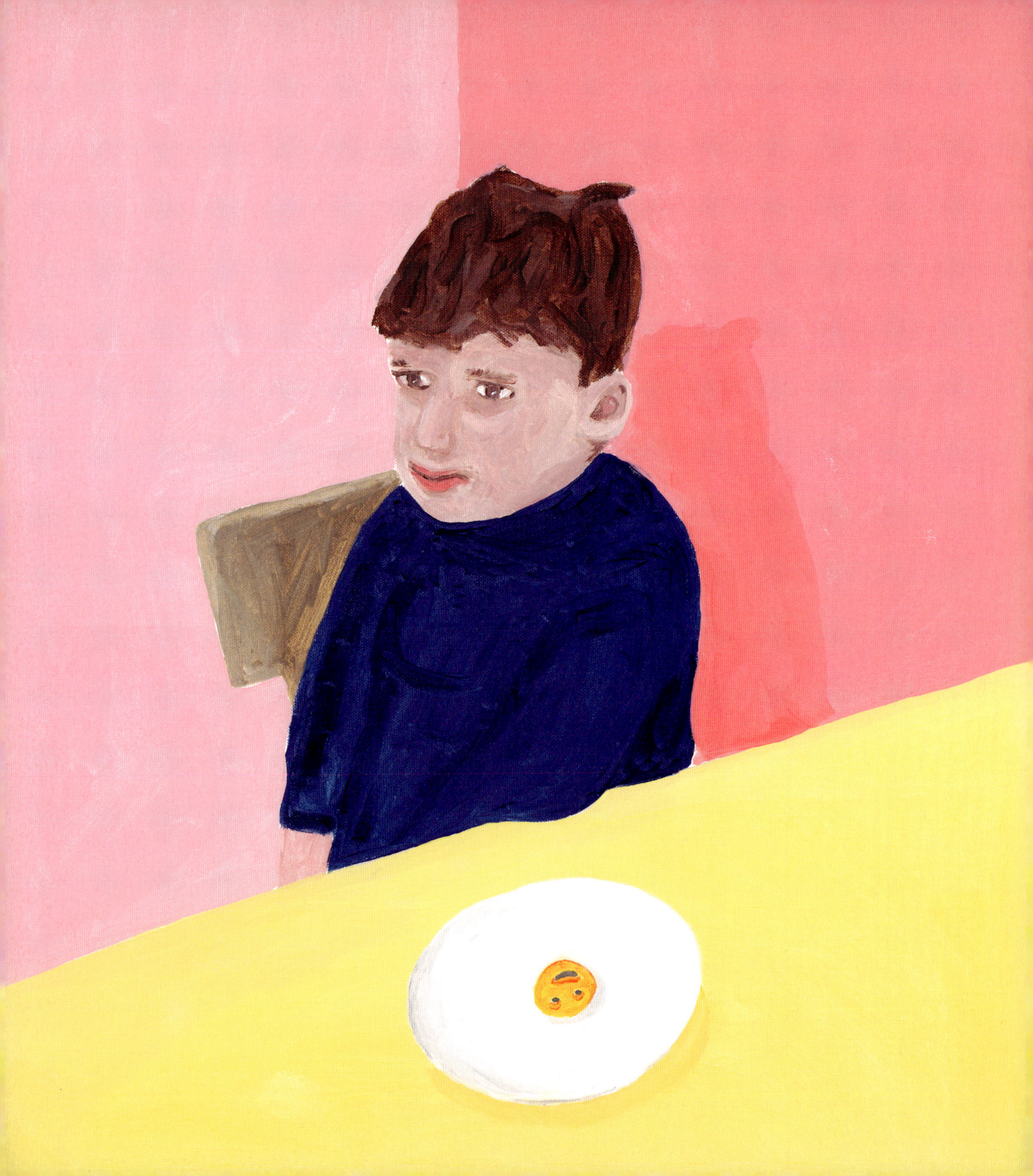

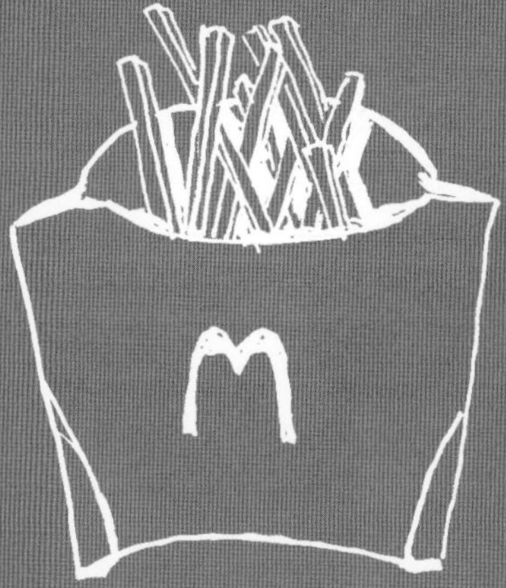

SHOW US YER TITS

In the dizzying world in which I live (show business), there is a long-held tradition that dictates that the respected older generation (sometimes known as 'has-beens') must pass on their wisdom to those young apprentices taking their first steps on the road to fame and fortune. Pop along to any showbiz get-together and you might very well see Jimmy Tarbuck showing Joel Dommett the best way to hold a microphone, Tom Jones telling Harry Styles how to hit a top C, or Dame Judi Dench explaining to Florence Pugh how to dispose of a cadaver without arousing the suspicion of the staff at an Ibis Styles.

I myself have enjoyed the non-taxable benefits of just such a mentoring process. It was back in late-2010, long before I began my celebrity life – a life in which I am unable to walk along the street for ten seconds without some ghastly muggle asking for a photograph (always refused), an autograph (always refused) or sexual advances (decided on a case-by-case basis) – that I had my first taste of being around a famo (aka famous person), and received valuable lessons that helped propel me to my current place in the celebrity stratosphere … nestled somewhere between Stacey Solomon, the bloke from the Kaiser Chiefs and Tim Vincent.

I was on my way to a gig (this is a technical term used by comedians, I believe it is short for 'giggle incident') at a club in the charming city of Norwich and had stopped on the charming high street to admire the wares in the charming window of Zavvi (now bankrupt). I heard a terrific commotion behind me. Looking around, I spotted a crowd of rough-looking youths following at a distance behind a man in an expensive overcoat. I could hear them repeatedly shouting the words 'Bean', 'Oi, Bean', 'Bean, over here' and other variations on the same theme. As the gentleman in the expensive overcoat neared me, I noticed it was none other than no less a personage than (i.e. it was) Rowan Atkinson, star of *Mr Bean*, *Blackadder* and that *Maigret* thing on ITV that didn't really catch on.

As Atkinson reached me, our eyes met, and he reached out in panic. 'You there, young woman,' he hissed. 'I'm getting hassle from these dickweeds. Can you get me to the nearest private members' club? I need to be protected from the hoi polloi.'[1]

1. Strictly speaking, since the word 'hoi' translates as 'the', Rowan saying 'the hoi polloi' was effectively the same as him saying 'the the polloi'. I was unable to tell him this at the time because I was only told it recently by Susie Dent, who was trying to distract me from an anxiety attack during a charity auction.

Fig. 57 *Show Us Yer Tits*, 2023, acrylic mixed with Stella Artois on repurposed copies of *Nuts*, 6 × 8ft.

Fig. 57

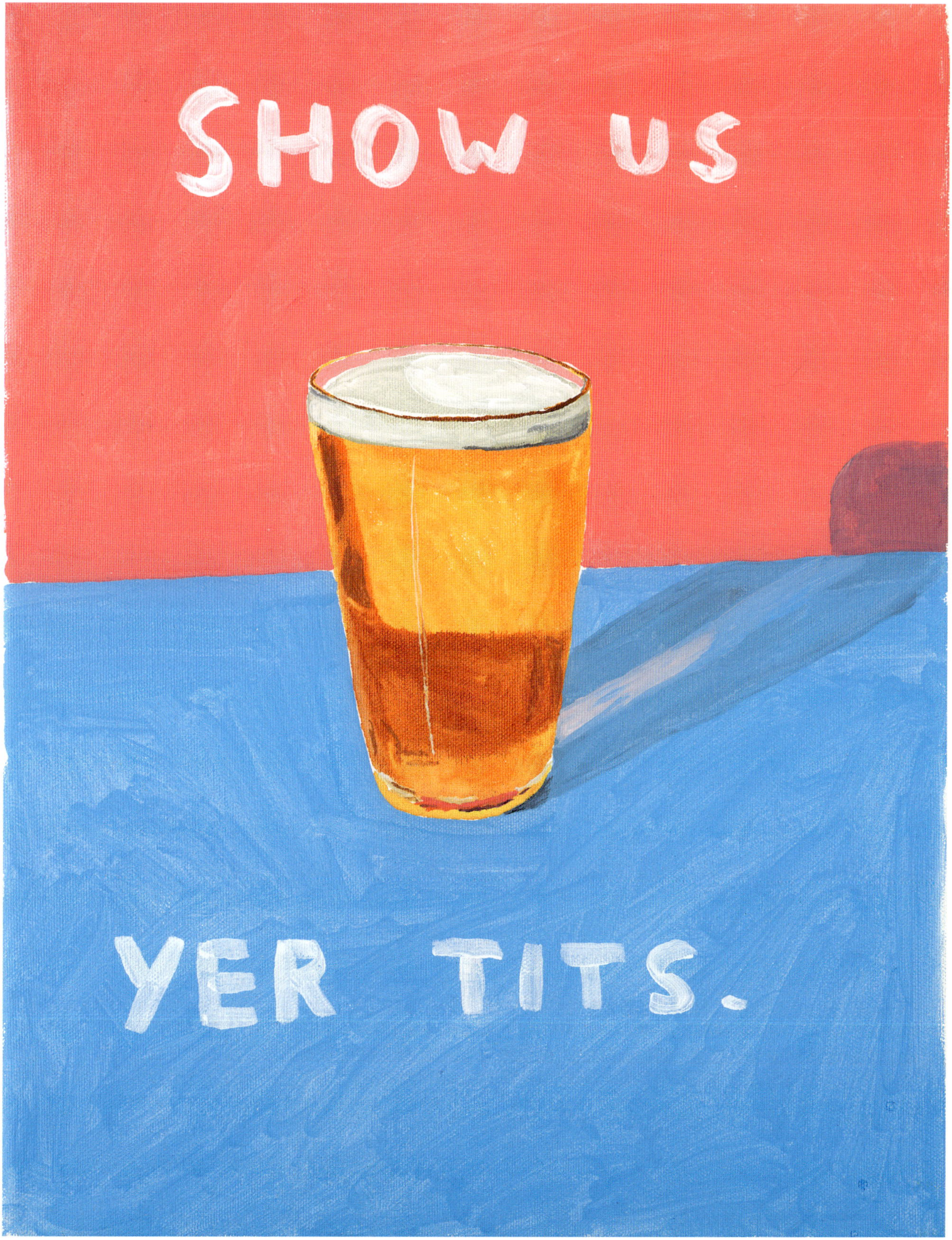

Not knowing the location of a private members' club in Norwich (or indeed anywhere), I took Rowan to the next best thing: a branch of Pizza Express. He nodded his head in satisfaction, clearly feeling that this was a sufficiently elite and safe establishment. Sure enough, the pursuing youths came no further than the threshold of the restaurant, repelled by middle-class values like demons by a line of salt.

Before long, we were ordering. Rowan steered us away from the food, saying it was 'for wankers', so I asked for a Magners, while he opted for a pint of Doom Bar ale. He stared at my drink.

'What you glugging that piss for?' he said, in a tone very unlike Mr Bean. I laughed awkwardly, unsure how to answer.

'I dunno … I like it, I guess,' I said.

'Rots your guts,' he said, drinking half his pint in one gulp. 'Rots your bloody guts.'[1]

I ignored Mr Atkinson's dig at my drink of choice[2] and changed the subject. 'It's a pleasure to meet you, sir,' I said, 'I'm a big fan.'

'Oh, really? Big fan, is it? OK then, what were the box office takings for the first *Johnny English* film?' he asked, finishing his pint.

'A hundred million?' A complete guess.

'One hundred and sixty point five million dollars, kid,' he said. 'Guess how much of that I saw?'

'I have no idea.'

He shook his head. 'Fucking loads of it.'

Atkinson had noticed that the man on the table next to us had gone to the bathroom, leaving his pint unattended. Effortlessly, he reached over, grabbed the glass and downed the contents in a single fluid motion, some of it spilling down the folds of his Ralph Lauren fleece, in deep emerald green. I stared, appalled, in my cardigan, purchased at a British Heart Foundation. The shape of his face seemed alien to the man I thought I knew – all the frivolity and childish joy of Bean was replaced with something altogether more complicated.

'What do you want to do with your life, kid?' He was slurring. My guess, he was six to eight pints down. God knows where he'd been before I'd bumped into him. A Zizzis? Ask Italian? Baguette World? Impossible to know.

'Well, as it happens, I've just started doing stand-up comedy. I have a gig tonight down the road.' It seemed odd, almost strangely arrogant, to be saying this to one of the most successful comedians the country had ever seen. I expect people feel like that when they say similar things to me today.

'You idiot.' He seemed genuinely annoyed. 'It's the hardest job in the world,[3] why would you want to get involved in something like that?'

1. In my late teens and early twenties, I had a remarkable capacity for original Magners cider. I wasn't that fussed by their more experimental options – the pear varieties or the 'summer fruits' all seemed to me to be the result of a product development team at head office who had got wildly above their station, the cider equivalent of when Coldplay started working with Brian Eno. And yet a classic crisp, cold, sugary pint of Magners was the sole alcoholic desire of my emerging adulthood. Don't get me wrong, I was aware of rival brands; there was the obvious and limp choice of a Strongbow (which I disregarded due to a dislike of archery), then Kopparberg who weasled their way onto the scene presenting themselves (wrongly) as the more refined Scandinavian choice, but whose cloying flavour I suspect played no small part in boosting the Leave vote, and of course there were Thatchers and Bulmers who seemed to me to be the seagulls following the Magners ship.

As I grew, so my tastes refined, my palate widened, and I sought more varied ways to gradually poison my liver and personal relationships. Gradually, silently, Magners slipped entirely out of favour, like a first love with whom I fell entirely out of touch, and the sight of whom simply fills you with feelings of wistful nostalgia, a sense of embarrassment and memories of premature ejaculation. Now I enjoy Moretti, Beavertown Neck Oil, Peroni, and anything that feels a bit special or premium. Unless it's after 10 p.m., in which case I'll settle for the contents of the drip tray.

2. At the time, I mean – I have dedicated a large footnote in this book to it (see above footnote).

3. It isn't.

Fig. 58 Magners Original.

Fig. 58

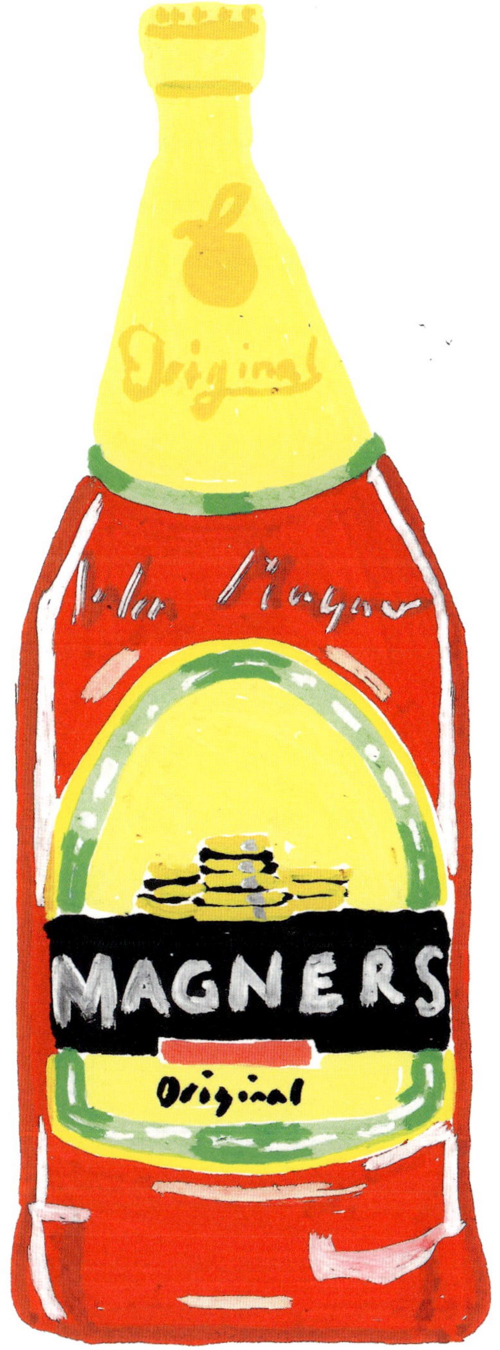

'I dunno … I really like watching stand-up and so I tried it and really enjoyed it.' This was the truth, but luckily I would come up with some more interesting lies when later asked the same question by Graham Norton or Jonathan Ross.

'You like it? Oh, that'll pass. That will pass, kid.' He shook his head. 'What's the act? What's your shtick?'[1]

I opted for the somewhat inaccurate category of: 'Gay stuff'.

'Oh, I see. "Gay stuff". Very in right now, isn't it? Very cool. Gay lads, very popular. Alan Carr. Graham Norton. Michael McIntyre. All that lot.' I didn't have the heart to tell Rowan Atkinson that Michael McIntyre has a wife and kids. It's the sort of thing that seems so unlikely when you say it out loud. 'I suppose if I invented Bean now, he'd be gay.[2] Probably have to be a shirt-lifter to get commissioned these days.' I noticed he now had a half-eaten plate of squid rings, while across the room a woman looked at the empty table in front of her.

It was at this point that the evening took a peculiar turn (up till then it had all been pretty unremarkable). 'Let's do some improv, kid. Test your reflexes.'

I had never done improv.

'I don't know, Rowan, it's not for me,' I replied, accurately. I find improv difficult because it is an entirely spontaneous art form, and shit.

'Just a quick one. For fun. Something to test ya. See if there's any meat on those comedy bones, lad. Any substance to ya!'

I went to take a sip of my drink for courage, but discovered he'd finished it.

'Yes, I've got it. You be a straight man. See how that works out for you. First time for everything!' He laughed for about four minutes, then resumed. 'And I'll be … I'll be … a buxom young woman mad for sex. Just a bit of fun!'

I thought with improv you needed a bit more of a scenario to bounce off, some sort of scene setting or motivating action, but me being a straight man and him being a big-titted woman was apparently all we needed. He waved me towards the restaurant vestibule, saying that I had to 'make my entrance', before further remarking that 'a moth-blaster like you should know how to do that'.

I walked into the vestibule, feeling a bit baffled. A member of the restaurant staff was standing by the front door, sliding a J-cloth around a hygiene-rating sticker.

'That Rowan Atkinson you're with?' the waiter asked.

'The same,' I answered. In retrospect an annoying answer.

'Of *Mr Bean*, *Blackadder* and that *Maigret* thing on ITV that didn't catch on?'

1. Having to describe my 'shtick' has always been something I have struggled with. I think, originally, I went with 'droll, camp storytelling', which I wasn't entirely happy with, mainly because it sounds awful. Like something you might hear trailed on Radio 4 while driving and crash your car to avoid. I suppose my 'shtick' has morphed over the years into something more anti-bureaucratic, and reluctantly political (this is largely a reaction to public opinion, and the repeated evidence that people prefer me talking about parking tickets rather than cock). I know now, as an accomplished painter, that stand-up is a completely worthless art form, and that despite all their fun and laughter, jokes cannot be beautiful and (like war or Howard Donald) ultimately achieve nothing. But in those days, I believed differently. And yet, I didn't have a pre-prepared description for my 'shtick'.

2. The more I thought about it, the more I thought that Mr Bean might actually have been gay (or as Atkinson put it repeatedly that evening, a 'moth-blaster', which is a new one for me) all along. After all, what is a reluctance to speak but a refusal to leave the closet in verbal form? You may argue that Bean identifies as straight: in some episodes he has a female companion who is apparently called Irma Gobb (sometimes credited as 'the girlfriend' – this is not my reductive terminology but that of the IMDb), but he treats her fairly dismissively, which I'm sure you'll agree is quite a gay thing to do. Admittedly, in the episode *Mr Bean Goes to Town* he does appear to become jealous when he sees her dancing with another man, but gay men in denial often find themselves in complicated psychological situations like this (this could well be the Mr Bean equivalent of the time Sir Elton John married a German woman). I could prepare a convincing thesis that Bean may actually be jealous of the fact that she gets to dance with a man, and I would offer the further evidence that Mr Bean sometimes has a twinkle in his eye, of a sort that suggests to me he absolutely loves giving hand jobs. Nevertheless, the likelihood of either Atkinson or his writing partner Richard Curtis coming clean that their hugely successful character is a homosexual seems pretty minimal, given the risks of damaging the lucrative legacy of their cash cow, and so I suppose we as a society will continue paying the price for their cowardice.

Fig. 59 Photographs of a different Pizza Express.

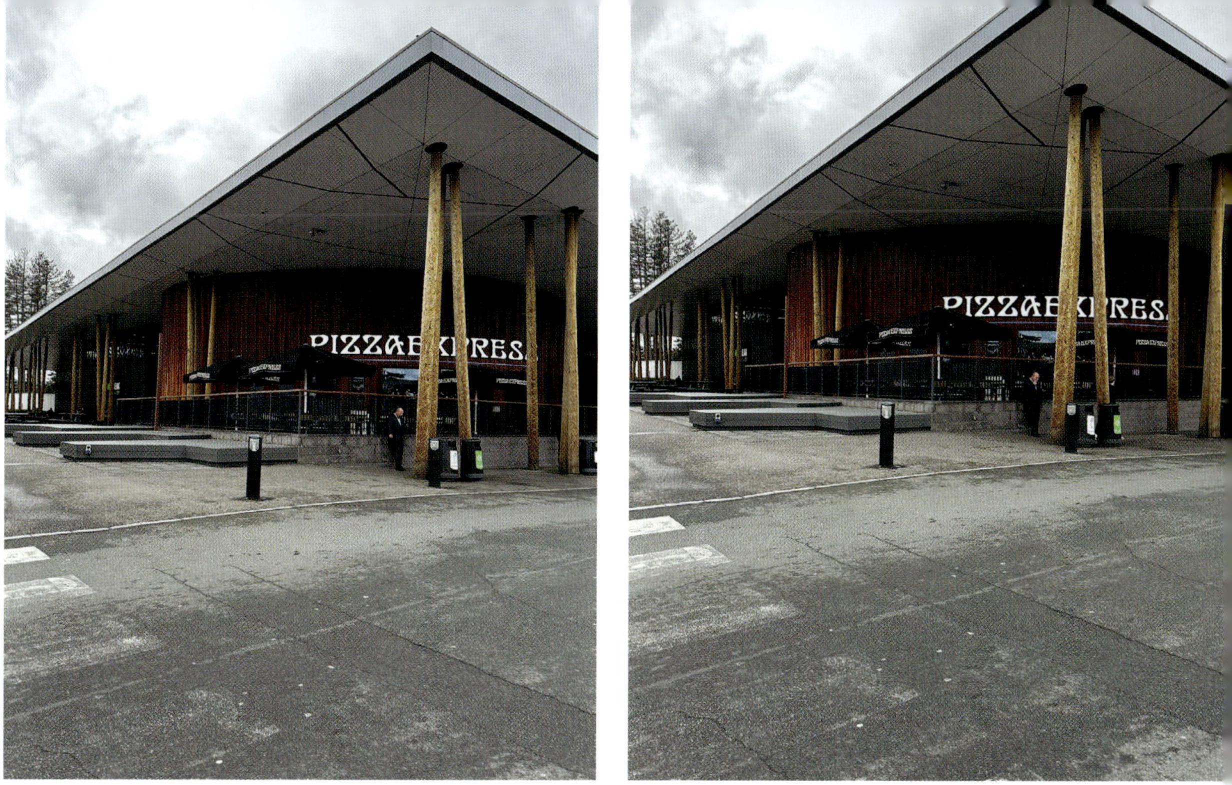

Fig. 59

I nodded. 'He's asked me to do an improv with him.'

'Years ago, I was working in a branch of Shoe Zone (*see* **Fig. 60**). Who should come in one day but Martin Shaw,' he said.

'Judge John Deed?' I exclaimed.

'The same,' he replied, also retrospectively annoying. 'As I was fitting him for a pair of brogues, I told him about my acting ambitions. He suggested we do an improv. He asked me to carry on fitting his shoes, but in the style of a furious spider who's just found out a second spider has eaten all of my spider children. I didn't know what to do, so I just said "Are these too tight?", but in a sort of hissing voice.'

'What happened?' I asked.

'Not much,' he answered. 'He just kicked me really hard in the face and walked out. Ever since, I've regretted not making the most of my big opportunity.'

I realised that, metaphorically, the waiter was giving me a message (he'd also literally given me a message). This was my opportunity to make an impression on Rowan Atkinson. I had to make sure I didn't blow it. I took a deep breath and walked back into the restaurant.

The first thing I saw was Rowan, standing in the middle of the floor with all the other diners staring at him. He had two fried eggs stuck to his chest in a simulation of breasts, some spaghetti as hair and a large sprig of basil between his legs for pubes. Chest puffed out and strutting on his tiptoes in lieu of high heels, thrusting his hips from side to side, he staggered towards me. In his drunken head he obviously thought he was moving gracefully, like a Victoria's Secret model or perhaps some sort of regal bird, but with the handicap of multiple Doom Bars he moved more like a cross between a duck and Theresa May. As he approached, he adopted his best attempt at a womanly voice, a grotesque and reductive impression that in this day and age would likely be considered a hate crime.

'A large glass of dry white wine please, gorgeous!' he said, winking and running his fingers lustfully through the basil sprig.

With the confidence of half a Magners on an empty 22-year-old stomach, I stood up and approached, arms bent at 45 degrees to suggest thick biceps, and legs far apart to suggest a big penis. 'Allo, darlin',' I said, in a sort of cockney pastiche, my own accent incapable of being seen as straight or masculine. 'Do you come 'ere often, babe?' It was a bit like Dick Van Dyke, only not quite as authentic.

'Oh yes, from time to time.' He fluttered his eyelids and flicked his spaghetti hair.

'Lovely lookin' lass, aren't ya? Lovely arse and face,' I said, pushing to the very limits of my powers of heterosexual flirtation and not yet aware of the ability to be retrospectively cancelled. 'Go on, love, show us yer tits.'

Fig. 60 Photographs of Shoe Zone (open and closed).
Fig. 61 A drawing of former Prime Minister The Right Honourable Theresa May.

Fig. 60

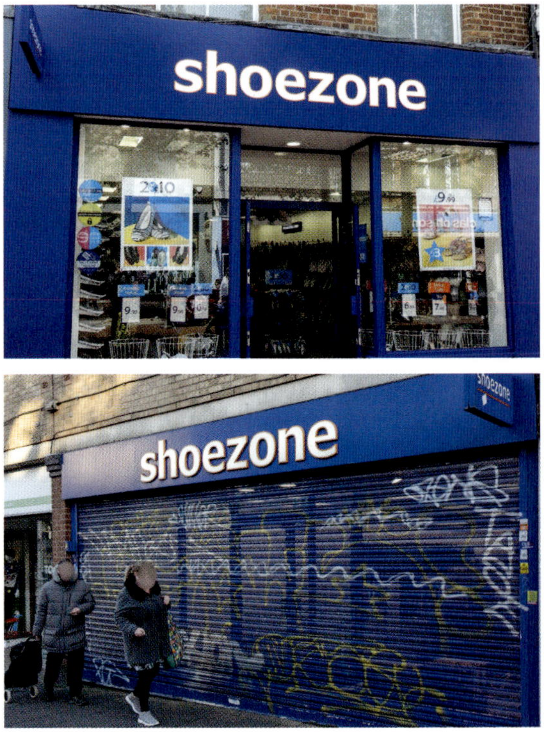

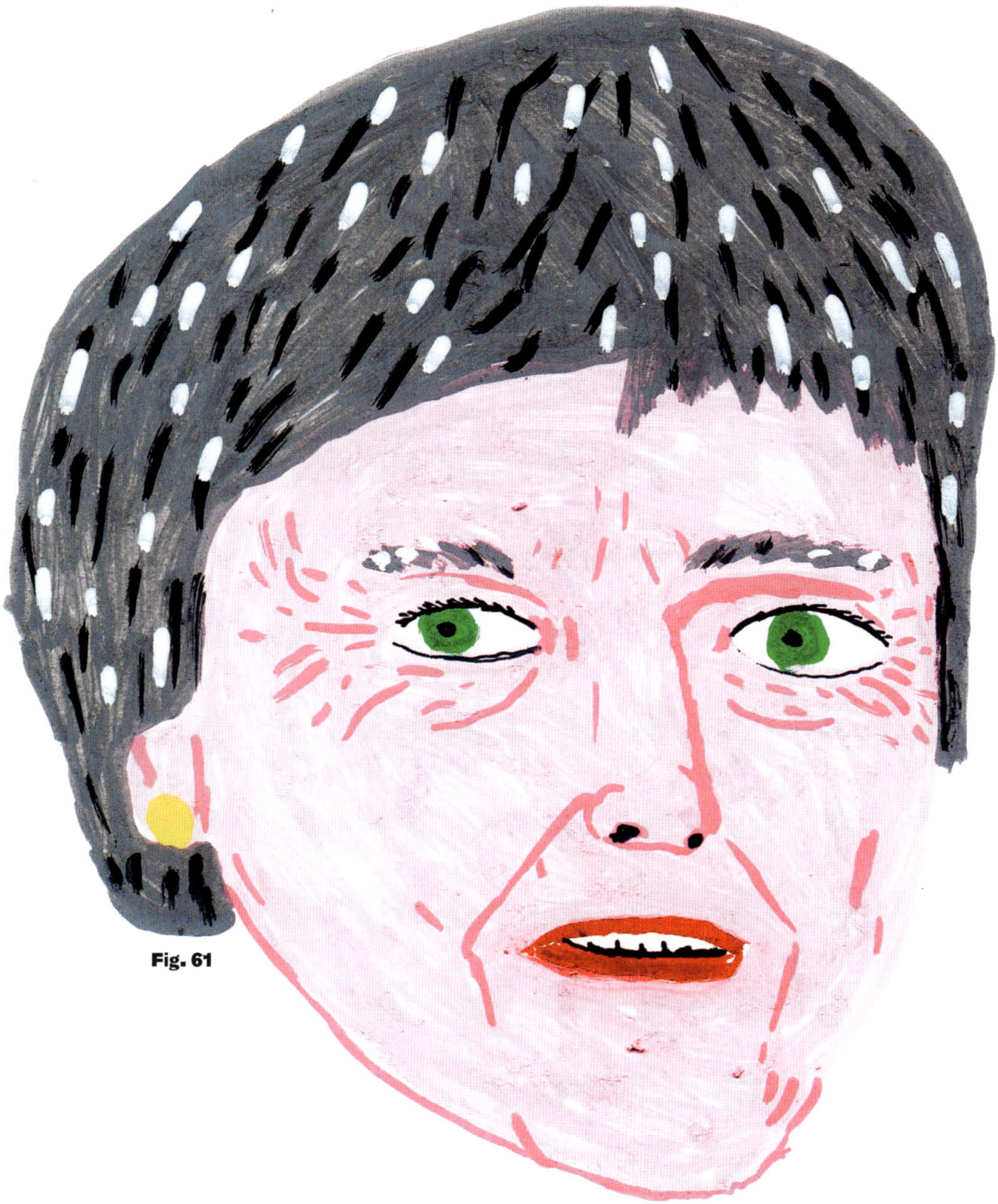

Fig. 61

He responded by squeezing one of his egg-breasts, forcing bright yellow yolk to spaff out of one of the ersatz nipples. It was equal parts a masterpiece of physical comedy, to rank alongside his gift-wrapping routine in *Love Actually*, and one of the most atrocious things I have seen in my entire life.

The next ninety seconds are a blur. I remember he staggered towards me, took me in his arms, pushed his head close to mine and said something quickly and aggressively. My therapist believes I have selectively deleted the words. All I know is that when I came round, I was on the floor, absent of trousers, covered in grated pecorino, and Rowan was receiving a standing ovation from the Pizza Express diners.

Years later he wrote to me – I don't know how he got my details, but I had my agent sack a few people to be on the safe side – to congratulate me on my success as a painter and to enquire about a commission. 'There was something you said to me, in that place in Norwich. Something about tits I think it was? I loved that. Can you put that on a painting?'

I did as requested. The painting is quite impressive in real life – one of my largest, about eight feet tall. Rowan put it in a beautiful ornate frame and apparently she hangs in the main bedroom of his South Oxfordshire home. We agreed that the price would remain between us, but let's just say he shouldn't have bragged so much about how much he got paid for *Johnny English*.

Fig. 62 Rowan Atkinson in character as Mr Bean (made clear by having slightly raised eyebrows and looking a bit dim).

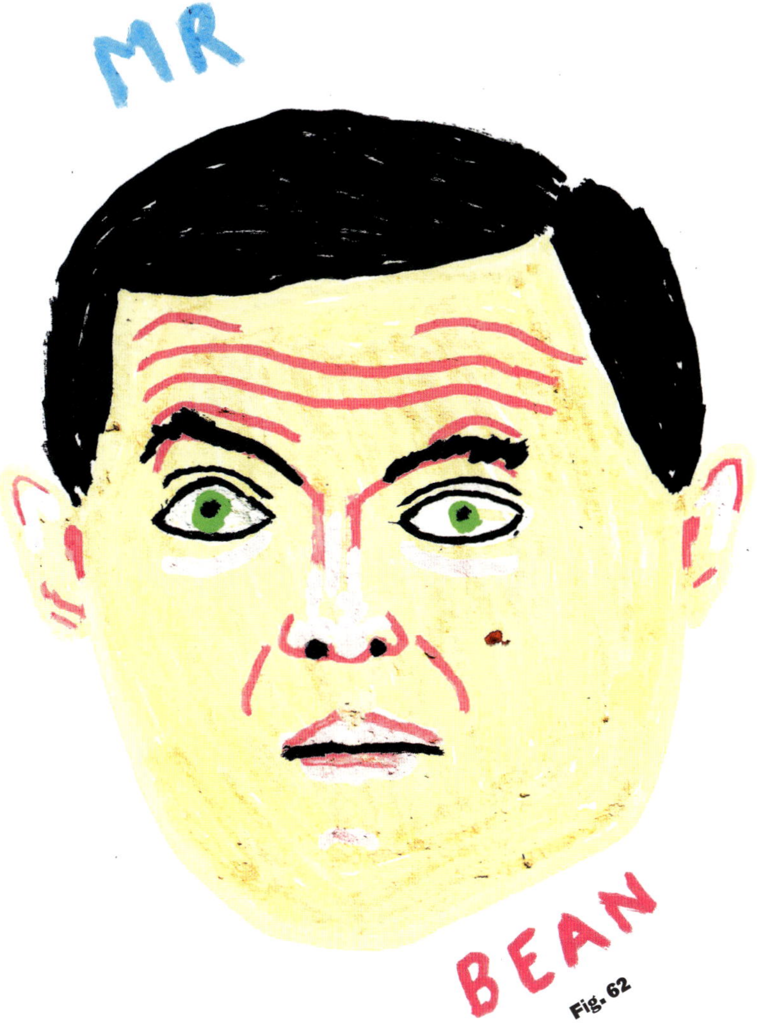

Fig. 62

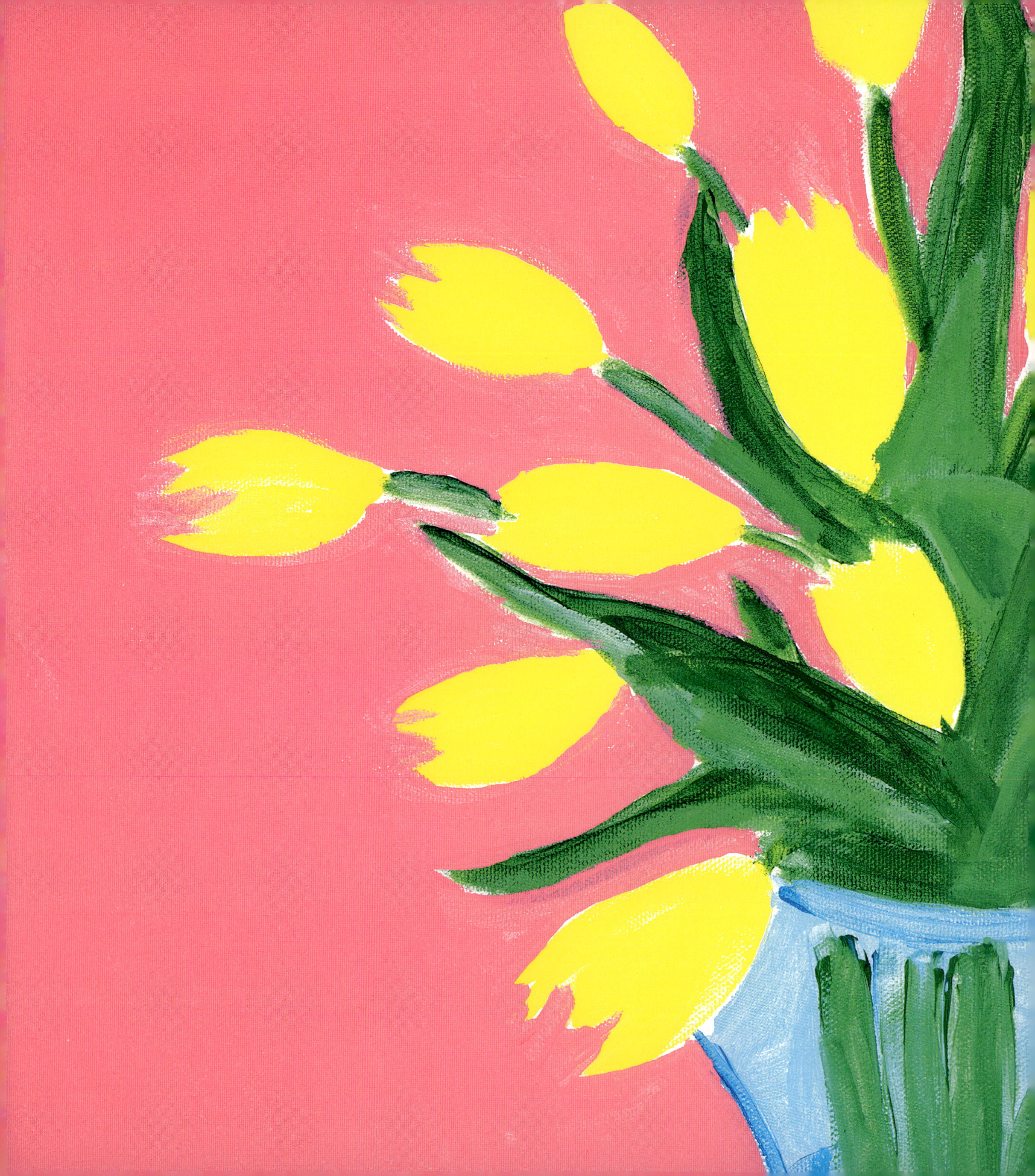

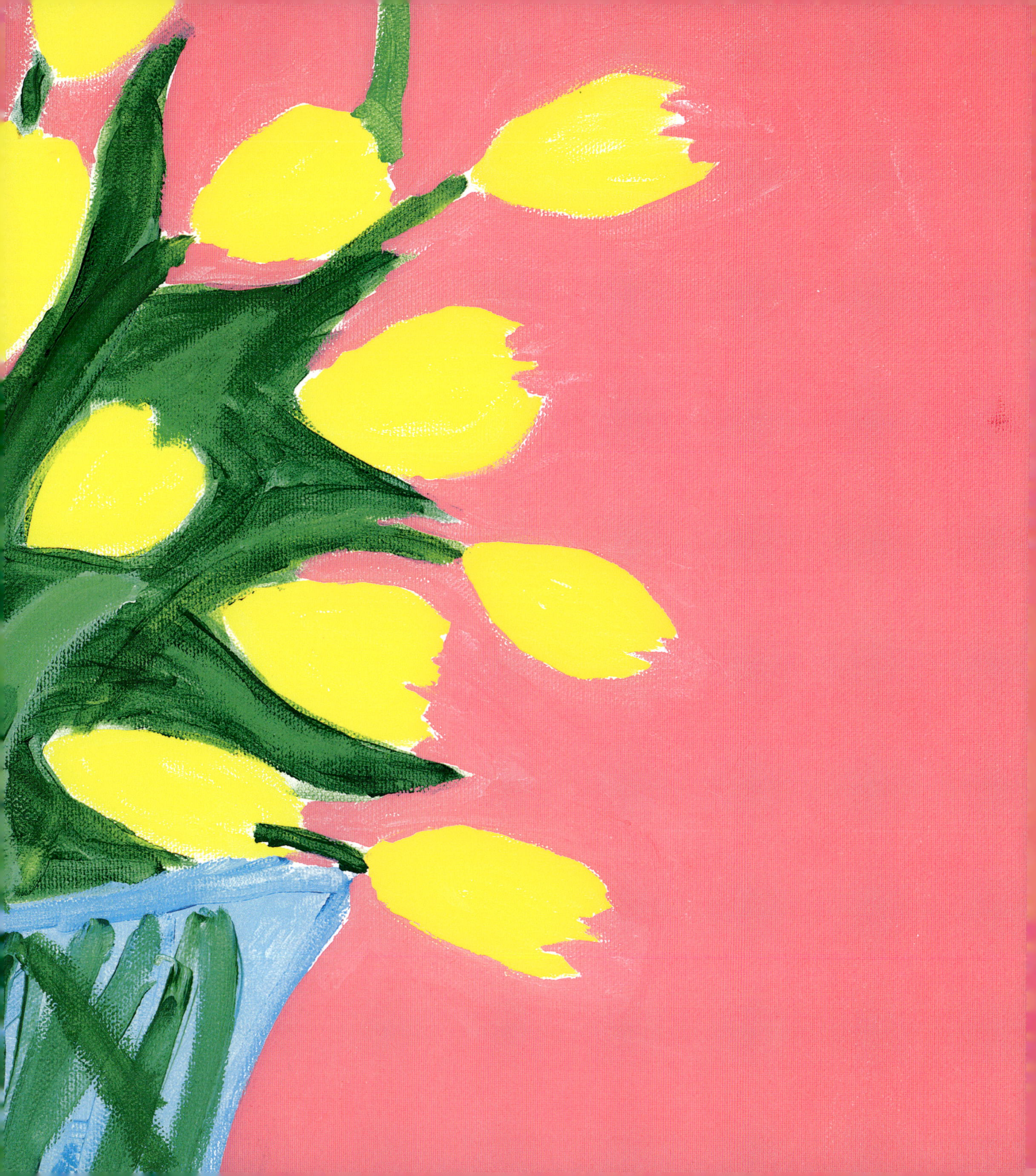

WARREN BUFFETT

Sometimes it is important to help those less fortunate than yourself (which in my case is everyone), and one such person who owes his present position in life entirely to me is the multibillionaire investment guru Warren Buffett.

Of course, these days, Warren Buffett is one of the richest men in the world, often placing in the top ten rich list, with a net worth at time of writing of well over $100 billion. I'd describe him as an old-school rich white bloke: he doesn't fill the sky with satellites so he can get more retweets or shag pop singers, and he's famous for his frugal, low-key lifestyle. He collects coupons in magazines, repairs his own perished underwear, refuses to use 'wasteful' toilet roll (preferring a rag or leaves), eats the gross bits of bell peppers and the skin on bananas, lives in a modest house and drives a Nissan Micra, taking it out of gear when going down big hills. Imagine the opposite of Paul Hollywood (apart from the wiping his arse with leaves bit).

However, this is only part of the story, because Warren Buffett's immense wealth is all thanks to me. Sure, Warren might claim that he was mad rich before I was even born (the expression he uses is 'pissing cash out of every pore'), but actually, if you look at his private accounts (with Nationwide), he spent years struggling to make progress in the business community. He found it difficult to raise venture capital, and often attracted mockery from fellow businessmen at investment lunches, due to the similarity of his surname to the style of luncheon being provided. 'Oi, Buffett (pronounced to rhyme with 'stuff it'),' they would shout, 'did you organise this buffet (not pronounced to rhyme with 'stuff it')?' I know this seems a feeble attempt at comedy, but you have to remember that businessmen are famously humourless, as illustrated by Steven Bartlett. This ceaseless bullying (ironically) buffeted Warren's confidence. Bereft of support, he was on the point of giving it all up. What he needed was a business partner with new ideas and money. Enter: me.[1]

At around this time, I was turning seven years old. My much-loved grandma (as opposed to the other one) gave me fifteen pounds as a gift. This was a sizeable sum of money back then, as Kwasi was yet to become chancellor. Naturally, like any other seven year old, given a free choice I would immediately have spent all the money on sweets

1. This sentence is a rare example of one colon protecting another colon.

Fig. 63 *Rich as Fuck*, 2024, cannabis-infused acrylic gouache on canvas board, 20 × 30cm.

Fig. 63

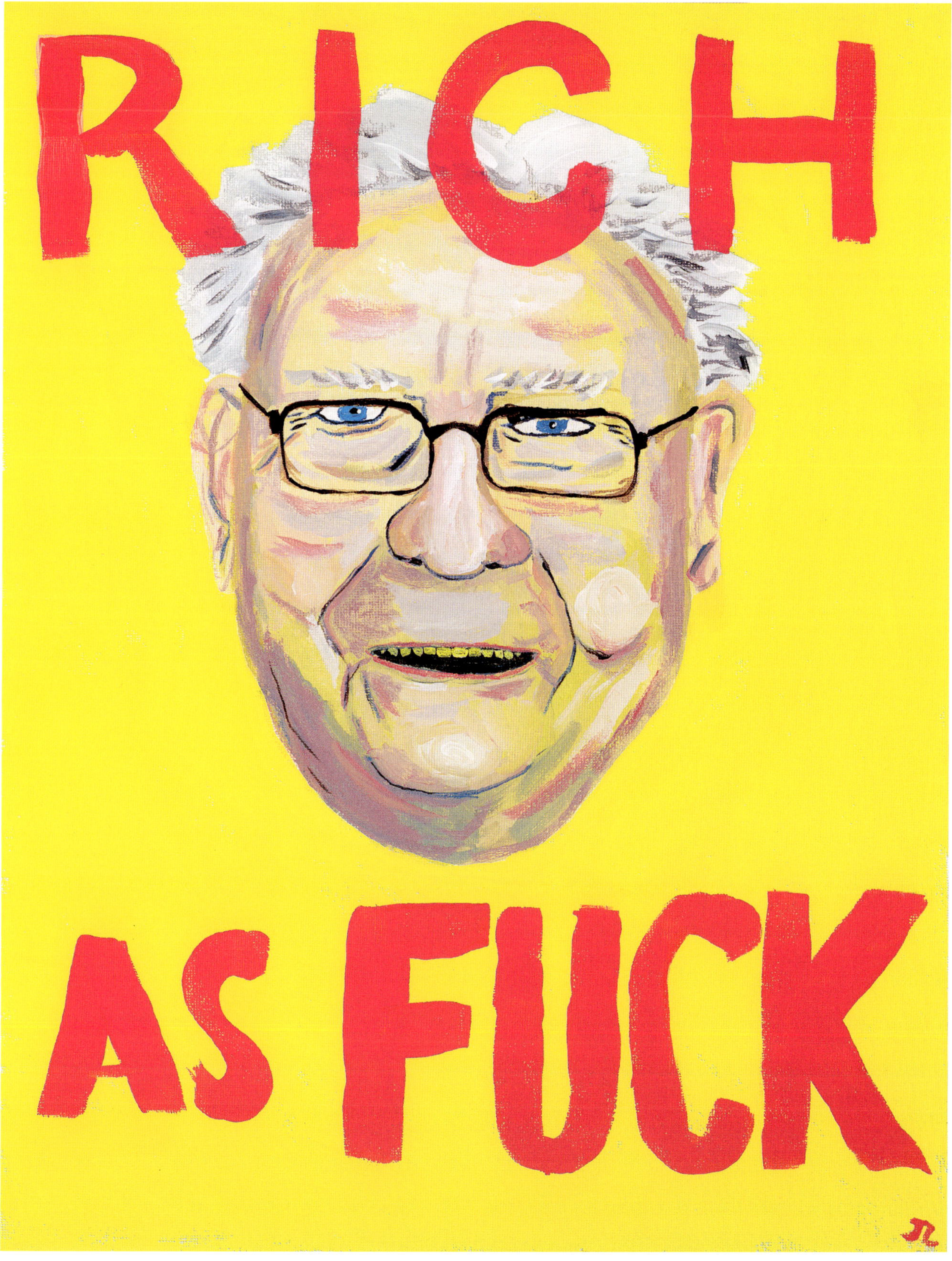

and WWE wrestling figurines. Grandma had a different idea. I remember her vividly, standing at the kitchen window, smoking a Dunhill and throwing darts at a passing child. 'Why don't you invest that money in a promising new business opportunity? Or spend it on whores?' she asked. I did not know how to make use of the whores at the time, so I opted for the former.

It transpired she had made the acquaintance of a young Warren Buffett during a recent visit to the Merry Hill shopping centre in Dudley. At that point, Warren was attempting to breathe new life into his career by running a pop-up nail-buffing stand manned by topless models, under the name Buffett's Buffting Buffings. Spotting my grandma as a potential sale, he had dashed up to her side and sweet-talked her into accepting a 'sample nail'. The idea being that once you compared the freshly buffed nail to your remaining nine, you'd be so stunned by the difference that you'd have no choice but to fork out (*see* **Fig. 64**) for the full treatment (performed by a far less attractive nail engineer in the back office).

Buffett had bitten off more than he could chew, buffing-wise. Decades of manual labour had eviscerated the surface of my grandma's nails to an extent that they proved impervious to any cosmetic treatment. My auntie Pat once remarked that, 'Applying nail polish to those is like creosoting a wooden fence.' Soon after this, auntie Pat sadly died.

All of Buffett's buffing had no effect on it whatsoever – Grandma's nail remained thoroughly unimproved. Warren was devastated, but she took pity on him, and struck up a conversation about his business, touching on his recent failures as well as his frustrated hopes and dreams. The upshot was that four days later she was dropping me off at his home.

Warren's abode was indeed modest and unpretentious – a tiny little shithole just off Shirley High Street.[1] You might think it odd that Grandma was so at ease leaving me with someone she barely knew, but it was different in those days and your parents and/or grandparents didn't mind dropping you off at a strange man's house and leaving you there for six to eight hours. The logic was that the decline of infant mortality during the twentieth century meant this was the only way left to ensure that only the strongest children survived.

Grandma pulled up in the Renault, leant over my lap to open my door, and pushed me out. I approached the house, looking back to see her skid and screech away enthusiastically. She had got out of the car by this point and was on foot, the screech sound coming from her knees.

1. Take the road opposite Big Johns and first or maybe second left.

Fig. 64 A fork. This is not the sort of fork you might use in the phrase 'forking out'.

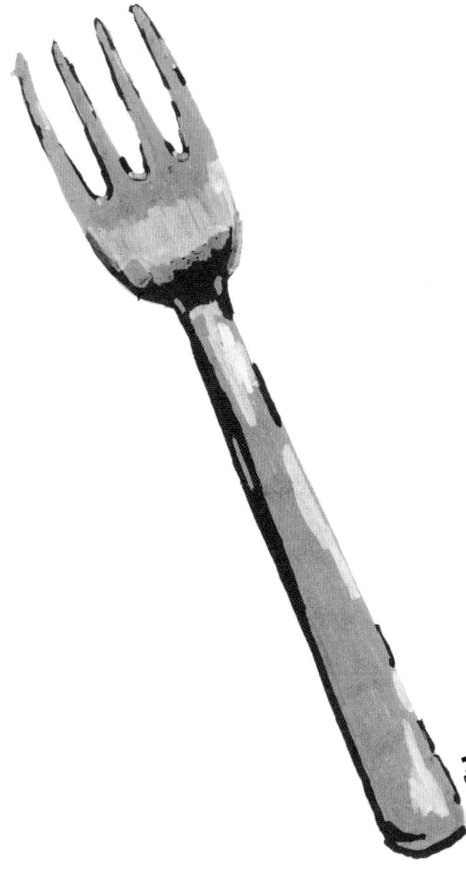

Fig. 64

Warren emerged with a ladle in one hand, a chicken drumstick in the other and a wide, gleaming smile on his face. I stared up at him. 'Come in then, you little twat!' he said. It was a hot August day and yet, for some reason, he was wearing a novelty Christmas jumper that said 'up to snow good'. The house smelt of Sudocrem and meat. I couldn't find the source of the Sudocrem, but the meat smell was definitely because he was cooking lots of meat. He later explained to me that he liked to cook all his meat for the month at once because it would 'save time'.

He sat me down in the kitchen and gave me a bottle of Newcastle Brown Ale. 'I'm only seven,' I pointed out. He nodded, looked in a drawer, and found a straw, which I accepted gratefully.

'So. Little businessman, are we?' he said, turning a gammon steak over on the hob. I plunged my straw into the bottle and took a sip. The taste was unpleasant, yet moreish, like a Pot Noodle if you removed the solids.

'Yeh, I heard you were the guy to talk to,' I said, abandoning the straw and taking a far more generous slurp.

'Oh yeh, kid, I'm big in business,' he said, filling a baking tray with approx. forty frozen nuggets and some frozen pineapple slices to go with the gammon. 'How much dough have you got to throw around?'

'Fifteen pounds,' I said casually, feeling like Deborah Meaden.[1]

'That'll do nicely.' Buffett was impressed by my casual display of wealth. 'I've got a new venture you'd be perfect for.'

He led me out into the garden, which was about the size of the cafes you sometimes see as part of a large ASDA. Generic unpleasant noise filled the air from a number of dogs that were being kept in crates, and what seemed to be a kestrel tethered to a concrete block. Occasionally a woman with a Birmingham accent would shout the word 'Brian' in anger.

'I'll show you what you should be spending your money on,' Warren whispered to me, ushering me forward. 'Seeds.'

'Seeds?' I queried.

'Seeds,' he responded.[2] 'I've got hundreds of plants growing here. A whole farm's worth. I'm sitting on a goldmine.' In front of us, I could see three impressive looking polytunnels with misty walls, dripping with hot condensation from the summer sun. 'Look,' he said, pointing inside.

I gasped. In stark contrast to the mess of his house, Buffett's tunnels were immaculately arranged; dozens upon dozens of virile tomato plants, in a dizzying array of varieties and colours. 'I sell them at the farmers' market,' he said proudly. 'Your investment could buy me quite a few more seeds!'

This was not at all what I had in mind. I may have only been seven, but I knew full well the return on a few tomatoes at the farmers' market would make me fuck all. 'Warren,' I said sternly, 'we need to talk.'

1. In the interests of accuracy, I should point out that I was probably unaware of Deborah Meaden at this point, given that the year was 1995 and she didn't join the *Dragons' Den* series until 2006. But I did look a lot like her at this age – and continued to do so until puberty.

2. This is an accurate account of the conversation, even though it makes for a repetitive read.

Fig. 65 A Polaroid of Newcastle Brown Ale.
Fig. 66 Newcastle Brown Ale.

Fig. 66

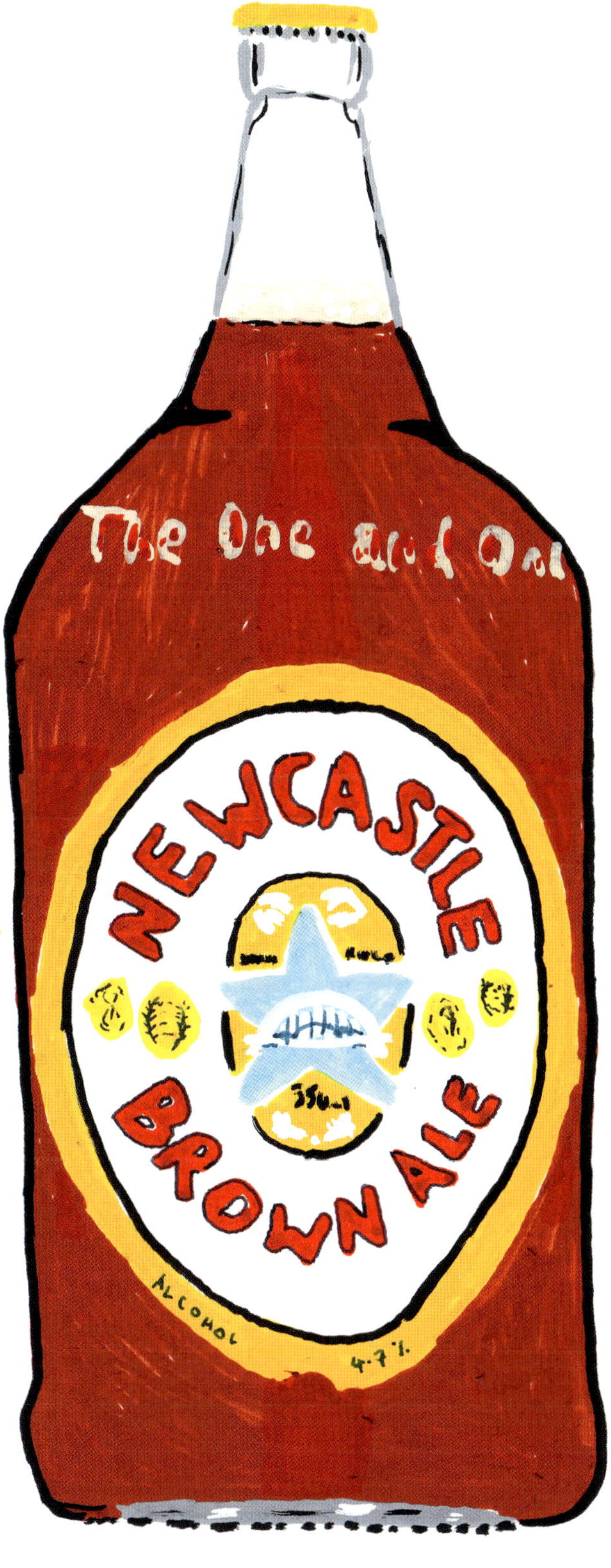

Fig. 65

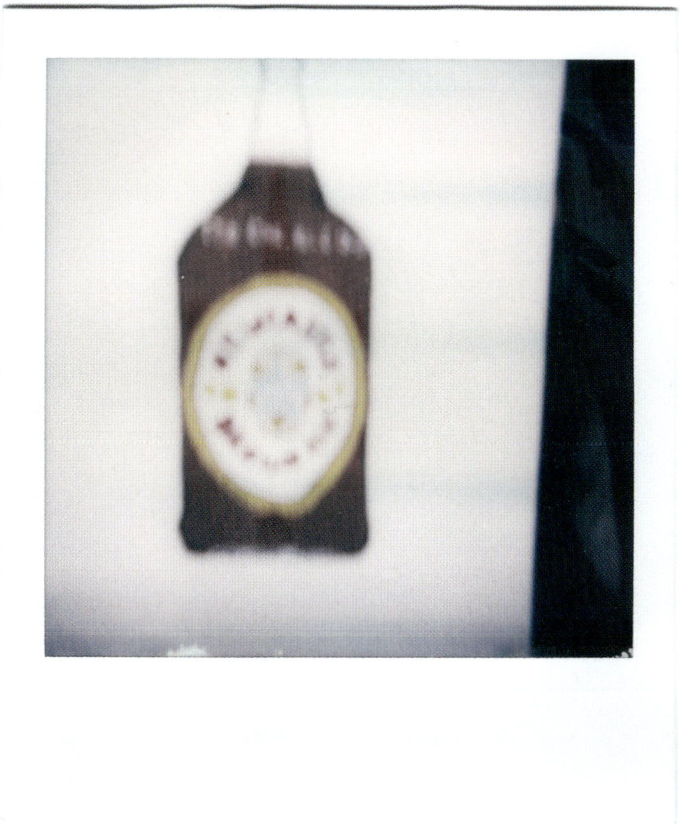

I took him back into the house and sat him at the table, swigging from the bottle of Newcastle Brown Ale as I did – I needed courage. 'The tomatoes are nice, Warren, don't get me wrong, but as a business idea it's dogshit.' An unattended pork knuckle burst into flames on the stove, and as Warren smothered the fire with a dampened tea towel, I broke through the miasma of singed meat with some real talk: 'You ever heard of hash, Warren?'

'Hash browns? Oh yes, I love them, I have them every morning with my eggs, a bit of saus—'

I cut the bastard off. This was the kind of simple misunderstanding whose weak comedic value I had always despised.

'No, Warren. Hash. Hashish?' He shook his head, perplexed. 'A bit of Mary Jane? A slice of the devil's lettuce? A bit of rope? Nice little brick of jazz cabbage?' Still nothing from the old man.

'Oh, come on, Warren, you know what I'm on about. A bit of boo boo bama? A whiff of the magic smoke? A short visit from the Reverend Green? Getting tickled by the golden ganja snake? A puff on a left-handed cigarette?' I had an alarmingly large vocabulary for my age.

'Oh! Tobacco?' he said. Idiot.

'Nearly, Warren! I'm talking about astro turf. A sniff of the blue sage. Lighting the Christmas tree? Going up nice and high in a space cake? Having a cuddle with Barbara Jean? Resting your head on a couple of Lime Pillows? Sharing a matchbox of Camberwell carrot?'

'Oh, you mean cannabis.'

'Yes, Warren, cannabis.'

By this point, Grandma had been dealing for several years – in fact, the fifteen pounds I was holding had been passed to her through the cranked rear window of the Renault just hours earlier.

'I'm a legitimate and honest businessman,' he said. 'I've never broken the law.' I later found out that, as we all have, he had downloaded the entire Sugababes back catalogue on LimeWire, so this was a lie.

I had to break it down for him. 'Listen, Princess. Stop twisting your knickers up and think about the score. Get this right and we could be pulling in hundreds of thousands a week.' The plan was gloriously, almost childishly simple. All we had to do was go to the farmers' market as usual and sell tomatoes. But whenever we sold to someone who looked like they might want a bag of weed, we slipped a little business card into their bag advertising 'special tomatoes'. (As it turned out, this was a bit too cryptic for the people of Birmingham, several of whom interpreted 'special tomatoes' as meaning those sweet Santini ones, so after a while we started writing 'special tomatoes (cannabis)').

Fig. 67 A picture I did of Warren Buffett in a chair.

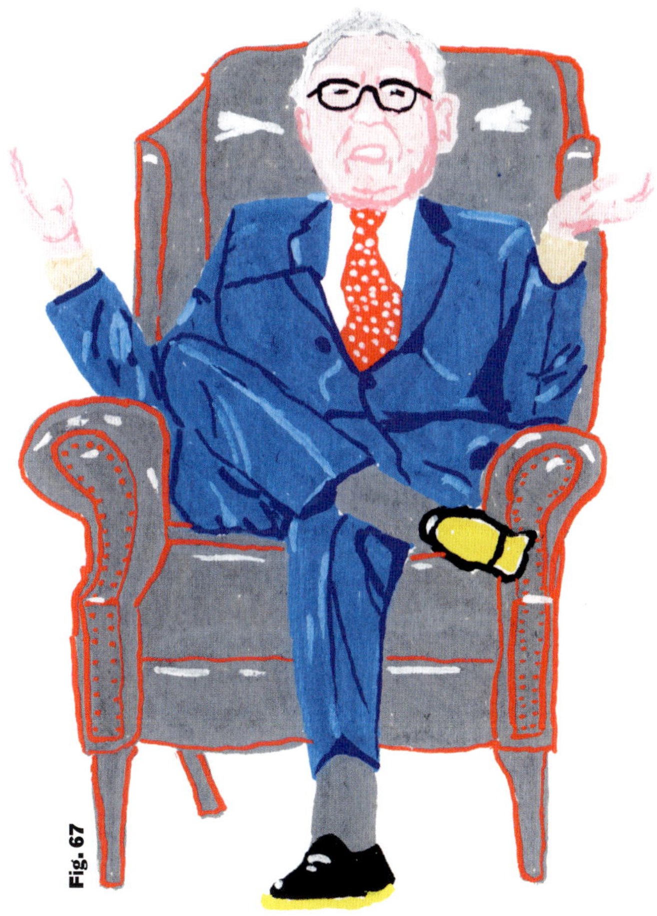
Fig. 67

Warren stood up from the table, walked out into the garden and emptied one of the polytunnels then and there. By the end of the day, the tomatoes had been replaced with high-grade cannabis plants. I was the Jesse Pinkman to his Walter White.[1] Grandma was delighted.

The stand was a huge success. We worked out who might want some weed by deciding if they moved slowly or wore hemp (shit) clothes. The business card smelt of weed. We had a loudspeaker on top of the stand playing 'Because I Got High' by Afroman. We also sold bongs. The clues were there for those able to interpret them.

The money was rolling in. But once you're in the game, you're always at risk from other players. I became increasingly paranoid, certain that my rivals were trying to rub me out. I started making Mother take me to Beavers in the car, and I'd keep my head below the window in case of drive-bys. Also, we'd started doing a school project about Roman Britain, and the daily requirement to colour in loads of centurions just added to the pressure I was under.

Eventually, I snapped. One day I was walking through the centre of Birmingham aimlessly, my mind full of strategies to stay alive and defeat my many enemies. Suddenly, I saw a police officer approaching me, his face a mask of pretend concern.

'Excuse me, son,' he said, which confused me because I wasn't his son. 'Are you lost?' I realised the question was a trick – I had been apprehended and had no choice but to confess.

'Warren Buffett sells cannabis from his tomato stand,' I said. The game was up.

Warren was arrested, tried and imprisoned for his crimes. This painting was done to assist the police in identifying him. Of course, we never spoke again but I felt a huge weight had been lifted. Years later, I read that he had become a billionaire. It looks like, for some people, prison is the making of them.[2] And so it seems for Warren – it's helped him go from being a failed entrepreneur to an investment guru and one of the most successful businessmen in the world.

NB: While writing this book, I became belatedly aware that the Warren Buffett I knew and Warren Buffett the multibillionaire investor are not, in fact, the same person. Mom tells me that the Warren Buffett I knew still lives off Shirley High Street, and she bumps into him in Iceland from time to time. He is apparently always keen to hear the latest news about me and my career, and on such occasions typically refers to me as a 'limp-wristed crook'.

1. This reference is imperfect as Buffett was not terminally ill and we were selling weed and tomatoes rather than meth, but it's my book and I'm sticking with it.

2. See also: Nelson Mandela, Martha Stewart, Jeffrey Archer.

Fig. 68 A Polaroid of me showing off my painting of Warren Buffett. Photograph by Margaret Mountford, formerly of *The Apprentice*.

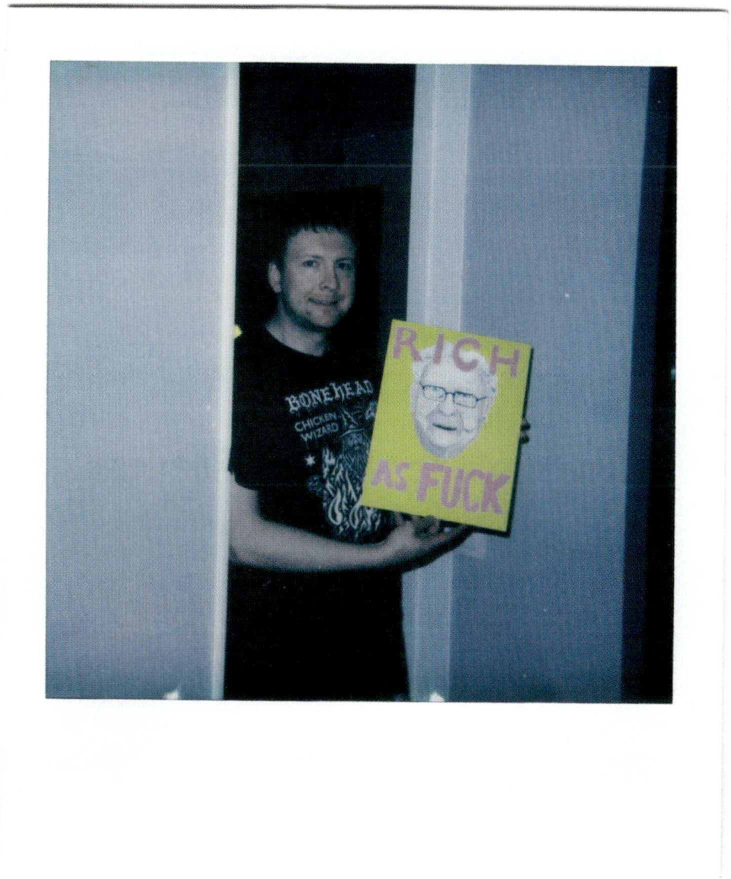

Fig. 68

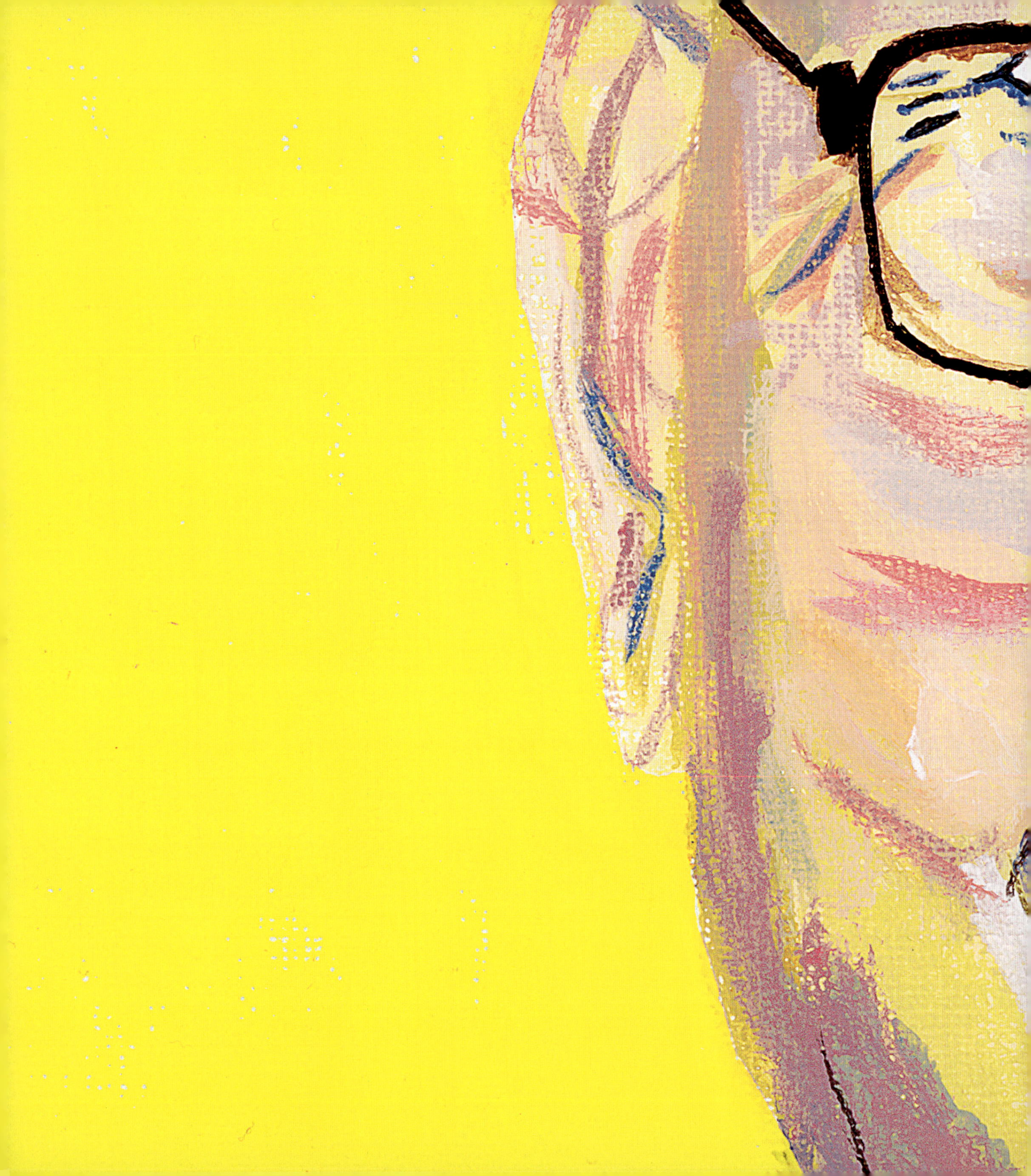

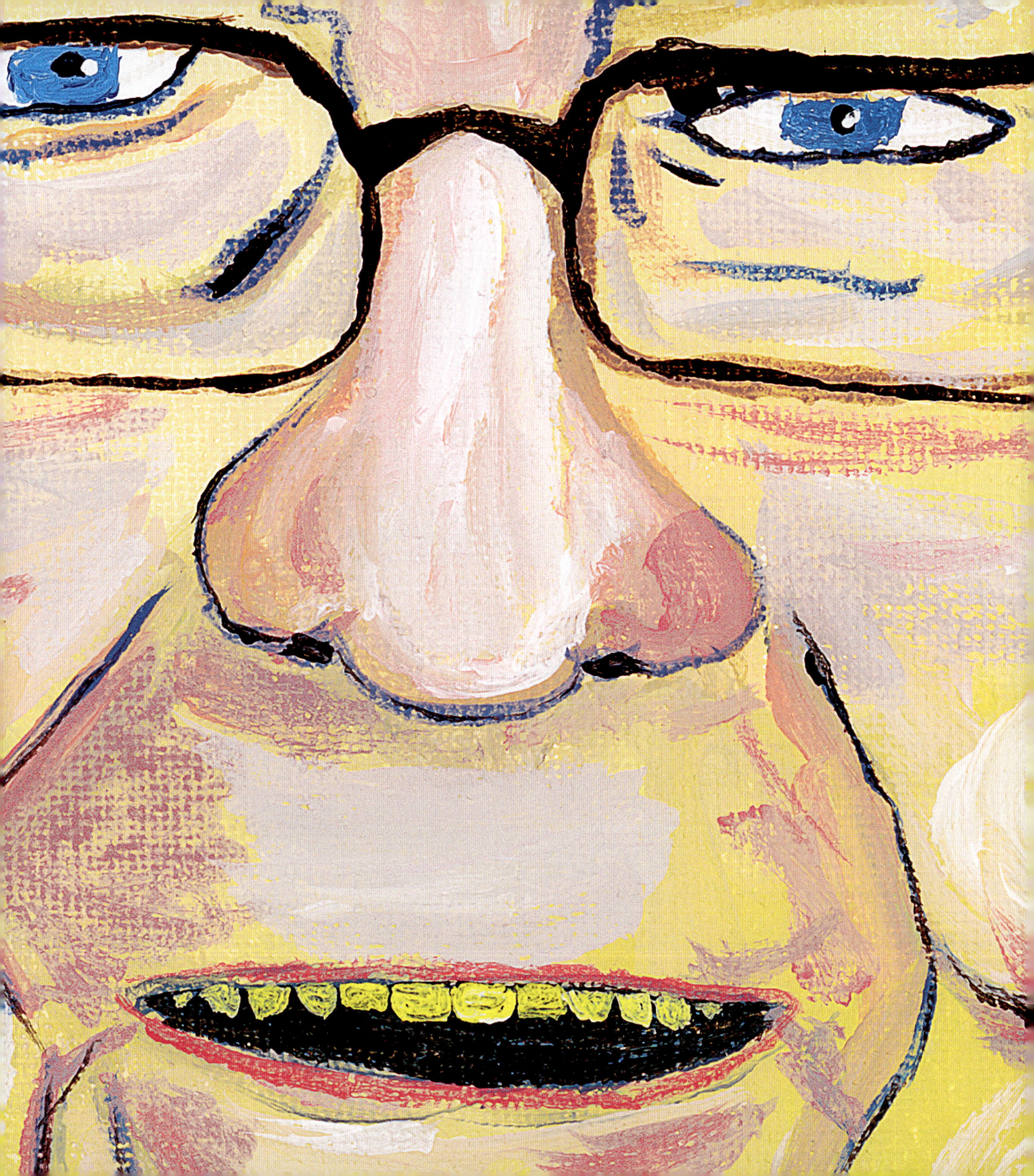

INCREDIBLE GIRTH

Britain was deep into the referendum campaign for leaving the EU and I was making a light-hearted appearance at a pro-Brexit conference in Wolverhampton. I didn't really give a shit how we voted either way because politics doesn't have any effect on celebrities, but they'd offered me thousands of pounds and a wallet made with British leather to do the talk, and I wasn't going to look a gift horse in the mouth. (To be honest, I have no desire to look any horse in the mouth, or any animal directly in the mouth, and now I think about it I don't know what a gift horse is. Regardless, I am not allowed to work with any animals till 2025 because, long story short, I tried to give my cat a vajazzle.)

Before the gig, I was stationed among the highest level of vote-leave-supporting celebrity talent, all of us clustered in a refreshment breakout space enjoying British produce like lemonade, olives, champagne and shish kebab. It was all the sort of people you would definitely trust with important decisions with unalterable consequences. People like Ringo Starr, John Cleese, Bernie Ecclestone, James Dyson, Morrissey, Elaine Paige and Liz Hurley.

Out of curiosity and sheer politeness, I attempted to chat to them all. I started with entrepreneur and inventor James Dyson, a vocal supporter of the campaign who argued 'It would mean better trade deals for Britain and less control from countries like Germany', when actually I'd just asked where the bathroom was. After I returned,[1] he mentioned he also wanted to leave because he once stayed in an Airbnb in Barcelona and he knew that it had been cleaned with a Henry even though he insists that one of his vacuums cleans every room he sleeps in. 'It's the classic lack of respect you get from that lot in Brussels,' he said. I lost him when I said that I loved his hand dryers but didn't know why he had hidden the word 'slut' in them (*see* **Fig. 71**), and he said, 'Ha! Good for you, bro!' while pretending to take a phone call from headquarters (now in Singapore).

I moved on to a fabulous chat with Liz Hurley, who kept having her champagne topped up while saying things like, 'We'll be drinking less of this when we leave!' to huge laughter in the room. She was obsessed with Angela Merkel, referring to her as 'Queen of Germany', and told a story where Merkel had said to Hurley that she was sorry, but she hadn't seen the fantasy romantic comedy *Bedazzled* (starring Hurley and Brendan Fraser, released in 2000) and couldn't promise that she

1. Just a piss.

Fig. 69 (lol) *Incredible Girth*, 2023, acrylic on pork cutlet, 12 × 15mm.

Fig. 69 (lol)

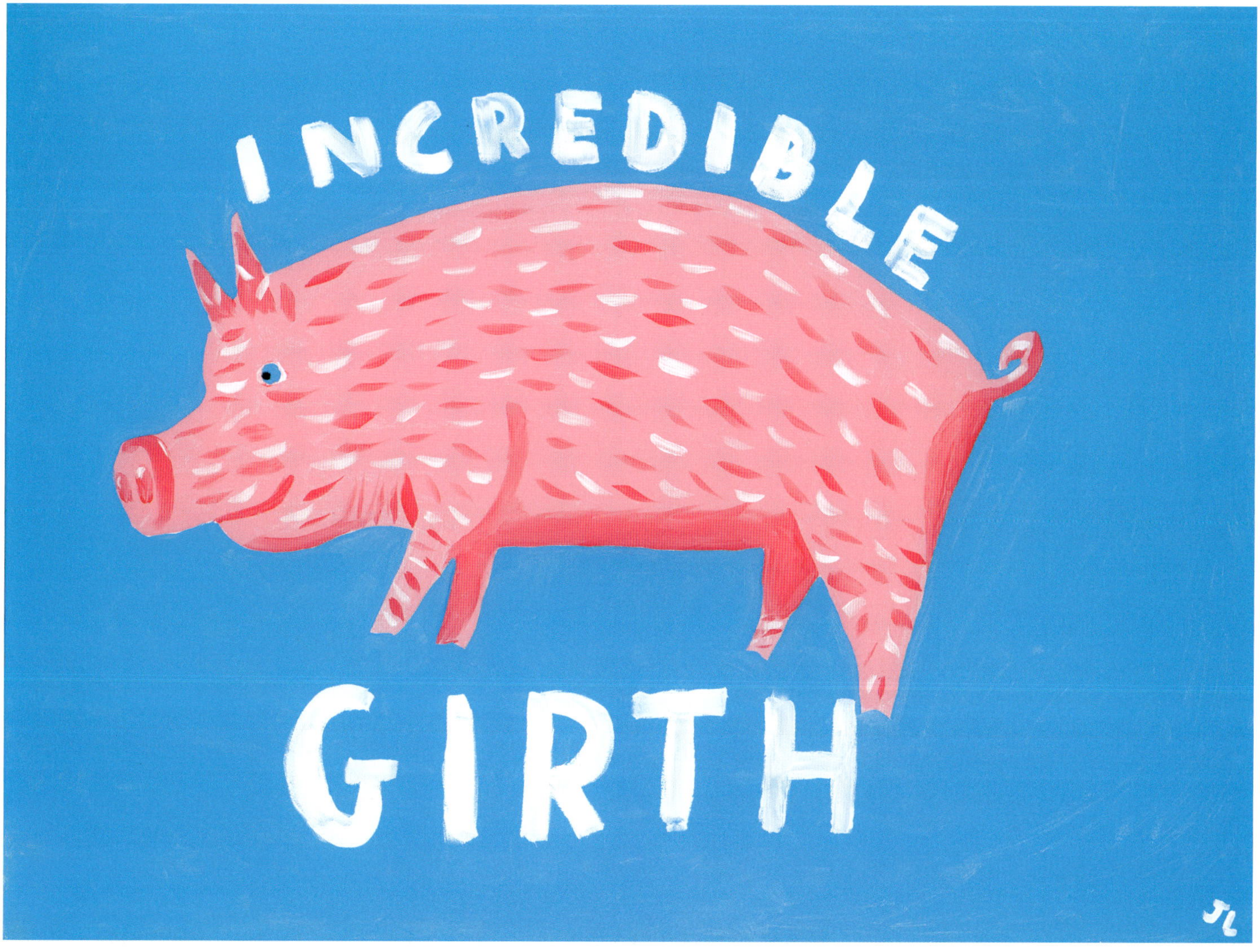

ever would. Liz seemed genuinely upset about it and couldn't let it go, telling me, 'Despite the reviews, it did well at the box office, and I just cannot believe Merkel won't agree to see it, even when I handed her a DVD and VHS of it that I had in my tote bag.'

John Cleese was absolutely hilarious. So, so funny, what a funny guy, saying he wanted to leave Europe even though he's always loved Europeans and that was very clear from the character of Manuel in *Fawlty Towers*. He then did an impression of him that was later described by some attendees as 'appalling'. I managed to both marry and divorce John at this event and now own the reproduction rights to *Life of Brian*.

Former chief executive of Formula One Bernie Ecclestone was the most animated of the guests, comparing Europe to 'an F1 car without any bloody wheels on', which most people laughed at but I didn't really get. 'Them pen-pushers in Bruges or wherever they are need to get some bleedin' indicators or they'll smash off their wing mirrors at this rate,' he said, while dragging a sofa across the room for some reason.

Morrissey sat in the corner drinking Shloer, at one point saying, 'Piss off, Portugal,' and was otherwise entirely unresponsive, just reading a Rupi Kaur poetry book and tutting. Elaine Paige was dressed head-to-toe in a Union Jack flag suit and was exactly as you'd imagine.

I got chatting to Ringo for a bit. 'People think I'm saying "peace and love",' he said, 'but actually sometimes I say "piss and love" just to see if anyone notices.' He sniggered. 'No one ever does.' This is why I consider him to be one of the most interesting and accomplished artists of our generation, a maverick who refuses to pander to the art world's petty demands for a work to either look nice or say something. Ringo broke that mould.

He gave me some great morsels that day. 'You gotta do your thing, man,' he said while eating a pork pie, 'and my thing is doing a quick drawing on MS Paint and then downloading it to a USB stick and then printing it and selling it on my website. You gotta just go with your heart, man, don't overthink it.'

Ringo's approach resonated with me. Of course, I respect people that can spend years on an artwork, pouring decades of their lives into one piece, but I just like to make things and get stuff done.[1] And we should all want to make things: the world is so full of violence and hatred, to make any art at all is an act of resistance. George Bush was once the US president that took the country into a messy and long war, but now he paints pictures of dogs. I was once told, 'It is impossible to paint and kick someone simultaneously,' but the recalcitrant in me proved otherwise and I am now banned from a branch of Cass Art.

1. Funnily enough, also how Bernie Ecclestone once described Hitler.

Fig. 70 An early etching of the Brexit pig.
Fig. 71 This is an image of a Dyson Airblade, which I believe includes a subliminal word. The pleasing curvature of the tubing on the vacuum to the far left (which looks to be the Big Ball model) makes a clear 'S'. Next, the iconic Ball Animal vacuum forms an 'L'. The next three Dyson products – the Air Purifier, 360 Vis Nav and the Cordless Vacuum, possibly a V8 – combine to produce a 'U'. A 't' is formed by a product which I am unable to confidently identify, but which I imagine may be one of their desk lamps. Finally, adding punctuation, the full stop (or maybe a comma) is the Supersonic Professional Hairdryer. All of this combined unmistakably produces the word: 'SlUt'.
Fig. 72 A map of the approximate location of Dyson's HQ.

Fig. 70

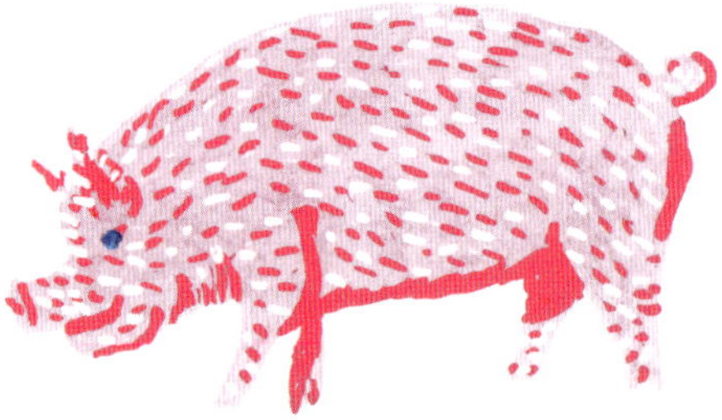

Fig. 71

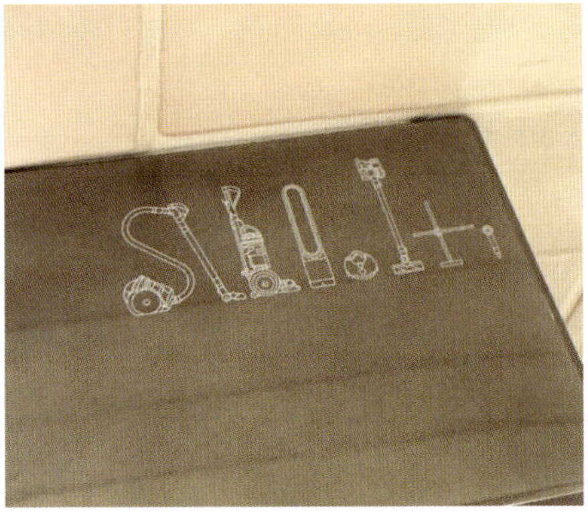

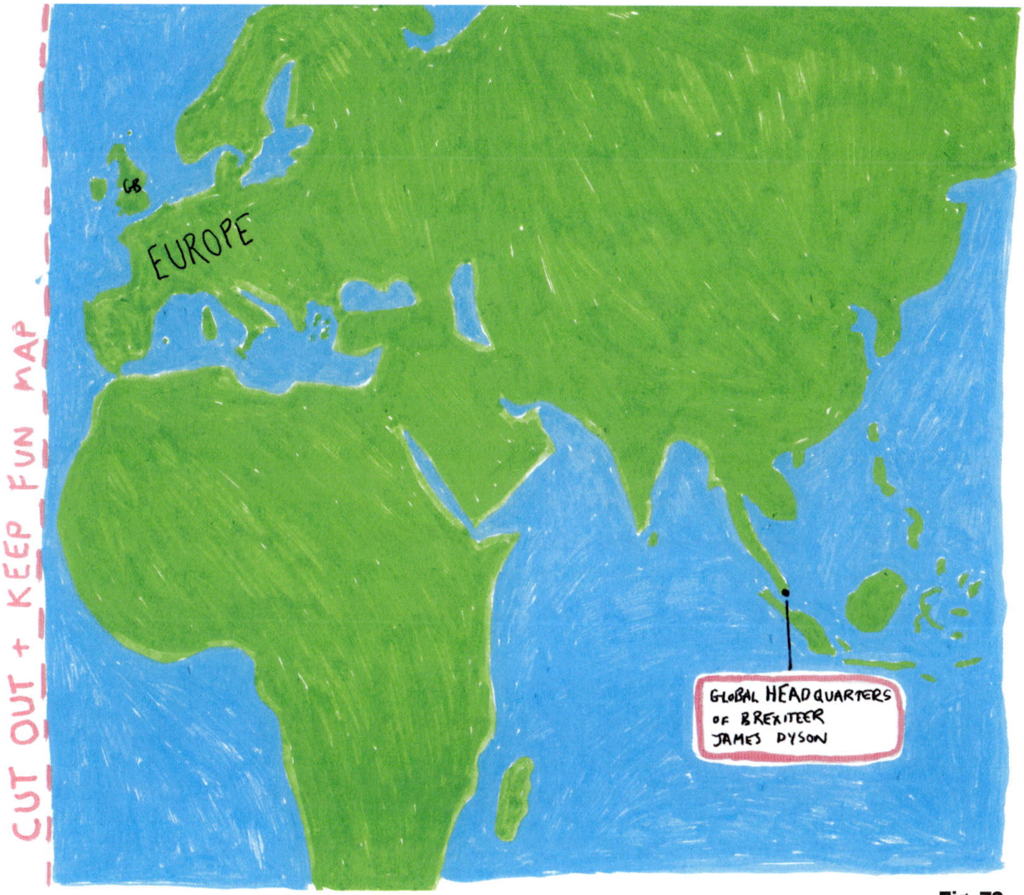
CUT OUT + KEEP FUN MAP
GB
EUROPE
GLOBAL HEADQUARTERS
OF BREXITEER
JAMES DYSON

Fig. 72

When I got Ringo onto the topic of Brexit, he became almost manic with delight. 'Oh, we gotta leave, man,' he kept saying, between bites of pork pie. 'We gotta get out. Get out there, man. Get outta that crazy place, man, do our own thing, man.' I nodded. 'Once we're out we can do whatever we want, man. We'll grow way bigger than we've ever dreamt, baby. We'll be crazy big. Insane weight to us, man. Big old slab. Wild size. Big old wild size. Incredible size, man. Incredible girth.'

I could have listened to him for some time (approx. four more minutes), but I was beckoned out of the room to do my performance. Easy money: I just did a few gags about how funny all the European accents sound, said 'vote leave' a bit, shook a few hands, then took the cash and British leather wallet in a bright blue envelope, and headed home.

It was pitch black when I returned (my direct debit with npower had elapsed). I sat in the orangery, pondering the day. The blank canvas I had placed on the easel that morning was staring at me. For some reason Ringo's phrase – 'incredible girth' – lingered in my mind. The phrase 'big old slab' did too but I haven't got round to doing anything with that one. I did this painting quickly, spontaneously, instinctively – channelling all the energy from those glorious and passionate Brexiteers. I imagined us, the United Kingdom, as a jolly fat pig, plump and juicy from an abundant harvest, living finally as our own people, off the fat of this green and pleasant land, with our glorious rotund bellies, an incredible size, wild size, big old slab, incredible girth.

Fig. 73 A Polaroid I took of the *Bedazzled* DVD and VHS in Liz Hurley's designer bag.
Fig. 74 A previously unpublished letter from Bill Gates of Microsuft to Ringo Starr.
Fig. 75 Ringo Starr's schedule (in his own words).
Fig. 76 Morrissey's schedule (in his own words).

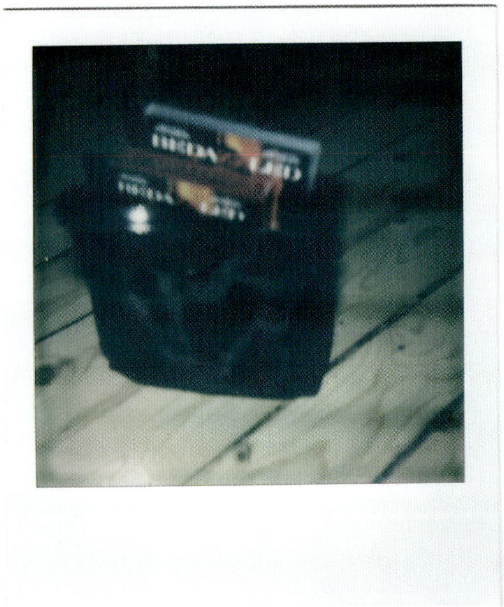

Fig. 73

Fig. 74

Microsuft
[redacted]

Tel: [redacted]
Fax: [redacted]

Microsuft

Mr Ringo Starr
[redacted]
UK

4th June 2023

Dear Ringo,

Wouldn't normally do this but happy to help on this occassion. The password for your Microsoft account is 'wowokyehwowpasswordwow'.

Might be worth changing it next time you login.

With Best Wishes.

Your friend,

Bill

Bill Gates

All contents of this letter are confidential and should not be reproduced in any way.

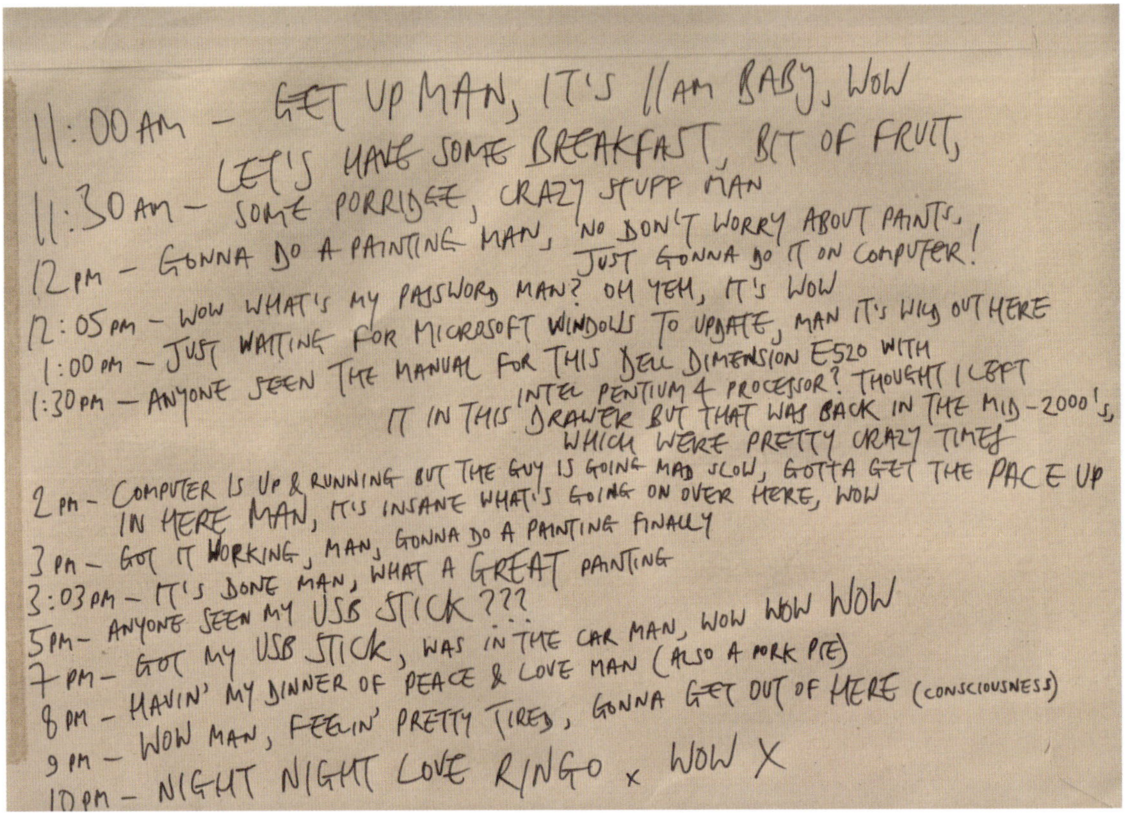

11:00AM – GET UP MAN, IT'S 11AM BABY, WOW

11:30AM – LET'S HAVE SOME BREAKFAST, BIT OF FRUIT, SOME PORRIDGE, CRAZY STUFF MAN

12PM – GONNA DO A PAINTING MAN, NO DON'T WORRY ABOUT PAINTS, JUST GONNA DO IT ON COMPUTER!

12:05PM – WOW WHAT'S MY PASSWORD MAN? OH YEAH, IT'S WOW

1:00PM – JUST WAITING FOR MICROSOFT WINDOWS TO UPDATE, MAN IT'S WILD OUT HERE

1:30PM – ANYONE SEEN THE MANUAL FOR THIS DELL DIMENSION E520 WITH INTEL PENTIUM 4 PROCESSOR? THOUGHT I LEFT IT IN THIS DRAWER BUT THAT WAS BACK IN THE MID-2000'S, WHICH WERE PRETTY CRAZY TIMES

2PM – COMPUTER IS UP & RUNNING BUT THE GUY IS GOING MAD SLOW, GOTTA GET THE PACE UP IN HERE MAN, IT'S INSANE WHAT'S GOING ON OVER HERE, WOW

3PM – GOT IT WORKING, MAN, GONNA DO A PAINTING FINALLY

3:03PM – IT'S DONE MAN, WHAT A GREAT PAINTING

5PM – ANYONE SEEN MY USB STICK???

7PM – GOT MY USB STICK, WAS IN THE CAR MAN, WOW WOW WOW

8PM – HAVIN' MY DINNER OF PEACE & LOVE MAN (ALSO A PORK PIE)

9PM – WOW MAN, FEELIN' PRETTY TIRED, GONNA GET OUT OF HERE (CONSCIOUSNESS)

10PM – NIGHT NIGHT LOVE RINGO x WOW X

Fig. 75

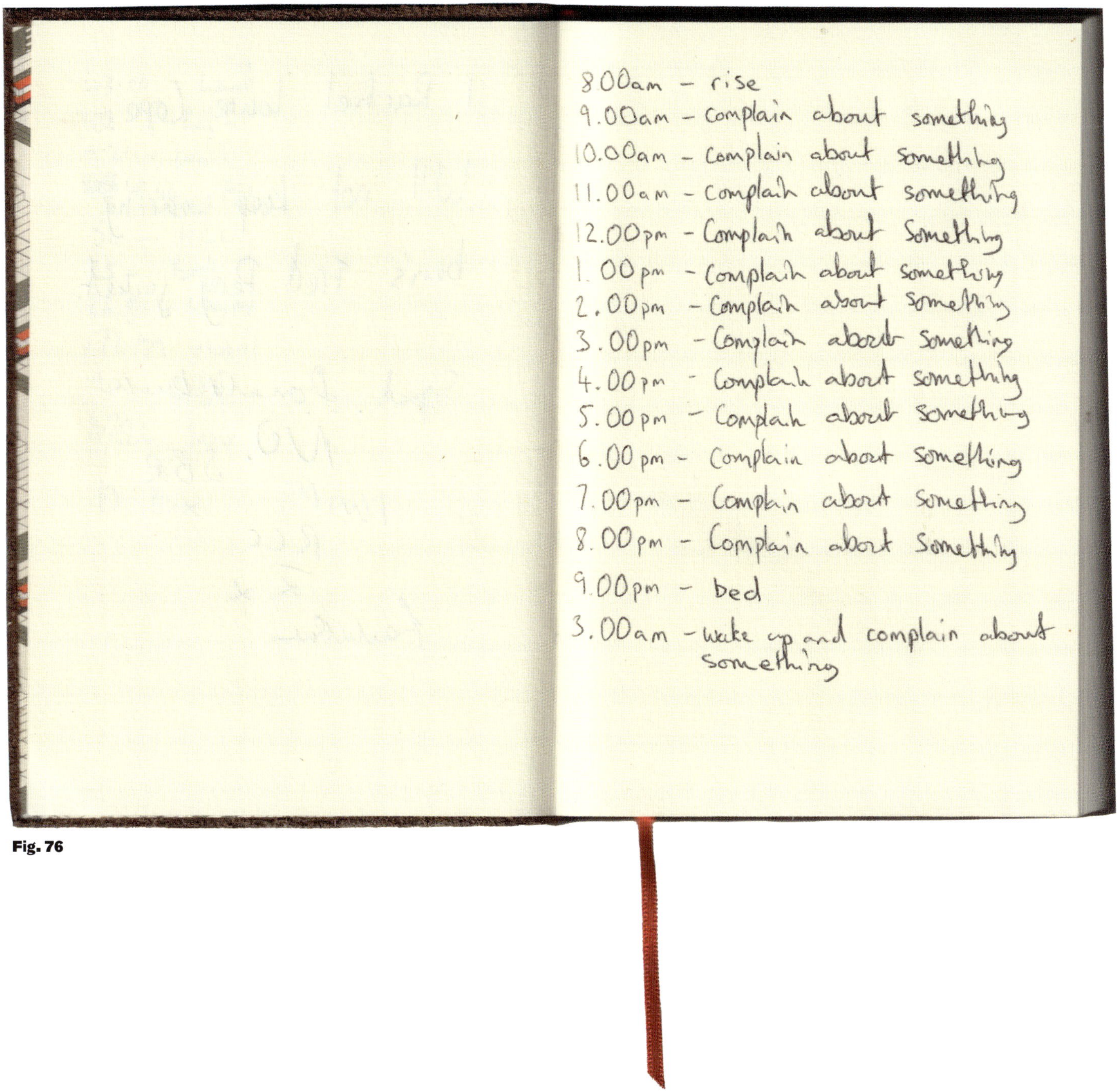
8.00am – rise
9.00am – complain about something
10.00am – complain about something
11.00am – complain about something
12.00pm – Complain about Something
1.00pm – complain about something
2.00pm – Complain about something
3.00pm – Complain about something
4.00pm – Complain about something
5.00pm – Complain about something
6.00pm – Complain about something
7.00pm – Complain about something
8.00pm – Complain about Something
9.00pm – bed
3.00am – wake up and complain about something

Fig. 76

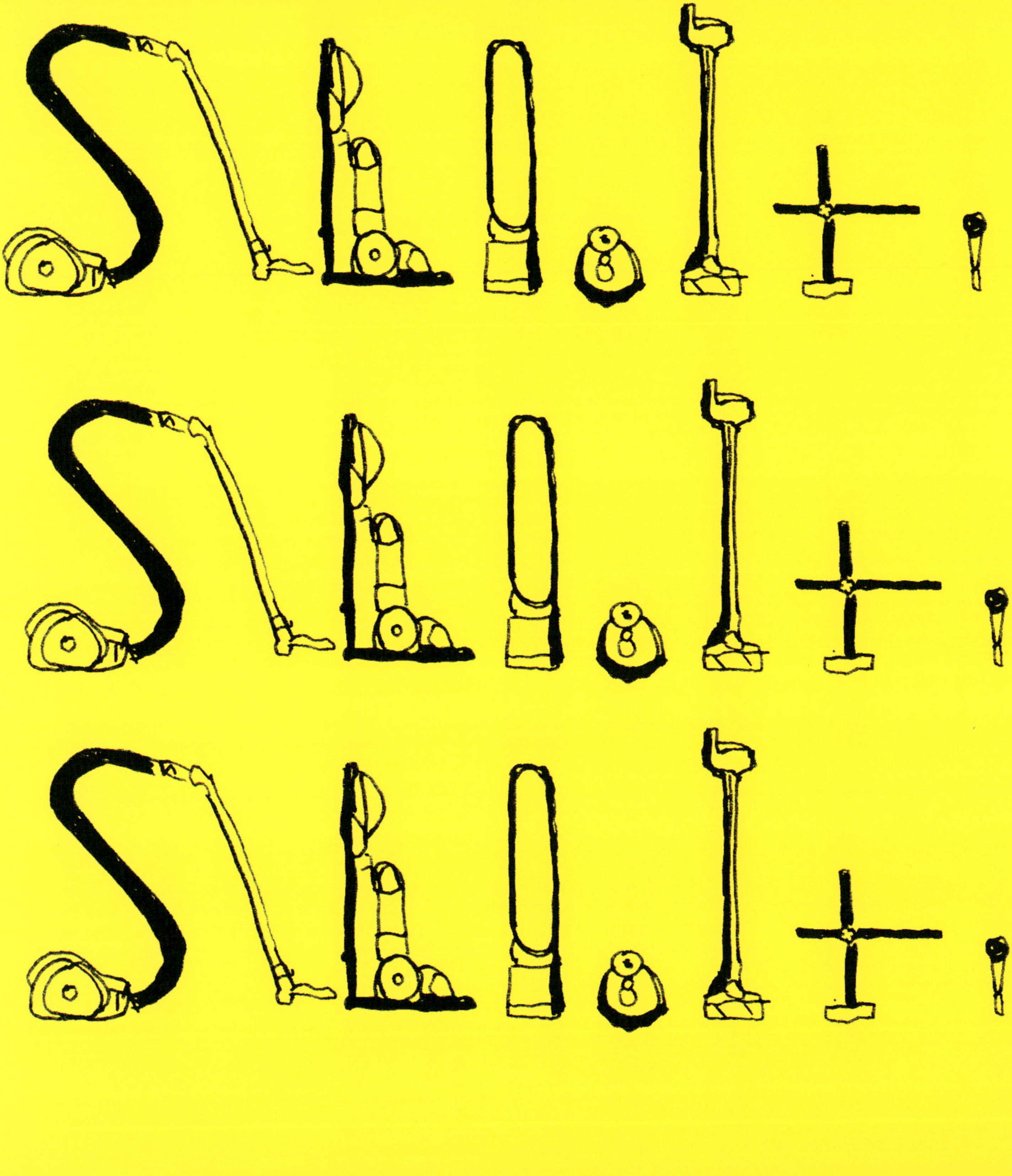

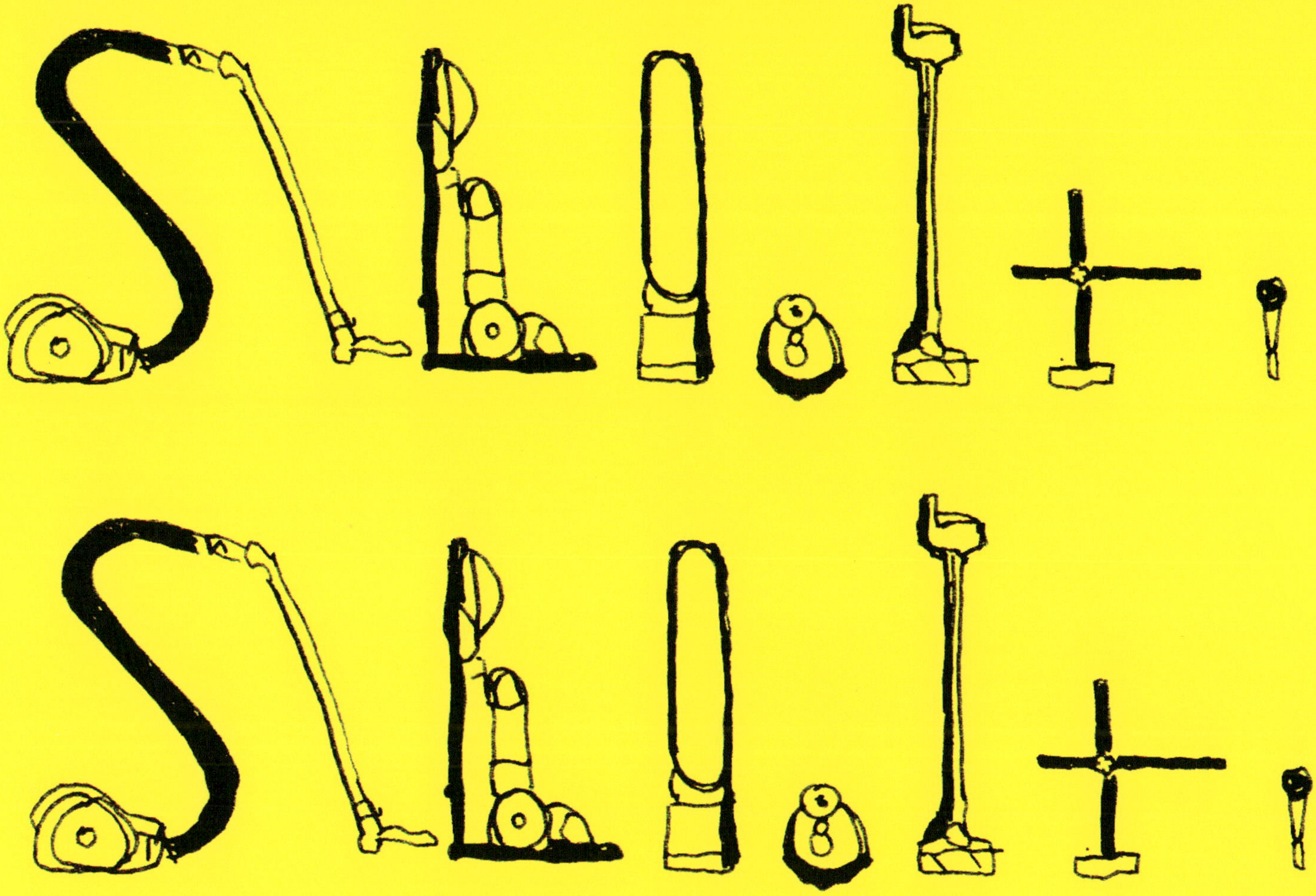

SLUt.

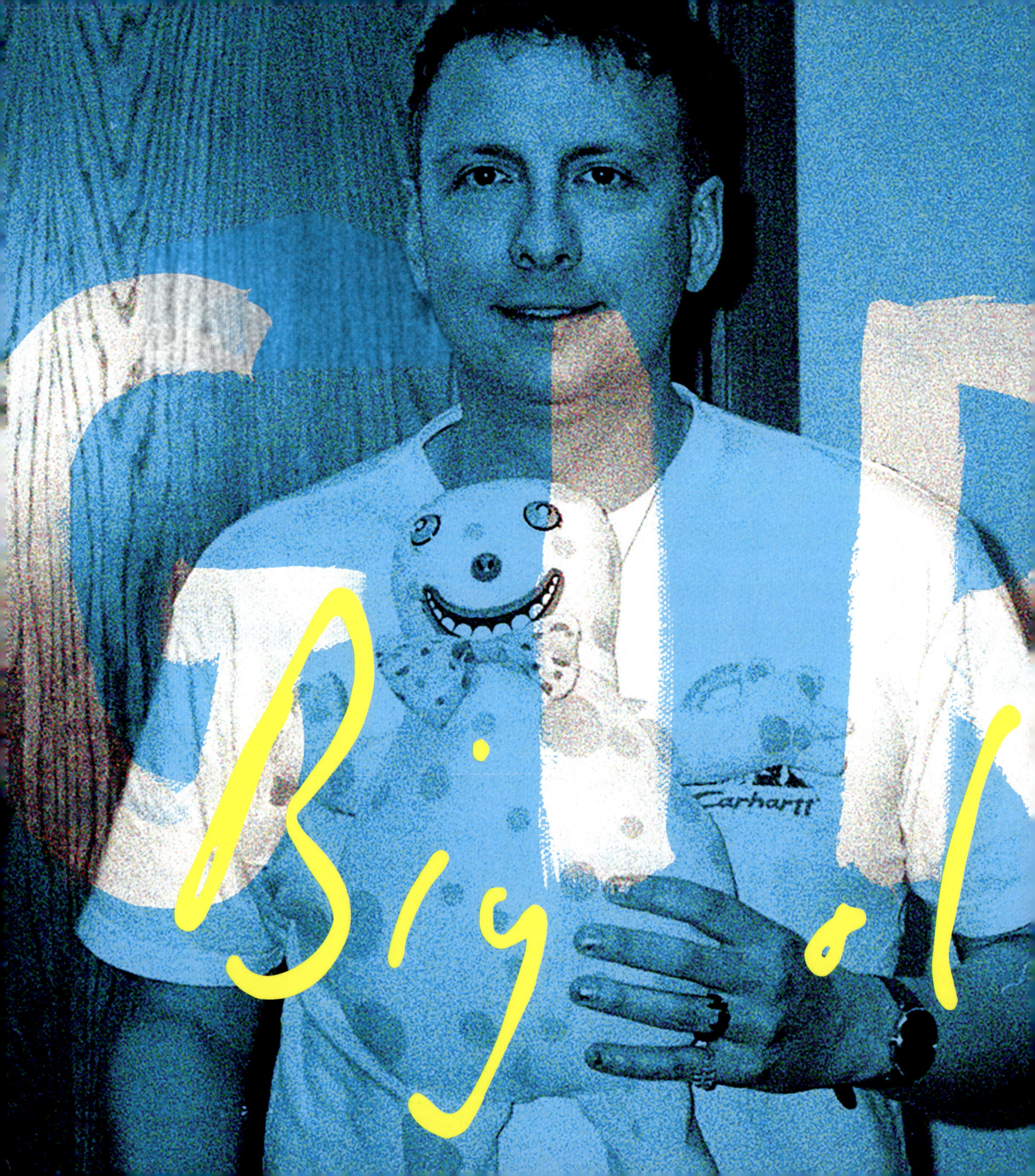
Big ol
Carhartt

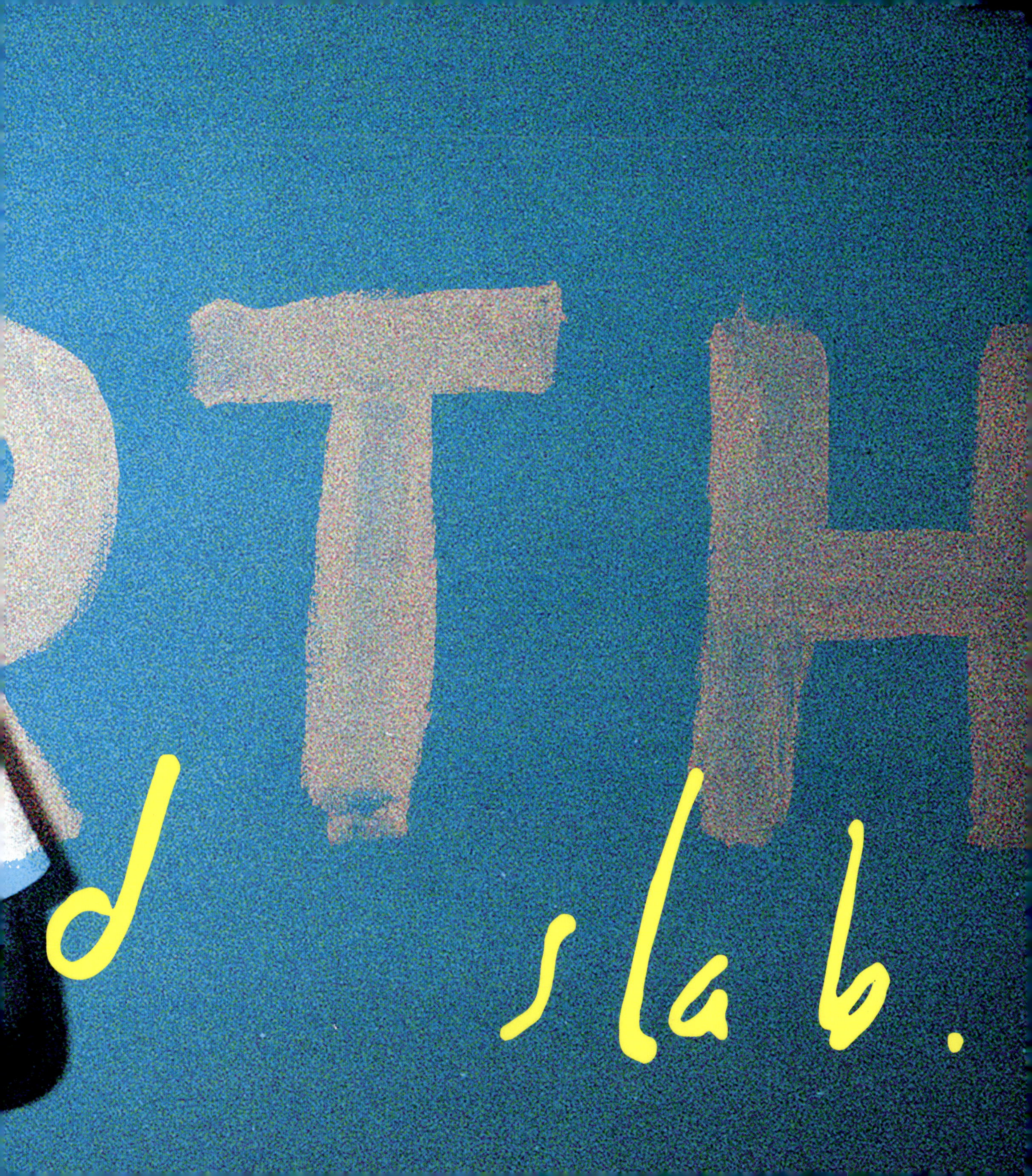

d slab.

YOU LOOK VERY NICE

Fig. 77 An early sketch that I sent to Ross Kemp. He replied, 'yeh ok'.
Fig. 78 *You Look Very Nice*, 2024, white paint and blood on pillowcase, 40 × 50cm.
Fig. 79 Texts between me and Ross Kemp.

I did say that I wouldn't publicly announce who this commission was for, but they haven't paid their invoice so I'm just going to go ahead and put it in print right here in my book: it's Ross Kemp.

I met him at hot yoga years ago and stupidly gave him my number. Now he's always texting, saying, 'How are the kids?' even though I've told him approximately twenty-five times that I don't even have kids, and sometimes he sends me memes which are just videos of little piglets and other creatures sprinting through farmyards (cats, shrews, XL Bully dogs).

One night, after sending me a video of a capybara eating a watermelon, he asked if we could FaceTime. I gave in. I thought I could ask him questions about his career, and started by enquiring as to what it was like to film *Ross Kemp on Gangs*. I couldn't believe it, but he said all the gangs were fake and played by actors and that, if you look closely, you can see a neo-Nazi played by a prosthetics-heavy Ian McKellen, and that one of the gangs in an early episode was just all the members of Steps in balaclavas. I asked him how he got away with it, and he said that if any journalists got wind of it, they got Claire from Steps to put her mask back on and kneecap them.

Anyway, I got a text from him one night saying he was doing up his bedroom at home and wanted to commission me to do a painting (or as he put it, 'Do one of your art things') for it that would make him feel good and boost his self-worth when he's trying on clothes. He said he doesn't normally struggle with self-confidence, but it can't hurt to have some sort of message that reminds him that he looks 'nice'. I asked him if he had any favourite colours or animals or objects, and he said pink was his all-time fave so maybe it could be a pig or a flamingo or something else pink. I did this piece in record time and sent him a picture, to which he replied, 'One sec,' and then never replied ever again. He doesn't respond to any messages whatsoever, even when I say things like, 'The kids are doing really well.' If anyone wants to buy it, I'll give it to you for the same price as agreed with Ross, which is £5,000 and lunch at a restaurant of his choice (he alluded to it being Pret).

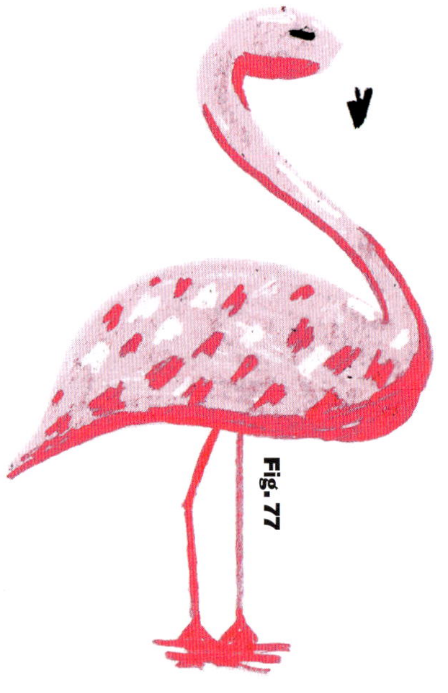

Fig. 77

Fig. 78

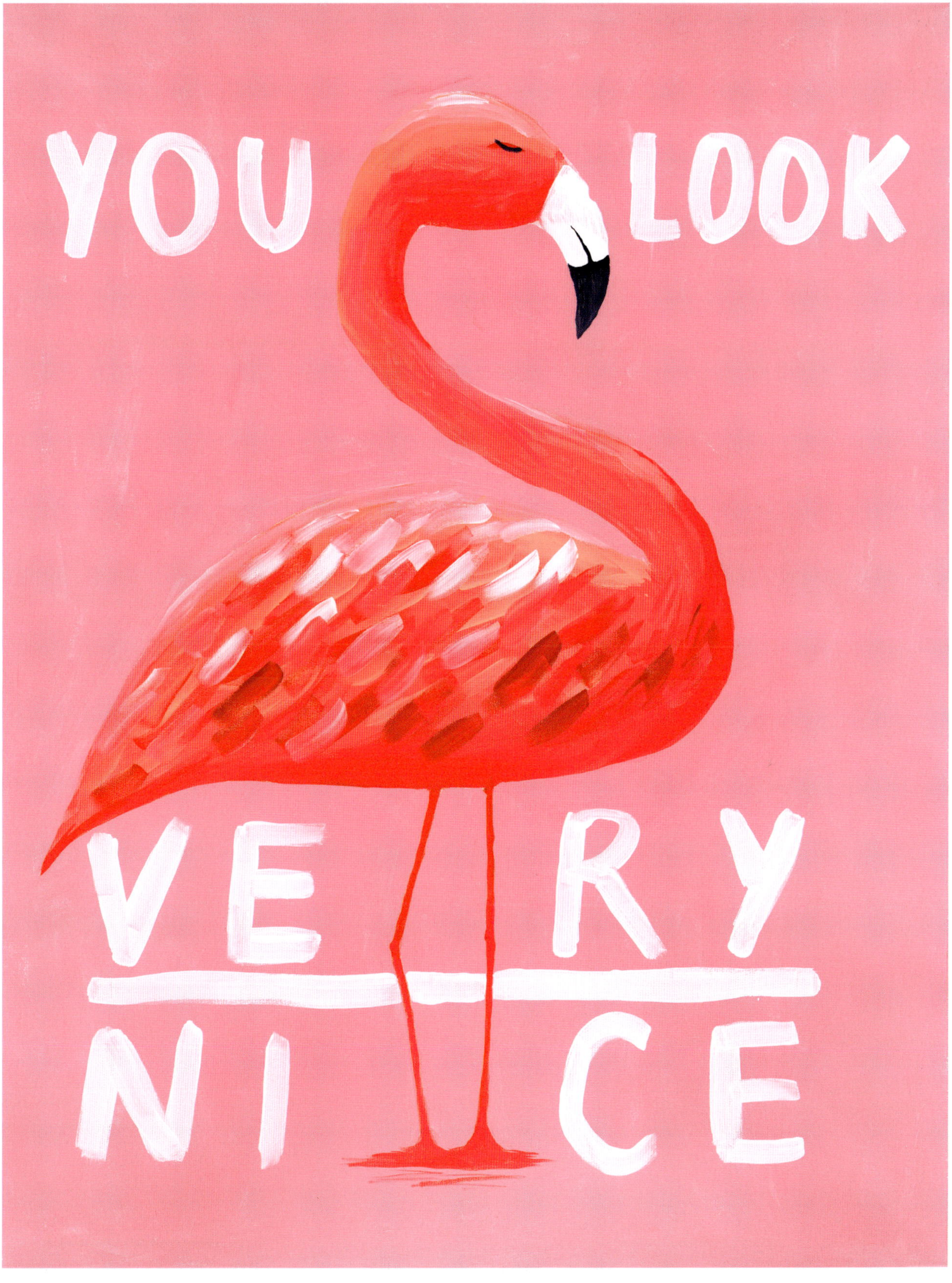

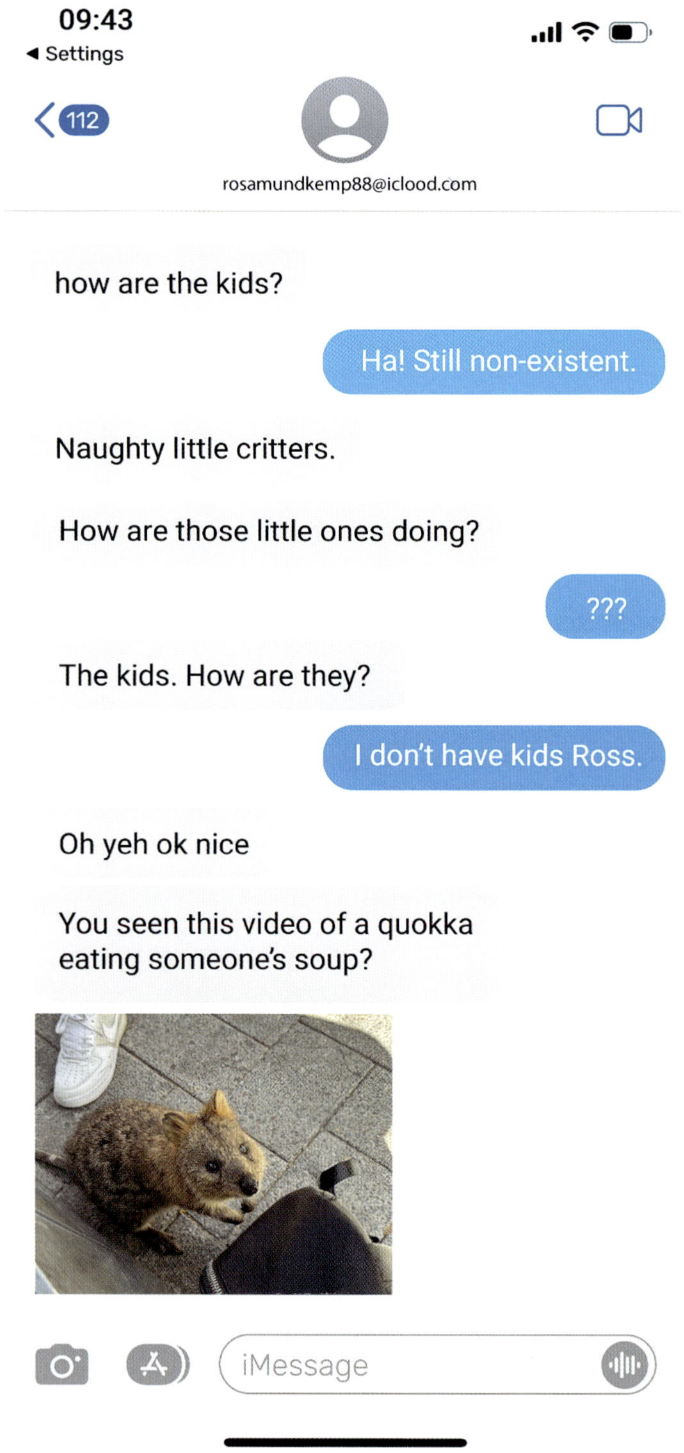
09:43
Settings
112
rosamundkemp88@icloud.com
how are the kids?
Ha! Still non-existent.
Naughty little critters.
How are those little ones doing?
???
The kids. How are they?
I don't have kids Ross.
Oh yeh ok nice
You seen this video of a quokka eating someone's soup?
iMessage

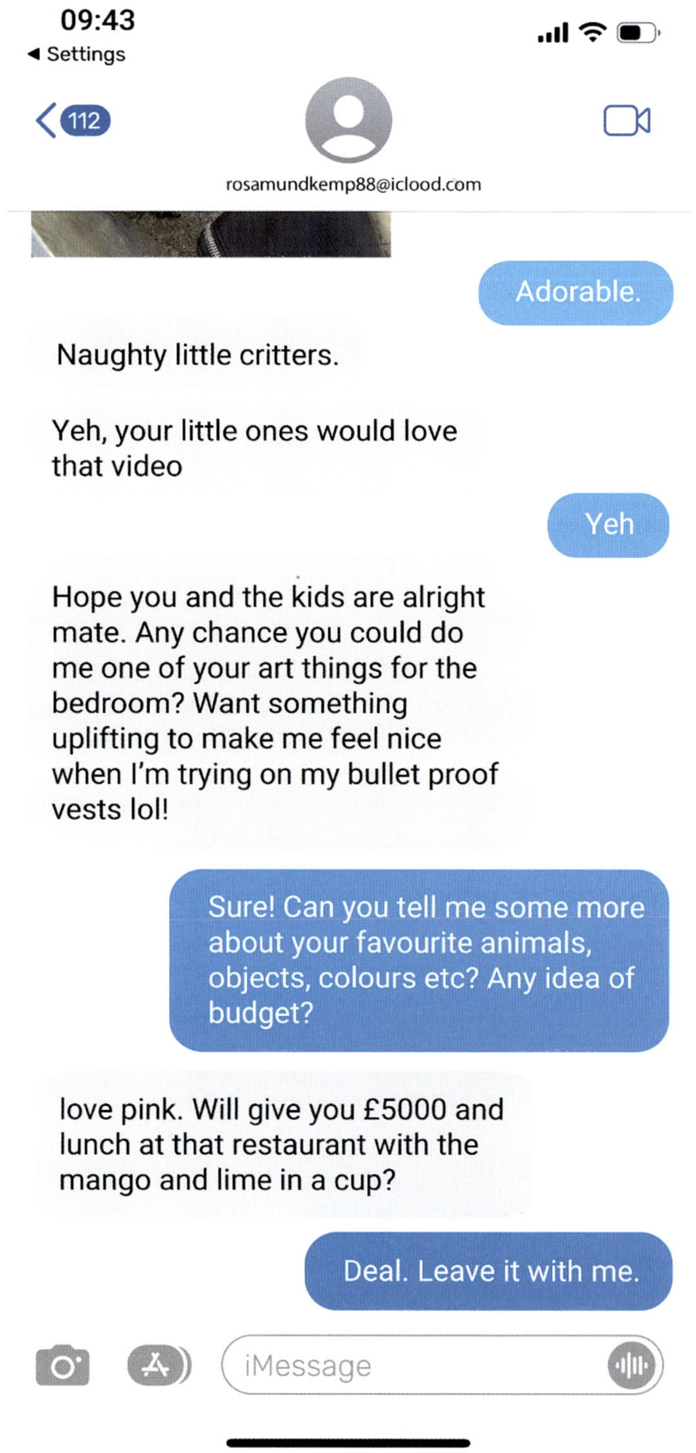
09:43
Settings
112
rosamundkemp88@icloud.com
Adorable.
Naughty little critters.
Yeh, your little ones would love that video
Yeh
Hope you and the kids are alright mate. Any chance you could do me one of your art things for the bedroom? Want something uplifting to make me feel nice when I'm trying on my bullet proof vests lol!
Sure! Can you tell me some more about your favourite animals, objects, colours etc? Any idea of budget?
love pink. Will give you £5000 and lunch at that restaurant with the mango and lime in a cup?
Deal. Leave it with me.
iMessage

Fig. 79

09:43

◀ Settings

112

rosamundkemp88@icloud.com

All done.

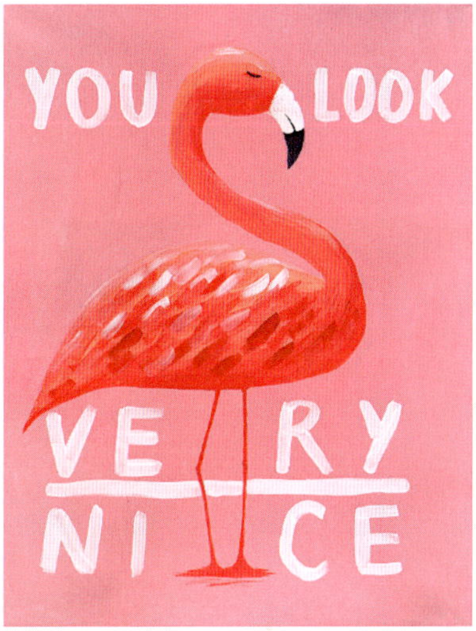

One sec

What do you think?

Hope you like the painting Ross? Can change it if you want?

Can you let me know whether you want this painting or not? Would love you to have it. The kids are doing really well and ask after you lots.

iMessage

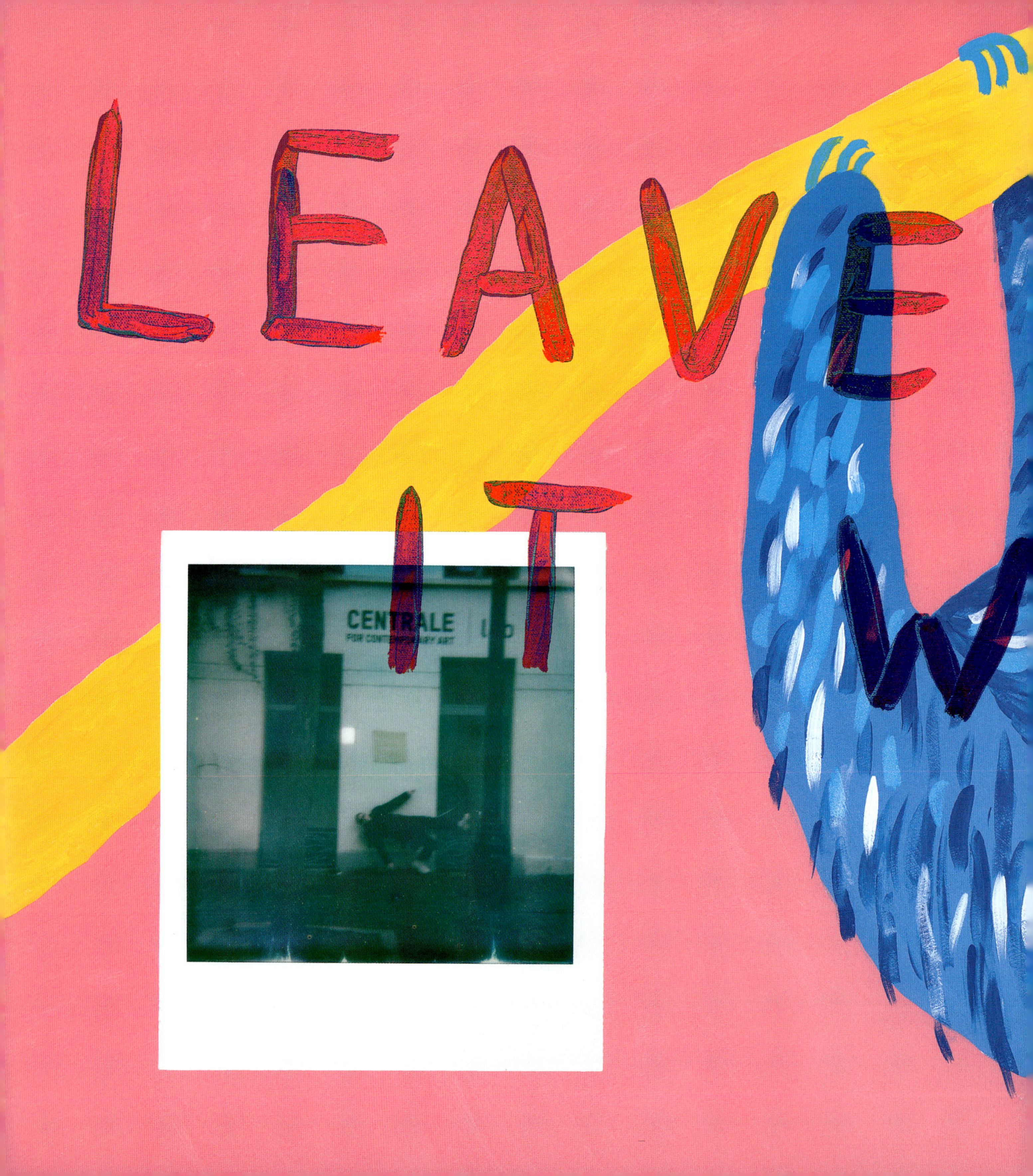
LEAVE
IT
W
CENTRALE

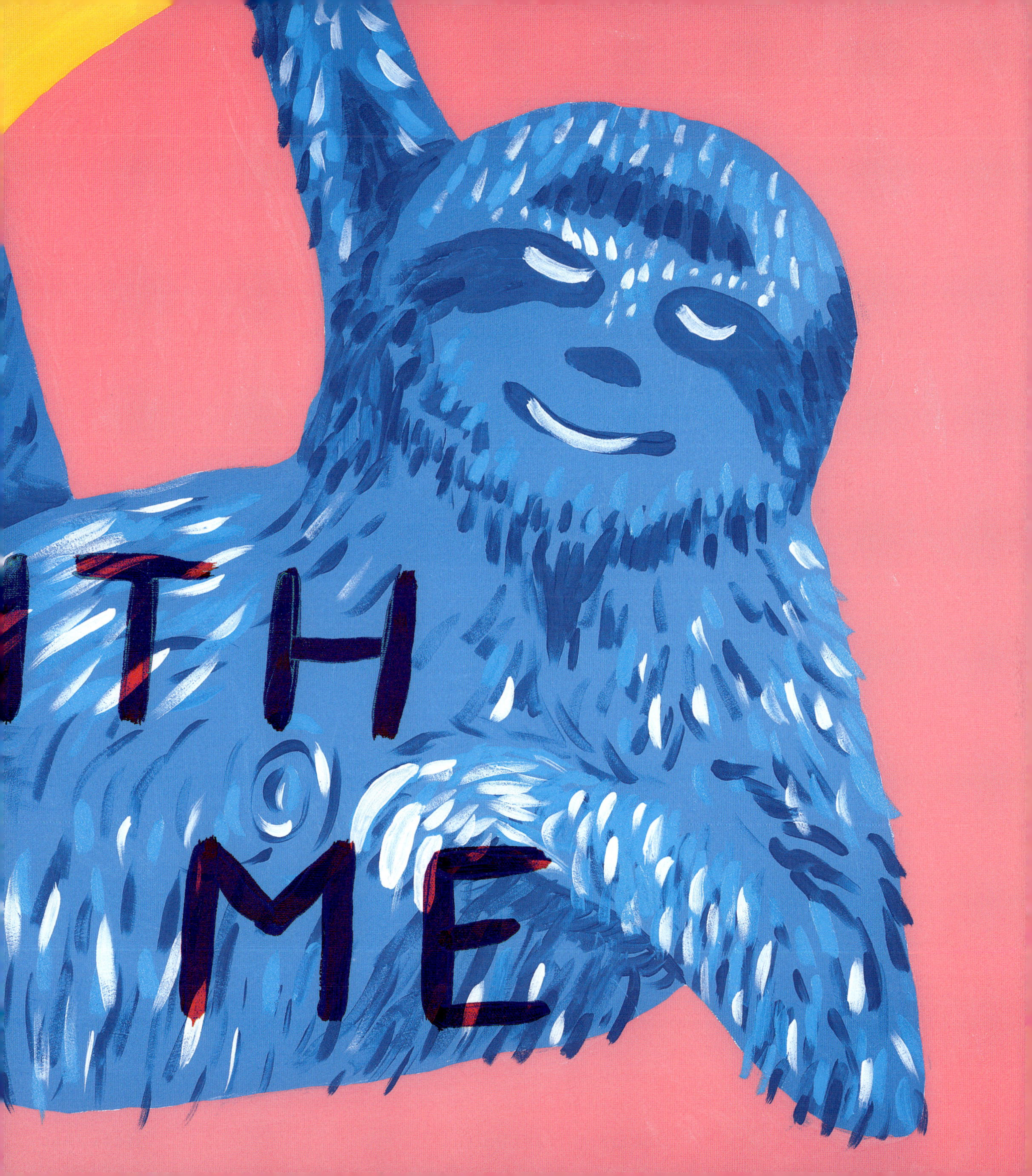
ITH
ME

VEGAN THUG

Fig. 80 The Deliciously Ella vegan dust ball, available in all stores very soon.
Fig. 81 *Vegan Thug*, 2024, watercolour (sans water) on water (sans water), 3 litres (sans litres).

A (rejected) brand identity I did for Eleanor Laura Davan Mills's (aka Deliciously Ella) new wellness company. She said she thought the hippo was sweet but, while she appreciates they are vegan, they are incredibly aggressive animals and she didn't want to encourage violence and just wants to quietly get on with selling balls of cacao and vegan dust.

Fig. 80

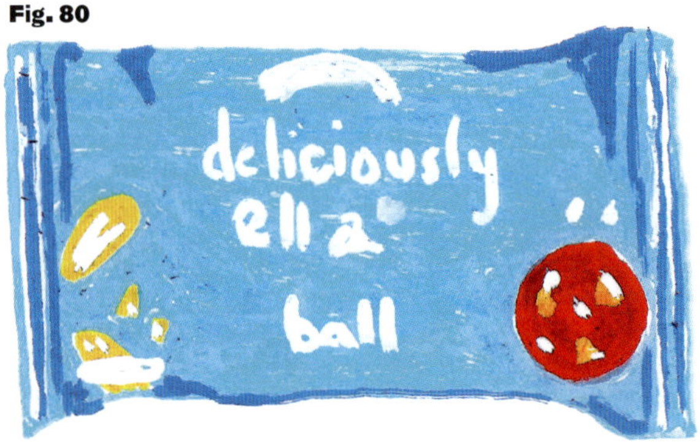

Fig. 81

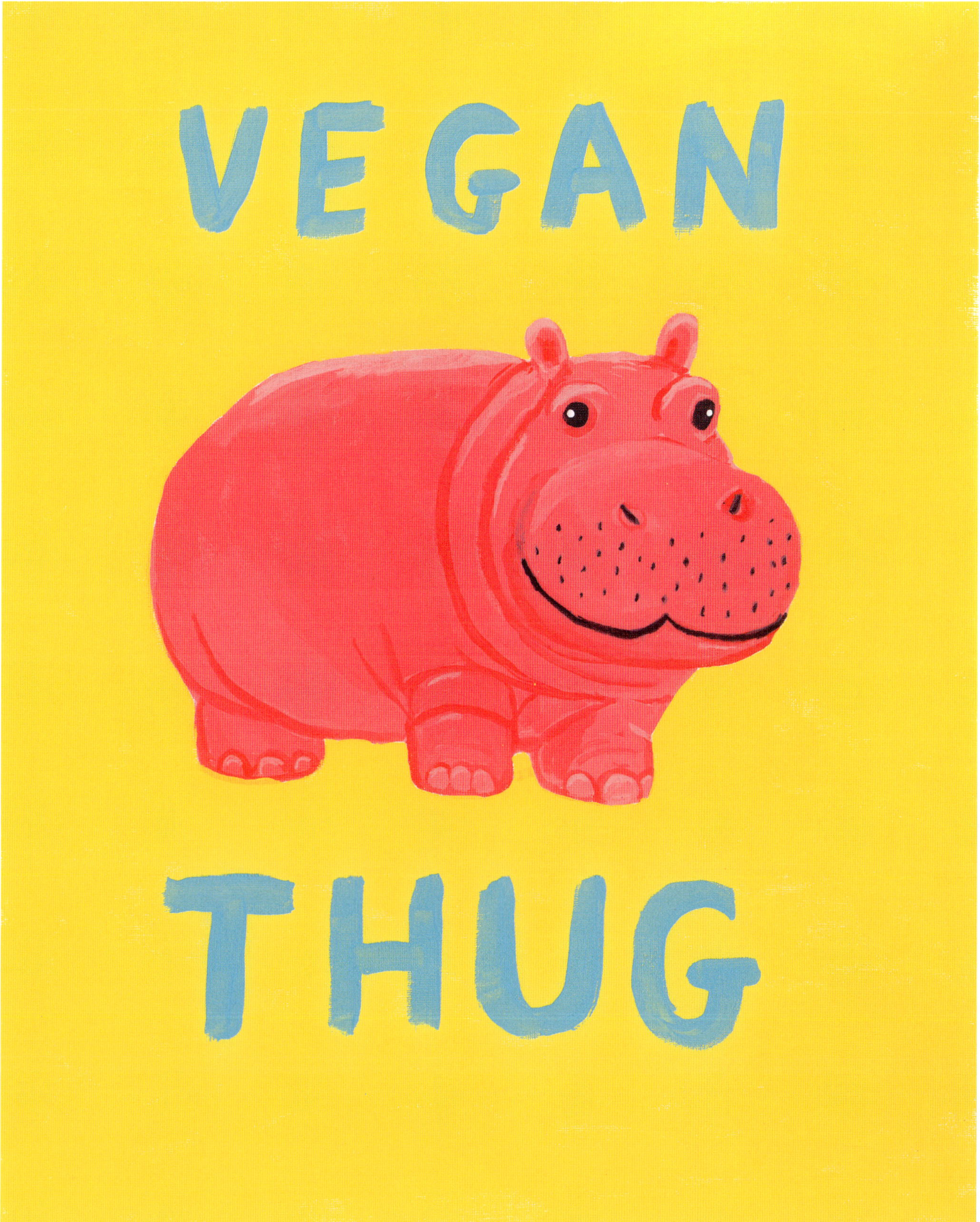

A CRISP GLASS OF PISS

Fig. 82 Keira Knightley's Nissan Qashqai before the accident.
Fig. 83 *A Crisp Glass of Piss*, 2023, Picpoul and Malbec on tablecloth, 1 × 2m.

I did this painting as a tongue-in-cheek gift for my long-time, close personal friend Keira Knightley, with whom I share an allotment in Tipton. If you don't know Tipton, it's a part of the Black Country, north-west of Birmingham; a place where grey prevails above all else, forcing the locals to bring colour through their personalities. I once went to a pub in Tipton and asked for a wine, to which the woman behind the bar replied, 'We day av it, I cun gow tescow if yam avin a bottle,' which is Black Country for 'We do not serve wine, but I can procure one from the local supermarket if you are planning on drinking a bottle'. I didn't want to trouble the woman, so had a warm pint of bitter.

Keira Knightley and I have been associates for a few years now, after I sold her a second-hand STANLEY FATMAX V20 18V Cordless Combi Drill with Kit Box (product code SFMCD711D11-GB) on Facebook Marketplace. Naturally, I didn't know I was selling to Kiera Knightley until she turned up at my house and said, 'I'm here for the STANLEY FATMAX V20 18V Cordless Combi Drill with Kit Box,' to which I said, 'Oh.' Unable to suppress my curiosity I asked her what she was using the FATMAX V20 for and she said, 'I've just taken on an allotment in Tipton and I'm securing some railway sleepers to create some raised beds.'

'I thought you lived in East London,' I said, letting it slip that I knew it was Keira Knightley.

'Well, gosh, yes, I do, but I come up every Thursday to tend to my allotment in Tipton. And I realised I couldn't do it on my own and needed a STANLEY FATMAX V20 18V Cordless Combi Drill with Kit Box.'

I handed it over and sent her on her way.

Long story short, Keira had a bump in her Nissan Qashqai on the A38 (Cat Deeley's private driver rammed into the back of her) and she redialled the last person she'd called on her phone for support: me. When I arrived, Deeley was listing off the American lawyers that she would employ if Knightley tried to press charges, while in the back of Deeley's Skoda sat Patrick Kielty who was crying and screaming. But Kiera was gracious and calm and explained she didn't want to get involved in any litigious proceedings and just wanted to get to her allotment in Tipton to use the STANLEY FATMAX V20 18V Cordless Combi Drill with Kit Box. Deeley calmed down when it transpired

Fig. 82

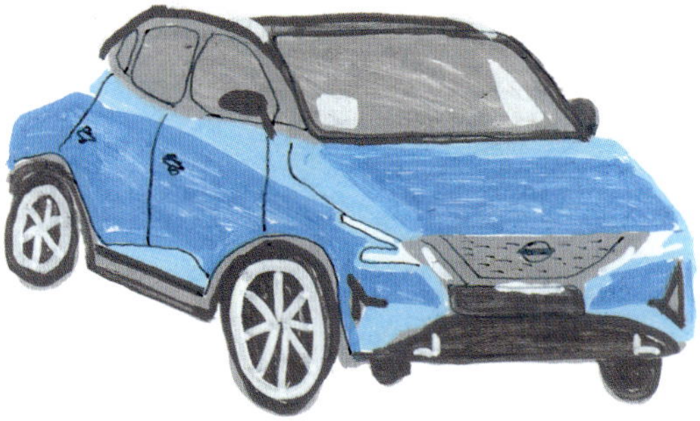

Fig. 83

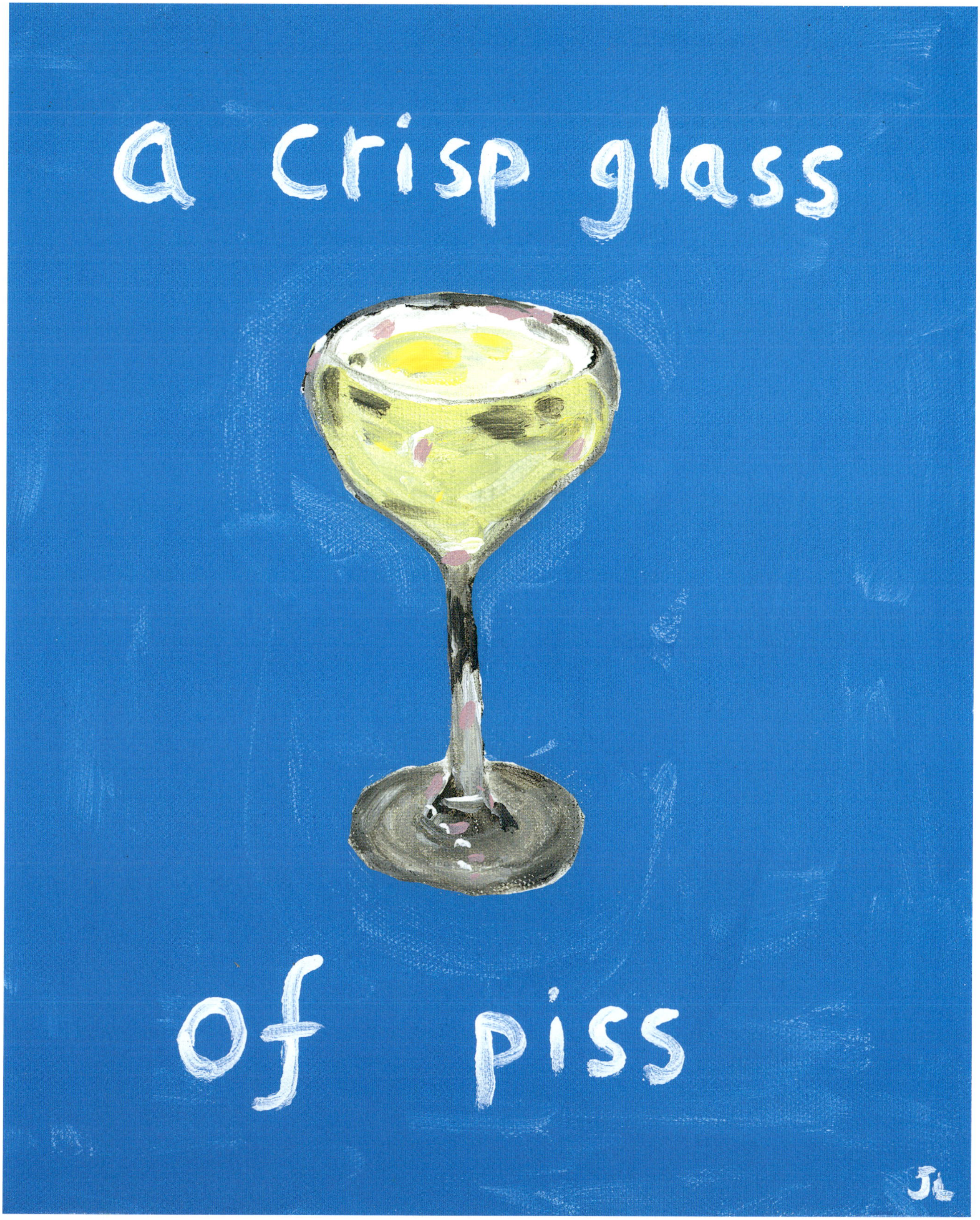

that they had the same chiropodist, and I offered to give them all a lift because both vehicles were a write-off. We dropped a far more cheerful and philosophical Deeley and Kielty[1] off at a Sandwell & Dudley train station and carried on to Tipton.

When we arrived at the allotment I was astonished at the size. At least the size of two football pitches, maybe more. 'It's huge,' I said, unoriginally.

'You get a lot more bang for your buck in Tipton,' said a self-satisfied Knightley. She wasn't wrong. The plot went on almost farther than the eye could see, but not farther than the eye could see, because the eye could see. Stacked up next to the entrance was an intimidating tower of the aforementioned railway sleepers, ready and waiting to be made into raised beds.

'Who's helping you with all this?' I asked.

'No one. Just little old me.' I knew the woman was ambitious from her giddying credit list, but this was too much.

I couldn't let her do it on her own, and yet I was torn. I was just about to be announced as the new host of *Strictly Come Dancing*.[2] I told the BBC I couldn't let Keira Knightley down and, for the time being, Tess Daly has clung onto the *Strictly* gig.

The next six months was non-stop, Tipton-based manual labour: dirty, dangerous, but ultimately thrilling. We assembled row after row of beautifully constructed raised beds, filling them with kale, rhubarb, lettuce, spinach, peas, raspberries, strawberries, leeks and more. At one point Keira turned to me and said, 'I feel so grateful, Joe.'

'That's lovely, Keira,' I replied. 'Are you grateful for the beauty of nature?'

'No, I am grateful for the STANLEY FATMAX V20 18V Cordless Combi Drill with Kit Box.'

I nodded in agreement.

With the first summer came a bountiful harvest, and Knightley began selling some of our yields to posh shops back in East London, claiming it was 'organic, British produce'. The last bit was accurate, but organic was a lie, as Knightley loves a pesticide and would drench each border in chemicals. Before long, she was spraying bug killer out of a modified Nerf Super Soaker. I realised she wasn't diluting it properly when I started finding various dead creatures on the plot – the volume was immense. I tried to put their corpses in the compost bin, but the smell became intolerable, and, in the end, I disposed of them in the Walsall Canal, which weirdly made the water clearer.

Harvests have come and gone, but the most unsuccessful was the year when Knightley decided we would become a vineyard. All the crops in the raised beds were replaced with vines, which she had been

1. I'd let Patrick play my Nintendo Switch to calm his nerves, but he'd let my Charmeleon evolve so now I was going to have to wait until level 48 to learn 'Fire Spin', which really fucked me off.

2. BBC bosses were in the process of sacking Tess Daly and felt I was the only capable replacement. They had become increasingly concerned about her behaviour and demands backstage. The main request they could no longer stomach was embedded in her contract from day one, and stated she would only go on set once a member of the production team had performed a 'humiliating prank' on one of Davina McCall, Emma Willis, Rochelle Humes or Zoe Ball. The pranks had been good fun at first apparently, mainly involving jumping out at them from behind sofas and doors, etc. But they'd become more elaborate as the years went on and a BBC crisis meeting was called after Willis told a journalist at the *Sunday Times Magazine* that she was being treated for PTSD after being covered in Bolognese and dropped into a cage with eighty starving seagulls.

Fig. 84 A drawing of a Bug Clear Gun! I did that everyone I have shown agrees looks just like a Bug Clear Gun!

Fig. 85 A drawing of Keira Knightley I did that everyone I have shown agrees does not look like Keira Knightley.

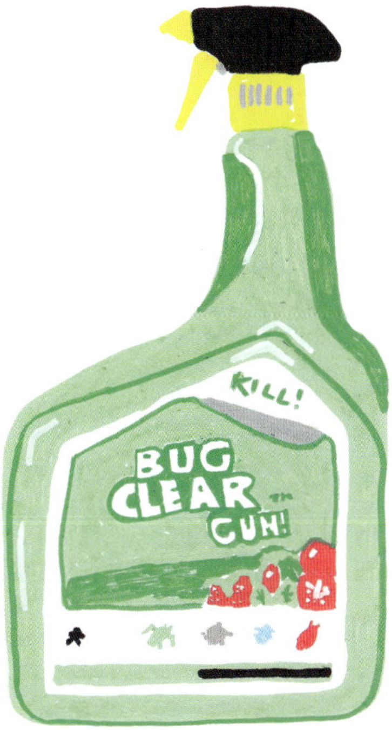

Fig. 84

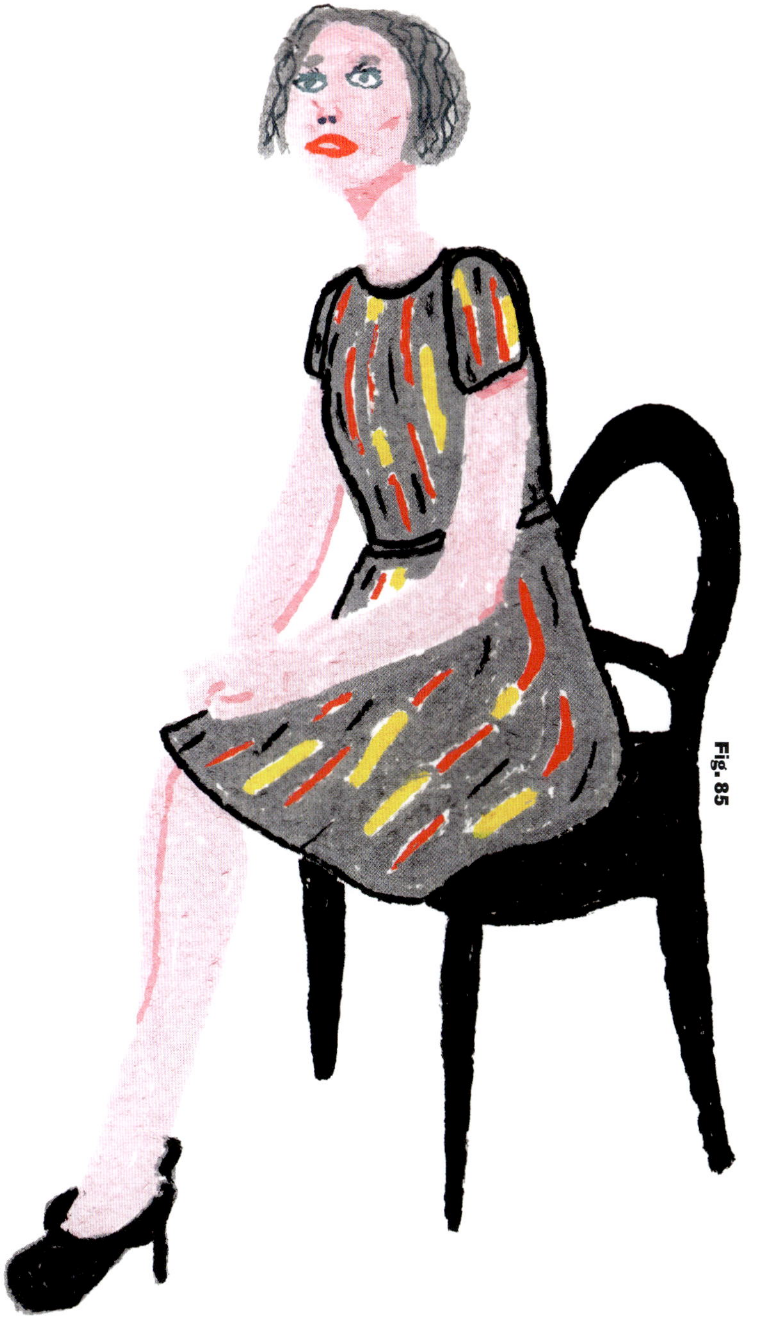
Fig. 85

gifted from her *Love Actually* co-star Andrew Lincoln in a Secret Santa. Tipton is not known for its hot summers, and the vines were disastrous from the start. By early summer they had all succumbed to powdery mildew, a disastrous fungal infection which reduces photosynthesis and impacts grape quality. Knightley went wild with the fungicide (another Secret Santa gift, from James McAvoy) and so we had a small harvest, but the resulting bottles of wine tasted, in her words, like 'a crisp glass of piss'. She wasn't wrong – the wine is impossible to drink and has the mouthfeel of porridge mixed with gravel, and a similar taste. I took her words and applied them to this painting, in the hope of using the artwork as an ironic label for the bottles.

Knightley and I recently parted ways after she accidentally killed a local milkman with a canister of Bug Clear, so we've handed the allotment over to Adrian Chiles who has been using it, in his words, to 'grow eggs'. He sold the remainder of the wine stock to Gary Barlow, who rebranded it in his own name, and you can get hold of the last remaining bottles at garybarlowwines.gov while stocks last.

Fig. 86 18V STANLEY V20 Cordless Brushless Hammer Drill with 4.0Ah Lithium Ion Battery.
Fig. 87 A vase of flowers from Keira's allotment: *A Glass of Slags*, 2020, acrylic on battering ram, 32 × 47cm.
Fig. 88 Me with a glass of wine (not Gary Barlow's wine).
Fig. 89 Me with raised bed (not raised bed at Keira Knightley's allotment).

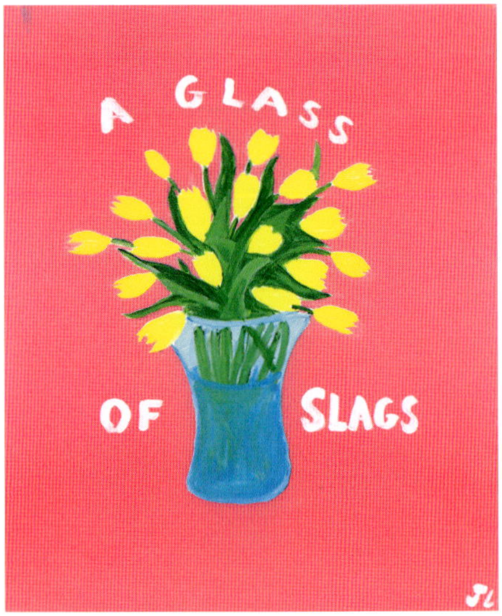

Fig. 87

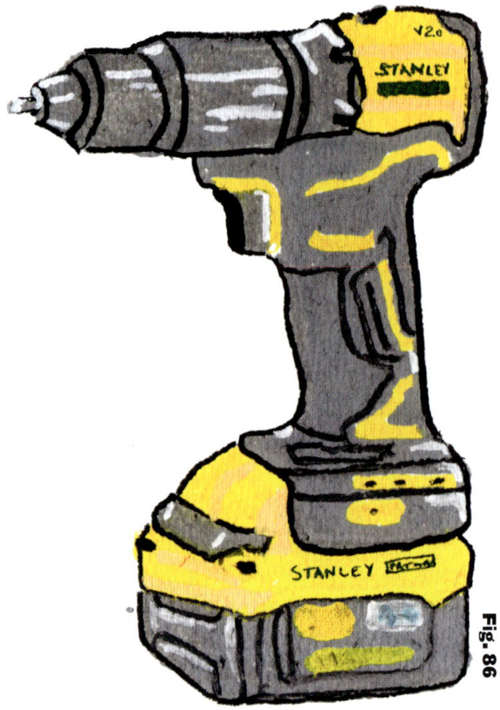

Fig. 86

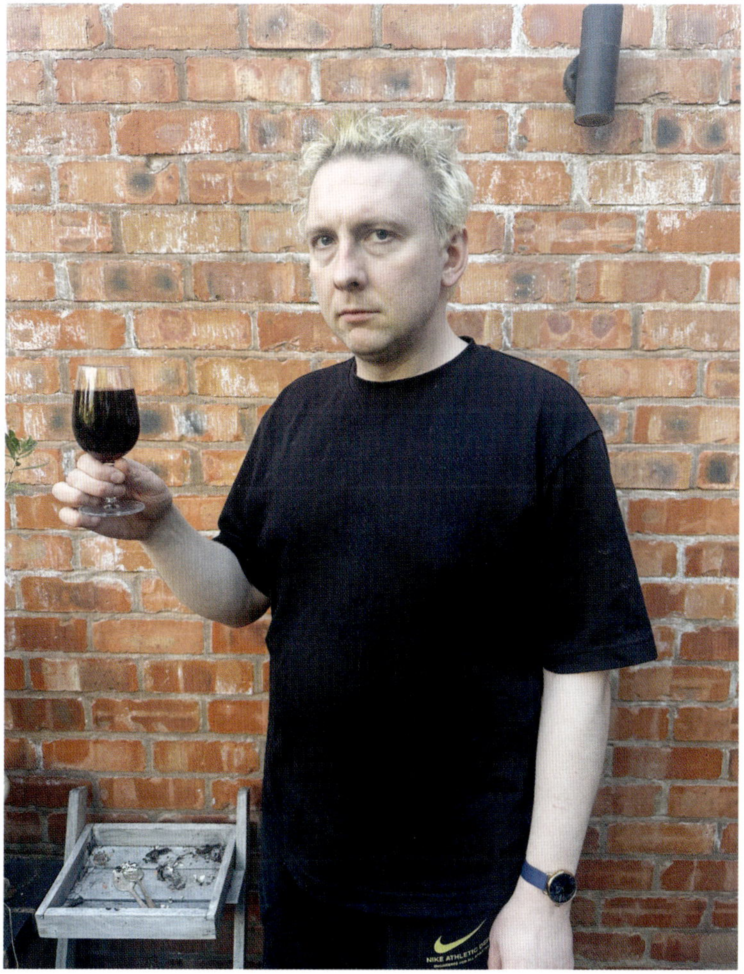

Fig. 88

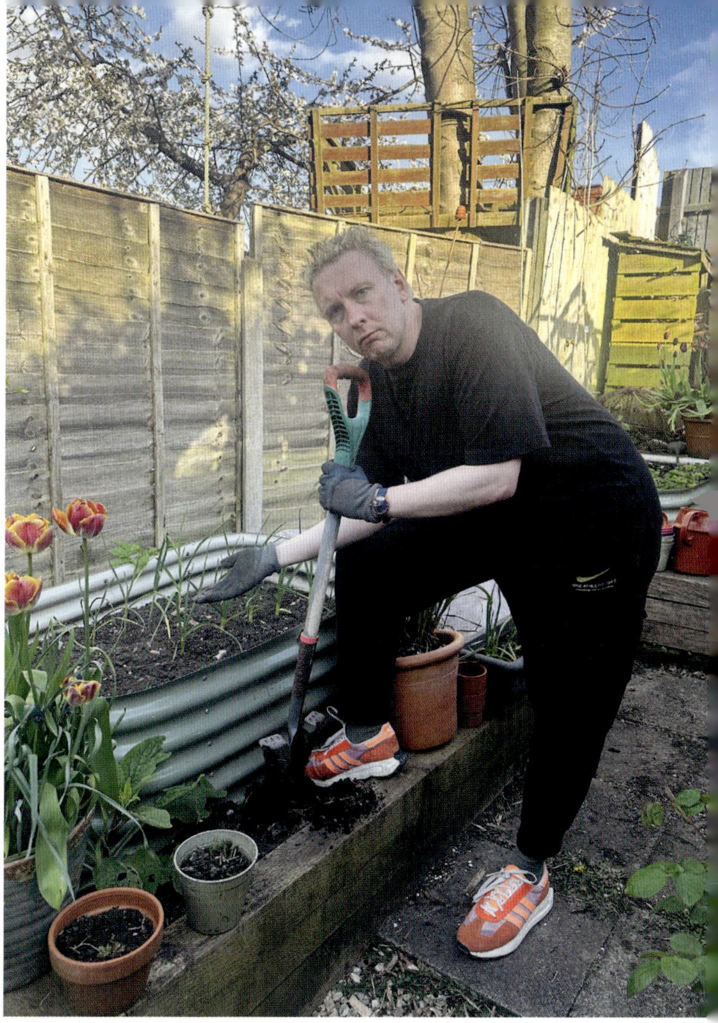

Fig.89

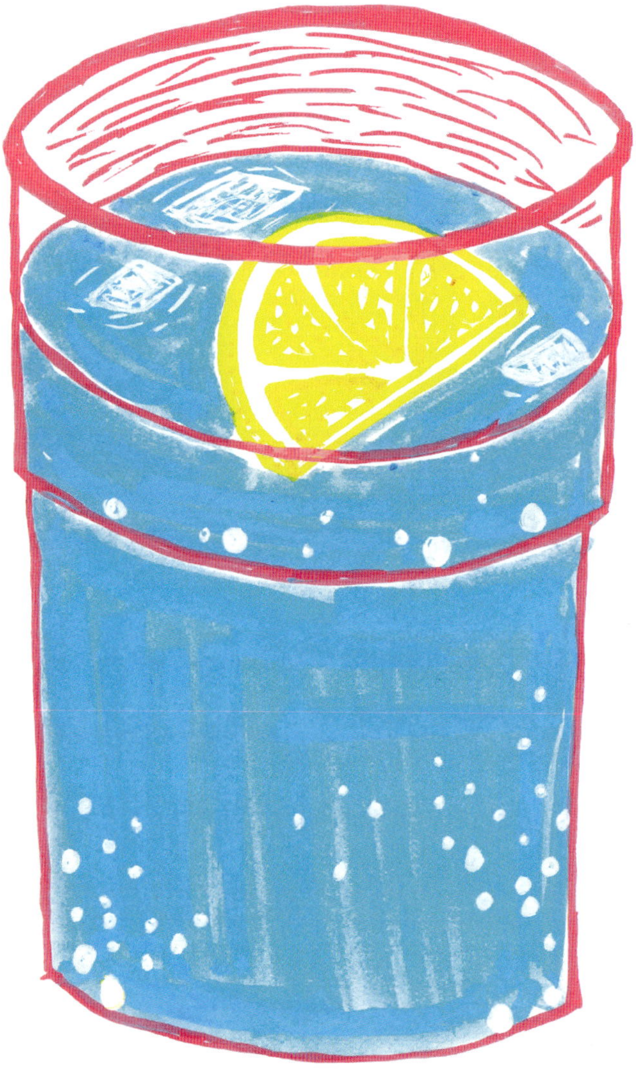

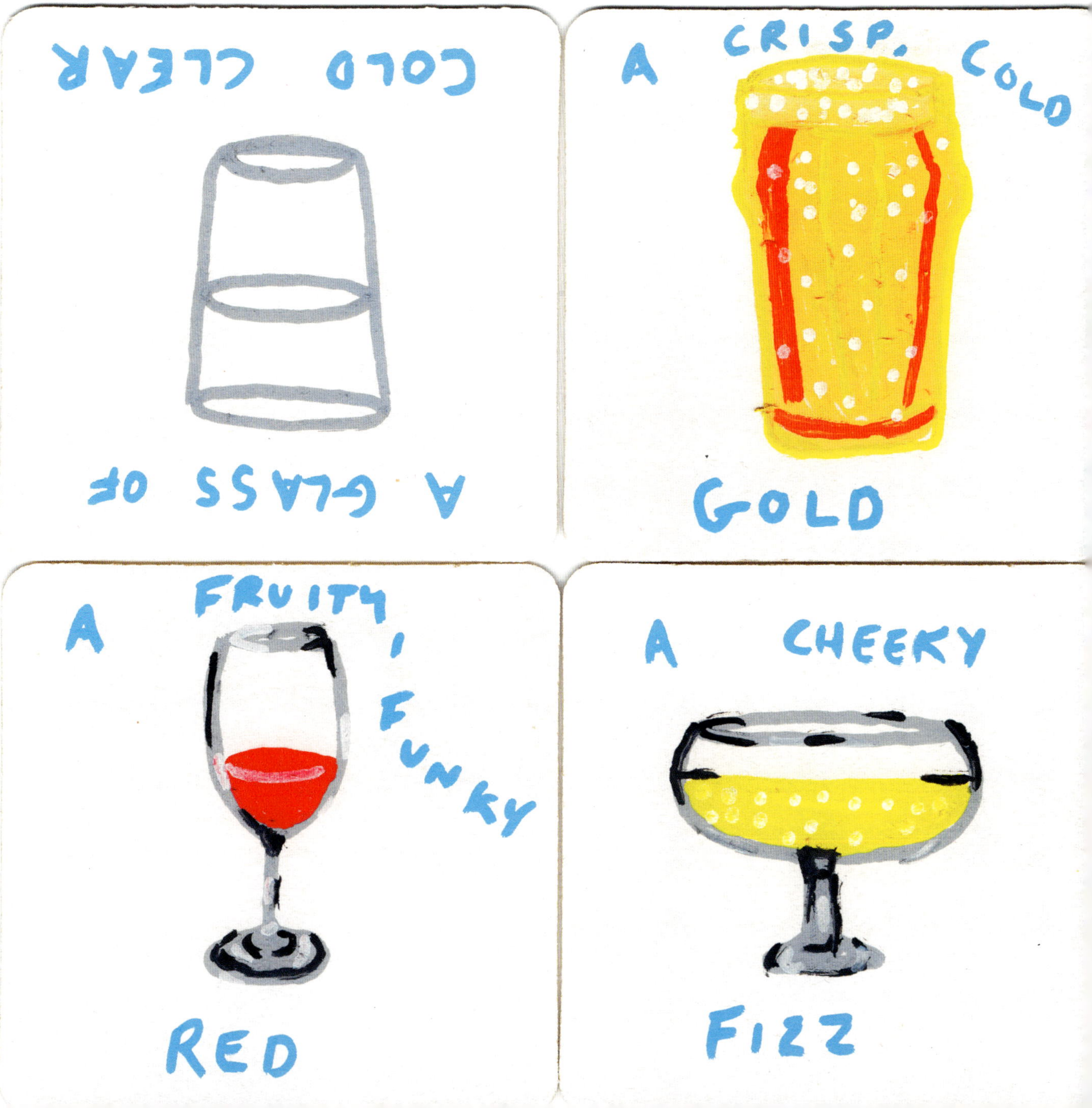
A GLASS OF
COLD CLEAR
A CRISP, COLD
GOLD
A FRUITY, FUNKY
RED
A CHEEKY
FIZZ

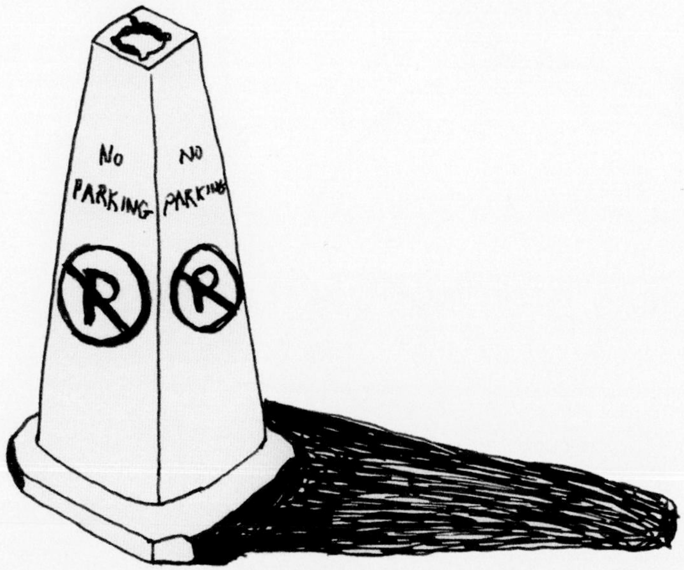
NO
PARKING
NO
PARKING

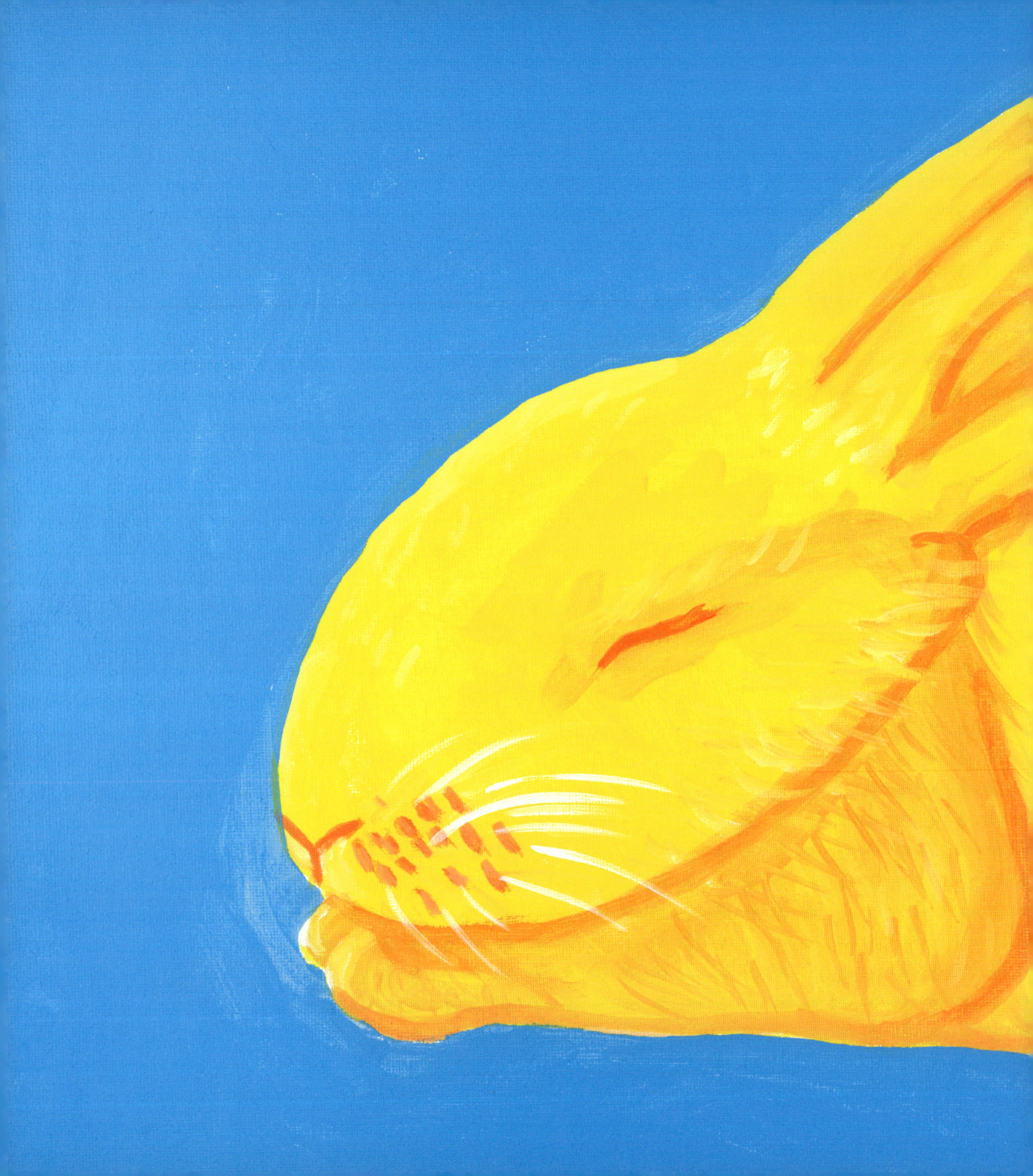

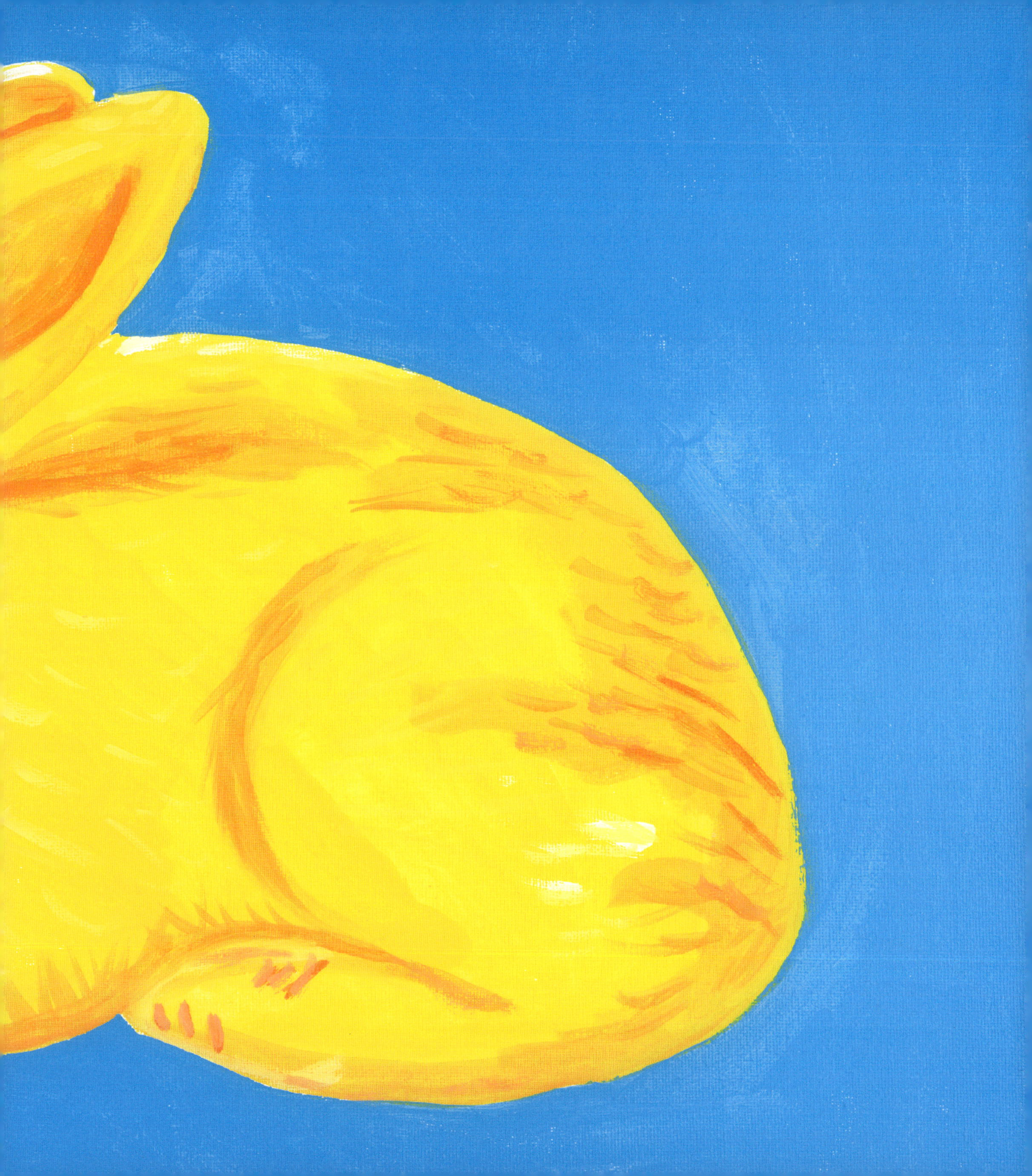

YOU SNOOZE YOU WIN

Fig. 90 Paula Vennells.
Fig. 91 *You Snooze You Win*, 2023, acrylic on dog, 12 × 14cm.

A commission for Paula Vennells, former chief executive officer of the Post Office.

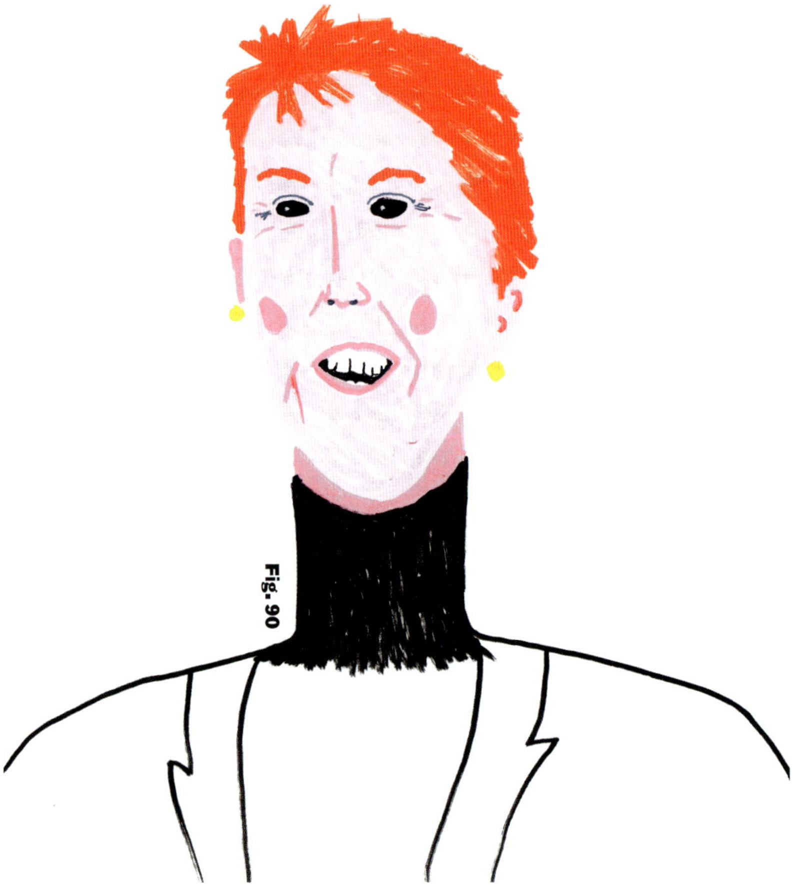

Fig. 90

Fig. 91

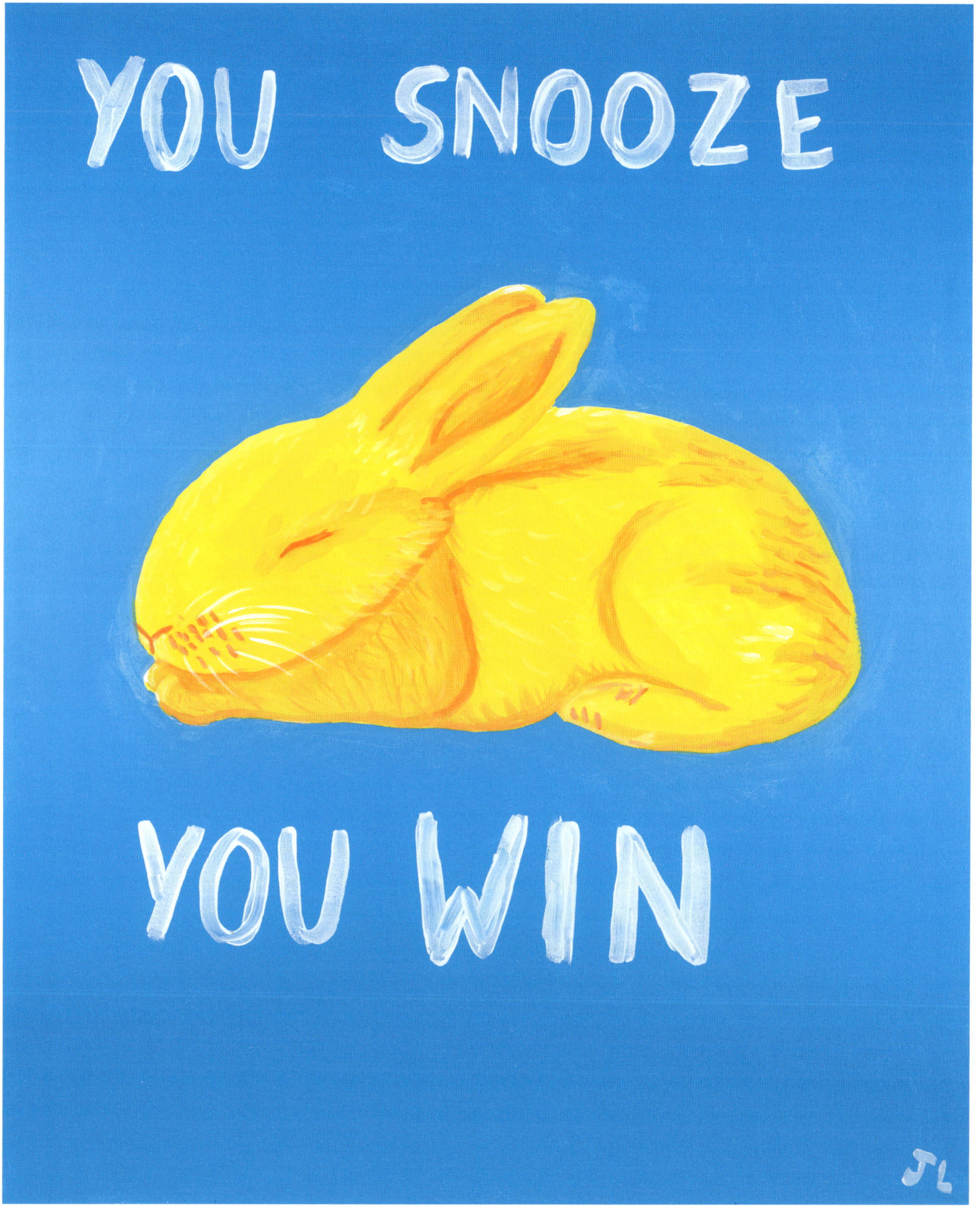

THÉRÈSE COFFEY

Fig. 92 *Thérèse Coffey*, 2023, acrylic mixed with ground beef on canvas board, 21 × 52mm.

I didn't go to Cadbury World expecting to meet Thérèse Coffey, but when I went to Cadbury World, I met Thérèse Coffey. It just goes to show that you never know what life has in store for you (what life had in store for me on this occasion was meeting Thérèse Coffey). At the time, she was the deputy prime minister (under Liz Truss; *see chapter Liz Truss*).

I was there solely because I promised Alison Hammond I'd look after her godson, a strange lad that she calls 'Little Jimmy'. Apparently she wasn't keen on having a godson, but when filming a competition segment for *This Morning* in Chester, she bumped into a family and they said, 'Will you be Little Jimmy's godmother,' and she said, 'Of course I will, babe,' not really meaning it and now every Tuesday they bring Little Jimmy to her house and say something like, 'May God bring you peace,' before driving away in a 2017 Citroen C4 Picasso (which is Alison's car but when they asked if they could borrow it she was unable to say 'no'). Privately, she told me she didn't really like Little Jimmy because he would push tables over in motorway service stations and tell strangers that she was his kidnapper, but she couldn't find a polite way of getting rid. I foolishly agreed to help out of misguided politeness – privately I hate the little dickhead.

It's hard to describe Little Jimmy. Words don't really encapsulate him. The first thing to note is we don't have an accurate age for him; we are guessing around seven because he is about four foot tall, but he has the hairy and beaten hands of an adult man, and a baritone voice which he uses to say 'Find them, we must find them' out of context at regular intervals. His head is smaller than that of an average seven-year-old boy, quite a lot smaller, probably the size of a mango. His eyes are bigger than you'd expect, yet his mouth is almost so small it is impossible to see – around the size of a five pence piece, maybe smaller – and his nose is probably about the right size but appears in some environments to be shiny, like a form of glazed ceramic. His ears are shaped like a cat; not like a cat's ears but in the actual shape of a cat, including tail. He only wears tracksuits by brands like Gucci or Balenciaga, and will not put on a pair of shoes unless they are second-hand bowling shoes, which are increasingly hard to purchase. He carries a Patagonia backpack, but refuses to reveal what is inside – if you try to open or even touch it, he takes your hand firmly and says, in that deep intimidating tone: 'He will punish you.' Sometimes the bag

Fig. 92

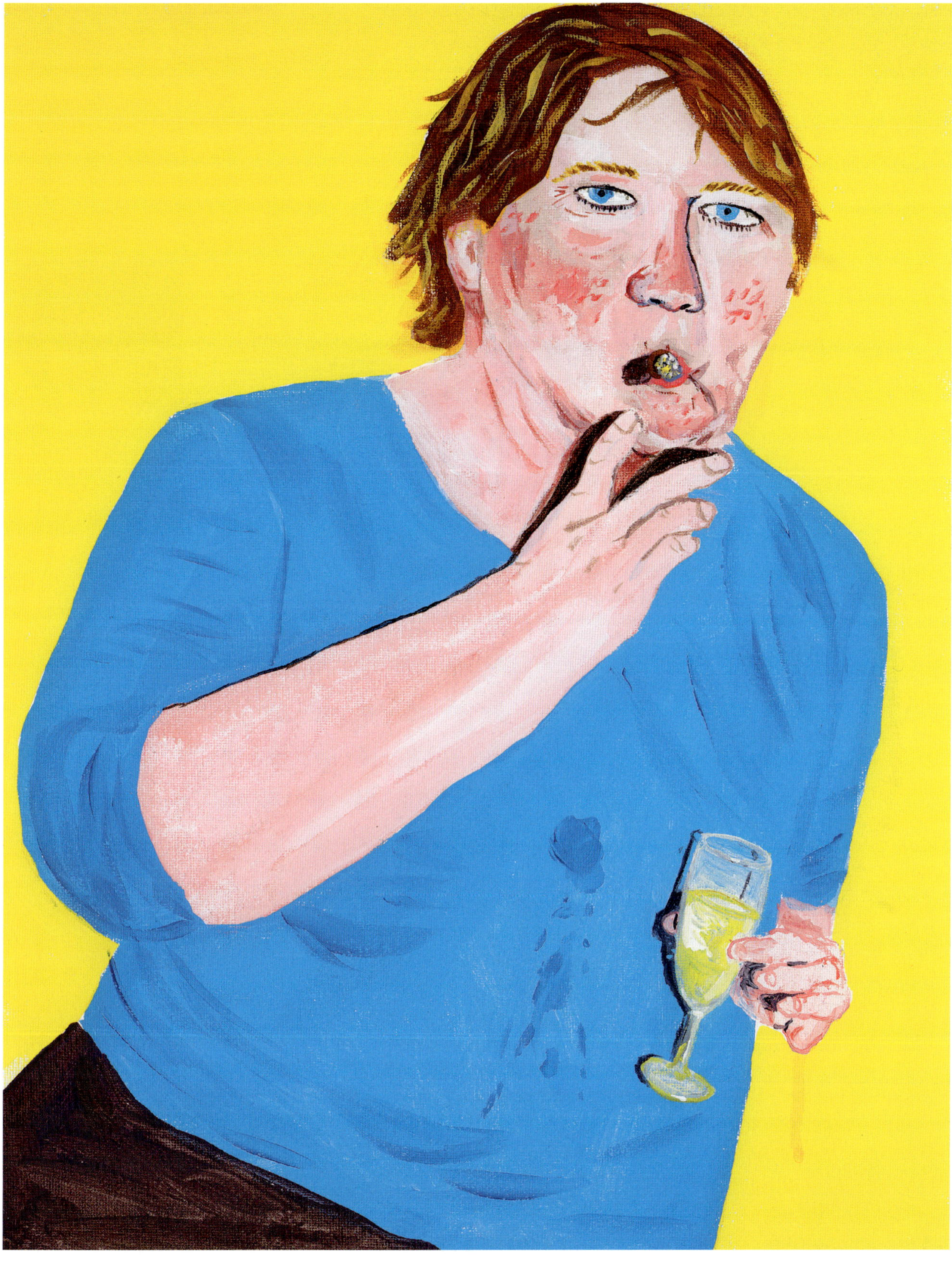

moves and makes noises. Alison told me that at Knutsford services, after telling the cashier at the Wild Bean Cafe that he was a hostage, he opened the bag and released what she described as 'thousands of locusts'.[1]

Thérèse Coffey was at Cadbury World because she'd been finding work a bit stressful and wanted to do something to get her mind off it for the morning. She'd been deputy prime minister for two weeks, and over that time plenty of people had offered her the advice that she wasn't very good at her job, which she'd taken quite personally. Perhaps, in hindsight, a solution to these critiques might have been to get on with doing some of the work that you would expect a deputy prime minister to do (reading documents, meetings with dignitaries, deputising for the prime minister, not going to Cadbury World, etc.), but we didn't have the benefit of hindsight at that time and so she was at Cadbury World.

Another key bit of info: in a stark change from her normal professional self, she appeared to be drunk. This wasn't end of the day, post-a-boozy-lunch drunk – this was 9 a.m. in the reception area of Cadbury World, absolutely fucking rat wankered, pissing into the wind, shitting off a bridge, spitting at children, finding a dog and telling it it's a prick, slapping a cat and calling it Margaret … drunk.

The moment she clocked me across the reception area of Cadbury World she started moving at pace, tripped over about three metres from me, got up slowly and said, 'Joe, I'm fruffn drunf.' (She knew my name as we are friends on LinkedIn.) Then, she turned her attention to Little Jimmy, grabbing him by the cheeks and saying, 'What a luvley lickle sausege an egg sannich,' which prompted him to immediately pinch the loose skin around the back of her elbows[2] with his big, blokey hands. 'Horrid little brat,' she said, recoiling, and then asked her security to arrest him, which they had to remind her was not within their remit, giving the impression they had to remind her frequently that she could not just demand the arrest of children. Little Jimmy's expression towards her was fascinating, a mixture of disgust and admiration, and when Coffey suggested we spin round Cadbury World together it was he who said, 'Yes, he will like that a great deal.'

Cadbury World is a Birmingham institution in the sleepy suburb of Bournville, just round the corner from the famous Cadbury factory and the slightly less well known Bournville Radio Sailing and Model Boat Club. There's also an appliance repair shop on Hazelwell Road where I once took my Hotpoint H55RM1110W1 Fridge in white to see if they could find out why it's not cooling properly; they said it was because I was overfilling it, which simply isn't true. The exhibit starts with a fact-dense section about the history of the company which,

1. Alison is prone to exaggeration, so I suspect it was more like hundreds.
2. This is also known as the weenus. Grow up.

Fig. 93 Little Jimmy's second-hand bowling shoes.
Fig. 94 Packaging design that was rejected by all the major chocolate brands: *A Moment on the Lips*, 2024, chocolate on pink Wayfair three-seater sofa, 12 × 24cm.

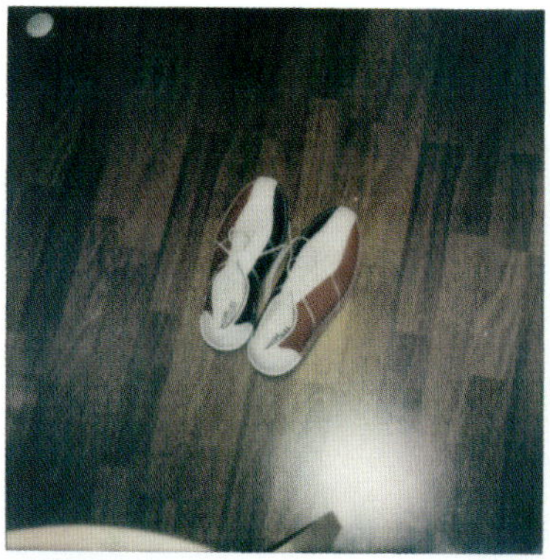

Fig. 93

Fig. 94

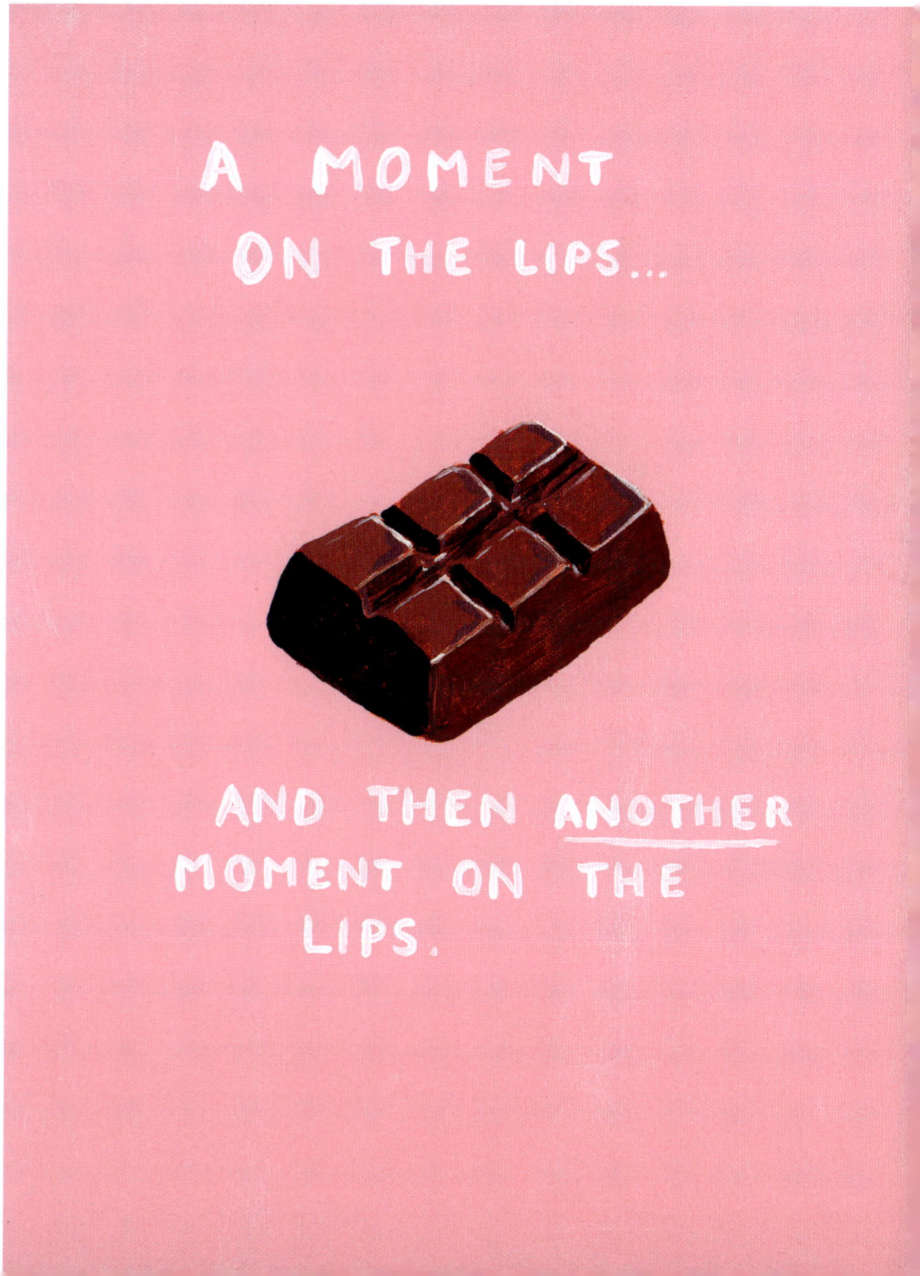

I'm not gonna lie, is boring as hell. I'm not alone in my feelings and I know that because, as we were going round it, the deputy prime minister, Thérèse Coffey, said: 'Who geevs a flayen fuck?' Not one person goes to Cadbury World because they are interested in history. That's like going to the GP because you love reading leaflets about the signs of a stroke.

To my surprise, Little Jimmy was, in fact, interested, and was captivated by the knowledgeable girl who escorted us round. As she talked about the original company structure and about how it has changed over the years, he started to nod his head, eventually adding things like 'Very interesting, very interesting indeed,' and licking his lips. Thérèse was growing increasingly impatient and clearly wanted some chocolate, which I knew very well they don't give you until much later. 'Hurr up,' she said at one point, which everyone ignored apart from Little Jimmy who looked at her furiously before saying, 'You will wait,' in a remarkably threatening tone. The Patagonia bag shuddered.

Things really ramped up when we got through to the room where they give you a little shot of melted chocolate which is deeply rich and moreish. Just as they handed Coffey the molten cup, an aide approached nervously, like you might approach an XL Bully, and whispered something to her about the prime minister of the Netherlands being on the line. Thérèse held the chocolate shot in one hand and the phone in the other.

'Pry minner,' she said to the device, holding it flat in her palm like they do on *The Apprentice*.

'Are you alone?' said a clearly concerned Dutch PM, over speakerphone.

'Ye, ye, all alone,' she replied, in a room of about thirty people.

'We are intercepting a terrorist incident,' he said coldly. 'I can't get hold of Prime Minister Truss.'

'Oh. Shees probree busy wiv the quinn, the quimm, the Kweeen,' coughed Coffey. 'Wat can I do te helf?'

The Dutch PM's voice became very concerned, almost militaristic. 'We believe there is an imminent attack on a British institution,' he said.

Thérèse nodded as if she was listening but was more focused on gesturing to me to take something out of her pocket. I slipped my hand into her M&S Collection Relaxed Single Breasted Blazer – 'We are not sure what the target is' – and pulled out a stubby bottle of cooking sherry. She then used the phone to point at the shot of melted chocolate. I poured a dash in, she smiled, and then gulped it right down with a swallowing noise that sounded like someone rapidly filling a drum with warm honey.[1]

'I unnerstan prim minner,' she said. 'Verry gud. We wil be in tush.'

'We are advising that you get to a safe house immediately,' he said.

1. I have actually filled a drum with warm honey to ensure the quality of the simile, and am proud to say it is bang on.

Fig. 95 Little Jimmy's hand print. You can see it is part hoof.
Fig. 96 A photograph I took of myself eating chocolate. It was rejected by the International Photography Awards on account of it being, in their words, 'bad'.
Fig. 97 A drawing I did of Thérèse Coffey.

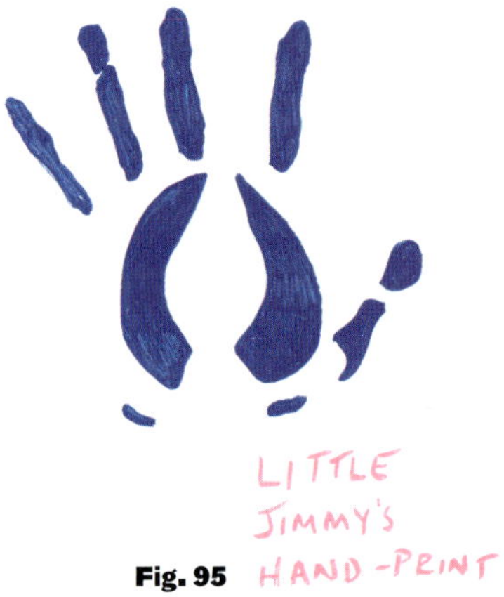

Fig. 95

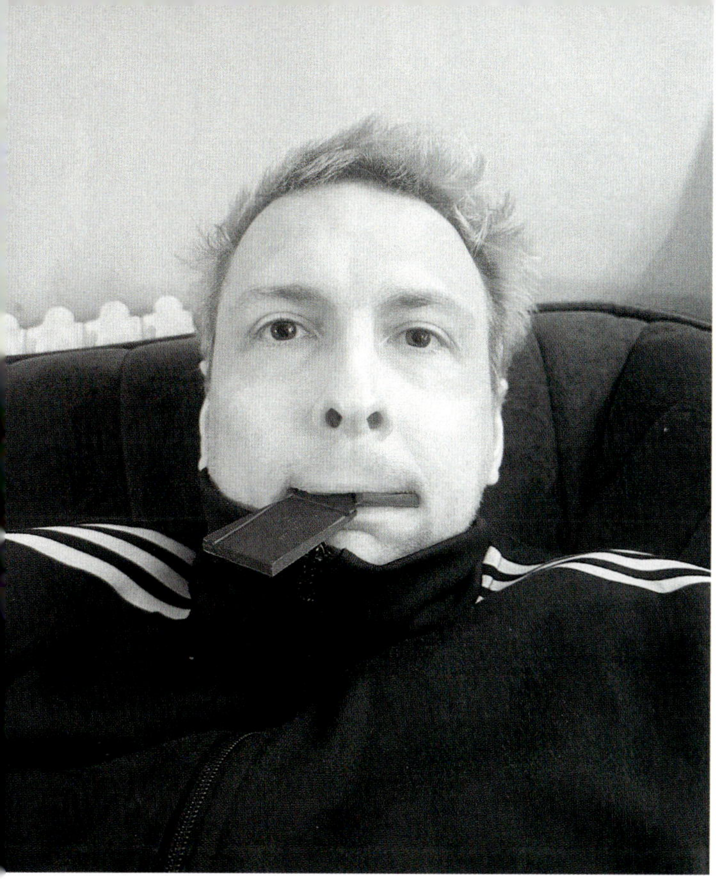

Fig. 96

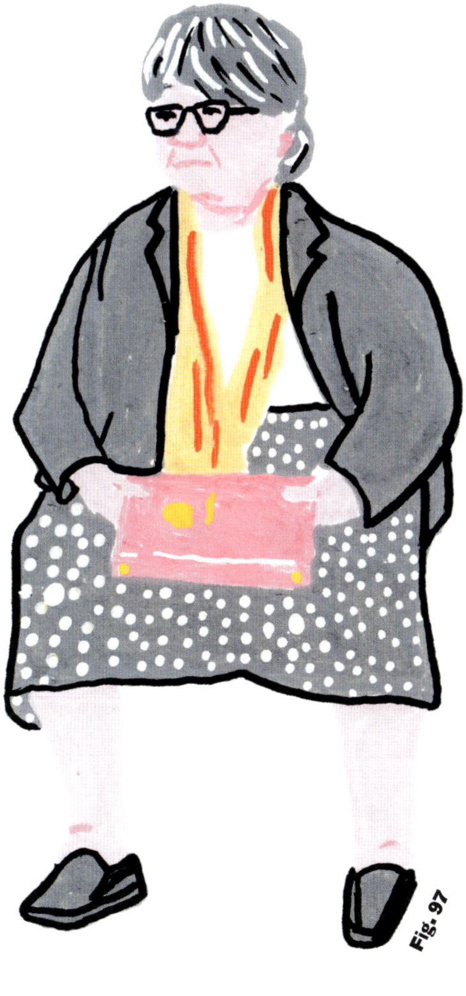

Fig. 97

At this exact moment, one of the Cadbury World guides loudly shouted: 'Cadbury actually started as a drinking chocolate business in 1824.'

'Deputy Prime Minister, you said you were alone,' came the voice.

'Oh yes. Thass is my adviserrr, we belief the attack iz comin from cadbree world,' she said, completely winging it.

'Very good,' he said.

'Gotta go, fanx babe,' she said, literally throwing the phone across the room, hitting a child in the neck.

Coffey's security detail thought it wise to evacuate, and we swiftly made our way to the emergency exit. We moved at an extraordinary and urgent pace; at one point one of Thérèse's men shouted 'Back away sir!' to a staff member dressed as a cocoa bean. Little Jimmy was visibly thrilled by the situation – his head was rocking side to side and he was shouting things like, 'It is happening,' and, 'You cannot stop it, you cannot stop the cocoa bean.' Realising we were going to leave at the nearest exit, Coffey insisted we take the ten extra minutes to get to the official exit because that's where you get all the free chocolate. In her defence, she did get four Freddos and a handful of Wispa Golds,[1] demonstrating an ability to maintain a clear head in stressful situations.

Finally, we were out of the building. Somehow the cocoa bean who security had previously pushed to one side was waiting for us. It was holding some sort of device in its hand. 'Don't move a muscle or I'll push the button,' said a male voice from inside the costume.

'Don be sur sillee, little cocoa bean,' said Coffey, 'lemme pass, i am the deputee leder of house of commoms.'[2]

'I fucking mean it,' said the cocoa bean, beginning to peel off its costume, 'the vest is loaded.'

Despite being running-under-a-donkey-and-pretending-to-be-a-carrot drunk, Coffey had called it right: the terrorist was indeed inside Cadbury World. The cocoa bean, now with Thérèse's guard's guns pointed at it, was shaking, terrified, yet determined. It started to remove the costume, but this required disconnecting the arms first before separating a line of Velcro at the back and literally wriggling out. This would be an undignified manoeuvre at the best of times, let alone while simultaneously holding a device connected to a live and loaded vest.

After I would guess about three minutes (a fairly accurate guess as I had managed to hum the entirety of 'Push the Button' by the Sugababes) of contorting, shimmying and eventually flailing, the man behind the bean was revealed. It was none other than radio legend Simon Mayo, wearing a Cadbury World branded vest that was enveloped with about a dozen cylinders. 'Don't move,' he said. 'You're live on the radio!'

1. She used Jimmy's hands so she got approximately thirty Wispa Golds.
2. This was inaccurate and a job she had held almost six years ago.

Fig. 98 Coffey's briefcase of Wispa Golds. This now resides in the V&A.

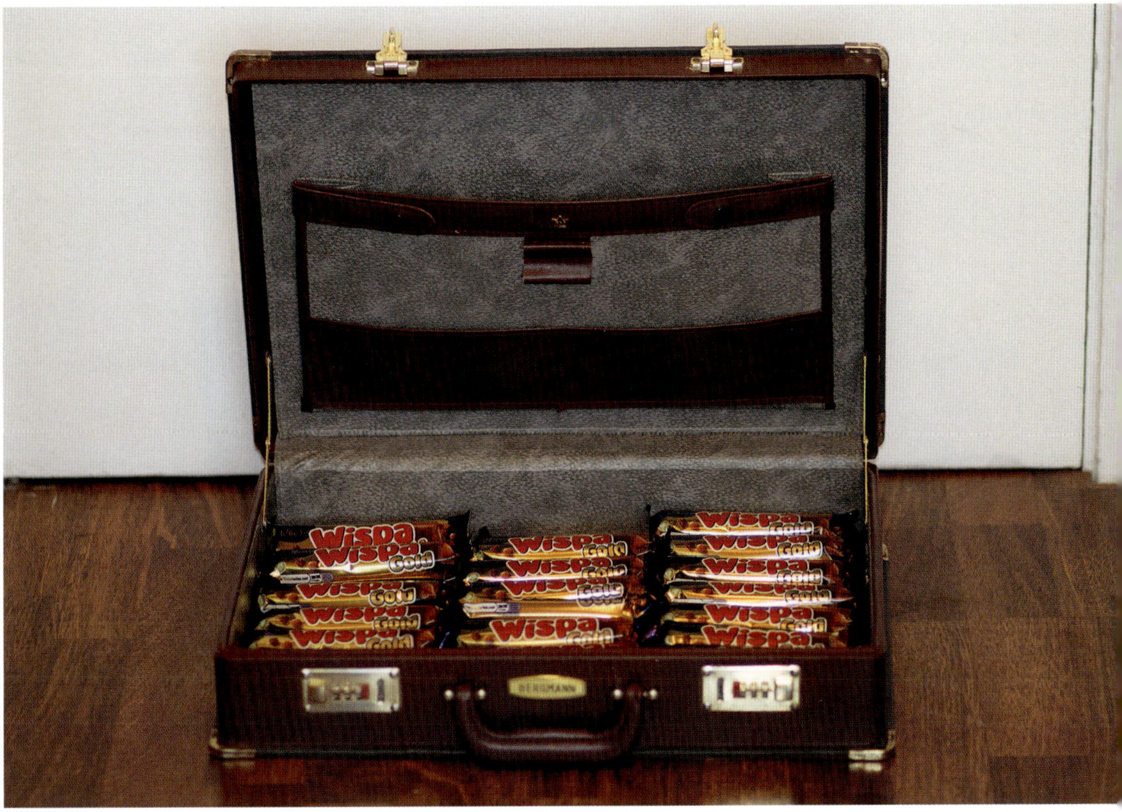

Fig. 98

At this point it was clear that it was a 'bit', but Little Jimmy lost all his fear, took off his backpack and placed it on the ground. It writhed, almost in anger. 'Do not make me release the wolf,' he said, confidently. 'I will not hesitate to remove the wolf.'

'Fuck off, pin head,' said Mayo, 'there's no way there's a wolf in there.' To be fair to Simon, the bag did not look big enough for a wolf.

Long story short, Mayo's 'bomb' cylinders were full of Smarties, but sadly Coffey's security panicked when he pressed the button releasing them and shot him nine times. He survived his injuries but had to take a few weeks off air – his sometime co-host Mark Kermode covered the slot, which Coffey later described as the most harrowing part of the ordeal. Alas, it was Little Jimmy who came away with the most scars, to his ego, which was completely obliterated when the 'wolf' was revealed to be a red panda from the local nature centre. It achieved nothing but a panicked shriek before biting one of Coffey's ankles and running into a nearby disabled toilet.

While we waited to give our statements to the police, I decided to calm my nerves by painting Coffey, who by this point was sipping a glass of champagne, smoking a cigar and shouting nuclear codes at passing children. In the confusion, she'd forgotten to top up the parking metre so her government Jaguar had been clamped. To avoid further delays she was bundled into a Creme Egg-shaped car (known as the 'Creme Egg Car') and driven away, while me and Jimmy got the bus back to Alison Hammond's so he could be picked up.

I later heard Simon Mayo was sued by Cadbury parent company Mondelez for bringing Smarties onto the property, which are in fact a Nestlé product. Coffey and I haven't interacted much since, although on one occasion she did erroneously send me a WeTransfer of all the pictures in her phone's camera roll – when I looked it was just thousands of screengrabs of the iPhone weather app.

Fig. 99 The famous Cadbury Creme Egg Car.
Fig. 100 A cover letter from Gary to Thérèse Coffey returning some of her documents.

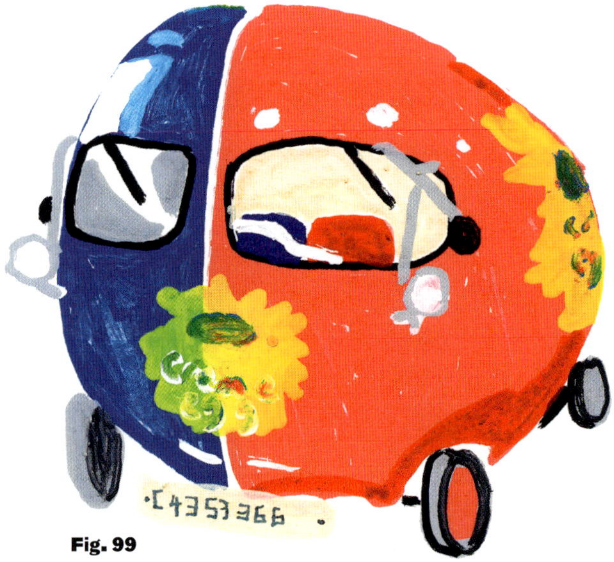

Fig. 99

Cadbry LAND

Therese Coffey
[redacted]

Cadbry Land
[redacted]

Reservations: [redacted]
Administration: +44 [redacted]
Facsimile: +44 (0[redacted]

Website: www.cadbryland4.gov

Dear Ms Coffey,

Thank you for your recent visit.

I hope you are ok given the circumstances of your visit and I am pleased to hear Mr Mayo is making good progress with his recovery.

Please accept the files sent with this letter ('Nuclear Codes 103NDKA', 'MI6 Agents: Real Names and Addresses' and 'Sarah Raven Autumn Bulb Catalogue') which were left on the side in our Aztec Jungle.

Best Wishes,
Gary

Fig. 100

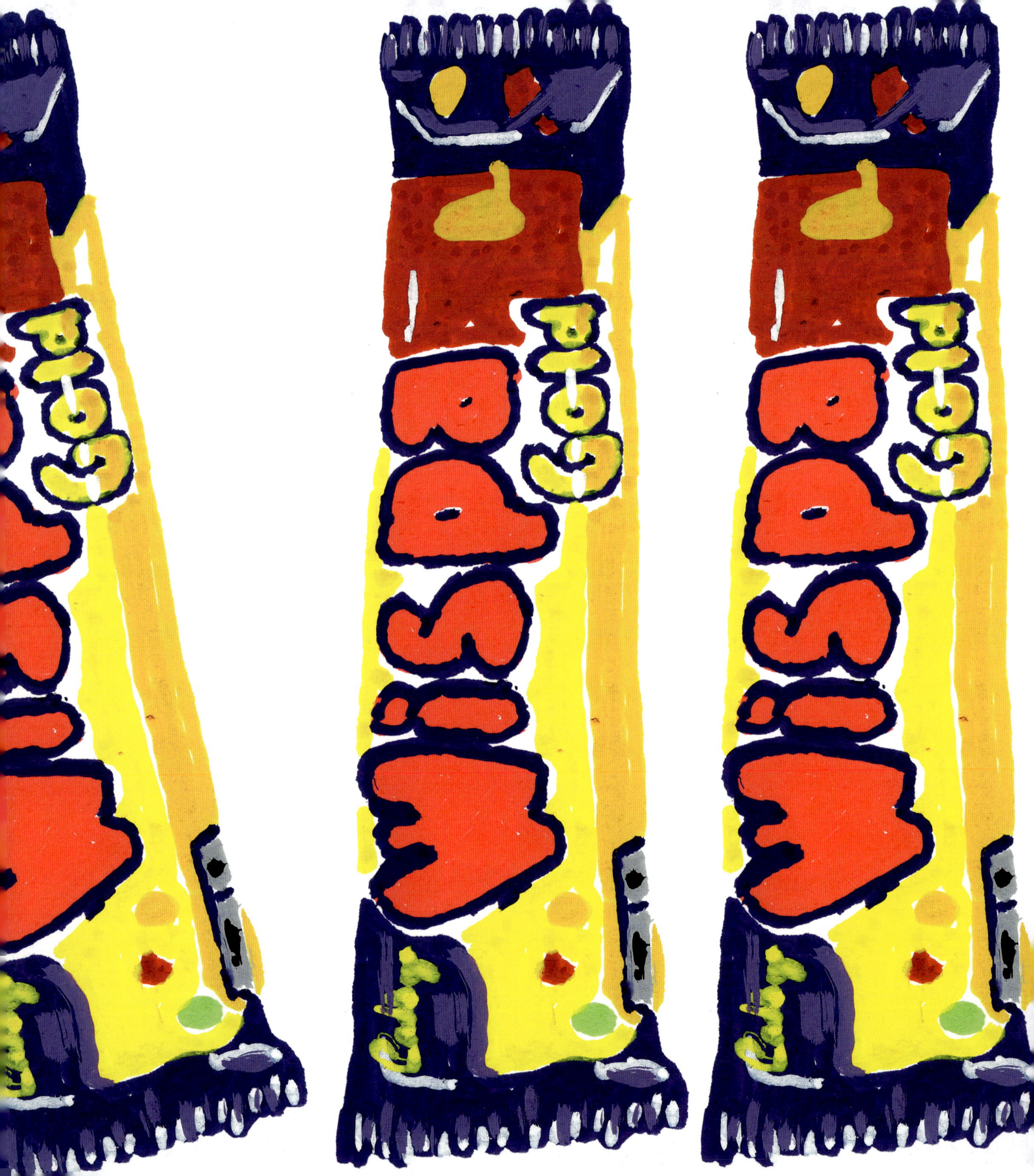
Wispa
Gold

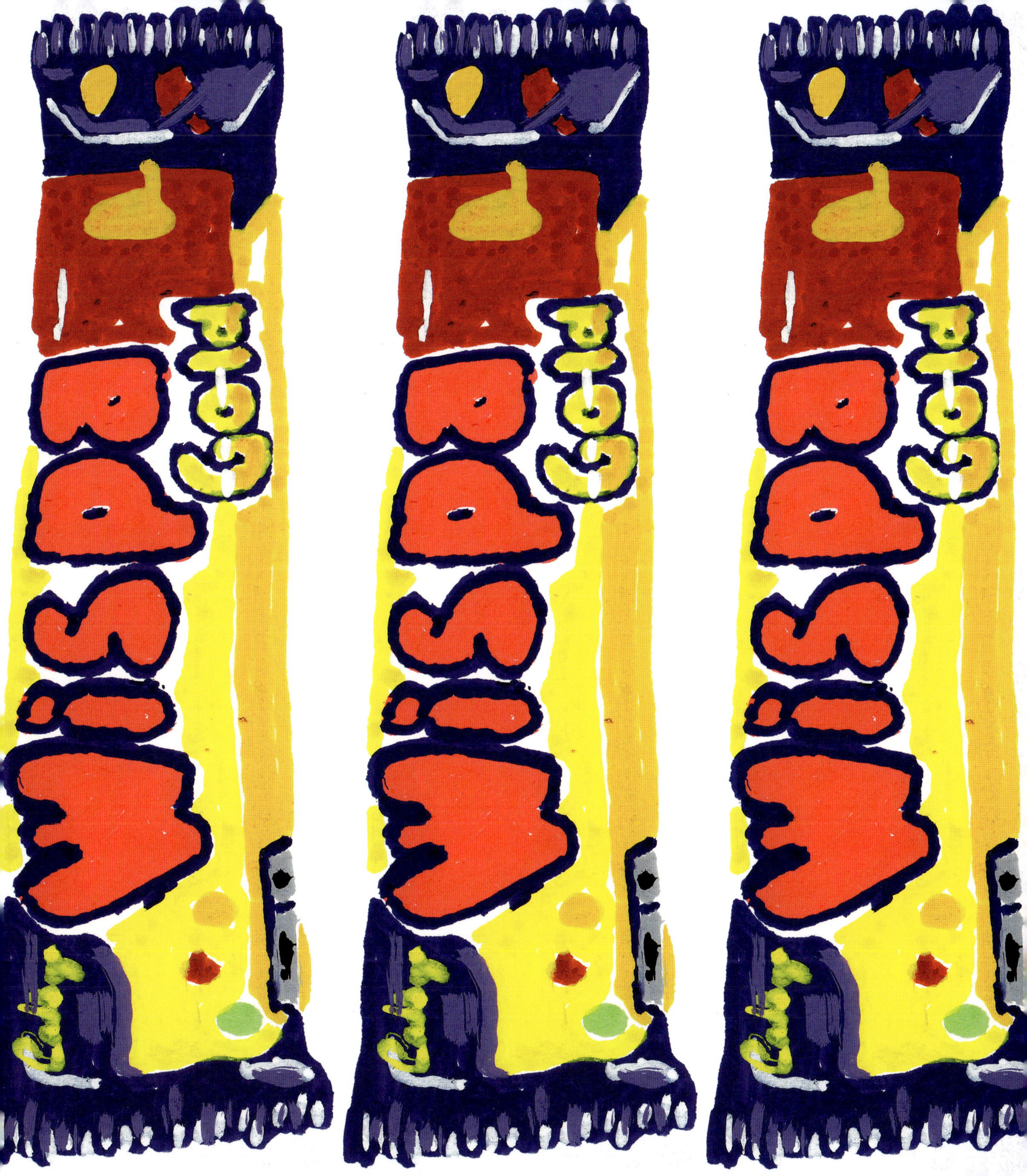
Wispa
Gold
Wispa
Gold
Wispa
Gold

A MOMENT
LIPS...
AND THEN
MOMENT ON

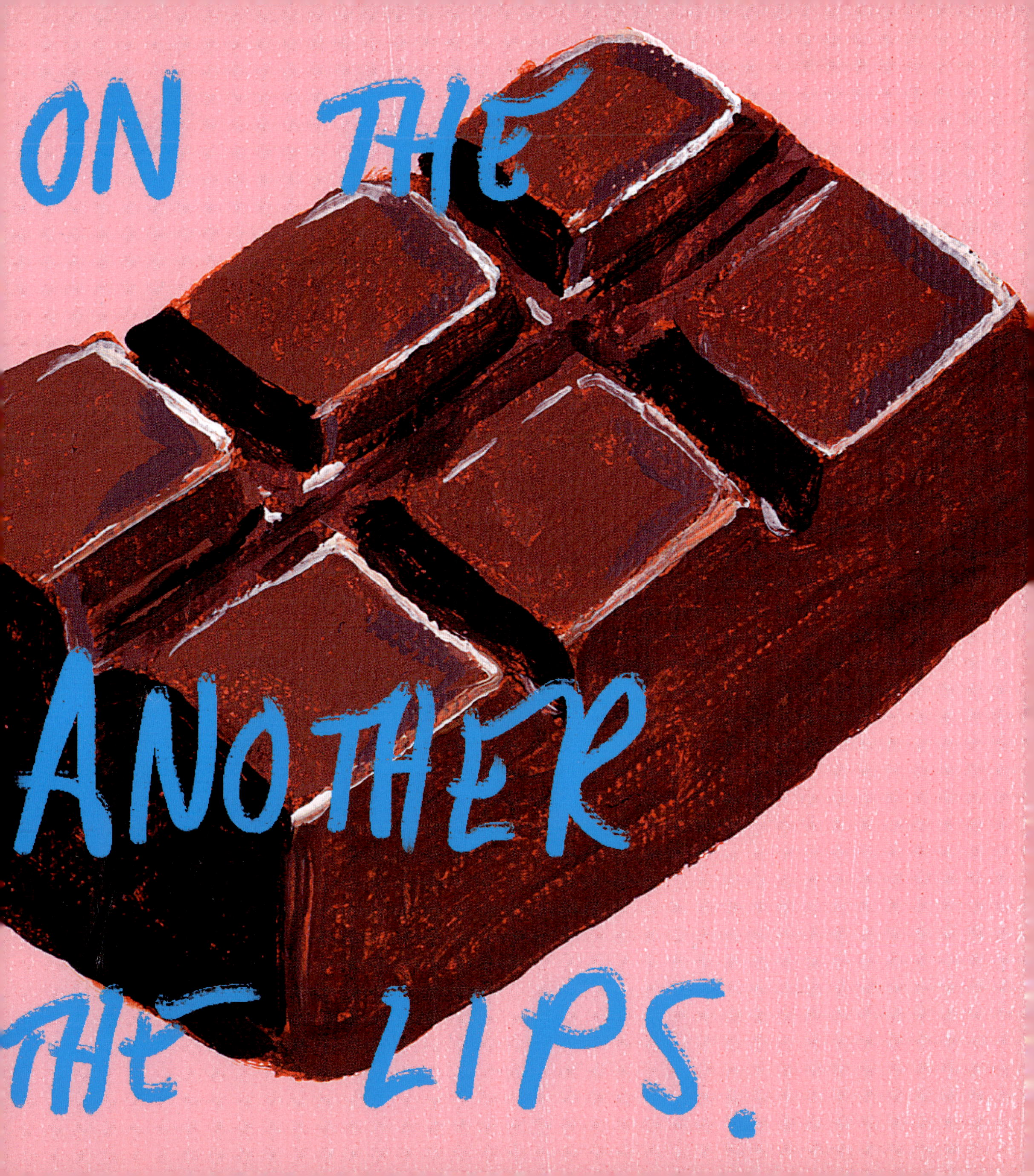
ON THE
ANOTHER
THE LIPS.

HUG ME

One Saturday I was taking a walk after my lunch (I had just been for a Toby Carvery and on three occasions gone back for additional potatoes) when I came across the SEA LIFE centre, and there was an advert outside that said 'Touch a crab!' and I thought to myself, 'Do you know what, there is nothing I would like more right now than to touch a crab'.

I stormed right on in there and approached the girl working on the desk, who behaved exactly like if you gave an adult woman the temperament of an aggressive cat.

'I saw the advert to touch a crab and I really wanna touch a crab,' I said.

She gave me a look as if I'd just flicked a wasp in her gob and said, 'No one on crab station until later, sorry.'

'How much later?' I said, not taking 'No one on crab station' for an answer.

'A good couple of hours,' she said, her gaze returning to the computer, which I'm fairly sure was open on a game of *Tom Clancy's Rainbow Six Siege*.

'I'll wait,' I said.

She looked back at me, before shouting, 'It could be three hours.' She clearly didn't want me to touch a crab, but sadly for this little lady she hadn't got the measure of the customer in front of her, me, and so I just lay down right there on the ground, taking off my shirt and balling it up as a pillow.

If there's one thing a triple portion of Toby Carvery potatoes gives you, it's the ability to lie down on the ground and fall asleep. I was out within seconds and woke up next to the otter enclosure, so I'm guessing she'd had security drag me away, which must've been quite the challenge 'cause when I eat potatoes, I get sweaty, and when I get sweaty, I get slippery.

Once I'd rubbed my eyes, I could see that there was a small queue next to the crabs and the people at the front of it were touching crabs, which I think I've made clear is all I intended to do.[1]

I got in the queue, and would you believe it,[2] in front of me lining up to also touch a crab was Steve who was in year eight with me at school. I fell out with Steve because he told everyone in our class that my shins looked like Barbara Windsor. In retaliation I tried to make a joke at his expense, but the best I could come up with was that his elbows looked like coat hangers, which elicited no laughter. I was humiliated, and when I got home Mom said to 'just ignore him' but also decided to add that my shins didn't look like Barbara Windsor at all, but more like Pauline Quirk.

1. Days after this I realised that the otter enclosure and the touch a crab station were both a considerable distance from the front desk, so either security lifted my lifeless body all that way, or there's a chance I didn't fall asleep but have blocked out certain memories, which does sometimes happen to me when I have potatoes from Toby Carvery.

2. I am asking you to believe it.

Fig. 101 A map of all the Toby Carvery establishments in the British Isles (correct at time of writing).

Fig. 102 A painting of one of the crabs I touched: *Hug Me*, 2024, acrylic on en suite, 23 × 42mm.

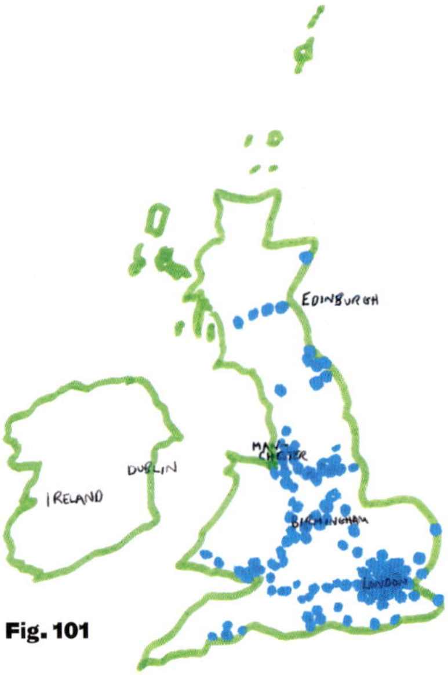

Fig. 101

Fig. 102

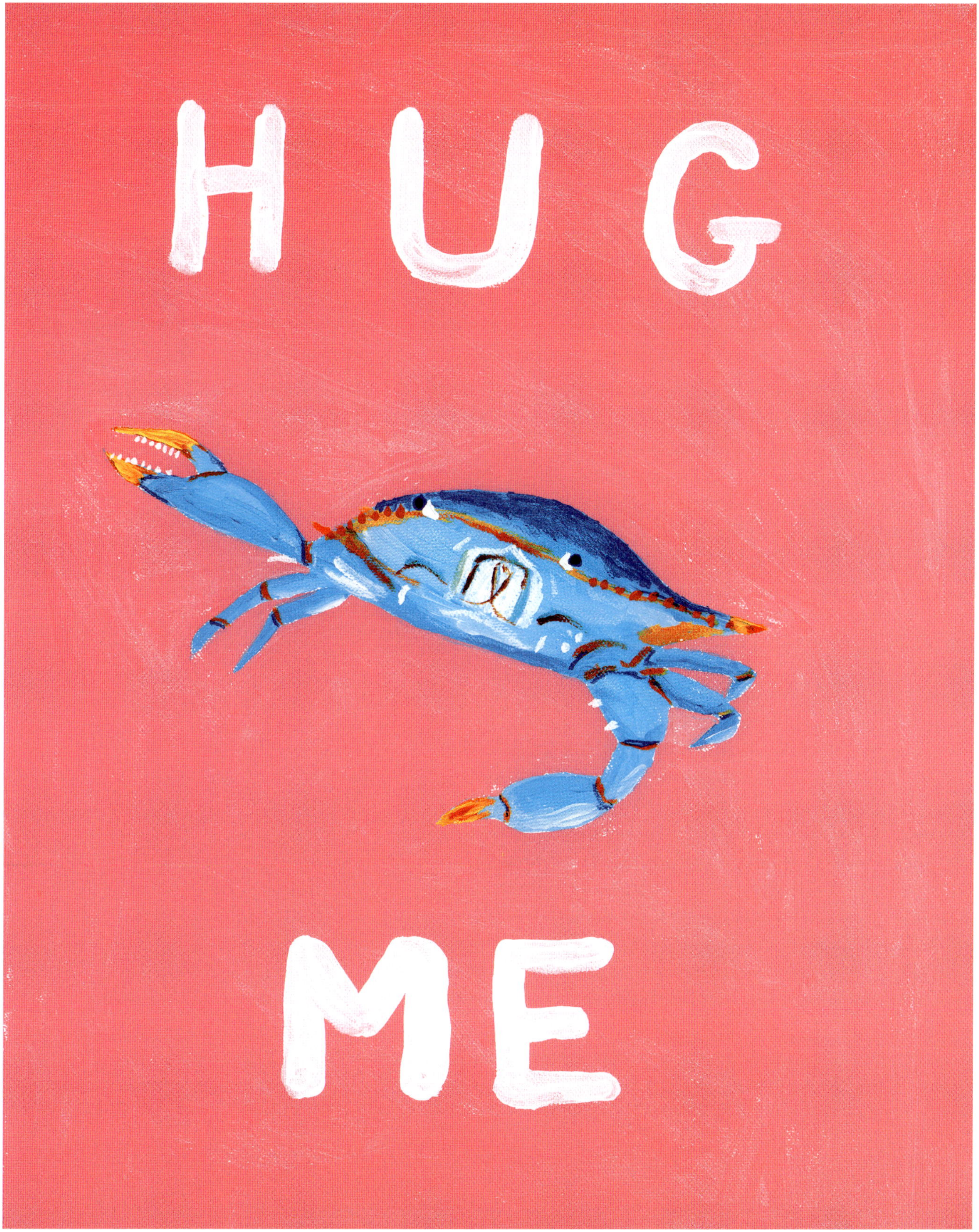

Fig. 103 *Body Goals*, 2024, charcoal on salad, 3 × 4in
Fig. 104 *Tom Clancy's Rainbow Six Siege* videogame, available on XBox One.

So, there I am, years later, in the SEA LIFE centre, all groggy and confused and not sure whether to be excited about touching a crab or annoyed that Steve from year eight is there with his coat hanger elbows. I thought I'd ignore him like Mom said, but eventually he turned round and said, 'Lycett! Bloody hell, you've aged!' Instinctively I felt I had to jab back at him.

'You look like you've had a fucking shit life, Steve,' I said, overreacting and misreading the situation all over again.

'Well, erm, yeh I suppose you're right, really.' He did an awkward laugh. 'I've only just recently received treatment for a serious autoimmune disease which incapacitated me for years, so I don't have a job or a home and I thought I'd cheer myself up and come and touch a crab with my son.'

He then introduced the sweetest little boy I have ever met, who looked like Mara Wilson (that actress they put in all the films for a while like *Matilda* and *Mrs Doubtfire*). The kid said, 'Daddy, who is that slippery man who just said you have had a shit life?'

Steve replied: 'He's an old school friend, Teddy, and now an accomplished artist, and he was only joking.'

'Yes, Teddy,' I added, 'just a joke. Haha!'

'Well, good to see you again, Joe,' Steve added in a devastatingly genuine way.

I watched as Steve and Teddy touched the crab, in awe at its texture. At one point Steve laughed and said to the guy holding it, 'Bloody hell, it feels like Barbara Windsor,' and in that moment I realised that's just a thing that he does, comparing everything to Barbara Windsor, and that neither my shins nor the crab nor any other thing Steve ever encounters is even remotely like Barbara Windsor. The guy could have met Barbara Windsor and said, 'Bloody hell, she looks like Barbara Windsor.'

I touched a crab and continued on through the SEA LIFE centre (I also saw a blob fish which I painted, *see* **Fig. 103**), but I was just so desperately sad; sad that Steve had endured such a shit life, sad that I then told him he'd had a shit life in front of his son, and sad that maybe his only crime was over-using Barbara Windsor as a reference.

Months later, I read in the paper that Steve was done for GBH, jailed for twenty years, and Teddy went into care. So, I was right about the fucker.

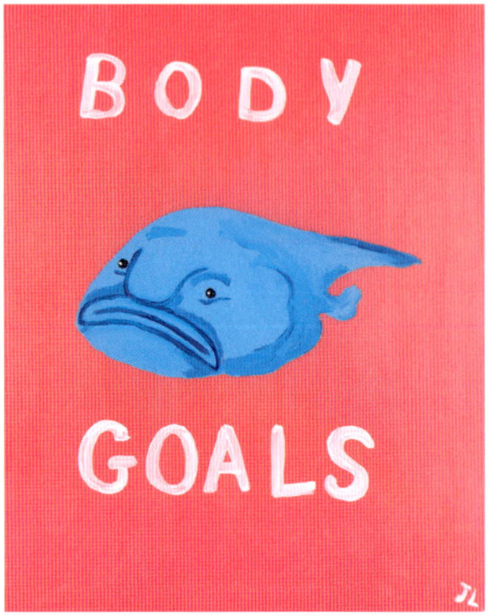

Fig. 103

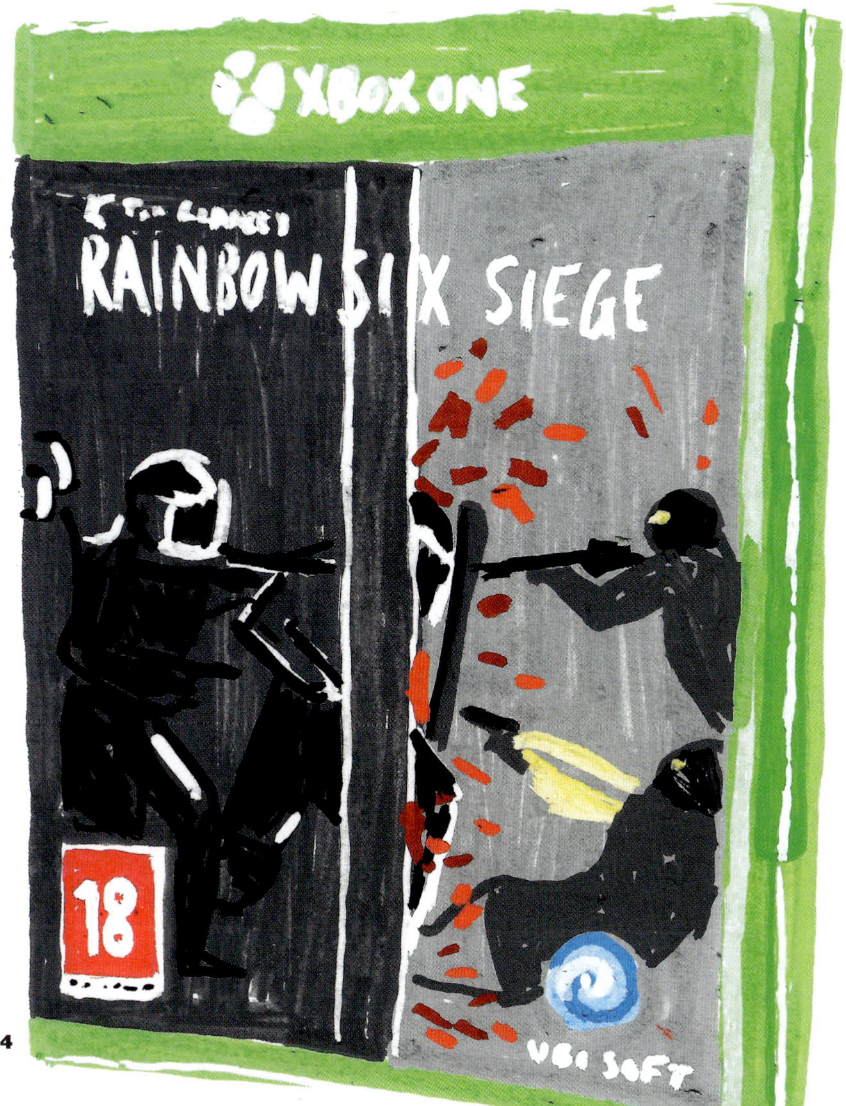

Fig. 104

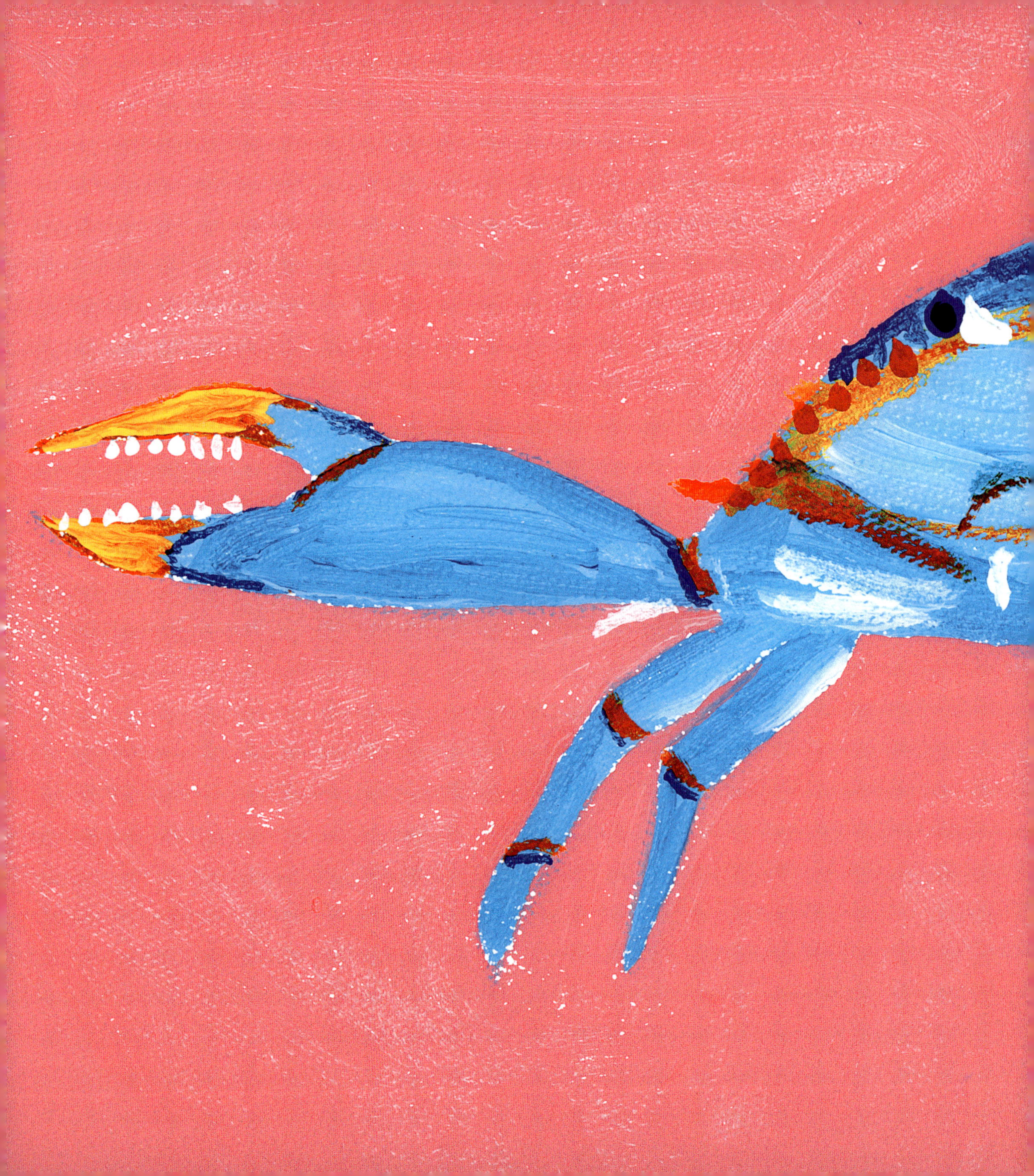

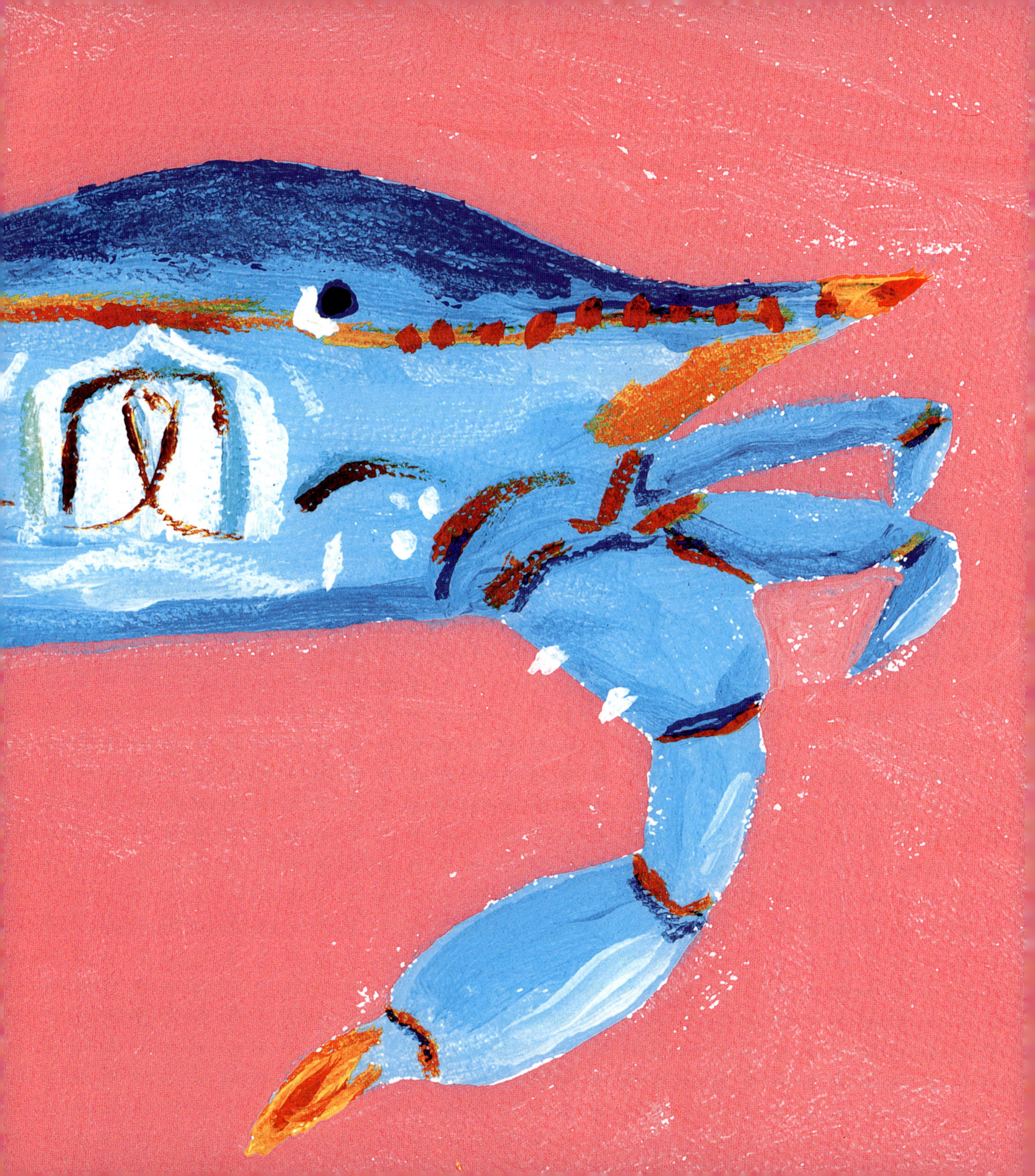

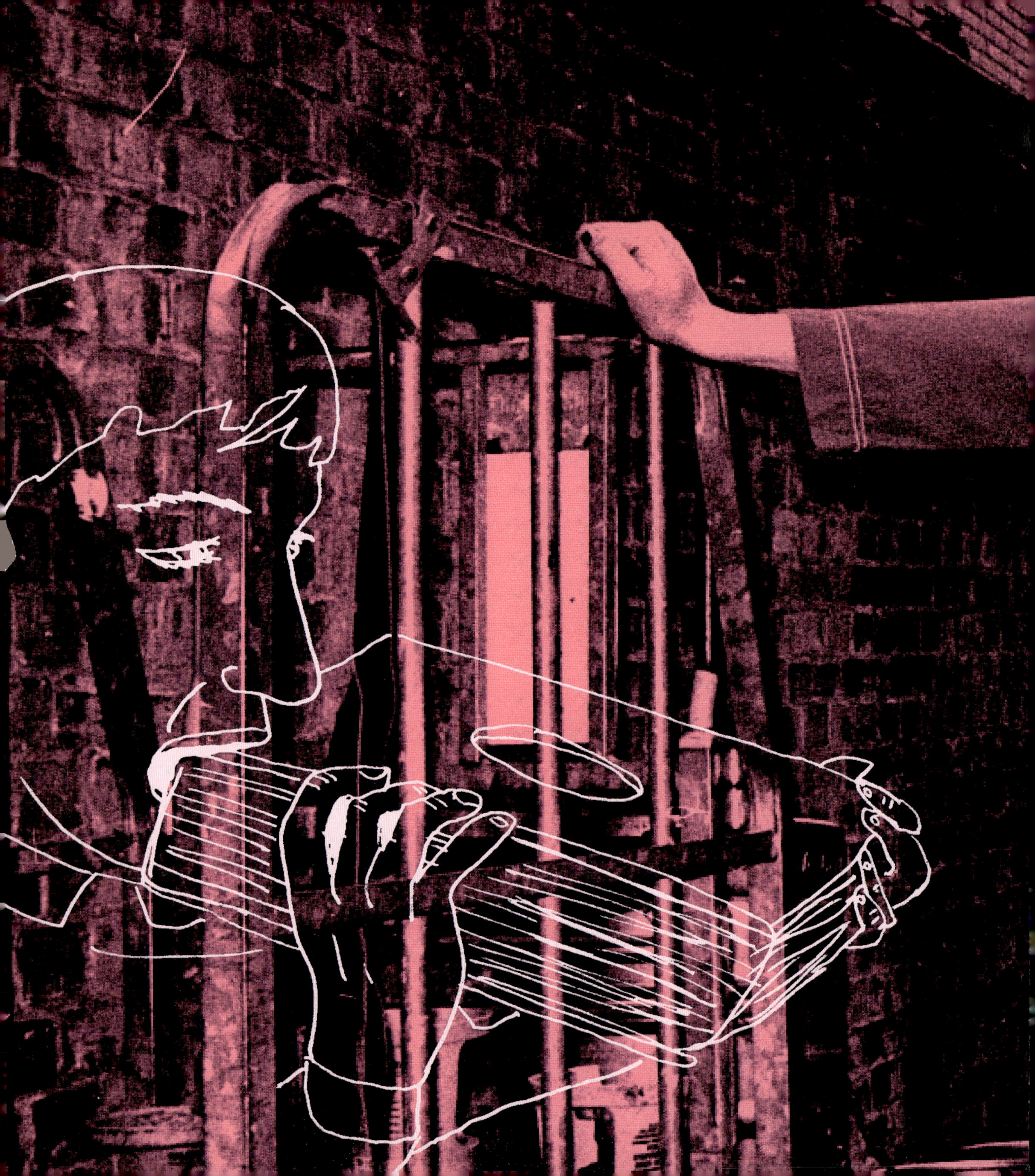

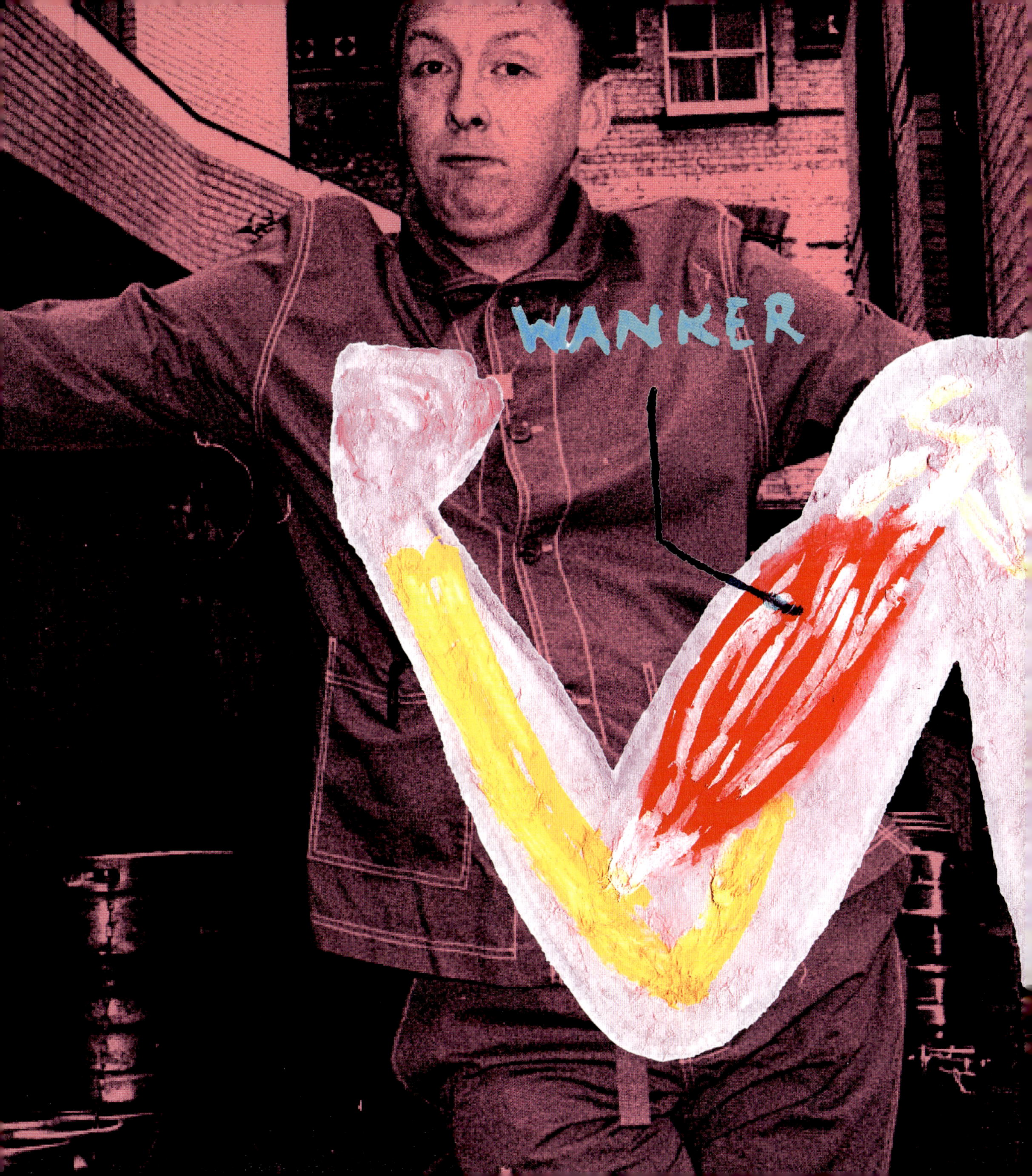
WANKER

PRITI PATEL

Excluding Liz Truss, Theresa May and Idi Amin, the politician I most admire is Priti Patel MP. She is a woman with bold, ambitious ideas, who works hard for her constituents, and all while being one of this country's most accomplished and versatile fly-tippers.

There's a small but growing community of what you might call 'professional fly-tippers' in the UK, of which I am proud to be a founding member. A great way to make a bit of extra pocket money, you approach a building site and offer to 'take some of this shite off your hands' in return for a not inconsiderable wedge of cash. It's a pastime that attracts a lot of MPs; they're always looking at ways of topping up their meagre salaries. They normally have insiders at large-scale building projects, and they love the thrill of taking home a fistful of tenners that they'll never have to declare.

I've worked with some of the best: I've dumped a school's worth of plastic chairs with Harriet Harman, dropped half a dozen dishwashers into the River Avon with David Davis, and poured a Citroen full of gravel off the south coast with the help of Grant Shapps. But the GOAT (Greatest Of All Tippers) is undoubtedly Priti Patel.

Nothing can prepare you for seeing her in action. The graceful efficiency, the skill, the sheer volume! I once heard she made eighteen tons of defunct double-glazing disappear in twenty minutes. The way the woman works is astonishing.

In the fly-tipping community she has mythical status but, despite my years in the business, I've encountered her only a handful of times. The first was in my early days, when I was but a young man, full of hope and promise and student debt. I was dragging two IKEA bags full of picture hooks through a forest just outside Bath. I thought I was alone, until a voice in the distance pierced the tranquil silence. I looked up to see Priti Patel and an assistant standing in a nearby clearing.

'Look at this chump,' said Patel. 'IKEA bags. What an amateur.' The assistant laughed, out of almost frightened obligation. I tried to make out who it was, and still can't be sure, but it appeared to be the actress that played Tracy Beaker in the children's TV series *The Story of Tracy Beaker*. Priti smiled, then entered the side door of a nearby motorhome, shouting from inside, 'Open her up.'

Beaker (I believe the actress is called Dani Harmer) walked to the back and meekly opened the doors. I couldn't see how it was done as my view was obscured, but all I know is that within three minutes I

Fig. 105 Added to this chapter simply because Whitty rhymes with Priti: *The Itty Bitty Titty Chris Whitty Committee,* 2020, acrylic on NHS pamphlet, 2 × 23cm.

Fig. 106 *Priti Little Thing*, 2024, dried blood and masonry paint on scrap metal, 18ft × 6mm.

Fig. 105

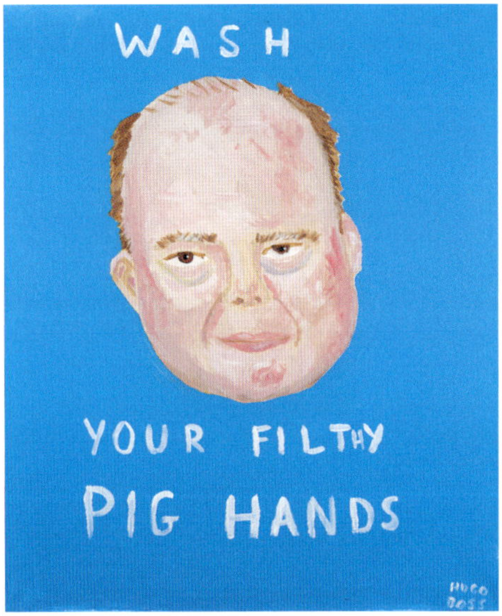

Fig. 106

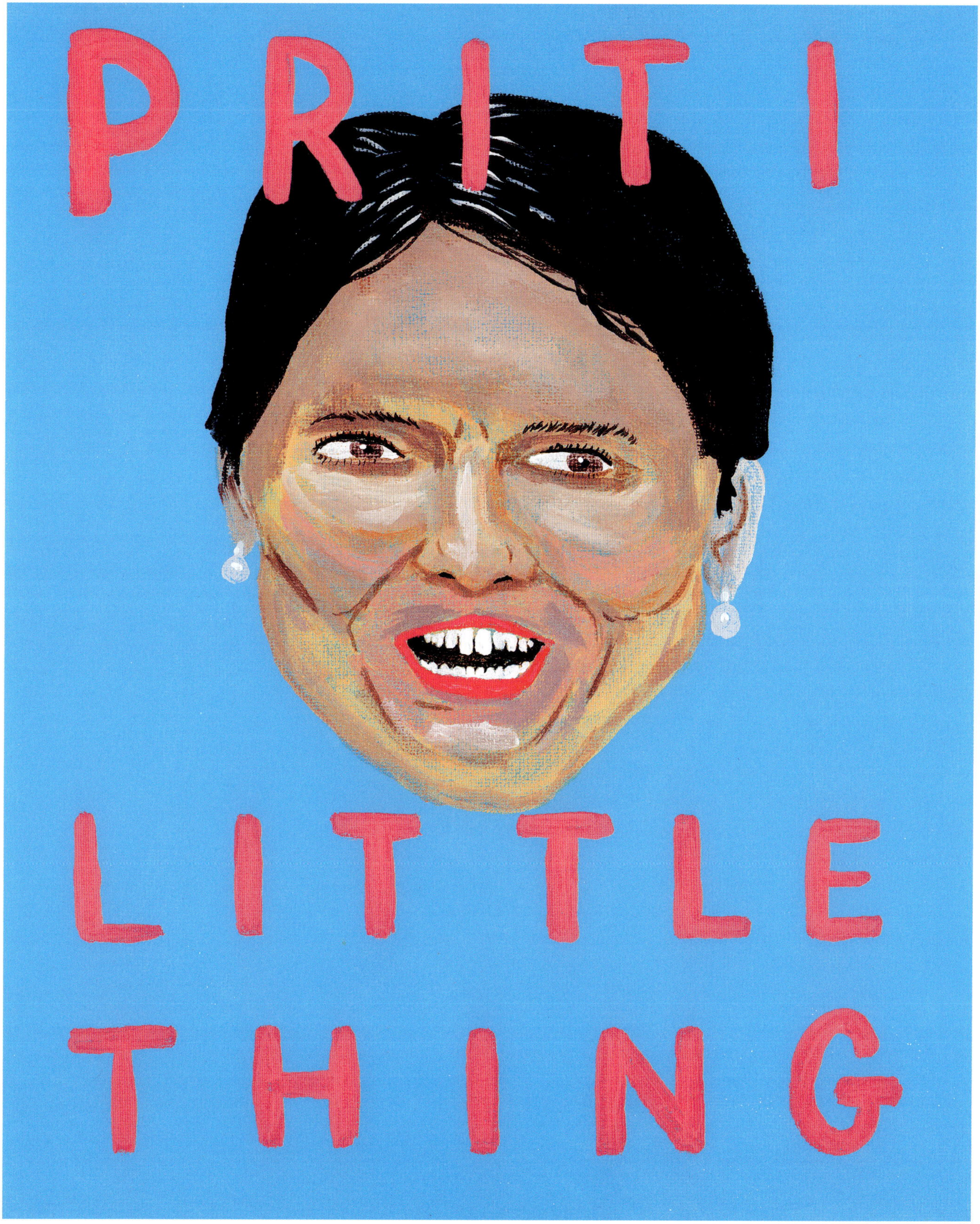

was standing alone in that forest in front of what must have been at least a thousand discarded laptops … Dells, ASUSs, Lenovos, ACERs, HPs – all piled up and abandoned.

I've since seen her empty that motorhome of floorboards, light fittings, bannisters and, on one occasion, fifteen tubes of underlay which slid out like warm Peperamis. She once asked me if I had any fridges I needed getting rid of as she was dumping a few dozen round the back of a hospice, but I was adamant I could fix the Hotpoint H55RM1110W1 Fridge in white.

The last time I saw her was in the grounds of a National Trust property in the Lake District. I had taken some time out of the fly-tipping game after a legal scare and was actually there in my capacity as an accomplished artist, looking to paint a pleasing vista. On the horizon I saw that unmistakable motorhome throwing up a haze of dust into the late afternoon sky.

Pulling up alongside me, I noticed she was alone and seemed very surprised to see me. 'Dumping for Cass Art now, are we?' she said, pointing at the large canvas I had under my arm.

'Oh, no, no,' I replied, 'I'm actually using this for one of my extraordinary paintings.'

'Right. Sure you are. Thought you'd been done?' she asked, taking a bite out of a full loaf of Soreen.

'Nearly,' I replied, 'got off on a technicality.'[1]

'Fair play,' she said, hopping out of the driver's seat and walking round to the back. 'Fancy giving me a hand?' Like alcohol and watching *The One Show*, you can take time away from fly-tipping, but it never really leaves you. The temptation was too much.

'Sure,' I said.

I'll never know how she managed it, or even how that motorhome took the weight, but inside was stacked high with reinforced steel joists. I counted at least thirty of them, thick metal blocks which she picked up and tossed out like chopsticks.

'Where's all this from?' I asked sheepishly.

'An immigration processing centre that I managed to get closed down. A double win for little Priti!'

Dumping accomplished, I took my shot: 'Might you sit for a portrait?'

'Eugh. You've got twenty minutes,' she said. 'I have to get back to parliament to vote in favour of legislation that will tear children away from their mothers.'

I nodded and began.

The resulting painting was purchased by Suella Braverman and thrown into some foliage off a slip road on the M25.

1. I convinced the judge I was doing an art project involving 'a Ford Transit full of plasterboard'.

Fig. 107 Soreen, as eaten by Priti Patel.
Fig. 108 The famous IKEA bag, which is well known to be stronger than any other known substance.

Fig. 107

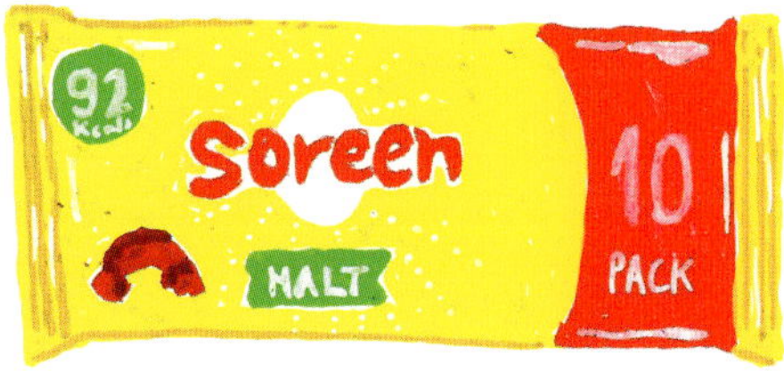

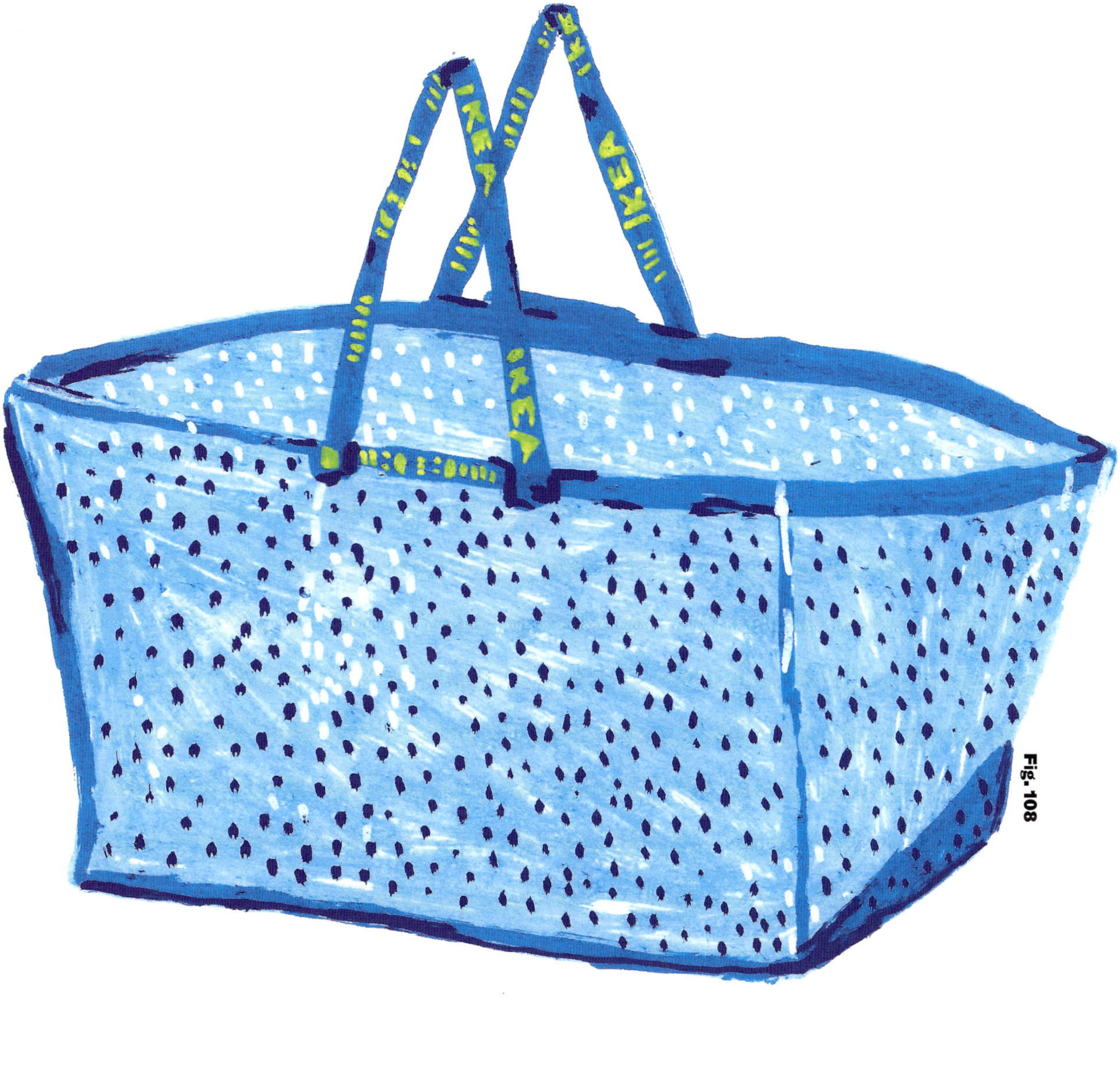

Fig. 108

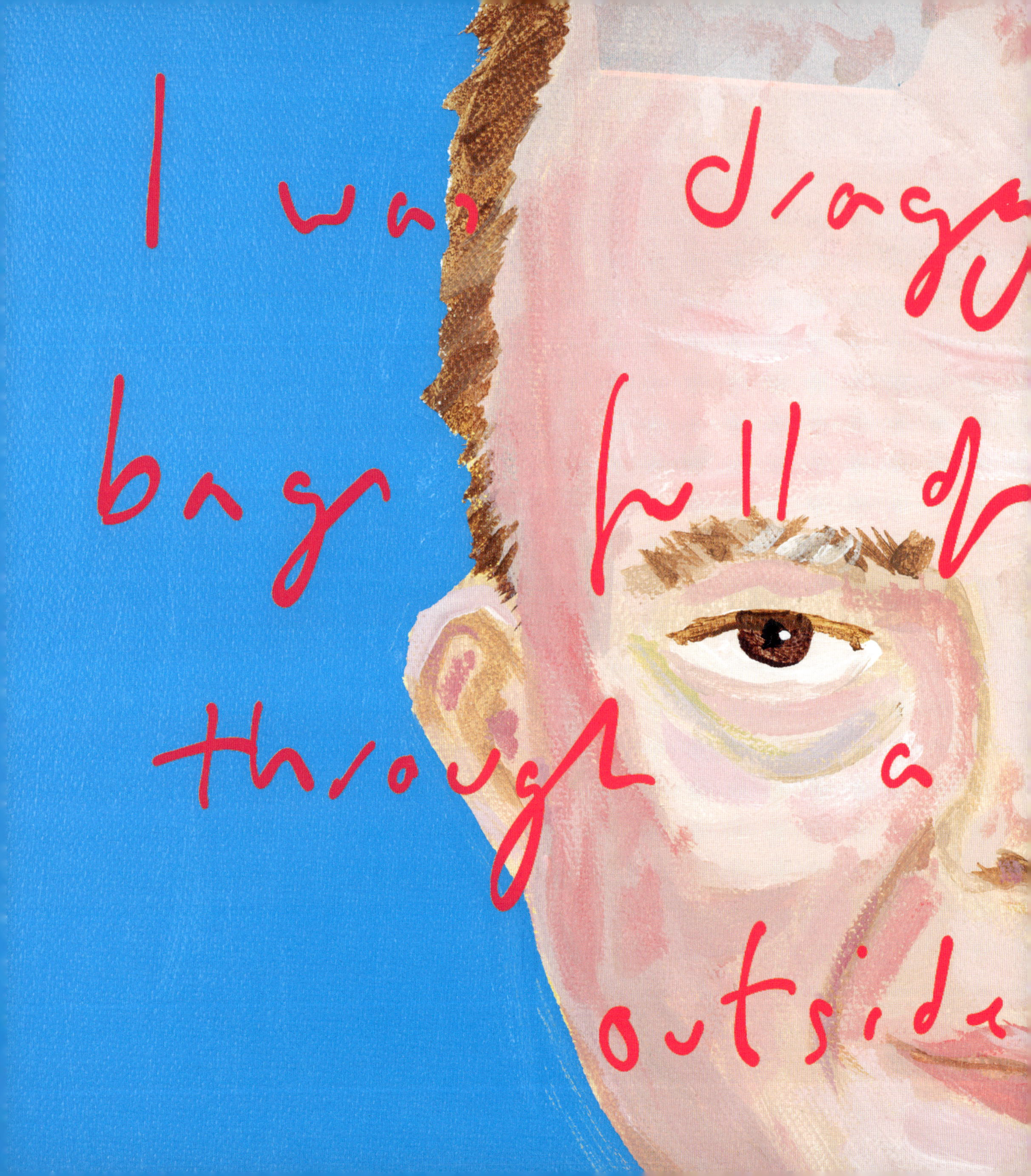
I was
through
a
outside

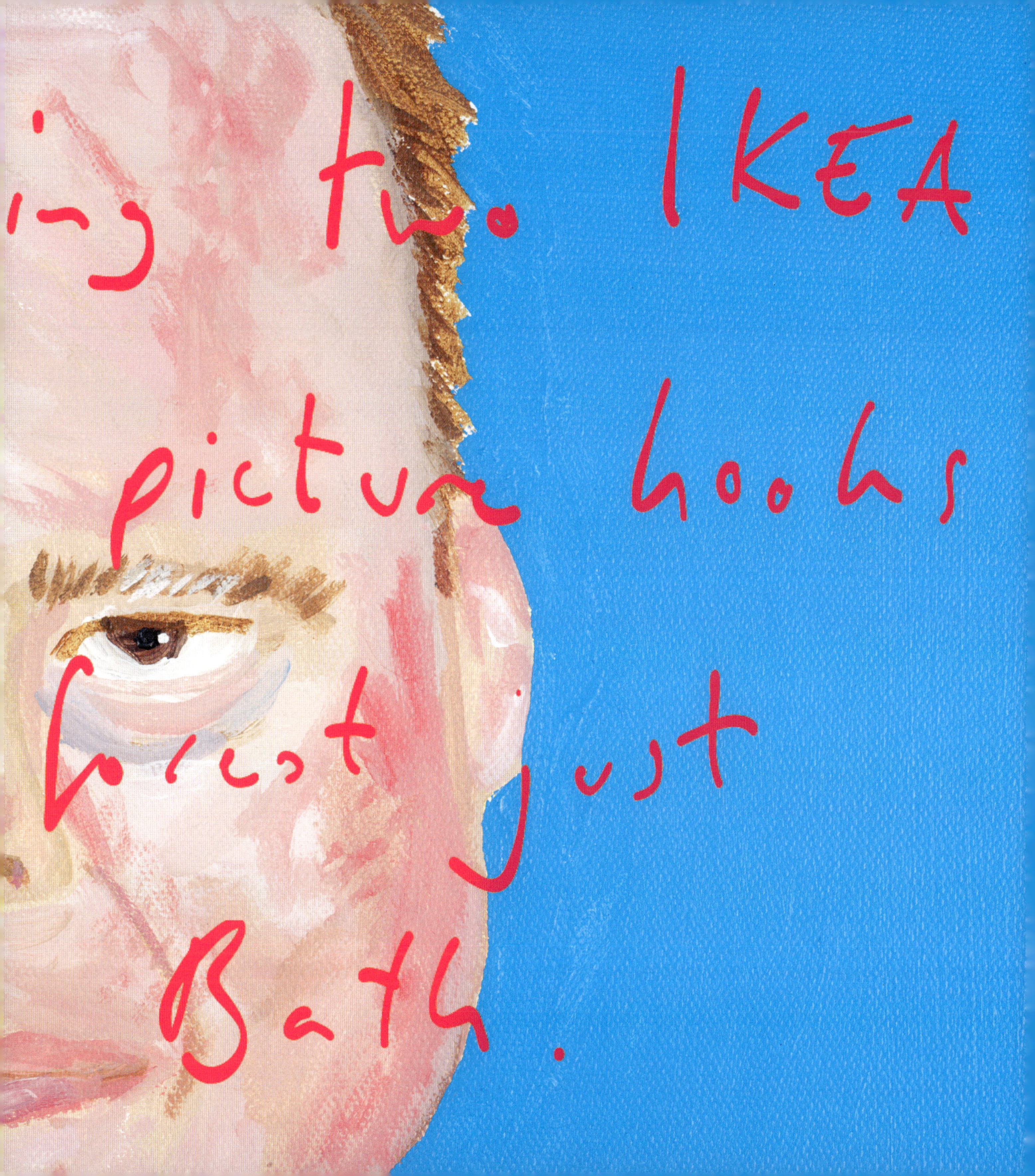
ing two IKEA
picture hooks
cost just
Bath.

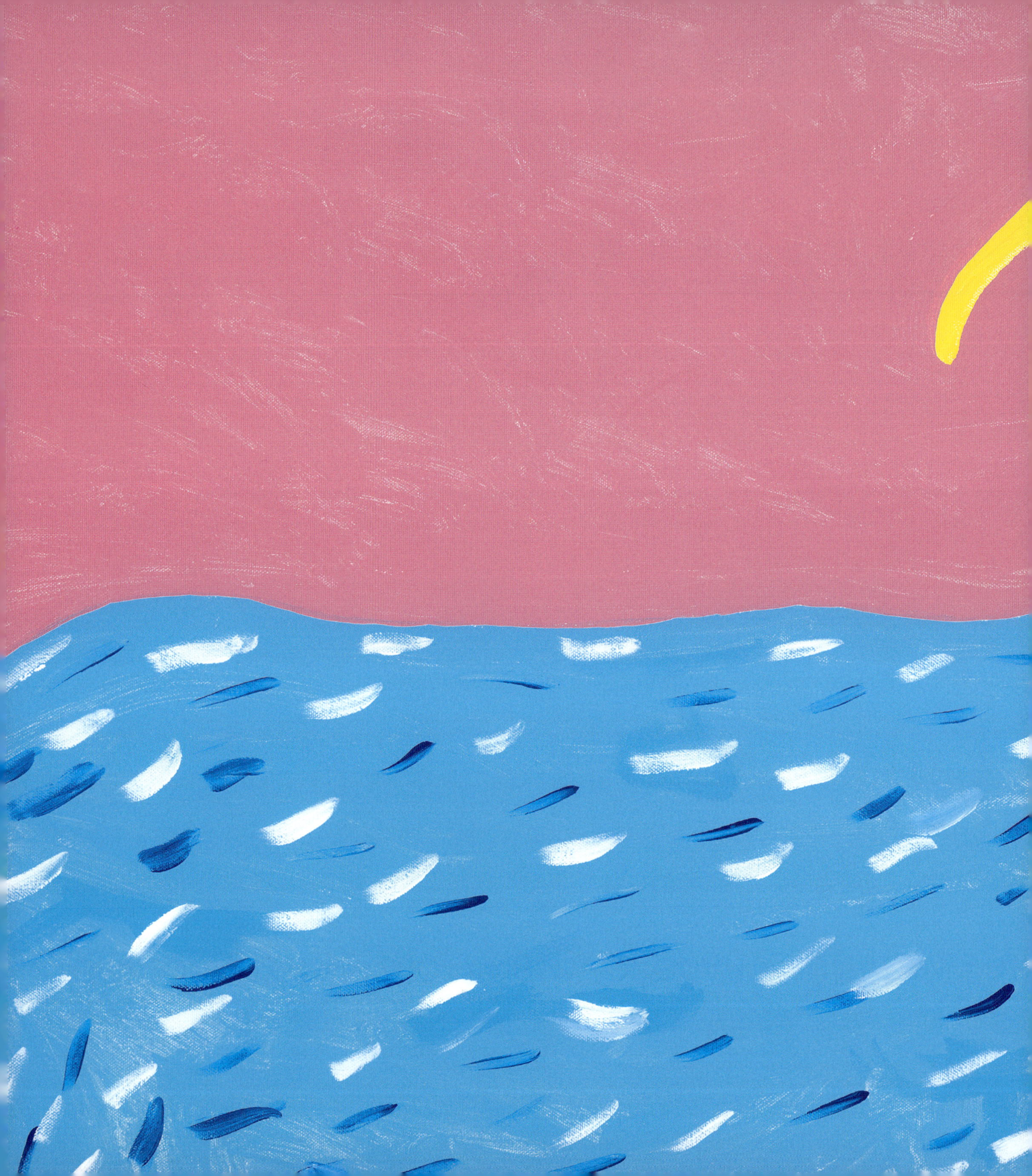

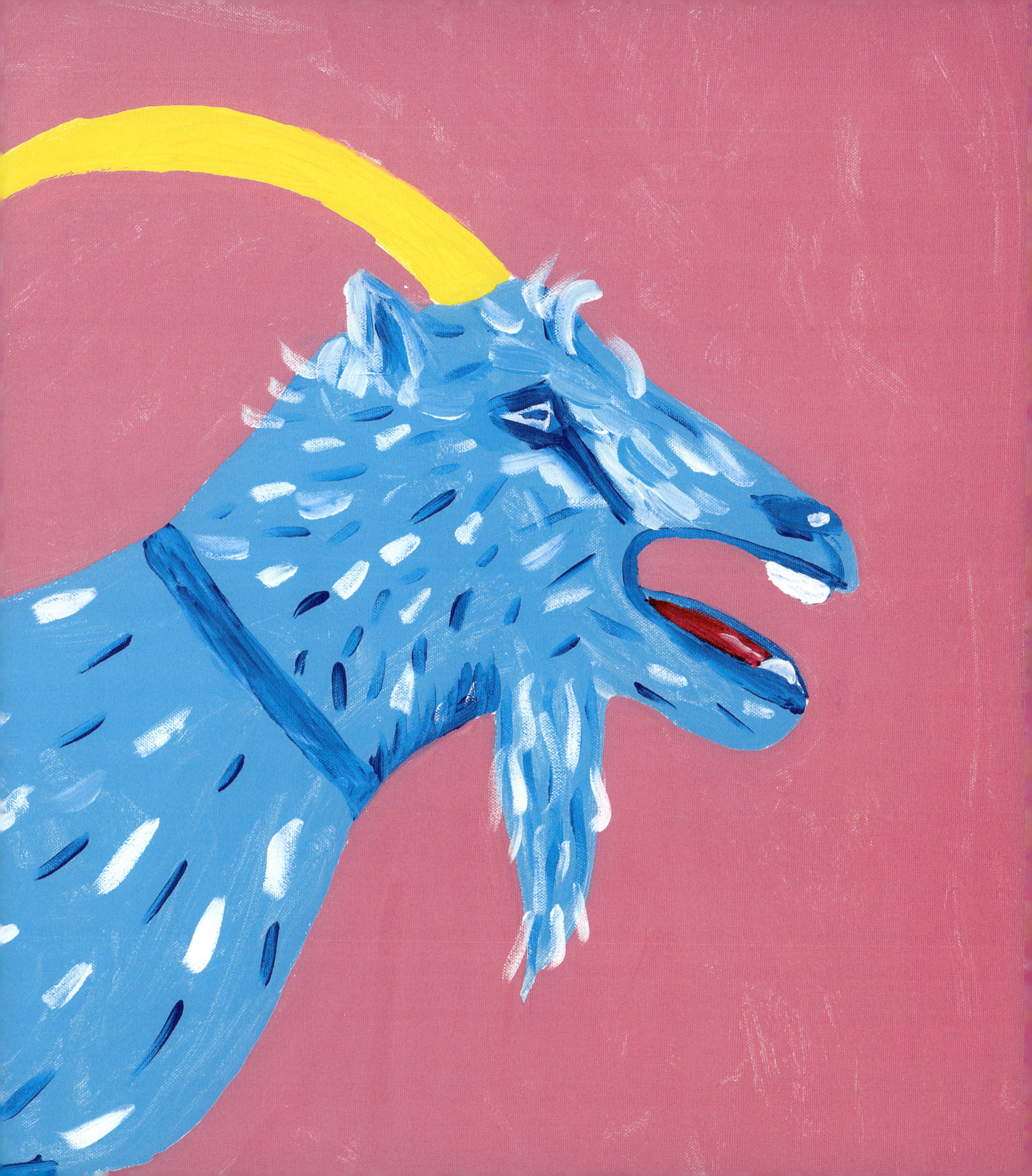

RO

POST-
OCOCO

Post-rococo

A CAT HAVING A LITTLE THINK WHILE RESTING ON A SKYLIGHT ON A HOT SUMMER'S DAY

I feel kind of vulnerable mentioning this, but I think it's important to speak your truth, so here we go, I'm just gonna do it: I'm mildly allergic to cats. It's taken me a long time to open up about this, but I figure others reading this will be suffering too and maybe this will bring them a little bit of hope.

If you are an unlucky sufferer, I'm sorry to admit that I'm not sure I can actually give you much hope because I have no cure. You will know full well that to have this condition (mild cat allergy) is a total nightmare. Whenever I get near a cat, which is all the time because I have a cat, I get runny eyes and a sniffly nose (unless I have a Benadryl or something that contains Loratadine). Sometimes it means I have to have a puff on my Salbutamol asthma inhaler (known to many by the brand name Ventolin), but it's not normally that bad, only if I go round someone's house who has a lot of cats, like an old widow or Richard Hammond. It's an unsustainable and awful condition and I wouldn't wish it on my worst enemy (who is Lenny Henry).[1]

'Why did you get a cat if you're so (mildly) allergic to cats?' you might ask me.

'Why don't you go and fuck yourself?' I might ask back. But then I will calm down eventually and tell you my story.

I was chugging my eighth shot of Jack Daniel's Tennessee Apple (aka JDTA) at a cocktail party at the country home of radio and television presenter Jeremy Vine. I'd spent most of the night trapped with Ken Bruce[2] – no relation to Fiona that we are aware of – who I usually like a lot, but the excitement of a wild showbiz party dimmed considerably when he pulled out a manual for a Hoover H-FREE 300 Pets HF322PT 3-in-1 Cordless Stick Vacuum Cleaner.

1. This isn't a question. I know who Lenny Henry is.
2. Who is Ken Bruce? Please send me a message on social media with any information.

Fig. 109 *A Cat Having a Little Think While Resting on a Skylight on a Hot Summer's Day,* 2022, Dreamies Creamy on canvas, 30 × 40cm.

Fig. 109

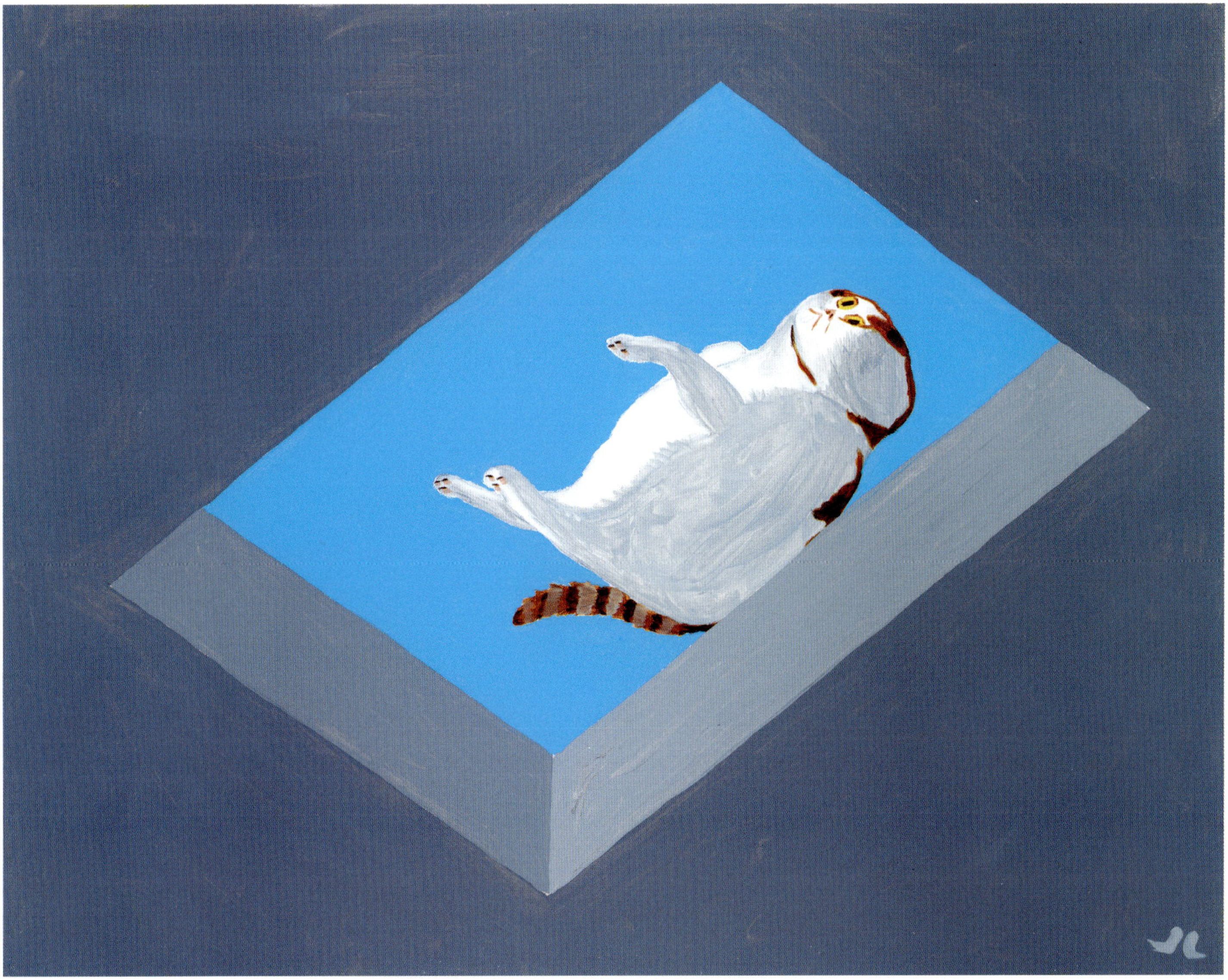

'Never thought I'd go bagless, never,' he said, sipping his chartreuse. 'And then along comes the Hoover H-FREE 300 Pets HF322PT 3-in-1 Cordless Stick Vacuum Cleaner and it changes everything. Do you have narrow spaces at home, Joe?' The question was loaded. I nodded my head and guzzled another JDTA.

'Quite a few narrow spaces, Ken, throughout the house.' His eyes lit up like eyes that have a light shining on them.

'I was hoping you'd say that. The Hoover H-FREE 300 Pets HF322PT 3-in-1 Cordless Stick Vacuum Cleaner is specifically designed for narrow corners. Lightweight, and with a detachable duster which you can put in the wash when you're done.' He got the detachable duster out of his pocket and I knew I had to get away, urgently. I made my excuses (needed a shit) and walked away.

I took another JDTA, made small talk with Skepta (Ken's plus one) and found myself on a sofa with Craig Charles. I was a little star-struck to be quite honest, as I've always admired the man and am a religious listener of his *Funk and Soul Show*. I pitched an idea to him once to do a spin-off called the *Funk and Soil Show* where he co-hosts with Alan Titchmarsh. I imagined the show would be Alan giving advice on how to tidy a potting shed while 'Cissy Strut' by The Meters plays in the background, Craig shouting, 'Feel the funk!' slightly off mic throughout. Craig had not responded to my email but his management thanked me for the interest but said that Craig was very busy.

Probably nine JDTAs down and my defences were in tatters. Craig could've asked me to rob a bank and I would've said, 'How high?' (It was loud and I would've misheard the question.) Alcohol paired with my reverence for the man meant I had no chance when he began our exchange immediately with, 'Lycett, fancy looking after a cat?'

'Sure, Craig! Tell me about it.' The cluster of radio producers around him began to laugh. I'd fallen into his trap.

'Well, it's your lucky day,' he slurred, placing his drink down and leaning over the sofa. What happened next tore the place apart. Craig lifted something that had been obscured from my view by the sofa arm. It was a cat box. And inside it was a cat.

I hadn't the heart to say that I am mildly allergic and so, once the party had ended (at midnight Jeremy announced, 'I've just tested positive … for get-the-fuck-out-of-my-house!'), me and the cat hitched a lift back to Birmingham with Vernon Kay.

'Ow'd you end up with the moggy, mate?' he asked.

'Craig gave it to me,' I said.

'Bastard did the same to me,' said Vernon, braking to 70 from 120 for a traffic camera.

Fig. 110 The Hoover H-FREE 300 Pets HF322PT 3-in-1 Cordless Stick Vacuum Cleaner.
Fig. 111 A Polaroid of me with the Hoover H-FREE 300 Pets HF322PT 3-in-1 Cordless Stick Vacuum Cleaner as taken by Bruno Tonioli.

A CAT HAVING A LITTLE THINK WHILE RESTING ON A SKYLIGHT ON A HOT SUMMER'S DAY

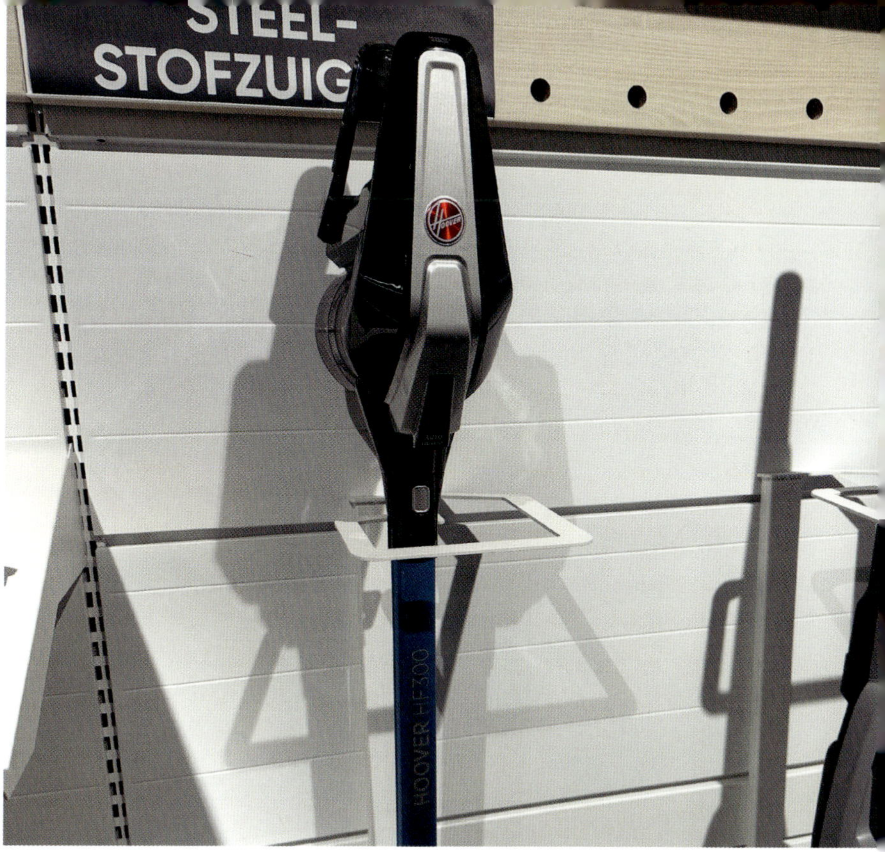

Fig. 110

Fig. 111

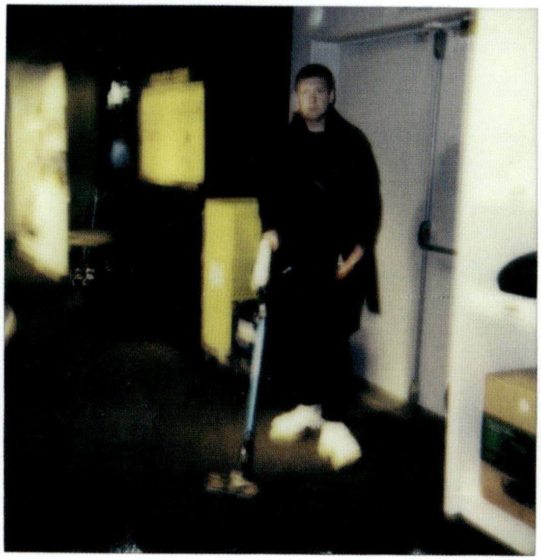

'He gave you a cat too?' I said, astonished.

'I wish! Let's just put it this way: I wouldn't normally choose to have a pet German Shepherd.'

Turns out it's a classic trick that Craig plays on newcomers at Radio 2 parties. Previous DJs have had guinea pigs, hamsters and even budgies thrust on them at parties. Poor Vanessa Feltz once got lumped with a terrarium full of exotic lizards.

I took it all in good humour and actually came to love that cat, which I named Craig in his honour. I paint him regularly, including this one of him in his favourite spot: on the kitchen skylight, basking in the sunshine, preferably after committing a small massacre of local rodents. Just like the man he's named after.

NB: Months later I learnt that Ken Bruce co-owns a second-hand vacuum shop that had recently taken a big order of knock-off Hoover H-FREE 300 Pets HF322PT 3-in-1 Cordless Stick Vacuum Cleaners (the rumour I heard stated it was approximately 15,000 units). With Craig's arrival, I was in the market for a vacuum that deals with pet hair, and the Hoover H-FREE 300 Pets HF322PT 3-in-1 Cordless Stick Vacuum Cleaner excels in that area, and Ken did me an exceptional deal.

Fig. 112 A stock photograph of a cat, for reference.
Fig. 113 Craig Charles's schedule (in his own words). It was made clear to me after he sent me this schedule that 'funk' is the word Craig uses for 'salt'.

Fig. 112

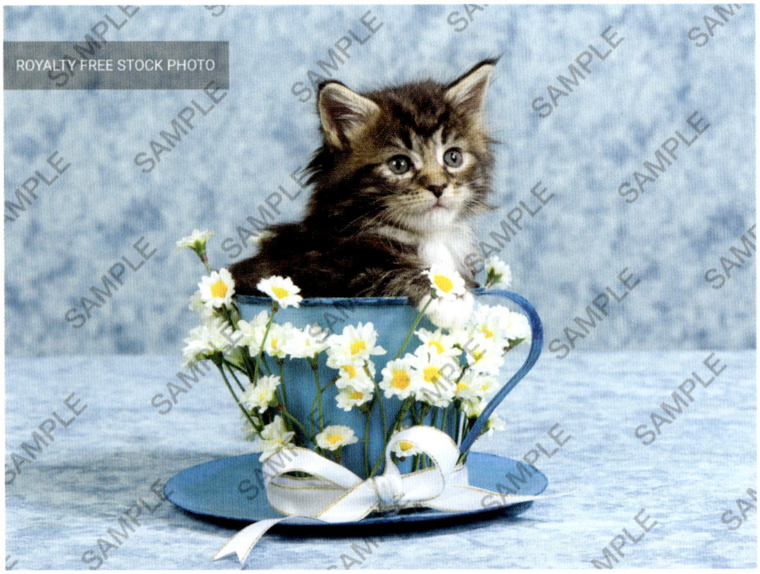

A CAT HAVING A LITTLE THINK WHILE RESTING ON A SKYLIGHT ON A HOT SUMMER'S DAY

Fig. 113

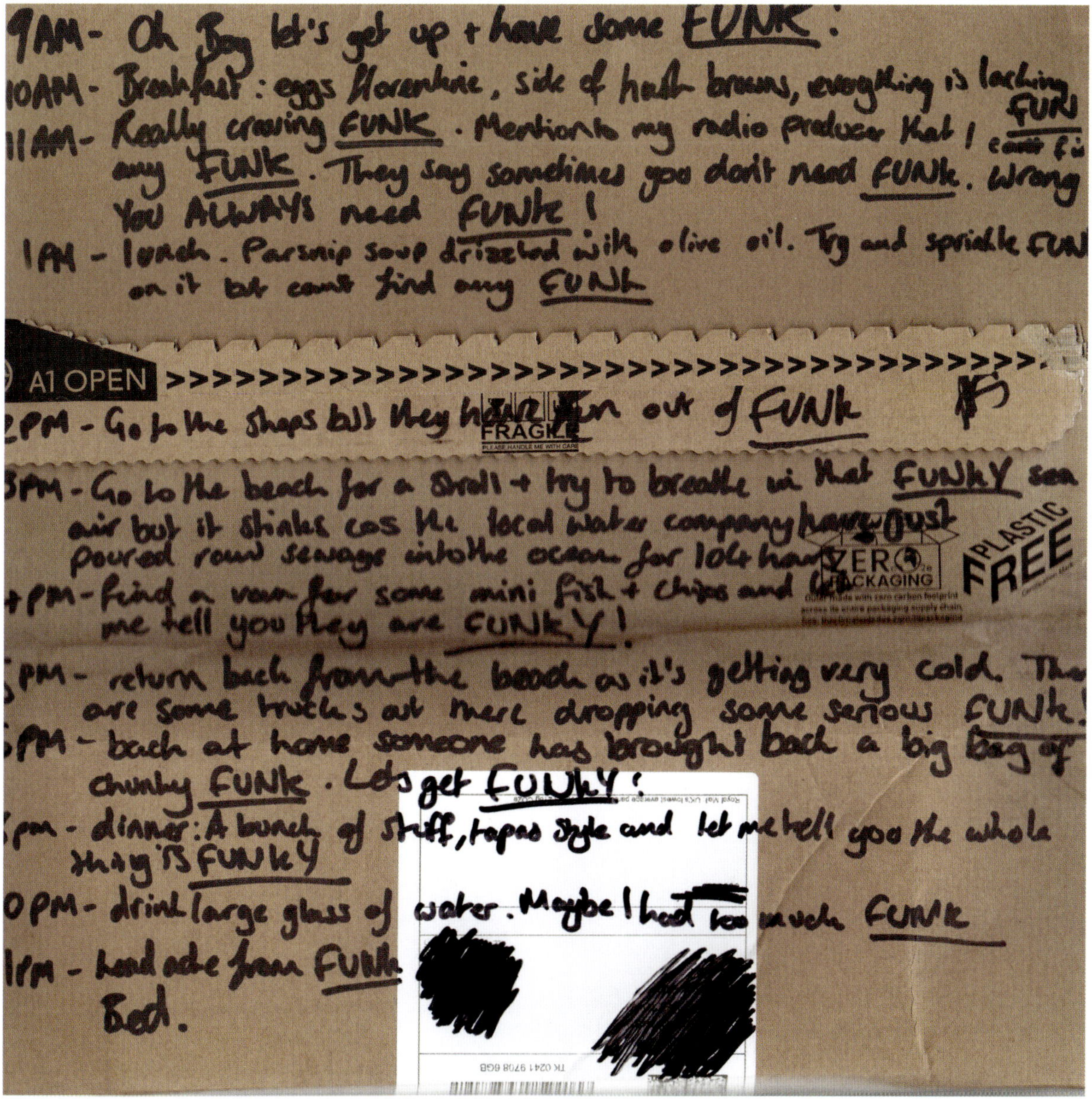
9AM - Oh Boy let's get up + have some FUNK!
10AM - Breakfast: eggs florentine, side of hash browns, everything is lacking FUN
11AM - Really craving FUNK. Mention to my radio producer that I can't find any FUNK. They say sometimes you don't need FUNK. Wrong You ALWAYS need FUNK!
1PM - lunch. Parsnip soup drizzled with olive oil. Try and sprinkle FUN on it but can't find any FUNK
A1 OPEN >>.
2PM - Go to the shops but they have run out of FUNK
FRAGILE
PLEASE HANDLE ME WITH CARE
3PM - Go to the beach for a stroll + try to breathe in that FUNKY sea air but it stinks cos the local water company have just poured raw sewage into the ocean for 104 hours
4PM - find a van for some mini fish + chips and let me tell you they are FUNKY!
ZERO PACKAGING
PLASTIC FREE
5PM - return back from the beach as it's getting very cold. There are some trucks out there dropping some serious FUNK!
6PM - back at home someone has brought back a big bag of chunky FUNK. Let's get FUNKY!
8pm - dinner: A bunch of stuff, tapas style and let me tell you the whole thing IS FUNKY
10PM - drink large glass of water. Maybe I had too much FUNK
11PM - headache from FUNK
Bed.
[redacted]
TK 0241 9708 6GB

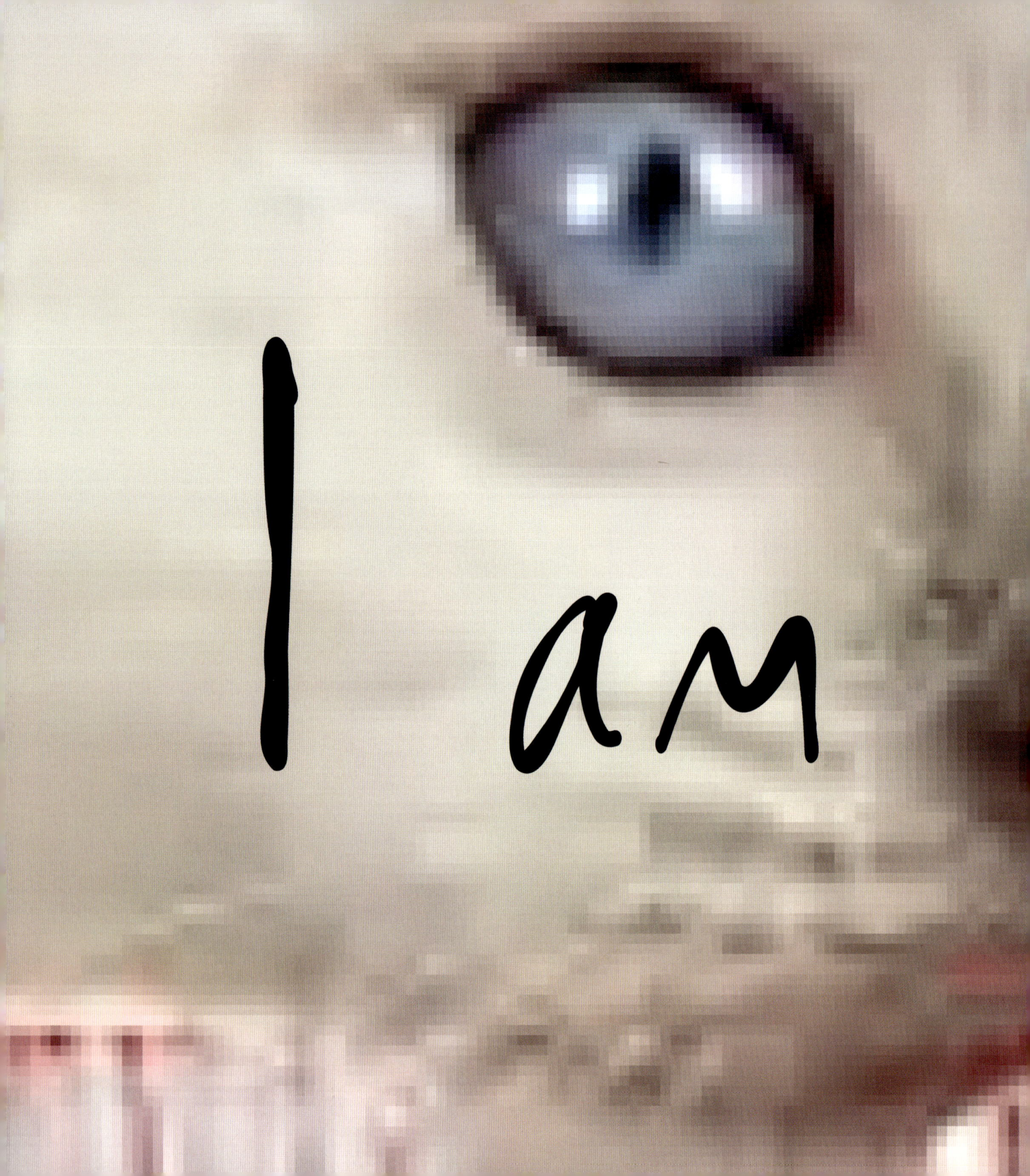
I am

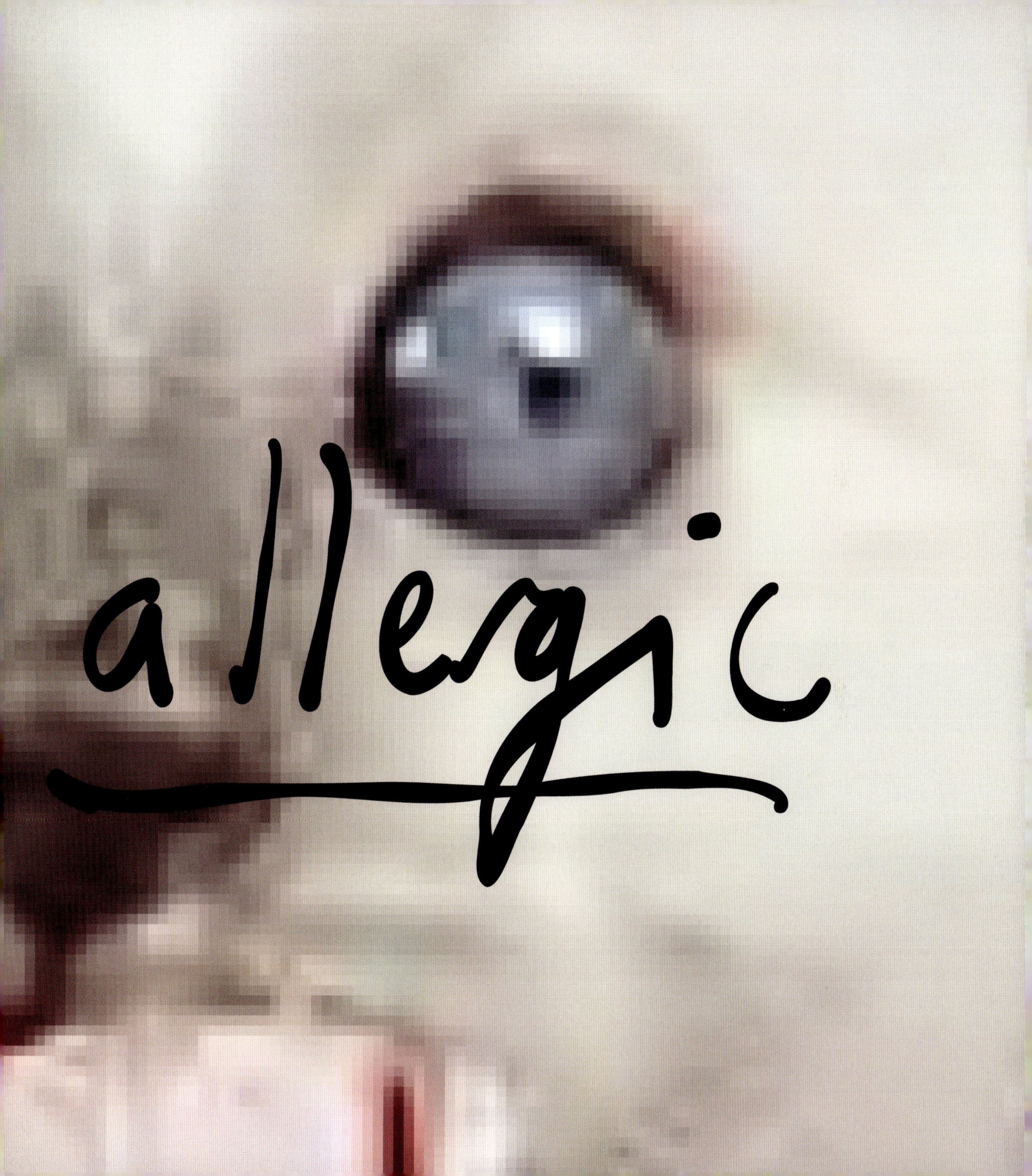
allergic

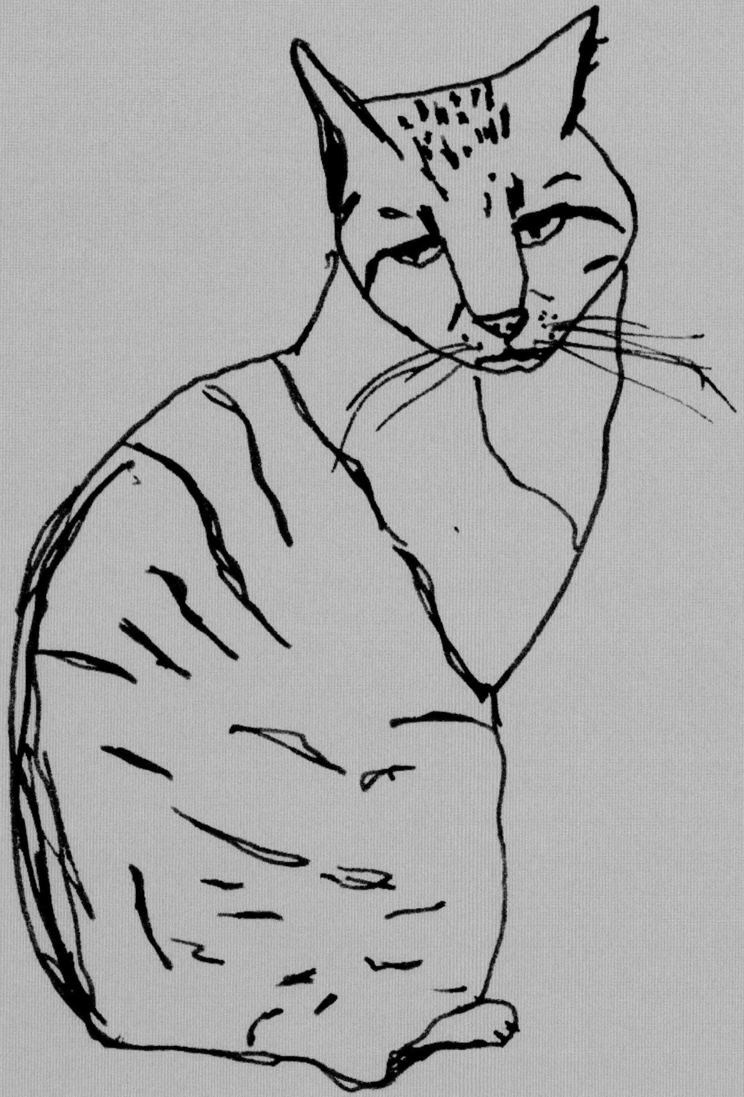

NADINE DORRIES

Fig. 114 A portrait I did of Nadine Dorries that was commissioned by [redacted] Rees-[redacted]
Fig. 115 *Judge a Book by Its Cover,* 2024, [redacted] on [redacted], [redacted] × [redacted] mm.
Fig. 116 Hanging with [redacted] backstage at the [redacted] Awards.

I met Nadine [redacted] at the [redacted] awards in [redacted]. She was there in her role as [redacted] for [redacted], and I was there supporting [redacted] [redacted] in her nomination for [redacted].

We were having [redacted] in the dinner hall, and I noticed Nadine across the room. [redacted], I approached and said, 'Hello, my [redacted] is Joe.'

'[redacted],' she said, [redacted].

'I wanted to ask you why you [redacted] me on [redacted]?' I asked.

'Oh, I didn't [redacted] [redacted]. My [redacted] is managed by [redacted].' I wasn't sure I believed her, but then her [redacted] came over to me to confirm [redacted].

At this point [redacted] came over and said, '[redacted]', to which Nadine responded, 'Actually, I think you'll find Boris is very [redacted] and the polls strongly support that. You can get [redacted].' I thought this was quite a [redacted] reaction, but she may have been referring to his penis. Nadine doubled down, explaining, 'If [redacted] says that [redacted] one more time, I will [redacted] until the fucking [redacted] is [redacted].'

I [redacted] her about the Hotpoint H55RM1110W1 Fridge in white but left [redacted] soon after and her security detail told me if I [redacted] then I could expect [redacted] to be [redacted]. I wish her all the best for the future.

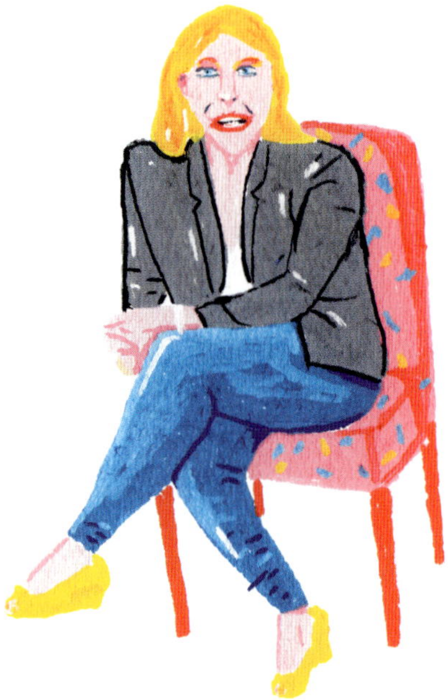

Fig. 114

Fig. 115

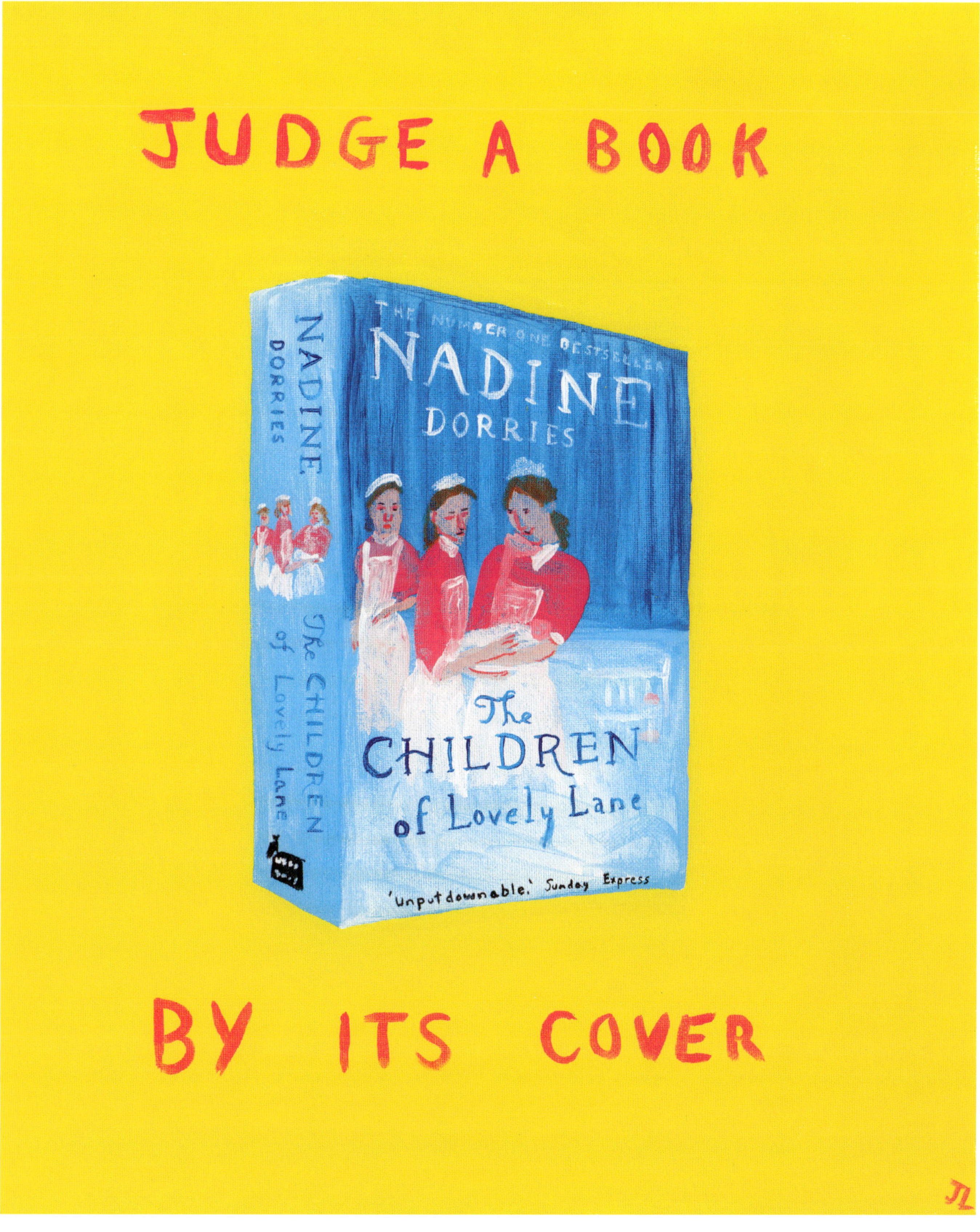
JUDGE A BOOK
NADINE DORRIES
The CHILDREN of Lovely Lane
NADINE DORRIES
The CHILDREN of Lovely Lane
'Unputdownable.' Sunday Express
BY ITS COVER

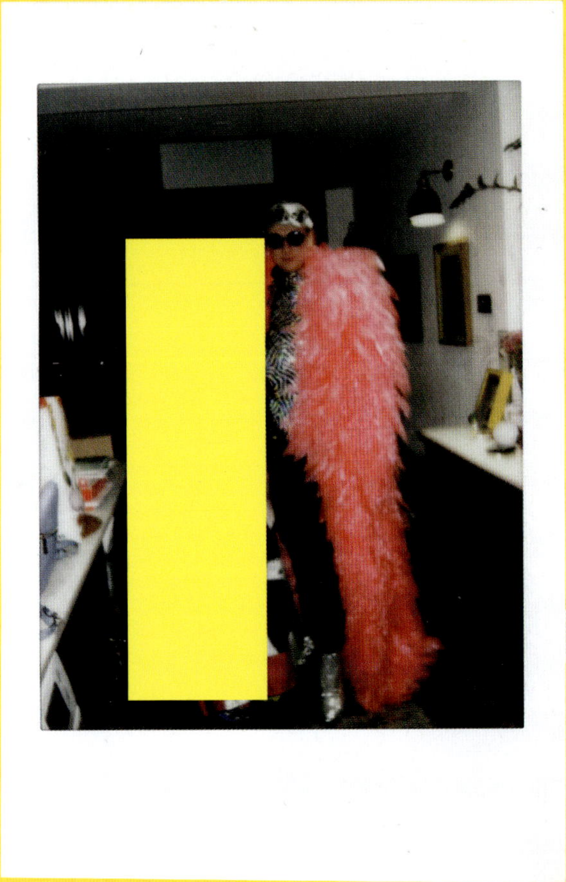

Fig. 116

Boris

very

— Nadine

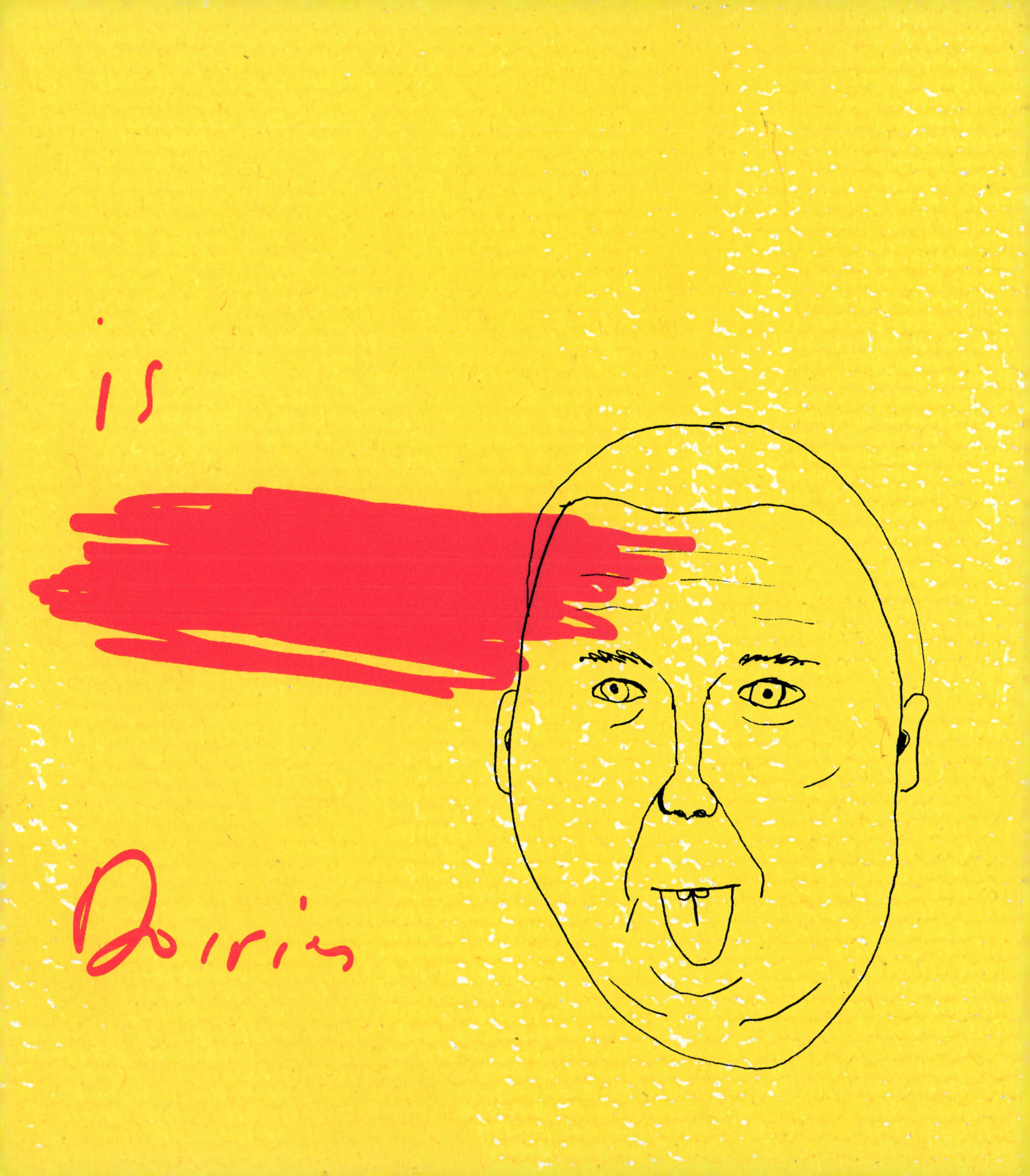
is
Boris

Do you know the human eye can see more shades of green than any other colour? Listen to me. Put that down. Did you hear what I just said?

GEORGE W BUSH

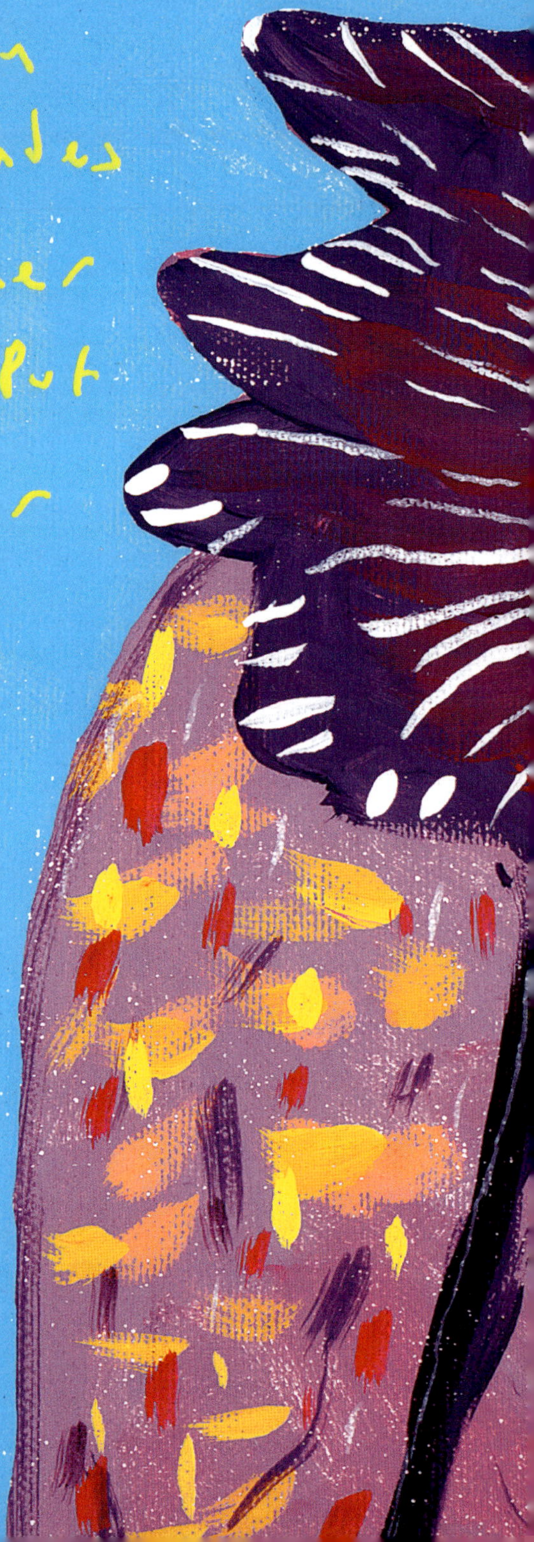

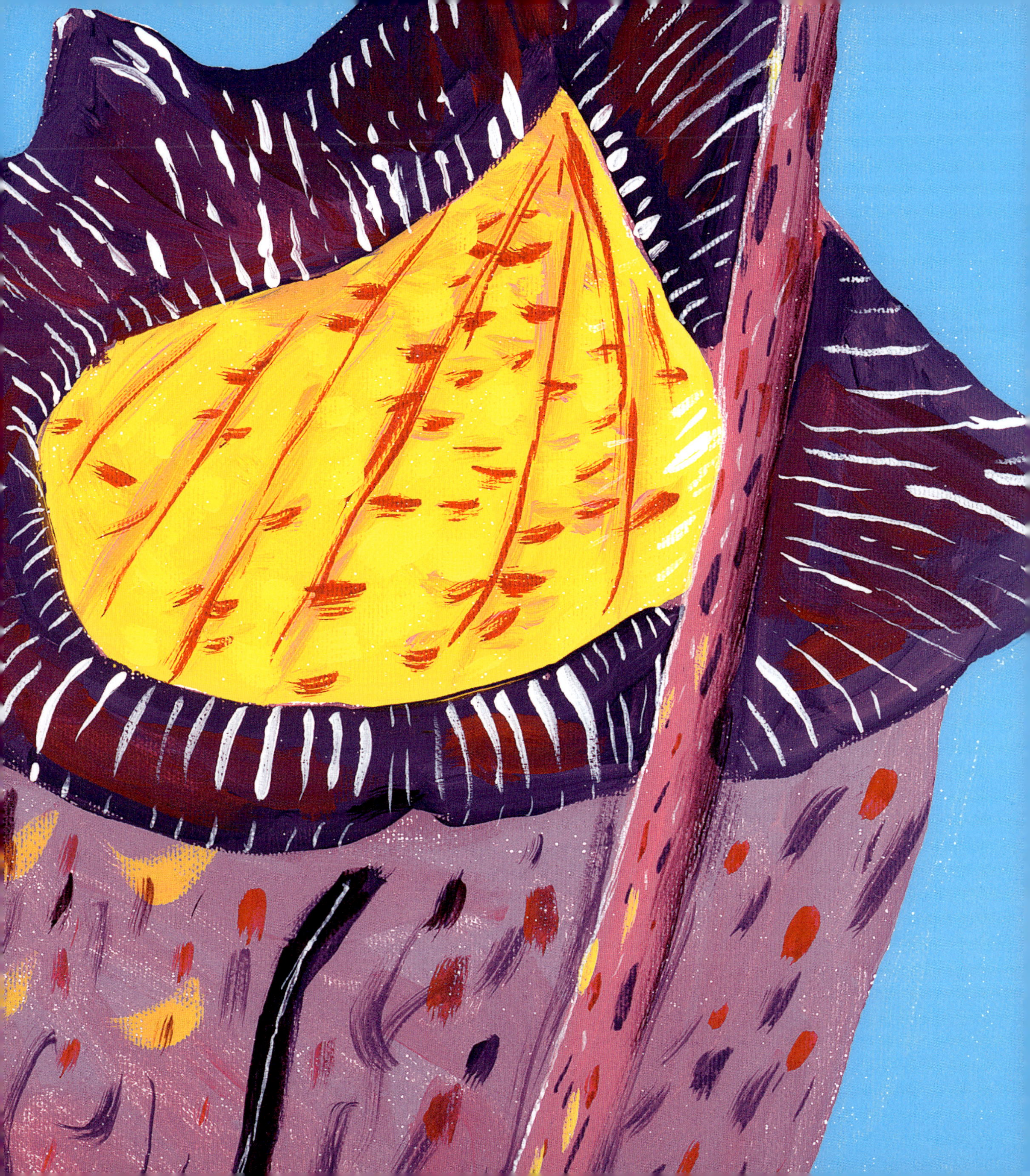

EAT SHIT

I have a confession. Back in 2020, in the heart of lockdown, the inhabitants of Number 10 Downing Street (i.e., our beloved government) were partying, in flagrant disregard of the strict stay-at-home rules they themself had imposed. At the time of writing, the official home of the prime minister remains the residence with the most fines for breaking these rules in the whole country. Like many, I condemned this behaviour publicly, saying that it seemed astonishing to me that so many people at the head of government could justify attending and/or holding booze-addled events when people were dying in the tens of thousands, often alone. Even more baffling to me (I said, when asked), was the long and slippery anal beads[1] of amnesiac ministers and elected MPs who were prepared to lie multiple times to the media, and therefore the public, about either that these events had been going on, or that they were in attendance. That they did it, that they lied about it, and that largely they got away with it, are all things that you might consider a national disgrace.

But, like Jesus and Osama bin Laden, I am not without my flaws.[2] I have been a hypocrite. I too have lied. Because during 2020 and 2021, I was also breaking the rules, almost on a daily basis, by holding wild and extravagant private events across England in the middle of the Covid lockdowns. These events, while never discovered by the British media, included some of the biggest names in show business, whom I will never name for moral reasons and also because of various legal restrictions and a letter from one saying they'd snap my legs 'like a pair of chicken drumsticks'. If I happen to write the names Tess Daly, Anne Robinson, Mr Motivator, Dannii Minogue, Chris Tarrant and Fiona Bruce in this paragraph that is pure coincidence and I am in no way saying that they were at these parties. If I also write the words 'naked conga' that is also irrelevant.

Anyway, at one bash in Kew Gardens, Fiona Bruce and I were given a tour of the glasshouses with a young horticulturalist called Jim. By doing so, Jim was taking great personal and professional risk, as Bruce is known to be erratic and physically unpredictable. I have changed his name to protect his identity and chose 'Jim' because it is far enough away from 'Tim', which may be his real name.

The glasshouses are extensive menageries which include every species of flora and fauna you could possibly imagine, unless you imagine ones that don't exist. Waterlilies, orchids, roses, cacti (and

1. I did not use the anal bead imagery when asked, this has just come to me.
2. People often wonder what it would be like to be without their flaws, but think far less often about what it would be like to be without their floors. In short: you would have nowhere to stand, or to put furniture; it would be a situation that is completely unsustainable.

Fig. 117 Boris Johnson's mixtape
Fig. 118 *Eat Shit,* 2023, acrylic on lizardskin, 12.4oz.

Fig. 117

Fig. 118

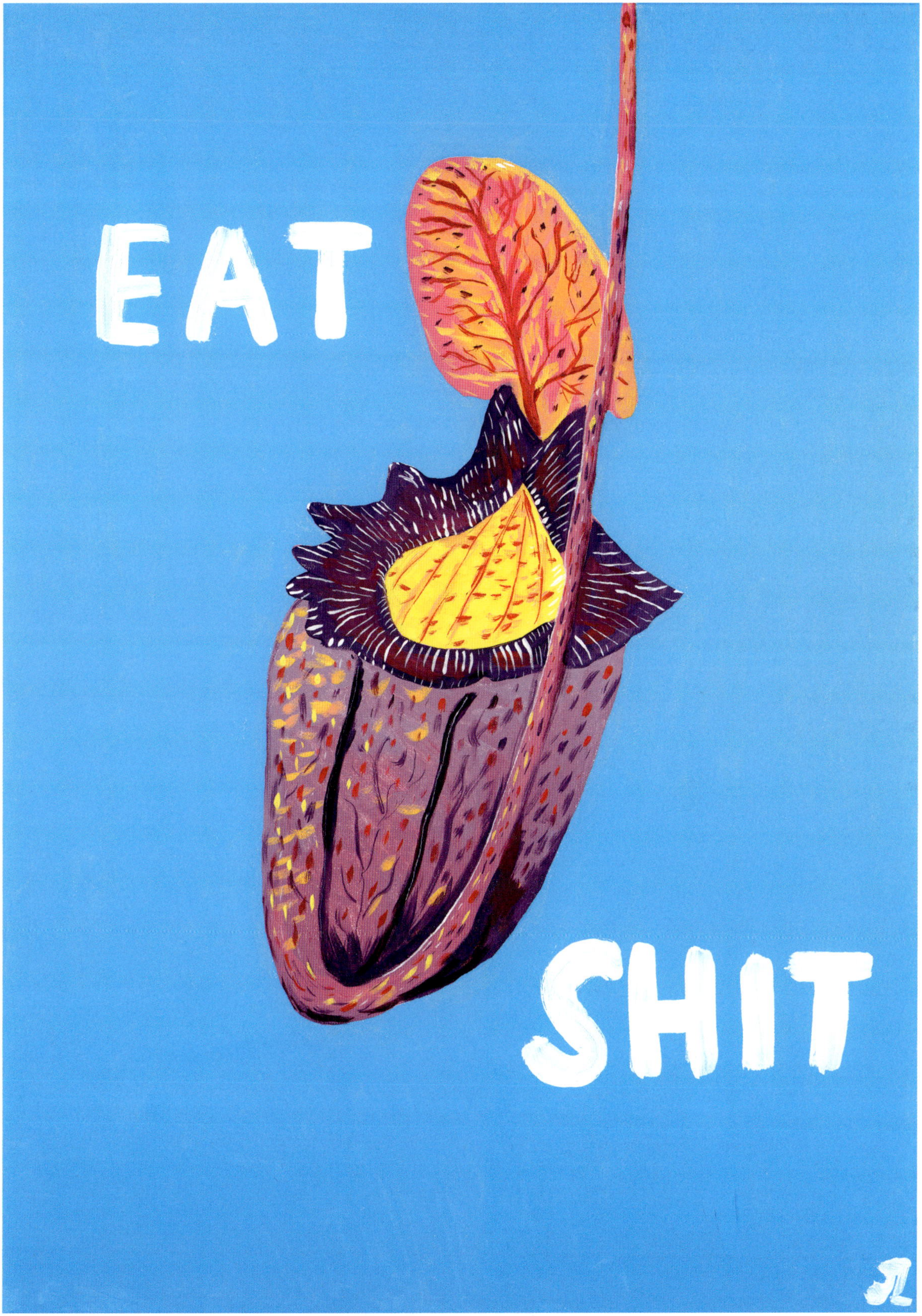

some of the shit ones as well like pansies and the ones you see on roundabouts in Tory-voting areas) – there is an almost unfathomable amount on display, a glorious testament to evolution. It made everything Monty Don has ever done seem, frankly, pathetic.

Many organisms have evolved alongside others in a symbiotic relationship. The most obvious of these relationships is Mel and Sue. The second most obvious is the flower and the bee. People often think this interaction is really cute, but I've always found it fairly humiliating that, to get a decent meal, bees have to put up with flowers spaffing on their back. We will never know which animals' backs Boris Johnson spaffed on to survive. I said this out loud to Jim and Fiona Bruce – Jim smiled a bit I think, and Fiona just pretended not to hear me, or perhaps did struggle to hear me over the bubbling of her shisha pipe.

Some plants have evolved in far more creative and complex ways to secure their survival. There's a plant with a bulbous root that has evolved with small channels throughout it; these mimic the tunnels of an ant nest, allowing any passing colony to easily set up home. The waste they leave there becomes the plant's fertiliser. It's strange to think of something needing piles of abandoned faecal matter to survive, until you remember the existence of GB News.

The plant Fiona was most drawn to was Nepenthes rajah, a type of pitcher plant that is native to Borneo. It evolved alongside mountain shrews, who like to lick the sweet nectar found in the lid. The nectar, while also being absolutely delicious, acts as a powerful laxative, prompting the shrew to take a big old dump right into the plant's gob. This dump acts as a nitrogen-rich fertiliser, so both the shrew and the plant get themselves a hearty meal.

'These guys,' said Jim joyfully, 'literally eat shit.'

I thought this was absolutely wonderful and quite beautiful, but Fiona's enthusiasm was on another level. 'What is it? The laxative?' she asked in that very Fiona Bruce way, gesturing towards it with her hand, as if probing a politician on *Question Time*.

'I'm not sure actually,' came Jim's response, 'but it sure is potent!'

'I need to know how much of it ...' she said, stuttering with excitement, 'how much of it ... that laxative ... that I can take away with me?'

'Oh, it can't be taken away, it's—' He was trying to be polite, but Fiona's excitement forced her to speak over him.

'I need to take it away with me, Jim. Tonight.' She was becoming very forceful. 'I will make it worth your while. Very, very lucrative.'

'Ah, but it's not for sale.' He wasn't backing down.

'I will change your life, young man. Do you know how long I've been in the television industry?'

Fig. 119 Nepenthes rajah specimen.

Fig. 120 The glasshouses at Kew Gardens. Later in the evening Tess Daley was found picking these leaves, muttering that she was going to feed them to Anton Du Beke.

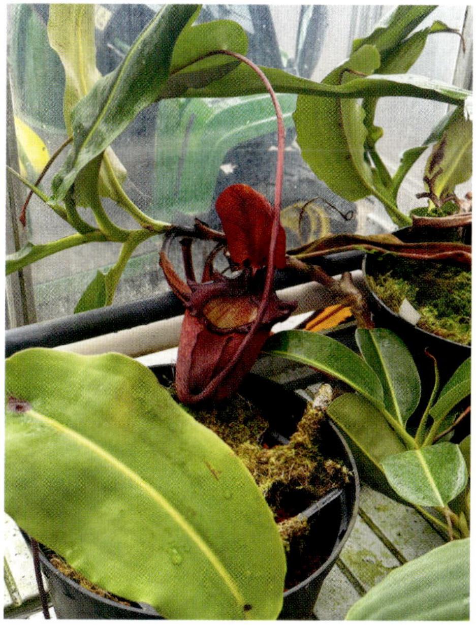

Fig. 119

Fig. 120

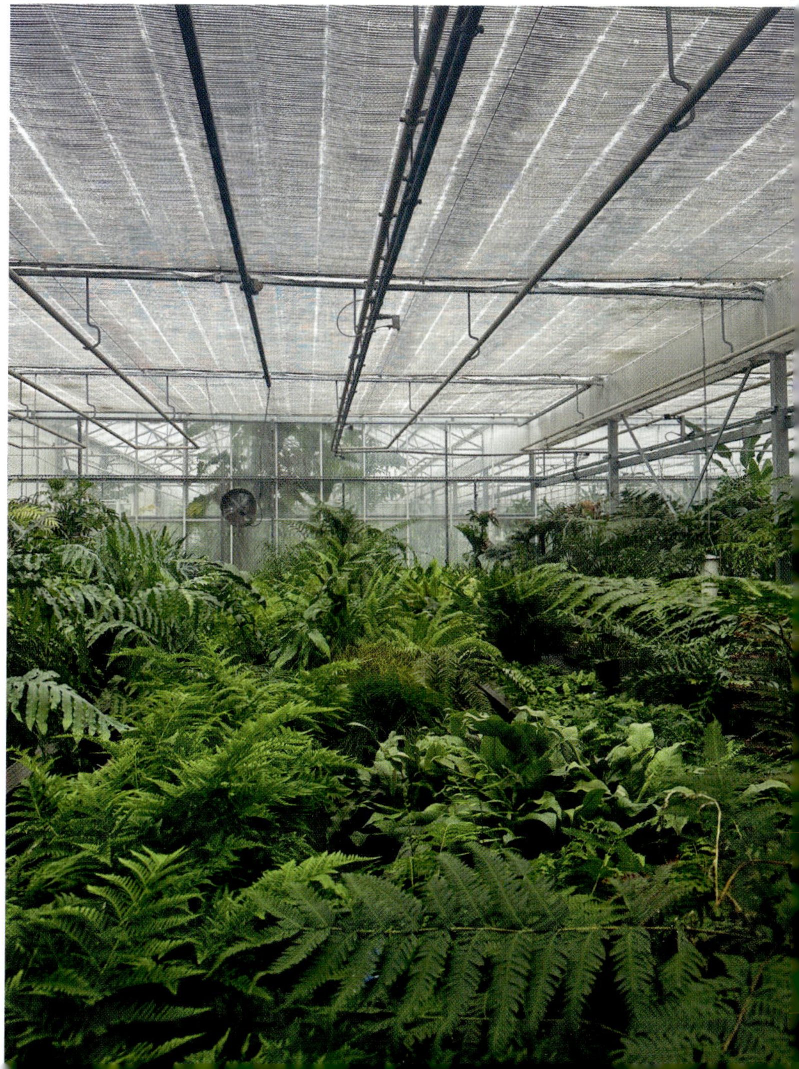

He shook his head. 'I'm sorry, I don't really watch television.'

'Longer than you've been having hot showers.' (That's not the correct phrase, but neither of us was brave enough to correct her.) 'And the one thing I have learnt through that extensive career, particularly on the *Antiques Roadshow*, is that everyone, EVERYONE, has a price.'

'I see,' he said.

'So. I ask again. How much for a swab of that sweet, delicious nectar?'

'I just can't …'

I felt awful for the lad. He was trying his best.

'Fifty grand. Fill up a small vile and I will give you fifty grand.'

He raised his hands as if to call some sort of time out.

'A hundred grand. Cash.'

'I'm sorry.' He shook his head once more.

I tried to soften the mood by saying, 'What do you even need that laxative for anyway? I don't want this party to be any more explosive for the British press than it already is!' Jim laughed, out of desperation more than anything. Fiona spun on her heels and jabbed her finger in my face.

'Maybe you should keep your nose out of it, pig boy.'

These words – which I have never been called before or since – were literally spat into my face. I knew this because a small cube of the smoked salmon blini canapés we had served earlier was projected into my eye. Reader, I have never been more scared in my life.

She spun back round and stormed out of the glasshouse, pushing over a couple of plant pots as she went and shouting something like, 'I will get it, it will be mine.' I looked at Jim and shrugged as if to say, 'What was all that about?' He returned a similar, concerned glance.

'Shall we continue?' he asked, unsure of how to proceed. I was genuinely interested so suggested we did, at least to take his mind off the whole debacle. But no sooner had we got into the tropical, jungle themed conservatory did we hear a clang, heavy footsteps, and the return of Bruce – this time with Mr Motivator for back-up.

'Just give her the laxative,' he said unconfidently, clearly also terrified. 'She's offering a good price.'

She was waving a thick envelope in the air that she had got out of her bag. 'I didn't want to have to do this, but here we are. Two hundred, two hundred grand. Unmarked notes.' She thrust it towards him. 'Don't make the biggest mistake of your life, Jim.'

No one could blame him, but I was surprised to see him take it. He managed to fill up about half a shot glass' worth of the stuff, with Bruce leering over him the whole time, salivating and whispering, 'All of it, every last drop.' After about twenty minutes of teasing as much out of the four or so specimens they had, he sealed the small ampoule and handed it to her.

Fig. 121 An artist's depiction of the money handed over by Fiona Bruce.

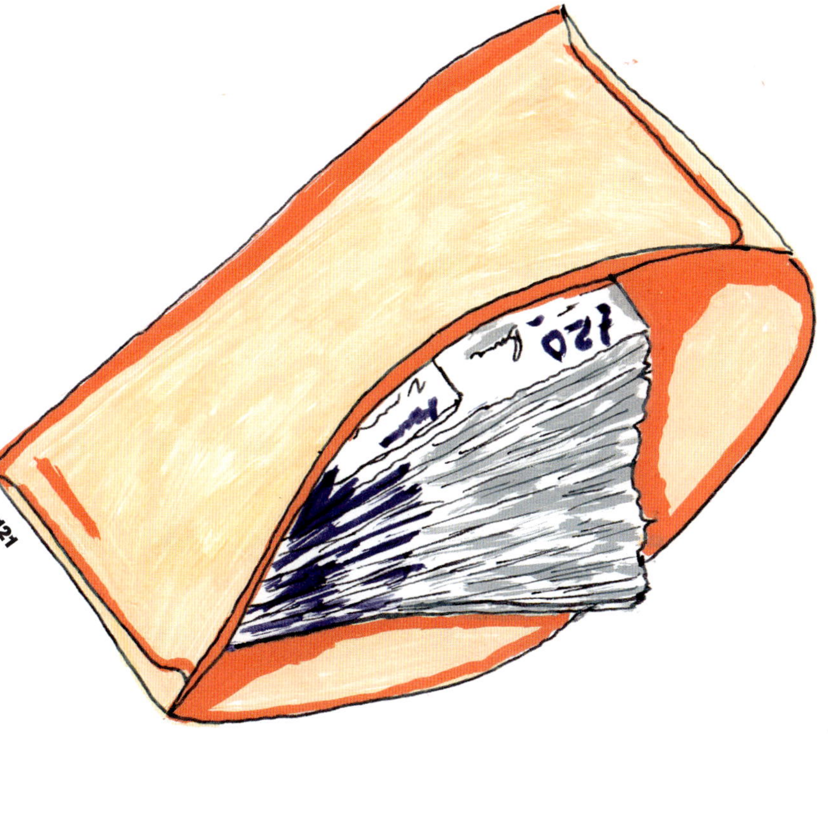

Fig. 121

'Good,' she said, her voice deeper than I have ever heard it before. 'Very, very good.'

I'll never be entirely sure what she wanted it for, but what I do know is that later that year, just before Christmas, everyone who attended the party received a beautifully packaged panettone, with a note that stated it was: 'Homemade, delicious and absolutely unique, using my secret ingredient. Love, Fiona'. Suspecting foul play, I left mine on the side until well into the new year, before chucking it out with the remaining festive leftovers. Months later, I read in an interview in one of the weekend supplements that Anne Robinson is a huge fan of panettone.

This painting is a tribute to that troubling chapter in the Covid lockdowns: a painting of the glorious Nepenthes rajah that evolved happily alongside a humble mountain shrew, and which I suspect Fiona Bruce used to give Anne Robinson the worst shits of her entire life.

Fig. 122 Given as a gift to Mr Motivator as an apology for his traumatic experience: *Leave It With Me*, 2023, acrylic on 4 × 4, approx. 4 × 4.

Fig. 123 The card sent with Fiona Bruce's home-made panettone. I am fairly sure the handwriting does not belong to Fiona, and suspect it may in fact belong to the TV chef Antony Worrall Thompson.

Fig. 124 Fiona Bruce's schedule (in her own words).

Fig. 122

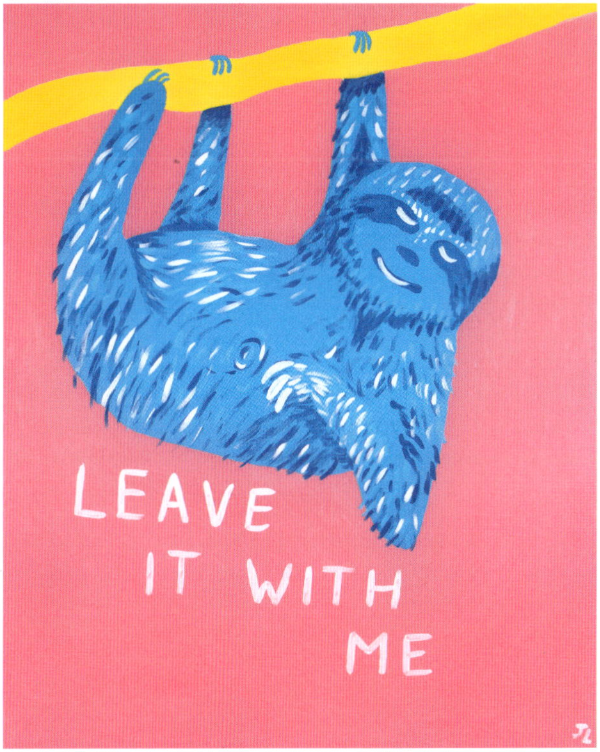

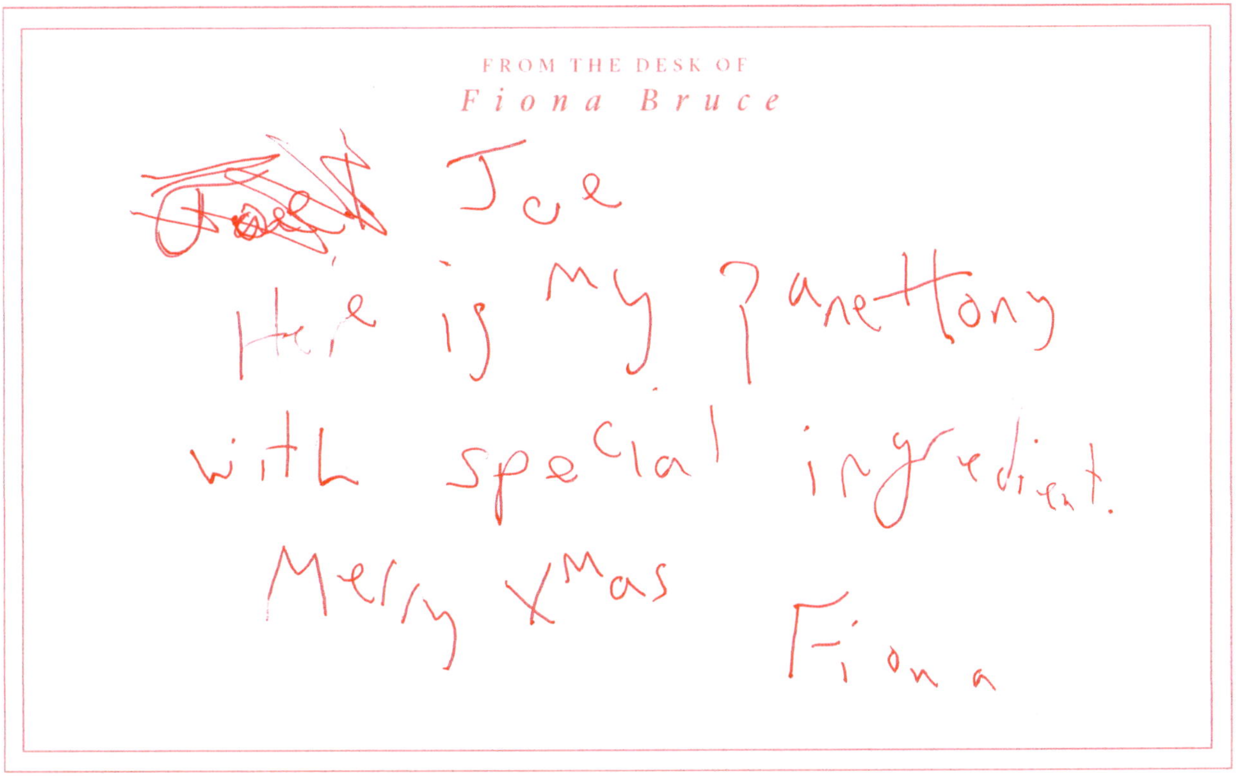
FROM THE DESK OF
Fiona Bruce

~~[illegible]~~ Joe

Here is my panettony
with special ingredient.
Merry Xmas
Fiona

Fig. 123

4pm now on Rita, queen of speed. While accelerating to 100 km/h in 2.5 secs send an imessage to Jane Hill with skull emoji

430 pm. hot donuts

5.00 pm I see Naga Munchetty has replied and try and read the message but lose my phone on a sharp bend on Runaway Mine Train

6 pm am told they cannot look for my phone until the park has closed for the day. I am furious

7 pm corn on the cob at Woodcutter Bar & Grill in silence

11 pm finally got phone back. It is sticky and smells of Fanta. Desperately send message to Sally Nugent explaining the horror of my day and asking if she's learnt to read autocue yet

11.30pm sleep

X but realise I'm blocked

Fig. 124

9am arrive at Alton Towers

9.30 am Start with a ride on Oblivion. In the queue I send a quick message to Victoria Derbyshire telling her that last night's interview with the Shadow Foreign Minister was 'subpar' but explain I am telling her this to be 'constructive'.

10.30 am Just being locked into the front of Nemesis, a short delay while they clean up sick so I send Clive Myrie a WhatsApp that includes the words 'betrayed' and 'kneecaps'

12pm quick Insta DM to Naga Munchetty in the queue for THI3TEEN saying how I watch her 'every morning' and have some thoughts

1pm lunch at Woodcutter's Bar & Grill, attempt to DM Mishal Husain on Twitter but realise I am blocked

3pm While enjoying Congo River Rapids send an email to BBC director general saying Reeta Chakrabarti microwaves eggs in the newsroom.

newsroom.

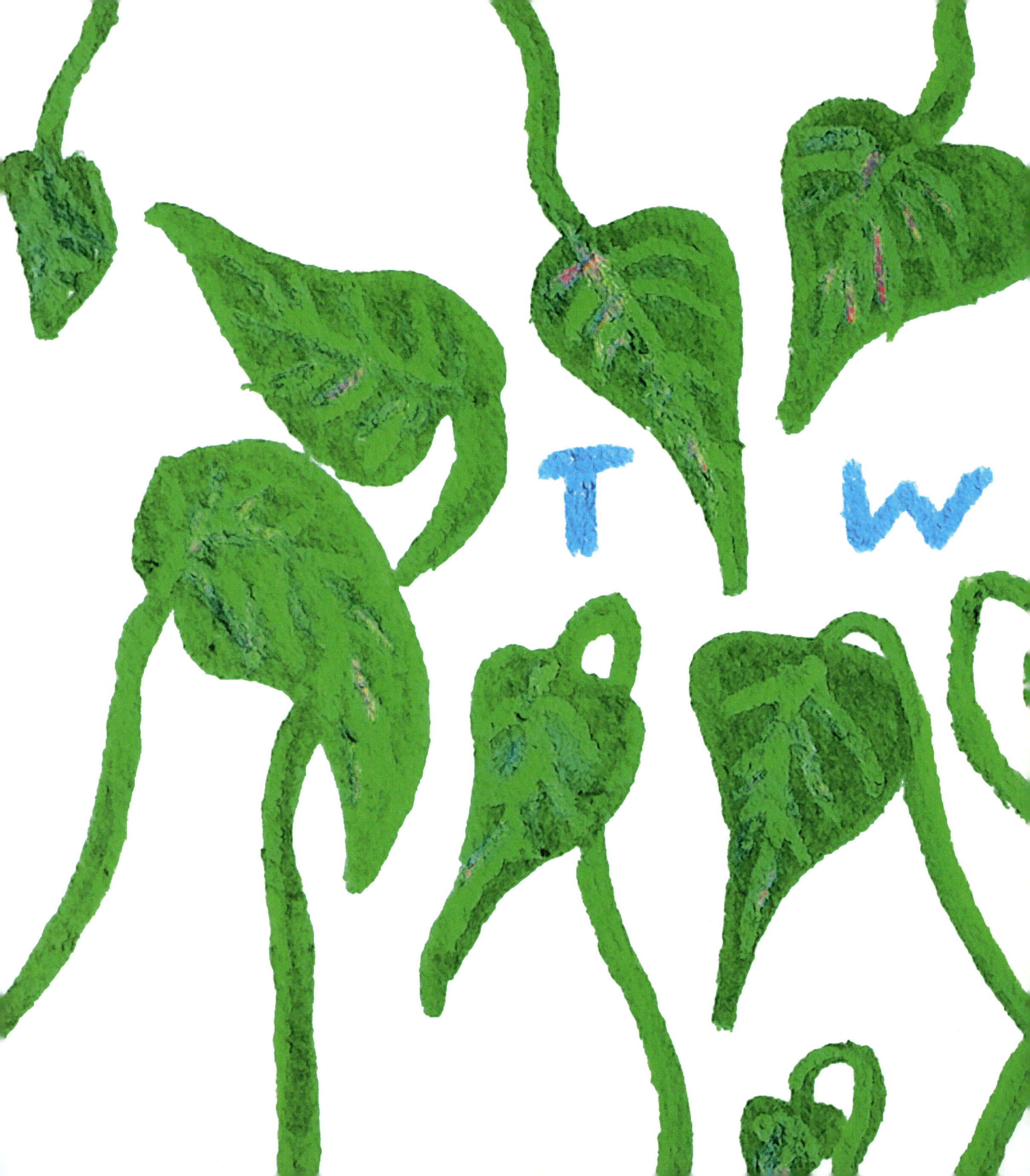
T
W

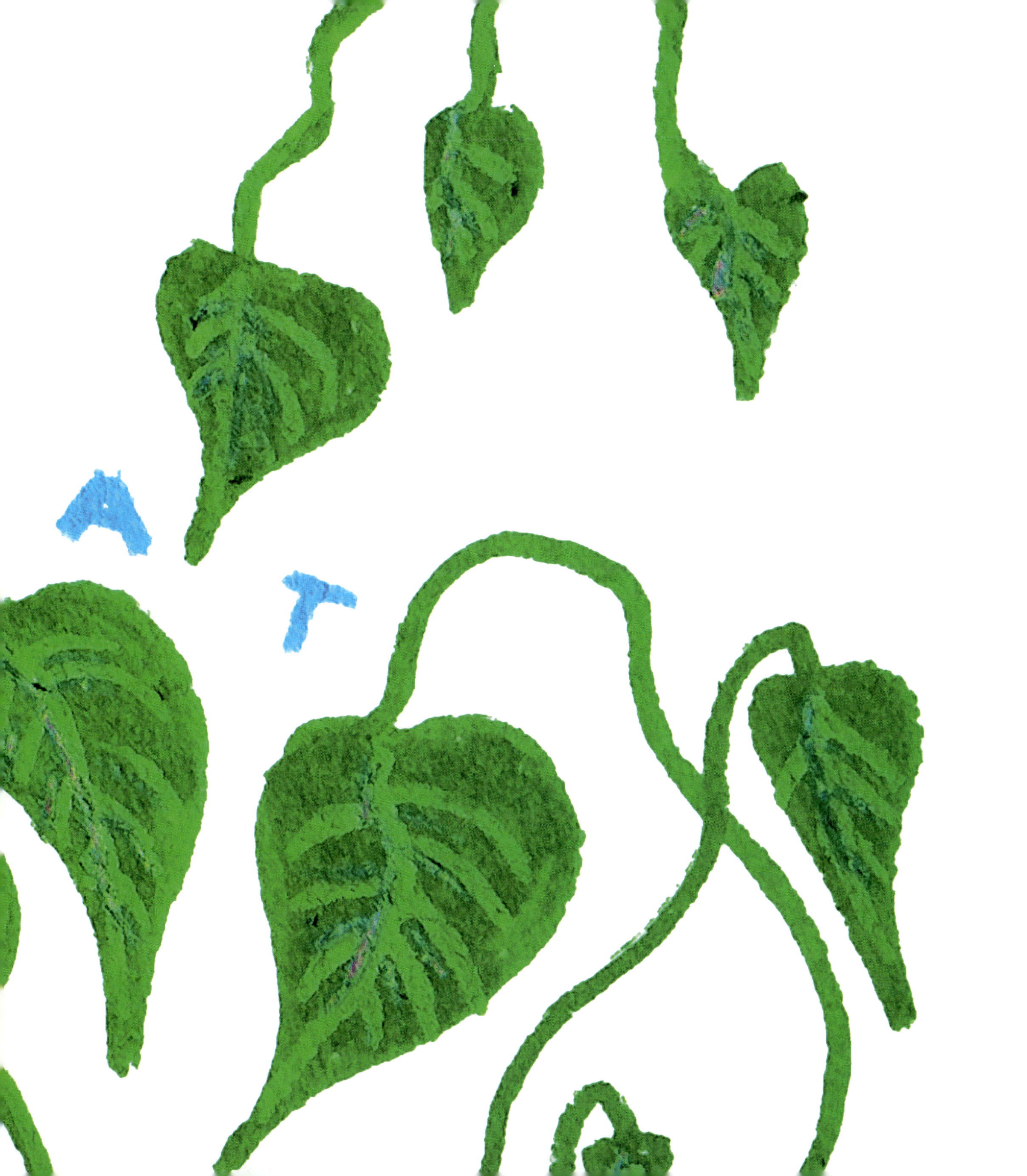
A
T

LIFE GAVE YOU LEMONS

Fig. 125 Tim Lovejoy's note to Simon Rimmer.
Fig. 126 *Life Gave You Lemons,* 2023, watercolour on owl, 14 × 23m.

This was a commission for *Sunday Brunch* star Tim Lovejoy. I heard he gifted it to Simon Rimmer for a birthday, with a card that read, 'I run this show, never forget that, kitchen bitch.'

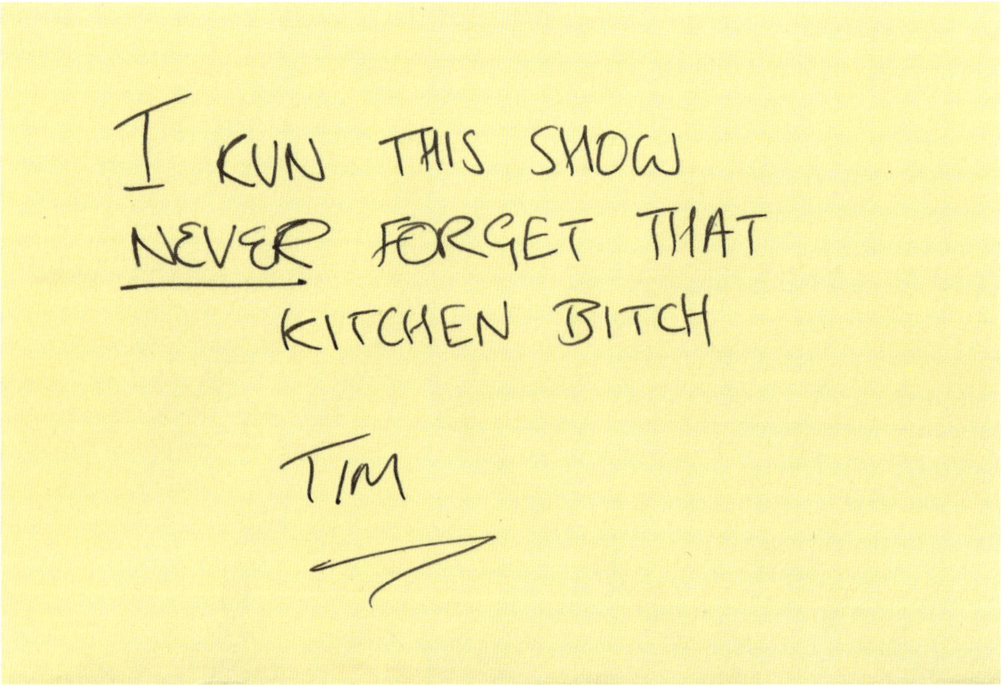

Fig. 125

Fig. 126

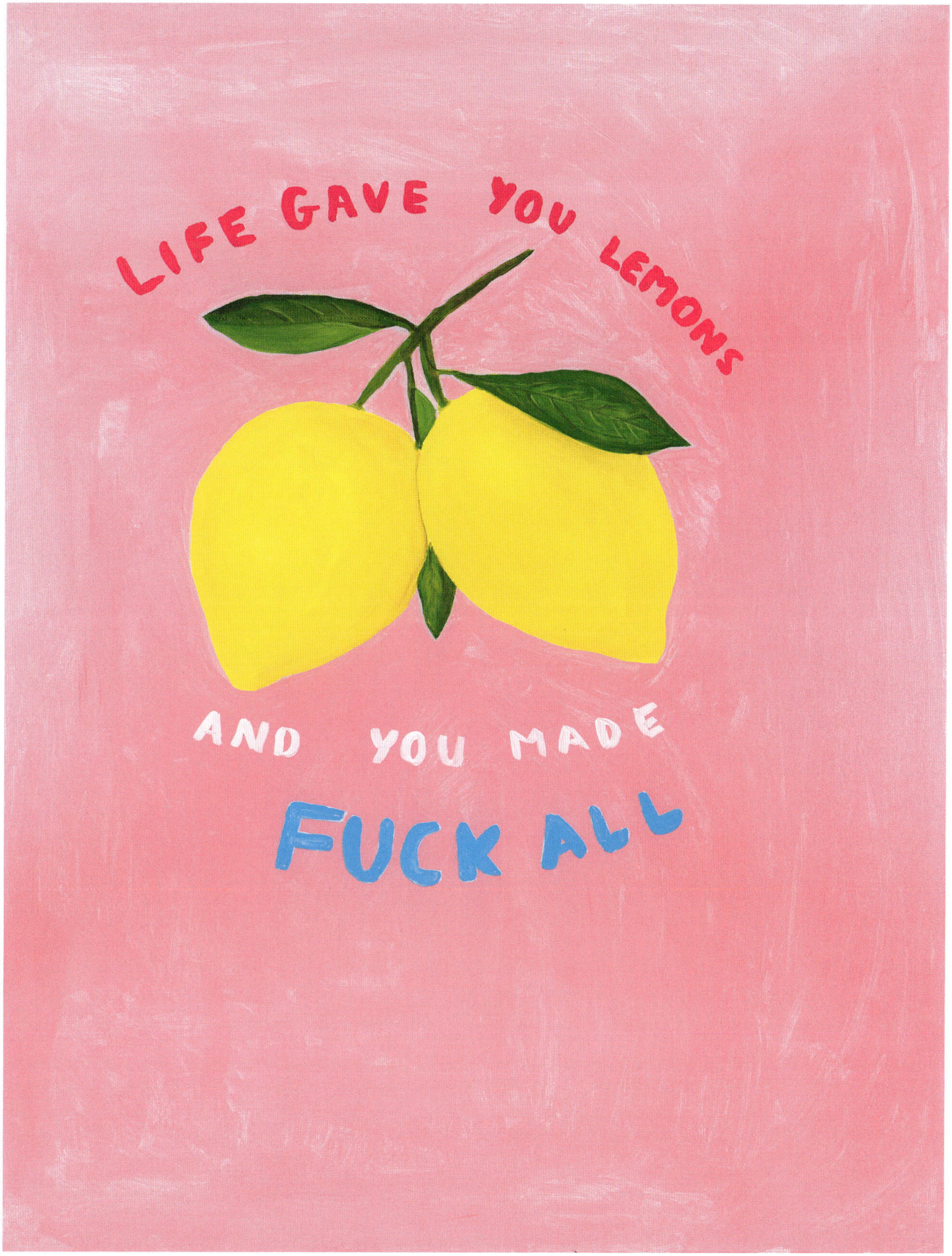

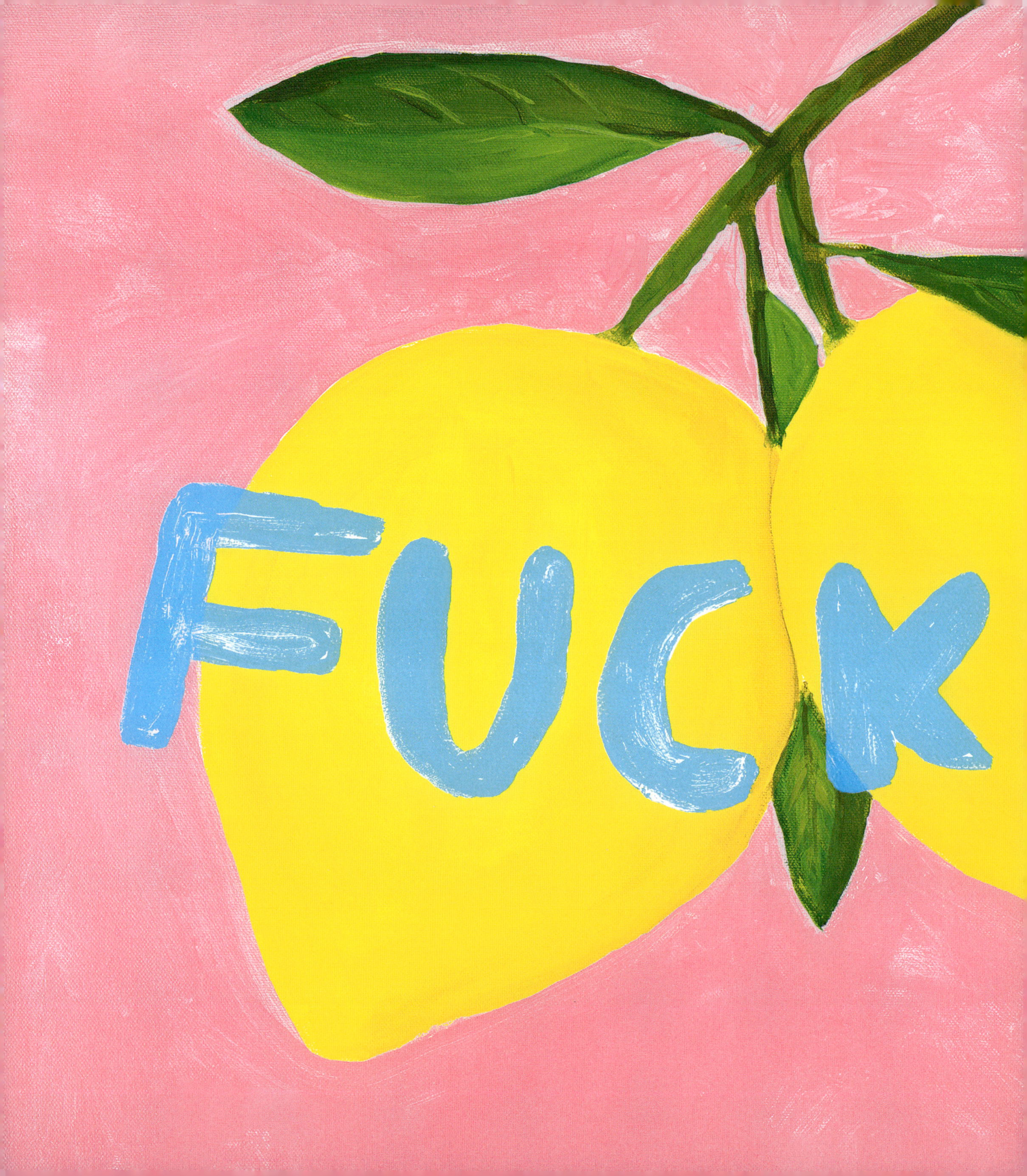
FUCK

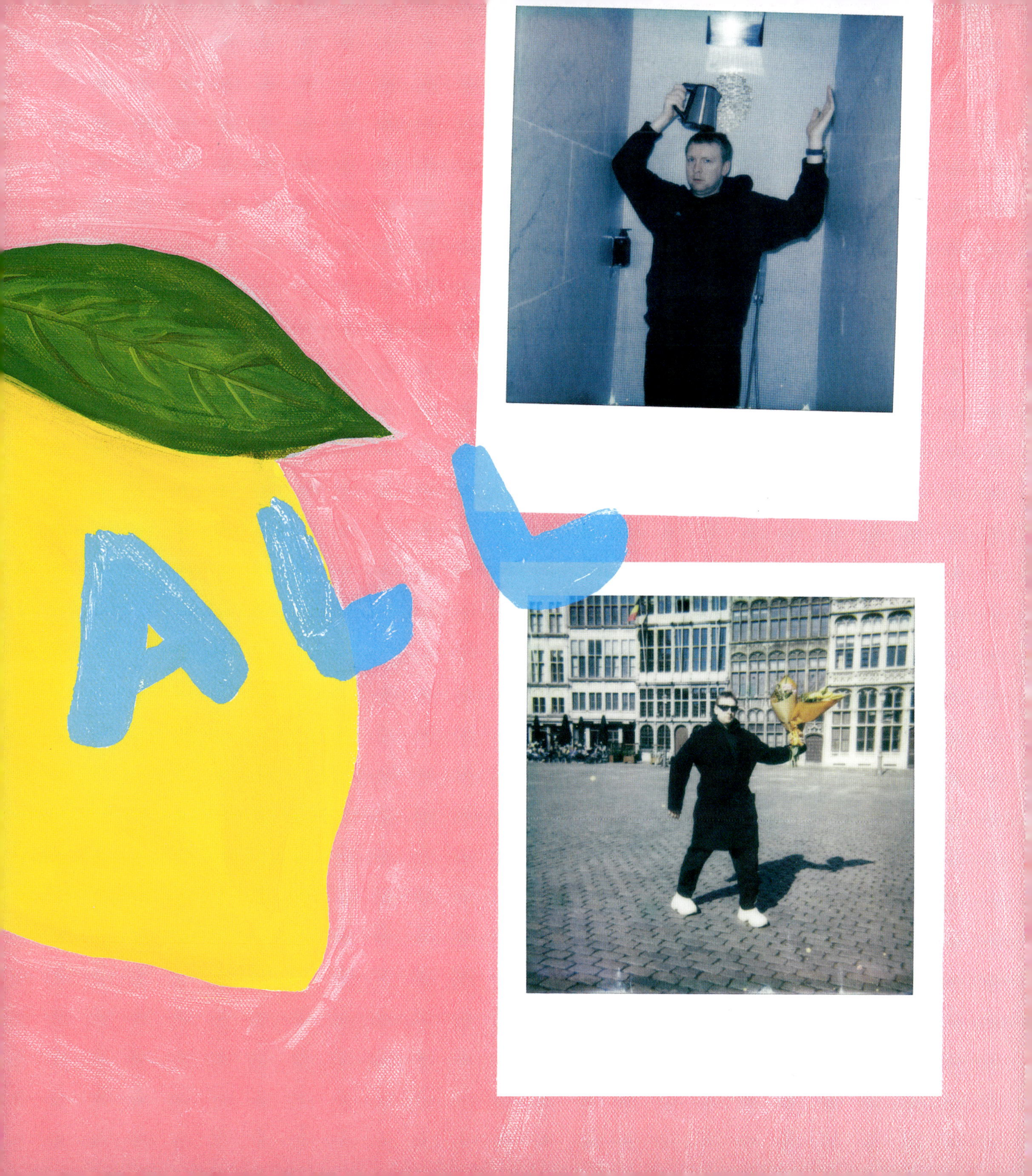
ALL

TONY ROBBINS

1. '*heat*' uncapitalised at their request.

Fig. 127 *Tony Robbins,* 2024, fake tan on bin, 32 × 48cm.

It's not every day a man dressed in all black knocks on your door and tells you he's going to take you to a secret tropical location in a private jet to meet his client, and that it will be 'worth your while financially, as in there will be money, a cash payment is what I mean'. That day was Wednesday, 34 June, I think, and like every Wednesday Dame Helen Mirren was sat in my kitchen, uninvited, drinking a glass of Fanta fruit twist and eating a bowl of chicken noodle soup and a Babybel.

'I have been called to a secret tropical location on urgent business,' I said, pouring my half-eaten portion of chicken noodle soup in with hers.

'This shit again,' I heard her say as I slammed the front door behind me. I knew full well that I would return to find all my crockery smashed and a 'deposit' in the tumble drier.

I've never been on a private jet before so didn't know there is a separate entrance at Birmingham Airport for dignitaries, rich people and drug kingpins. Dame Helen has repeatedly mentioned the VIP entrance at Heathrow in what I take to be a form of bragging, but I know she refuses to travel from Birmingham Airport because she finds the mood of the security staff to be unpredictable. Also, someone working in the Burger King there once called her 'Judi' and she had a breakdown.

Most people would have been delighted to have the unique and luxurious experience of a private entrance. I did try to enjoy it but, if I'm honest, I was annoyed, because when I get a flight I really like to stop off and get some magazines from WHSmith, browse the bathroom miniatures in Boots and have a couple of plates of tapas at the All Bar One (I call it the 'microwave medley'). Instead, they just walked us straight onto the private jet where they only had copies of yacht magazines and stuff about cars – neither of which are for me because I like a *heat* magazine,[1] *Homes & Gardens*, *Closer*, *TV Times* and a tasteful porno. I also like to adopt the WHSmith checkout machine's suggestion that I suddenly buy a 400g bar of Dairy Milk for no apparent reason, but on this occasion was forced to eat the Charbonnel et Walker luxury chocolates on board.

Unimpressed with the magazines, I was forced to talk to the dude in all black; a look I normally associate with Johnny Cash, Death and Rylan. I asked him what his name was and where we were going and who we were going to meet (some people would have asked these questions prior to boarding a flight, but you need to factor in how grateful I was for an excuse to get away from Helen Mirren).

Fig. 127

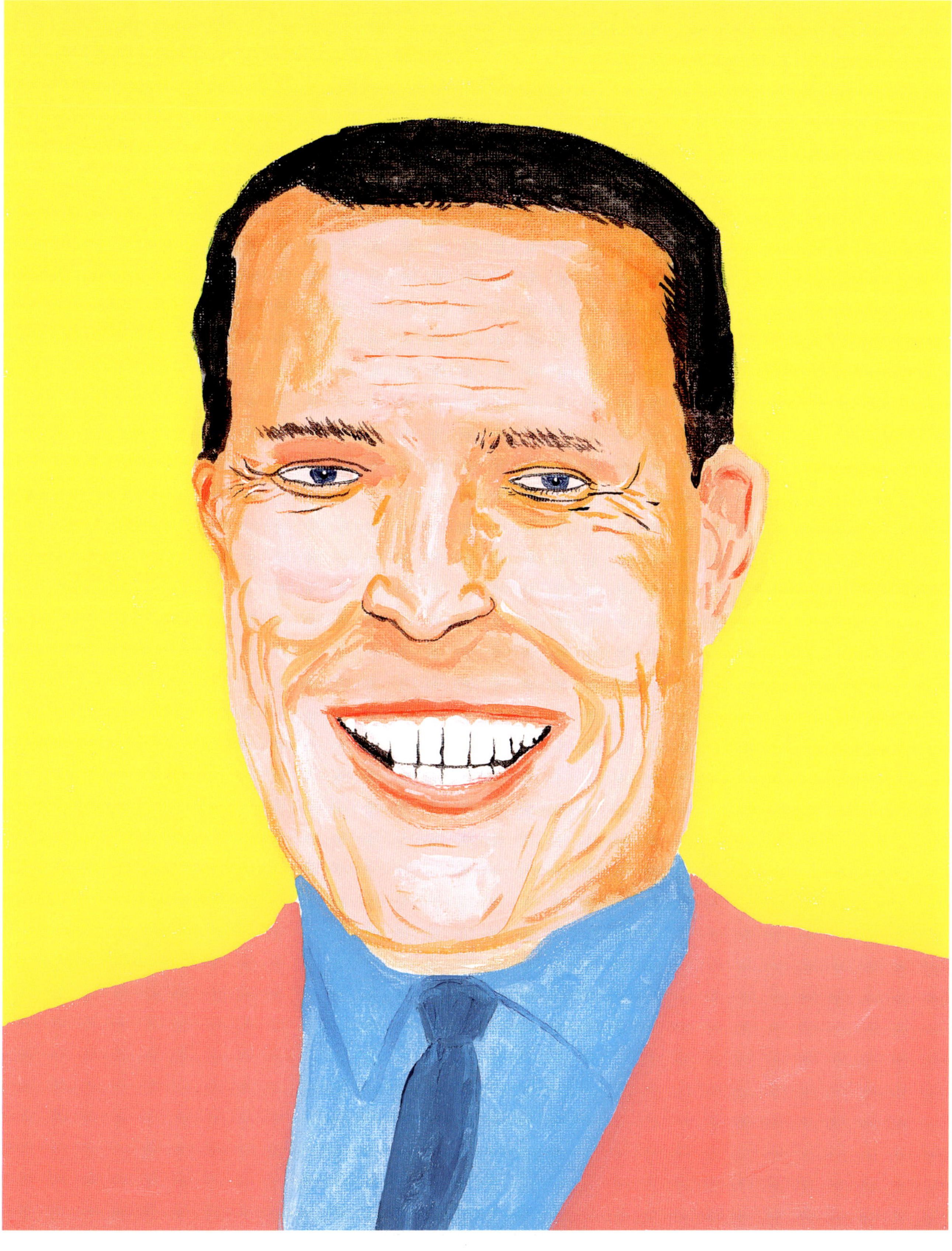

He was a man of medium height with a bald head[1] and those glasses that supposedly become sunglasses in sunlight but in practice turn to a dark ash in the meagre presence of a tea light. What I'm saying is, he is the sort of man TK Maxx would see coming. He refused to tell me anything and just said 'Call me JPEG', which clearly wasn't his real name. Anyway, I knew we were in Fiji 'cause JPEG obviously forgot to tell the pilot to keep quiet and so when we landed he said 'Welcome to Fiji' really loudly and from that I worked out we were in Fiji. For the experienced traveller, interpreting these clues becomes second nature.

We drove silently[2] in a blacked-out Mercedes Vito for some time, perhaps forty minutes,[3] with me in the back seat and JPEG up front with a driver who said his name was MP4. Cerulean beaches, cerulean palm trees and adorable cerulean wooden huts passed by. It is possible some of this detail may be inaccurate, as I was wearing tinted glasses, the colour of which was cerulean. Soon, we arrived at a large hotel resort with several cerulean sports cars lined up in a crescent moon driveway, which appeared to me to be cerulean.[4]

I was still trying to work out who it was I was supposed to be meeting; from my deductions, I'd narrowed it down to someone who was rich and who also lived at a resort in Fiji. Of the available possibilities, it all seemed too elaborate for Gwyneth Paltrow and not elaborate enough for Natalie Cassidy. JPEG walked me beyond a neat marble reception area where a very well-dressed and attractive woman said, 'Welcome, Mr License. My name is PDF, anything I can do to help, just ask.' I had worked it out – everyone's names had been replaced with file types. This was reassuring, as I had begun to worry I was suffering from some sort of extended neurological episode involving cerulean.

I was led down a narrow stone path lined with green palm trees to a large white beach hut and sat down on a wicker chair looking out over the cerulean ocean (I had removed my glasses by this point but the ocean is naturally cerulean). JPEG handed me a small cup of a mystery drink (which I'm fairly sure was a warm glass of Gary Barlow wine, with its unmistakable mouthfeel of paint thinner) and said, 'Don't move, he'll be through shortly.' He then just stood and looked out at the sea with his hands behind his back, whistling the theme tune to *Byker Grove*. The guy was weird as fuck.

A buggy driven by a gorgeous blonde[5] pulled up, and off the buggy stepped someone I instantly recognised as Tony Robbins, the richest, best and most famous motivational speaker in the world.[6]

'A million thanks to you, ZIP,' he said to the blonde, as she sped away. 'The ass on that!' he said to JPEG as she drove away. 'What an ass. Ten out of ten ass.'

1. I mean that his own head was bald, not that he was travelling with a separate bald head somehow in his possession, rolling in his hand luggage like a bowling ball made of flesh and bone – I know that might seem so obvious that it's not worth pointing out but I find clearing these things up well in advance saves me from having to answer confused letters later.

2. We weren't speaking, but the car was making a noise.

3. On reflection, I think it might've been forty-five minutes.

4. For the benefit of any untrained, non-artists reading this book: blue. (*see* **Fig. 128**)

5. For the avoidance of doubt, the blonde was an adult woman, as opposed to any other type of blonde (animal, beer, brownie).

6. Reader, I'll be honest, I didn't instantly recognise him, as although he is the most famous motivational speaker, this still doesn't make him all that famous in absolute terms – it's a bit like being the most interesting person in Formula One. Luckily, while I was staring at him wondering who the fuck this was, I heard JPEG behind me saying under his breath, 'Here he comes, Tony Robbins, still the richest, best and most famous motivational speaker in the world.' I can't tell you how useful it was to have JPEG coming out with that information at that moment, as if we were in a BBC historical drama.

Fig. 128 A helpful guide to differentiate between cerulean and blue.

Fig. 129 An artist's depiction of Fiji. The artist is me.

Fig. 128

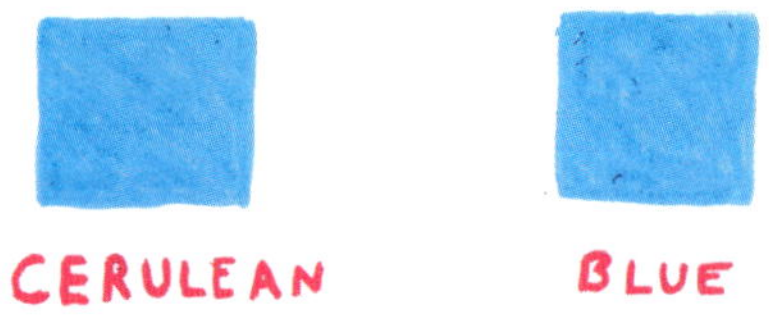

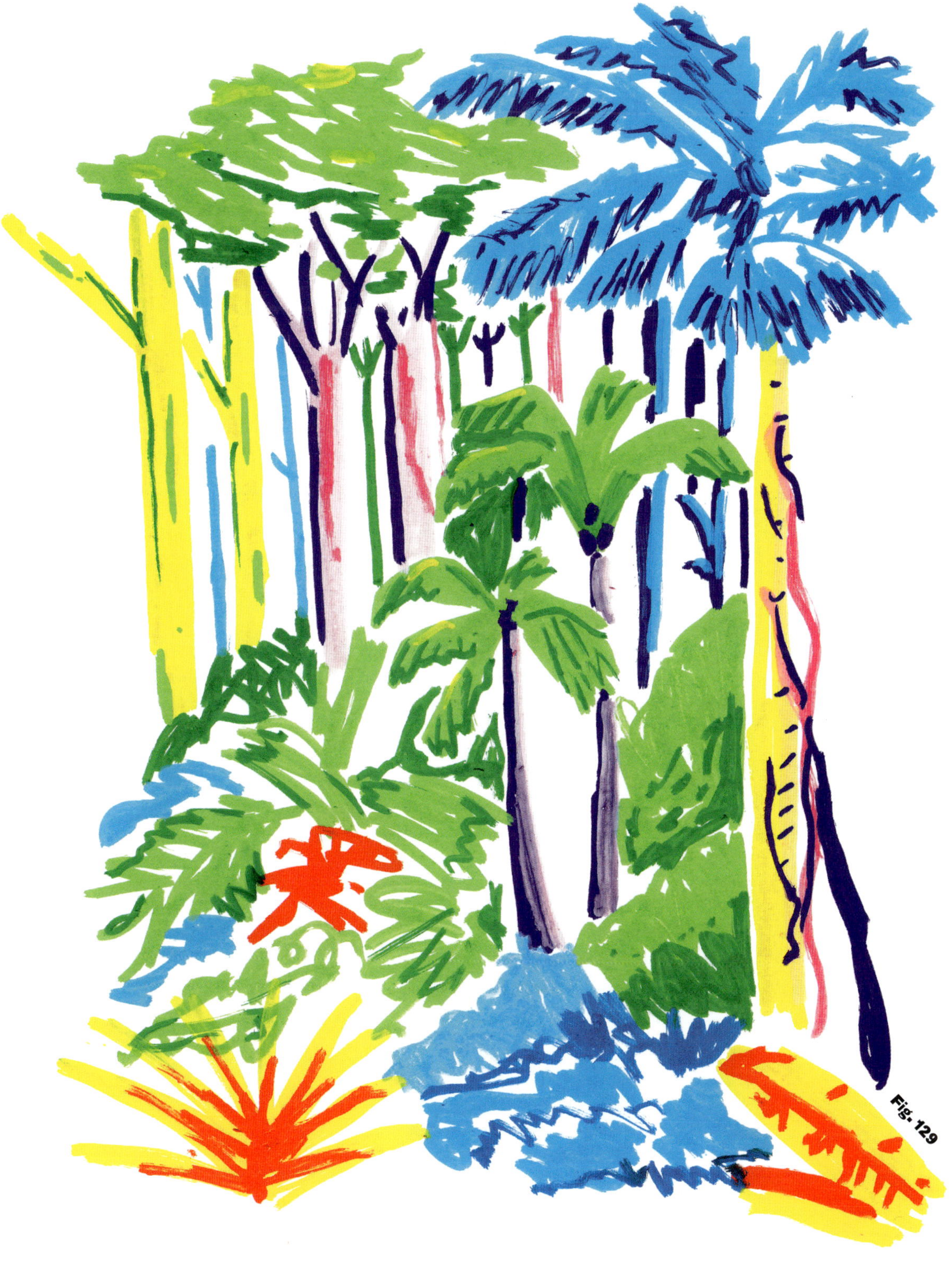

Fig. 129

I was torn about this, as I dislike objectifying women, but also I hadn't been looking at ZIP's ass when I had the chance, and it sounded like I had missed a really nice ass (or as we respectfully call them in Britain: arse).

Tony took gigantic strides towards me – so gigantic he had to swivel his body from side to side a little to accommodate them. He sighed and sat in one of the wicker chairs opposite. I was nervous: people with large strides often have that effect on me and I once had a panic attack going round a Westfield with Helena Bonham Carter (she has the gait of a yokozuna grand champion (or two-legged cheetah)). He looked deep into my eyes from a really close distance, basically as close as the optician gets, but without the little puff of air to check for glaucoma. It was intimidating 'cause if you don't know what Tony Robbins looks like, imagine the head of Gaston from *Beauty and the Beast* but on the body of a manager of a Topps Tiles who's got a platinum membership to David Lloyd.

'Wow, man, wow,' he said, 'handsome guy.' He sat back and stroked his chin, which took him a while 'cause it's about the size of an iPad mini.

'You want to change your life. That's beautiful, man,' he said, becoming almost emotional.

'Yeh … well … er …' I replied awkwardly. I had not come to change my life. I had come because JPEG told me it would be 'worth [my] while, financially [as in there will be money, a cash payment is what I mean].'

'I think there's been a misunderstanding,' I said.

'I hear you, I hear you very loud and very clear, man. Look out there, man, at the sea,' he was pointing at the sea. 'Amazing, isn't it?'

'Yeh, I s'pose,' I replied, even though it wasn't that amazing, it was just the sea (it had remained cerulean).

'Your mind and body are like the sea, man.' I nodded, humouring him the way you would an armed terrorist or Michael McIntyre. 'What I'm saying is: it's deep. You're a deep guy, I can tell that.'

'Yeh. Yeh, I am deep, I suppose,' I said, realising in that moment that I am not deep.

'Also, that sea is pretty calm right now, like you are calm, man. But sometimes I bet I'm right in saying that you get pretty angry, man.'

I nodded. 'And sometimes I eat a lot of prawns and there are a lot of prawns in the sea,' I added, further deepening the realisation that I am not deep.

'Yeh, that's true, haha, good one, man,' he laughed.

'And sometimes, Shell or BP spill millions of litres of oil into my mouth—'

'That's enough, now,' he said. I had gone too far.[1]

We chatted for perhaps twenty minutes,[2] but every five minutes or so a model would pass by, Tony would say something lurid to them and

1. As with so many things, when it comes to drawing direct comparisons between yourself and the sea, the secret is moderation.

2. On reflection it was probably thirty.

Fig. 130 A lifesize scan of an iPad mini to help give you a sense of what someone with a chin like an iPad mini might look like.

Fig. 130

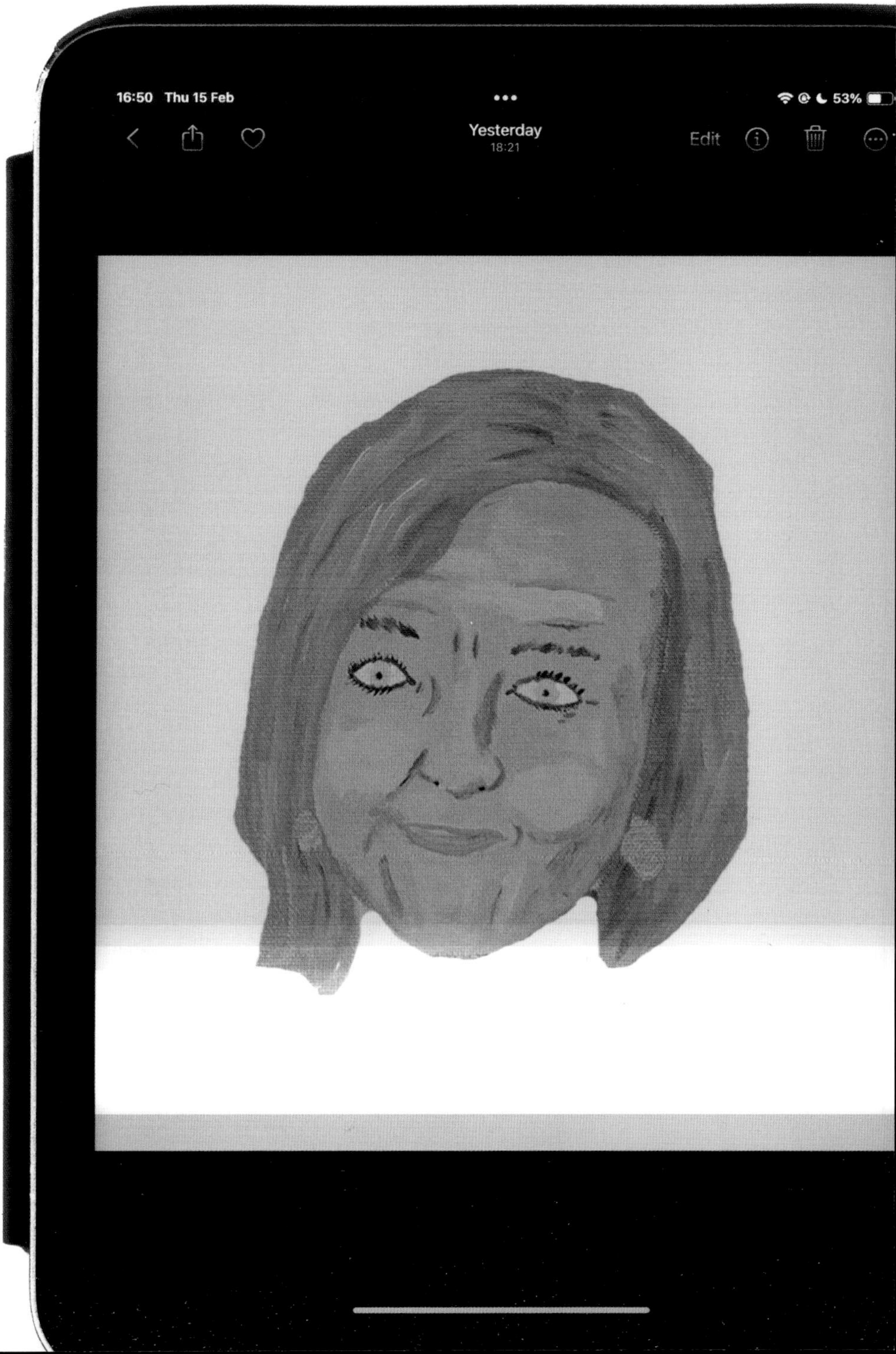

that would prompt a giggle or an 'Oh, Tony'. I made a mental note of their names: WAV, HTML, TXT and CSV.

'Why have you brought me here?' I finally asked. 'To paint your portrait?' I couldn't imagine why else he would bring me to Fiji at such expense. Much like the continued existence of the streaming service BritBox, the whole thing was baffling.

'Oh god, no way, man, you paint like you've never seen a living creature before.' I was undeniably hurt (it's only just occurred to me that I could have denied it, but it's too late now). 'I just want you to change your life. I want you to want to change your life. Do you want to change your life?' I was confused by the number of times he had said the word 'want'.

'Sorry, just to clarify, are you asking me if I want to change my life, or if I want me to want to change my life?'

'What I want to know is, if you want you to want to change your life?' he said.

'Well, I think I want to change my life, maybe,' I said, 'but I don't think I want to want to change my life.'

'No, you do want to want to change your life,' he said, 'because you can't want to change your life without wanting to want to change your life.'

'No, I don't want that,' I said.

'Sorry, which bit don't you want?' he said.

'Who wants to know?' I replied.[1]

He lost patience at this point and called JPEG over, instructing him to take me to my room. He accidentally called him Keith and then followed it up with, 'Sorry, I mean JPEG, that's what I meant to say, not Keith, JPEG I mean.' It was a pretty uncomfortable thing to watch and I loved every second.

JPEG spoke into a radio and PDF appeared almost immediately on a buggy. 'Ah, PDF, my favourite tits in all of Fiji,' said Tony.[2] He looked at me: 'We'll change your life, Joe. And you'll want to change it. And you'll want to want to change it. It'll take as long as you want it to take.'

'Will it take longer than five days?' I asked. 'As I have an appointment with a chiropodist on Wednesday.' He ignored this perfectly reasonable question. Changing your life is all very well, but without effective treatment a verruca can make it not worth living.

He stretched his arms to the sky, and then ran, literally ran, to the sea and jumped straight in, fully clothed. He moved across the water like a torpedo if that torpedo was a man.[3] He emerged on the other side, close to a hut that I was later told was where Tony did his 'one on one wealth sessions'. He shook the hand of who I could tell at a glance was Michael Le Vell, the actor who portrays Kevin Webster in *Coronation Street*.

1. I did mention that there was one thing I wanted to change in my life, which was that my Hotpoint H55RM1110W1 Fridge in white wasn't cooling properly, and I would be interested if he could help. He said he would look into it, but never got back to my thirty emails about it.

2. I would advise younger readers that this isn't an expression you should use in everyday conversation, especially not with elderly relatives or the support staff in a GP surgery.

3. I've been asked by Tony's legal team to clarify that 'torpedo' has nothing to do with the similar sounding word 'pedo'.

Fig. 131 A picture I did of Tony Robbins in a chair.

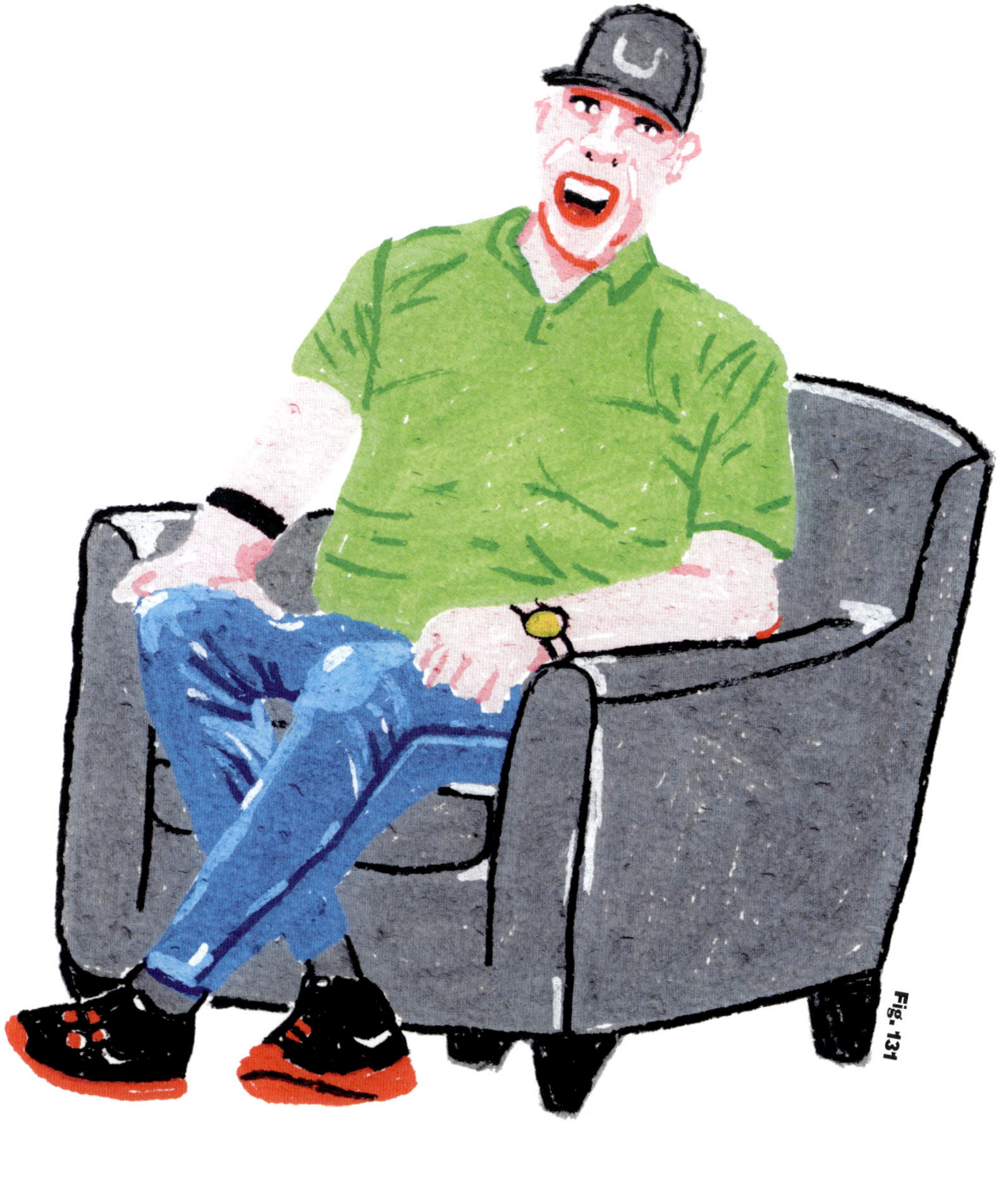

Fig. 131

The room they put me up in was absolutely fine, but they only had an annoying Nespresso Krups Pixie XN304T40 Coffee Machine in cerulean finish (I had put my glasses on again), which uses pods that dribble a mouthful of coffee into a little shot glass. I had just had a long journey (see above, paragraphs 1–9 inclusive) and wanted nothing more than a cup of tea, so I called reception and thirty minutes later was handed one by a man called GIF (it later transpired his real name was Geoff so this one at least was less of a stretch).

I sipped the tea, sitting at the desk, contemplating how I could interpret Tony's words into a painting (I know this isn't what Tony was after, but I was feeling spiteful). Suddenly, without much thought, I took out a small canvas (I always keep several concealed about my person, like a Scotsman does with knives) and began to paint, from memory, focusing mainly on his iPad mini-shaped chin. Lost in my creative process, it felt like I'd been working for hours, perhaps days, but when I was finished I looked at my phone and I had actually been working for just under seven minutes.

Creatively spent and desperately hungry, I noticed night was falling, so I went down to the restaurant and sat with JPEG. We shared a glass of scotch[1] and some mozzarella sticks, waiting for Tony to arrive so I could unveil his painting. I'd covered it with one of the restaurant serviettes, which JPEG explained they'd bulk-bought following the collapse of Little Chef. The place was busy – TXT was sat drinking some sort of spritz with ZIP and I think CSV (but I am not great with names, and it could well have been WAV). I looked across the water and noticed the silhouette of a swimmer interrupting the reflected moonlight, moving fast towards us. It was Tony Robbins, the richest, best and most famous motivational speaker in the world. Moments later he was on land, his Hugo Boss mixed-material trainers with EVA-rubber outsole squelching loudly as he approached. He drew no attention to the fact that he was entirely soaked, but when he sat down he crossed his legs and some of the shoe water flicked out in a big fan, scattering over me and JPEG (some of it went into my mouth, resulting later in a brief stay in a Tropical Disease Unit).

'It's time to change your life, Joe, starting with that name of yours. Joe comes with a lot of … baggage.'

'Stalin?' I asked.

'I was thinking Pasquale,' he said firmly. Several of the people in the restaurant winced. 'So, we're going with something different.' He stroked his chin again, looked out at the sea, then laughed and said, 'I've got it. Your new name is MOV.'

1. It might have been more sensible just to have one each.

Fig. 132 A drawing I did from memory of what I remembered Tony Robbins to look like when he was angry.

Fig. 132

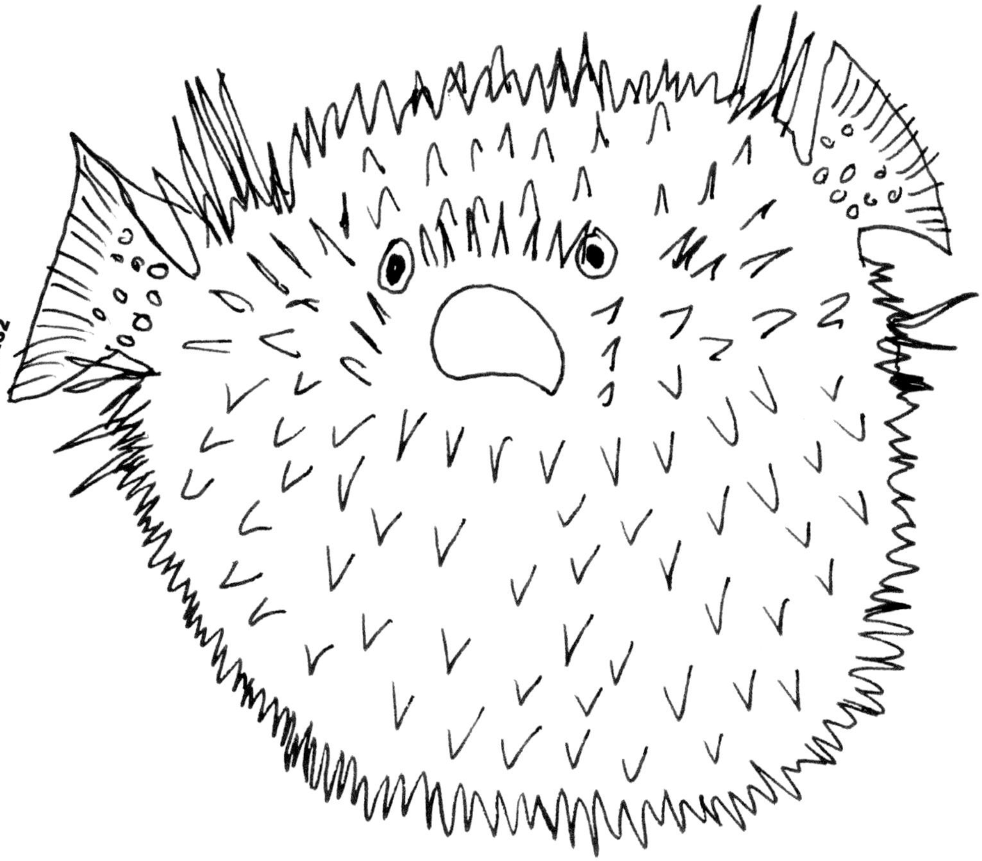

He offered it up like it was a beautiful and precious gift, like a nice bowl, or the secret of eternal life, or some salad spoons. 'MOV? As in QuickTime File Format? No way,' I said. I hated it. 'Can't I have something else?'

The man was not up for negotiating.

'What about ePUB? No one has had ePUB yet,' added JPEG, trying to help.

'I'm not going to be fucking ePUB,' I spat back.

I sat in silence for a short while, fuming. I felt I was the recipient of a profound injustice, like Nelson Mandela or Baroness Michelle Mone. Then suddenly, I spotted a flaw in the whole set up. 'Hang on just a moment,' I said, 'why don't you have a filename?' The place went silent. I'm sure someone gasped (due to shock or possibly asthma).

'What?' he replied, his brow much furrowed.

'Why do you get to be Tony?' I said, doing the stupid thing of doubling down when a situation gets awkward, a bit like Putin in Ukraine. 'We're all giving up our names. You could be MOV or ePUB?'

Tony uncrossed his legs, spraying more foot-warm water into the air. Some of it landed in WAV's drink; she nervously giggled. 'This isn't about me,' he said, 'we're here for you. JPEG, get me a Twix.' The conversation was over. 'A Twix. Now, you fucker.' JPEG moved, and fast.

I didn't feel he deserved to see the painting after rechristening me in such a disappointing fashion, but I was proud of it and wanted him to see it (I was also fishing for compliments, because I am very insecure and crave praise even from people I despise). His reaction was unexpected. He cried.

Now this is not the first time people have cried when seeing one of my paintings (sometimes they are weeping so aggressively they can't even gasp out words like 'No!' and 'Why?'), but Tony cried in a way that suggested he was releasing years, maybe decades, of emotion. No one could console him, not even JPEG when he brought the Twix. I don't know if you've ever seen a grown man with an iPad mini-shaped chin crying and eating a Twix at the same time, but I can tell you that it's a mad thing to see. Also, I suspect it wasn't an official Twix, as JPEG brought the two fingers over in some kitchen roll, not in the instantly recognisable and reassuring gold sleeve.

'ePUB, it's the most beautiful thing I've ever seen in my life. I feel I am looking at the face of God,' he said, wiping away the last of the tears with his already wet sleeve (in the process just making his wet face more wet).

'Wrong,' I said, accepting my fate as ePUB. 'You are looking at the face of Tony Robbins, the richest, best and most famous motivational speaker in the world.'

Fig. 133 The rare Twix white.

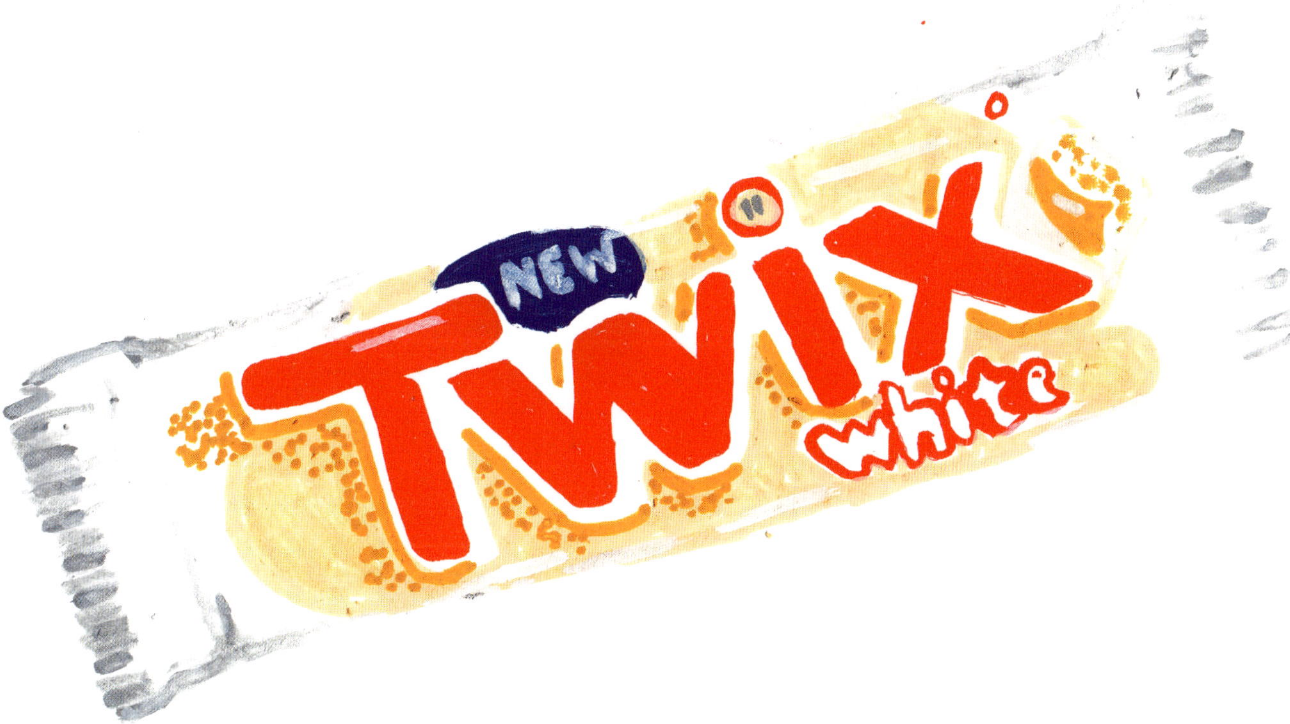

Fig. 133

I suggested a price which I thought was fair ($80 mil, minus what it would've cost him to fly me out, plus labour), but he somehow persuaded me that I didn't need paying for my talents and that I could earn way more anyway by joining his one on one wealth training sessions with Michael Le Vell. I was a bit dubious because Michael reckoned he'd been doing them for three years and had considerably less wealth now than when he started, but I thought I'd give it a go. There was some OK advice like 'don't exchange your money at the airport 'cause you'll get a bad rate' and 'use coupons', but basically it was total horseshit, so I sold the painting to Michael Le Vell who then subsequently gifted it to Beverley Callard. She was holding a lit Benson & Hedges superking while putting it up and the painting, and her flat, were entirely destroyed in a merciless inferno. Luckily no one was hurt (Bev escaped by vaulting out through the VELUX, like Beth Tweddle on some sort of meth) and she had good insurance, got an eye-watering payout, and rebuilt the flat. She bunged me a couple of mil to recreate the painting exactly, which wasn't too difficult as I can usually see it every time I close my eyes.

NB: If you don't know who Tony Robbins is then what have you been doing with your life, man? He's the bomb!! Tony Robbins is the richest and best motivational speaker in the world. The guy literally became a multimillionaire through doing three key things every morning and you can too! Change Your Life Today![1]

1. Some of this chapter was written in consultation with Tony Robbins's representatives, who agreed I could include the rest of this chapter as long as I published some of the above promotional information.

Fig. 134 A picture of me on the beach in Fiji or maybe Bournemouth by Harry Griffin.

Fig. 135 This picture was taken on the same day as **Fig. 134**, so I'm pretty sure it's Bournemouth.

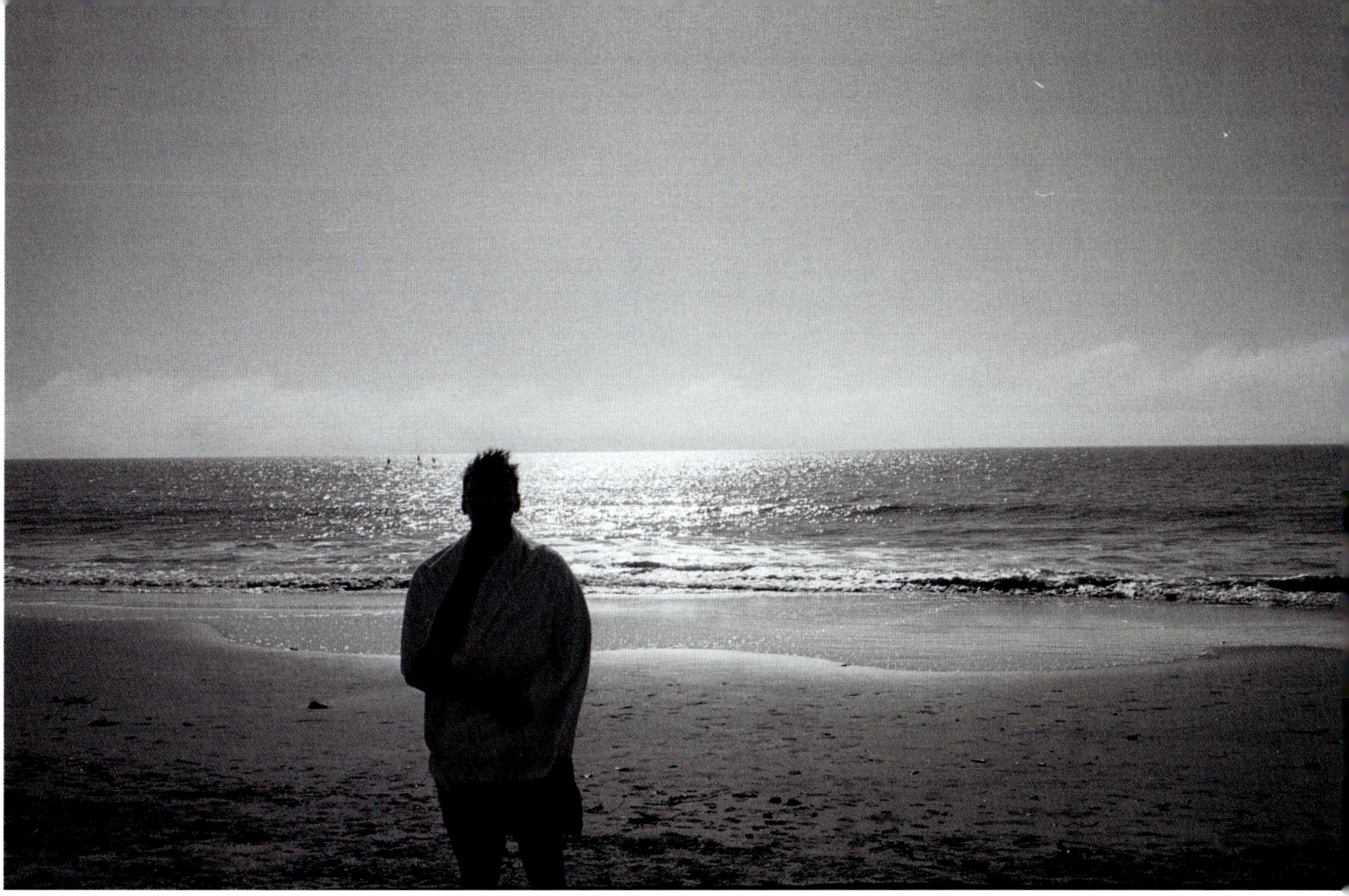

Fig. 134

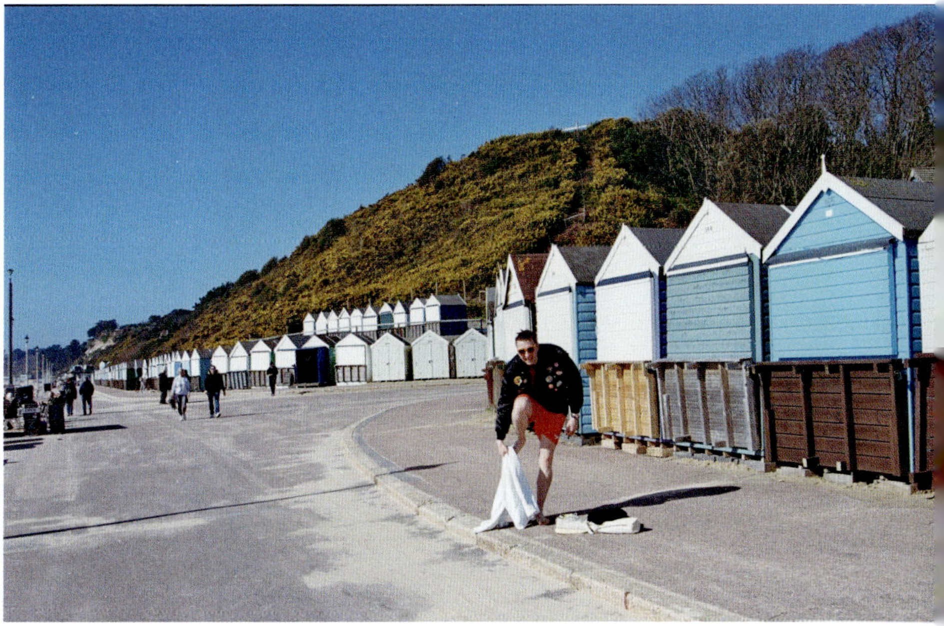

Fig. 135

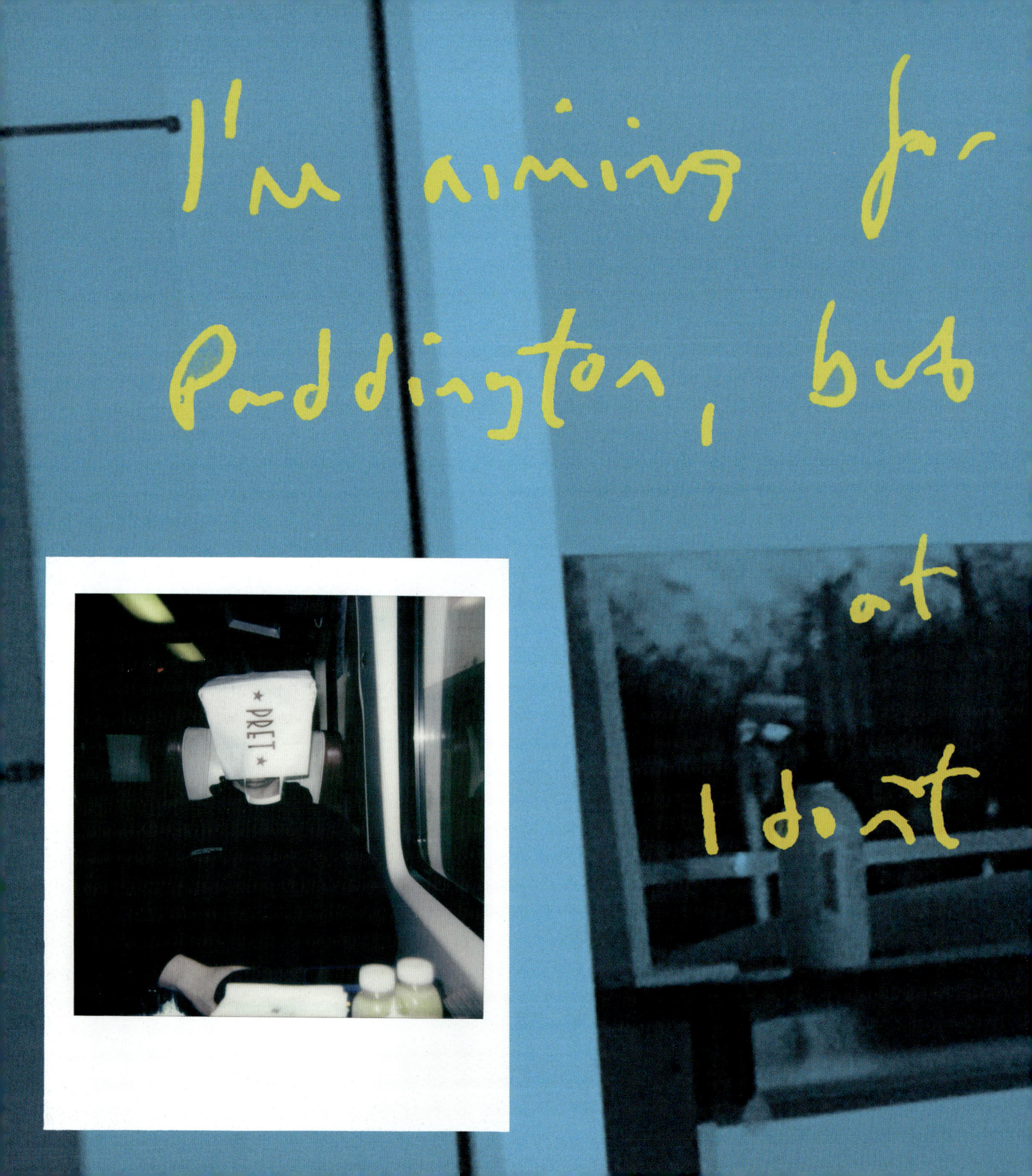
I'm aiming for
Paddington, but
at
I don't
PRET

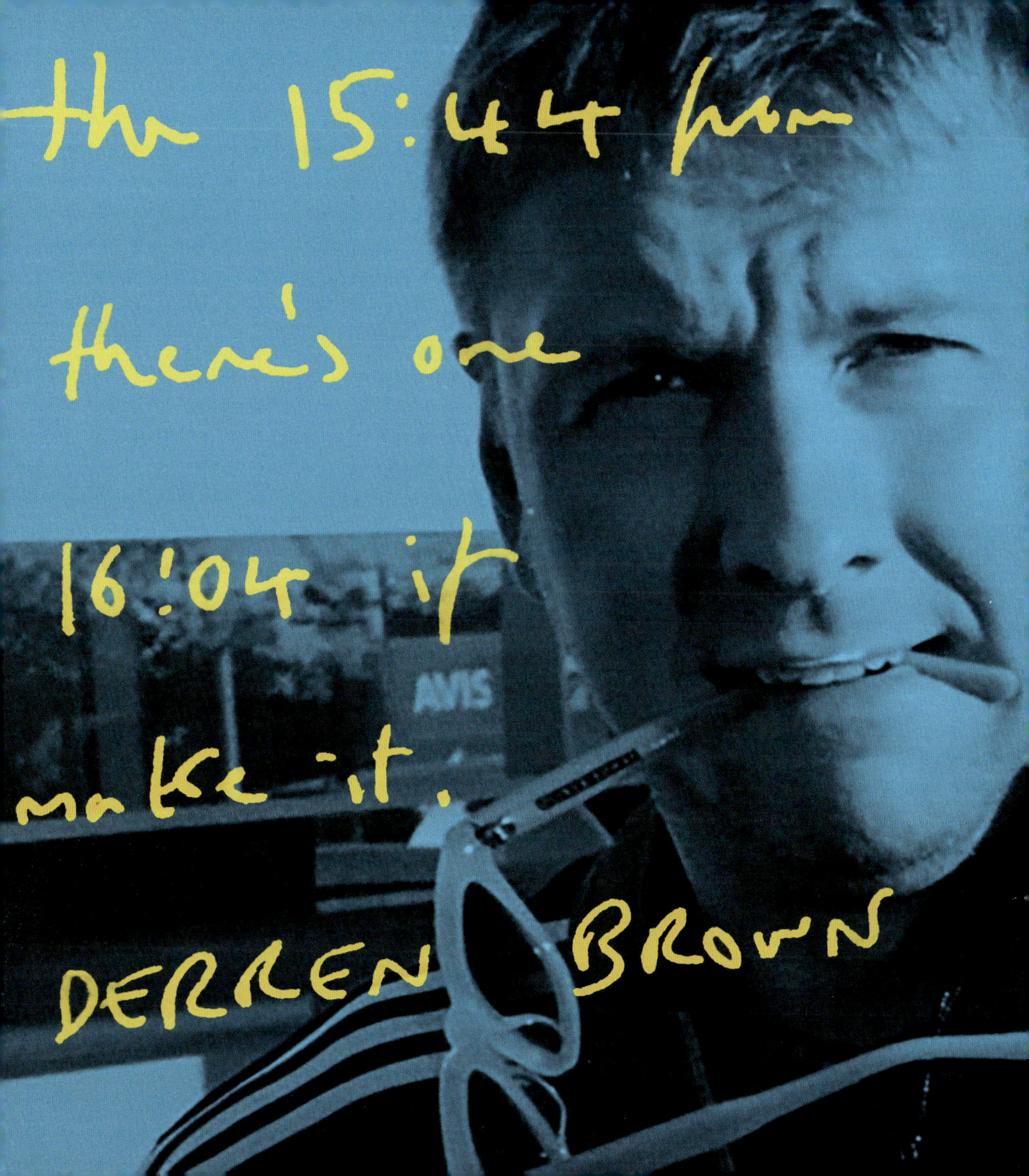
the 15:44 from
there's one
16:04 if
make it.
AVIS
DERREN BROWN

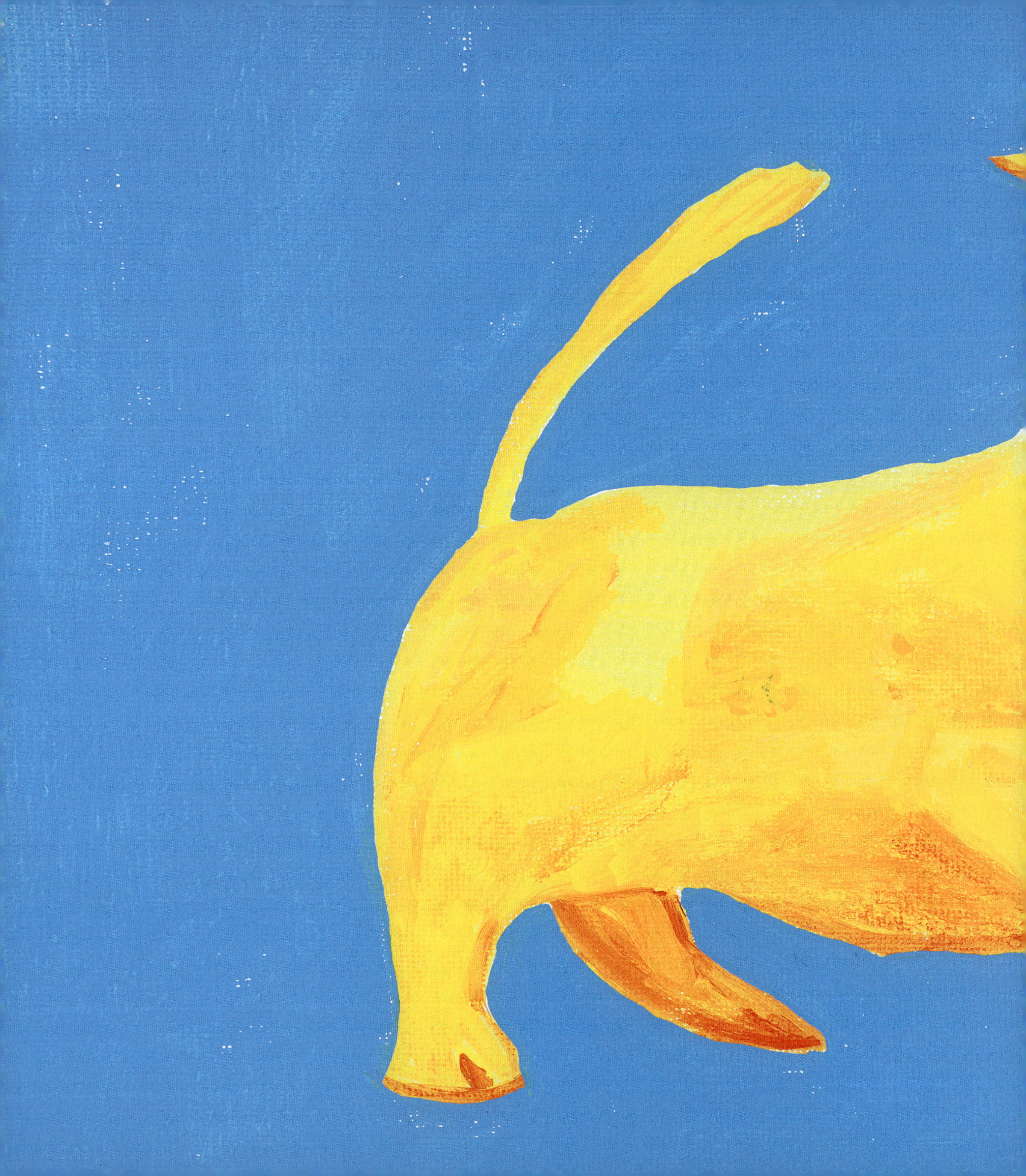

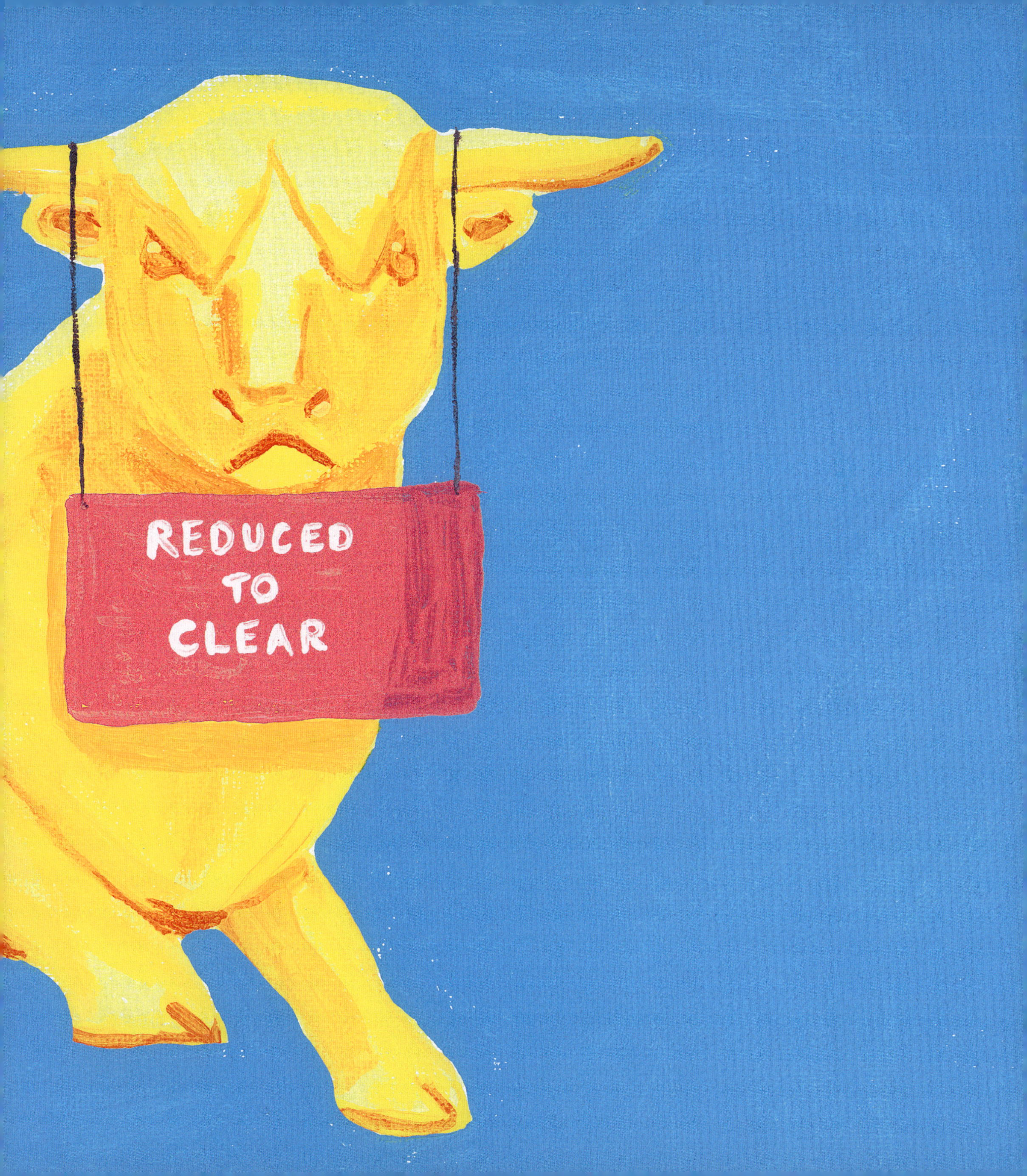
REDUCED
TO
CLEAR

THIS YEAR WILL ALSO BE SHIT

Fig. 136 SCART cable.
Fig. 137 *This Year Will Also be Shit,* 2022, gouache on feather, 10 × 10mm.
Fig. 138 *Susan Boyle,* 2024, pen on Days Inn bedsheet, 10 × 10m.

One New Year's Eve, I was invited to a house party at Eric Cantona's house. He'd invited all of his favourite people from show business and football: Paul Gascoigne; the guy who plays Charlie from *Casualty*; Paul Scholes; Joss Stone; Alan Shearer; Diana Vickers from *The X Factor* 2008; Ryan Giggs; Jessie J; Sol Campbell; Susan Boyle; Robbie Fowler; and me.

I'd never met Eric Cantona before, but it turned out neither had most of the other guests, footballers aside (apart from Alan Shearer who claimed to me that he has never ever met another football player). Regardless, I really liked him – he was courteous, gentle, interested and just wanted everyone to have a nice time. For example, when at one point Jessie J suggested all the singers do a number together, prompting Susan Boyle to have a panic attack, Eric quietly lit a lavender incense stick, told Susan that she was under no pressure to do anything, and asked Charlie from *Casualty* to escort Jessie into a taxi for her own good.

Everyone was having a great time; Eric was wearing Diana Vickers's wild pink coat and handing out shots, Vickers was getting on marvellously with Paul Gascoigne, telling him how Ruth Lorenzo still sends her messages even though she hasn't replied in years, and Sol Campbell was telling Joss Stone that extra virgin olive oil is great added to a yoghurt. I was getting great advice from Paul Scholes about my Hotpoint H55RM1110W1 Fridge in white that I just could not manage to get cold, who said based on what I'd told him it was almost certainly a faulty compressor. What I'm saying is, the party was a riot!

Then, just before midnight, Jessie crashed back in, blind drunk and holding an LCD TV under her arm that she'd prised off the wall of a kebab shop. She started pointing and jabbing into everyone's faces, saying that all the guests there were 'pricks', that Susan Boyle was 'a spineless coward' and that 'this year was shit, every year is shit, and so this year will also be shit'.

'Cannae be as shite as yer fuckin' albems,' said Susan Boyle, reanimated from a recent snakebite.

'Who's got a fucking SCART lead?' squealed Jessie, ignoring Boyle's jibe.

Alan Shearer managed to get Jessie to go outside again by convincing her he'd seen another LCD TV in a nearby carpark, the clock struck midnight, and everyone hugged and kissed and said Jessie J was wrong and in fact the next year would be fantastic.

The next year was 2020, a shit year, so Jessie J was actually bang on.

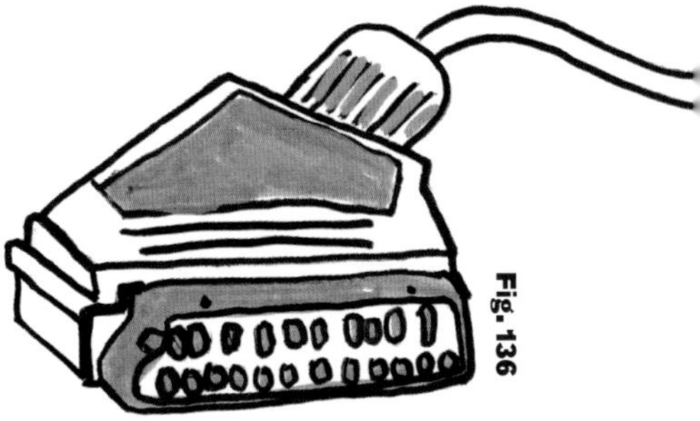
Fig. 136

Fig. 137

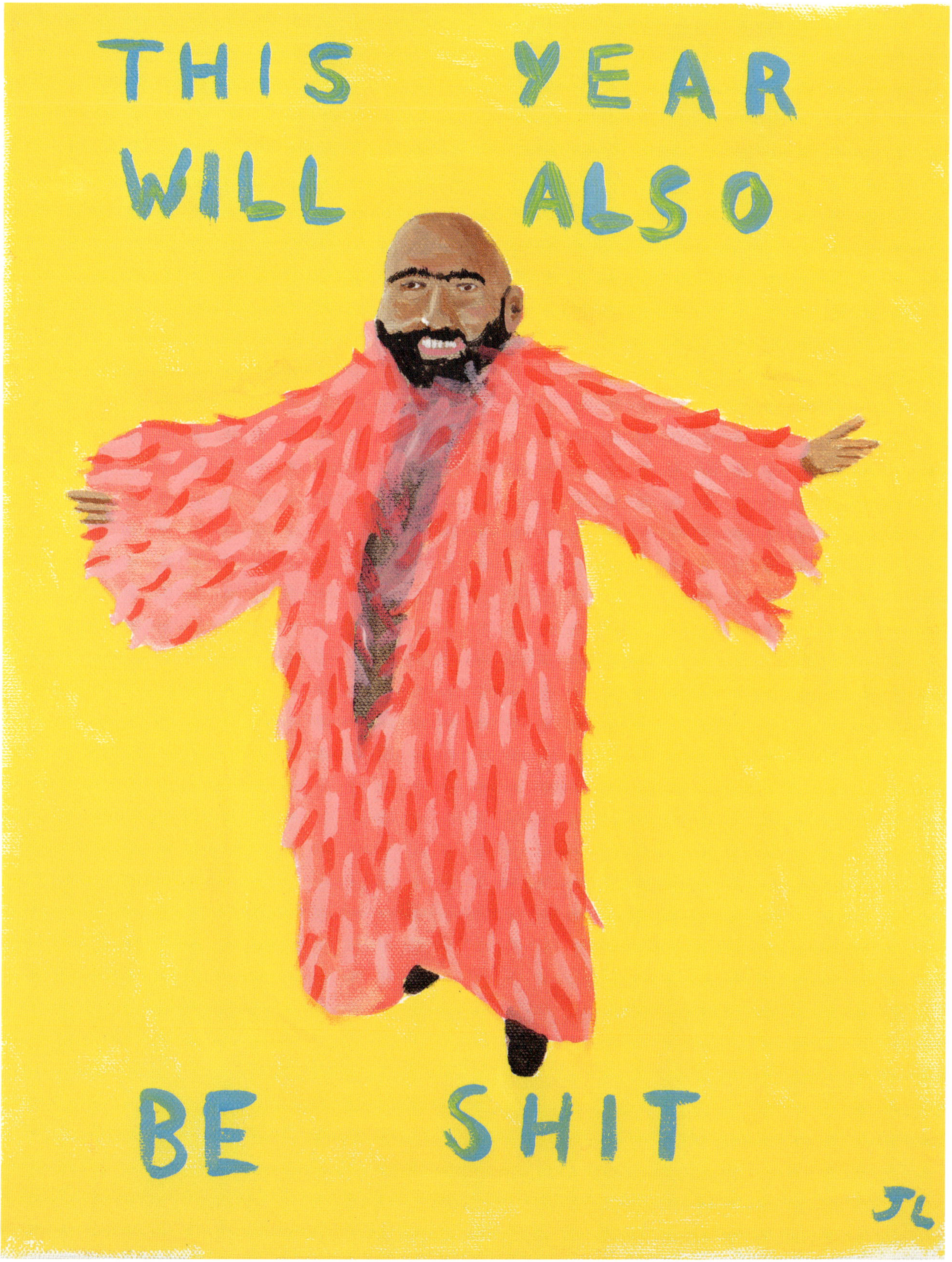

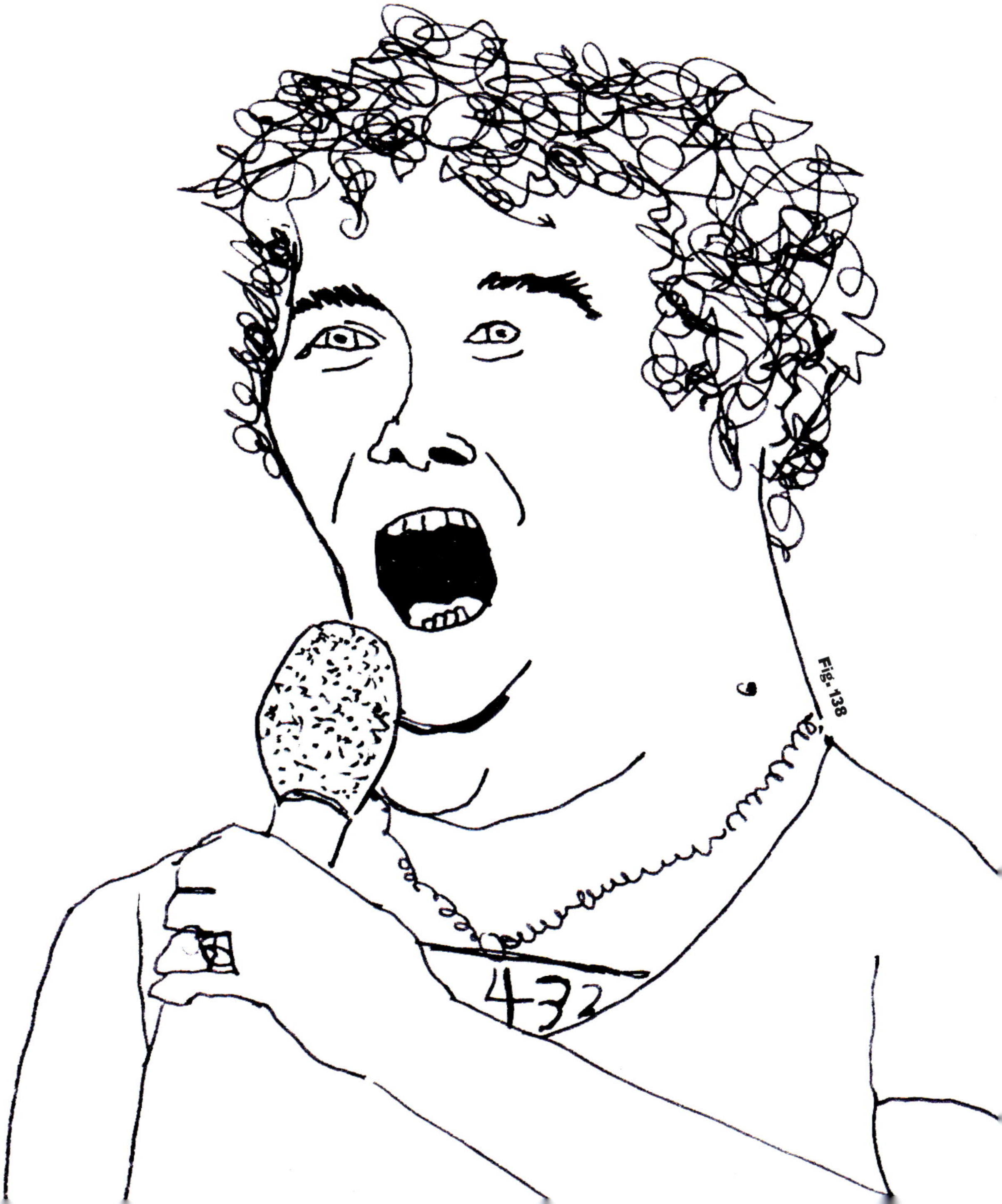

Fig. 138

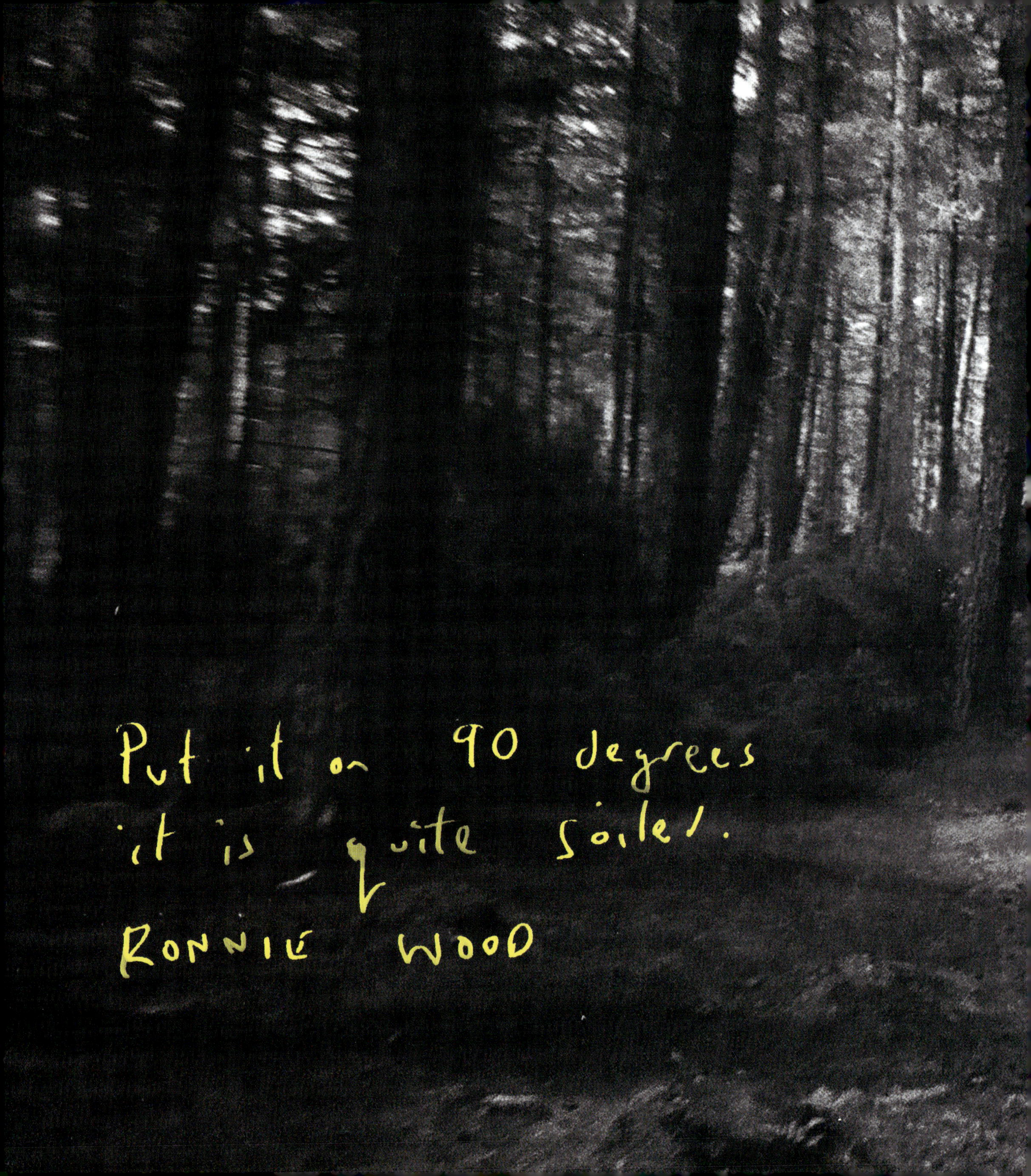
Put it on 90 degrees
it is quite soiled.
RONNIE WOOD

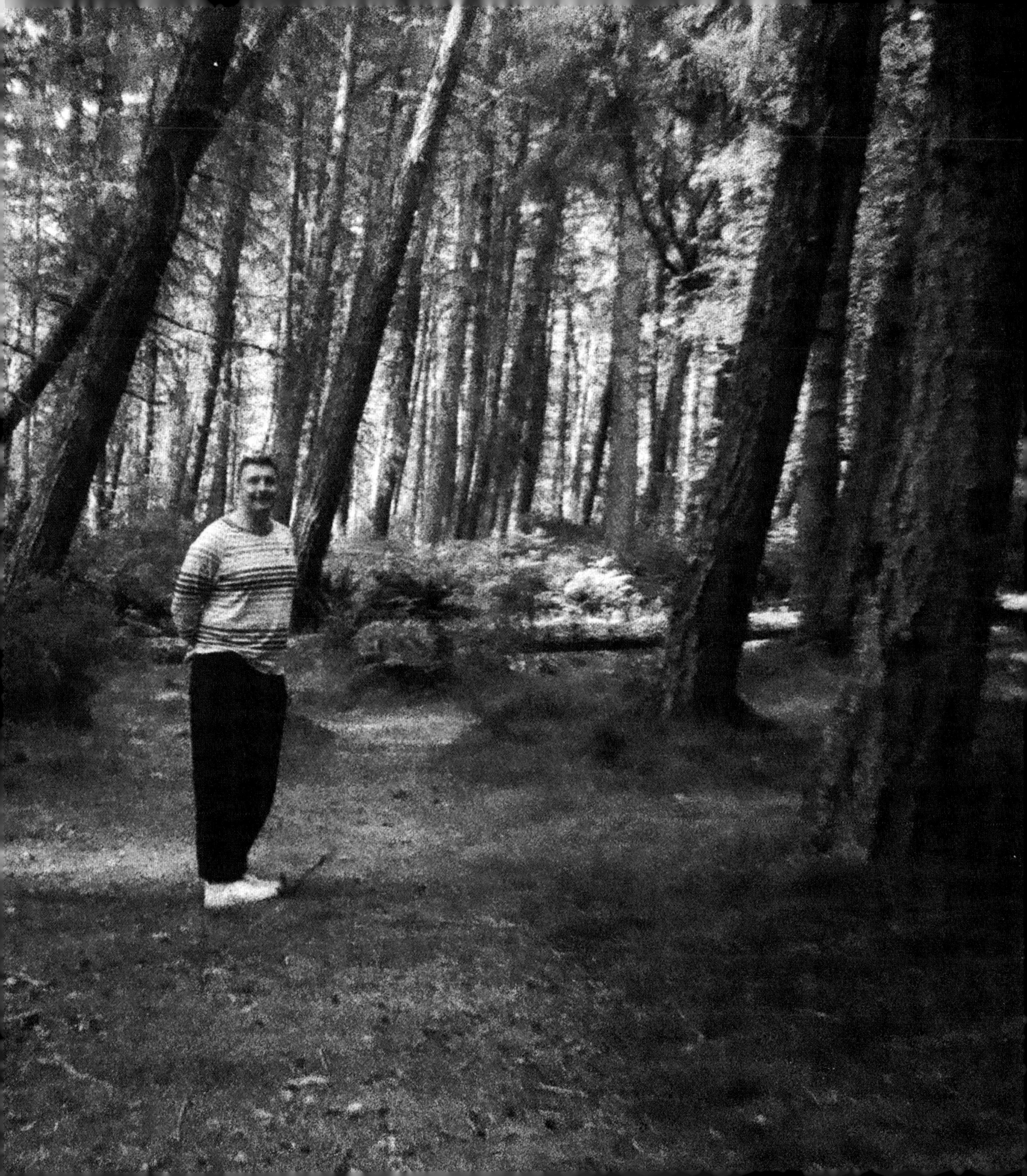

SIR ELTON JOHN

Like everyone who becomes a celebrity, I am close personal friends with Sir Elton John. Not many people know this, but once your Instagram following goes over 500,000 you get an email from his PA asking if you might want to pretend to be friends. Once you're over 750,000 you are allowed to say 'close' and after 1,000,000, 'close personal'. I like being close personal friends with Elton because he can get you exclusive Ocado delivery slots, but the downside is that I am financially devastated.

Not only are Sir Elton John and I close personal friends, but we are also equal shareholders in a holiday let in Skegness. It's a small, one-bedroom cottage just back from the coast, about the size of an average Timpsons.[1] There are a mere two rooms – a bedroom/kitchenette and a shower room – with a small driveway and a raised flower bed filled with dahlias and novelty statues of gnomes with their genitalia out (Elton's idea).

The fiscal nightmares began when we had the property completely knocked down and rebuilt exactly as it was before we knocked it down. This seemed like a strange thing to do to me, as it was a new build and was structurally absolutely fine, but Elton assured me (during an incoherent phone conversation which, on reflection, was my fault for calling him while he was on stage in Malmo) that being able to say it was 'entirely restored' would make it more attractive to renters and future buyers. The whole thing cost about £800k in addition to the £200k that we spent on buying the property, plus an extra £400k for the solicitor fees (I'd suggested using a local firm for low cost and ease, but even though she doesn't do conveyancing Elton insisted on using Erin Brockovich because he liked the film; he had originally asked for Julia Roberts, but she declined).

I tried in vain to keep costs down on the fixtures and fittings, but Elton had other ideas. 'Harry and Meghan sold us an armchair,' he told me on one call. 'Isn't it just gorgeous!' The chair was perfectly OK.

'Yes, it's nice,' I said through gritted mouth and teeth, which was quite challenging.[2] 'How much did you get it for?'

'Only thirty!' I was massively relieved. Elton could tell this because I did a sigh delineating relief, through my aforementioned gritted mouth and teeth. 'Yeh, I'm pleased with that, too. Thirty grand is really good for a chair once owned by a prince and princess!' My relief dissolved. Later that evening I googled it and discovered that the thing was off Wayfair and retails at £74.99.

1. And funnily enough it does have a key cutting machine in it, which was previously owned by Nicholas Lyndhurst.

2. I always grit my mouth and teeth in the winter months to prevent accidents.

Fig. 139 An average-sized Timpsons.
Fig. 140 *Pansexual,* 2023, acrylic on diamonds, 38 × 47m.

Fig. 139

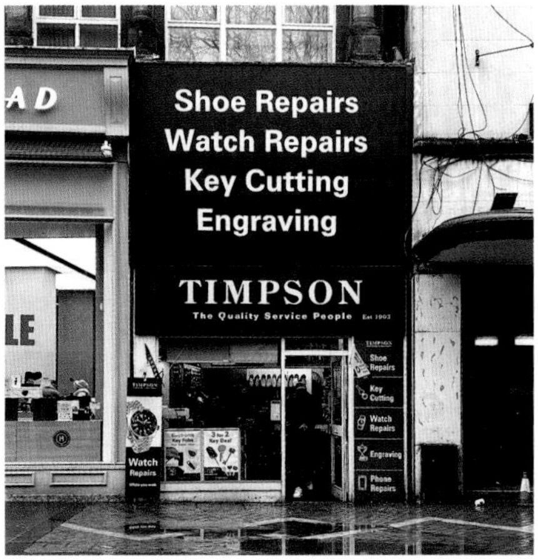

Fig. 140

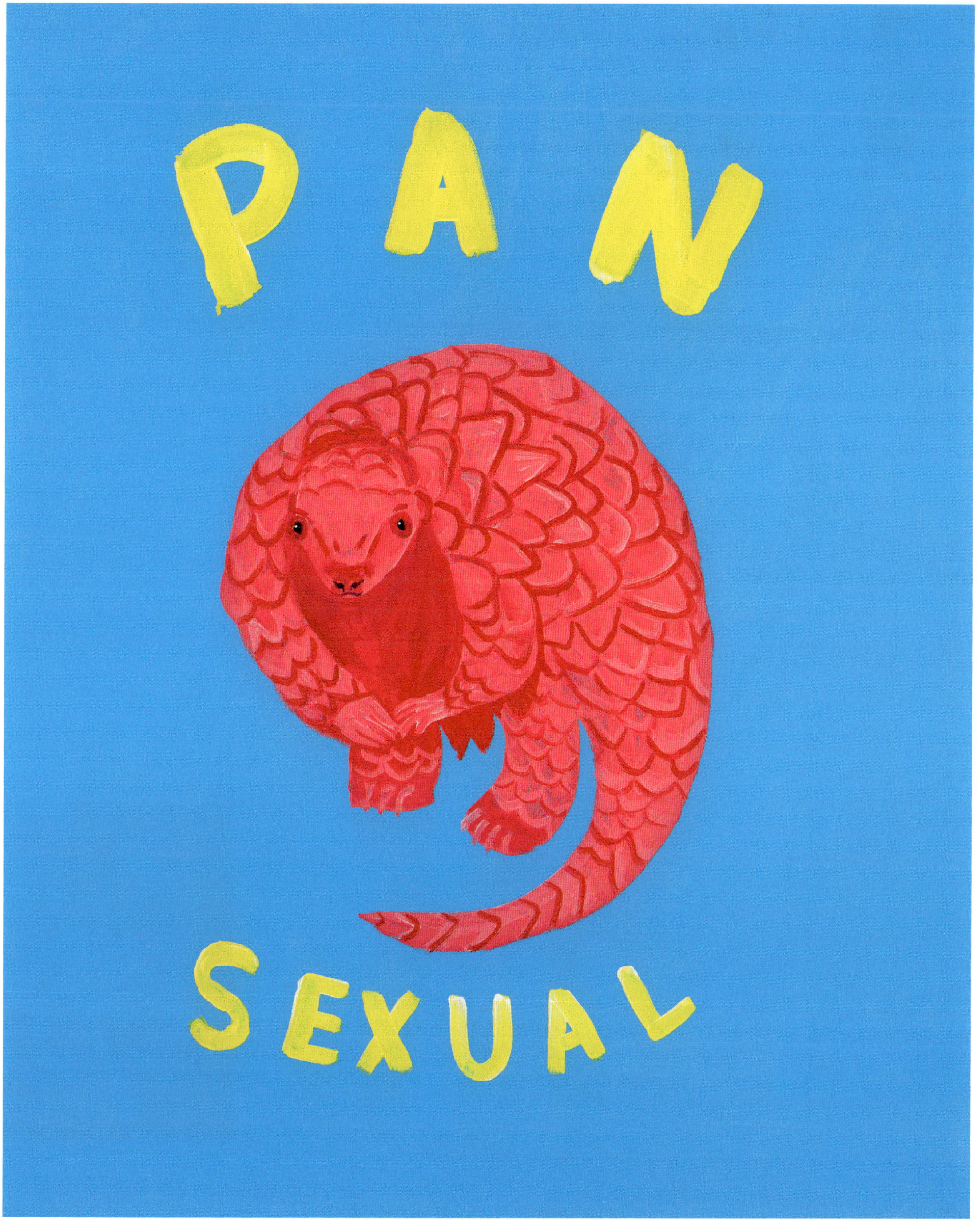

It was when Elton announced he would not allow a single item that hadn't been previously owned by a well-known public figure to pass the threshold into the property that I knew I was in trouble. Everything in there had to be direct from a top celeb or won at a charity auction, in furious bidding wars with either Elton or one of his associates (David Furnish or Sting). The full list includes: a toothbrush holder previously belonging to Drake; Rod Stewart's chopsticks; Uri Geller's blanket; a coffee grinder from Judi Dench; Peter Capaldi's fish tank (filled with dead eels); a bag of various charging cables from Idris Elba; Naomi Campbell's sandwich press; Sacha Baron Cohen's patio heater; and twenty heavy-duty clear plastic storage boxes formerly owned by Emma Watson (the boxes were labelled 'EMMA'S STUFF – DO NOT TOUCH'). The total bill for these items was in the millions. There wasn't even really a patio to put Sacha's heater on and Emma Watson's boxes are in the attic, empty.

The celebrities also had to be of a certain level. When I enthusiastically told Elton that Nick Knowles had sold me some wooden salad servers, he went silent. Then they mysteriously went missing. I was gardening months later and found them half-buried near the fence, with clear burn marks like someone had tried and failed to ignite them with a Zippo. I offered up my Hotpoint H55RM1110W1 Fridge in white, telling Elton, 'It's not cooling brilliantly, but it will do the job.'

'Keep your fucking Hotpoint, Dame Shirley Bassey has given me a Smeg.'

When Elton announced in an email that he had arranged for the walls to be painted by hand by Damien Hirst 'for his usual rate', I finally intervened. 'Could we set up a Zoom call,' I asked. An email from an assistant explained that Elton 'doesn't do Zoom calls'. Further enquiries revealed he was only available on Microsoft Teams.

'Darling, these things can get expensive, but you do want it to be nice, don't you?' he said to me, patronisingly. He was using one of those unconvincing virtual backgrounds on Microsoft Teams to make it look like he was in a cafe sitting with Ian Beale, when I knew really he was in Donatella Versace's spare room.

'Yes, Elton, I want it to be glorious, but it's only a small holiday let in Skegness, I'm just not sure we need Damien bloody Hirst to do it by hand!'

'OK, OK, Joe. I get it,' he was beginning to strop. 'I'll cancel Damien. We only paid him a 10 per cent deposit. Shall I ask Tracey instead?'

'Tracey?' I asked.

'Emin.'

I lost my rag.

Fig. 141 Idris Elba's charging cables.
Fig. 142 Damien Hirst's plans for the painting works. He claimed he had been planning this for years and that this preparatory drawing was done in 1994 but I had literally just watched him tear it from a Filofax with '2023' embossed in the cover.

Fig. 141

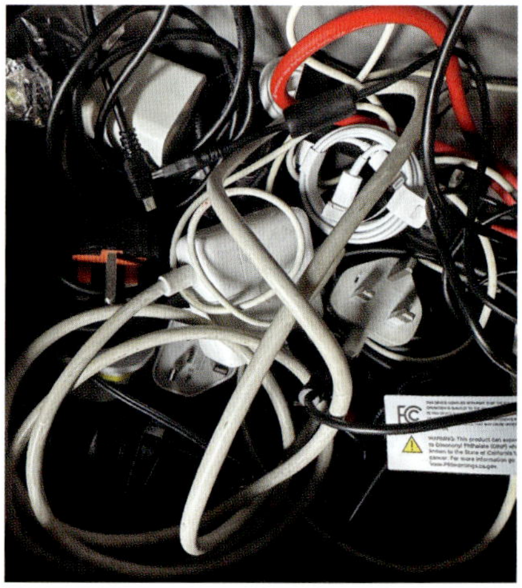

Fig. 142

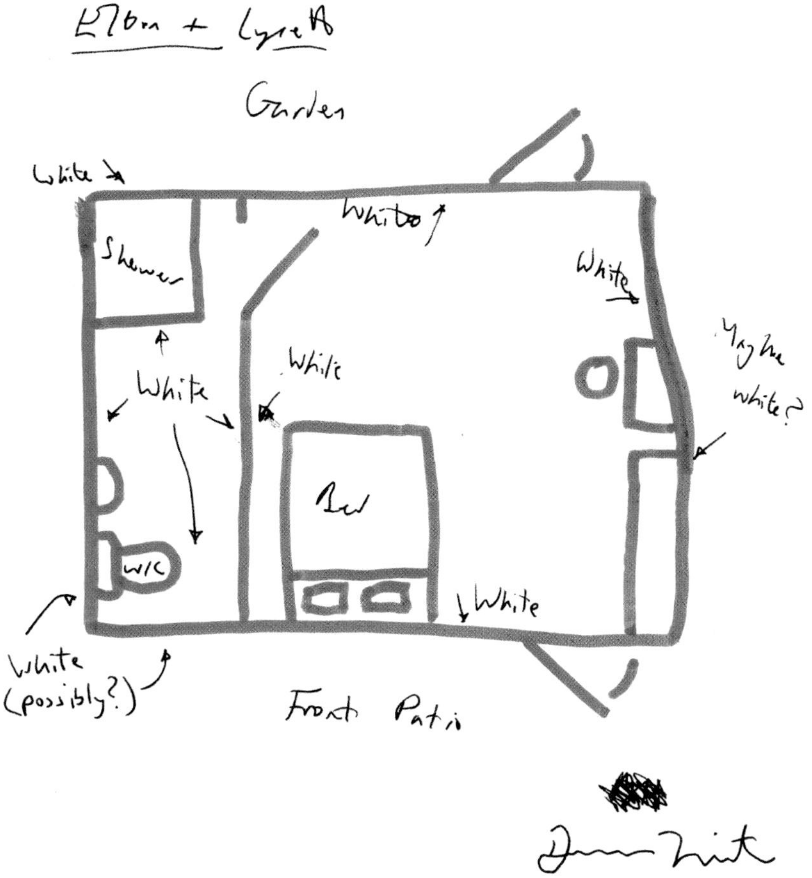
Garden
White
Shower
White
Bed
W/C
White (possibly?)
Maybe white?
Front Patio

Elton began arguing with me that owning things that were 'second hand' was good for the environment, but I pointed out that among the second-hand items he'd bought was a helicopter previously owned by Tom Hanks, Celine Dion's collection of white rhino tusks and a lump of depleted uranium that had, for some reason, been in Oprah's garage.

It was not really about the money. I could probably have leveraged a bit of capital to cover most of the expenditure in normal circumstances; but at the time I had dedicated all of my earnings to supporting a global charity for sick and injured snails, which was struggling to get funding due to no one giving a shit about snails. But I know a thing or two about how much art costs, and I knew the thing was getting out of control.

Eventually, I arrived at what I believed to be the perfect solution. 'Elton, I will paint the walls. I can do it for a fraction of the price, and it will be at least 30 per cent better as art than either Hirst or Emin.'

He pretended to be reverential about my art, saying, 'Darling, you're too good to do a job like this.' But I know he isn't a fan of my work because on Microsoft Teams I once heard him talking to David Furnish when he thought his microphone wasn't live, saying that my stuff is 'what happens if you give a toddler too much praise'. 'What do you mean by that?' replied Furnish. 'It's fucking shit,' said Elton. I began to join the dots.

In the end, we agreed to stick with Hirst because the 10 per cent deposit already amounted to around £250k pre-VAT and we figured a sensational attention-grabbing work might at least draw in some holiday goers. Hirst's genius idea was to 'paint it all white, clean, classic, timeless'. The guy really is a visionary. Due to scheduling conflicts, he was unable to do it himself so sent one of his staff to do it in his place. Amazingly, the staff member he sent was Handy Andy, former *Changing Rooms* star, so we got the Hirst/Handy double whammy of celeb interior design involvement. Andy told me that Hirst had given him strict instructions to use Farrow & Ball paints, but he'd managed to colour match at B&Q for a fraction of the price. I didn't tell Elton and I never will.

Despite the savings from Handy Andy, I was still down massively, so to scrape back some of the spiralling finances I asked Elton if I might be able to paint his portrait. He agreed, as long as I 'turned back the clock about forty years' and 'sold it at a celebrity auction'. He sat for a few hours and rejected all of my attempts (three) as he said I made him look like Deirdre Rachid. Despairing, he said 'paint this', and produced a live pangolin from his jacket pocket, which he said he'd bought from a Saudi prince. He loved the painting, and I immediately sent it to be auctioned.

Fig. 143 A Zippo lighter (with flame).
Fig. 144 Me with a tin of Crown Contract Quick Dry Gloss Brilliant White paint (1L).

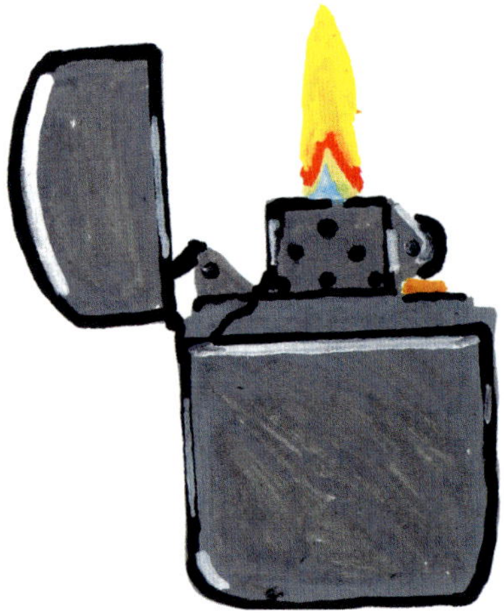

Fig. 143

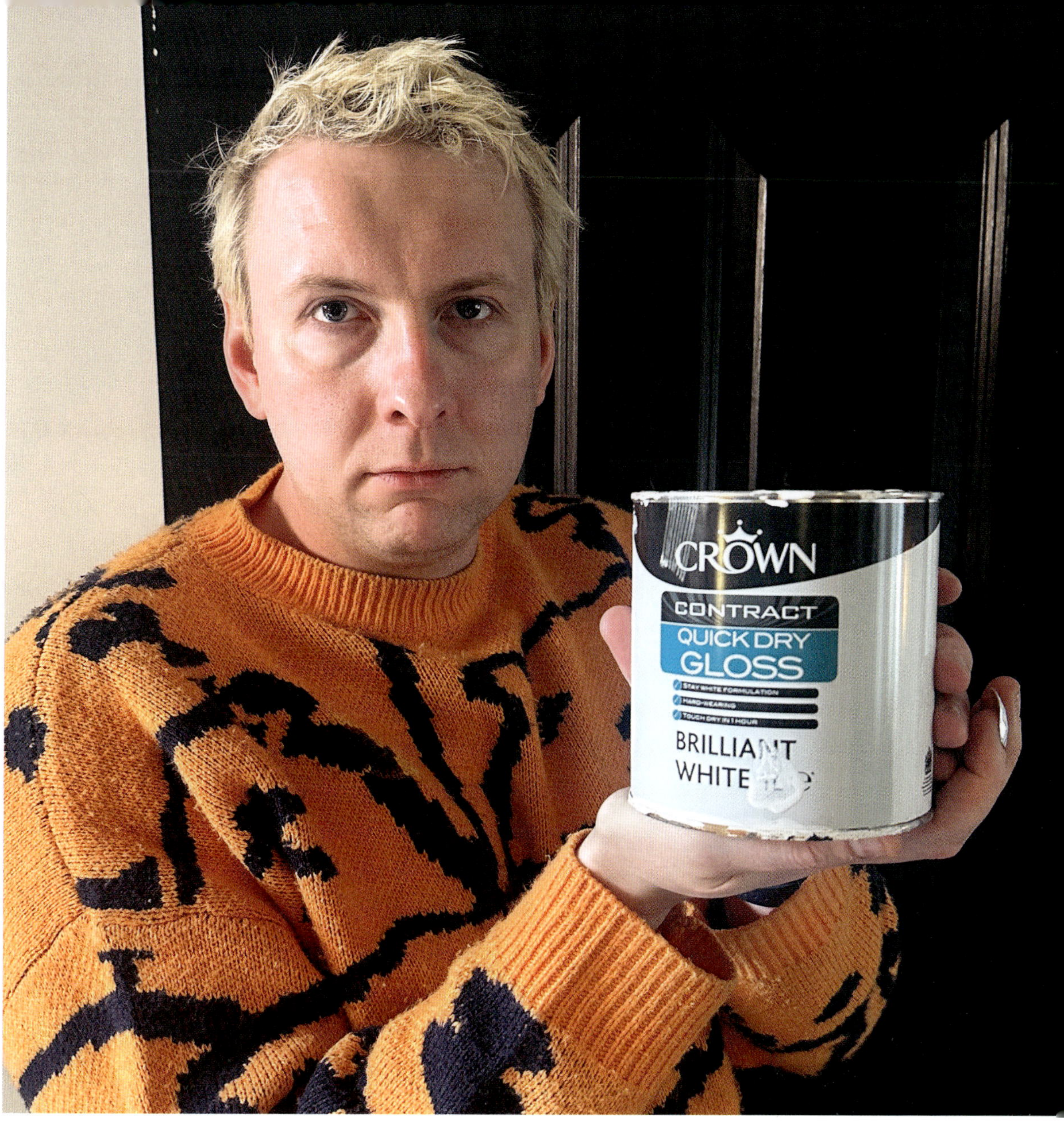

Fig. 144

Infuriatingly, my art agent (Neil Buchanan) messed up and despite the piece pulling in 400,000, the auction was held in Uzbekistan so the currency was Uzbekistani Som, which amounts to a little over £25 GBP.

NB: Once we'd installed the Baxi 830 2 Gas/LPG Combi Boiler in white (a gift from Juan Carlos I, King of Spain), Elton listed the property on Airbnb but used the term 'luxury cottaging', which attracted the wrong crowd (mainly football players and various members of the *Britain's Got Talent* on- and off-screen team), and most of the priceless furniture has been destroyed or extraordinarily stained. Airbnb soon banned us, but you can find it on local Skegness websites and it has availability pretty much all of the time – apart from Easter weekend when Elton uses it to host an egg hunt for Will and Jada Pinkett Smith's kids.

Fig. 145 One of my paintings of Elton, which he described as 'looking like a cross between all of the cast members of *Last of the Summer Wine*'.

Fig. 146 Elton John's schedule (in his own words).

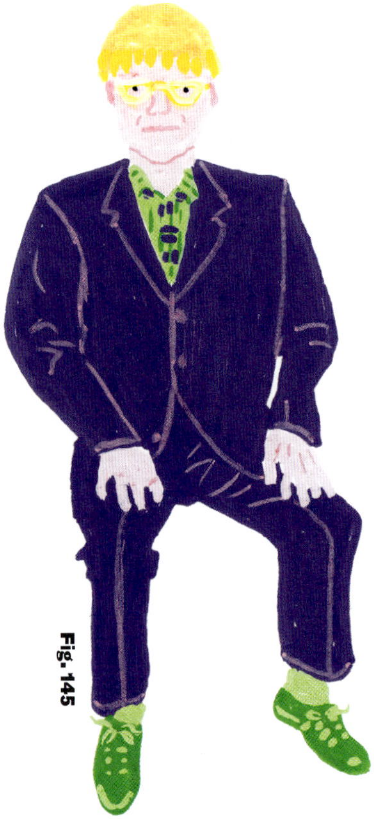

Fig. 145

Fig. 146

9am — RISE and exchange WhatsApp messages with Craig Cash.

10am: breakfast (crumpets) while messaging various members of the Backstreet Boys.

11am - massage while emailing Bill Clinton.

12pm - WhatsApp exchange with Lil Nas X but only using emojis.

1pm - LUNCH - (bread) while taking a video call with Eminem.

2pm - NAP.

3pm - Wake from nap, text 'you just popped into my head' to Malala.

4pm - Send various messages to Malala explaining that you got her number from Bill Gates at a fundraiser + that you didn't mean to disturb.

5pm - play piano for a bit.

6pm - LONG voice note session with Nigel Havers

7pm - DINNER (fish), ignore instagram DMs from Stephen Mulhern.

9pm - BED, after quick text exchange with the Pope

EVERYONE
DESERVES
A CHANCE

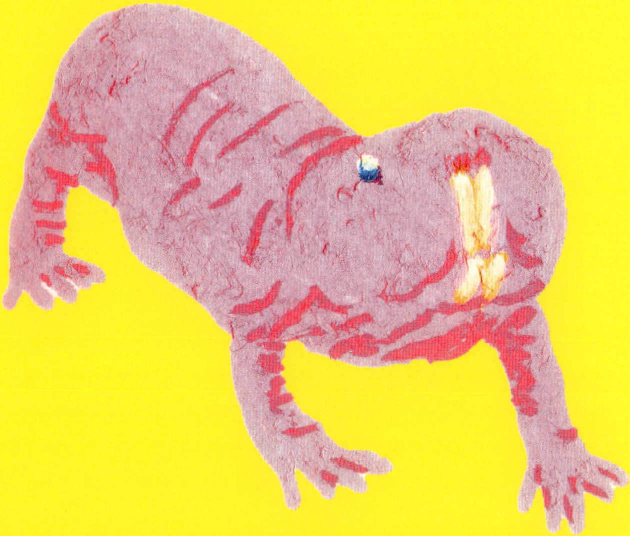

AMOL RAJAN

It was the middle of the early part of a late-summer early evening, with all that that brings: warm wood tables under orange skies; children returning to school; sleeping lovers in uneasy embraces; abandoned allotments; having to turn the diary over to October in a couple of weeks; Starbucks releasing the pumpkin spice latte;[1] the quiet sense of coming change. I sat in the silence in the doorway of the orangery, sipping in the stillness, and a Pepsi Max (maximum taste, zero sugar), when I noticed BBC journalist and new *University Challenge* host Amol Rajan had sent me a private message on Snapchat: 'Fancy an on-camera chat?'

I wasn't interested. I had neither anything to promote nor a requirement to make a public apology. I offered a compromise.

'Off-camera chat, and only if I can paint you,' I replied.

'Deal,' responded Rajan.

It wasn't till late October that we could find a gap in our respective schedules, and also he claimed he wouldn't sit for portraits outside of a full moon. We agreed we'd do it at his place so as to capture him in his natural habitat. Turns out Rajan has lived in the Premier Inn on the Euston Road for the last ten years. 'I was only meant to be here for a couple of nights, but they have everything I need: great location, free cleaning, unlimited tea and coffee, and the duvet is really heavy so I never fall out of bed.'

'Fair play,' I said, trying to hide my disgust at the arrangement.

At first, he was assigned a room on the second floor, but after a couple of years they took pity on the bloke and upgraded him to a suite, which is basically the same set-up but with an extra couple of square feet, a fridge and a wipe-clean chair. I was immediately drawn to the fridge, asking if it was a Hotpoint.

'No, I think it's Hisense. Why do you ask?'

'Oh, well, just because I'm having an issue with the cooling on my Hotpoint H55RM1110W1 Fridge in white,' I said.

'I'm sorry, that's awful. Is it cooling at all?' he asked, with deep concern.

'Not really,' I said, becoming tearful.

'You should try cleaning the condenser coils at the back. They can get a bit dirty over time and so the fridge can't efficiently release heat,' he replied, helpfully.

'May I use your facilities?' I asked, trying to distract from my pain, gesturing towards the en-suite/wet room.

'Absolutely!' He hurried over and turned the light on for me, a congenial act.

1. Or, as Starbucks marketing call it: PSL season. This sounds, to me, like an incurable disease of the bladder.

Fig. 147 A drawing of a can of Pepsi Max (maximum taste, zero sugar).
Fig. 148 *Amol Rajan,* 2024, acrylic gouache on backpack, 22 × 45mm.

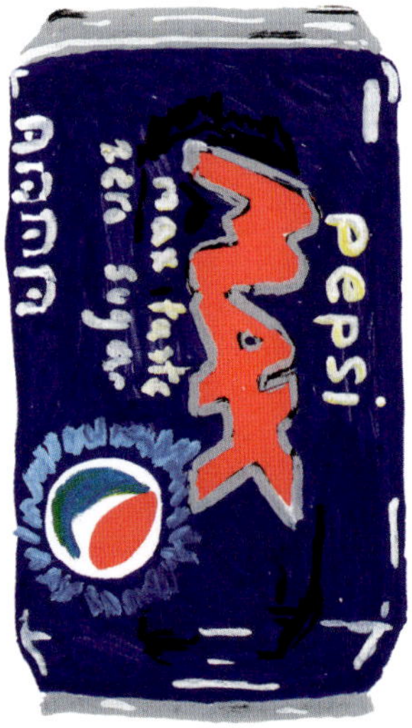

Fig. 147

Fig. 148

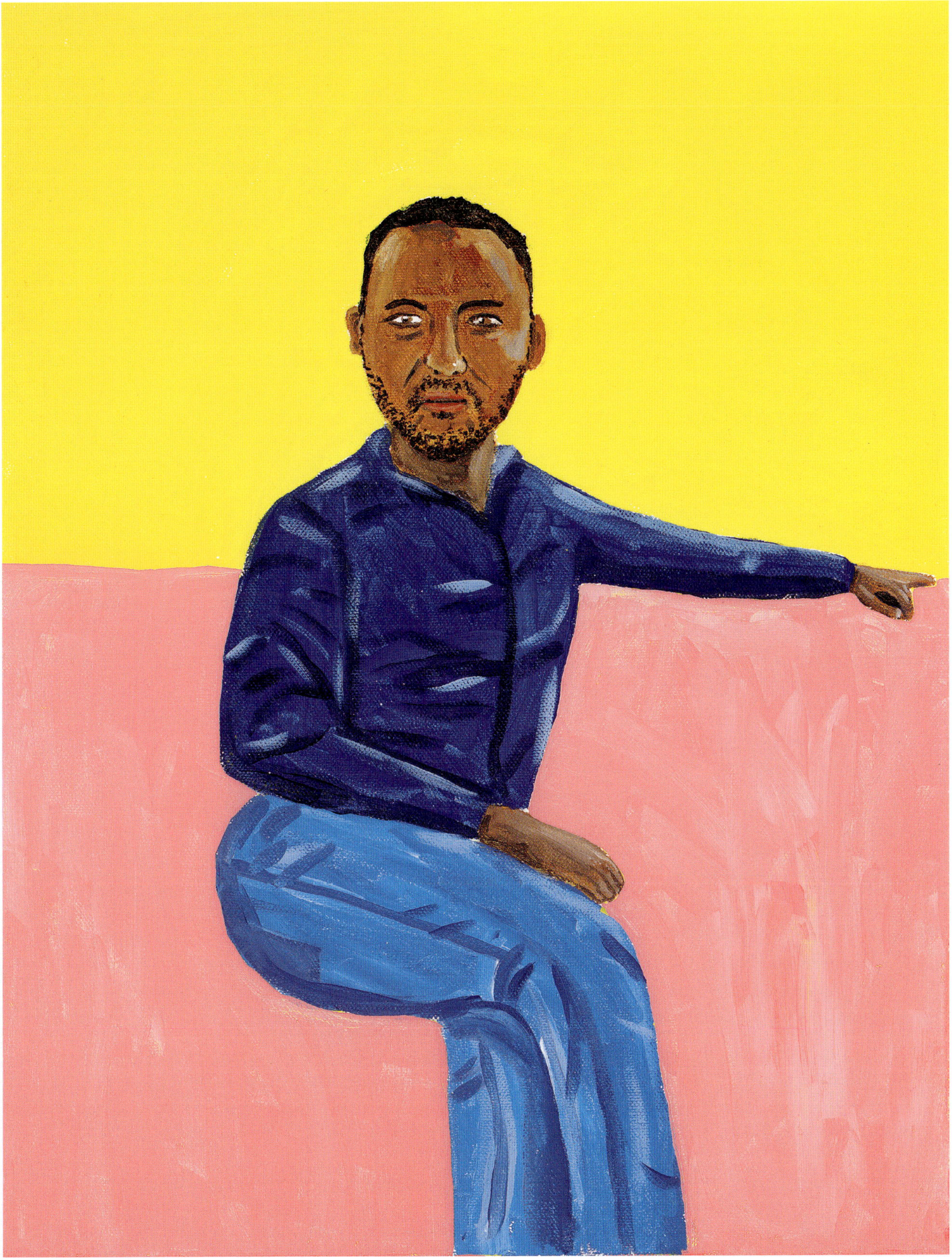

I closed the door behind me and noticed the room was a little different to your standard Premier Inn. I've stayed in enough to know how one looks. Everything was as expected, aside from a small wooden corner cabinet that Rajan must have had installed for extra storage. On it were dozens of different types of men's antiperspirant. There were classics like the Right Guard Sport Original Aerosol spray, the Dove Men+Care Extra Fresh antiperspirant stick and the Nivea Men Cool Kick 48H antiperspirant. But then were the altogether more interesting, unusual and premium offerings like Aesop's deodorant roll-on, Lab Series Antiperspirant Deodorant stick and the Old Spice High Endurance Original Scent Men's Antiperspirant & Deodorant.

I must have been looking longer than I realised as there was soon a tap on the MDF door: 'Everything OK in there?'

'Just a moment, Amol, I was looking at the deodorant cabinet,' I said, as he unlocked the bathroom from the outside somehow and came in.

'Oh yes, it's fantastic, isn't it? I've been collecting them for years!' His enthusiasm was adorable. 'My favourite is this one, you must try it.' He rubbed a bit of Gucci Guilty Deodorant Stick (70g) on my wrist. 'Smell,' he said, almost conspiratorially.

'Nice,' I said. It was fine.

'Like sea air and lemon groves,' he said, closing his eyes to enjoy it. 'Anyway, we'd best get on with this painting. I'm interviewing Ant from Ant and Dec in a couple of hours.' I raised my eyebrows. 'Sorry, I'm interviewing "Tony" from Ant and Dec.' I nodded at his correction.

We moved back into the bed/sitting room, even though I hadn't used the toilet and felt too awkward to ask to go again, and he took to[1] the chair. I tried to ask him what it was like interviewing some of the most famous and revered people in the world – Greta Thunberg, Bill Gates, Phillip Schofield – but he would always manage to change the subject to Jeremy Paxman.

'Have you ever met Jeremy Paxman?' was his first question,[2] but subsequent questions included: 'Do you think Jeremy Paxman has seen any of my episodes of *University Challenge*?', 'Has Jeremy Paxman read any of my journalistic blogs on the BBC News site?' and 'Do you think Jeremy Paxman will see this painting?'

'I don't think he'll be interested, truthfully,' I said, truthfully.

'Oh no, no, no, that won't do,' he said, fretting. 'No, no, no.'

He was clearly very worried that Paxman (the previous host of *University Challenge*) might disapprove of his work.

'Look, Amol,' I said, 'of course when you take over a job from someone it's natural to worry about what they think of your approach. When I was hosting *The Great British Sewing Bee*, I contemplated

1. Or, 'sat in'.
2. I hadn't.

Fig. 149 A Polaroid of me drawing a can of Pepsi Max (maximum taste, zero sugar).
Fig. 150 A Polaroid of a small selection of Amol's male deodorants.

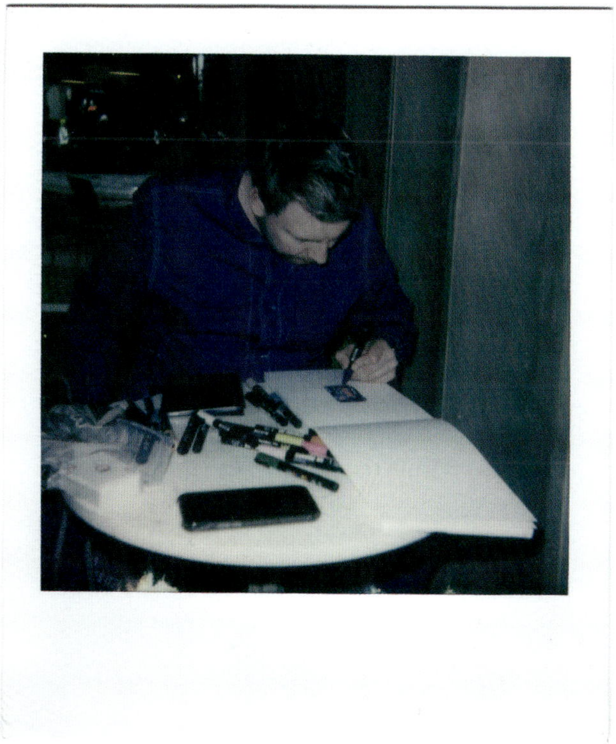

Fig. 149

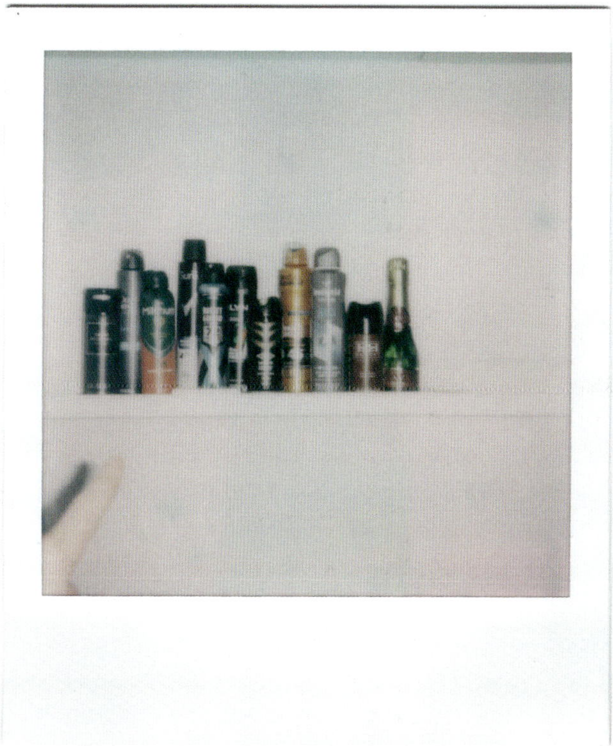

Fig. 150

what Claudia Winkleman made of me, and similarly what Richard Ayoade thinks of me hosting *Travel Man*, but you can't get bogged down in it.'

'Have you heard from either of them?' he asked.

'Neither of them has watched my series as far as I'm aware. In fact, Winkleman told me that she "couldn't be fucked",' I said. He sat in silence for a little while after this, contemplating my words, which was helpful as it allowed me to focus on the portrait and, also, I was finding him boring.

I used a little artistic licence to achieve the final result. For example, the colours of the room were not yellow and pink, and Amol wasn't wearing the blue shirt in the painting but a t-shirt that read 'Running Late Is My Cardio'. I noticed he had a few slogan t-shirts hanging up next to his Premier Inn iron and ironing board set. There was 'This Shirt Was Clean Yesterday', 'I Don't Snore, I Dream I'm a Motorcycle' and 'I'm Not Gay But $20 is $20'.

I was all about finished when his phone rang. I could see from the screen that it was his sometime *The One Show* co-host Alex Jones. 'I've got to take this,' he said, swiping to answer.

'Babe, can't speak for long, we're just in the middle of a VT about some fucking farm or something,' she said. I realised that it was 7.15 p.m. and they were live on air.

'Who's hosting with you?' asked Rajan.

'Jermaine,' she said, 'he's doing my nut in. Listen, babe, I bumped into Jeremy Paxman today.' Amol's eyes widened.

'Oh my god, what?' he said.

'Yeh, he was in the corridor,' she said, clearly understanding how important this information was going to be to Amol.

'What did he say?'

'Oh shit, babe, the VT is ending, will text you after the show.'

'No!' he shouted. 'No, no, no!' The words came out more like a wail of a bereaved dog – a despairing, guttural cry – than that of an esteemed BBC presenter.

Our session was over, Rajan could not focus on anything but *The One Show*, which he was staring at as if he were an elderly person and the LED TV screen was the windscreen of their car, his eyes about ten centimetres from the display, trying to surmise through the nuances of Alex's performance what Jeremy Paxman said to her in the corridor earlier that day. He would only avert his gaze to also constantly try to call her mobile. 'Why isn't she fucking answering?' he kept saying, knowing full well it was because she was live on BBC One. At one point, I noticed her shuffle on her chair as if to suppress the buzzing of the device.

Fig. 151 One of Amol's beloved t-shirts.
Fig. 152 *The One Show* sofa.

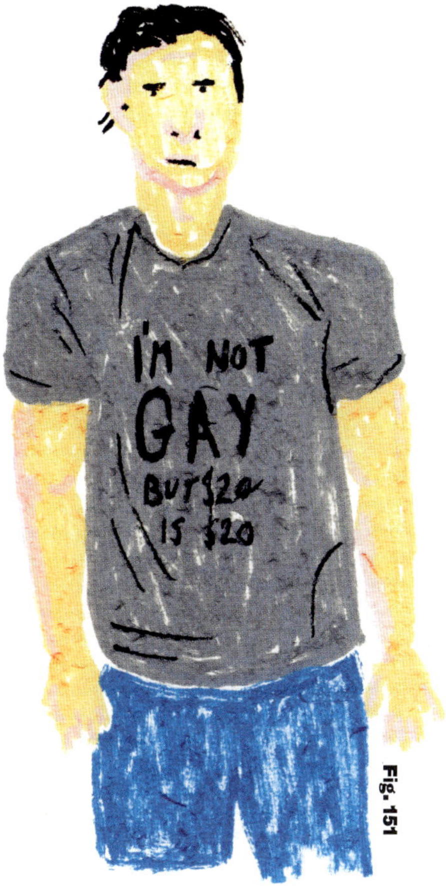

Fig. 151

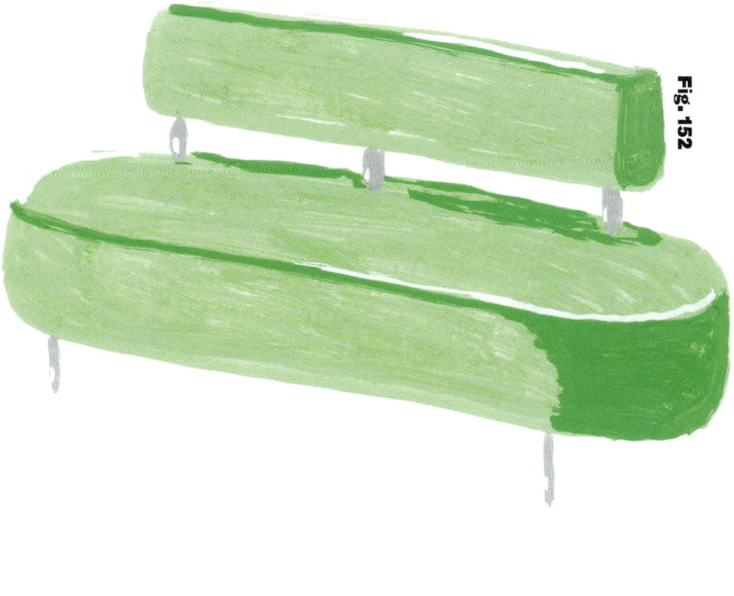
Fig. 152

Once the show had come off air there was a ten-minute pause (so unbearable for Amol that at one point he went into the bathroom and threw a Body Shop roll-on deodorant at the wall) until she finally rang back, and told him that Paxman had been very nice about him and said he'd not seen all of the new episodes of *University Challenge* but what he had seen he'd thought were 'terrific'.

'Which episodes? Did Jeremy Paxman say which episodes?' asked a now fully erratic Rajan.

'He didn't say, babe,' replied Jones, clearly regretting the whole thing.

Rajan walked me out of the Premier Inn, shaking the hands of everyone he met on the way as if he were a victorious sportsman. The reactions on their faces suggested this was quite out of the ordinary and in fact one of the staff at the 'Thyme'[1] restaurant said, 'What's got into you?', which he ignored.

Months later, I had the great fortune of bumping into Jeremy Paxman in Toolstation. I was picking up a Drayton TRV4 Classic Thermostatic Radiator Valve 15mm Angled with Lockshield and he was getting a spring doorstop. I asked him if he had watched any of Rajan's work and he said he hadn't seen a 'single frame' of *University Challenge*, 'even when I was hosting the damn thing', and when I pressed him on what he'd said to Alex Jones in the corridor he just said, 'Never heard of the woman.'

This painting is kept in the private collection of the late Italian PM Silvio Berlusconi, alongside his other worthless paintings and six life-size posters of Kelly Brook.

1. Thyme is one of the many onsite restaurants provided by the Premier Inn brand. Depending on the branch, you might find: Bar + Block Steakhouse; Beefeater; Brewers Fayre; Table Table; Cookhouse + Pub; Whitbread Inns; The Kitchen; Hub Lounge Café Bar; Hub Proven Dough Deli + Bar; and The Social. Each of them offers a slightly alternative take on the same theme, which is what you might describe as 'meals that are absolutely fine'.

Fig. 153 A drawing of the sort of radiator you might use a Drayton TRV4 Classic Thermostatic Radiator Valve on.

Fig. 154 The Drayton TRV4 Classic Thermostatic Radiator Valve, a stunning feat of radiator engineering. Photograph by Clive Myrie.

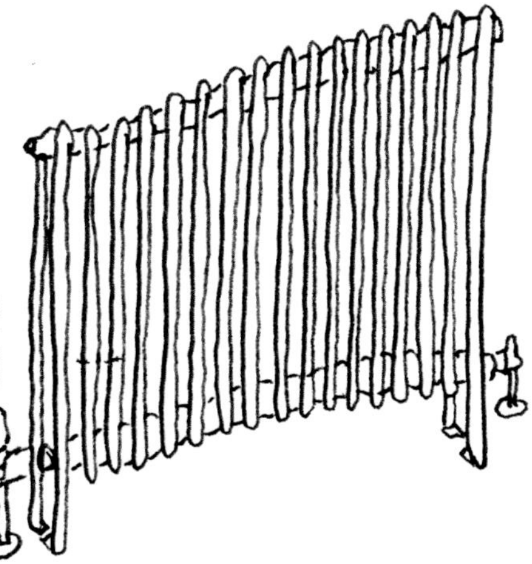

Fig. 153

Fig. 154

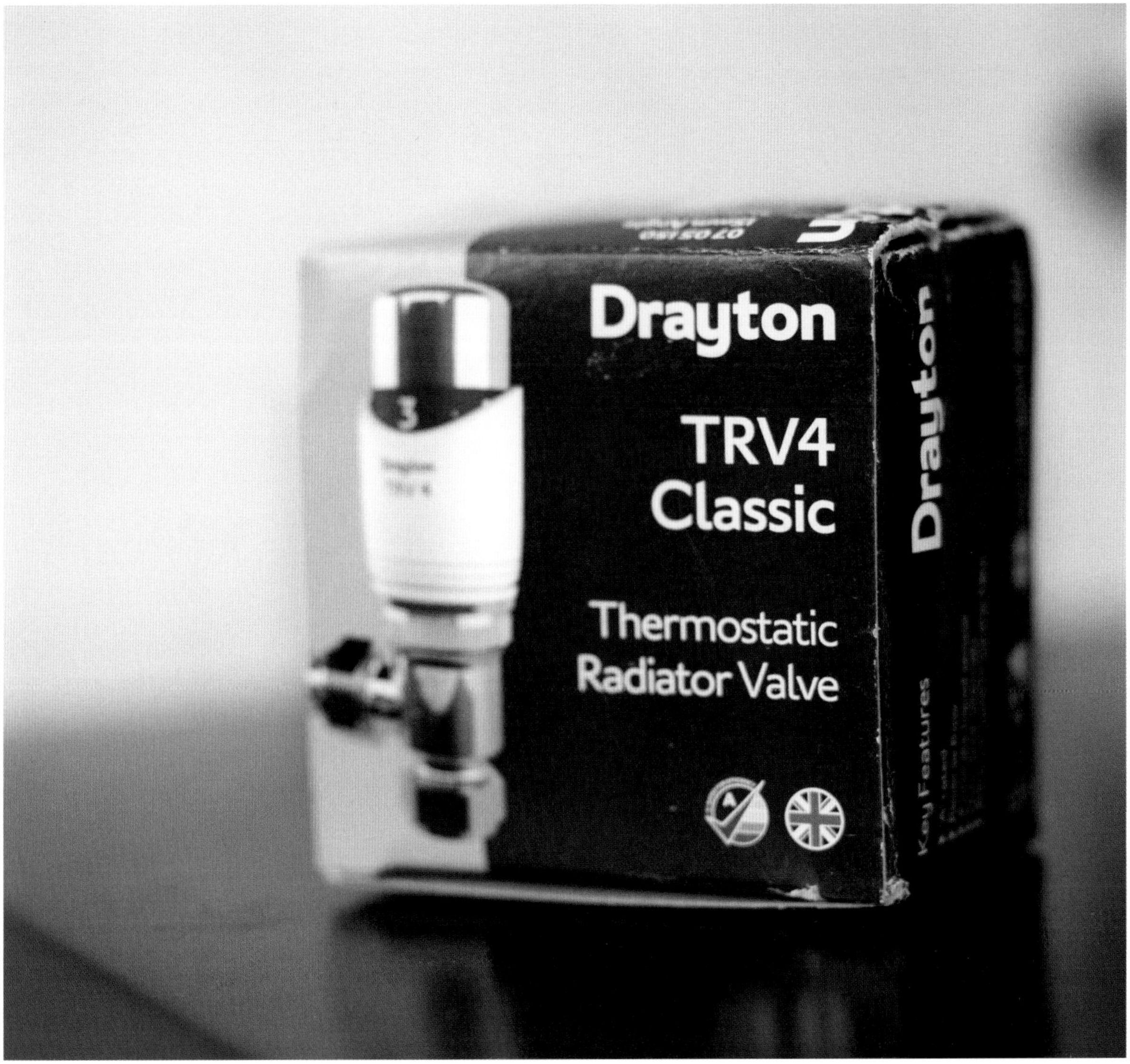
Drayton
TRV4
Classic
Thermostatic
Radiator Valve
Drayton
Key Features

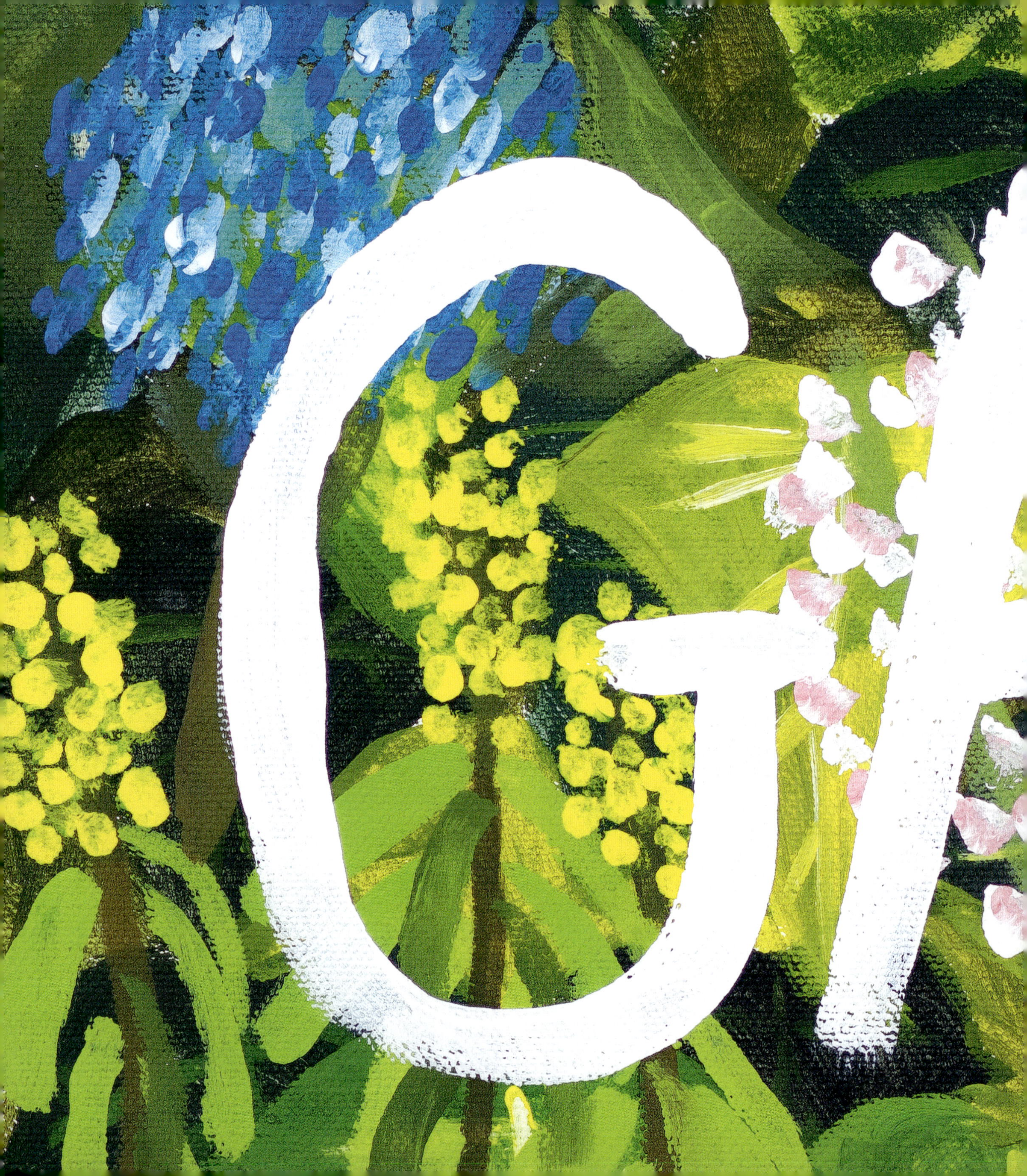

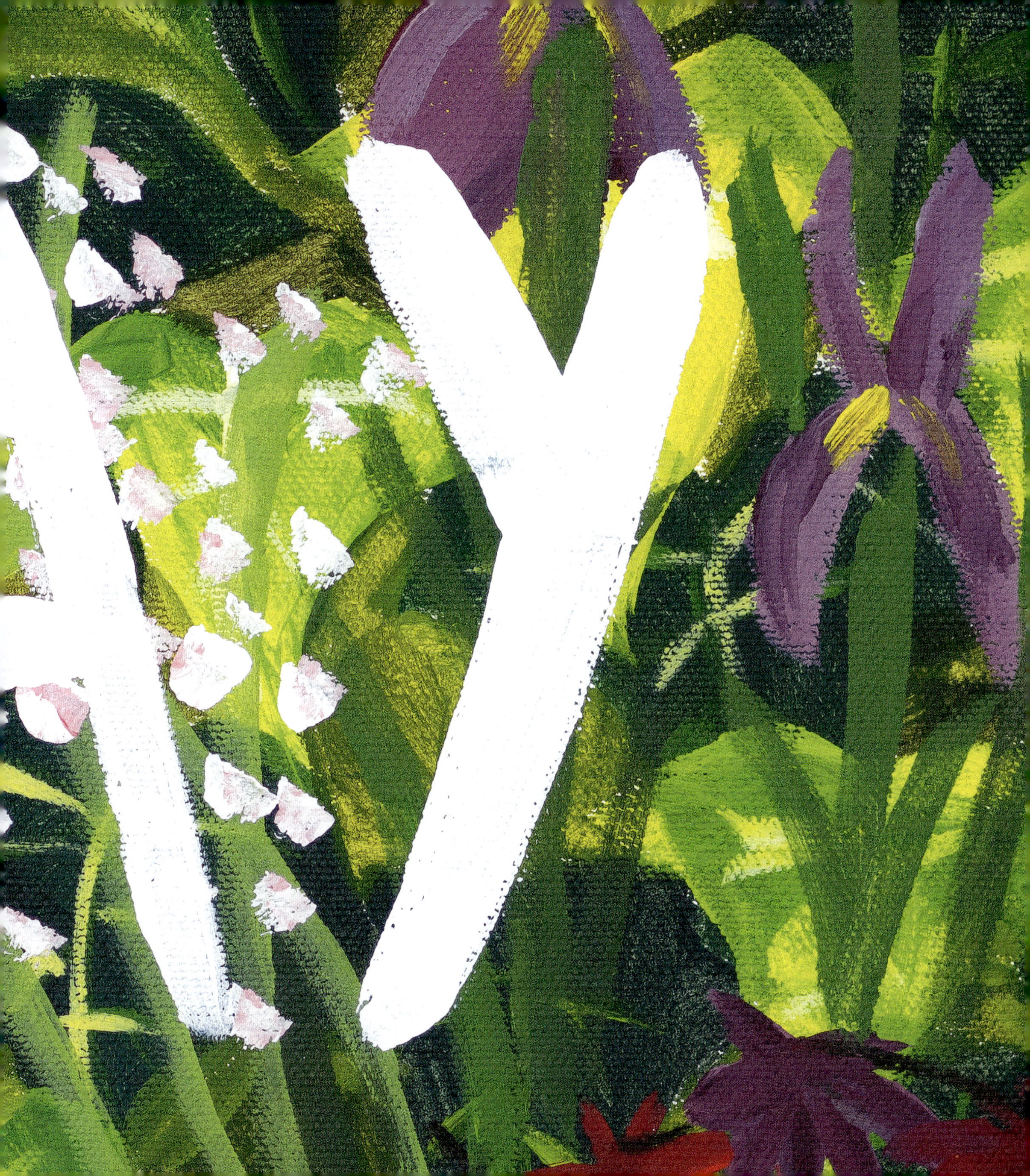
Y

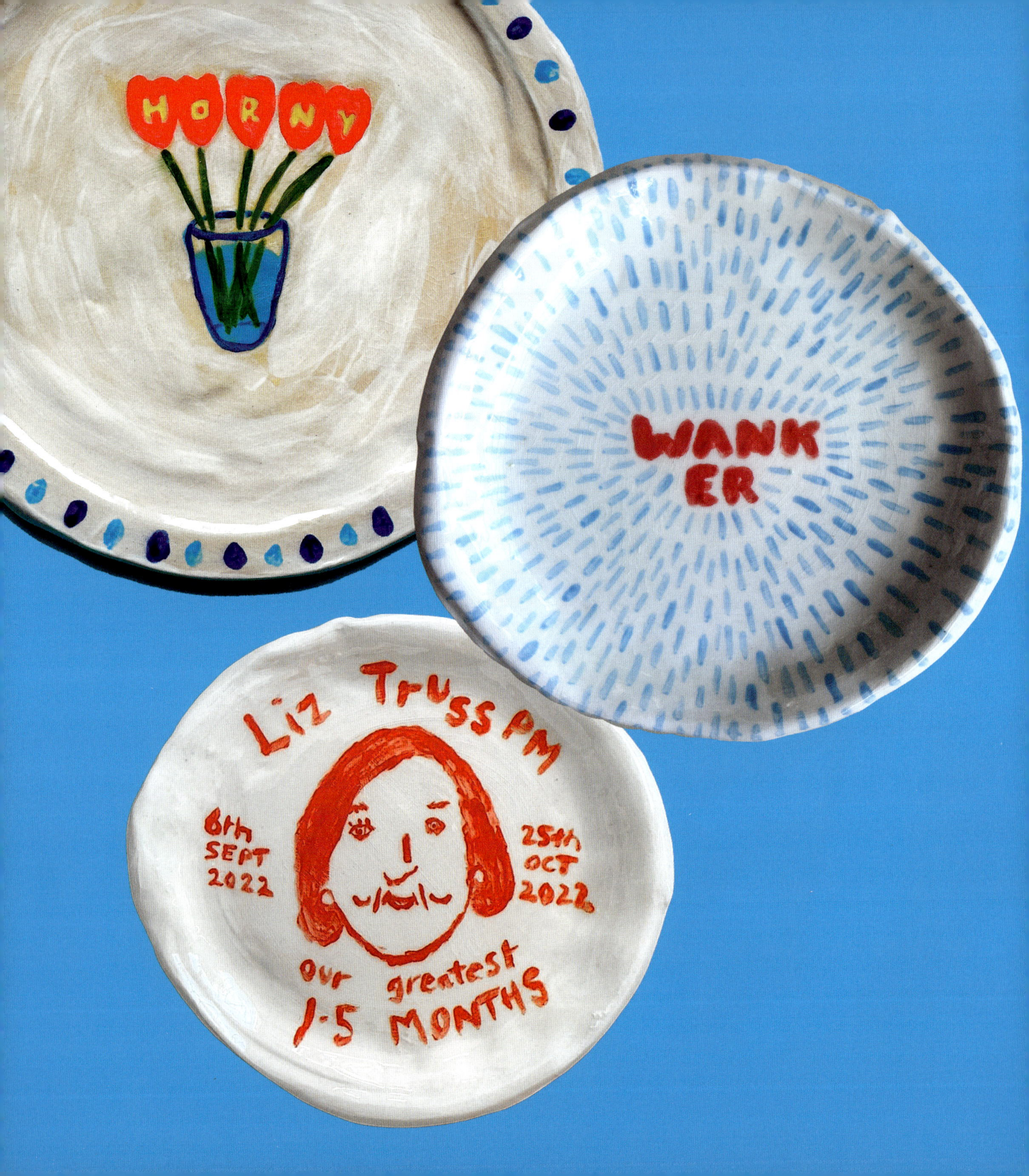
HORNY
WANK
ER
Liz Truss PM
6th
SEPT
2022
25th
OCT
2022
our greatest
1.5 MONTHS

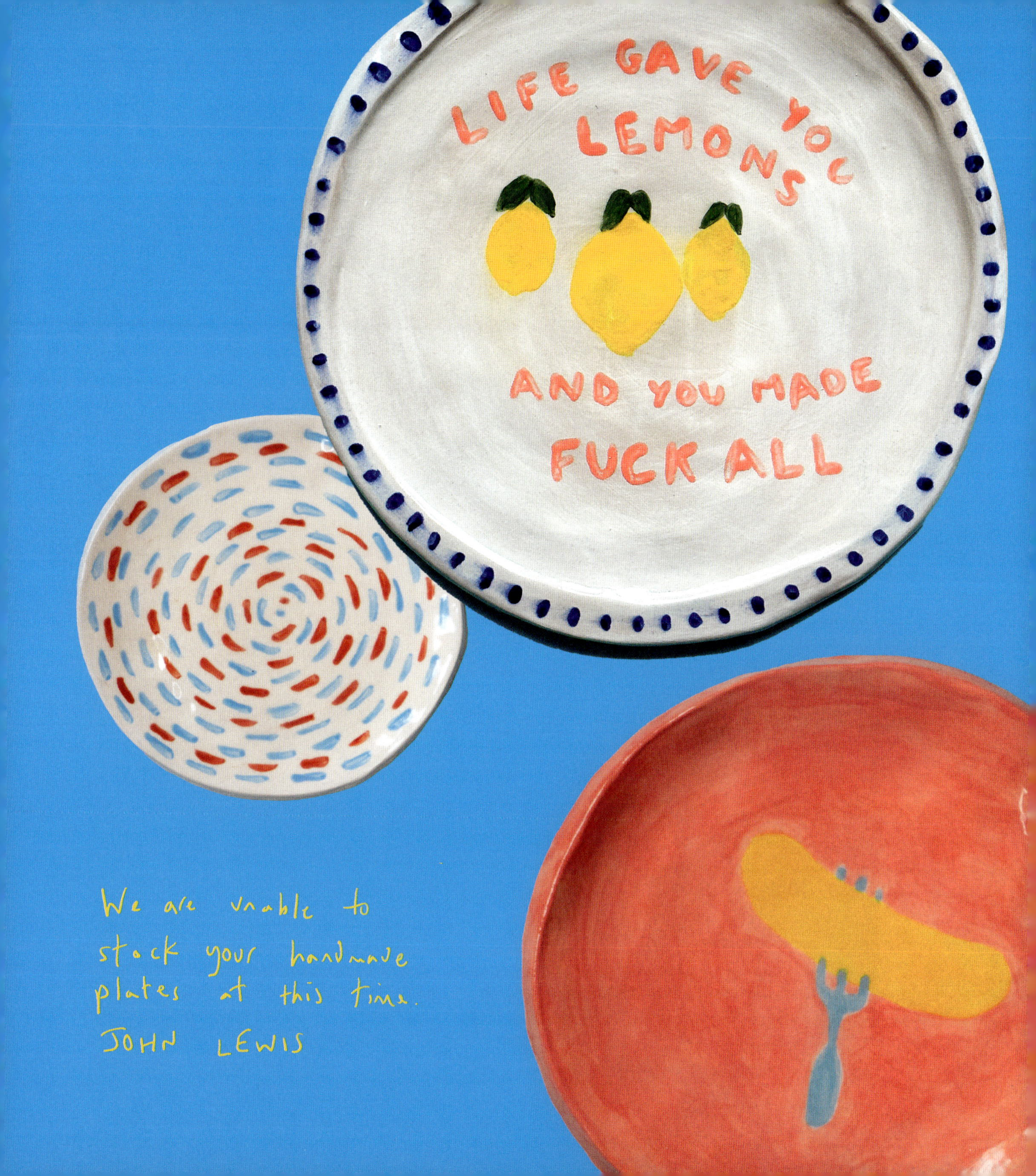
LIFE GAVE YOU LEMONS
AND YOU MADE FUCK ALL
We are unable to stock your handmade plates at this time.
JOHN LEWIS

JACK GREALISH

Fig. 155 *Jack Grealish,* 2024, acrylic, grass and melted sock on football, 30 × 30cm.

The day Great Aunt Shirley left us (died) is seared in my memory forever. A black and hopeless day, where clocks resigned and acid sunbeams found no beauty, revealing only nature's shadows and heaven's disappointments. I lost track of my purpose and my heart forgot to beat. The only light in that endless gutter of grief was the Premier League footballer Jack Grealish.

My great aunt Shirley was like a mother to me, nurturing and stoic, but also like a father because she was obsessed with golf and left shits in the bowl the size of a small dog. I had watched her deteriorate – slowly at first, over years, and then at considerable pace in those final, hopeless days.

She had been in Birmingham's Queen Elizabeth Hospital (known as 'the QE' to locals, pronounced 'quee') for eight days, in and out of consciousness, when the doctor, rushed and forlorn, told us that she was nearing the end of her life. The words were incomprehensible (because he was, as many staff are at the QE, on cocaine). A sadness that could have torn plaster from those grey walls filled the room but was soon dispersed by audible excitement outside in the wider ward; the sounds of tittering, doctors scrambling for their phones, and patients climbing from their death beds. 'Omg,' came one voice. 'Look, Sandra, it's Jack Grealish!'

Grealish was there on a visit to see some sick children and show them footballs and how nice he looked in his kit. He'd loved it so much, he vowed to visit every ward, stopping and taking photographs with whoever asked. He was charming, handsome, thoughtful and, dare I say it, pretty fit.

I knew I had to risk it, to potentially not be by her side as she died, in the hope that she might have the opportunity, even for the briefest of moments, to meet Jack Grealish. I stepped out into the ward and approached, tentatively. I was expecting aggression, but far from being intimidating, his presence was like a soft and luxurious blanket – warm and really nice to run your palm over. 'Jack,' I said, 'my great aunt Shirley is dying. You are her favourite footballer. Might you sit with us a while?'

'It would be my great honour,' he replied, bowing his head all the way to the floor. I asked if he was being sarcastic, to which he said, 'Probably September,' and we entered.

Cousin Liz was quickly removed to make space for Grealish because, like the rest of the family, Shirley thought Liz was a loser. 'Go and get a coffee, and while you're there maybe see if you can get a life,' said my uncle Tim, handing her a fiver and his Costa Coffee Club loyalty card. 'If you don't get a stamp, don't come back.'

Fig. 155

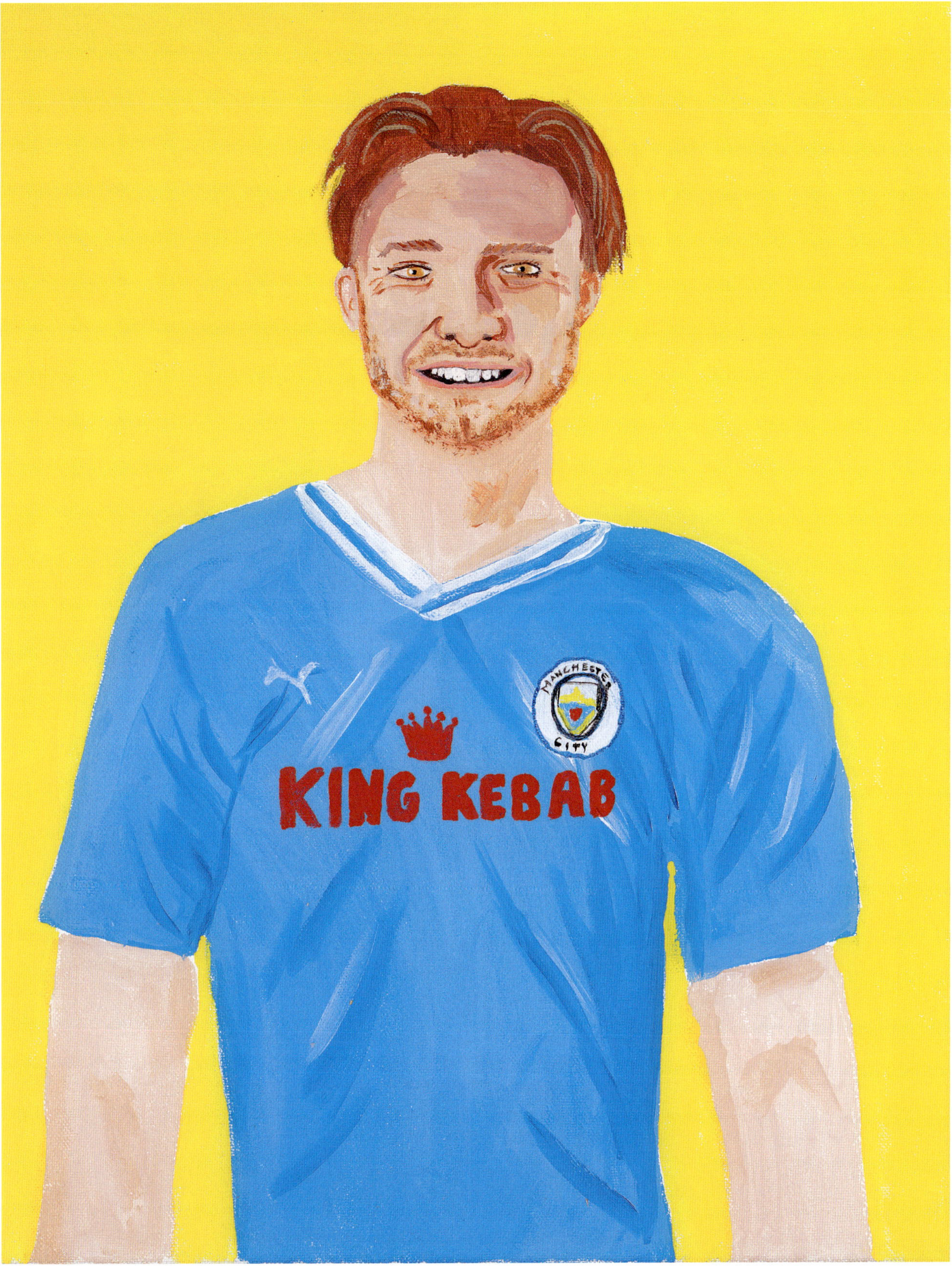

'Great Aunt Shirley,' I whispered. 'It's your favourite football player, Jack Grealish.' She stirred, opened her eyes and began to cry.

'My favourite footballer is Frank Lampard,' she said.

Far from being hurt, Jack took hold of Shirley's hand and leant in to speak to her. 'I'm sorry I'm not Frank Lampard. If there was any way I could become Frank Lampard, to still your pain and soothe your soul, please know, Shirley, that I would do it for you.' She smiled.

'You are a kind boy,' she said, and dropped a tab of acid that had been provided by the hospital caretaker.

'There, there, sweet Shirley,' he said, taking her hand and softly rubbing the back of it with his thumb. 'I know you are frightened. But let us not dwell on graves and grief. Death is not to be feared. You reach your hand out into the abyss and what do you feel? There is nothing to feel but love. Wherever, whatever next, it will not and cannot be without love. Remember, my dear Shirley, the words of Dylan Thomas: "Though lovers be lost love shall not".'

Shirley's mouth had begun to curl into a contented smile, from his words but also probably 'cause of the tab of acid. 'Thank you, Jack Grealish,' she whispered. 'Thank you for everything.'

'Don't thank me, I have told you nothing you did not already know yourself,' he purred. 'Are you comfortable? Do you need anything?'

'There is one thing you can help with,' she said, raising her finger. 'My nephew, the irritating effeminate one,' – she was now pointing the finger at me – 'his Hotpoint H55RM1110W1 Fridge in white is just not cooling properly. A real man would be able to fix it, but he is a limp-wristed arse bandit with no applicable skills. Might you be able to restore it?'

'Interesting,' said Grealish, stroking his chin, 'is it a faulty thermostat or dirty condenser coils?'

'Neither, I believe,' I said.

'And you've checked the compressor and not overfilled the fridge?'

'Correct,' I said. 'I have tried everything.'

'I will have it working by morning.'

Hearing those words, calmly and peacefully, Great Aunt Shirley slipped away (died). Jack stayed with us, silent unless spoken to, fixing my Hotpoint H55RM1110W1 Fridge in white, which I had brought to the bedside.

We said our goodbyes to Shirley's brittle body, and once I had kissed her on her cold and sunken forehead, Jack took hold of the back of my head with his palms and looked into my eyes. 'Joe, I have fixed your Hotpoint H55RM1110W1 Fridge in white. The refrigerant was leaking because of a faulty valve,' he said. 'When a mountain appears

Fig. 156 The Costa Coffee Club card, which gets you one free coffee for every ten coffees. If you have one large coffee a day, by the end of the year you'll have amassed roughly enough free coffee to fill a small wheelbarrow. This fact has not been independently verified.
Fig. 157 A diagram of Jack Grealish's brain.

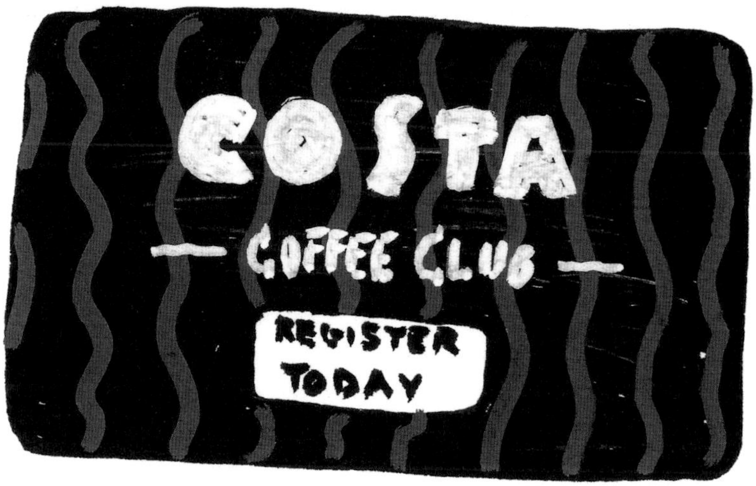

Fig. 156

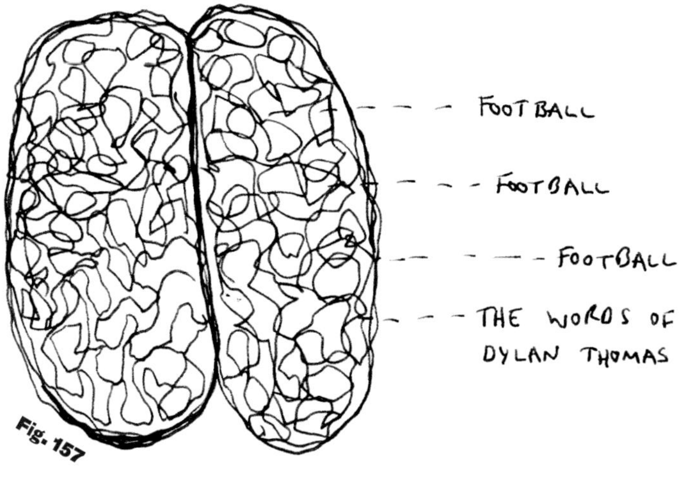

Fig. 157

unassailable, you will find a way. This is as true of your fridge as it is with your sadness. Remember that grief is the price of love, and the price of the replacement valve will be £65 plus VAT. Shirley's life, your life, the life of a Hotpoint H55RM1110W1 Fridge in white, even my life – they are all transient. But so is sorrow. It will pass. All of us are destined to return home one day, to see out the rest of the seasons, listen closely to the morning dew, smell faint winds of rice and wine, take earth and ash in our fists, sip in the light of the moon. Do not despair, dear Joe. We have been shown the truth of all life: that is, eternity is meaningless.'

And with that, he slipped away (left quietly).

As he walked out, I heard him say to one of his minders: 'Let's get out of this shithole, it smells like a fucking human abattoir.'

Fig. 158 A small etching I did of a seated Jack Grealish on a toilet wall in a Harvester just outside Swindon.

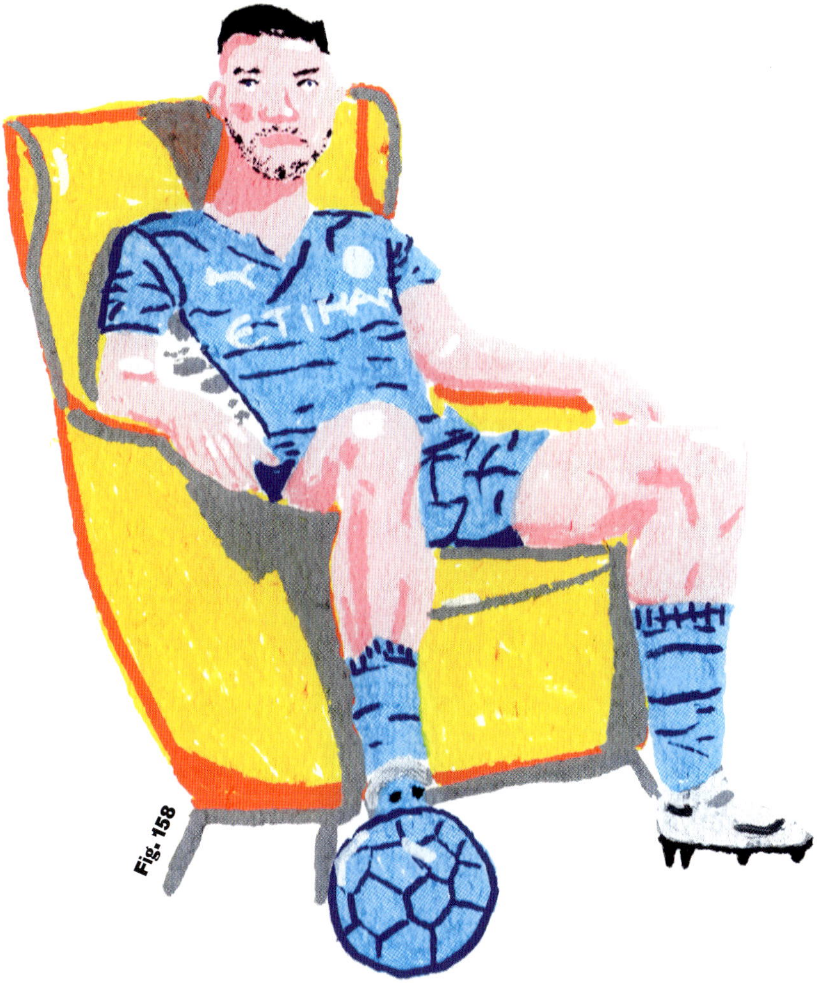

Fig. 158

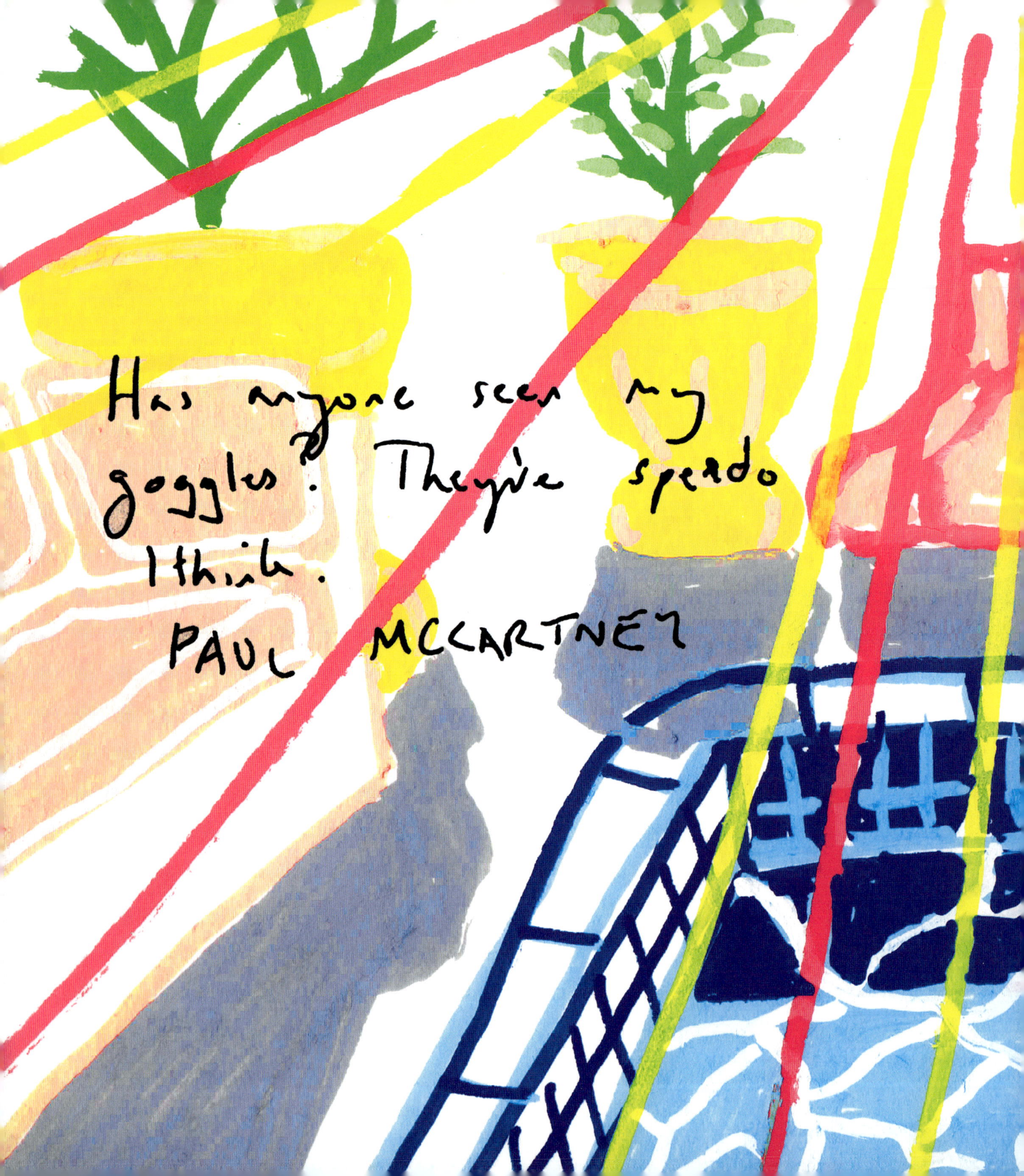
Has anyone seen my goggles? They're speedo I think.
PAUL MCCARTNEY

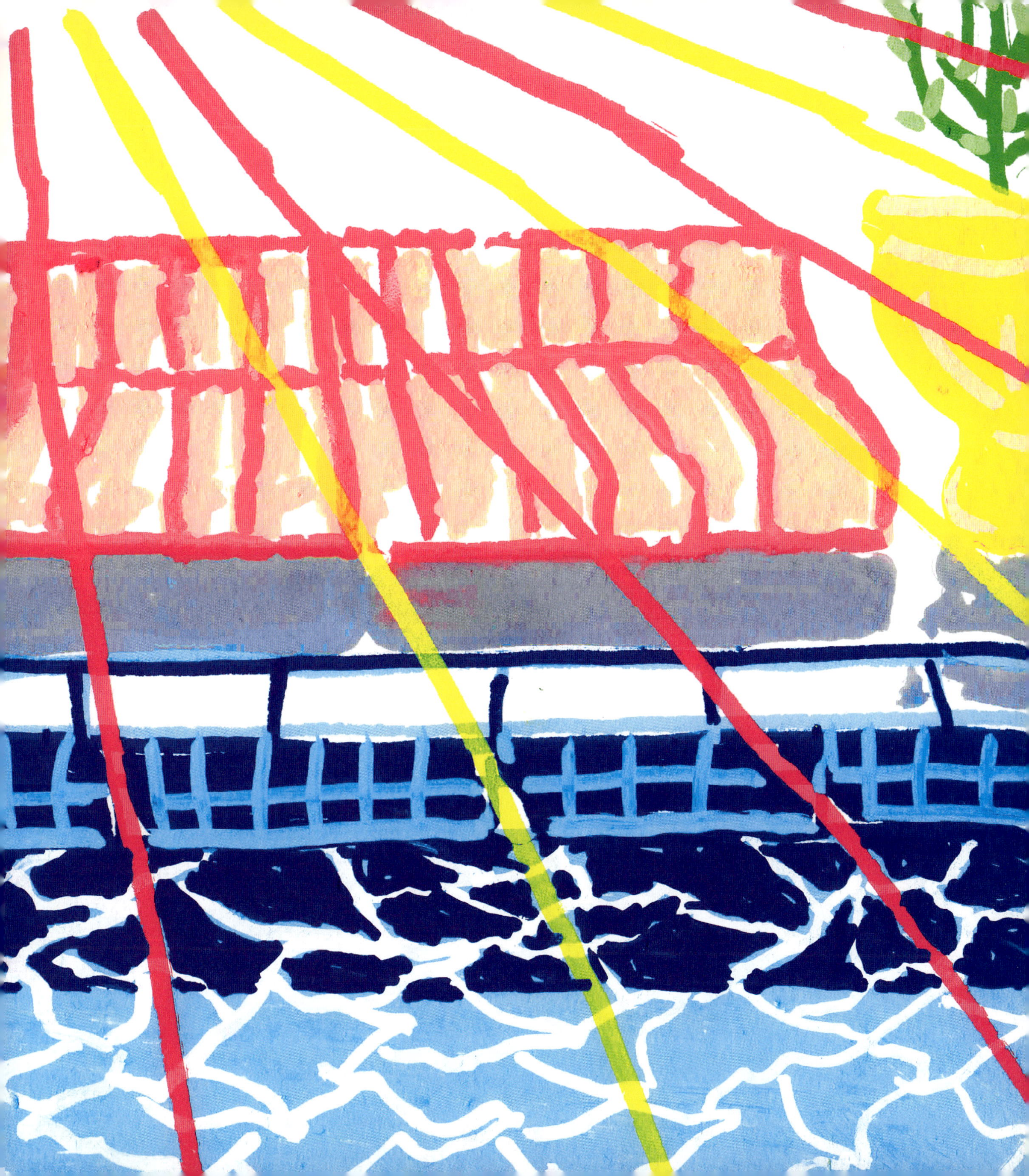

JOE LYCETT'S SCHEDULE

Fig. 159 My schedule (in my own words).

I thought long and hard about how to end this book. I read it through about six times, and each time I said to myself: 'It is perfect.' But then, on seventh reading, I realised that there was one thing missing. I have asked my subjects to make themselves vulnerable by sharing their daily schedules – a glance into their innermost lives – and yet you know nothing of mine. So, to conclude this book, I bring you a day in the life of little old me.

Fig. 159

Joe Lycett – Schedule

12:30pm — rise

1:00pm — morning paper, right wing publications ONLY (Telegraph, Daily Mail) with black coffee prepared in De'Longhi Eletta Explore ECAM 450.86.T Bean to Cup Coffee Machine in titanium black.

2:00pm — return to bed to send emails, some aggressive, on my 2020 Apple MacBook Air 13.3" Retina Display, M1 processor, 8GB RAM, 256 GB SSD in space grey.

3:00pm — indoor cycling session on NordicTrack Commercial S15i spin bike.

3:25pm — bath with bottle of 2015 Champagne Louis Roederer, Rosé Vintage, Brut.

5:30pm — lunch, at home but sourced from The Delaunay/The Wolseley/Nando's: beetroot carpaccio; halloumi sticks and dip; fettucine alfredo; half a chicken (mango+lime); still water; Sancerre; Coke Zero; Malbec; peri-peri salt on filet au poivre; Gâteau Opéra aux Truffles et Café d'Arabica; and a Wispa Gold.

8:00pm — diazepam

8:05pm — alprazolam

8:10pm — lorazepam

8:15pm — nitrazepam

8:20pm — marzipan

8:25pm — temazepam

8:30pm — spam

9:00pm — Joe Lycett is ready to paint

11:00pm — paint voraciously while downing pints of Birra Moretti

3:00am — finishing touches while downing shots of Patrón XO Cafe Tequila Coffee liquer (discontinued)

4:00am — television (old episodes of 'In The Night Garden') with dinner; dominoes pizza, but with original toppings scraped off and replaced, by a Michelin star chef, with crème fraiche base, thinly sliced prosciutto di Parma, lobster tail medallion, fresh figs, and a drizzle of aged port reduction

5:00am — send spring loaded glitter bombs to estate agents to relax.

6:00am — sleep.

I have a saying: 'these days everyone is obsessed with their phone. What they don't realise is their phone is obsessed with them.'

Pretty neat.

YOKO ONO

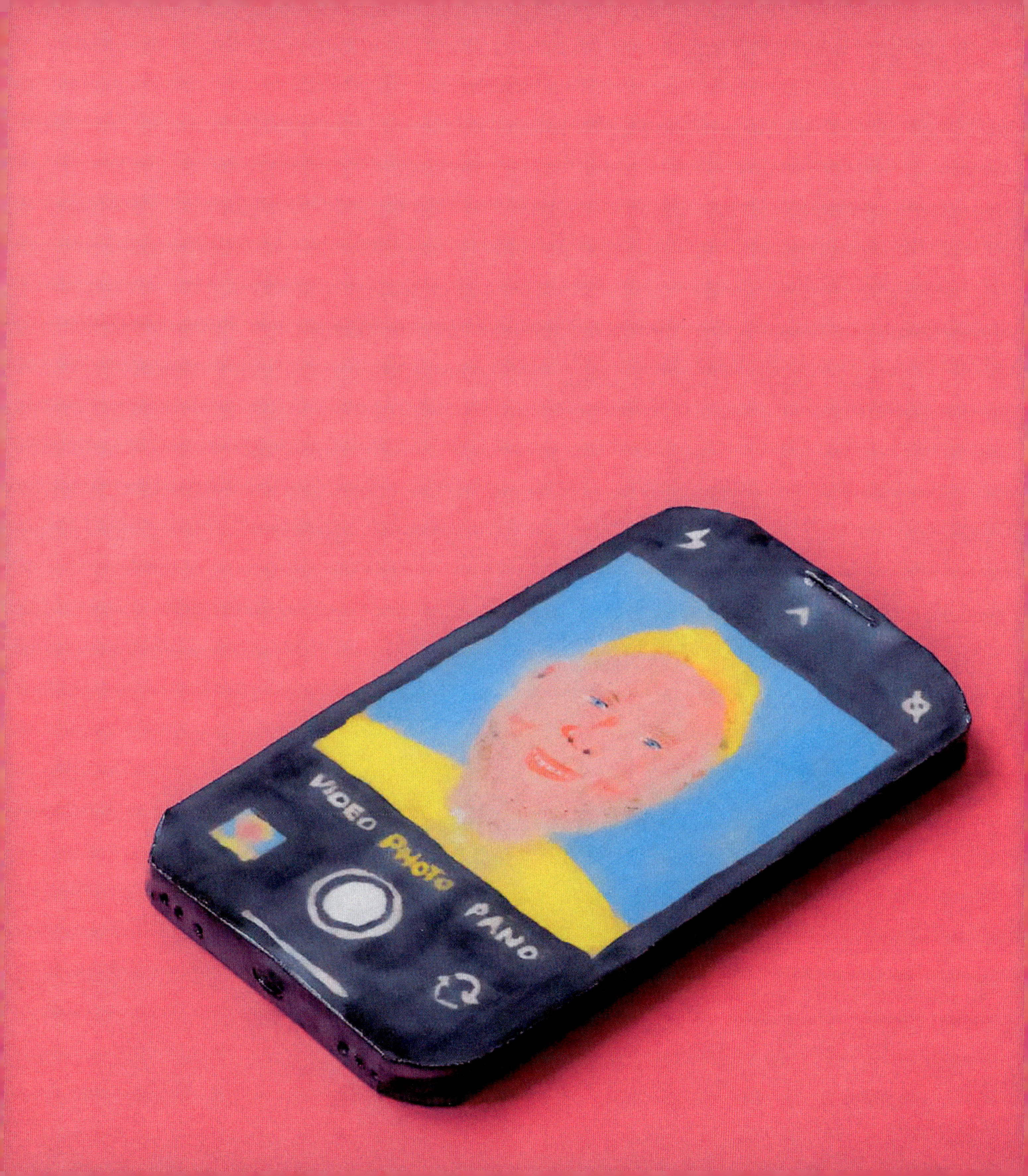
VIDEO
PHOTO
PANO

Q&A WITH BANKSY

Fig. 160 A chair from the foyer of a Radisson Blu.

Banksy is an internationally recognised street artist and entrepreneur. To celebrate the release of Art Hole, *he agreed to sit with me in the foyer of a Radisson Blu to discuss the art world, anonymity and what the future holds.*

JOE: Wow, I had no idea.
BANKSY: Yeh, everyone says that.

JL: Who else knows who you are?
B: Well, obviously the other boys do, although not Lee 'cause you can't trust him with anything. But Simon and Duncan have kept it to themselves, by and large – although Duncan did once tell Shaznay from All Saints, which really fucked me off.

JL: Well, I really didn't expect it. It's a pleasure to meet you ... again. You are arguably the most important artist of our generation. Why keep your identity secret?
B: Well, Joe, as you well know, if you're known for one thing then people in the UK don't let you do anything else. I saw it with my friend Lesley Joseph. She was very well known for being in the ITV sitcom *Birds of a Feather*, but most people don't know that she's also a world-class engineer specialising in Unmanned Aircraft Systems (UAS). When she applied to be on the R&D team at Airbus to develop powerful attack drones – a role she was born to do – the management said they couldn't see past the character of Dorien Green and refused to hire her. As I developed as an artist, I realised that my work in the band could potentially muddy the waters, and so Banksy was born.

JL: That's so interesting. Daft Punk told me a similar thing. They didn't want to reveal their identities in case it conflicted with their presenting jobs on *I'm a Celebrity ...* and *Saturday Night Takeaway*. Tell me, what's your process?
B: Well, I'm not really politically minded, so I generally just have a flick through things like the *New Statesman* or Owen Jones's Twitter to see what's winding up the lefties. Then, I'll have a brainstorming session on Zoom with my team (which consists of the other lads without Lee, half a dozen comedy writers, my business manager and approx. thirty lawyers) and see what we can come up with. Then, I'll do a mock-up on my iPad, print out a stencil, chuck a balaclava on and get out there.

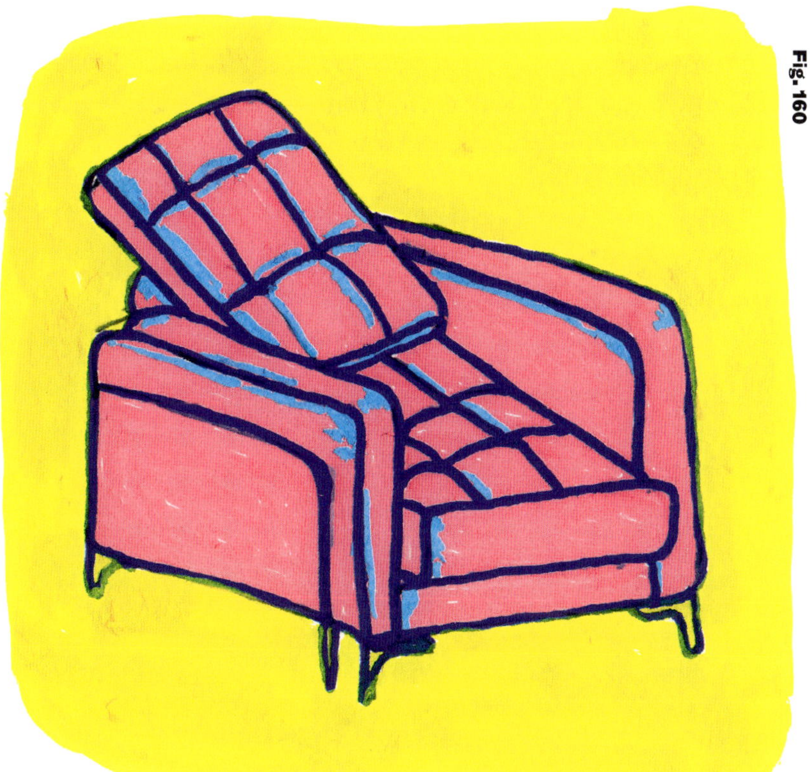

Fig. 160

JL: Fascinating. So, it was a deliberate choice to appeal to a left-wing audience?
B: I did make some art for right-wing people for a while, but I got bored of doing landscapes of the south of France and Maggie Thatcher on horseback. One day I did some graffiti on one of my client's houses in Chelsea, but I didn't use Farrow & Ball Elephant's Breath so they paid someone to clean it off. Then I did one on a left-winger's wall, and they said, 'Very interesting, very interesting indeed,' and asked a journalist from *The Observer* to come and do a piece on it. It just seemed like the most commercial prospect.

JL: Your work does sometimes get damaged, stolen or destroyed, but you once tried to shred your own work straight after it had been auctioned. Why?
B: Mate, the best way to get the price of something up is to get *The Economist* to write an article about it. Everyone thinks you're dead clever. And don't forget, due to artists' resale rights, every time one of my works gets resold I get about 3 per cent. The original sold for about a million. The shredded version went for 25 million. I'll let you work out the maths.

JL: OK, so if the original sold for a million and you got 3 per cent that's £30k, and then the second sale was 25 million so that's £750k. So, in total, you're looking at about £780k.
B: I wasn't expecting you to actually work out the maths. But yeh.

JL: Has anyone ever got close to finding out your identity?
B: Foolishly, one night I was doing a piece on a wall in London and had forgotten to put my balaclava on. I spotted someone taking photos of me and realised I had to distract them, so I pissed against a cashpoint to quell the rumours. I never finished that piece, which was going to be a caged gorilla making Pret sandwiches.

JL: What does the future hold?
B: I'm taking a break from art to work on the new album and a tour. Then I'll probably do something really thought-provoking like release a load of doves onto the forecourt of a Shell garage.

JL: Thank you for your time, Antony.

Fig. 161 An early Banksy sketch of a gorilla making Pret sandwiches.

Fig. 161

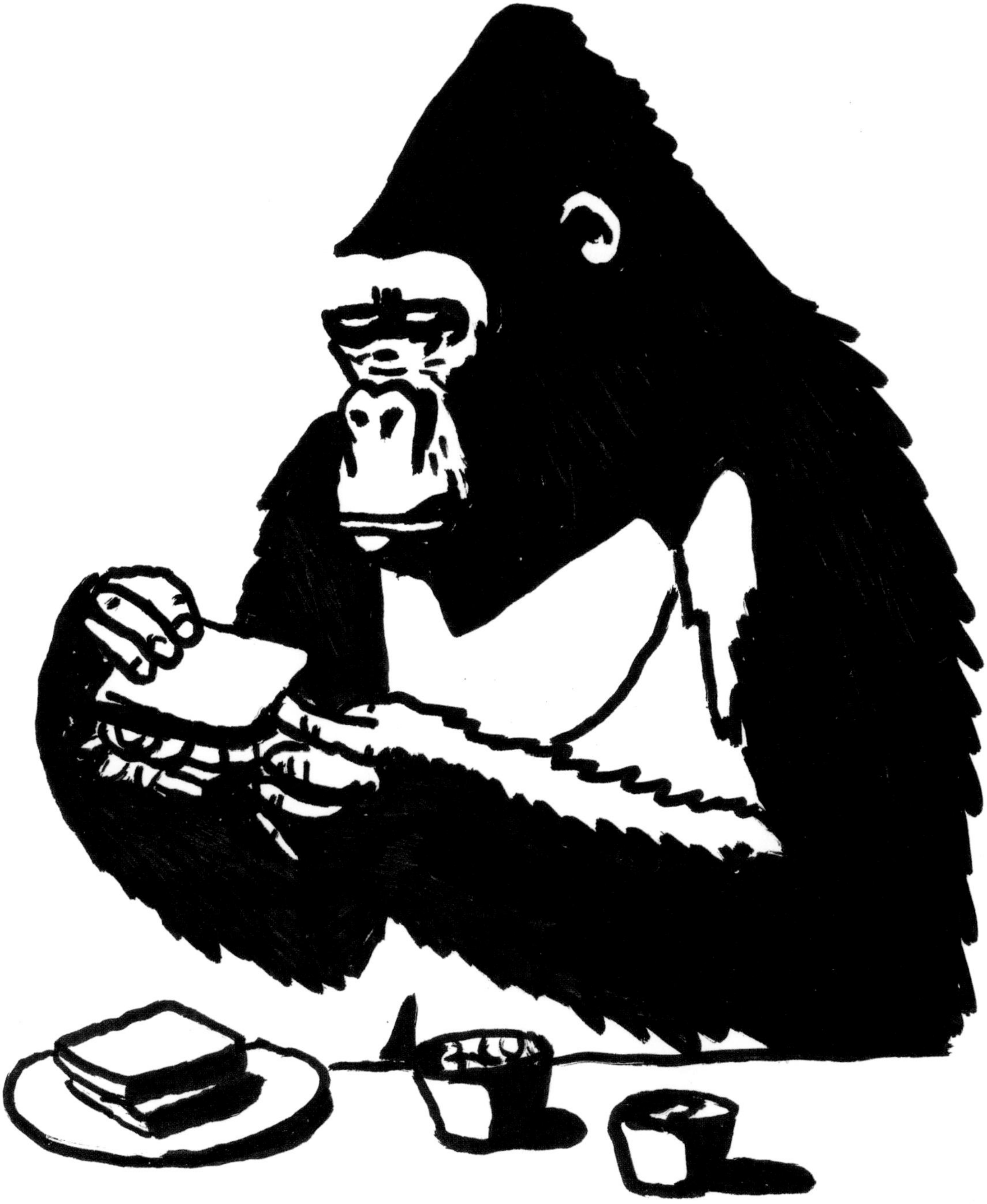

APPENDIX

Fig. 162 *Appendix,* 2023
acrylic on a piece of shit,
20 × 30mm.

I wasn't sure what to put on the appendix page so I have included a painted diagram of an actual human appendix. The appendix shown is inflammed, which is a condition otherwise known as appendicitis.

At first I wasn't sure how to depict this, but then realised that a useless and obsolete thing that can become catastrophically toxic at a moment's notice is also a great way to describe the politician Sir Jacob Rees-Mogg. The resulting painting also appears to be toxic as it has made most of the people I've shown it to feel physically unwell.

Fig. 162

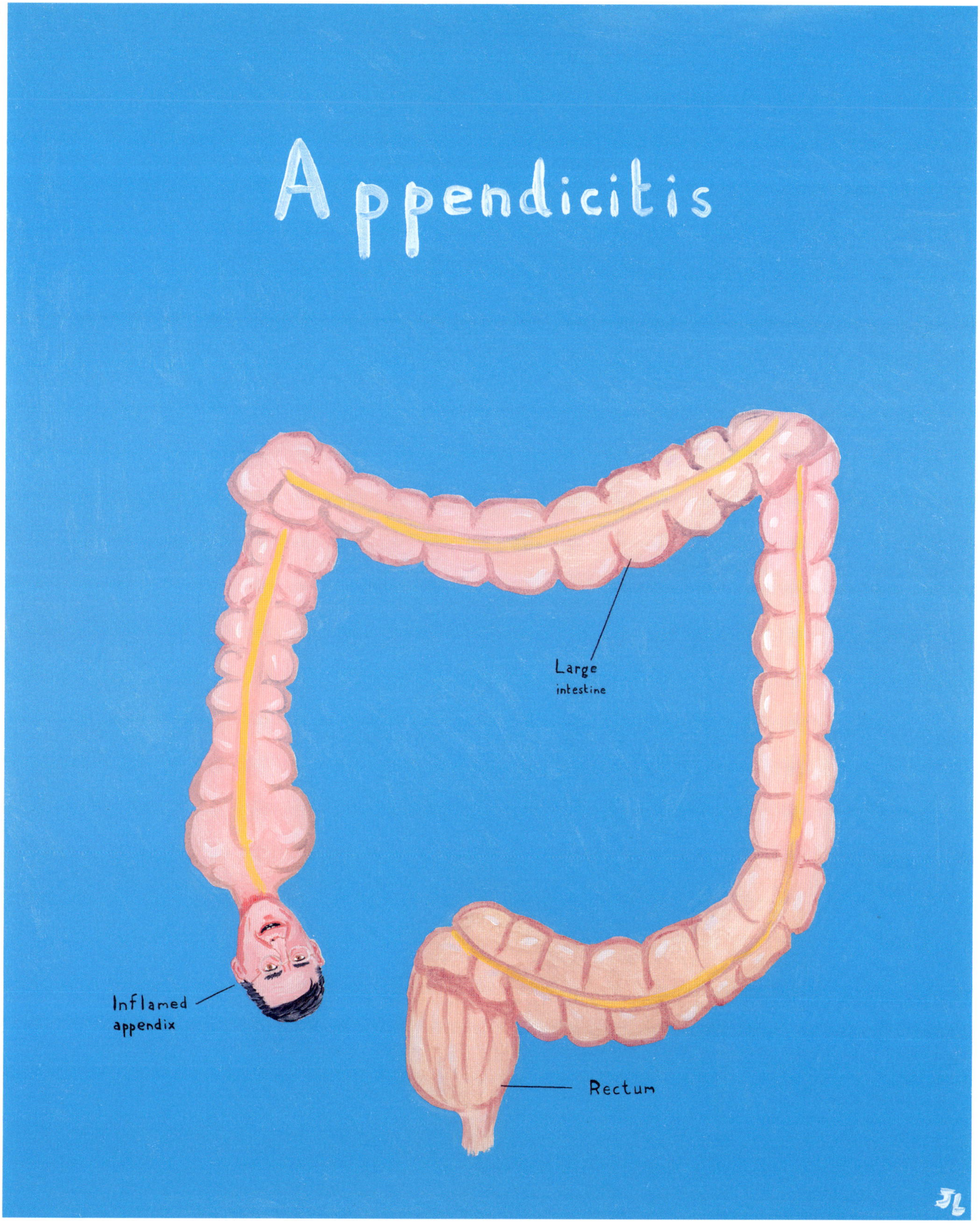

Appendicitis
Large intestine
Inflamed appendix
Rectum
JL

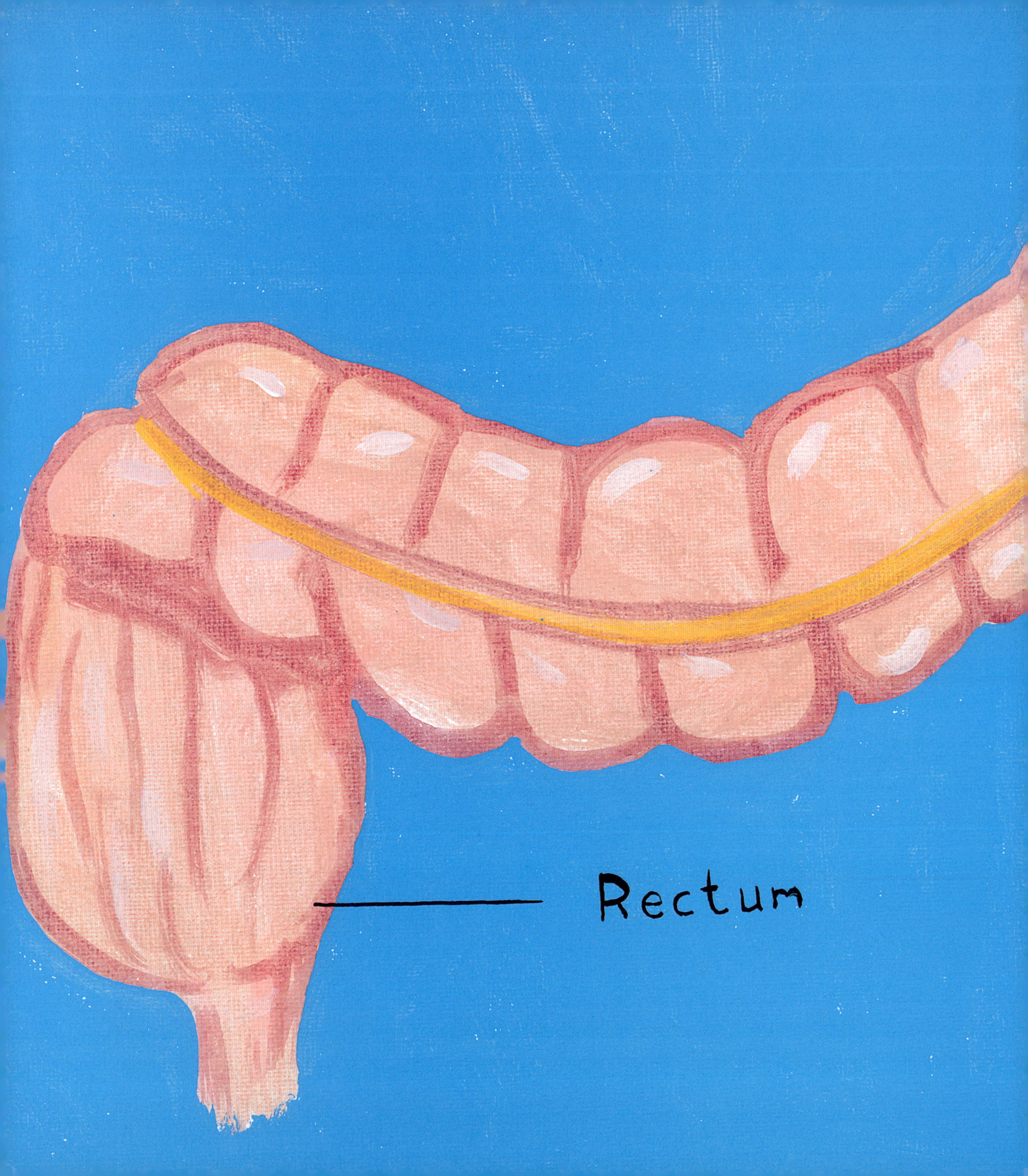
Rectum

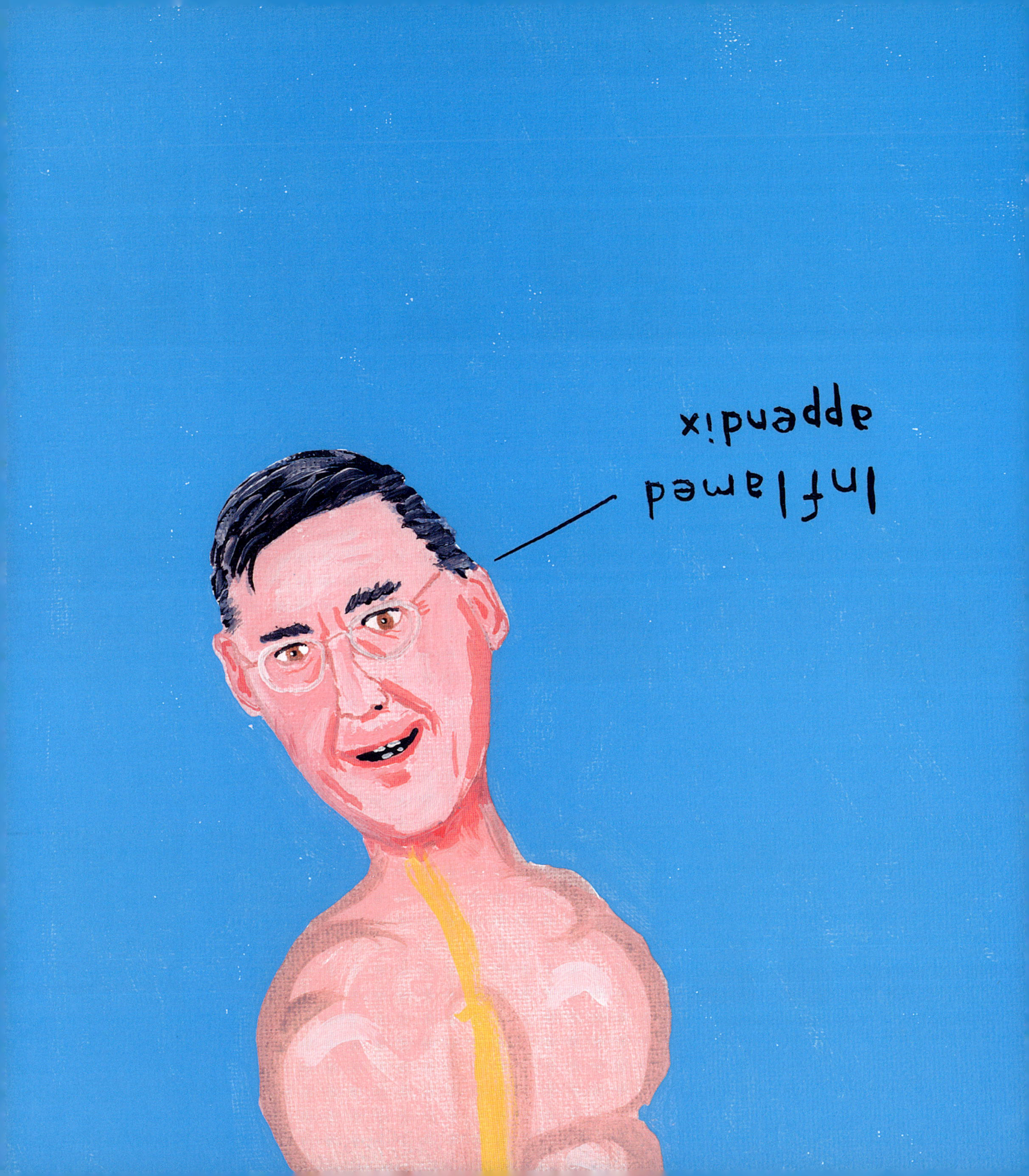
Inflamed
appendix

INDEX OF PAINTINGS

PORTRAIT WORKS IN ORDER OF APPEARANCE:

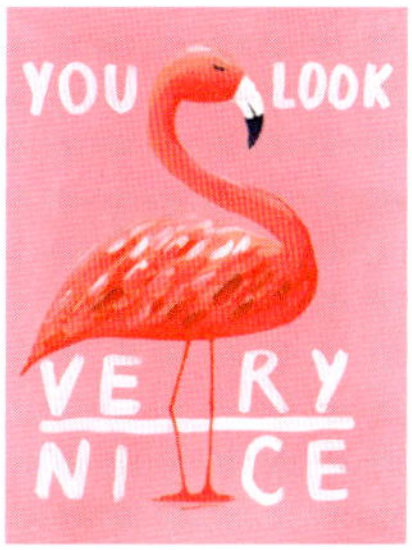

You Look Very Nice, 2024,
white paint and blood
on pillowcase,
40 × 50cm.
pg.161

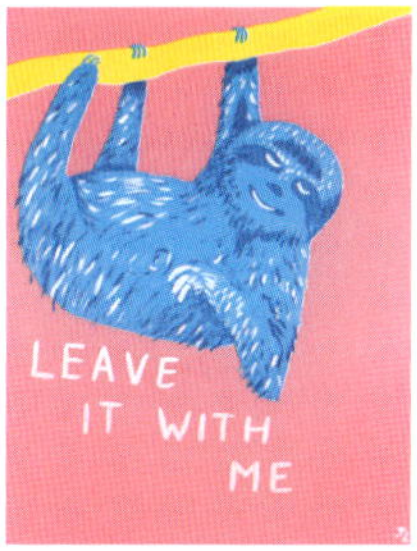

Leave It with Me, 2023,
acrylic on 4 × 4,
approx. 4 × 4.
pg.164–5 (detail) & 237

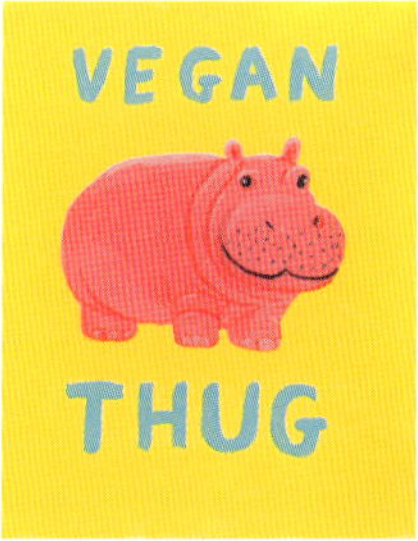

Vegan Thug, 2024,
watercolour (sans water)
on water (sans water),
3 litres (sans litres).
pg.167

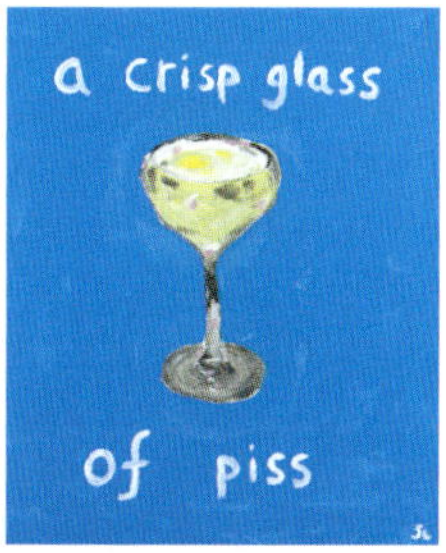

A Crisp Glass of Piss, 2023,
Picpoul and Malbec
on tablecloth,
1 × 2m.
pg.169

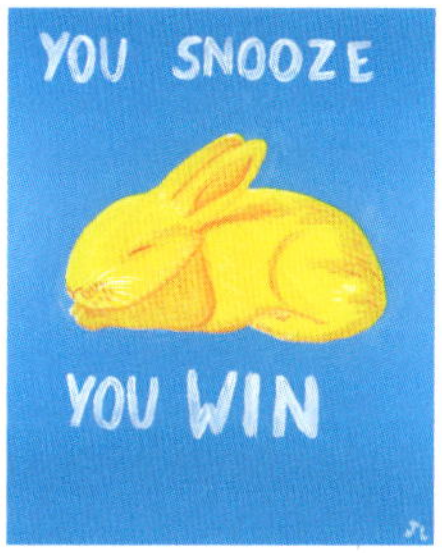

You Snooze You Win, 2023,
acrylic on dog,
12 × 14cm.
pg.178–9 (detail) & 181

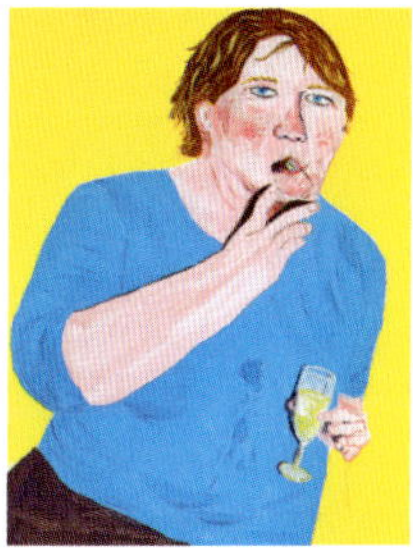

Thérèse Coffey, 2023,
acrylic mixed with ground
beef on canvas board,
21 × 52mm.
pg.183

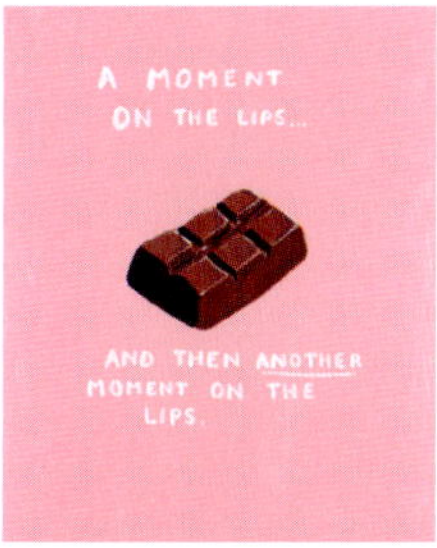

A Moment on the Lips, 2024,
chocolate on pink Wayfair
three-seater sofa,
12 × 24cm.
pg.185 & 194–5 (detail)

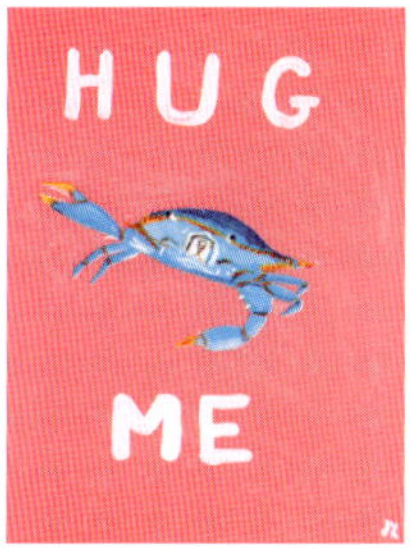

Hug Me, 2024,
acrylic on en suite,
23 × 42mm.
pg.197 & 200–1 (detail)

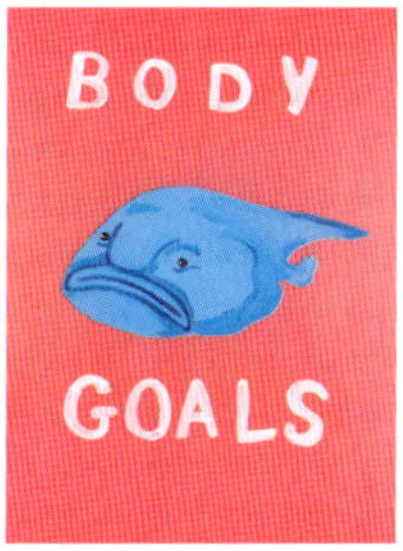

Body Goals, 2024,
charcoal on salad,
4 × 3in.
pg.198

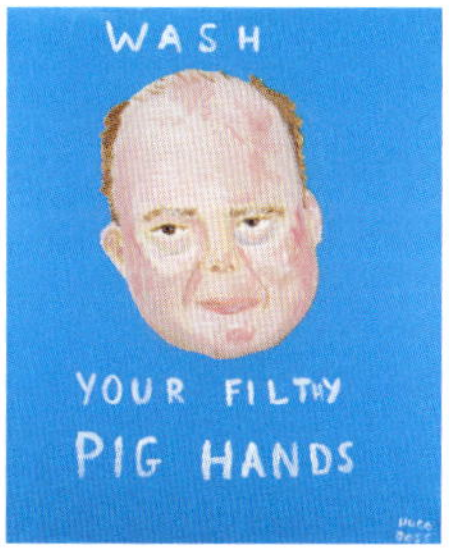

The Itty Bitty Titty Chris Whitty Committee, 2020,
acrylic on NHS pamphlet,
12 × 23cm
pg.204 & 208–9 (detail)

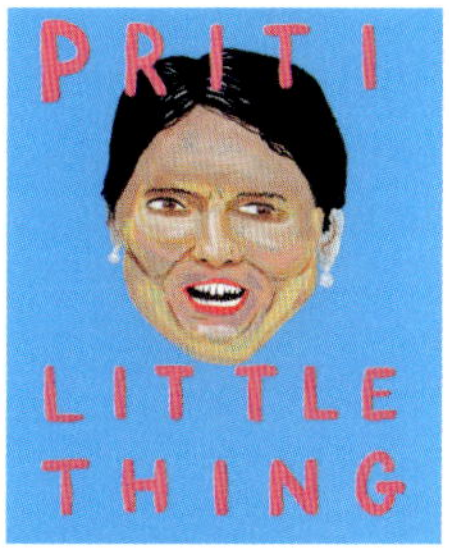

Priti Little Thing, 2024,
dried blood and masonry
paint on scrap metal,
18ft × 6mm.
pg.205

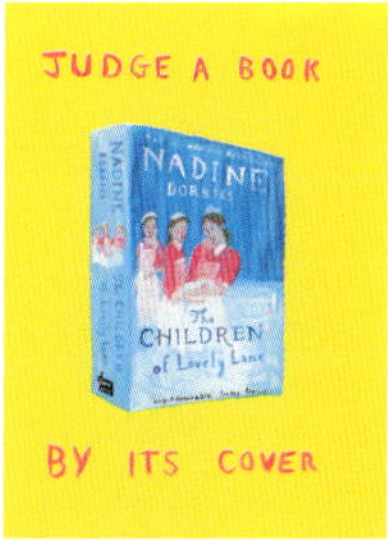

Judge a Book by Its Cover, 2024
[redacted] on [redacted],
[redacted] × [redacted]mm.
pg.225

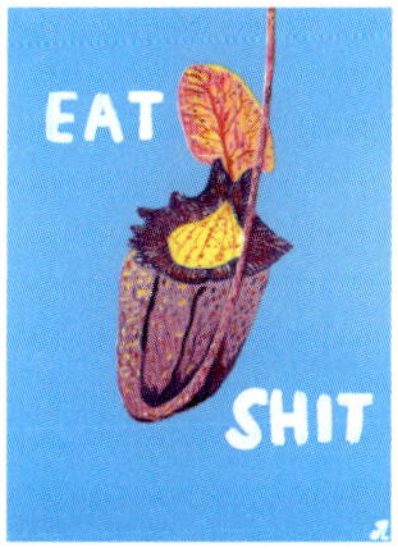

Eat Shit, 2023,
acrylic on lizardskin,
12.4oz.
pg.228–9 (detail) & 231

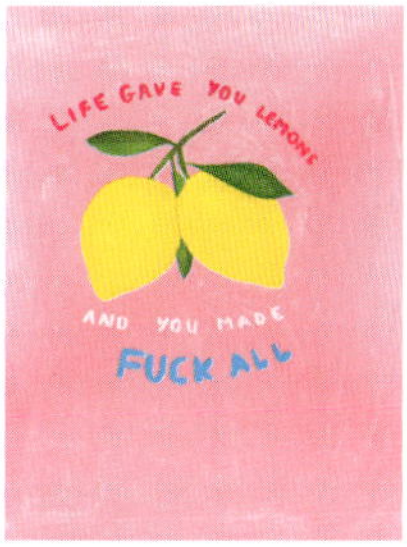

Life Gave You Lemons, 2023,
watercolour on owl,
14 × 23m.
pg.243 & 244–5 (detail)

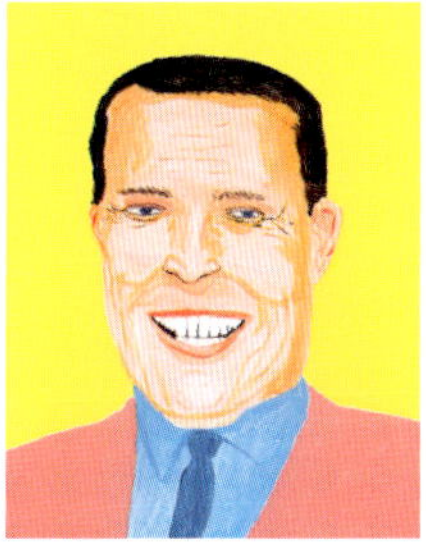

Tony Robbins, 2024,
fake tan on bin,
32 × 48cm.
pg.247

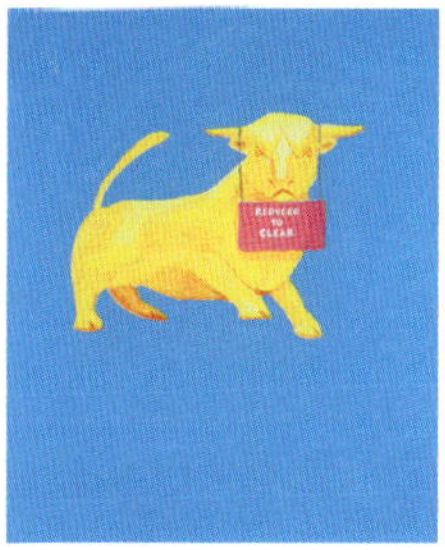

Reduced to Clear, 2024,
piss on shit,
23ml × 14g
pg.262–3 (detail)

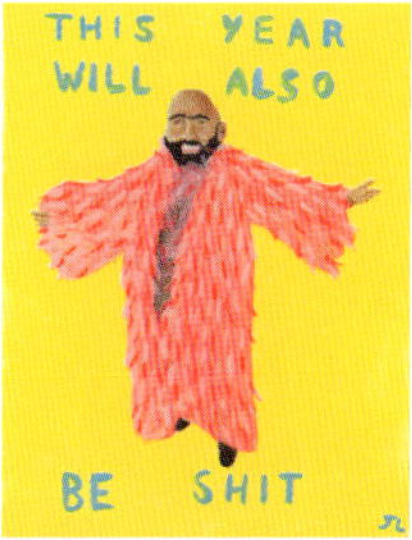

This Year Will Also Be Shit, 2024,
gouache on feather,
10 × 10mm.
pg.265

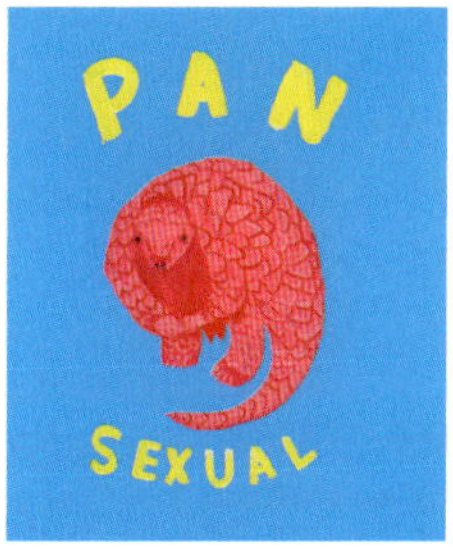

Pansexual, 2023,
acrylic on diamonds,
38 × 47m.
pg.271

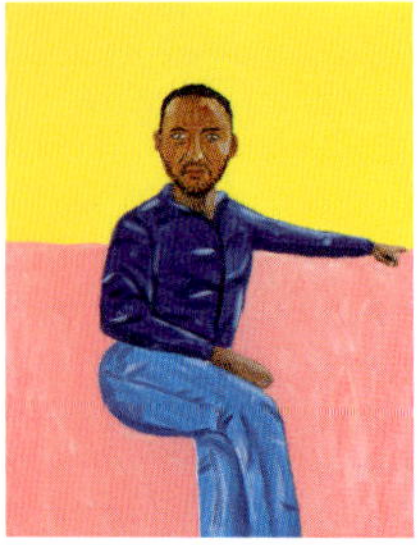

Amol Rajan, 2023,
acrylic gouache on
backpack,
22 × 45mm.
pg.281

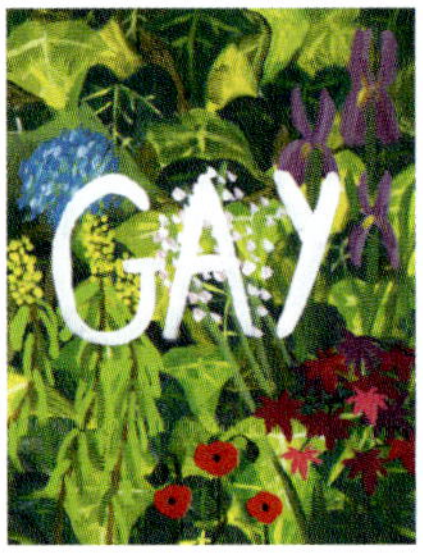

A Portrait of Your Dad, 2023,
acrylic on your dad,
2 × 7in.
pg.288–9 (detail)

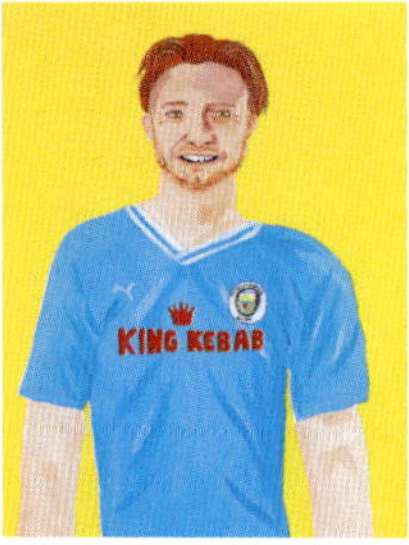

Jack Crealish, 2023,
acrylic grass and melted
sock on football,
30 × 30cm.
pg.293

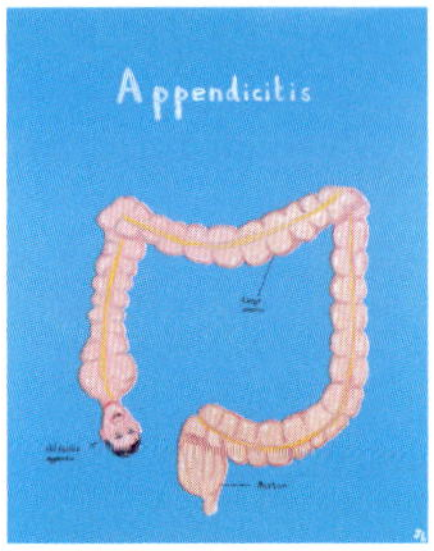

Appendix, 2023,
acrylic on a piece of shit,
20 × 30mm.
pg.309 & 310–11 (detail)

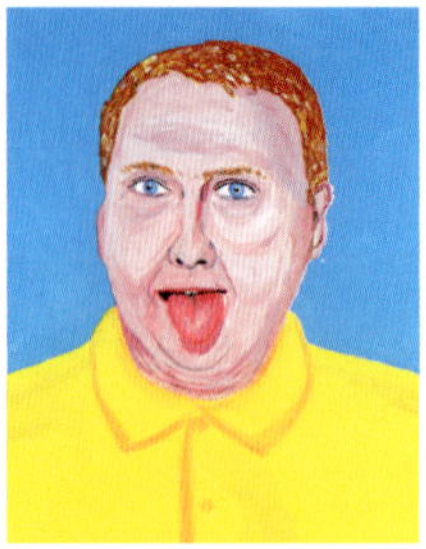

Self-Portrait, 2024,
acrylic on raw
chicken breast,
23 × 45cm.
pg.316

LANDSCAPE WORKS IN ORDER OF APPEARANCE:

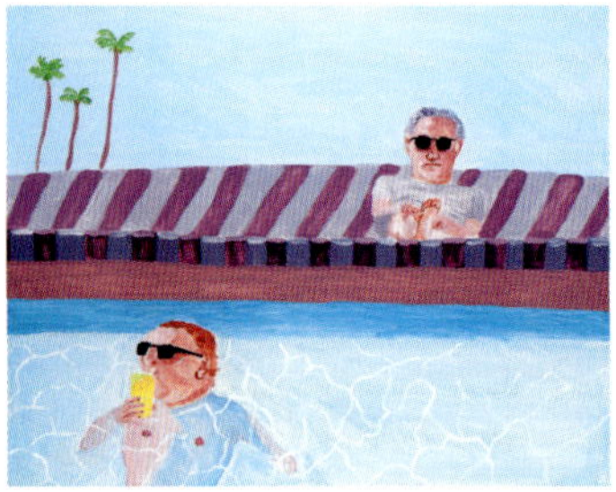

I drink a crisp, cold glass of lager in a pool in Los Angeles while Cary Lineker looks on in disgust, 2020,
acrylic on bonnet of Vauxhall Corsa,
approx. 1 × 3mm.
pg.25 & 30–1 (detail)

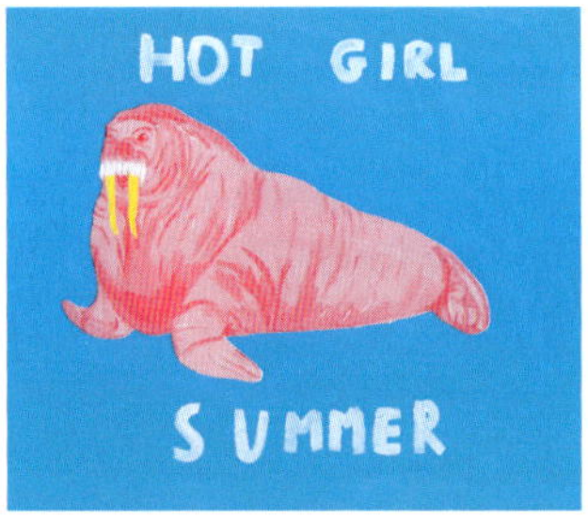

Hot Cirl Summer, 2023,
acrylic on number 11 bus stop,
152 × 121cm.
pg.73 & 74–7 (detail)

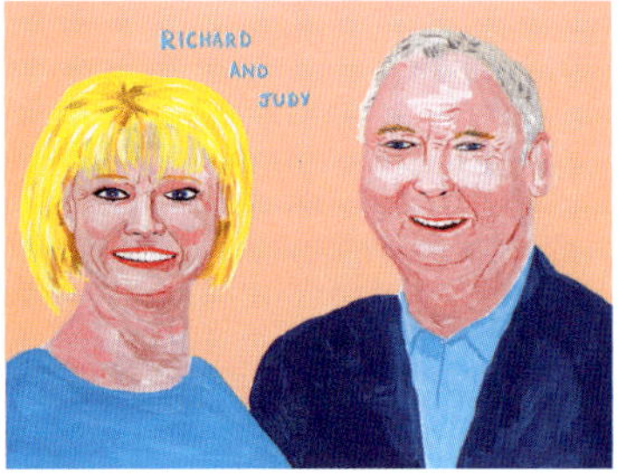

Eamonn & Ruth, 2024,
burnt butter on toasted brioche,
about the size of a 20 pence piece.
pg.89

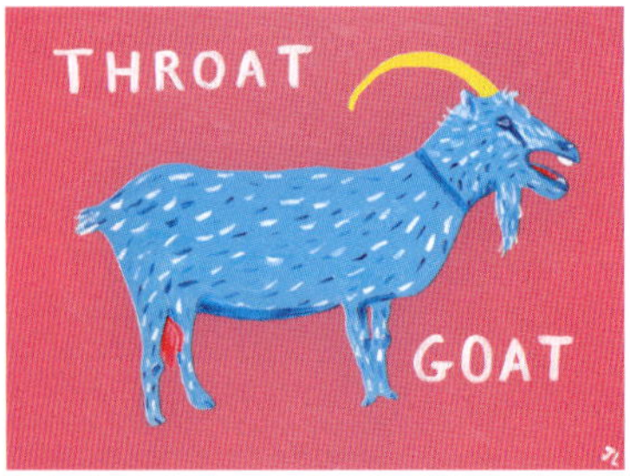

Throat Coat, 2023,
oil on goat,
84 × 17ft.
pg.121 & 210–11 (detail)

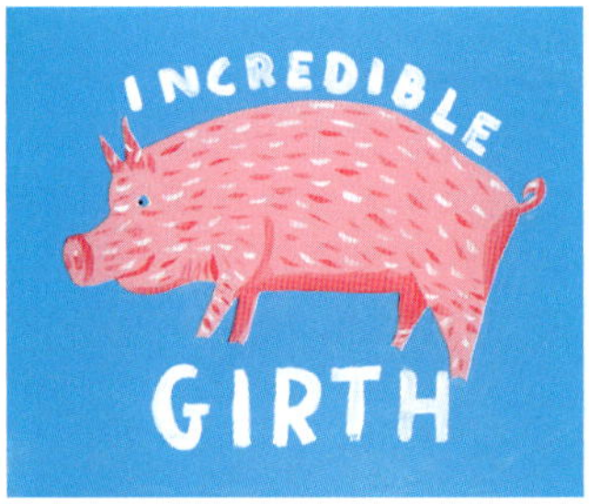

Incredible Cirth, 2023,
acrylic on pork cutlet,
12 × 15mm.
pg.149 & 158–9 (detail)

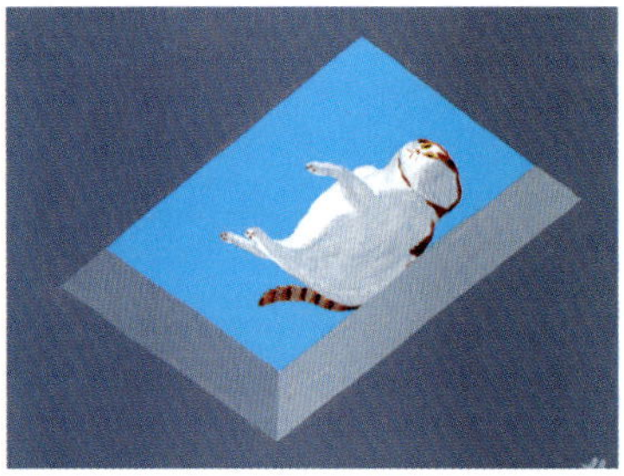

A Cat Having a Little Think While Resting on a Skylight on a Hot Summer's Day, 2022,
Dreamies Creamy on canvas,
30 × 40cm.
pg.215

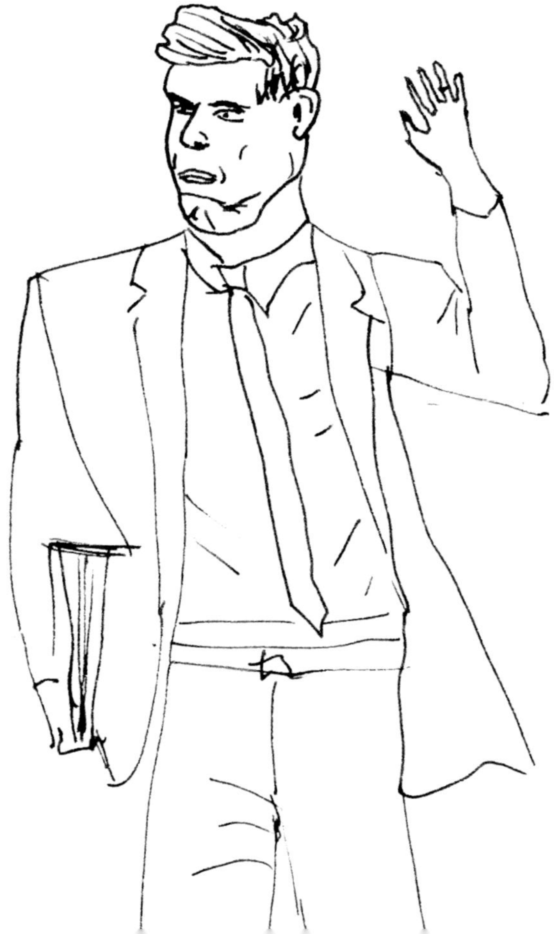

ABOUT THE AUTHOR

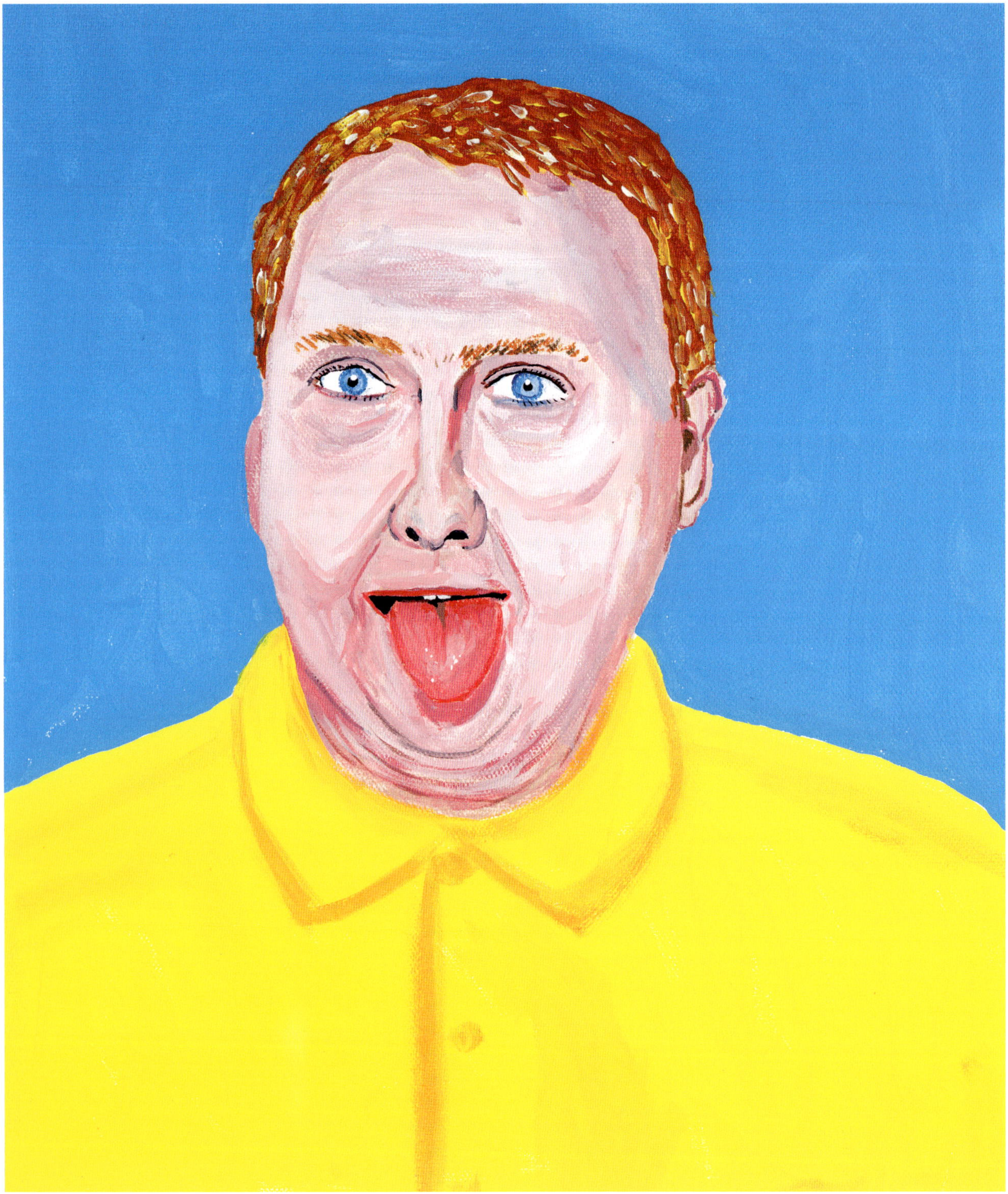

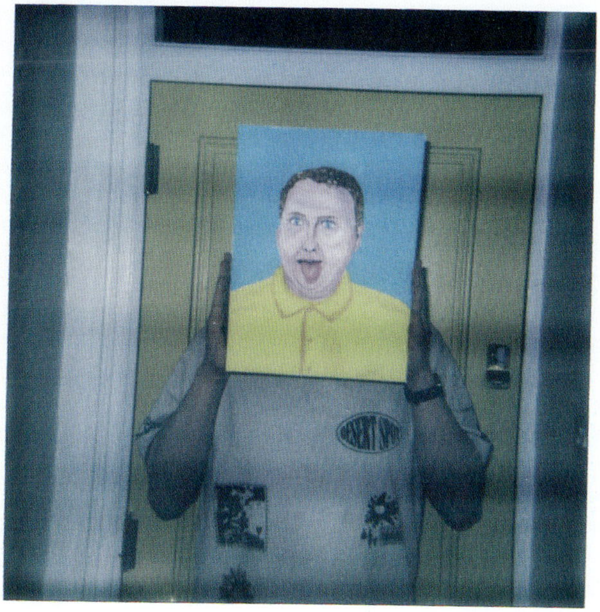

Joe Lycett, born in England, is a celebrated broadcaster and journalist renowned for his coverage of major sporting events including the Olympic Games and horse racing. His engaging and knowledgeable commentary has not only won the hearts of the British public but has also earned him accolades such as the BAFTA Special Award and the RTS Presenter of the Year.

Beyond his broadcasting achievements, Joe is an ardent advocate for animal welfare and an outspoken supporter of LGBTQ+ rights. His charm, wit and depth of knowledge in sports, particularly in horse racing and rugby, reflect a lifelong passion that began in childhood, influenced by his father, a horse trainer. Off the air, Joe enjoys playing golf and is an accomplished amateur jockey, having participated in charity races. His unique blend of humor, empathy and professionalism makes him a beloved figure both on and off the screen.

Make sure you change this bio and don't just copy and paste it into the book, Joe. I've used Clare Balding's bio as a placeholder.

ACKNOWLEDGEMENTS

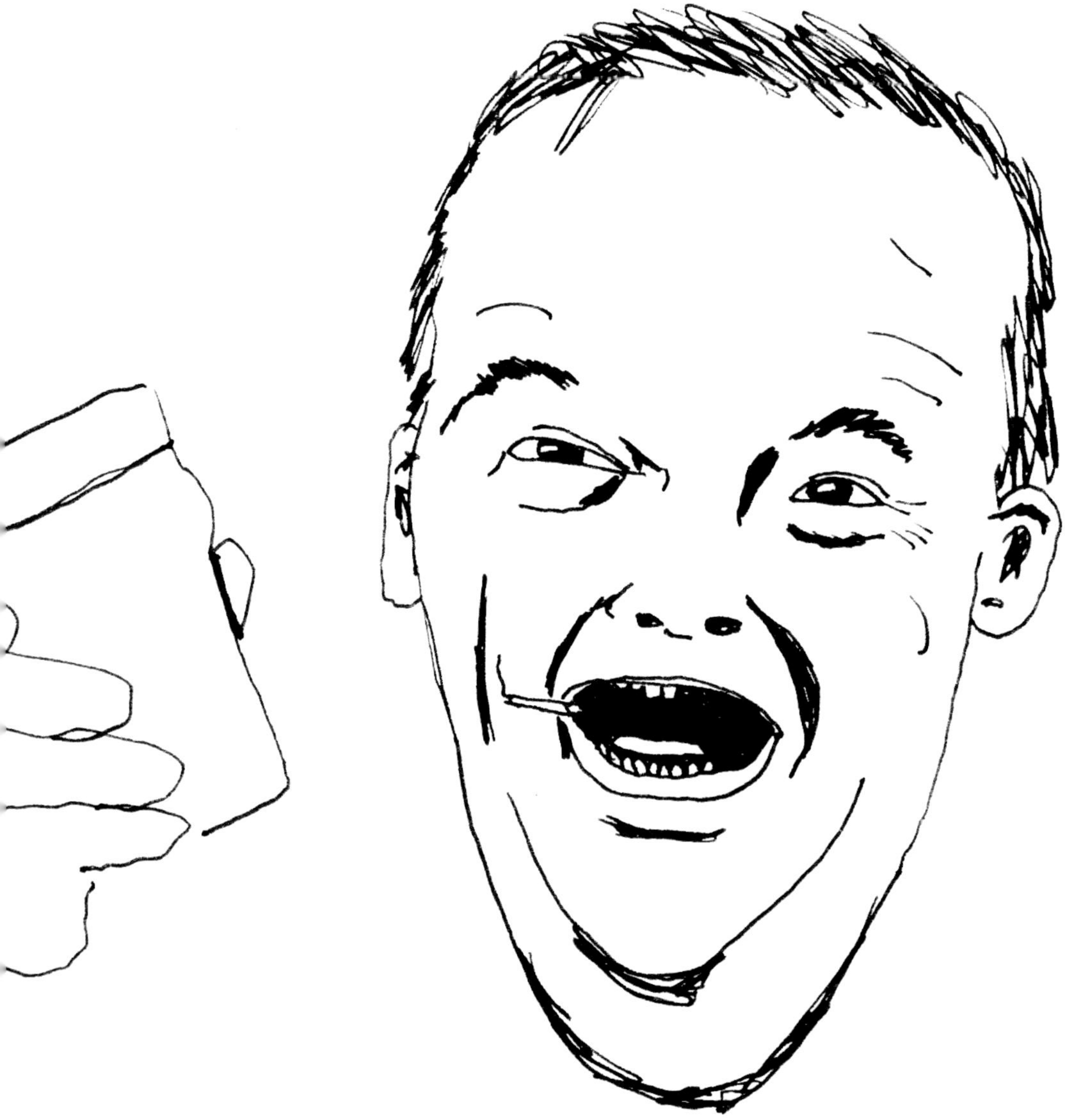

Endless thanks to:

Billie Temple, Lucy Kane, Aidan Butler, James Kettle and Rhik Samadder for their lending considerable hours, work, guidance, additional jokes, ideas and general encouragement to this stupid book.
Adam Langstaff, Ben Kane, Chris Sawyer, James Kettle, Mom & Dad, Caitlin Albery Beavan, Trevor Wensley and Denise for writing the schedules.
Anna Valentine, Georgia Goodall, Lucy Horrocks, Cait Davies, Francesca Pearce, Hennah Sandhu, Sian Smith and all at Orion.
Clare Hoban for doing a merciful legal read, Georgia Goodall for her brilliant copyediting, and Steve Burdett for his fabulous proofreading.
Denise for her help with many things, and photography.
Harry Griffin for the photography additions.
Simon & Karen at Kaleidoscope for scanning all the paintings.
Imogen for the book modelling.
The Epson scanner for all the additional scanning.
Hannah Chambers and all at Chambers Management
Yaz, the real subject of the *This Year Will Also Be Shit* painting, but who also looks like Eric Cantona.
Phil Harris, the real subject of the Mick Hucknall/Patsy Palmer painting, who looks nothing like any of them.
Elva Donnelly for her Timothée Chalamet/Timmy Mallett idea.
Dion Kitson, Jonny Gent, Alan Thorpe, Jenny Beavan, Josh Charles, Mr Bingo, Robbie Williams and Greg James for their help and encouragement.
Will Wood and all the team at Multitude Media.
Mom, Dad, Beth and Fitz for their support.
Thank you to Monica Debitcard for deadline management.

First published in Great Britain in 2024 by Trapeze,
an imprint of The Orion Publishing Group Ltd
Carmelite House, 50 Victoria Embankment, London EC4Y 0DZ
An Hachette UK Company

1 3 5 7 9 10 8 6 4 2

A CIP catalogue record for this book is available from the British Library.

ISBN (Hardback) 978 1 3987 2492 1 / **ISBN** (eBook) 978 1 3987 2493 8 / **ISBN** (Audio) 978 1 3987 2494 5

Art Direction, design & layout: Joe Lycett and Billie Temple
Creative: Joe Lycett, Billie Temple, Lucy Kane, Aidan Butler, James Kettle and Rhik Samadder
Photography: Joe Lycett, Denise, Harry Griffin and Lucy Kane
Editorial: Anna Valentine and Georgia Goodall
Production: Lucy Horrocks, Sian Smith, Chris Singleton and the team at F1 Colour

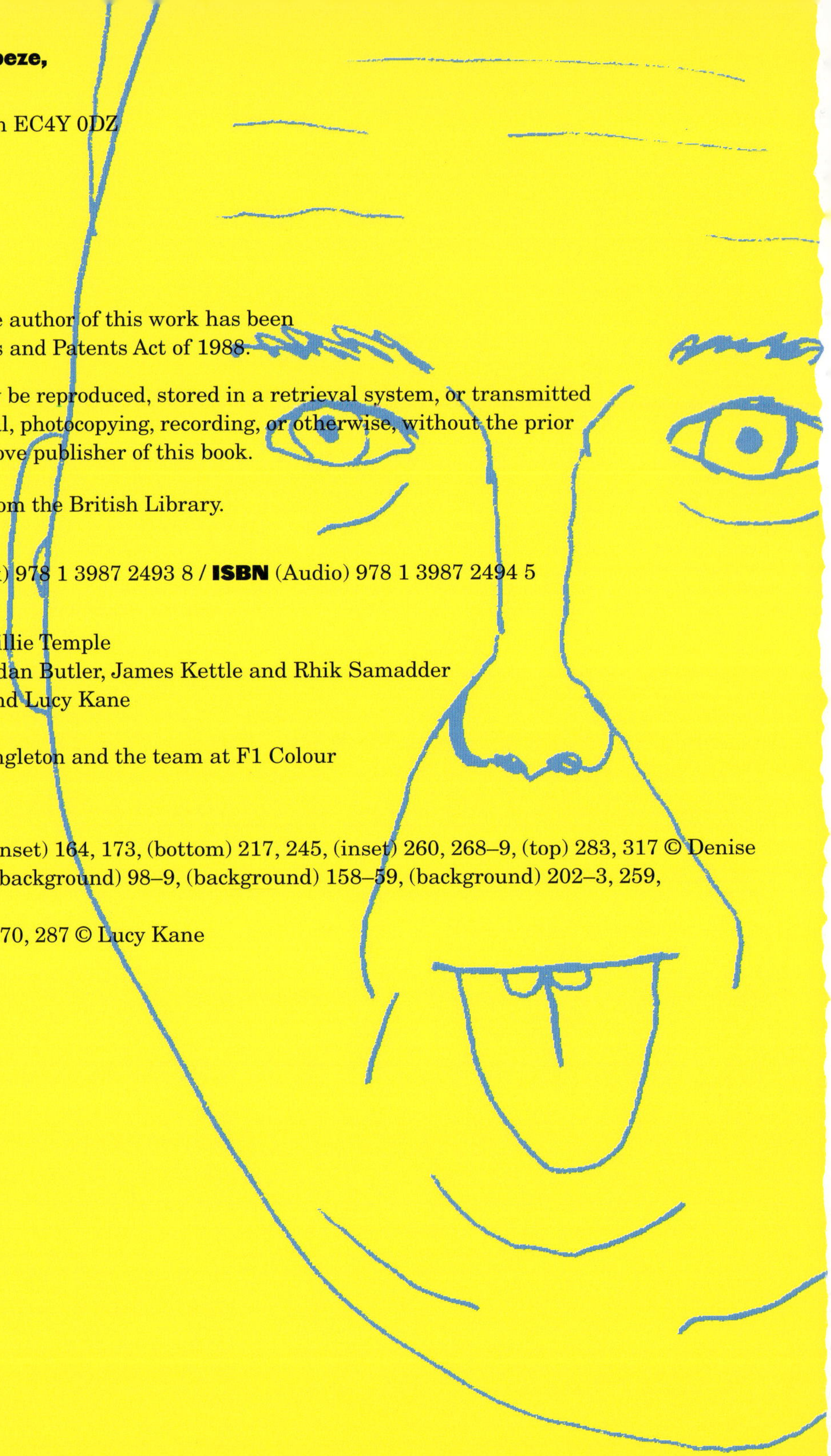

Printed in Italy by Printer Trento S.R.L

FSC www.fsc.org MIX Paper | Supporting responsible forestry FSC® C104740

www.orionbooks.co.uk
www.joelycett.com

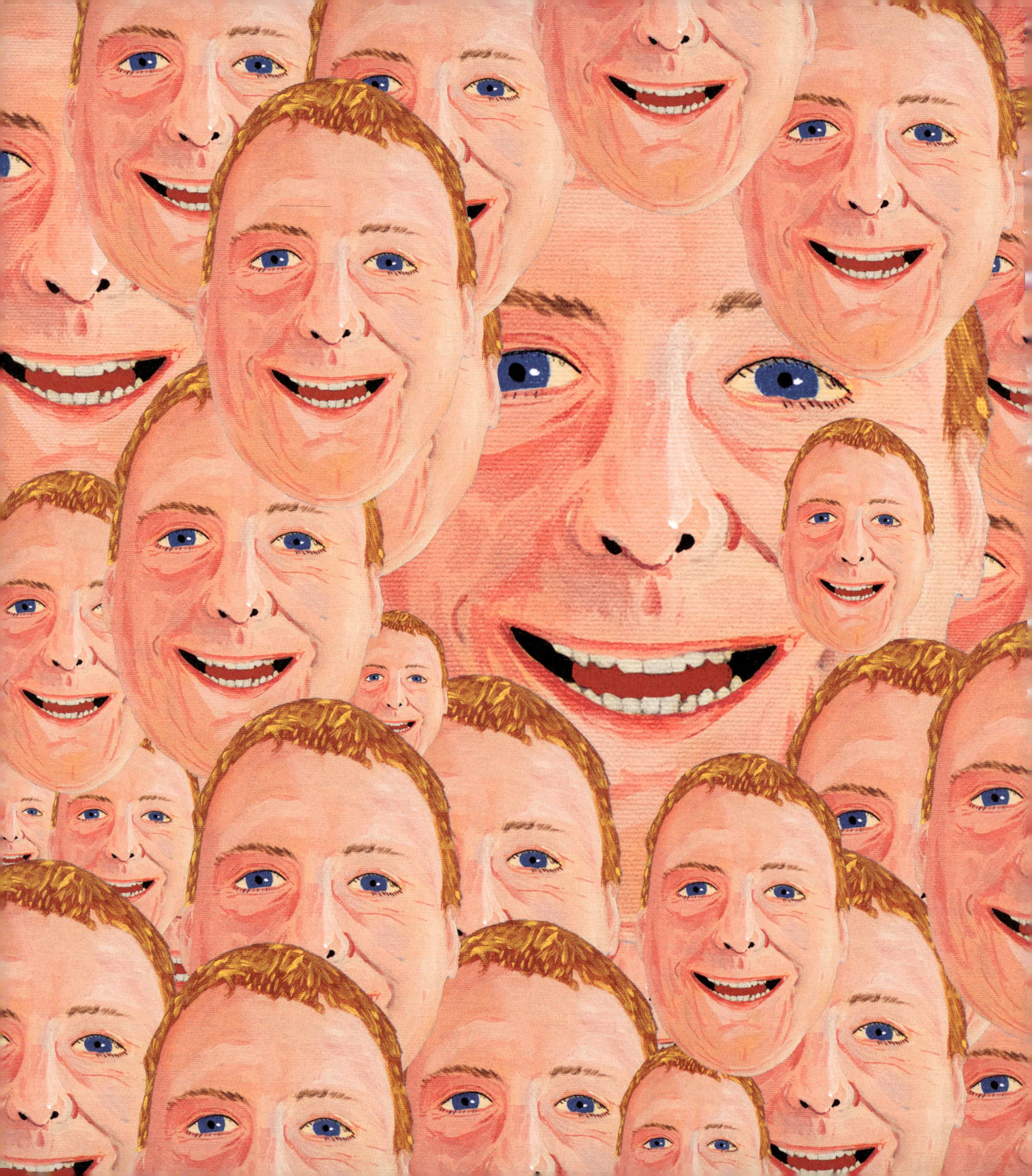